Johannes Brahms

An Annotated Bibliography of the Literature from 1982 to 1996

with an Appendix on Brahms and the Internet

Thomas Quigley

in collaboration with Mary I. Ingraham

The Scarecrow Press, Inc.
Lanham, Md., & London
1998

SCARECROW PRESS, INC.

Published in the United States of America
by Scarecrow Press, Inc.
4720 Boston Way
Lanham, Maryland 20706

British Library Cataloguing in Publication Information Available

Library of Congress Cataloging-in-Publication Data

Quigley, Thomas, 1954—
    Johannes Brahms : an annotated bibliography of the literature from 1982 to 1996 with an appendix on Brahms and the Internet / Thomas Quigley, in collaboration with Mary I. Ingraham.
        p.   cm.
    Includes bibliographical references and indexes.
    ISBN 0–8108–3439–1 (cloth : alk. paper)
    1. Brahms, Johannes, 1833–1897—Bibliography.   I. Ingraham, Mary   I.   II. Title.
    ML134.B8Q53   1998
    016.780′92—dc21   97–41925
                                                                CIP
                                                                MN

Johannes Brahms (last known photograph before his death).

Contents

Contents vii

Contents

Acknowledgments

Although mine is the only name on the title page, there have been many individuals who have supported this work. I hope that by mentioning them here, some of my appreciation can be expressed for all that they have done.

It was my life-partner Ernest de Beaupré, who kept at me to get going on this (second) volume and who has supported my work all the way. Thanks too for all his help on gathering information, and his advice on how to handle matters as they arose. He has stood by me throughout this project; his unflagging encouragement and respect for my single-mindedness have been vital to the work's completion.

The groundwork for this bibliography was greatly facilitated by the information sources and documentation readily available in the Metropolitan Vancouver area. I would like to acknowledge the extensive resources of the University of British Columbia Library (Ruth Patrick, Director) and to salute Music Librarians Hans Burndorfer, former Head, now retired, and Kirsten Walsh, current Head, for building the strongest music research collection in Western Canada. I also want to thank John Cull and his staff from the Fine Arts and Music Division at the Vancouver Public Library, plus other Public Library sections, notably Newspapers and Magazines, for all their help. What couldn't be found locally was made available through the efforts of the Interlibrary Loan Staff of the Vancouver Public Library (Debra Jabs, Senior Library Assistant).

I am grateful to librarians and staff at those North American institutions that I visited in search of Brahmsiana. William Sgrazzutti, formerly of the University of Calgary Music Library, and the staff of the Art Department at Seattle Public Library paved the way for short, intense, but very productive visits, to their institutions. "The Great Brahms

Bibliographical Adventure" vacation cum research trip of Fall 1995 would not have been the success it was, without the assistance of Don Roberts, Deborah ("Debbie") Campana, on leave and acting Head Music Librarian respectively, and Michael Nealon, Public Services Assistant, at Northwestern University Music Library; William McClellan, Music Librarian, and Marlys Scarbrough, Library Operations Assistant, at the Music Library, University of Illinois at Urbana-Champaign; and at the Library of Congress Music Division, Jon Newsom, then acting Chief, now confirmed in his position, William Parsons, Music Specialist and the Readers Services Staff, particularly Charles Sems, Marcus Haynes, Stephen Soderberg, and the Deck Attendants. These people helped me on-site as well as by pre- and postvisit e-mail. Also to be noted in the Adventure's context is assistance received from staff in the Performing Arts, Main, and Newspaper and Current Periodical Reading Rooms at the Library of Congress; from Phil De Sellem, who selfishly appointed himself our Library of Congress Guide; and from staff in Northwestern University's University Library, the Main and Undergraduate Libraries at the University of Illinois at Urbana-Champaign, the Main Library at the University of Illinois at Chicago, University of Chicago's Regenstein Library, and from Linda A. Naru, Director of Member Services, and Michelle Carver, Reading Room Coordinator, at the Center for Research Libraries.

Many thanks are due those colleagues who heeded my calls for information and responded with additional suggestions for literature to be included in this work. The comprehensiveness of the bibliography owes much to the effort of Styra Avins, Andrea Massimo Grassi, Kurt Hofmann, and Dillon Parmer. I also want to thank colleagues in several Brahms societies for their support: George Bozarth and Virginia Hancock of the American Brahms Society and Isamu Yagi of the Japan Brahms Society. Local Brahms scholar Mary Ingraham has been a great booster as well, and her interest in Brahms information on the Internet is responsible for my decision to include World Wide Web-related information sources in this volume. Jürgen Neubacher kindly served as electronic sounding-board during final stages. I was fortunate to have opportunities to present on my work-in-progress at several library- and musicology-related events in British Columbia and Washington State. "Hedgehogs of Merit" go to Kirsten Walsh and John Cull (CAML Conference Committee) for their encouragement to present at the Canadian Association of Music Libraries, Archives and Documentation Centres 1996 Conference (Vancouver, BC), and to Calvin Elliker (University of Michigan Music Library), Bibliography Roundtable

Coordinator, MLA , and JoAnn Taricani (Music Department, University of Washington), Programme Coordinator, PNW-AMS, for including me in their programmes at the Music Library Association 1996 Conference (Seattle, WA), and the 1996 Annual Meeting of the Pacific Northwest Chapter of the American Musicological Society (Seattle, WA), respectively.

The support of my family, friends, and coworkers in the various library units where I've worked over the last 13 years has been a great encouragement. My brother Michael generously shared his expertise in computer and Internet matters. Ken Quandt and the "NJ boys," Martin ("Marty") Lomax and Carmen Palogruto, were unabashed enthusiasts.

My final thanks go to Christian Brandstätter Verlag (Wien) for allowing me to use their photograph of Johannes Brahms for the frontispiece and to Martina Paul for her assistance in procuring that release.

Introduction

This work is the second volume I have compiled that documents literature written about Johannes Brahms and his music. As with its predecessor,[1] the objective here is to provide a comprehensive, systematic guide to this wealth of information; the goal is not only to accurately and consistently report basic bibliographic information on this literature, but also to attempt to establish historical-bibliographic relationships between different publications by the same author, when the items have common topics or themes. Full access to the work's contents is available via the extensive cross-referencing and indexing apparatus that have been supplied. A checklist of consulted bibliographic aids is also included, so that users can ascertain the sources of cited references and gain a sense of the work's magnitude and coverage. Two appendixes round out the volume: one looks ahead, discussing Brahms information on the Internet; the other looks back, reviewing my use of two significant historical indexing projects in music literature.

The publication dates of information cited in this volume fall, in the main, between December 1982 and March 1996. I have also included references from earlier times that I wasn't previously aware of; in addition, research trips to examine the WPA Music Index (Northwestern University) and the Library of Congress Music Division inhouse periodical index unearthed a significant number of earlier citations hitherto unknown, and these too have been included in this work.[2] The Répertoire International de la Presse Musicale [RIPM] Series[3] was not reviewed for possible Brahms references. The main source for Brahms literature up to 1982 remains my previous volume.[4]

This bibliography includes published and unpublished items appearing in a variety of formats, including monographs, serials, dissertations,

Congress proceedings, letters to the editor, etc. The following types of materials, however, are not usually cited in this work:

1. Audio-visual items—filmstrips, 8mm and 16mm films, video-tapes, audiocassettes, phonorecordings and compact discs. Users interested in information about resources in this format are advised to consult such bibliographic aids as the Library of Congress catalogs for music and film, *The Video Source Book,* and *The Classical Video Guide.*[5]
2. Multimedia products and computer software developed for the educational and home computer markets. Users interested in these resources should consult *The Music Index* or *Readers' Guide*[6] for information on what is available.
3. Reviews of performances, audiocassettes, phonorecordings, and compact discs. Users interested in this information should consult McCorkle's *Johannes Brahms: Thematisch-Bibliographisches Werkverzeichnis* and Koch's *Brahms-Bibliográfia* for reference to reviews of performances occurring during Brahms's lifetime, and the *Music Index* for more recent performance or recordings' reviews.[7]
4. Reviews of music editions other than those for first editions.
5. Book reviews or reports, unless they are critiques presented out of context, e.g. as a periodical article.
6. Concert programme, phonorecord or compact disc liner notes.
7. Public lectures or lecture-recitals given in partial fulfillment of degree requirements.
8. Lexical works, such as general and specialized encyclopedias or biographical dictionaries (relevant lexical works are cited as bibliographic aids in the "Checklist of Examined Indexes and Other Bibliographic Aids").
9. Abstracts of proceedings at society and chapter meetings.
10. Works in which reference to Brahms is diffuse or scant. Works in this category include general music histories, genre surveys, analytical overviews of the Romantic period, etc.

Exceptions to the above exclusions can be made when, in my opinion, an item makes a significant contribution to the information available on its topic, or when the item has a historical-bibliographic connection with material cited in this work.

The bibliography is divided by subject into seven main parts, reflecting the major topics of the literature. Sections within each part are devoted to more specific areas of interest and can be further subdivided into more specific subjects yet again. In instances where sections/subsections contain a large number of references, lists of entry numbers have been compiled that further group entries by theme. These lists are located at a section's/subsection's beginning. The scheme of parts and sections is the same as for the previous volume, with the addition of new subsections in Parts I.C. and VI.B.

Material that addresses more than one topic is cited in the subject area it primarily discusses. Cross-references are made from other appropriate subject areas to this entry. These cross-references are recorded by entry number and are listed at the end of a section/subsection. The use of an entry number in this bibliography refers to the entire entry, unless otherwise indicated.

Entries within each section/subsection are filed alphabetically word by word, with authored and anonymous items interfiled in one author/title sequence. There are two significant exceptions to this rule. Citations in which authorship is indicated only by initials are filed alphabetically by first letter, letter by letter; serial citations for which only a periodical name is known are filed alphabetically at the beginning of their section/subsection, word by word.

Each entry in the bibliography consists of the following:

1. A principal bibliographic citation with an entry number. Standardized formats for bibliographic citations are based on Turabian's *A Manual for Writers of Term Papers, Theses, and Dissertations* and the University of Chicago *Manual of Style.*[8] The formats used in this work, however, intentionally contain more detail than is normally found in academic bibliography because my experience with verifying information indicates that the more information provided for users, the better. Emphasis is on literal transcription of information following the *Anglo-American Cataloguing Rules* (2nd ed.);[9] errors in unverified information are not corrected. Editorial commentary is used only to clarify information or to cast references in the standard formats used in such bibliographic aids as Union Lists of Serials and National Bibliographies.

Entry numbers continue on from the last number of my previous volume.[10] Entries for material issued in multivolume sets, each volume having its own complex publication history, are constructed so that individual volumes are treated as subentries within the main entry. Capital letters are added to the entry number—i.e., 39A, 39B, 39C, 39D—to flag this situation.

Information is provided in the original language of the publication, following its normal rules of capitalization except when otherwise indicated in the source. Title translations are not generally provided. Romanization of titles in the Cyrillic alphabet follows the Library of Congress transliteration system.

The author has attempted to examine a broad base of material in order to describe the literature within its physical context; i.e., monographs within a larger edition span, articles within the whole serial volume. Material not seen at all is indicated by an asterisk sign (*) before the entry number. Question marks (?) are used within entries to alert the user to problems encountered in trying to locate the item from available citations, or to significant discrepancies that occur in the reporting of the citation in different bibliographic sources. A dagger (†) after a person's name indicates that that person is dead. Editorial brackets within titles of citations are transcribed as double bracket sets: "[]" is transcribed as "[[]]."

2. *Collation information.* This information is provided so that the user has some indication of *apparatus criticus* and other features present in a reference. In entries where material on Brahms is only a portion of the entire reference, as for example, an article in a Festschrift or Congress proceeding, the collation applies only to the Brahms section itself or to features that relate to the section, e.g., an index for the whole volume. The abbreviations used in the collation are as follows:

a. *ill.*—illustrations, including photographs or works of art.
b. *facsim.*—facsimiles of Brahms's handwriting either in prose or music.
c. *mus.*—musical examples taken from Brahms's compositions: these can range from a few bars to an entire work.
d. *fig.*—figures, tables, graphs, charts, diagrams, schematics, plans.
e. *ind.*—index.
f. *notes*—documentation, footnote or endnote references, bibliography.
g. *discog.*—discography.

3. *Publication history.* The various editions and issues in which an item may have appeared in print are detailed here. This information may not be comprehensive, because it is only based on physical evidence or references from the bibliographic sources examined.

4. *Annotation.* An annotation is provided when the title alone is not sufficient explanation or when it is necessary to describe content, point of view, or intended audience. It can be a quotation from the item itself, a paraphrase, a quotation from other sources, or information obtained

directly from the author; in the last two instances, the source is provided in editorial brackets. Standardized vocabulary is used to lessen discrepancies in information interpretation.

Names of cities and geographic points in Germany and in states within the former Habsburg Empire are not usually translated into English. German words that the author considers to be familiar terminology in Brahms studies are also not translated. RISM sigla are used, whenever possible, for institutions referred to in entries. Annotations only apply to the citation directly above the annotation.

5. *Bibliographic-historical remarks.* The purpose of the information reported in this section of the entry is to make users aware of other resources related by author or content, and to flag bibliographic relationships between different references. Users thus have the fullest access to information from a variety of points of view and from a variety of literary forms. As many as five different kinds of remarks are possible; unless otherwise indicated below, arrangement is alphabetical by author/title:

a. *reprint.* Exact duplication of text, though not necessarily in the same format as the original. Arrangement is chronological by date of publication.

b. *translation.* The equivalent of the original text, but in a different language. Arrangement is alphabetical by language.

c. *excerpt.* Portion of the text, in either its original language or in other languages.

d. *other.* A literary relationship exists between the principal entry and another reference, though not in the sense of (a) or (b). Examples include ensuing discussion of a principal entry's topic; articles that condense, elaborate, incorporate, or rework information from the principal entry; letters to the editor that refer back to the principal entry.

e. *report/review.* Articles summarizing or criticizing the content of a principal entry. Such materials are secondary literature once removed and as such, would not usually merit inclusion in a bibliography. However, they do provide information that can be used to ascertain whether items not available locally are relevant to one's research. They are included in this bibliography in a subordinate position to their subject, the principal entry, in order to avoid any confusion as to their bibliographic worth.

Lower-case Roman numerals are used to distinguish more than one reference within each kind of remark. Each reference can, in turn, become a principal entry, with its own publication history, annotation, and bibliographic-historical remarks. To eliminate redundancy, basic information is given subsequent to the principal entry only when there are changes.

Remarks that refer to material in my earlier volume[11] cite its entry number there and provide a shortened citation. This citation is intended as an aid for those users who may not have the other volume available to them.

Notes

1. Quigley, Thomas, *Johannes Brahms: an annotated bibliography of the literature through 1982.* With a Foreword by Margit L. McCorkle. Metchen, NJ and London: The Scarecrow Press, 1990.

2. See Dena J. Epstein, "The Mysterious WPA Music Periodical Index" *Notes* 45/3 (3.1989) pp. 463–82; and Gillian B. Anderson, "Unpublished Periodical Indexes at the Library of Congress and elsewhere in the United States of America" *Fontes artis musicae* 31/1 (1.-3.1984) pp. 54–60 for details on these two indexes; I also made presentations on my work at the Music Library Association 1996 Conference (Seattle, WA) and Canadian Association of Music Libraries, Archives and Documentation Centres 1996 Conference (Vancouver, BC). See also Appendix B.

3. Répertoire International de la Presse Musicale Series. H. Robert Cohen, General Editor. Published under the auspices of the International Musicological Society and the International Association of Music Libraries, Archives and Documentation Centers. vol. [1]– . Ann Arbor, MI: UMI, 1988– .

4. See note 1.

5. U.S. Library of Congress, *Library of Congress Catalog: Music and Phonorecords.* Washington, D.C.: Library of Congress, 1953– . [Subtitle varies: *Music, Books on Music, and Sound Recordings* (1973–).] U.S. Library of Congress, *Library of Congress Catalog: Films.* Washington, D.C.: Library of Congress, 1953– . [Subtitle varies: *Motion Pictures and Filmstrips* (1954–1972); *Films and Other Materials for Projection* (1973–78); *Audiovisual Materials* (1979–).] *The Video Source Book* and its *Supplement,* Professional volume, 16th ed. Syosset, N.Y.: National Video Clearinghouse, 1995. *The Classical Video Guide.* Michael Scott Rohan, ed. London: Gollancz, 1994.

6. *The Music Index.* 1– . 1949– . Detroit: Information Services Incorporated, 1949– . [publication information varies]; *The Music Index 1979–1993 on CD-ROM.* [Warren, MI:] Harmonie Park Press, 1996. *Readers' Guide to Periodical Literature.* vol. 1– . 1900– . Minneapolis: The H.W. Wilson Company, 1905– . [place of publication varies]; *Readers Guide Abstracts Index.* [database] n.p.: The H.W. Wilson Company.

7. Margit L. McCorkle, *Johannes Brahms: Thematisch-Bibliographisches Werkverzeichnis*. Herausgegeben nach gemeinsamen Vorarbeiten mit Donald M. McCorkle †. München: G. Henle Verlag, 1984. Lajos [Louis] Koch, "Brahms-Bibliográfia," *A Fővárosi könyvtar évkönye* 12 (1942), pp. 65–149; Monograph "Sonderabdruck": Koch, *Brahms-Bibliográfia/Brahms-Bibliographie*. Budapest: Budapest Székesfőváros házinyomdája, 1943. *The Music Index.* 1– . 1949– . Detroit: Information Services Incorporated, 1949– . [publication information varies]; *The Music Index 1979–1993 on CD-ROM.* [Warren, MI:] Harmonie Park Press, 1996.

8. Kate L. Turabian, *A Manual for Writers of Term Papers, Theses, and Dissertations*. 5th ed. Revised and Expanded by Bonnie Birtwhistle Honigsblum. (Chicago Guides to Writing, Editing and Publishing) Chicago: University of Chicago Press, 1987. University of Chicago Press, *The Chicago Manual of Style*, 14th ed. Chicago and London: University of Chicago Press, 1993.

9. Michael Gorman and Paul W. Winkler (eds.), *Anglo-American Cataloguing Rules*, 2nd ed. Chicago: American Library Association; Ottawa: Canadian Library Association, 1978.

10. See note 1.

11. See note 1.

Checklist of Examined Indexes and Other Bibliographic Aids

This list includes sources examined for information on Brahms, and sources used to verify that information. It should be pointed out that a significant amount of the literature in this bibliography is a result of information noted and followed up from the materials themselves. Items in this list are referred to by their siglum in the bibliography. Unless otherwise indicated in the annotation, all serial materials have been consulted up to 3.1996.

Encyclopedias and Dictionaries

S001. *Die Musik in Geschichte und Gegenwart.* 14 vols. Kassel und Basel: Bärenreiter-Verlag, 1949–68.

S002. *Die Musik in Geschichte und Gegenwart. Supplement.* 2 vols. [=*Die Musik in Geschichte und Gegenwart.* vols. 15, 16] Kassel [et al.]: Bärenreiter-Verlag, 1973–79.

S003. *The New Grove Dictionary of Music and Musicians.* Stanley Sadie, ed. 20 vols. London: Macmillan Publishers Limited, 1980.

S004. *Riemann Musiklexikon.* 12. völlig neubearbeitete Auflage. Wilibald Gurlitt, ed. 3 vols. Mainz: B. Schott's Söhne, 1959–67. [vols. 1,2 = Personenteil; vol. 3 = Sachteil, begonnen von

Wilibald Gurlitt fortgeführt und herausgegeben von Hans Heinrich Eggebrecht].

S005. *Riemann Musiklexikon. Ergänzungsband. Personenteil.* Carl Dahlhaus, ed. 2 vols. Mainz: B. Schott's Söhne, 1972–75.

Bibliographies

National and Trade

S006. Biblioteca Centrala de Stat. *Bibliografia Romaniei. Carti, albume, harti.* vols 17–39. [Bucuresti] : Biblioteca Centrala de Stat, 1968–1990.

S007. Biblioteca nazionale centrale di Firenze. *Bibliografia nazionale italiana. Catalogo alfabetico annuale.* 1– . 1958– . Firenze: Author, 1961– . [publisher varies].

S008. Biblioteca nazionale centrale di Firenze. *Catalogo cumulativo 1886–1957 del bollettino delle pubblicazione italiane.* 39 vols. Nendeln: Kraus Reprint, 1969.

S009. Bibliothèque nationale du Québec. *Bibliographie du Québec.* Quebéc: Bibliothèque nationale du Quebéc, 1968– . 1– .

S010. Bibliothèque nationale (France). *Bibliographie nationale française. Livres.* [Paris: Bibliothèque Nationale, Office général du livre,] 1990– . no. 1– . (vol. 179– .)

S011. *Books in Print PLUS.* Canadian ed. [CD-ROM] [New Providence, NJ:] R.R. Bowker. Consulted up to 11.1996.

S012. Brinkman, Carel Leonhard. *Brinkmans cumulative catalogus.* 1846– . Leiden: A.W. Sijthoff's Uitgeversmaatschappij, 1846– . [title, publication information varies].

S013. *The British National Bibliography.* 1950– . London: Council of the British National Bibliography, Ltd., 1951– . [publisher varies].

S014. *Deutsche Bibliographie.* Herausgegeben und bearbeitet von Deutschen Bibliothek. Frankfurt a.M. 1971– . Frankfurt a.M.: Buchhändler-Vereinigung GmbH, 1971– . Consulted up to 1995.

S015. *Gesamtverzeichnis des deutschsprachigen Schrifttums (GV)*

1700–1900. Bearbeitet unter der Leitung von Peter Geils und Willi Gorzny. [editors vary] 160 vols. München [et al.]: K.G. Saur, 1979–87.

S016. *Gesamtverzeichnis des deutschsprachigen Schrifttums (GV) 1911–1965.* Herausgegeben von Reinhard Oberschelp. Bearbeitet unter der Leitung von Willi Gorzny. Mit einem Geleitwort von Wilhelm Totok. 150 Bde. [Bde. 1–82:] München: Verlag Dokumentation, 1976–79; [Bde. 83–150:] München [et al.]: K.G. Saur, 1979–81.

S017. Library of Congress. *The National Union Catalog.* 1970– . Totowa, NJ: Rowman and Littlefield, 1970– . [publisher varies].

S018. Library of Congress. *The National Union Catalog. Pre-1956 Imprints.* 685 vols. London, Chicago: Mansell Information/Publishing Limited, 1968–1980.

S019. Palau y Dulcet, Antonio. *Manual del librero hispano-americano; bibliografia general espanola e hispano-americana desde la invencion de la imprenta hasta nuestros tiempos, con el valor comercial de los impresos descritos.* 2. ed. corr. y aumentada por el autor. 30 vols. [Vols. 9–28: Revisado y anadido por Agustin Palau [Baquero]]. Barcelona : A. Palau, 1948. [imprint varies].

S020. *Slovenska narodna bibliografia. Seria A: Knihy.* Martin : Matica slovenska. 20– . 1969– . Consulted vol. 30–47 no. 4. 1979–1996.

Union Lists and Guides to Periodicals and Newspapers

S021. *British Union-Catalogue of Periodicals.* James D. Stewart [et al.], eds. 4 vols. London: Butterworths Scientific Publications, 1955–58.

S022. Fellinger, Imogen. *Verzeichnis der Musikzeitschriften des 19. Jahrhunderts.* (Studien zur Musikgeschichte des 19. Jahrhunderts 10) Regensburg: Gustav Bosse Verlag, 1968.

S023. Hagelweide, Gert. *Deutsche Zeitungsbestände in Bibliotheken und Archiven=German Newspapers in Libraries and Archives.* Herausgegeben von der Kommission für Geschichte des Parlamentarismus und der politischen Parteien und dem Verein Deutscher Bibliothekare e.V. (Bibliographien zur Geschichte des

Parlamentarismus und der politischen Parteien 6) Düsseldorf: Droste Verlag, 1974.

S024. Library of Congress. *Library of Congress Catalogs: Newspapers in Microform. Foreign Countries. 1948–1972.* Washington, D.C.: Author, 1973.

S025. Library of Congress. *Library of Congress Catalogs: Newspapers in Microform. United States. 1948–1972.* Washington, D.C.: Author, 1973.

S026. *New Serial Titles. A Union List of Serials Commencing Publication after December 31, 1949.* 1950– . Washington, D.C.: Library of Congress, 1973– . [publication information varies].

S027. *Union List of Serials in Libraries of the United States and Canada.* 3rd ed. Edna Brown Titus, ed. 5 vols. New York: The H.W. Wilson Company, 1965.

Library Catalogs

S028. Center for Research Libraries. *Catalogue: Newspapers.* 2nd ed., cumulated. Chicago: Author, 1978.

S029. Center for Research Libraries. *Catalogue: Serials.* 2 vols. Chicago: Author, 1972.

S030. Center for Research Libraries. *Catalogue: Serials. First Supplement.* Chicago: Author, 1978.

S030.5. *Outlook.* [database] [Updated Edition] [Victoria, Canada:] BC [British Columbia] Electronic Library Network and Library Services Branch, BC Ministry of Municipal Affairs, 8.1996.

S031. *Worldcat.* [database] [Dublin, OH:] OCLC. Consulted up to 8.12.1996.

Subject Bibliographies

S032. Angermüller, Rudolph, and Johanna Senigl. *Mozart-Bibliographie, 1986–1991 mit Nachträgen zur Mozart-Bibliographie bis 1985.* Kassel et al.: Bärenreiter, 1992.

S033. Baron, John H. *Chamber Music. A Research and Information Guide.* (Music Research and Information Guides 8; Garland Reference Library of the Humanities 704) New York and London: Garland Publishing, Inc., 1987.

S034. Birch, Courtney. *Russian Literature on Music in the Music Library of the University of Virginia. A Handlist of Holdings to June 1989.* Charlottesville, VA: The University of Virginia, 1989.

S035. Birnbaum, Clemens, and Horst Albert Scholz. *Einführung in die Musikliteratur. Eine kommentierte Bibliographie.* 2. überarbeitete und erweiterte Auflage. Berlin: n.p., 1991.

S036. Browne, Richmond. *In Theory Only* 3/7–11 (10.1977–2.1978) viii, 170 pp. Cover Title: "Index of Music Theory in the United States 1955–1970".

S037. Dell'Antonio, Andrew and Geoffrey Chew. "Dissertation Abstract Bulletin" http://www.rhbnc.ac.uk/Music/Archive/Disserts/index.html. Consulted up to no. 8 (1.3.1996).

S038. Diamond, Harold J. *Music Analyses. An Annotated Guide to the Literature.* New York: Schirmer; Toronto: Collier Macmillan Canada; New York et al.: Maxwell Macmillan International, 1991.

S039. *Doctoral Dissertations in Musicology.* 7th North American edition; 2nd International edition. Edited by Cecil Adkins and Alis Dickinson. Philadelphia: American Musicological Society, International Musicological Society, 1984.

S040. *Doctoral Dissertations in Musicology.* Second Series, First cumulative edition. Edited by Cecil Adkins and Alis Dickinson. Philadelpha: American Musicological Society and The International Musicological Society, 1990.

S041. *Doctoral Dissertations in Musicology. December 1988–November 1989.* Edited by Cecil Adkins and Alis Dickinson. n.p.: American Musicological Society and The International Musicological Society, 1990.

S042. *Doctoral Dissertations in Musicology. December 1989–November 1990.* Edited by Cecil Adkins and Alis Dickinson. n.p.: American Musicological Society, International Musicological Society, 1991.

S043. *Doctoral Dissertations in Musicology. December 1990–November 1991.* Edited by Cecil Adkins and Alis Dickinson. n.p.: American Musicological Society, International Musicological Society, 1992.

S044. *Doctoral Dissertations in Musicology. December 1991–November 1992.* Edited by Cecil Adkins and Alis Dickinson. n.p.: American Musicological Society, International Musicological Society, 1993.

S045. *Doctoral Dissertations in Musicology. December 1992–November 1993.* Edited by Cecil Adkins and Alis Dickinson. n.p.: American Musicological Society, International Musicological Society, 1994.

S046. "Doctoral Dissertations in Musicology-Online" http://www.music.indiana.edu/ddm/. Consulted on 10.12.1996.

S047. Fasman, Mark J. *Brass Bibliography. Sources on the History, Literature, Pedagogy, Performance, and Acoustics of Brass Instruments.* Bloomington and Indianapolis: Indiana University Press, 1990.

S048. Filler, Susan M. *Gustav and Alma Mahler. A Guide to Research.* (Garland Composer Resource Manuals 28; Garland Reference Library of the Humanities 738) New York and London: Garland Publishing Inc., 1989.

S049. Gooch, Bryan N.S., and David Thatcher. *A Shakespeare Music Catalogue.* Odean Long, Associate Editor. Incorporating Material Collected and Contributed by Charles Haywood. 5 vols. Oxford: Clarendon Press, 1991.

S050. Graber, Kenneth. *William Mason (1829–1908). An Annotated Bibliography and Catalog of Works.* (Bibliographies in American Music 13) Warren, MI: Harmonie Park Press, 1989.

S051. Grasberger, Renate. *Bruckner-Bibliographie (bis 1974).* (Anton Bruckner Dokumente und Studien 4) Graz: Akademische Druck- und Verlagsanstalt, 1985.

S052. Gray, Michael. *Classical Music Discographies, 1976–1988: a bibliography.* (Discographies 34) New York, Westport, London: Greenwood Press, 1989.

S053. Gray, Michael H., and Gerald D. Gibson. "Bibliography of Discographies. Classical Music — 1980–1985" *ARSC [Association for Recorded Sound Collections] Journal* 17/1–3 (1985) pp. 53–120.

S054. Green, Richard D. *Index to Composer Bibliographies.* (Detroit Studies in Music Bibliography 53) Detroit: Information Coordinators, 1985.

S055. Heintze, James R. *Igor Stravinsky. An International Bibliography of Theses and Dissertations, 1925–1987.* (Detroit Studies in Music Bibliography 61) Warren, MI: Harmonie Park Press, 1988.

S056. Helms, Siegmund, and Reinhold Schmitt-Thomas. *Musikpädagogische Literatur 1977–1987. Eine Auswahlbibliographie.* Regensburg: Gustav Bosse Verlag, 1988.

S057. Hinson, Maurice. *The Pianist's Reference Guide. A Bibliographical Survey.* Los Angeles [Van Nuys]: Alfred Publishing Co., Inc., 1987.

S058. Hinson, Maurice. *The Piano Teacher's Source Book. An Annotated Bibliography of Books Related to the Piano and Piano Music.* 2nd ed. Melville: Belwin Mills Publishing Corp., 1980.

S059. Jackson, Roland. *Performance Practical, Medieval to Contemporary. A Bibliographic Guide.* (Music Research Information Guides 9; Garland Reference Library of the Humanities 790) New York and London: Garland Publishing Inc., 1988.

S060. Lee, Eun Young. "Index to Masters Theses for Music Degrees in Korea (1956–1990)" *Currents in Musical Thought* 1 (1991) pp. 483–616.

S061. MacBrien, Nathan and LuAnn Ausloos. "Beethoven Bibliography Database (BBD)" Ira F. Brilliant Center for Beethoven Studies, San Jose State University. [Database maintained in the State University's Library Catalog] Consulted on 10.12.1996.

S062. Namenwirth, Simon Michael. *Gustav Mahler. A Critical Bibliography.* 3 vols. Wiesbaden: Otto Harrassowitz, 1987.

S063. Ossenkop, David. *Hugo Wolf. A Guide to Research.* (Garland Composer Resource Manuals 15; Garland Reference Library of the Humanities 747) New York and London: Garland Publishing Inc., 1988.

S064. Palmieri, Robert. *Piano Information Guide. An Aid to Research.* (Music Research and Information Guides 10; Garland Reference Library of the Humanities 806) New York and London: Garland Publishing Inc., 1989.

S065. "Performance Practice Bibliography" in *PPR—Performance Practice Review* 1–. (1987–). Consulted up to 6/2 (1993).

S066. Rast, Nicholas. "A Checklist of Essays and Reviews by Heinrich Schenker" *Music Analysis* 7/2 (7.1988) pp. 121–32.

S067. "Register of Australian undergraduate theses in music" *Musicology Australia* 8–. (1985–). Consulted up to 18 (1995).

S068. "Register of theses on musical subjects accepted for higher degrees and research projects on music subjects in progress for higher degrees at Australian and New Zealand universities" *Studies in music* 1–. (1967–). Consulted up to [26] (1992).

S069. Saltonstall, Cecilia D., and Henry Saltonstall. *Books about Chamber Music and Other Books of Related Interest.* New York: Amateur Chamber Music Players, Inc., 1986.

S070. Schulz, Ferdinand F. *Pianographie. Klavierbibliographie der lieferbaren Bücher und Periodica sowie der Dissertationen in deutscher, englischer, französischer und italienischer Sprache.* 2. verbesserte und erheblich erweiterte Auflage. Recklinghausen: Piano-Verlag, 1982.

S071. Seaton, Douglass. *The Art Song. A Research and Information Guide.* (Music Research and Information Guides 6; Garland Reference Library of the Humanities 673) New York and London: Garland Publishing Inc., 1987.

S072. Stock, Karl F., Rudolf Heilinger, and Marylène Stock. *Mozart-Bibliographien. Selbständige und versteckte Bibliographien und Nachschlagewerke zu Leben und Werk Wolfgang Amadeus Mozarts, seines Vaters Leopold Mozart und seiner beiden Söhne.* (Bibliographieverzeichnisse großer Österreicher in Einzelbänden) Graz: Stock & Stock, 1991.

S073. Vondenhoff, Bruno, and Eleonore Vondenhoff, eds. *Ergänzungsband zur Gustav Mahler Dokumentation, Sammlung Eleonore Vondenhoff. Materialen zu Leben und Werk* (Publikationen des Instituts für Österreichische Musikdokumentation 9) Tutzing: Hans Schneider, 1983.

S074. Vondenhoff, Bruno, and Eleonore Vondenhoff, eds. *Gustav Mahler Dokumentation, Sammlung Eleonore Vondenhoff. Materialien zu Leben und Werk.* (Publikationen des Instituts für Österreichische Musikdokumentation 4) Tutzing: Hans Schneider, 1978.

S075. Walter, Horst. "Haydn-Bibliographie 1973–1983" *Haydn-Studien* 5/4 (12.1985) pp. 205–93.

S076. Walther, Hermann. *Bibliographie der Musikbuchreihen 1886–1990.* (Catalogus musicus XII) Kassel [et al.]: Bärenreiter, 1991.

S077. Wenk, Arthur. *Analyses of Nineteenth- and Twentieth-Century Music: 1940–1985.* (MLA Index and Bibliography Series 25) Boston: Music Library Association, 1987.

Indexing and Abstracting Services

General

S078. *ArticleFirst.* [database] [Dublin, OH:] OCLC. Consulted up to 8.12.1996.

S079. *Book Review Digest.* [database] n.p.: The H.W. Wilson Company. Consulted 1.1983–11.1996.

S080. *Canadian Business and Current Affairs Index.* [database] [Toronto: Micromedia Limited.] Consulted 1982–9.1996.

S081. *[ProQuest] Dissertation Abstracts Ondisc.* [CD-ROM] Ann Arbor: University Microfilms International, 1989– . Consulted 1861–9.1996 [5 discs].

S081.5. The Electronic Newstand, Inc. http://www.enews.com/

S082. *FastDoc.* [database] [Dublin, OH:] OCLC Online Computer Library Center Inc. Consulted up to 8.12.1996.

S083. *[ProQuest] General Periodicals Ondisc.* [CD-ROM] Research I ed. 1986– . Ann Arbor: University Microfilms, Inc., 1987– . Consulted 1986–6.1995.

S084. *Infotrac.* [database] Foster City, CA: Information Access Co. Consulted up to 11.1996.

S085. *Internationale Bibliographie der Zeitschriftenliteratur aus allen Gebieten des Wissens = International Bibliography of Periodical Literature covering all Field of Knowledge = Bibliographie internationale de la litterature periodique dans tous les domaines de la connaissance.* 1– . 1963– . Osnabrück: Felix Dietrich Verlag, 1965– . Consulted up to 1995.

S086. *Readers Guide Abstracts Index.* [database] n.p.: The H.W. Wilson Co. Consulted 1.1983–9.1996.

S087. *UnCover.* [database] Consulted Fall 1988– .

Subject

S088. *Applied Science and Technology Index.* [CD-ROM] [New York:] The H.W. Wilson Company; [Norwood, MA:] Silverplatter Information. Consulted up to 9.1996.

S089. Arneson, Arne Jon. *The Music Educator's Journal: Cumulative Index 1914–1987. Including the Music Supervisors' Bulletin and the Music Supervisors' Journal.* Stevens Point: Index House, 1987.

S090. *Art Index.* 1– . 1929– . New York: The H.W. Wilson Company, 1933– .

S091. [Instituto de Bibliografía Musical.] *Artículos sobre música en revistas españolas de humanidades.* 1–.(1982–). Consulted no. 1.

S092. *British Humanities Index.* Version 4.0. [CD-ROM] [London:] Bowker-Saur Ltd. Consulted 1992–1996.

S093. Cohen, H. Robert, Sylvia L'Ecuyer Lacroix, and Jacques Léveillé. *Les Gravures musicales dans l'Illustration 1843–1899.* Préface by Barry S. Brook. 3 vols. (La Vie musicale en France au dix-neuvième siècle. Etudes et documents) Québec: Les Presses de l'Université Laval, 1983.

S094. Eagle, Charles T. and Donald Hodges. "C.A.I.R.S.S. [Computer-Assisted Information Retrieval Service System] for Music" University of Texas at Austin Library. TELNET: 129.115.50.1 [the Library]. Consulted in 10.1996.

S094.5. *The Education Index.* [database] n.p.: The H.W. Wilson Company. Consulted 6.1983–1.1997.

S095. Hassen, Marjorie, and Mark Germer. *American Musicological Society: Index to the Papers, Bulletin, and Journal, 1936–1987.* n.p.: American Musicological Society, 1990.

S096. *Humanities and Social Sciences Index.* [database] n.p.: The H.W. Wilson Company. Consulted 2.1983–9.1996.

S097. "*Journal of the Arnold Schoenberg Institute.* Series I. Index to Volumes I–VIII (1976–1984)" *Journal of the Arnold Schoenberg Institute* 9/1 (6.1986) pp. 114–23.

S098. *Library Literature.* [database] n.p.: The H.W. Wilson Company. Consulted 12.1984–11.1996.

S099. *MLA Bibliography.* [database] [Norwood, MA:] Silverplatter International N.V. Consulted 1981–8.1996.

S100. "MTO—Music Theory Online Dissertation Index" http://boethius.music.ucsb.edu/mto/docs/diss.index. Consulted on 10.12. 1996.

S101. McIntosh, R.D. "Music Education Resource Base including the Canadian Music Index" University of Victoria. http://www.ffa.ucalgary.ca/merb/. Consulted up to 10.1996.

S102. *muse (MUsic SEarch).* [CD-ROM] Baltimore, MD: National Information Services Corporation. Consulted 1969–1993.

S103. *The Music Index.* 1– . 1949– . Detroit: Information Services Incorporated, 1949– . [publication information varies].

S104. *The Music Index 1979–1993 on CD-ROM.* [Warren, MI:] Harmonie Park Press, 1996.

S105. Music Research Information Network. *Register of Music Research Students in Great Britain and Northern Ireland, with Thesis Subjects and General Areas of Study.* Christchurch: The Author, March 1988.

S106. Music Research Information Network. *Register of Music Research*

Students in Great Britain and Northern Ireland 1988. [Supplement.] Christchurch: The Author, June 1988.

S107. *PsycLIT. Chapters & Books.* [database] [Norwood, MA:] American Psychological Association and Silverplatter International N.V. Consulted 1.1987–6.1996.

S108. *PsycLIT. Journal Articles.* [database] [Norwood, MA:] American Psychological Association and Silverplatter International N.V. Consulted 1.1974–12.1989; 1.1990–6.1996.

S109. *RILM Abstracts of Music Literature.* [database] n.p.: Rilm Abstracts. Consulted up to 9.1996.

Newspaper Indexes

S110. *Canadian NewsDisc.* [CD-ROM] (Infomart on CD) [Don Mills, ON: Southam Electronic Pub.] Consulted up to 7.1996.

S111. *The New York Times [Index].* [database] [New York:] The New York Times Company. Consulted 1.1994–8.12.1996.

Indexes to Material in Collections

S112. *The Columbia Granger's World of Poetry.* [CD-ROM] [New York:] Columbia University Press, 1995.

Miscellaneous

S112.5. ABC Bücherdienst GmbH. http://www.telebuch.de. Consulted up to 2.1997.

S113. Amazon.com Books [Bookstore on the World Wide Web]. http://www.amazon.com.

S114. *The American Brahms Society Newsletter* 1–. (1983–). Consulted up to 14/1 (Spring 1996).

S115. "Books Recently Published" *Notes.* Consulted up to 53/1 (9.1996). [compilors vary].

S116. *Cum notis variorum. Newsletter of the Music Library, University of California (Berkeley)* nos. 1–136(?). (3.1976–10.1989). Consulted 3.1982–10.1989.

S117. Green, Alan. "In the Pipeline: Research in Music Librarianship" *MLA [=Music Library Association] Newsletter.* Consulted up to issue no. 106 (9.–10.1996).

S118. Green, Alan. "Members' Publications" *MLA [=Music Library Association] Newsletter.* Consulted up to issue no. 107 (11.–12.1996).

S119. [Library of the JBS [Japan Brahms Society]. "Brahms Bibliography" Part 1– .] in *Akai Harinezumi [=] Zum roten Igel* no. 18– . (1988–). Consulted up to Part 8 (1995) [in no. 25].

S120. *Music Reference Services Quarterly* 1– . (1992–). Consulted up to 4/4 (1996).

S121. "Pepper Music Network." http://www.jwpepper.com. Consulted 11.1996.

S122. "Publications Received" *Journal of the American Musicological Society.* Consulted up to 49/2 (Summer 1996).

S123. "Recent Publications in Music" *Fontis artis musicae.* Consulted up to 42/4 (10.–12.1995). [compilors vary].

Part I

Historical and Research Information

A. General Studies—Life and Works

All material in this section discusses Brahms's life and music in general, or reviews materials that do. Annotations are only provided when this isn't the case, when additional types of information are included, or when comment is necessary regarding material's presentation or significance.

1. Monographs and Dissertations

Chronology included: 3211, 3217.
Juvenile literature: 3208, 3213.

3198. *The Hour* (New York) [1] (1880). Report on 117? (H. Deiters. "Johannes Brahms." (1880)). [from compiler]
   (a) *reprint: "Johannes Brahms" *Musical Record* (Boston) [no. ?] (11.1880) p. 115.

3199. Audiberti, Marie-Louise. *Brahms. Un génie ordinaire.* (Collection biographique) Paris: Plon, 1991. 293, [1] pp. ill., facsim., notes. Focuses on the life and Brahms's milieu; includes comments on Brahms the man and composer.

3200. *Boltz, Paula Maria. "The Life and Times of Brahms As Reflected in Selected Solo Vocal Works: Supplementary to a Full Recital of

His Songs" M.A. diss., Texas Woman's University, 1970. 92 pp.
ill., notes.

3201. *Brahms, Johannes. *Johannnes Brahms: Life and Letters.* Styra
       Avins, comp. Oxford: Oxford University Press, 1997. 784 pp. ill.,
       mus. Brahms's life as seen through a comprehensive collection of
       over 550 letters, linked with narrative passages. First comprehen-
       sive English language collection of Brahms's letters. [from pub-
       lisher's catalogue]
       (d) Avins, Styra. " "A Jolly End to My Summer." Gustav Wendt
       and the Clarinet Sonatas" *The American Brahms Society
       Newsletter* 9/2 (Autumn 1991) pp. 6–7. facsim. only. Presents
       a postcard from Brahms to Gustav Wendt, Bad Ischl, 9.1894,
       on the occasion of meeting Mühlfeld and regarding Op. 120;
       includes an overview of the friendship of Brahms and Wendt.

3202. *Bruyr, José. *Brahms.* ([Collections microcosme.] Solfèges 25)
       Paris: Editions du seuil, 1991. 186 pp. ill., mus., ind., discog. Re-
       issue of 6 (J. Bruyr. *Brahms.* (1965)). [from S031]
       (b) *Japanese translation by Osamu Honda (of 1965 edition?):
       [Brahms.] (Eien no ongakuka 12) Tokyo: Hakusuisha, 1970.
       291 pp.

3203. *Carëva, Ekaterina. "Iogannes Brams" Ph.D. diss., Istoriia muzyki,
       Gosudarstvennaia Konservatoriia Moskva, 1990.
       (d) *Carëva. (Klassiki mirovoĭ muzykal'noĭ kul'tury) Moskva:
       Muzyka, 1990. 46 pp. notes. Analyses Brahms the man and
       composer; includes selected translations of Brahms's letters.
       [from S102]

3203.5. *Componistenreeks Brahms.* (Toonkunst: muziek en opera 924)
       Bloemendaal: Uitgeverij Gottmer/Becht/Aramith, 1987.

3204. *Cristani, Alberto. *Invito all'ascolto di Johannes Brahms.* (Invito
       all'ascolto 26) Milano: Mursia, 1996. 332 pp. ind., notes.

3205. *Davies, Marion. "Brahms" Mus.M. diss., Oberlin College, 1931.
       3, 97, 3 pp. ill., mus., notes.

3206. *Erhardt, Ludwik. *Brahms.* 1. vyd. Hilda Holinova, trans. Ján
       Krížik, ed. Bratislava: Opus, 1986. 296 pp. ill., notes. Slovak
       translation of 19 (Erhardt. *Brahms.* (1969) (?)).

3207. Geiringer, Karl, in collaboration with Irene Geiringer. *Brahms.*
His Life and Work. 3rd edition, revised and enlarged with a New
Appendix: "Brahms as a Reader and Collector." "Paperback edition. (Da Capo Press Music Reprint Series; Da Capo Paperback)
New York: Da Capo Press, 1982. xv, 397, [14] pp. ill., notes. Reissue of 25 (K. Geiringer. *Brahms. His Life and Work.* 3rd ed., revised and enlarged (1982)).
     (c) Geiringer, Karl. "Johannes Brahms. The Man and the Artist"
     (The Brahms Sesquicentennial [1, 2]) *Ovation* 4/4,5 (5.,6.;
     1983) pp. 12–16, 20–22. ill. An excerpt from 25 (K. Geirin-
     ger. *Brahms. His Life and Work.* 3rd ed., revised and enlarged
     (1982)).

3208. *Goss, Madeleine, and Robert Haven Schauffler. *Brahms. Un
maestro en la música.* (Coleccion austral 670) Buenos Aires:
Espasa-Calpe, Argentina, S.A., 1947. Juvenile literature: historical fiction. Translation of 28 (Goss. *Brahms. The Master.* (1943)).
[from compiler]
*also: Madrid: 1947.

3209. *Grasberger, F[ranz]. *Iogannes Brahms.* V.G. Shnitke, trans.
Moscow: Muzyka, 1980. 71 pp. Translation of 30 ? (Grasberger.
Das kleine Brahmsbuch. (1973)). [from compiler]

3210. Höcker, Karla. *Johannes Brahms: Begegnung mit dem Menschen.*
Mit 79 zeitgenössischen Bildern, Notenbeispielen und Dokumenten sowie einem Geleitwort von Dietrich Fischer-Dieskau.
Berlin: Erika Klopp Verlag, 1983. 275, [2] pp. ill., facsim., mus.,
fig., ind., notes. Focuses on the life and Brahms's milieu; includes
discussion on the musical forms that Brahms composed in, and information on monies received for each work. Based on standard
literature.
*"Ungekurzte Ausgabe": Mit zahlreichen Abbildungen. n.p.:
Deutscher Taschenbuch, 1986. 277 pp.
     (b) *Finnish translation by Seppo Heikinheimo (of ? Ausgabe):
     Johannes Brahms: vapaa vaeltaja. Rajamaki: Hellas-Piano,
     1984. 207, [44] pp. ill., notes.

3211. Hofmann, Renate, and Kurt Hofmann. *Johannes Brahms.
Zeittafel zu Leben und Werk.* (Publikationen des Instituts für
Österreichische Musikdokumentation 8) Tutzing: Hans Schnei-
der, 1983. vi, 286, [8] pp. ill., ind. A chronology of Brahms from

time of his parents' birth until his death, dating both life events
and composing activity; includes list of first performances for his
works. Based on standard literature.

3212. Holmes, Paul. *Brahms: His Life and Times.* (Midas Life and
Times of the Great Composers) Southborough, Kent: The Baton
Press, 1984. 163 pp. ill., facsim., ind., notes. Much use of the
Briefwechsel as source material; Brahms the man is an important
part of this work.
  *American edition: New York: Hippocrene Books, 1984.
  *also: (The Illustrated Lives of the Great Composers) London,
  New York: Omnibus Press, 1987.
  (b) *Chinese translation by Chih-hao Kuo (of ? edition): Holmes.
  Pu-la-mu-ssu. Ti 1 pan. (Wei ta tso chu chia chun hsiang i shu
  sheng huo 8) Tai-pei shih: Chih ku wen hua ku fen yu hsien
  kung ssu, 1995. xiii, 207 pp. ill., mus.

3213. *Ikeda, Riyako. *Sarang kwa konoe: Puraamsu.* ([Junior Music Li-
brary] 13) Soul: Segwang Omak Chulpansa, 1984. 152 pp. ill.
[from S031]

3214. *Johannes Brahms.* Imogen Fellinger, ed. (Wege der Forschung
[no. ?]) Darmstadt: Wissenschaftliche Buchgesellschaft, 1986 (?).

3215. *Johannes Brahms: Leben und Werk.* Christiane Jacobsen, ed.
Wiesbaden: Breitkopf & Härtel, 1983. 200 pp. ill., facsim., fig.,
ind. Life and works with individual chapters by different authors.
Contains: 3410, 3445, 3519, 3637, 3945, 4096, 4273, 4443, 4465,
4656, 4762, 4770, 5012, 5015, 5028, 5037, 5108, 5143.d.ii.,
5389.

3216. Keys, Ivor. *Johannes Brahms.* Portland: Amadeus Press, 1989.
viii, 310 pp. ill., facsim., mus., notes. Based on primary source
materials and standard literature; includes comments on Brahms's
worth and style.
  also: London: Christopher Helm, 1989.
  (e) i) report (on Portland edition): Brodbeck, David [Lee]. "Two
  New Brahms Biographies" *The American Brahms Society
  Newsletter* 9/1 (Spring 1991) pp. 7–8. Includes review of
  3217.
  (d) expanded: *Notes* 48/1 (9.1991) pp. 86–90.
  (e) ii) report (on Portland edition): Mellers, Wilfred. "Fortitude

without Faith" *Times Literary Supplement* no. 4,537 (16.–22.3.1990) p. 285. Includes review of 3217.

3217. MacDonald, Malcolm. *Brahms.* 1st American ed. [(Master Musicians)] New York: Schirmer Books, 1990. xiii, [1], 490 pp. ill., facsim., mus., ind., notes. Includes 5 appendixes: chronology, works list, guide to persons, "Who wrote the A major Trio?". Significantly different approach taken in studying Brahms the composer and his place in music history.
*Paperback edition: 1993. xiii, 490, 8 pp. ind., notes only.
*also: London: J.M. Dent & Sons Ltd., 1990. [448, 8 pp.]
*1st Paperback edition, revised with updatings: (The Dent Master Musicians) 1993. xiii, 490, [8] pp. ill., mus., ind., notes only.
(e) reports (of New York edition): see 3216.e.

3218. *May, Florence. *Johannes Brahms. Die Geschichte seines Lebens.* Foreword by Carl Dahlhaus. München: Matthes & Seitz, 1983. ix, 308, 357, [6] pp. ill., notes, discog. New edition of 48.b. (F. May. *Johannes Brahms.* (1911)).

3219. *Molnár, Antal. *Brahms.* 2. kiad. (Zenei kiskönyvtár) Budapest: Gondolat, 1983. 217 pp. ill., ind. New edition of 53 (Molnár. *Johannes Brahms.* (1959)).

3220. Röttgers, B. "Max Kalbeck: Johannes Brahms" *Neue Musik-Zeitung* 29/9 (6.2.1908) pp. 195–98. mus., notes. Report on 39B (M. Kalbeck. *Johannes Brahms. II. Erster Halbband. 1862–1868.* (1907)).

3221. *Rostand, Claude. *Brahms.* (Collection les indispensables de la musique) Paris: Edition Fayard, 1990. 725 pp. notes. New issue of 76.d. (?) (Rostand. *Brahms.* (1978)).
(b) *Italian translation by Paolo Donati (of 76.d.?): Rostand. *Brahms.* Milano: Rusconi, 1986. 742 pp. ill., ind.

3222. *Ryu, Yon-hyong. *Buramsu : susung ui anae Kullara yosawa ui yonjong.* (Umak chunchu mungo. Segye umakka ui chakpum kwa insaeng ' 7) Soul : Umak Chunchusa, 1993. 206 pp.

3223. Schmelzer, Hans-Jürgen. *Johannes Brahms. Zwischen Ruhm und Einsamkeit. Eine Biographie.* Mit einem Werkverzeichnis und acht Bildtafeln. Tübingen: Heliopolis, 1983. 300 pp. ill., facsim., notes. Focuses on Brahms the man and his milieu.

3224. *Schmidt, Christian Martin. *Johannes Brahms*. Mit 48 Noten-beispielen und 23 Abbildungen. (Reclams Musikführer) Stuttgart: P. Reclam, 1994. 356 pp. ill., mus., ind., notes. Related (?) to 5044.

3225. Terenzio, Vincenzo. *Lettura di Brahms*. Bari: Mario Adda Editore, 1985. 103 pp. mus., notes. Focuses on the works; includes comment on the Brahms "school."

3226. Thomas, Wolfgang. [Wolfgang Alexander Thomas-San-Galli] "Johannes Brahms. Von Max Kalbeck" *Der Merker* (Wien) 3/2 (1.1912) pp. 75–77. Review of 39C (M. Kalbeck. *Johannes Brahms. III. Zweiter Halbband. 1881–1885.* (1912)).

3227. "A True Brahms Estimate" *Musical Courier* 62/11 (Whole no. 1616) (15.3.1911) p. 23. Reports on 23 (J. Fuller-Maitland. *Brahms.* (1911)).

3228. Walker, Ernest. "Richard Specht's "Brahms"" *Monthly Musical Record* 60/714 (2.6.1930) pp. 167–68. notes. Report on 82.b. (R. Specht. *Johannes Brahms.* (1930)).

3229. Walker, Ernest. "Walter Niemann's Brahms" *Monthly Musical Record* 60/712 (1.4.1930) pp. 103–04. notes. Review of 61.b. (W. Niemann. *Brahms.* (1929)).

3230. *Wirth, H[elmut]. *Johannes Brahms. Lebensbericht mit Bildern und Dokumenten.* Kassel: n.p., n.d. (?)

3231. Woerner, Gert, comp. *Kleine Bettlektüre für alle, die Brahms lieben.* Bern, München: Scherz Verlag, 1983. 118 pp. notes. Anecdotal biography; consists of excerpts from 4.d. (L. Berger. *Von Menschen Johannes Brahms.* (1959)); 39.a. (M. Kalbeck. *Johannes Brahms.* (1976)); 618.a. (J.V. Widmann. *Johannes Brahms in Erinnerungen.* (1898)); 765.d. (K. Huschke. *Frauen um Brahms.* (1936)); 984.a. and 1266 (K. Huschke. *Unsere Tonmeister unter Einander.* (1928)); 959 (*Klaus Groth und die Musik.* (1933)); 968.a. (E. Hanslick. *Aus meinem Leben* (1894)); 991 (R. Heuberger. *Erinnerungen an Johannes Brahms.* (1971)); 1170 (B. Litzmann, ed. *Clara Schumann.* (1902–08)); 1179 (C. Schumann. *Clara Schumann. Johannes Brahms.* (1927)); 1292 (Brahms. *Jo-*

hannes Brahms und Mathilde Wesendonck. (1943)); and Klaus Mann. *Symphonie Pathétique. Ein Tschaikowsky-Roman.* (München: Ellermann Verlag, 1979).
See also 3297, 3712, 3739, 3743, 3832, 3904, 4132.
See also "Brahms in Fiction" in Part VI.B.

2. Serial and Section Materials

Humorous literature: 3236, 3240, 3243, 3273.5.
Juvenile literature: 3242, 3257, 3260, 3266.

3232. *Musical Courier* 25 (10.10.1892) p. 6.

3233. *Musical News* (London) 40 (1911) pp. 265–66.
(a) *reprint: *The Musical Leader [and Concertgoer]* 21/22 (1911) pp. 24–25.

3234. *Wiener Signale* 2 (1878/79) p. 323. ill.

3235. Abbiati, Franco. "Poesia di Brahms" in Abbiati. *Storia della musica. [Vol. 4.] L'Ottocento.* Milano: Officine Grafiche Aldo Garzanti, Editore, 1957. pp. 631–46. ill., facsim., mus., notes. Focuses on the works and Brahms the composer.
[reworked:] in Abbiati. *Storia della musica. [Vol. 3.] L'Ottocento.* (Collezione maggiore Garzanti) Officine Grafiche Garzanti, 1967. pp. 675–94. mus. omitted.

3236. Barber, David W. "Brahms" in Barber. *Bach, Beethoven, and The Boys. Music History As It Ought To Be Taught.* [Preface by Anthony Burgess] Toronto: Sound and Vision Publishing Ltd., 1986. pp. 90–92. ill., notes. A "witty and irreverant" look at life, focuses mostly on pre-1862.

3237. Becker, Heinz. "Brahms, Johannes" in *The New Grove Dictionary of Music and Musicians.* Stanley Sadie, ed. London: Macmillan Publishers Limited; Washington, DC: Grove's Dictionaries of Music Inc.; Hong Kong: Peninsula Publishers Limited, 1980. vol. 3, pp. 155–90. ill., facsim., notes. Includes comments on Brahms the man and his interest in early music.
(b) *Italian translation [(of above or of d.i. (?))] : Becker. "Brahms" in Becker and Deryck Cooke. *Maestri del tardo*

romanticismo: Brahms, Bruckner. (Guida alla musica) Milano: Ricordi; Firenze: Giunti, 1992. pp. 7–63.

(d) i) *amended: Becker [and Margit L. McCorkle]. "Johannes Brahms" in Deryck Cooke, Heinz Becker, John Clapham, and Eric Sams. *The New Grove Late Romantic Masters: Bruckner, Brahms, Dvořák, Wolf.* ([The New Grove Dictionary of Music and Musicians] The Composer Biography Series) London: Macmillan, 1985. pp. [75]–201. Paperback ed.: 1985. adds ind. McCorkle is responsible for the revision of the works list, she assists Becker in amending article's body.

also: New York and London: W.W. Norton & Company, 1985.

*Paperback edition: 1985

(b) *German translation (of ? edition): Becker. *Brahms.* (The New Grove—Die großen Komponisten) Stuttgart: J.B. Metzlersche Verlagsbuchhandlung, 1993. 264 pp.

(d) ii) Becker. "Johannes Brahms" in *Heritage of Music. Volume III. The Nineteenth-Century Legacy.* Michael Raeburn, Alan Kendall, Series Editors; Heinz Becker, Martin Cooper, Consultant Editors, vol. III. Oxford, New York: Oxford University Press, 1989. pp. 183–209. ill. (also p. [182]), facsim. (also before title page). Discusses life up to 1860's, then jumps to just before death.

(d) iii) parody: see 3243.

3238. *Bekker, Peter O. E., Jr. *The Romantic Era.* (The Life, Times & Music Series) New York: Friedman/Fairfax Publishers, 1992. 72 pp. ill., ind., notes.

3239. *Bertelsmann Konzertführer: Komponisten und ihre Werke.* Christoph Hahn and Siegmar Hohl, eds. Gütersloh: Bertelsmann Lexikon, 1993. 639 pp.

3240. Borge, Victor, and Robert Sherman. "Johannes Brahms" in Borge and Sherman. *Victor Borge's My Favorite Comedies in Music.* New York [et al]: Franklin Watts, 1980. pp. [72]–[[82]]. notes. Gives the highlights of Brahms's life, with many anecdotes.

*also: New York: Dorset Press, 1980.

* issue: 1992.

*1st Paperback edition (of Dorset Press edition): New York: M. Evans, 1994.

3241. *"Brahms" in *Classic Composers*. Anna Maria Mascheroni, ed. Leicester, England : Magna Books, 1991. ill.

3242. *Brownell, David. *[A Coloring Book of] Great Composers: from Brahms to Bartok*. Santa Barbara: Bellerophon Books, 1984. 48 pp.

3243. Burnham, Howard, and Richard Butterworth. "Your Highness Brahms (1833–1897)" in Burnham and Butterworth. *Grones Dictionary of Music or A Golden Treasury of Musical Rubbish or Misleading Lives of the Great Composers*. [Foreword by Fritz Spiegl. Richard Butterworth, illus.] Ampleforth: Emerson Edition, 1978. pp. 15–16. ill. A highly irreverent and pun-filled overview of Brahms's life.

3244. *Confalonieri, Giulio. "Tre romantici introversi" in *Guida alla musica* Bd. II. Milano: Casa editrice academia, 1953. ind. Discusses Mendelssohn, Schumann and Brahms. [from S031]

3245. *Della Corte, Andrea, and Guido Pannain. *Storia della musica*. 2 vols. Torino: Unione tipografico-editrice torinese, 1936.
   *2. ed.: 3 vols. 1942.
   *issue: 1944.
   *3. ed. molto amplicata: 1952.
   *4. ed. riv. e amplicata: "Brahms e gli ultimi ottocentisti" in vol. 3. 1964.

3246. Deppisch, Walter. "Das Leben eines großen Tonsetzers" *Die Welt* Hamburg-Ausgabe nr. 106 (7.5.1983) "Geistige Welt" (7./8.5. 1983) p. [I]. ill. Focuses on life pre-1862.
   (b) *Spanish translation: Deppisch. "La Vida de un gran compositor" *Humboldt. Zeitschrift für die iberische Welt* 24/79 (1983) pp. 68–72.

3247. Dunwoody, Michael. "From "The Brahms Suite"" *The Antigonish Review* no. 89 (Spring 1992) pp. 49–51. A set of 6 poems: poet sees himself as Brahms at various stages in Brahms's life; poems also reflect on Brahms and Clara Schumann and the experience of Brahms's music.

3248. *Gal, Hans. "Brahms" in *La musica*. 2 parts in 6 vol. Edited by Guido Maria Gatti and Alberto Basso. [Torino:] Unione tipografico-editrice torinese, 1966–1971. in *Parte Prima. Enciclopedia storica.* vol. 1, pp. 557–93. ill., mus., facsim.

3249. Gal, Hans. "Brahms, Johannes" Annalisa Gersoni, trans.; bibliography and works catalogue edited by the editor. in *Dizionario enciclopedico universale della musica e dei musicisti. Le biografie.* Alberto Basso, ed. Torino: UTET, 1985. vol. 1., pp. 651–75. notes, works list (pp. 660–73). Includes comments on Brahms the artist and composer and his historical position.

    (d) *revised (?): in *Dizionario degli interpreti musicali (musica classica e operistica).* (I Dizionari TEA-UTET) Milano: TEA, 1993. adds discog. [from *Fontes artis musicae* 43 (1996) p. 56]

3250. "Giovanni Brahms" *Gazzetta musicale di Milano* 34/11 (16.3. 1879) pp. 97–98. Includes comment on Brahms's style and a descriptive analysis of Op. 68.

3251. Gray, Anne. "Johannes Brahms" in Gray. *The Popular Guide to Classical Music.* Secaucus, NJ: Carol Publishing Group, 1993. pp. 63–65. ind., notes. "A Birch Lane Press Book." Focuses on life before 1860; includes comments on style, Brahms the man, and the symphonies and piano concertos.

    Paperback ed.(?): Secaucus, NJ: 1996. "A Citadel Press Book." also: London: Hale, 1994.

3252. Hall, Charles J. *A Nineteenth-Century Musical Chronicle. Events, 1800–1899.* (Music Reference Collection 21) Westport, CT and London: Greenwood Press, 1989. [10], 374 pp. ind. Charts musical events year-by-year, in the context of political, social and cultural history. Within each year there are births, deaths, biographical highlights, music written and more. The *New Grove Dictionary of Music and Musicians* [see 3237 for citation] is the authority for music history information.

3253. Holmes, Robert, with additions by Bruce Carr. "Johannes Brahms" in 5255.5. pp. [3–40, 61–66.] ill., facsim., notes.

3254. *Hutchings, A.J.B. "The Nineteenth Century" in *Classical and Romantic.* Alec Robertson and Denis Stevens, eds. (The Pelican History of Music 3; Pelican Books A494) Baltimore: Penguin Books, 1968. mus., notes.

(a) *reprint: Harmondsworth, Middlesex: Penguin, 1978. adds discog.
*reprint with revised bibliography: Harmondsworth, Middlesex; New York: Penguin Books, 1980. adds ind.
*another issue: 1986.

(b) *Spanish translation (of ? edition): *Desde el clasicismo hasta el siglo XX.* (Historia general de la música 3; Colección fundamentos 5) Madrid: Ediciones ISTMO, n.d.
*7. edition: 1985.

3255. *Iliuţ, Vasile. *De la Wagner la contemporani, volumul 1: muzica germană şi austriacă in a doua jumătate a secolului al XIX-lea.* (SC »Universul«) Bucureşti: Editura musicală a uniunîi compozitorilor şi muzicologilor din România, 1992. 267 or 270 pp. mus., notes.

3256. Jack, Adrian. "Johannes Brahms" (Composer of the Month) *BBC Music Magazine* 3/2 (10.1994) pp. 27–31. ill., facsim., notes., discog. Includes timeline, and comments on Brahms's place in music history, Brahms the composer and his influence into the 20th century.

3257. *"Johannes Brahms" in *Composers.* Lori Vidmar, ed. [Montrose, CO: Morgan Elementary School, 1989.] Juvenile literature. [from compiler]

3258. "Johannes Brahms" *The Etude and Musical World* 15/2 (2.1897) p. 42. ill. Includes comments on his reception, his standing and his style.

3259. *"Johannes Brahms" in *The Immortals of Music: Biographic Stories of the World's Greatest Composers and Conductors.* Willam S. Meyerson, comp. and ed. [n.p., 19–?].

3260. "Johannes Brahms" in *Johannes Brahms 1833–1897. Gustav Mahler 1869–1911.* Reference edition. (The Great Composers. Their Lives and Times) Freeport, NY: Marshall Cavendish Corporation, 1990. pp. 6–84. ill., facsim., mus., ind., notes. Focus is on appreciating the music, with listening guides for Opp. 68, 77 and 83. Includes comments on Brahms and Clara Schumann, the "New German School of Music" controversy, and biographies of Brahms interpreters von Karajan, Haitink, and Szeryng (but nothing on them performing Brahms's works). The background

Part I

section on the times includes articles on German immigration to the United States, Bismarck, and the rise of middleclass tourism.

3261. *"Johannes Brahms" Josephine Upson Cady, trans. *Music Review* (Chicago) 3 (10.1893) pp. 12–14. Excerpts in translation of 149 (?) (R. Heuberger. *Deutsche Kunst- und Musikzeitung* (Wien) (1893)). [from compiler]

3262. *"Johannes Brahms" *Presto* (Chicago) 11/19 (7.3.1895) p. 11.

3263. [Diaz, George L.] "Johannes Brahms" in *Tragedies & Triumphs. Portraits and Profiles of the Greatest Composers.* Hialeah, FL: The Author, 1989. pp. 60–[61]. ill. Focuses on life before 1862.

3264. *Kendall, Alan. *The Chronicle of Classical Music: an Intimate Diary of the Lives and Music of the Great Composers.* London: Thames and Hudson, 1994. 288 pp. ind., notes, discog.

3265. *Kobbe, Gustav. "Johannes Brahms" *Looker-On* 4 (1.1897) pp. 549–65.

3266. *McLeish, Kenneth, and Valerie McLeish. "Brahms" in McLeish. *The Oxford First Companion to Music.* Oxford: Oxford University Press, 1982. p. [F7] ill., mus. issues: 1982–84, 1986. Includes listening suggestions; for children.

3267. *Meilensteine der Musik.* Hans A. Neunzig, ed. 3 Vols. Dortmund: Harenberg Verlag, 1991. ill., facsim. Work is arranged chronologically; Brahms entries include excerpts from contemporaries' writings on Brahms as marginalia.
Vol. 2 (Wolfgang Sandner wrote pp. 73–75, all the rest by Neunzig): pp. 29–30, 54–60, 66–68, 73–75, 79–82, 105–08, 128–31, 191–93. Discussions of Opp. 8, 15, 45, 56a, 68, 98, 121, Ungarische Tänze [McCorkle WoO 1]; comments on Brahms and Schubert, Beethoven; Brahms and Biblical texts; Brahms's last days.
Vol. 3 (by Neunzig): "Johannes Brahms" in "Komponistenporträts" pp. 242–43. Includes comment on Brahms's place in music history.

3268. *Mila, Massimo. "Johannes Brahms. (1833–1897)" in Mila. *Cent'anni di musica moderna.* Torino: EDT, 1992. pp. 65–76. Another issue of 178.a.a. (Mila. (1981)).

3269. Morris, Lydia T. "Johannes Brahms. Born 1833." in Morris. *Fa-*

mous Musical Composers. Being Biographies of Eminent Musicians. London: T. Fisher Unwin, 1891. pp. [255]–256. ill. [p. 254]. Focuses on life up to the 1860's.

3270. Neunzig, Hans A. "Johannes Brahms" in Neunzig. *Lebensläufe der deutschen Romantik. Komponisten.* München: Kindler Verlag GmbH, 1984. pp. 191–230. ill. Focuses on life, mostly on Brahms and Clara Schumann.

3271. "1833-The Real Brahms-1897" (The Etude Master Study Page) *The Etude* 31/1 (1.1913) pp. 25–26. ill., facsim., notes. Includes comments on Brahms the man; Brahms as pianist and teacher (Brahms as teacher from 48? (F. May. *The Life of Johannes Brahms.* (1905))); and a suggested Brahms programme.

3272. *Pinter, Lotte. "Johannes Brahms—Aufstieg eines Genies" *Chormagazin. Mitteilungen des Österreichisches Arbeitersängerbundes* 2 (1983) pp. 2–4.

3273. *Searles, Beatrice. *History of the Piano. Its Music and Its Composers.* [1st ed. n.p., 19–?].
2nd edition: "Johannes Brahms (Germany) 1833–1897". Phoenix: Central District, Arizona State Music Teachers Association, 1987. pp. 27–28. Focuses on pre-1850's, with overview by genre and remarks on style; includes comment on Brahms the man. Does not focus on piano music.

3273.5. Shannon, John R. *One Does Not Spell Mozart with a "T." Histerical Dischords in Music.* Frank J. Rocca, illus. Chapel Hill: Hinshaw Music, 1983. [2], 115 pp. Brahms: pp. 92, 94–95, 103. ill., notes. A "blooper" history of music; includes comments on Brahms the man and composer.

3274. Smith, Delos. "Brahms" in Smith. *Music In Your Life: The Lives of the Great Composers.* 1st edition. New York: Harper & Brothers Publishers, 1953. pp. 117–21. Focuses on Brahms the man. *issues: 1954–57.

3275. Stuckenschmidt, H[ans]. H[einz]. "Johannes Brahms 1833–1897" in *Die großen Deutschen. Neue Deutsche Biographie.* Bd. 4. Willy Andreas and Wilhelm von Scholz, eds. Berlin: Propyläen=Verlag, 1936. pp. 148–63. ill., facsim. Includes description of the musical world when Brahms first emerged as a composer.

(a) reprint: Stuckenschmidt. "Ein Leben in romantischen Visionen: Johannes Brahms" in Stuckenschmidt. *Schöpfer klassischer Musik. Bildnisse und Revisionen.* Berlin: Siedler Verlag, 1983. pp. 139–62.

3276. Swafford, Jan. "Johannes Brahms" in Swafford. *The Vintage Guide to Classical Music.* 1st ed. New York: Vintage Books, 1992. pp. [290]–305. ill., notes. Includes comment on Brahms the man and composer and descriptive analyses of Opp. 34, 36, 45, 68, 83, 90, 115.

3277. *T͡Sytovichy, Tamary. *Muzyka Avstrii i Germanii XIX reka.* [Music of Austria and Germany in the 19th Century] (Istoriia̐ zarubezhnoĭ muzyki) Moskva: Muzyka, 1990. 525 pp. ill., mus., ind.

3278. Venditti, Rodolfo. "Johannes Brahms (1833–1897)" in Venditti. *Piccola guida alle grande musica.* 1. ed. Torino: Sonda, 1993. vol. 3, pp. [139]–80. ill., notes, discog. Includes comments on style (in general, also focuses on lieder), his place in music, Brahms and Wagner, and descriptive comments on Opp. 45 and 77.

See also 3428, 3430, 3432.5., 3498, 3501, 3523, 3630, 3639, 3641, 4047, 4049, 4052, 4066.d., 4091, 4098, 4134, 4224, 4278, 4459.5.d., 4662, 4681, 4761.5, 4768, 5017, 5044, 5452, 5454, 5492.
See also I5, I9, I14, I21, I26, I27, I29, I32, I46, I48 in Appendix A.

B. Brahms Study

1. General Appreciation

3279. Apthorp, William Foster. "Brahms" in Apthorp. *By the Way. Being A Collection of Short Essays on Music and Art in General taken from the Program-Books of the Boston Symphony Orchestra[, 1892–1897]. Vol. II: About Musicians.* Boston: Copeland and Day, 1898. pp. 31–43. Discusses why Brahms's music seems so unapproachable and intellectual and exhorts reader to persevere and see through to the emotion and passion.
(a) reprint (from program-books or from book?): "Apthorp on Brahms" *The American Brahms Society Newsletter* 13/2 (8.1995) pp. 7–8.

3280. *Beaujean, A. "Kennen Sie Brahms?" *HiFi Stereophonie* 22 (6.1983) pp. 586+.

3281. *Berron, Linda. "¿Te gusta Brahms?" in Berron. *La cigarra autista : relatos.* 1. ed. (Coleccion vieja y nueva narrativa costarricense 9) San Jose, Costa Rica : Editorial Universidad Estatal a Distancia, 1992.

3282. "Bis, Bis Brahms!" *Musical Courier* 95/24 (Whole no. 2488) (15.12.1927) p. 38. Pushes for more performances of the smaller and lesser known works.

3283. *Eisler, Edith. *Classical Pulse!* [no. 8] (2.1995).

3284. *Feger, Hubert. "Zum Vergleich strukturanalytischer Verfahren" *Musikpsychologie* 6 (1989) pp. 106–08. Reviews and compares results obtained by two different analytic approaches [see d.], as applied to an experiment where subjects were asked to judge videotaped performances of Brahms and Chopin piano music. [from S102]

(d) i) *Schlosser, Otto, and Klaus-Ernst Behne. "Die clusteranalytische Auswertung eines Musik-Video-Experiments" *Musikpsychologie* 6 (1989) pp. 109–21. Results as obtained by cluster analysis. [from S102; see main entry]

(d) ii) *Wille, Rudolf. "Formale Begriffsanalyse diskutiert an einem Experiment zum Musikerleben im Fernsehen" *Musikpsychologie* 6 (1989) pp. 121–32. Results as obtained by formal concepts analysis. [from S102; see main entry]

3285. Garden, Neville. "Brahms, Johannes (1833–1897)" in Garden. *Bloomsbury Good Music Guide.* (Bloomsbury Reference) [London:] Bloomsbury, 1989. pp. 29–30; also et passim. An overview of his music, with suggestions for other composers' music if one likes Brahms's.

3286. *Grove, George, Sir. *St. James's Gazette* (London) [12] (12.5. 1886). A general appreciation of Brahms's genius. [from 3796]

3287. Hemming, Roy. "Johannes Brahms" in Hemming. *Discovering Music. Where to Start on Records and Tapes, The Great Composers and Their Works, Today's Major Recording Artists.* New York: Four Winds Press, 1974. pp. 139–44; also et passim. Basis for book is performers' opinions; includes comment on Brahms's worth;

descriptive comments and recommended recordings for Opp. 68, 77, 83; briefer remarks and fewer recommended recordings for Opp. 15, 45, 73, 90, 98, 102. Brahms et passim in interviews with performers and comments on performers' affinities for individual composers.

(d) adapted and updated: *Discovering Great Music. A New Listener's Guide to the Top Classical Composers and Their Masterworks on CDs, LPs and Tapes.* New York: Newmarket Press, 1988. pp. 60–64; also et passim. Adds more recordings for Opp. 68, 77, 83; drops Op. 45 and has fewer recommended recordings for Opp. 73 and 98.

*issues: 1990, 1991.

2nd ed.: *Discovering Great Music. A New Listener's Guide to the Top Classical Composers and Their Best Recordings.* 1994.

3288. Katz, Larry. "Brahms Discovered, Brahms Revealed" *Boston* 83/3 (3.1991) p. 22. On discovering Brahms for the first time; discusses his style, suggests chamber music as an introduction to Brahms's music.

3289. Keller, Hans. "Resistances to Brahms" [Keller, trans.] *The Spectator* 241/7840 (7.10.1978) pp. 23–24. Discusses the psychology of our artistic response to Brahms's music. Uses the Wagners' reactions to show the depth of Brahms's music and the difficulties in understanding it.

(a) reprint: Keller. in Keller. *Essays on Music.* Christopher Wintle, ed., with Bayan Northcott and Irene Samuel. Cambridge: Cambridge University Press, 1994. pp. 60–62. ind., notes.

3290. Kraeft, Norman. "When My Time Comes" [The Author, n.d.] Poet describes how he will miss Brahms's music when he dies; includes comment on Brahms's modesty.

3291. Marcotte, Gilles. "Johannes B." *Liberté* 36/3 (Whole no. 213) (6.1994) pp. 152–54. Writer describes what hearing Brahms's music evokes for him; includes comments on Brahms as a German and Brahms and the Schumanns.

3291.5. *"Methodendiskussion" *Musikpsychologie* 6 (1989) pp. 106–32. Contains 3 items; see 3284 for description. [from compiler]

3291.8. *Oestreich, James R. "Brahms: always lovable, always fathomless" *The New York Times* 145 (4.10.1996) p. B1. ill.

3292. *Oestreich, James R. "Brahms and Schubert, all day, all the time" *The New York Times* 145 (8.9.1996) p. H61. ill.

3293. *Souza, Maria R., and Cecilia Camacho. "Alteracoes nos estados subjetivos de pessoas idosas em decorrencia da audicao musicale—A LEP como instrumento de pesquisa" *Psicologia* (Caracas) 11/3 (11.1985) pp. 53–62. Reports on a study of mood changes on adults who listened to a 10 minute excerpt from the works of Brahms and Tchaikovsky. [from S108]

3294. Walsh, Michael. *Who's Afraid of Classical Music? A Highly Arbitrary, Thoroughly Opinionated Guide to Listening to—and Enjoying!—Symphony, Opera, and Chamber Music.* New York [et al]: Simon & Schuster Inc., 1989. 227 pp. ind.
"Interlude: Schumann and Brahms": pp. 67–72. Brahms: pp. 69–72. Includes comments on Brahms the musician, his early and late days, and anecdotes about Brahms the man and Brahms and the Schumanns.
"The Basic Repertoire—And Beyond": pp. 94–158. Brahms: pp. 97–98, 111–12, 140. Section is arranged by genre. Includes descriptive analyses of Opp. 8, 73, 78, 83.
p. 191: assessment of good Brahms recordings.

See also 3247, 3260, 3570, 4181.d., 4457, 4555, 4643, 4925, 5017, 5223.
See also "Commemorative Pieces" and "Evaluation" in Part VII.

2. Classroom Study

3295. *Becker, Peter. "Musik als Medium im Unterricht: Ein Problemskizze" *Musik und Bildung* 19/7–8 (7.–8.1987) pp. 559–68. A general consideration of music education and music as a medium of instruction; examples of applications include Brahms works. [from S102]

3296. *Danfelt, Edwin Douglas. "The Clarinet Choir: A Means of Teaching and Performing Music" Ph.D. diss., University of Rochester, 1965. 2 vols. mus. [entire vol. 2], notes. Op. 18, 3rd movement is one of the examples. [from S031]

3297. *Meyer, Heinz. *Begegnung mit Johannes Brahms.* (Lese- und Arbeitshefte für den Musikunterricht in der Sekundarstufe I) Frankfurt am Main: Verlag Moritz Diesterweg, 1986. 48 pp. ill., mus.

3298. Schmidt, H[ugo]. W[olfram]., and A[loys]. Weber. "Johannes Brahms" in Schmidt and Weber. *Die Garbe. Vom Leben und Schaffen deutscher Musiker. Musikkunde für höhere Lehranstalten Klasse 4–8.* (Schmidt/Weber. *Die Garbe* 2) Köln: P.F. Tonger Musik Verlag, 1942. pp. 457–72. ill., facsim., mus. [Op. 19 no. 4], ind., notes. Focuses on the works, with a survey by genre; includes excerpts from the literature.

See also 3487, 3768, 4800, 4816, 5467.

3. Musicological Research

3299. Bozarth, George S. "Brahms Research in North America. Scholars Mark Sesquicentenary" *The American Brahms Society Newsletter* 1/1 (Spring 1983) pp. [1–2]. ill. Overview of previous decade's Brahms research; includes comments on upcoming commemorative events and publications in 1983.

(b) German translation: Bozarth. "Moderne Brahms-Forschung in Nordamerika" *Österreichische Musikzeitschrift* 38/4–5 (4.– 5.1983) pp. 252–53. ill. omitted.

3300. Bozarth, George S. "Brahms's "Liederjahr of 1868"" *The Music Review* 44/3/4 (8./11.1983) pp. 208–22. fig., notes, appendixes. Uses modern research methods to refute Kalbeck's claim for an outburst of song composition in 1868. Songs come from Opp. 33, 46–49, 57–58. Appendixes include list of extant holographs and criteria for study of manuscript paper.

(d) i) see: 3400.

(d) ii) see: 2040 (Bozarth. "The 'Lieder' of Johannes Brahms— 1868–1871 . . . " (1978)).

3301. Bozarth, George S. "A New Collected Edition for Brahms" *The American Brahms Society Newsletter* 6/1 (Spring 1988) pp. [4–8]. facsim., mus. Uses Brahms song source study (examples from Op. 33) to show shortcomings of current collected edition and to answer the question of why a new edition is needed.

(d) see: 2040 (Bozarth. "The 'Lieder' of Johannes Brahms— 1868–1871 . . . " (1978)).

3302. Fellinger, Imogen. "Zum Stand der Brahms-Forschung" *Acta musicologica* 55/2 (7.–12.1983) pp. 131–201. notes. Review of research focusing on 1945– , although overview of earlier work is included. Systematic listing by topic, 544 entries; includes comment on research lacunae.

(d) i) continued: Fellinger. "Das Brahms-Jahr 1983. Forschungsbericht" *Acta musicologica* 56/2 (7.–12.1984) pp. 145–210. notes. Review of 1983 activities and writings, done in same format as main entry. 379 entries.

(d) ii) condensed: Fellinger. "Neuere Brahms-Forschung in Europa" *Österreichische Musikzeitschrift* 38/4–5 (4.–5.1983) pp. 248–52. Brief prosaic survey of research and writings from 1945– ; includes comment on 1983 commemorative activities and research lacunae.

3303. Frisch, Walter [M.]. "Afterthoughts on the Brahms Year" *The American Brahms Society Newsletter* 2/1 (Spring 1984) pp. [1–2]. ill. Reflects on 1983's output—few dazzling revelations, lots of enrichment and consolidation. Also discusses the merit of reviving "lost" works like the Missa canonica [McCorkle WoO posthum 18]. Comments on the latter point are in response to 4859.

3304. Korsyn, Kevin. "Brahms Research and Aesthetic Ideology" *Music Analysis* 12/1 (3.1993) pp. 89–103. mus., notes. Uses 5480 to attempt a critique of assumptions behind current wave of Brahms research—is the discipline limiting what can be asked?

3305. "Schluβdiskussion" in *Brahms und seine Zeit*. (Hamburger Jahrbuch für Musikwissenschaft 7) [for full citation see 5428] pp. 273–79. A roundtable discussion concerning areas of current Brahms research, and areas that need to be addressed.

See also 3316, 3402, 3432.5, 3434, 3441, 3686.e., 3739, 3743, 3803, 3832, 3967, 3974, 4148, 4515, 4605, 4757, 4793.d.e., 4842.d., 4859, 5027, 5293, 5348, 5436, 5462, 5480.

C. Research Tools

See also "Creative Process" in Part V.C.

1. Bibliography

Contains significant compilations of Brahms literature. Includes references that refer to conference papers and works-in-progress.

The American Brahms Society Newsletter Checklists (by serial year):

1984: 3306, 3316
1985: 3310
1986: 3315, 3320
1987: 3308, 3319
1990: 3314
1991: 3309, 3323
1992: 3324, 3325
1993: 3311, 3312
1994: 3313, 3326
1995: 3317, 3327
1996: 3328

3306. Bozarth, George S. "Brahms Publications of 1983" *The American Brahms Society Newsletter* 2/1 (Spring 1984) pp. [2–4]. facsim. Surveys recently published materials, focuses on 6 monographs; includes an overview by topic.

3307. Bozarth, George S. "Four papers on Brahms . . ." *The American Brahms Society Newsletter* 3/2 (Autumn 1985) p. [10]. Reports on 5 Brahms papers to be given at the joint SMT/AMS meeting, Vancouver, Canada, November 1985.
(d) see: 3320.

3308. Bozarth, George S. "News and Comment" *The American Brahms Society Newsletter* 5/1 (Spring 1987) p. [10]. Reports on 14 items, arranged by format.

3309. Bozarth, George S. "Other Recent Brahms Publications" *The American Brahms Society Newsletter* 9/1 (Spring 1991) pp. 9–10. reports on 11 items, arranged by genre.

3310. Bozarth, George S. "Publications of 1984–85" *The American Brahms Society Newsletter* 3/2 (Autumn 1985) pp. [6–9]. ill. Annotated list of 8 items, plus comment on 10 other titles both published and forthcoming. Includes news of an unpublished letter, Clara Schumann to Brahms, 6.5.1891.

3311. Bozarth, George S. "Recent Brahms Publications" *The American Brahms Society Newsletter* 11/1 (Spring 1993) pp. 9–10. 17 items, arranged by format.

3312. Bozarth, George S. "Recent Brahms Publications" *The American Brahms Society Newsletter* 11/2 (Autumn 1993) pp. 8–9. 18 items, arranged by format.

3313. Bozarth, George S. "Recent Brahms Publications and Recordings" *The American Brahms Society Newsletter* 12/2 (8.1994) pp. 8–10. 30 items, arranged by format.

3314. Bozarth, George S. "Recent Publications" *The American Brahms Society Newsletter* 8/1 (Spring 1990) pp. 8–10. 23 items, arranged by format.

3315. Bozarth, George S. "Recent publications received . . ." *The American Brahms Society Newsletter* 4/2 (Autumn 1986) p. [10]. 7 items, arranged by format.

3316. [Hancock, Virginia Lee.] "Brahms Research in Progress" *The American Brahms Society Newsletter* 2/2 (Autumn 1984) p. [10]. 15 items, mainly dissertations.

3317. Brodbeck, David [Lee], and George S. Bozarth. "Brahms Studies and Other Recent Brahms Publications and Recordings" *The American Brahms Society Newsletter* 13/1 (Spring 1995) pp. 8–9. 18 items, arranged by format; includes report on vol. 1 of 5498.

3318. DeVenney, David. "Writings on the Choral Music of Johannes Brahms" *American Choral Foundation. Research Memorandum Series* no. 139 (9.1985) pp. [1]–7. ind. 99 items; annotated list, focus is on secondary scholarly literature.

3319. Hancock, Virginia [Lee]. "Recent Writings on Brahms" *The American Brahms Society Newsletter* 5/2 (Autumn 1987) p. [10]. 4 items.

3320. [Hancock, Virginia Lee.] "In Abstract" *The American Brahms Society Newsletter* 4/1 (Spring 1986) pp. [4–6].
"Dissertations, Recent and In Progress": p. [4]. 6 items.
"Papers at AMS/SMT Vancouver": pp. [4–6]. facsim. 5 items; annotations adapted from conference programme book abstracts.

3321. Kross, Siegfried. *Brahms-Bibliographie.* Tutzing: Hans Schneider, 1983. 285 pp. ind. 2,736 entries covering 1847–mid 1983. Claims to replace 241.a. (L. Koch. *Brahms-Bibliográfia. Brahms-Bibliographie.* (1943)) but is limited in coverage and has ineffective apparati.

(e) announcement: "New Brahms Bibliographies" *The American Brahms Society Newsletter* 1/2 (Autumn 1983) p. [7]. Also discusses 3322.

3322. Quigley, Thomas. *Johannes Brahms: an annotated bibliography of the literature through 1982.* With a Foreword by Margit L. McCorkle. Metuchen, NJ and London: The Scarecrow Press Inc., 1990. xxxix, 721 pp. ill., ind., notes. 3,197 entries covering mid 1849–1982.

(d) Quigley, Thomas. "Johannes Brahms and Bibliographic Control—Review and Assessment" *Fontes artis musicae* 30/4 (10.–12.1983) pp. 207–14. notes. Discusses problem of bibliographic control for Brahms literature. Reviews past attempts then focuses on 241.a. (L. Koch. *Brahms-Bibliográfia. Brahms-Bibliographie.* (1943)) and 243 (I. Lübbe. "Das Schrifttum über Johannes Brahms in den Jahren 1933–1958" (1960))

(e) i) report: Bozarth, George S. "A Comprehensive Bibliography for Brahms" *The American Brahms Society Newsletter* 9/1 (Spring 1991) p. 8.

(e) ii) announcement: see 3321.e.

3323. [Bozarth, George S.] "Recent Brahms Publications" *The American Brahms Society Newsletter* 9/2 (Autumn 1991) p. 10. 30 items, arranged by format.

3324. [Bozarth, George S.] "Recent Brahms Publications" *The American Brahms Society Newsletter* 10/1 (Spring 1992) p. 8. 14 items, arranged by format.

3325. [Bozarth, George S.] "Recent Brahms Publications" *The American Brahms Society Newsletter* 10/2 (Autumn 1992) pp. 9–10. 22 items, arranged by format; includes reviews of 5480.

3326. [Bozarth, George S.] "Recent Brahms Publications" *The American Brahms Society Newsletter* 12/1 (Spring 1994) p. 6. 6 items.

3327. [Bozarth, George S.] "Recent Brahms Publications and Recordings" *The American Brahms Society Newsletter* 13/2 (8.1995) pp. 9–10. 17 items, arranged by format.

3328. [Bozarth, George S.] "Recent Brahms Publications and Recordings" *The American Brahms Society Newsletter* 14/1 (Spring 1996) pp. 9–10. 13 items, arranged by format.

3329. Schubert, Giselher. "Brahms-Bibliographie" *Musik und Bildung* 15/5 (Bd. 74) (5.1983) pp. 14–16. 125 items; reviews important literature published 1950– .

3330. Weiβ, Ursula, and Ursula Mederer. *Johannes Brahms. Zum 150. Geburtstag. Bestandskatalog der Stadtbibliothek Koblenz.* (Bildung, Information, Dokumentation. Verzeichnisse der Stadtbibliothek Koblenz 32) Koblenz: The Stadtbibliothek, 1983. [4], 4–23 pp. 181 items; all materials in library's collection.

3331. [Bozarth, George S.] "The Writings of Carl Dahlhaus on Brahms" *The American Brahms Society Newsletter* 7/2 (Autumn 1989) p. 6. Analyzes 8 items, arranged by publication date. Includes brief 1–2 pp. references.

3332. [Bozarth, George S.] "The Writings of Karl Geiringer on Johannes Brahms" *The American Brahms Society Newsletter* 7/1 (Spring 1989) p. 5. 25 references, arranged by publication date.
      (d) augmented: Hancock, Virginia [Lee]. "Mr. [Thomas] Quigley has kindly . . ." *The American Brahms Society Newsletter* 7/2 (Autumn 1989) p. [12]. 6 additional items.

See also 3299, 3302, 3347, 3382, 3432.5, 3622, 3912, 3914, 3927–29, 4455, 4479, 5058, 5224, 5478.e., 5497.
See also I25, I28, I30, I38, I40, I46 in Appendix A.

2. Discography

Contains compilations and comparative studies of recordings of Brahms's music.

Basic overall collection lists: 3339, 3341, 3346.5, 3369, 3371, 3372.
Record review serials: 3333, 3364, 3367.

3333. *CD Review Digest—Classical* 1–3/1 (1.1987–1.1989). Voorheesville, NY: The Peri Press.
      (d) i) *continued by: *CD Review Digest* 3/2–7/4 (Summer/Fall 1989—Winter 1994) Voorheesville, NY: The Peri Press.
          (d) *continued by: *Schwann CD Review Digest Annual—Classical* 8– . (1995–) Santa Fe, NM: Stereophile, Inc.
      (d) ii) *cumulated yearly into: *CD Review Digest Annual—*

Classical 1–4 (1983–87–1990) Voorheesville, NY: The Peri Press, 1988–1990.

3334. *Ardoin, John. *The Fürtwangler Record*. Discography by John Hunt. Portland: Amadeus Press, 1994. 376, [12] pp. ind., notes., discog.

3335. Bart, Jan van. *Discografie van het Concertgebouworkest*. Zutphen: De Walburg Pers, 1989. 120 pp. ind. Includes 53 items that cover 16 Brahms works.

3336. Basart, Ann P. "Brahms, Johannes" in Basart. *The Sound of the Fortepiano. A Discography of Recordings on Early Pianos*. With a Foreword by Edwin M. Good. (Fallen Leaf Reference Books in Music 2) Berkeley: Fallen Leaf Press, 1985. p. 58. Notes recordings of op. 39, nos. 15, 16, on an 1864 Streicher.

3337. "Best of Music" *Time* Canadian edition. 136/28 (31.12.1990) p. 34. ill. One of the "Top Ten of 1990" compact discs picked is of Brahms's 3 violin sonatas.
American edition: p. 42.
(e) report: Bozarth, George S. ""There are half a dozen or so . . ."
. ." *The American Brahms Society Newsletter* 9/1 (Spring 1991) p. [12].

3338. *Brahms, Johannes. *Brahms Edition*. [Recording series; title from containers. Alternate title = *Works*. 1983] Various performers. Deutsche Grammophon, 1983. DGG 2740 275 – DGG 2740 280, DGG 2741 018 – DGG 2741 019. 62 records in 8 containers. Portions previously released. Durations, program notes in German, English, and French, and texts of vocal works with translations in containers. [from S031]
(e) i) review: ab. [A. Briner] "Brahms-Edition" *Neue Zürcher Zeitung* nr. 106 (7./8.5.1983) p. 68. Discusses the notes that accompany this recordings collection.
(e) ii) review: Barker, John W. "The Nuclear Brahms. The Latest Complete Works Project from Deutsche Grammophon" *American Record Guide* 47/5 (7.1984) pp. 2–17. ill., facsim.
(e) iii) review: Bozarth, George S. "All Brahms enthusiasts . . ." *The American Brahms Society Newsletter* 3/1 (Spring 1985) p. [12]. Comments on the work and wonders why it omits the Studies [McCorkle Anhang Ia, nr. 1] and the solo quartet version of Op. 103.

(e) iv) *review: Davis, Peter G. "Brahms Bonanza" *New York* 16
(8.8.1983) pp. 62+.

(e) v) review: "Deutsche Grammophon hyllar Brahms—Et dig-
nande smörgåsbord där inget fattas" *Musikrevy* 38/5 (1983)
pp. 222–23.

(e) vi) review: Goldsmith, Harris. "A Brahms Birthday Bash"
High Fidelity 33/12 (12.1983) pp. 80–83. ill. Discusses instrumental works' recordings.

(d) continued: Crutchfield, Will. "In Praise of Brahms's
Songs" *High Fidelity* 34/1 (1.1984) pp. 68–70, 72. ill.
Discusses vocal works' recordings.

(e) vii) review: see 3354.

(e) viii) review: R.L. "The Brahms Edition" *Gramophone* 60/720
(5.1983) pp. 1241–43. ill.

3339. "Brahms, Johannès (1833–1897)" in *Dictionnaire des disques [de
Diapason]. Guide critique de la musique classique enregistrée.*
1ère éd. (Bouquins) Paris: Robert Laffont, 1981. pp. 171–210.
ind. 238 items cover 68+ works; arranged by genre.
Nouvelle édition revue et augmentée [2ème édition]: 1984. Adds
compact discs and "basic list" of 100 items. Brahms: pp.
173–212, 1004 (CD's), [1019] ("basic list"). 259 items cover
61+ works; arranged alphabetically by work's title.
Nouvelle édition revue et augmentée [3ème édition]: *Dictionnaire
des disques et des compacts [de Diapason-Harmonie]. Guide
critique de la musique classique enregistrée.* 1988. Brahms:
pp. 144–87. 135 items cover 71+ works; arranged by genre.

3340. *"Brahms Violin Sonatas CD Round-up" *The Strad* 107/1275
(1.7.1996) p. 738+.

3340.5. *Cargher, John. *The Good Classical CD Guide.* Melbourne : A.
O'Donovan, 1994. 190 pp. ind.

3341. "Classical" in *All Music Guide. The Best CDs, Albums & Tapes.
The Experts' Guide to the Best Releases From Thousands of
Artists in All Types of Music.* Michael Erlewine, ed. San Fran-
cisco: Miller Freeman Inc., 1992. pp. 621–715.
BGT ["Blue" Gene Tyranny], PM [Peter Meyer], and MKS [Mary
Scanlan]. "Johannes Brahms 1833–1897": pp. 633–35. 78
items cover 55 works; includes comments on Brahms the
composer, and evaluations of performances.

3342. *Classical Music on CD; the Rough Guide*. Matthew Boyden and Jonathan Buckley, eds. London: The Rough Guides, 1994. x, 465 pp.

3343. *Clough, Francis [F.], and G.J. Cuming. *The World's Encyclopedia of Recorded Music*. London: Sidgwick & Jackson, in association with the Decca Record Corp., and in the U.S.A., the London Gramophone Corp., [1952]. xvi, 890 pp. Includes First supplement (4.1950–5.–6.1951).
   (a) *reprint (of all 3 volumes, see below for 2 and 3): Westport, CT: Greenwood Press, 1970.
   (d) *Clough, Cuming and A.E. Hughes. *The World's Encyclopedia of Recorded Music. 2nd Supplement (1951–52)*. London, [New York]: 1952. 262 pp.
   *another issue: 1953.
   (a) reprint (of which issue?): see 3343.a.
   (d) *Clough, Cuming and Hughes. *The World's Encyclopedia of Recorded Music, Third Supplement (1953–1955)*. London, [New York]: Sidgwick and Jackson, in association with . . . Decca and London Records, 1957. xxvi, 564 pp.
   *another issue: 1966.
   (a) reprint (of which issue?): see 3343.a.

3344. Cohn, Arthur. "Johannes Brahms (1833–1897)" in Cohn. *Recorded Classical Music. A Critical Guide to Compositions and Performances*. New York: Schirmer Books; London: Collier Macmillan, 1981. pp. 269–88. ind. Describes and evaluates the best recordings of Brahms's music, 88 items cover 75 works.

3345. "Definitive Classical Library" by *CD Review* Staff. (The Basic 50) *CD Review* 7/3 (11.1990) pp. 36–37. Opp. 77 and 90 make this list of "sure-fire choices for a killer classical collection." A compilation to encourage further musical exploring.

3346. *Farneth, David Paul. *An Index to Commercial Recordings of Brahms Songs Held by the Indiana University Music Library*. [Bloomington: The Music Library,] 1977. 36 pp.

3346.5. *Freed, Richard. "The Basic Repertoire" *Stereo Review* 48 (6.1983) pp. 52+ .

3347. Gilardoni, Bruno, and Françoise Malettra. "Brahms a ecouter et a

lire. Les Valeurs sûres" *Diapason* (Paris) no. 283 (5.1983) p. 36.
A discography of 16 items (Gilardoni) and a bibliography of 6
items (Malettra) (5 in French, 1 in German).

3347.5. *The Good CD Guide.* [1st ed.] Harrow : General Gramophone
Publications in association with AKAI (UK) Ltd.,1987. x, 198 pp.
ind. "Reviews of the best classical compact discs you can buy."
[from S031]

> [4th ed.:] *The Good CD Guide 1991.* Harrow : General Gramo-
> phone Publications in association with Quad Electro-
> acoustics, 1990 l, 550 pp. ill.

> [5th ed.:] *The Good CD Guide, 1992.* General Gramophone Pub-
> lications, 1991. 679 pp. ind.

> [6th ed.:] *The Good CD Guide, 1993 : reviews of the best classi-
> cal compact discs you can buy.* General Gramophone Publi-
> cations in association with Quad Electroacoustics, 1992. 927
> pp. ill.

> [[8th?] ed.:] *The Gramophone Good CD Guide.* 1994–95. 2 vols.
> General Gramophone, 1994–95.

> [9th ed.:] *The Gramophone Classical Good CD Guide.* Harrow,
> Middlesex : New York : Gramophone Publications, Ltd.,
> 1996.

> 10th ed.: *Gramophone Classical Good CD Guide.* Introduction
> by David Mellor. Gramophone in association with B&W
> Loudspeakers, 1996.

3348. Greenfield, Edward, Robert Layton, and Ivan March. "Brahms,
Johannes (1833–97)" in Greenfield, Layton, and March. *The Penguin Cassette Guide.* March, ed. (Penguin Handbooks) Harmondsworth: Penguin Books Ltd., 1979. pp. 111–31. 85 items
cover 34+ works. Compares versions, makes recommendations.
Continues 3351.

Supplement: Greenfield, Layton, and March. *The New Penguin
Stereo Record and Cassette Guide.* March, ed. No series.
Penguin Books, 1982. Brahms: pp. 160–84. 124 items
cover 63+ works. Compares versions, makes recommendations.

(d) continued (from 1982 Supplement): Greenfield, Layton,
and March. "Brahms, Johannes (1833–97)" in Greenfield,
Layton, and March. *The Complete Penguin Stereo Record
and Cassette Guide.* March, ed. (Penguin Handbooks)

Harmondsworth: Penguin Books, 1984. pp. 200–35. 181 items cover 122+ works. Compares versions, makes recommendations.

(d) continued: see 3349.

3349. Greenfield, Edward, Richard Layton, and Ivan March. "Brahms, Johannes (1833–97)" in Greenfield, Layton, and March. *The Penguin Guide to Compact Discs, Cassettes and LPs.* (Penguin Handbooks) [No editor] Harmondsworth: Penguin Books, 1986. pp. 192–221. 104 items cover 55+ works. Compares versions, makes recommendations. Continues 1984 edition in 3348.

(d) continued: Greenfield, Layton, and March. "Brahms, Johannes (1833–97)" in Greenfield, Layton, and March. *The New Penguin Guide to Compact Discs and Cassettes.* March, ed. (Penguin Handbooks) London, New York: Penguin Books, 1988. pp. 204–36. 162 items cover 66+ works. Compares versions, makes recommendations.

*Supplement: 1989. Greenfield, Layton, and March. *The New . . . . Cassettes. Yearbook 1989.* March, ed. Brahms: pp. 82–95. 61 items cover 44+ works. Compares versions, makes recommendations.

Revised and updated edition (of 1988 ed.): Greenfield, Layton and March. *The Penguin Guide to Compact Discs.* March, ed. 1990. pp. 195–223. 169 items cover 78+ works. Compares versions, makes recommendations.

Supplement (to 1990 ed.): Greenfield, Layton, and March. *The Penguin Guide to Compact Discs and Cassettes. Yearbook 1991/2.* March, ed. (Penguin Handbooks) Harmondsworth: Penguin Book Ltd., 1992. pp. 95–116. 95 items cover 60+ works. Compares versions, makes recommendations.

New edition (follows 1990 ed.): 1992. March, Greenfield, and Layton. *The Penguin Guide to Compact Discs and Cassettes.* March, ed. Brahms: 185–215. 187 items cover 70+ works. Compares versions, makes recommendations.

(d) i) *Greenfield, Edward, Robert Layton, and Ivan March. *The Penguin Guide to Bargain Compact Discs and Cassettes.* (Penguin Handbooks) London, New York : Penguin Books, 1992.

New edition (follows 1992 ed.) ["now fully revised and up-dated"]: 1994. Brahms: pp. 195–226. 223 items cover 63+ works. Compares versions, makes recommendations.

(d) ii) supplement: see 3350.

3350. *Greenfield, Edward, Robert Layton, and Ivan March. *The Penguin Guide to Compact Discs. Yearbook 1995*. Ivan March, ed. London; New York: Penguin Books, 1995. Supplement to 1994 edition in 3349. [from compiler]

3351. Greenfield, Edward, Ivan March, and Denis Stevens. "Brahms, Johannes (1833–1897)" in Greenfield, March, and Stevens. *The Stereo Record Guide*. [Foreword by Percy Wilson] Ivan March, ed. 9 vols. n.p.: The Long Playing Record Library Ltd., 1960–74.

vol. 1: pp. 54–64. 23 items cover 21 works.

vol. 2: pp. 356–68. 53 items cover 22 works.

vol. 3: pp. 723–33. 99 items cover 42 works.

vol. 4: pp. 1165–76. 101 items cover 50 works. Includes mono-aural catalogue numbers.

vol. 5: pp. 117–33. 136 items cover 52 works. Adds Robert Layton.

vol. 7: pp. 1132–48. 90 items cover 58 works. Omits Denis Stevens, omits monoaural catalogue numbers.

(d) Greenfield, Edward; Richard Layton; and Ivan March. "Brahms, Johannes (1833–97)" in Greenfield, Layton, and March. *The Penguin Stereo Record Guide*. Ivan March, ed. (A Penguin Handbook) Harmondsworth: Penguin Books, 1975. pp. 197–224. 159 items cover 61 works.

issue: 1976.

2nd edition: 1977. (Penguin Handbook) Brahms: pp. 199–229. 184 items cover 81+ works.

Supplement: see 3348.

3352. Hernon, Michael. *French Horn Discography*. (Discographies 24) New York, Westport, London: Greenwood Press, 1986. xiv, 291, [1] pp. ind. Brahms: pp. 7, 67–70, 82, 104, 200. 48 items cover 5 works. Includes arrangements for various ensembles; includes citations for record reviews.

3353. *Ho, Allan B[enedict]. "Music for Piano and Orchestra: The Recorded Repertory" [manuscript] Lexington: University of Kentucky, 1983. 125 pp.

3354. Höslinger, Clemens. "Das Brahms-Werk auf der Schallplatte"
      Österreichische Musikzeitschrift 38/4–5 (4.–5.1983) pp. 292–93.
      Reviews current recordings, focuses on 3338.

3355. *Hunt, John. *Giants of the Keyboard: Kempff, Gieseking, Fischer,
      Haskil, Backhaus, Schnabel. Discographies.* [London: J. Hunt,]
      1994. 371 pp. ill., facsim.

3356. [Johnson, Stephen.] "Johannes Brahms Violin Sonatas" (Collec-
      tion) *Gramophone* 73/866 (7.1995) pp. 38–40. ill., discog. Offers
      a guide to 18 recordings of Opp. 78, 100, and 108; movement-by-
      movement comparison with good and bad comments. Includes
      overall recommendations.

3357. Kolodin, Irving. "The Best of Brahms on Disc" (The Brahms
      Sesquicentennial [3]) *Ovation* 4/6 (7.1983) pp. 20–21, 41–43. ill.
      Includes historical as well as contemporary recordings. 95 items
      cover 61 + works; includes "deletes".

3358. Kolodin, Irving. "Brahms, Johannes (1833–1897)" in Kolodin.
      Orchestral Music. (The Guide to Long-Playing Records 1) New
      York: Alfred A. Knopf, 1955. pp. 36–41. 41 items cover 15 works.

3359. Kowar, Helmut; Franz Lechleitner; and Dietrich Schüller. "Zur
      Wiederherausgabe des einzigen Tondokuments von Johannes
      Brahms durch das Phonogrammarchiv" *Das Schallarchiv* 14
      (12.1983) pp. 16–23. notes. English abstract: p. 23. Discusses the
      history of the Brahms recording, its provenance and how it was
      restored for re-release on *Johannes Brahms und sein Freun-
      deskreis.* Various performers. [for full citation see 3609]
      (b) English translation: Kowar, Lechleitner, and Schüller. "On the
          Re-Issue of the Only Existing Sound Recording of Johannes
          Brahms by the Phonogrammarchiv" *Phonographic Bulletin*
          no. 39 (7.1984) pp. 19–22. omits notes. Updated version of
          original article.
      (e) report: Bozarth, George S. "Brahms on Record" *The
          American Brahms Society Newsletter* 5/1 (Spring 1987)
          pp. [5–9]. ill. Also reports on 5157. Includes: "Record-
          ings of Brahms's Works by the Composer and by Mem-
          bers of His Circle": pp. [8–9]. Notes recordings by 11
          contemporaries; this list expands on 5157's list.
      (d) Kowar, Helmut. "Zum Fragment eines Walzers, gespielt von

Johannes Brahms" in *Brahms-Kongress Wien 1983*. [for full citation see 5431] pp. 281–90. notes. Speculates that the waltz Brahms plays is Josef Strauss's Op. 204. (d) see: 3638.

3360. *Lacas, Pierre-Paul. "Requiem allemand de Brahms" *Diapason* (Paris) no. 224 (1.1978) pp. 54–55.

3361. Laster, James. "Brahms, Johannes (1833–1897)" in Laster. *A Discography of Treble Voice Recordings*. Metuchen, NJ and London: The Scarecrow Press, Inc., 1985. pp. 14–18. 44 items cover 21 works.

3362. Leclercq, Fernand, and Serge Martin. "Les Symphonies de Brahms. Discographie critique" (Dossier du mois) *Harmonie-Opera Hi-Fi Conseil* 19/28 nouvelle serie (2.1983) pp. 28–40. ill. [also issue cover], fig., notes. Includes comments on Brahms the composer and as a follower of Beethoven, and descriptive comments on each symphony. Looks at conductors, focusing on Furtwängler, Klemperer and Solti, and compares versions within each symphony (39 items total). Includes comment on Schoenberg's orchestration of Op. 25.

3363. Libbey, Ted. *The NPR [National Public Radio] Guide To Building A Classical CD Collection*. Introduction by Mstislav Rostropovich. New York: Workman Publishing, 1994. xiii, [1], 498 pp. ill., ind. Brahms: pp. 36–43, 217–23, 311–19, 371–73, 419–21. 17 items cover 20 works. Includes descriptive comments and some background on each work, suggestions for additional listening, comments on recommended recordings and on Brahms the composer.

3364. *Maleady, Antoinette O. *Record and Tape Reviews Index*. [Vols. 1–4 (1971–74)] Metuchen, NJ: The Scarecrow Press, Inc., 1972–75.
(d) *continued: Maleady. *Index to Record and Tape Reviews. A Classical Music Buying Guide*. [vols. 1–7 (1976–82)] San Anselmo, CA: Chulainn Press, 1977–83.
    (d) *continued in part as: *Fanfare Index*. Frances Jenkins, ed. vol. 8– . (9.1984–) Seattle: Seagulls Enterprises, 1985– .

3365. Miller, Philip L. "Brahms, Johannes (1833–1897)" in Miller. *Vocal Music*. (The Guide to Long-Playing Records 2) New York: Alfred A. Knopf, 1955. pp. 48–55. ind. 19 items cover 13+ works.

3366. Molkhou, Jean-Michel. "Beaux Arts Trio: On The Record. The Complete Discography of the Beaux Arts Trio" *The Strad* 106/1263 (7.1995) pp. 692–93. Brahms: p. 692. 9 items.

3367. Myers, Kurtz. *Index to Record Reviews*. 5 vols. Boston: G.K. Hall & Co., 1978–1980.
   "Brahms, Johannes": vol. 1, pp. 218–54. c. 700 entries for 401 works; also vol. 5 [5index for composite entries], pp. 39–43 [12 columns of references]. Based on material originally published in Notes between 1949–1977.
   (d) Myers. *Index to Record Reviews 1978–1983*. Boston: G.K. Hall & Co., 1985.
   "Brahms, Johannes": pp. 70–80. c. 230 entries for 45+ works; also pp. 611–13 [=index for composite entries; 5 columns of references]. Based on material originally published in *Notes* between 1978–1983.
   (d) Myers. *Index to Record Reviews 1984–1987*. Boston: G.K. Hall & Co., 1989.
   "Brahms, Johannes": pp. 33–42. c. 180 entries for 120+ works; also pp. 358–59 [=index for composite entries; 1 1/2 columns of references]. Based on material originally published in *Notes* between 1984–1987.

3368. *"Overview: Brahms: Symphonies and Piano Concertos" *American Record Guide* 52/3 ([5./6.] 1989) pp. 8–9.

3369. *Parker, Bill. *Building A Classical Music Library. A Concise Guide To Building Your Personal Record Collection*. [cover title=*Minnesota Public Radio's Guide To Building A Classical Music Library*.] St. Paul: Minnesota Public Radio, Inc., 1981. 152 pp. ind.
   *Revised ed.: 1985. *Building A Classical Music Library*. [cover title=*A Concise Guide To Building A Classical Music Library*.] 232 pp.
   *3rd ed., fully revised: 1994. No different cover title. Minneapolis: Jormax Publications. xv, 286 pp.

3370. *Reverter, Arturo. *Brahms*. (Guias scherzo 3) Barcelona : Peninsula, 1995. 276 pp. notes.

3371. Rosenberg, Kenyon C. "Brahms, Johannes 1833–1897" in Rosenberg. *A Basic Classical and Operatic Recordings Collection for Libraries*. Metuchen, NJ & London: The Scarecrow Press, Inc., 1987. pp. 37–43. 31 items cover 29 works; includes comment on

Brahms's reception by Shaw, and Brahms the composer. Distinguishes essential items from others and includes prices.

3372. Rosenberg, Kenyon C. "Brahms, Johannes 1833–1897" in Rosenberg. *A Basic Classical and Operatic Recordings Collection on Compact Discs for Libraries: A Buying Guide.* Metuchen, NJ & London: The Scarecrow Press, Inc., 1990. pp. 146–52. 32 items cover 34 works; includes comparative remarks on performances, CD timings.

3373. Schonberg, Harold C. "Brahms, Johannes 1833–1897" in Schonberg. *Chamber and Solo Instrument Music.* (The Guide to Long-Playing Records 3) New York: Alfred A. Knopf, 1955. pp. 59–68. 61 items cover 45 works; includes comments on performance and recording quality.

3374. Sitsky, Larry. "Brahms, Johannes" in Sitsky. *The Classical Reproducing Piano Roll. A Catalogue-Index.* (Music Reference Collection 23) New York [et al.]: Greenwood Press, 1990. vol. 1, pp. 67–76. 124 references to works, 353 performances noted in total; includes comment on who recorded the roll, whether it was original solo piano or an arrangement.

3375. *Song on Record. [Vol.] 1. Lieder.* Alan Blyth, ed. Cambridge [et al.]: Cambridge University Press, 1986. ind. Surveys different interpretations of vocal works.
    Steane, John [B.]. "Brahms Ten Songs": pp. 195–209. Discusses Opp. 32 no. 9, 43 nos. 1 and 2, 84 no. 4, 86 no. 2, 91 nos. 1 and 2, 96 no. 1, 105 nos. 1 and 2, 106 no. 1.
    Blyth, Alan. "Brahms Vier ernste Gesänge": pp. 187–94. Discusses Op. 121.

3376. Stahl, Dorothy. "Brahms, Johannes (1833–1897)" in Stahl. *A Selected Discography of Solo Song.* (Detroit Studies in Music Bibliography 13) Detroit: Information Coordinators, Inc., 1968. pp. 6–8. Discography is alphabetical by song title, 54 Brahms titles included.
    (d) Stahl, Dorothy. "Brahms, Johannes (1833–1897)" in Stahl. *A Selected Discography of Solo Song: Supplement, 1968–1969.* (Detroit Studies in Music Bibliography 13 Supplement) 1970. pp. 8–12. Includes 61 Brahms song titles; covers recordings released from 12.1967–1.1970, plus omissions from base volume.

Revised edition (of 1968 and 1970 editions): Stahl, Dorothy. *A Selected Discography of Solo Song: A Cumulation through 1971.* (Detroit Studies in Music Bibliography 24) 1972. pp. 20–24. Includes 66 Brahms song titles; includes recordings still available from previous editions, and new recordings released since 1969.

(d) Stahl, Dorothy. *A Selected Discography of Solo Song. Supplement. 1971–1974.* (Detroit Studies in Music Bibliography 34) 1976. pp. 14–15. 38 Brahms song titles; includes recordings released since 1971.

(d) Stahl, Dorothy. *Discography of Solo Song. Supplement, 1975–1982.* (Detroit Studies in Music Bibliography 52) 1984. pp. 21–24. 45 Brahms song titles.

3377. Svejda, Jim. "Brahms, Johannes (1833–1897)" in Svejda. *The Record Shelf Guide to the Classical Repertoire.* Rocklin, CA: Prima Publishing & Communications, 1988. pp. 54–66. 24 items cover 14 works. Includes CD's, recordings and audiocassettes.

2nd ed. [revised and expanded]: 1990. pp. 70–84. 29 items cover 34 works. Items dropped if superceded or discontinued; recordings virtually excluded unless exemplary and not available in other formats.

3rd ed. [revised and expanded]: 1992. pp. 75–90. 31 items cover 42 works. Recordings no longer included; first CD cuts.

*4th ed. [revised and expanded]: 1995. *The Record Shelf Guide to Classical CDs and Audiocassettes.*

*5th ed. [revised]: 1996. ind.

3378. Vroon[, Donald R]. "Overview: Brahms" *American Record Guide* 57/3 (5./6.1994) pp. 57–61. 50 items cover 18+ works. Includes deleted items and symphony sets.

3379. *Zeisel, Georges. *L'Avant-scène opera, operette, musique* no. 53 (6.1983) pp. 114–29. Discography of the symphonies. [from S031]

See also 3287, 3294, 3382, 3432.5, 3626, 3895, 3971, 4036, 4038, 4090, 4100, 4154, 4156, 4359, 4389, 4402, 4459.5, 4460.5, 4461, 4483, 4489.5, 4555, 4559, 4569, 4570, 4573, 4620, 4629, 4790, 4815, 4817, 4821, 5017, 5046, 5086, 5164, 5167, 5173, 5174, 5191, 5413.
See also "Bibliography" in Part I.C.
See also I9, I21, I23, I24, I33–I37, I42, I43, I45, I46 in Appendix A.

3. Editions

a. Collected Editions

This subsection is arranged in reverse chronological order by edition publication date.

3380. *Brahms, Johannes. *Werke.* Johannes Brahms Gesamtausgabe e.v., ed., with the Editorial Board in Kiel, in conjunction with the Gesellschaft der Musikfreunde, Vienna. (Johannes Brahms Gesamtausgabe. Series I–) München: G. Henle Verlag, 1996– .
    (e) i) *Kieler Nachrichten* (6.6.1991).
    (b) English translation: "The New Kiel Edition of Brahms' Works will run to 60 Volumes" *The German Tribune* 30/1472 (23.6.1991) p. 10. Reports on objectives of new Brahms Gesamtausgabe.
    (e) ii) Bozarth, George S. "Word has reached . . ." *The American Brahms Society Newsletter* 3/1 (Spring 1985) p. [12]. Reports that funding for new Brahms Gesamtausgabe has been secured.
    (e) iii) Hancock, Virginia [Lee]. "Recently the ABS [American Brahms Society] received . . ." *The American Brahms Society Newsletter* 8/2 (Autumn 1990) p. 10. Reports that new Brahms Gesamtausgabe has been accepted into the German Scholarly Editions Programme.
    (e) iv) [Hancock, Virginia Lee.] "Progress Towards A New Brahms Edition" *The American Brahms Society Newsletter* 4/2 (Autumn 1986) pp. [3–4]. An account of initial work towards a new Brahms edition—founding of a Society and details on a 3 year pilot project.
    (e) v) Webster, James. "The New Critical Edition" *The American Brahms Society Newsletter* 9/2 (Autumn 1991) p. 5. Presents a progress report.

3381. [Brahms, Johannes. *Sämtliche Werke.* Ausgabe der Gesellschaft der Musikfreunde. [Hans Gal and Eusebius Mandyczewski, eds.] 26 Bde. Leipzig: Breitkopf & Härtel, [1926–27] [= 272]].
    (a) i) *reprint (of Bde. 5 and 6): Brahms. *Complete Concerti in Full Score.* Hans Gál, ed. New York: Dover, 1981. xvii, 332 pp. Includes English translation of Revisionsberichte; Stanley Appelbaum, trans.

(a) ii) *reprint (of Bd. 3): Brahms. *Three Orchestral Works in Full Score*. From the Breitkopf & Härtel Complete Works Edition. Hans Gál, ed. New York: Dover, 1984. 100 pp. Includes English translation of Revisionsberichte; [Stanley Appelbaum, trans.?].

(a) iii) reprint (of Bd. 8): Brahms. *Quintet and Quartets for Piano and Strings*. From the Breitkopf & Härtel Complete Works Edition. Hans Gál, ed. New York: Dover Publications, Inc., 1985. vi, 298 pp. Contains English translation only of Revisionsberichte; Stanley Appelbaum, trans.

(a) iv) *reprint (of Bd. 17): Brahms. *German Requiem in Full Score*. From the Breitkopf & Härtel Complete Works Edition. Eusebius Mandyczewski, ed. New York: Dover, 1987. xvi, 192 pp. ill. Contains English translation of Revisionsberichte, and work's text in both German and English translation; [Stanley Appelbaum, trans.?].

(a) v) reprint (of Bd. 9): Brahms. *Complete Piano Trios*. New York: Dover Publications, Inc., 1988. vi, 281 pp. Contains English translation only of Revisionsberichte; [Stanley Appelbaum, trans.?].

(a) vi) reprint (of Bd. 10): Brahms. *Complete Sonatas for Solo Instrument and Piano*. New York: Dover Publications, Inc., 1989. vi, 202 pp. Contains English translation only of Revisionsberichte; [Stanley Appelbaum, trans.?].

(a) vii) reprint (of Bd. 16): in: *Organ Works: Johannes Brahms, Felix Mendelssohn & Robert Schumann*. From the Breitkopf & Härtel Complete Works Editions. New York: Dover Publications, 1991. iii–viii, 166 pp. Brahms: pp. v–viii, 1–55. Includes reprints of Mendelssohn. *Felix Mendelssohn Bartholdy's Werke. Serie 12: für Orgel*. Julius Rietz, ed. (Leipzig, 1875 (?)) and Schumann. *Werke. Serie 8: für Orgel*. Clara Schumann, ed. (Leipzig, 1881). Contains English translation only of Revisionsberichte and chorale texts for Brahms section; [Stanley Appelbaum, trans.?].

(c) *excerpt (of Bd. 19): Brahms, Johannes. *Alto Rhapsody, Song of Destiny, Nänie, and Song of the Fates in Full Score from the Complete Works Edition*. n.p.: Dover, 1995. 118 pp. [Contains English translation only of Revisionsberichte and vocal texts; Stanley Appelbaum, trans.?] [from compiler]

(d) *index: Rumberger, Marian Stewart. "Contents List for Johannes Brahms *Sämtliche Werke*, Leipzig, Breitkopf & Härtel. Including References to the Payne-Eulenburg Partitur Editions" n.p., 1937. iii, 56 pp.

See also 3301, 3383, 4435.d.

b. Editing, Popular Editions, and Publication Rights

Contains bibliographies of Brahms's works and comments on the editing of Brahms's music by others and the ending of copyright limitations on the original editions.

3381.5 Antonicek, Theophil. "Brahms-Ausgaben der letzten Jahre" *Österreichische Musikzeitschrift* 38/4–5 (4.–5.1983) pp. 289–91. Reviews the various editions of Brahms's music, including those that contain arrangements of works for unusual instrument groupings.

3382. *A Basic Music Library. Essential Scores and Books.* Music Library Association Committee on Basic Music Collection, comp. Pauline Shaw Bayne, ed. Chicago: American Library Association, 1978. vii, 173 pp. ind. Selects the best available editions, work is arranged by genre. Includes books on Brahms, too.
*2nd edition: adds Robert Michael Fling as ed. 1983. vii, 357 pp.
*3rd edition: *A Basic Music Library: Essential Scores and Recordings.* Elizabeth Davis, coordinator. 1996. 550 pp. Includes nearly 7,000 recordings.

3383. Bozarth, George S. "Brahms's Posthumous Compositions and Arrangements: Editorial Problems and Questions of Authenticity" in *Brahms 2* [for full citation see 5481] pp. 59–94. mus., fig., notes., appendixes. A survey of the publication history of the posthumous compositions with an exploration of respective editorial problems. Strongly refutes the theory that the Op. 78 arrangement as a cello sonata is by Brahms.
Appendix A: "Revised Readings for the *Brahms Werke* Edition of the *Choralvorspiele,* Op. 122 nos. 1–7 . . .": pp. 86–88.
Appendix B: "Revised Readings for the *Brahms-Werke* (sic) Edition of 'Regenlied,' WoO [posthum] 23": p. 88.
Appendix C: "Revised Readings for the Hieckel Edition (G. Henle Verlag) of Brahms's Scherzo for Violin and Piano for the 'F.A.E.' Sonata, WoO [posthum] 2 . . .": pp. 88–89.
Appendix D: "Editorial Problems in the *Brahms Werke* Edition of the Sarabandes in A minor and B minor (WoO [posthum] 5),

the Gigue in B minor (WoO [posthum] 4), the Preludes and Fugues in A minor and G minor (WoO [posthum] 9 and 10) and the Cadenzas for the Mozart Concertos, K. 453, 466, and 491 (WoO [posthum] 13–15)": pp. 90–94.

3384. Bozarth, George S. "Breitkopf is also in the process . . ." *The American Brahms Society Newsletter* 7/1 (Spring 1989) p. 10. facsim. Compares editing of Op. 119/1 as seen in Breitkopf and Henle editions.

3385. C.S. [Cesar Saerchinger] "Tuning In With Europe" *Musical Courier* 95/24 (Whole no. 2488) (15.12.1927) p. 38. Discusses the Berne convention in relation to Brahms editions; includes comment on current opinions of Brahms.

3386. Deutsch, Otto Eric. "The First Editions of Brahms. [Part 1]" [Introduction translated by Percy H. Muir] in *Eighteenth- and Nineteenth-Century Source Studies* (The Garland Library of the History of Western Music 8) New York: Garland Publishing Inc., 1985. pp. 1–21. notes. Reprint of portion of 275 (Deutsch. *Music Review* 1/2 (5.1940) pp. 123–43).

3387. Devriès, Anik, and François Lesure. *Dictionnaire des éditeurs de musique français. Volume II. De 1820 à 1914.* (Archives de l'édition musicale française. IV/2) Genève: Éditions Minkoff, 1988. 510 pp. Brahms: pp. 77, 171, 208, 292. Provides historical and bibliographical details on French publishers who published editions of Brahms music.

3388. *[Harvard University.] Houghton Library. *The Haverlin/BMI Collection of Music in the Houghton Library, Harvard University.* Barbara Mahrenholz Wolff, comp. Cambridge: Harvard University Library, 1996. [10] pp. ill. Exhibition catalogue; includes information on 18 editions of Brahms. [from *Notes* 52/4 (6.1996) pp. 1137–38] (e) *report: Petrozzello, Donna. "BMI donates gift of music to Harvard" *Broadcasting & Cable* 126/10 (4.3.1996) p. 36.

3389. "Johannes Brahms (1833–1897)" in Österreichische Nationalbibliothek. Musiksammlung. *Katalog der Sammlung Anthony van Hoboken in der Musiksammlung der Österreichischen Nationalbibliothek. Musikalische Erst- und Frühdrucke. Band 4: Johannes Brahms. Frédéric Chopin.* Bearbeitet von Karin Breitner und Thomas Leibnitz. Herausgegeben vom Institut für Österreichische Musikdokumentation. Tutzing: Hans Schneider, 1986. pp. [1,2,] 3–74. ill., facsim., ind., notes. Cites and describes 174 first and early Brahms editions, with editorial description and comment if warranted.

3390. *Charles Scribner's Sons. *First Editions, Johann Sebastian Bach, Ludwig van Beethoven, Johannes Brahms.* (Catalog no. 119) [New York:] Scribners, 1930. [28] pp. *issue: 1939.

3391. Simeone, Nigel. "Early Brahms Editions: Some Notes and Queries" *Brio* 24/2 (Autumn/Winter 1987) pp. 59–63. notes. Examines variant issues, as held by British Library as copyright deposit copies, to see the bibliographical questions they bring up; starts by looking at the work of Otto Erich Deutsch (275; *Music Review* 1/2,3 (1940)) and Kurt Hofmann (277; *Die Erstdrucke der Werke von Johannes Brahms.* (1975)).

3392. "Die Simrock-Volksausgabe" *Deutsche Militär-Musiker-Zeitung* 31/14 (2.4.1909) pp. 176–77. Announces the publication of a new Brahms music edition that will be half the cost of the regular edition.

3393. *"Ein Spaziergang durch vergriffene Jahrgänge der Musik" *Die Musik* (Berlin) 25 (10.1932) pp. 22–40.

3394. "Urgåvor av Brahms Musik—Från Breitkopf & Härtel till Henle" *Musikrevy* 38/5 (1983) pp. 220–21. facsim., mus. Reviews publishers of Brahms editions (from first through Henle) looking at attention to urtext.

See also 3381.d., 3401, 3410, 3412, 3427, 3429, 3914.

See also "Bibliography," "Textual Criticism," and "Works—Catalogues and Indexes" in Part I.C.; individual publishers in Part III.B.2.; and "Creative Process" in Part V.C.

4. Manuscripts and Manuscript Studies

See also "Creative Process" in Part V.C.

a. Autograph Facsimiles

Contains cross-references to complete facsimiles.
See 3400, 4068, 4238, 4325, 4368, 4534, 4647, 4720, 4834.

b. Manuscripts—Music and Letters

Contains descriptions of Brahms's manuscripts and lists exhibitions featuring Brahms's manuscripts of his own works or his copies of others' works. Includes comments on the process of tracing dispersed manuscripts. Cross-references are made to discussions of individual manuscripts.

Places where manuscripts are:
Austria: 3413, 3419.
Belgium: 3416.
England: 3421.
Germany: 3399, 3405, 3407, 3411, 3412, 3415, 3418.
Poland: 3399.
Russia: 3399.
United States: 3395, 3396, 3404, 3405, 3408, 3414, 3417, 3420.

Reports of manuscripts at auction (by reporting year)—
1983: 3399, 3406 (includes 1981 and 1982).
1987: 3422.
1991: 3403.
1993: 3409.
1994: 3397.
1995: 3398.

3395. Ambrose, Jane P. "Brahms and the Hamburg Frauenchor: An American Footnote" *The American Brahms Society Newsletter* 5/2 (Autumn 1987) pp. [3–5]. ill., facsim. Describes the provenance of the Frauenchor's Stimmenhefte at Smith College and the work done with the Hefte by Sophie and Henry Drinker, Jr.

3396. *Auman, Elizabeth H. "Living treasures: from Brahms to the Gershwins; the Music Division's special collections" *Library of Congress Information Bulletin* 49 (16.7.1990) pp. 258–63.

3397. Bozarth, George S. "Brahms at Auction" *The American Brahms Society Newsletter* 12/2 (August 1994) pp. 7–8. Describes Brahms manuscripts and letters up for sale in Berlin (19 items) and London (10 items), and how these items relate to Brahms's work and situation at their time.

3398. Bozarth, George S. "Brahms at Auction" *The American Brahms Society Newsletter* 13/1 (Spring 1995) p. 9. Provides details on

Brahms manuscripts and letters up for sale in Basel (6 items), Vienna (3 items) and Berlin (9 items).

3399. Bozarth, George S. "Brahms Manuscript Discoveries" *The American Brahms Society Newsletter* 1/2 (Autumn 1983) pp. [7–8]. Describes auctions and autograph sales in the U.S. and Europe, and manuscript discoveries (and their backgrounds) in Poland, Russia and Germany. Includes discussion of a previously unknown solo song "Die Müllerin" [McCorkle Anhang III nr. 13].

3400. Bozarth, George S. "Brahms's Lieder Inventory of 1859–60 and Other Documents of His Life and Work" *Fontes artis musicae* 30/3 (7.–9.1983) pp. 98–117. mus., notes. Detailed discussion of the lieder inventory with full transcription, and comments on dates of compositions; includes descriptions of relevant Brahms documents, including his Werkverzeichnis, the Ischl Testament, Notebooks, drafts for the works, the catalogue of his library, etc. with physical descriptions, locations and provenances, contents summary, their histories and location of available facsimiles.
    (d) i) corrections: "The following corrections need to be made . . ." *Fontes artis musicae* 31/2 (4.–6.1984) p. 129. mus.
        (e) report: "George Bozarth writes that . . ." *The American Brahms Society Newsletter* 2/2 (Autumn 1984) p. [8]. Includes corrections for 4714, 4716, and repeats corrections for 3401.
    (d) ii) see: 3300.

3401. Bozarth, George S. "The First Generation of Brahms Manuscript Collections" *Notes* 40/2 (12.1983) pp. 239–62. notes, appendix. Reconstructs the history and contents of a number of the most important collections (friends, acquaintances and publishers) and when possible comments on how items came into these collections and where they went when the collections were dispersed. Appendix details contents of the collections (86 items).
    (d) correction: "Falling flats and missing sharps . . ." *Notes* 40/4 (6.1984) p. 769. This correction is also in 3400.d.i.e.

3402. Bozarth, George S. "In conjunction . . ." *The American Brahms Society Newsletter* 3/2 (Autumn 1985) p. [10]. Advises that Brahms Archive at the University of Washington is gathering information on primary sources for Brahms correspondence.

3403. Bozarth, George S. "In June 1990 . . ." *The American Brahms Society Newsletter* 9/1 (Spring 1991) p. [12]. Reports on manuscripts offered for sale in 1990 (1 item) and 1991 (2 items).

3404. Bozarth, George S. "The Library of Congress . . . " *The American Brahms Society Newsletter* 6/2 (Autumn 1988) p. [10]. Reports on Library acquisitions of manuscripts (3 items) and correspondence (8 items) with details on provenance and items' descriptions.

3405. Bozarth, George S. "Manuscript Migrations" *The American Brahms Society Newsletter* 11/2 (Autumn 1993) p. 4. Provides details on 4 formerly private manuscript collections that are now housed at the Brahms-Institut (Lübeck) and US-NYpm.

3406. Bozarth, George S. ""New" Brahms Manuscripts. Recent Auctions Produce Rich Yield" *The American Brahms Society Newsletter* 1/1 (Spring 1983) pp. [4–5]. Discusses auctions 1981–83 which had significant Brahms materials (manuscripts, correspondence); focuses on purchases relating to Opp. 3 and 61, McCorkle WoO posthum 18, Brahms-Keller correspondence.

3407. Bozarth, George S. "Updating the Brahms Catalogue" *The American Brahms Society Newsletter* 4/1 (Spring 1986) pp. [7–8]. Reports on Brahms manuscript migrations (3 items: 1 to the Heinrich Heine Institut, Düsseldorf, 2 to new private collectors) and newly discovered items (1). See 3414 for description of 1 item.

3408. Bozarth, George S.; with the assistance of Elizabeth H. Auman and William C. Parsons. *The Musical Manuscripts and Letters of Johannes Brahms (1833–1897) in the Collections of the Music Division, Library of Congress.* [Introduction by Donald L. Leavitt.] Washington, DC: [The Library of Congress,] 1983. 22 pp. 112 manuscripts; 4 collections of letters; 3 single letters. Description includes collation, significant features; for letters it includes background of recipient, whether published or not, number of items in collection.

3409. "Brahms on the Auction Block" *The American Brahms Society Newsletter* 11/1 (Spring 1993) pp. 8–9. Reports on manuscript of Op. 69 no. 9 and 5 items of correspondence on sale; includes comments on provenance and description.

3410. Fellinger, Imogen. "Autographe, Drucke und Ausgaben" in

Johannes Brahms: Leben und Werk [for full citation see 3215] pp. 75–77. Reviews these materials for what they show about creative process. Covers sketches, manuscripts, and editions; also includes works by other composers that Brahms edited and his arrangements. (d) related to: 5499.5.

3411. Hancock, Virginia [Lee]. "Simrock Treasure Trove Goes to Brahms-Institut Lübeck" *The American Brahms Society Newsletter* 13/2 (Autumn 1995) p. 5. facsim. Reports on acquisition of 32 copyists' manuscripts from Fritz Simrock estate. General comments on provenance and on these manuscripts' role in the creative process. (d) see: 3412.

3412. *Hofmann, Kurt, and Renate Hofmann. "Katalog der Stichvorlagen" in *32 Stichvorlagen von Werken Johannes Brahms.* [Introductory Remarks by Jörg Auckenthaler.] (Patrimonia 107) Kiel: KulturStiftung der Länder, 1995. pp. 22–58 (total pp.: 63pp.) ill., facsim. A detailed catalog of this Brahms-Institut (Lübeck) collection; volume also includes 3977 and 5109.

3413. Leibnitz, Thomas, and Agnes Ziffer. *Katalog der Sammlung Anton Dermota. Musikhandschriften und Musikerbriefe.* (Publikationen des Instituts für Österreichische Musikdokumentation 12) Tutzing: Hans Schneider, 1988. ix, 190 pp. Brahms: pp. 15–21. facsim. Descriptions, transliterations and background for 12 items; includes manuscripts, sketches, photographs and correspondence.

3414. Locke, Ralph P., and Jurgen Thym. "New Schumann Materials in Upstate New York: A First Report on the Dickinson Collection, with Catalogues of its Manuscript Holdings" *Fontes artis musicae* 27/3–4 (7.–12.1980) pp. 137–61. Brahms: pp. 142, 148–49, 151, 156. notes. Story of the collection and catalogue with descriptive annotations: 2 manuscripts and 2 postcards Clara Schumann to Brahms, 1890 and 1895 (1895 item in 1179 (C. Schumann. *Clara Schumann. Johannes Brahms. Briefe . . .* (1927))). (e) report: see 3407.

3415. Marx, Hans Joachim. "Johann Matthesons Nachlaβ. Zum Schicksal der Musiksammlung der alten Stadtbibliothek Hamburg" *Acta musicologica* 55/1 (1.–6.1983) pp. 108–24. Brahms: p. 111. Discusses where these manuscripts were located during World War II.

3416. *Musee Royal de Mariemont. *400 lettres de musiciens au Musee Royal de Mariemont.* Malou Haine, ed. (Collection musique/ Musicologie) Liège: Editions Pierre Mardaga, 1995. 596 pp. ill.

3417. "The Music Division of the Library of Congress . . ." *Notes* 45/2 (12.1988) pp. 262–63. Brahms: p. 263. Reports on materials received from Hans Moldenhauer estate; notes that manuscripts for Opp. 65a, 46 no. 1 and 50 had been previously received.

3418. *(?)*Musik, enthält wertvolle Bücher, Musikalien, Autographen und Andere aus den Bibliotheken.* (Katalog 3) Heinrich Reif-Gintl and Wilhelm Pfannkuch, eds.(?) Berlin: R. Hartwig, 1991(?). 299 pp.

3419. Österreichische Nationalbibliothek. Musiksammlung. *Katalog der Handschriften.* Vienna: Olms Microform, [1983]. 106 microfiche + booklet. Brahms: 15th sheet, frames 97–141. This is literally filmed card catalogue cards. 80 items, including manuscripts, correspondence, arrangements of Brahms's works by others, especially Max Reger. Information provided includes manuscript type, collation, and location no.
Booklet: Brosche, Gunter. *Musiksammlung der Österreichischen Nationalbibliothek und ihr Handschriftenkatalog.* (Die Europäische Musik [I, Katalog der Musikhandschriften 1]) 29 pp. facsim. Brahms et passim.

3420. "Restoration Office Uses New Technique To Complete Brahms Preservation Project" *Library of Congress Information Bulletin* 42/45 (7.11.1983) pp. [377]–79. ill. Announces completion of preservation project involving Brahms manuscript collection; focuses on revision done as overlays by Brahms, all separated from original manuscripts.

3420.1. 32 *Stichvorlagen von Werken Johannes Brahms,* see 3412.

3421. Thomason, Geoffrey. "The Brodsky Archive at the RNCM [Royal Northern College of Music]" *Brio* 22/2 (Autumn/Winter 1985) pp. 46–49. Brahms: p. 48. Indicates that correspondence between Brahms and Brodsky (1891– ?) is part of collection with details on selected items.

3422. [Bozarth, George S.] "Updating the Brahms Catalogue" *The American Brahms Society Newsletter* 5/1 (Spring 1987) p. [9]. Reports on recent offering of 3 manuscripts at auction.

See also 3300, 3301, 3424.e.v., 3432.5, 3491, 3492, 3509, 3533, 3644,

3703, 3711, 3909, 3911, 3914, 4095, 4131, 4151, 4158, 4160,
4198, 4238.d., 4262, 4285, 4365, 4373, 4377, 4435, 4458, 4479,
4513, 4534, 4540, 4575, 4588, 4605, 4618, 4654, 4713, 4714,
4716, 4717, 4797, 4823, 4830, 4854, 4856, 4971, 5080, 5109,
5111, 5112, 5158, 5160, 5292, 5429, 5430, 5435, 5462.
See also I10 in Appendix A.

c. Textual Criticism

Contains comparisons of editions of Brahms's music with relevant manuscript sources, or manuscript-to-manuscript comparisons. Cross reference is made to studies of individual works.

See 3301, 3383, 3394, 4131, 4151, 4160, 4198, 4262, 4435.d., 4467,
4513, 4540, 4542.d., 4605, 4647, 4720, 4793.d.e., 5158, 5160,
5462.
See also "Autograph Facsimiles", "Manuscripts—Music and Letters" in
Part I.C. and "Creative Process" in Part V.C.

5. Works—Catalogues and Indexes

3423. Brook, Barry S. "Brahms, Johannes, 1833–1897" [with annotations by Donald M. McCorkle] in Brook. *Thematic Catalogues
in Music. An Annotated Bibliography including printed, manuscript, and in-preparation catalogues; related literature and reviews; an essay on the definitions, history, functions, historiog-
raphy, and future of the thematic catalogue.* (RILM
Retrospectives 1) Hillsdale, NY: Pendragon Press, 1972. pp.
32–34. 8 items.
  *2nd ed.: Brook, and Richard J. Viano. *Thematic Catalogues in
  Music. An Annotated Bibliography.* (RILM Retrospectives 4)
  Stuyvesant, NY: 1995.

3424. McCorkle, Margit L. *Johannes Brahms. Thematisch-bibliographisches Werkverzeichnis.* Herausgegeben nach gemeinsamen
Vorarbeiten mit Donald M. McCorkle †. München: G. Henle Verlag, 1984. lxxvii, [3], 841 pp. ill., mus., ind., notes. Includes complete listing of extant and lost music and manuscripts (includes
arrangements); also music editions. Includes information on works'
origin and creative process, first performance and publication.

Serves as foundation for determining composer's intent as regards to definitive texts and discusses textual relation between manuscripts, manuscripts-editions. Includes information on previous thematic catalogues, publication history of works, history of Brahms's music manuscripts.

(d) i) "Brahms Catalogue a Major Contribution" *University Affairs/Affaires universitaires* [26/2] (2.1985) p. 15. ill. Report on presentation of work to Canada Council.

(d) ii) "The Completion of an 18-year research project . . ." *UBC Reports* 30/17 (19.9.1984) p. 7. Report on launch of catalogue in Germany.

(d) iii) "Work on Brahms Wins German Order of Merit" *The Vancouver Western News* 56/2 (19.2.1986) p. 5. ill. Reports on awarding of Order to McCorkle for her achievement.

(d) iv) see: 5111 and 5112.

(e) i) report: Ackermann, Felicitas. "Zum 150. Geburtstag: Margit McCorkle und die Werke des Johannes Brahms. Ein Sonderbericht" *Pazifische Rundschau* 19/359 (28.5.1983) p. 8. ill., mus. Gives an explanation of the catalogue's purpose and describes the history of the project; written for a general audience.

(e) ii) report: Brolinson, Per-Erik. "Mönstergill förteckning över Brahms verk" *Musikrevy* 40/1 (1985) pp. 37–38. ill., facsim.

(e) iii) *report: Fierz, Gerold. "Rochenschaft über eines komponisten Lebenswerk. Zu einem Verzeichnis von Johannes Brahms' Kompositionen" *Schweizer Monatshefte für Politik, Wirtschaft und Kultur* 65/7–8 (1985) pp. 700–01.

(e) iv) announcement: Hancock, Virginia [Lee]. "In a future issue . . ." *The American Brahms Society Newsletter* 3/1 (Spring 1985) p. [10].

(e) v) report: Kaffsack, Hans-Jochen. "Brahms' Köchel heißt McCorkle und kommt aus Kanada. Erstes Werkverzeichnis im September" *Hamburger Abendblatt* [37] (31.7.1984) p. [?]. Gives background of the project; includes comment on where the autographs are located and the process used to find them.

(e) vi) announcement: McCorkle, Margit L. "Completion of the New Brahms Catalogue" *The American Brahms Society Newsletter* 1/1 (Spring 1983) p. [5]. Describes its audience and the work involved.

(e) vii) [Banham, Jim.] "17-year Research Project Nears Completion" *UBC Reports* 28/8 (17.3.1982) p. 6. ill. Reports on project's history and the completion of the catalog.

(a) i) reprint: "17 Years of Research Results in First Catalogue of Brahms's Work" (UBC Reports) *Alumni Chronicle* [=*UBC Alumni Chronicle*] 36/3 (Fall 1982) pp. 17–18.

(a) reprint: *B.C.L.A. [British Columbia Library Association] Reporter* 26/3 (11.1982) pp. 18–19.

(a) ii) reprint: "UBC Research Team Nears Completion of Landmark Project on Music of Brahms" in *Basic Facts About UBC's Faculty of Arts*. [Vancouver: UBC Faculty of Arts and UBC Department of Information Services, 1982.] pp. 4–5.

(e) viii) Stevens, Agnes. "The Love of Her Life" *The Vancouver Courier. Datebook* (25.12.1985) pp. 15–16. ill. Focuses on McCorkle's personal interest in Brahms; includes comment on the project and the catalogue.

See also 3400.

6. Miscellaneous

Contains works that exist solely to provide access to Brahms's works, or to present Brahms in a larger context by the use of timeline and systematic information grouping.

3425. *Blackmore, A.S.G. *An Index of Composers*. 1. Impression. Bradford-on-Avon, Wiltshire: Saracen Publications, May 1993.
2. (Revised and enlarged) Impression: June 1993. [4], [3–6], 7–220, [3], 222–322 pp. Contains 4 indexes: composers alphabetical by last name; composers in chronological order by birth year; composers in chronological order by death year; composers in alphabetical order by country of origin.

3426. Drone, Jeanette M[arie]., and Mark A. Crook. "Brahms, Johannes" in Drone and Crook. *Indexes to the Established Titles, Variant Titles, Obsolete Uniform Titles, and Work Numbers in the Library of Congress Name-Authority File for the Works of Bach, Beethoven, Brahms, Haydn, Mozart, Schubert, Tchaikovsky, Telemann*. (Research Report Series #OCLC/OR/RR-88/3) Dublin, OH: Office of Research, OCLC Online Computer Library Center, Inc., 1988. Part III [=32 pp.]. Provides access to title data in the

Library of Congress Name-Authority File that are difficult to re-
trieve or unavailable in current OCLC Authority File.

3427. Fuszek, Rita M. "Brahms, Johannes (1883 (sic) –1897)" in Fuszek.
Piano Music in Collections. An Index. Detroit: Information Coordinators, 1982. pp. 96–97. Access for 15 piano works in 74 collections, includes piano arrangements of non-piano works and
transpositions, including those not authorized by Brahms.

3428. Gilder, Eric, and June G. Port. *The Dictionary of Composers and
Their Music. Every Listener's Companion: arranged chronologi-
cally and alphabetically.* New York & London: Paddington Press
Ltd., 1978. [1–9], 12–406, [1–25] pp.
  "Brahms, Johannes/1833–1897/Germany": pp. 49–51. This is in
    an alphabetical listing of composers by last name, with
    works' titles arranged in chronological order by when writ-
    ten, with note of composer's age at time work written.
  Brahms: pp. 263–94. Chronological survey by when works writ-
    ten, in context of time period and other composers' works.
  Brahms: [3rd paging sequence] [pp. 11–12]. Timeline by com-
    posers' lives.
  *[2nd revised edition?]: 1985. Gilder, Eric, only. *The Dictionary
    of Composers and Their Music: A Listener's Companion.*
    New York: Holt, Rinehart, and Winston, 1985.
  also: Newton Abbott, London: David & Charles, 1985. 592 pp.
    "Brahms, Johannes": pp. 64–66; [survey:] pp. 403–31; [time-
    line:] p. 588.

3429. Goleeke, Thomas. *Literature for Voice. An Index of Songs in Collections and Source Book (sic) for Teachers of Singing.* Metuchen,
NJ and London: The Scarecrow Press, Inc., 1984. [2,8,] 223 pp.
ind. Includes 53 references for Brahms's songs. Includes particulars on key, range for each song.

3430. Greene, Frank. *Composers on Record. An Index to Biographical In-
formation on 14,000 Composers Whose Music Has Been Recorded.*
Metuchen, NJ and London: Scarecrow Press, 1985. xxxi, 604 pp.
Brahms: p. 69.

3431. Hancock, Virginia [Lee]. "Mary Ingraham . . ." in Hancock. "Editor's Notes" *The American Brahms Society Newsletter* 14/1
(Spring 1996) p. [12]. Announces World Wide Web site for
Brahms and advises on site for Clara Schumann.
  (d) see: 3432.5.

3432. Hermil, Hélène. *Musique. 10,000 Compositeurs du XIIe au XXe siècle. Repertoire, chrono, ethnique.* Saint Mandé: Production et distribution G.R.E.M. [Groupe de Recherches et d'Etudes Musicales], 1983. [2], 842, [4], xx pp. Brahms: pp. 91, 533, 555. Consists of 2 lists: composers arranged alphabetically by name with dates, mention of works, and composers grouped alphabetically by country (Brahms in Austria and Germany).

    mise en jour Été 1983 à Décembre 1984: 1985. Brahms: p. 65. Adds more works.

3432.5. Ingraham, Mary I[sabel]. "Johannes Brahms WebSource" [World Wide Web (Internet) site] [URL:] <http://www.mjq.net/brahms/> . February 1998. Includes biographical information and a works list; an "Image Gallery"; information on Brahms Societies, Scholars, Festivals and Special Events; audio clips from recordings; and an annotated "Webography" of Web resources.

3433. Murray, Sterling E. "Brahms, Johannes (1833–97)" in Murray. *Anthologies of Music: an annotated index.* (Detroit Studies in Music Bibliography 55) Detroit: Information Coordinators, Inc., 1987. pp. 49–51. Volume indexes 33 anthologies; includes reference to 43 works.

    2nd ed.: (Detroit Studies in Music Bibliography 68) Warren: Harmonie Park Press, 1992. Brahms: pp. 60–63. Volume indexes 40 anthologies; includes reference to 58 works.

3434. Perone, James E. *Musical Anthologies for Analytical Study.* (Music Reference Collection 48) Westport CT, London: Greenwood Press, 1995. vii, [5], 2–182 pp. ind. Volume indexes 41 anthologies; includes reference to 83 Brahms works.

3435. *Poroila, Heikki. *Yhtenaistetyt Brahms ja Chopin: teosten yhtenaistettyjen nimekkeiden ohjeluettelo.* [Catalogue of works with uniform titles—Brahms and Chopin] (Suomen musiikkikirjastoyhdistyksen julkaisusarja 45) Helsinki, Vantaa: Suomen musiikkikirjastoyhdistys, 1994. 66 pp.

3436. Rabson, Carolyn. "Brahms, Johannes" in Rabson. *Orchestral Excerpts. A Comprehensive Index.* (Fallen Leaf Reference Books in Music 25) Berkeley: Fallen Leaf Press, 1993. pp. 36–40. Volume indexes 200+ collections; 23 excerpts for Brahms works.

3437. Vincent, David M. *A Percussionist's Guide to Orchestral Excerpts*. Columbia, SC: Broad River Press, Inc., 1980. 71 pp. A guide to excerpts in 41 volumes and 2 record sets, arranged by instrument. 16 excerpts for Brahms works.

See also 3211, 3252, 3346, 3374, 3381.d., 3683, 3849, 3936, 4110, 4635, 4636, 4642.d., 4653, 4682, 4754, 4763, 4771, 4931, 5103.

See also I49 in Appendix A.

Part II

Brahms Himself

Contains materials that focus on specific periods in Brahms's life; places he visited in his travels; comments he made about other countries; and his personality, physical condition and relationships with other people in general.

A. Life

This section is arranged chronologically.

1. Family History, Childhood (1833–1853), and Links to Hamburg

Brahms in Hamburg: 3438, 3441, 3442, 3445.
Genealogy: 3443.

3438. *Hamburger Correspondent* [119] Supplement (2.5.1849) p. [?].
Review of solo piano recital by Brahms, 14.4.1849. [from b.]
(a) reprint: in 4061.a. pp. 100–01.
(b) English translation by Styra Avins: "Concert of the Pianist J. Brahms" in Avins. "The Young Brahms: Another View" *The American Brahms Society Newsletter* 11/2 (Autumn 1993) p. 5. ill., notes. Review shows that Brahms's talent was recognized early on, in contrast to picture we get from Schumann of the young but anonymous person met with complete indifference in his home town.

3439. *"The Birthplace of Brahms" *American Organist* (New York) 17 (10.1934) p. 463.

3440. "Brahms" *Musical Courier* 45/19 (Whole no. 1180) (5.11.1902) p. 30. Relates anecdotes from 39A.d.i. (M. Kalbeck. *Deutsche Rundschau* (1902)) and 1096 (S. Münz. *Römische Reminiscenzen und Profile*. (1900)).

3441. Hofmann, Kurt. "Johannes Brahms in Hamburg" in *Brahms und seine Zeit*. (Hamburger Jahrbuch für Musikwissenschaft 7) [for full citation see 5428] pp. 21–32. notes. Looks at various events and either provides documentation for them or refutes them.

    (d) i) Hofmann, Kurt. *Johannes Brahms und Hamburg. Neue Erkenntnisse zu einem alten Thema mit 29 Abbildungen*. Reinbek: Dialog-Verlag, 1986. 96, [1] pp. ill., fig. notes. A thorough look at Brahms's life in Hamburg, including his triumph in later years. Includes information on works written and first performed in Hamburg, as well as Hamburg's recognition of him. Includes unpublished letter Christiane Brahms to Johannes, 26.1.1865.

    (d) ii) *Hoffman [Hofmann], Kurt. "Johannes Brahms' Wirken in Hamburg bis zum Jahre 1862: Eine biografische Standortbestimmung" in *Johannes Brahms: Leben, Werk, Interpretation, Rezeption*. [for full citation see 5453] pp. 14–25.

    (d) iii) Hofmann, Kurt. "Neue Aspekte zum Verhältnis Brahms und Hamburg" in *Brahms-Kongress Wien 1983*. [for full citation see 5431] pp. 269–80. notes. Comments on Brahms and Cossel, and Brahms as a child, presents background on Brahms's attempt for the post of conductor in 1862, surveys performances of Brahms's works, discusses the award Brahms was given in 1889. Also includes comment on reaction to Brahms's death and reports on commemorative events to date.

3442. Hofmann, Kurt. "Marginalien zum Wirken des jungen Johannes Brahms" *Österreichische Musikzeitschrift* 38/4–5 (4.–5.1983) pp. 235–44. ill., facsim., notes. Overview of period up until 1853, with details on Brahms in Winsen, Brahms and Joachim, Brahms and Reményi.

3443. *Johnsen, W. "Die Vorfahren von Johannes Brahms [Parts 1–2]" *Brunsbüttelkooger Zeitung* 2. Folge (6.,8.; 5.1933).

3444. Maguire, Helena M. "Johannes Brahms" *The Etude* 23/11 (11.1905) pp. 452–53. Discusses Brahms's childhood; includes comments on what he was like as a child, his home life, Brahms at school.

3445. Petersen, Peter. "Von Hamburg nach Wien" in *Johannes Brahms: Leben und Werk*. [for full citation see 3215] pp. 20–22. Discusses Brahms's bitter links with Hamburg, the city's attempts to honor him after the fact; includes overview of life up to 1862.

3446. Rachlin, Ann. *Brahms*. Susan Hellard, illus. (Famous Children) [Hauppauge, NY:] Barron's, 1993. [21] pp. ill. Juvenile literature; focuses on Brahms at 6–10 years old, with emphasis on his early musical training with Cossel and Marxsen.
  *also: (Fun With Music) n.p.: Childrens Press, 1993.
  (b) *French translation by Myrian De Visscher (of Hauppauge edition): (Enfants célèbres; Gamma jeunesse; Héritage jeunesse) Paris: Éditions Gamma; Saint-Lambert, Que.: Éditions Héritage, 1994.

3447. Tapper, Thomas. "Brahms as a Boy" *The Etude* 21/7 (7.1903) p. 270. Describes Brahms's musical prowess up to age 10 and his training with Cossel.

3448. *Wiepking, Henny. "Wo ging Johannes Brahms zur Schule?" *St. Georger Blätter* (Hamburger Stadtteil-Zeitung) (Frühjahr 1966). Reprint of 358.e.ii. (Wiepking. *Vom Jungfernsteig zur Reeperbahn* (1962)).

See also 3236, 3237.d.ii., 3246, 3247, 3251, 3263, 3269, 3425, 3432, 3522, 3570, 3646, 3652, 3668, 3732, 3865, 3866, 3932, 4030, 4054, 4057, 4061, 4100, 4459, 4478, 5009, 5047, 5066, 5169, 5226, 5239, 5313, 5324.
See also "Brahms Family" in Part III.B.; and "Memorial Activities" in Part VII.

2. In Transition (1853–1862)

3449. *Göttinger Zeitung* (21.,25.;3.1911). Describes Brahms, Remenyi and Joachim in Göttingen in 1853. [from 3441.d.i.]

3450. "Liszt, Remenyi and Brahms" *Music* (Chicago) [14/3] (7.1898)

p. 304. ill. Discusses a portrait of these three and speculates that the figure thought to be Brahms may not be him at all.

3451. Schram, Willi. *Johannes Brahms in Detmold.* Neu herausgegeben und mit Anmerkungen versehen von Richard Müller-Dombois. (Beiträge zur westfälischen Musikgeschichte 18) Hagen: Kommissionsverlag v.d. Linnepe, 1983. [2], viii, 64, [7] pp. ill., notes. Reprint of 380 (published in 1933) with new notes and more local history research. Includes 3554.

3452. *Sink, Gina Martha. "Brahms, The Crucial Years, 1853–1865" M.Mus. diss., Kansas State University, 1979. 37 pp. mus., notes.

3453. *Specht, Richard. "[A Rhineland Pilgrimage]" *Musik-Kultur* 4 (1929) pp. 89–97. Excerpt of 82 (Specht. *Johannes Brahms.* (1928)) in Swedish translation (?). [title from WPA index; annotation from compiler]

See also 3236, 3237.d.ii., 3246, 3251, 3264, 3269, 3275, 3395, 3401, 3445, 3522, 3562, 3604, 3662, 3665, 3668, 3671, 3715, 3838, 3866, 3938, 3947, 3950, 3952, 3956, 3958, 3960, 3961, 3987, 4054, 4057, 4100, 4285, 4325, 4459, 4478, 4517, 4782, 4864, 4947, 5008, 5009, 5143.d.iv., 5212, 5274, 5367, 5415, 5440, 5461, 5469.

3. Brahms and Vienna (1862–1894)

Brahms and the Rote Igel: 3472.
Involvement with Viennese Institutions: 3455, 3456, 3460, 3464, 3477, 3480.

3454. Banks, Paul. "Vienna: Absolutism and Nostalgia" in *The Late Romantic Era. From the Mid-19th Century to World War I.* Jim Samson, ed. (Man and Society) Englewood Cliffs, NJ: Prentice Hall, 1991. pp. 74–98. Brahms: pp. 85–90, 97–98. fig., ind., notes. Describes Vienna during Brahms's times; includes comments on Brahms the man and on Brahms and Bruckner.
*also: (Man & Music) London: Macmillan, 1991.

3455. Biba, Otto. "Brahms in Wien" in *Brahms und seine Zeit.* (Hamburger Jahrbuch für Musikwissenschaft 7) [for full citation see 5428] pp. 259–71. notes. Describes characteristics of Viennese musical life when Brahms came to Vienna, and his involvement with various musical societies.

(d) related to: 5449.5.

3456. Biba, Otto. "Brahms und die Gesellschaft der Musikfreunde in Wien" in *Brahms-Kongress Wien 1983*. [for full citation see 5431] pp. 45–65. notes. Surveys important sources and details for Brahms's involvement with the Gesellschaft, 1862–1897. Looks at his role both when he was conductor and afterwards, the activities he was involved in.

3457. Biba, Otto. "Brahms-Gedenkstätten in Wien" *Österreichische Musikzeitschrift* 38/4–5 (4.–5.1983) pp. 245–47. notes. Traces where Brahms lived, places he frequented, memorial sites.

3458. Biba, Otto. "Johannes Brahms und die Musikstadt Wien" in *Musikbuch in Österreich. Eine Chronik in Daten, Dokumenten, Essays und Bildern.* Gottfried Kraus, ed. 1. Auflage. Wien: Verlag Christian Brandstätter, 1989. pp. 253–57; also et passim. ill. Describes Vienna at the time of Brahms; includes comment on his circle and activities.

3459. Botstein, Leon. "Time and Memory: Concert Life, Science and Music in Brahms's Vienna" in *Brahms and His World*. [for full citation see 5478] pp. 3–22. notes. Atttempts to understand Brahms the composer better by looking at the character of Viennese musical culture and contemporary scientific thought and its impacts on music.

3460. Brahms, Johannes. *Mit den Gedanken in Wien. With My Thoughts in Vienna. 5 Briefe/5 Letters. Faksimiles/Facsimiles.* Mit Erläuterungen von/With Commentaries by Otto Biba. Eugene Hartzell, trans. Wien-München: Doblinger, 1984. 27 pp. [pp. 5–16 are the German; pp. 17–27 are the English translation] All letters are at A-Wgm; includes short introduction on Brahms and Vienna. Letters are Brahms to Franz Flatz (between 1864–67); Johann Peter Gotthard (1868); Gesellschaft der Musikfreunde's Board of Directors (1876, 1896); Johann Herbeck (1876).

3461. *Brincker, Jens. *Wien: Drommeby og undergangsstad—Musik, mennesker og kultur omkring 1900.* Herning: Systime, 1993. 144 pp. ill., mus., fig., ind., notes. Discusses characteristic aspects of Viennese music culture, based on analyses of music by composers of the time. [from S109]

3462. C.M. "Besuch bei Cölestine Truxa, der Hausfrau von Johannes Brahms" *Neues Wiener Journal* 41/14,170 (4.5.1933) pp. 5–6. Reports details on Brahms at home, his routines in Vienna; includes comments on Brahms the man.

3463. Endler, Franz. "Johannes Brahms" in Endler. *Musik in Wien— Musik aus Wien. Eine kleine Wiener Musikgeschichte.* (Österreich-Thema) Wien: Österreichischer Bundesverlag, 1985. pp. 81–89. ill. Discusses Brahms and his circle in Vienna, Brahms the man. There are many anecdotes. Includes comment on his influence.

   (b) English translation by Leo Jecny: Endler. "Johannes Brahms" in Endler. *Vienna. A Guide to Its Music and Musicians.* Foreword by Leonard Bernstein. Reinhard G. Pauly, General Ed. Portland: Amadeus Press, 1989. pp. 53–58.

3464. Floros, Constantin. ""Orchester-Werke gehörten eigentlich den Philharmonikern." Brahms, Bruckner und die Wiener Philharmoniker" in *Klang und Komponist. Ein Symposion der Wiener Philharmoniker. Kongressbericht.* Otto Biba and Wolfgang Schuster, eds. Tutzing: Hans Schneider, 1992. pp. 157–65. notes. Discusses Brahms's relation to the Wiener Philharmoniker: its playing of his works, his reception in Vienna. Contrasts Brahms's situation to Bruckner's, also both as composers for the Philharmoniker sound.

3465. Fridberg, Franz. "Personal Recollections of Johannes Brahms" *Musical Courier* 38/5 (1.2.1899) p. 21. Report on 935 (Fribberg (sic). *Berliner Tageblatt* (18.12.1898)). Describes how unpopular Brahms was in Vienna at first; includes anecdotes of meeting with Brahms, Brahms and Bülow, Brahms in his later years.

3466. "Geiringer Scholar Awarded National Grants" *The American Brahms Society Newsletter* 14/1 (Spring 1996) p. 5. Notice of award to Margaret Notley, who's doing research on Viennese musical culture and Brahms's "Late Style" (1882–1892).

3467. *Grieser, Dietmar. "Johannes Brahms" in Grieser. *Wien : Wahlheimat der Genies.* Munchen : Amalthea, 1994. ill.

3468. Herttrich, Ernst. "Brahms-Aufführungen in Wien - Rezensionen und Materialien" in *Brahms-Kongress Wien 1983.* [for full citation see 5431] pp. 229–45. facsim., notes. Discusses appearances of Brahms's work in Vienna and how they were received; appearances of Brahms as pianist and how he played; and Brahms's work as a conductor (of Bach) and how he performed it.

3469. *Keller, James. "Beethoven, Brahms, and Bruckner Slept Here" *Travel & Leisure* 25/10 (10.1995) pp. 133+ .

3470. Kretschmer, Helmut. "Brahms, Johannes" in Kretschmer. *Wiener Musikergedenkstätten*. Felix Czeike, ed. Wien: J & V Edition, 1988. pp. 26–30. ill., ind. Lists locations/addresses in Vienna that have a Brahms connection: residences, grave, statue, museum.

3471. Kretschmer, Helmut. "Die Stadt Wien in der zweiten Hälfte des 19. Jahrhunderts—Wahlheimat von Johannes Brahms" in *Brahms-Kongress Wien 1983*. [for full citation see 5431] pp. 301–08. notes. Describes the Vienna of Brahms's time, especially when he first arrived. Focuses on the political and overall cultural scene.

3472. *Kromnitzer, Josef. "Das Gasthaus der Berühmtheiten" *Österreichische Volkzeitung* (Summer 1916).

3473. Mailer, Franz. "Musik in den Wiener Gast- und Unterhaltungsstätten zur Brahmszeit" in *Brahms-Kongress Wien 1983*. [for full citation see 5431] pp. 361–65. Describes Vienna's musical life (classical and popular) when Brahms arrived: institutions, programming, prominent composers and conductors.

3474. Morton, Frederic. *A Nervous Splendor: Vienna 1888/1889*. 1st edition. Boston, Toronto: Little, Brown and Company, 1979. x, 340 pp. ill., ind., notes. Brahms: pp. 161–67; also et passim. Describes Brahms's daily routines and contrasts Brahms with Bruckner, sees Brahms as an element in Vienna's mosaic. Time period covered is 7.1888–20.4.1889.

3475. Nebehay, Christian M[ichael]. "Johannes Brahms 1833–1897" in Nebehay. *Wien speziell - Musik um 1900: Wo finde Ich Berg, Brahms, Mahler, Schönberg, Hauer, Wolf, Bruckner, Strauss, Zemlinsky, Webern. Leben und Werk/Gedenk- und Wirkungsstätten/Museen und Sammlungen in Wien*. Wien: Christian Brandstätter Verlag & Edition, 1984. pp. III/1–III/24. ill., facsim., mus. Pinpoints places of interest in connection with Brahms.

3476. *Pisk, Paul A. "Johannes Brahms en Weenen" *[De] Muziek* (Amsterdam) 7 (5.1933) pp. 340–42.

3477. Planyavsky, Alfred. "150 Jahre Wiener Philharmoniker" (Ein Stück europäischer Musik- und Orchestergeschichte. 2) *Das Orchester* (Hamburg) 40/11 (1992) pp. 1298–1305.
"Brahms und Bruckner": p. 1298. Traces early performances of Brahms's works (1860–1870's).

3478. Stefan, Paul. "Vienna's Gifts to Brahms, Her Adopted Son" *Musical America* 53/9 (10.5.1933) pp. 8, 34. ill. Discusses its attractions for Brahms, his activities, his last days.

3479. *Weber, H. "Brahms als k[aiser-]. u[nd]. k[öniglicher]. Komponist" *Jahrestagung der Gesellschaft für Musikforschung Marburg* (1983).

3480. Witeschnik, Alexander. *Musizieren geht übers Probieren oder Viel Harmonie mit kleinen Dissonanze. Die Geschichte der Wiener Philharmoniker in Anekdoten und Geschichten.* Wien: Paul Neff Verlag, 1967. 212 pp. Brahms: pp. 42–47. ill. Relates anecdotes from the late 1880's.
*im text ungekurzte Ausgabe: ([Deutscher Taschenbuch Verlag] 622) München: Deutscher Taschenbuch Verlag, 1969.
*2. Auflage: 1970. (dtv Taschenbücher 622) 156 pp. ill.
*4. Auflage: 1975. ([Deutscher Taschenbuch Verlag] 622) adds facsim.

See also 3432, 3440, 3445, 3452, 3522, 3523, 3646, 3653.6, 3668, 3670, 3671, 3679, 3695, 3703, 3710.d., 3711, 3721, 3725, 3727, 3729, 3735, 3740, 3741, 3786, 3787, 3796, 3800, 3808, 3809, 3820, 3830, 3844, 3847, 3848, 3863, 3866, 3945, 4012, 4054, 4253, 4292, 4481, 4541, 4887, 4940, 5143.d.v., 5305, 5319, 5350, 5381, 5405.
See also "Last Years, Death, Nachlaß (Legacy), and Testament" in Part II.A.; and "Memorial Activities" in Part VII.
See also I32 in Appendix A.

4. Last Years, Death, Nachlaß (Legacy), and Testament (1894–1902)

Last Days (8.1896–4.1897): 3501, 3505, 3510, 3513.
Death and Funeral: 3484, 3494, 3499, 3503, 3507, 3511.
Obituaries/Death Notices: 3481, 3483, 3486, 3488, 3500, 3504.
Nachlaß: 3484, 3489, 3491–93, 3495–97, 3509, 3516.

3481. *Chicago Tribune* (?.4.1897).
    (a) *reprint: *Presto* (Chicago) 13/564 (15.4.1897) p. 10.

3482. *The Independent* (New York) (1897).
    (a) *reprint: Stevenson, E. Irenaeus. "Johannes Brahms 1833–1897" *Musical Courier* 35 (20.10.1897) p. 13.

3483. *Musical Courier* 34 (7.4.1897) pp. 19–20. Obituary. [from WPA index]

3484. *Musical News* (London) 15 (6.8.1898) p. 121. Reports on disposition of Nachlaβ and events following death. [from WPA index]

3485. *Nachrichtenblatt des Reichskommissars für die Wiedervereinigung Österreichs mit dem Deutschen Reich* no. 28 (27.1.1939).

3486. *Presto* (Chicago) 13/563 (8.4.1897) p. 9. Obituary. [from WPA index]

3487. Bäβler, Hans. "Das Leiden und Sterben als theologisch-musikalisches Problem" *Musik und Bildung* 19/11 (Bd. 78) (11.1987) pp. 831–37. Brahms: pp. 834–36. ill., facsim., mus., notes. Looks at how Brahms felt about his own death, looks at Opp. 105 and 121 in particular. For planning a music lesson on this topic.

3488. *Bergheim, Gaigg von. "Johannes Brahms" *Die Reichspost* (Wien) (6.4.1897) p. 1. Obituary. [from compiler]

3489. Biba, Otto. "New Light on the Brahms Nachlass" in *Brahms 2*. [for full citation see 5481] pp. 39–47. notes. Relates the entire history of the Nachlaβ, from 1891 until final resolution in 1915, using primary source documents. Also discusses dispersal of estate and its current whereabouts.

3490. "Brahms Again" *Musical Courier* 37 (26.10.1898) p. 25.

3491. "Brahms Legacies" *Musical Courier* 44/17 (Whole no. 1152) (23.4.1902) p. 21. Reports on the disposition of the manuscripts and advises that there are still lawsuits ongoing in regards to the disposition of the letters addressed to Brahms.

3492. *"Brahms Manuscripts" *Musical Courier* 42 (13.3.1901) p. 30.

3493. *"Brahms Relics" *Musical Courier* 10[40]/4 (27.7.1900).

3494. *"Brahms' Death Day" *Musical News* (London) 32 (6.4.1907) pp. 329–30.

3495. *"Brahms' Estate" *Presto* (Chicago) 13/566 (29.4.1897) p. 11.

3496. "Brahm's (sic) Will" *Musical Courier* 43/11 (Whole no. 1120) (11.9.1901) pp. 24–25. Contains an English translation of Brahms's testament (1871 letter to Simrock) and describes the lawsuits that are going on.

3497. *"Brahms's Will" *Presto* (Chicago) 15/630 (28.7.1898) p. 5.

3498. De Eisner. "Giovanni Brahms" *Gazzetta musicale di Milano* 52/15 (15.4.1897) pp. 220–21. ill. Memorial article, overview of life and works and comment on style.

3499. *"Death Bed and Funeral of Brahms" *Presto* (Chicago) 13/565 (22.4.1897) p. 9.

3500. "Death of Brahms" *The Etude and Musical World* 15/5 (5.1897) p. 123. Obituary.

3501. Franken, Franz Hermann. "Johannes Brahms (1833–1897)" in Franken. *Die Krankheiten großer Komponisten. Bd. 2. Wolfgang Amadeus Mozart. Carl Maria von Weber. Gioacchino Rossini. Franz Schubert. Gaetano Donizetti. Johannes Brahms.* (Taschen-bücher zur Musikwissenschaft 105) Wilhelmshaven: Florian Noetzel Verlag »Heinrichshofen-Bücher«, 1989. pp. 245–89. ill., notes. Reviews Brahms's life from a medical history point of view, focuses on the last year of his life.

3502. [Ellis, Horace.] "Frau Cosima Wagner as a Brahms Student" *Music* (Chicago) [14/3] (7.1898) p. 321. Report on 443.c.ii. (J.B.K. *Musical Opinion and Music Trade Review* (1897–98)).

3503. "The Funeral of Brahms . . ." *The Etude and Musical World* 15/6 (6.1897) p. 146. Describes the event.

3504. "Giovanni Brahms" *Gazzetta musicale di Milano* 52/14 (8.4.1897) p. 211. Announcement of Brahms's death.

3505. *Hanslick, Edward [Eduard]. "Brahms' Last Days" *Musical Courier* 34 (5.5.1897) p. 17. Report/English translation of ex-cerpts of 443 (E. Hanslick. *Neue freie Presse* (Wien) (1897)). [from compiler]

3506. *Heyse, Paul. "Johannes Brahms†" in (?) Heyse. *Neue Gedichte und Jugendlieder*. Berlin: Hertz, 1897.

(a) reprint: in Heyse, Paul. "Frühling am Gardasee (1897)" in Heyse. *Gesammelte Werke*. 3. Reihe. Bd. V. Stuttgart-Berlin-Grunewald: J.G. Cottasche Buchhandlung Nachfolger, Verlagsanstalt Hermann Klemm A.G., 1924(?). pp. 393–94. Poem on Brahms's death and its impact on music scene.

3507. *Hirschfeld, Robert. "Johannes Brahms" *Neue musikalische Presse* [=*Internationale Musik- und Instrumenten-Zeitung*] [6] (4.4.1897) p. 1.

3508. *Hirschfeld, Robert. "Zum 3. April" *Neue musikalische Presse* [=*Internationale Musik- und Instrumenten-Zeitung*] [7] (3.4.1898) pp. 1–2.

3509. "It is reported to "La Bibliofilia" that . . ." *Music* (Chicago) [19/5] (3.1901) p. 536. Reports on the number of musical items (editions, books, manuscripts) in Brahms's library.

3510. "Mme Celestina Truxa . . ." *Le Guide musical* 49/28–29 (12. et 19.;7.;1903) pp. 540–41. Report on 526 (C. Truxa. *Neue freie Presse* (Wien) (7.5.1903) Morgenblatt). Describes Brahms's last day.

3511. *"On Deathbed" *Presto* (Chicago) 13 (19.11.1896(?)) p. 9.

3512. *"The Passing of Brahms" *Musical Courier* 34 (19.5.1897) pp. 11–12.

3513. *Perger, Richard v. "Brahms' letzte Tage" *Deutsche Militärmusikerzeitung* 30 (1908) pp. 467–68.

3514. *Piening, Karl Theodor. "Johannes Brahms' letztes Pfingstfest" *Weser-Zeitung* (Bremen) (4.6.1933).
(a) i) *reprint: *Westfälische Zeitung* (4.6.1933).
(a) ii) reprint: in 3884 pp. 128–32. Recounts the private music festival organized by the Weyermann's in May 1896. Reports on who attended, what was played, Brahms's activities.

3515. *Revers, Henri, and Alfred Kaiser. "Johannes Brahms" *La Revue blanche* 12 (1897) pp. 461–66.

3516. Smekal, Richard. "Unbekanntes von Johannes Brahms. Reliquien und Briefe aus seinem Nachlaß" *Die Musik* (Berlin) 22/10 ([7.1930]) pp. 794–95. Reprint of 519 (R. Smekal. *Neues Wiener Journal* (1930)).

3517. *"Word-Picture of Brahms" *Presto* (Chicago) 15/663 (16.3.1899)
        p. 7.

See also 3237.d.ii., 3247, 3267, 3400, 3401, 3425, 3441.d.iii., 3465,
        3470, 3478, 3648, 3665, 3668, 3729, 3838, 3919.d.i., 3953, 4052,
        4626, 4732, 4940, 5209, 5371, 5388, 5443.

B. Brahms the Traveller

The "Specific Countries" subsection is arranged alphabetically by country name. Cross references include reference to national attitudes towards
Brahms and his music.

1. General Remarks

3518. *Birt, Theodor. *Auf Reisen. Ein Ferienbuch.* Leipzig: Quelle &
        Meyer, 1924. xi, 178 pp.

3519. Kneif, Tibor. "Konzertreisen und Sommeraufenthalte" in *Jo-
        hannes Brahms: Leben und Werk.* [for full citation see 3215] pp.
        36–39. fig. Gives overview of concert tours, 1840–1880; also
        overview of summer stays and table showing which works writ-
        ten during which summer stay.

3520. *Philharmonia; guida alle città dell'Europa musicale.* Valerio
        Tura and Roberto Verti, eds. (Collana) Bologna: Calderini, 1993.
        xiv, 597 pp. Describes 58 concerthalls and includes tourist infor-
        mation on each city cited. [from S031]

See also 3605.

2. Specific Countries

Australia

3521. *Australian Musical News* [=*Music and Dance*] [1–53 (1911–
        1953)].

Austria

General Remarks: 3522, 3523, 3531.
Altaussee: 3524.

Bad Ischl: 3525, 3532.

Gmunden: 3528–30.

Mürzzuschlag: 3527.

Pörtschach: 3526.

Wien: See "Brahms and Vienna" and "Last Years, Death, Nachlaβ (Legacy), and Testament" in Part II.A.

3522. Asshauer, Sigrun, and Henning Berkefeld. *Johannes Brahms. Symphonische Sommer.* Fotografiert von Sigrun Asshauer and Henning Berkefeld. Erzählt von Hans A. Neunzig. München, Wien: Mahnert-Lueg [bei Langen Müller], 1983. 143 pp. ill., notes. Focuses on summer destinations in Germany and Austria, presented in chronological order. Discusses activities, circle of friends, pieces written at each. Also includes an overview of Brahms's life up to 1872.

3523. *Brusatti, Otto. *Alles schon wegkomponiert.* 1. Auflage. St. Pölten: Niederösterreichisches Pressehaus, 1991. 181 or 198 pp. ill. Highlights specifically Austrian elements in the life and works of Brahms and 13 other composers. [from S102]

3524. *Ebert, Wolfgang. *Johannes Brahms in Altaussee.* Wien: Author, 1982. 10 pp. ill., facsim. Describes his visits in 1867, 1880, 1882. [from S102]

3525. *Eyckmans, Jozef. *Brahms in Bad Ischl.* Brussel: Manteau, 1974. 51 pp. Collection of poems. [from S031]

3526. *Fuchs, Anton. *Auf ihren Spuren in Kärnten. Alban Berg, Gustav Mahler, Johannes Brahms, Hugo Wolf, Anton Webern.* Klagenfurt: Kärtner Druck- und Verlagsgesellschaft, 1982.
2. geänderte Auflage: "Johannes Brahms. Auf seinen Spuren in Kärnten" 1988. pp. 37–53. ill., facsim. Describes Brahms in Pörtschach, 1877–79: works written, circle of friends, activities. Reprint of 536 (Fuchs. *Die Brücke* (Klagenfurt) (1976)).

3527. *Fuchs, Ronald. *Brahms in Mürzzuschlag.* Wien: Doblinger Verlag, [1985].
(d) Fuchs. "Brahms in Mürzzuschlag" *The American Brahms Society Newsletter* 4/1 (Spring 1986) p. [7]. ill. Reports on May 1985 festival and its activities; includes comment on Brahms's visits in 1884, 1885.

3528. *Prillinger, Elfriede. "Anregung und/oder Auslösung: Das Salzkammergut als Anziehungspunkt für Musiker" in *Bruckner Symposion: Musikstadt Linz—Musikland Oberösterreich*. Linz: Anton-Bruckner-Institut, 1993. p. 273–281. notes. Discusses the attraction of the Salzkammergut to musicians. [from S109]

3529. *Prillinger, E[lfriede]. "Aus Gmundens Kurlisten, Gäste- und Tagebüchern. Beziehung und Auswirkung am Beispiel Miller-Aichholz und Brahms" *Oberösterreich. Kulturzeitschrift* no. 3 (1983) pp. 29–35.

3530. *Prillinger, E[lfriede]. "Brahms in Gmunden - Geschichte einer Freundschaft. Aus der berühmten Sammlung Miller-Aichholz im Kammerhofmuseum Gmunden" *Salzkammergut-Zeitung* no. 30 (28.7.1983) p. 19.

3531. *Scheller, Erich. "Sternstundenreise auf den Spuren von Friedrich Hebbel und Johannes Brahms nach Österreich vom 15. bis 22. Mai 1993" *Jahresgabe der Klaus-Groth-Gesellschaft* 35 (1993) pp. 151–154. ill.

3532. *Spitzer, Daniel. "Aus Ischl" (18.8.1889). [originally published in one of the major Viennese newspapers]
(a) i) *reprint: Spitzer. "Aus Ischl" in Spitzer. *Letzte Wiener Spaziergänge*. Wien: Verlag der literarischen Gesellschaft, 1894.
(a) *reprint: in Spitzer. *Wiener Spaziergänge. III*. Max Kalbeck and Otto Erich Deutsch, eds. (Spitzer. Gesammelte Schriften 6) München: Georg Müller, 1914.
(a) ii) reprint: Spitzer. in Spitzer. *Wiener Spaziergänge*. Gustav Brenner, ed. (Gesamtausgabe der Wiener Spaziergänge 7) Wien: Verlag Haase, [1967]. pp. [260]–67. Brahms: pp. 266–67. Describes meeting Brahms in Ischl, his activities, how he looks.

See also 3646, 3774, 3882, 3902, 4979, 5073, 5323, 5372, 5416, 5419, 5439, 5454, 5465, 5466.
See also I32 in Appendix A.

Brazil

See 4035.

Czech Republic

3533. Nouza, Zdeněk. "Beobachtungen zu Brahms' Stellung im Tschechischen Musikleben seiner Zeit" in *Brahms-Kongress Wien 1983*. [for full citation see 5431] pp. 405—[425]. ill., facsim., notes. Reports on instances when Brahms's music was performed and the reaction to it, discusses his connections with other Czech composers (Dvořák, Suk, Martinů), Brahms mss. in Czech locations.

See also 3745, 4388.

Denmark

3534. Martner, Knud. "Johannes Brahms i København" *dmt. Dansk Musiktiddsskrift* 57/6 (1982/83) pp. 248–51, 253–54. ill. Describes concert tour Brahms and Stockhausen made to København in 1868; also mentions Nielsen visiting Brahms in Wien, 11.1894.

See also 4061.

England

3535. Musgrave, Michael. "Brahms and England" in *Brahms 2*. [for full citation see 5481] pp. 1–20. ill., notes. Surveys performing of Brahms's music in England and the reaction to it; traces reaction of English critics/composers/academics from Brahms's times to the present. Includes letter from Grove to Brahms (1884) and Cobb to Brahms (1876).

3536. (?)*Music in England, 1885–1920: as recounted in Hazell's Annual*. Edited with illustrations, introduction and index by Lewis Foreman. London: Thames Publishing, 1994. viii, 121 pp.

3537. "The music of Brahms . . ." *The Musical Times* 38/651 (1.5.1897) pp. 305–06. Describes early performances of Brahms's music in England in chronological order; includes a list of "first" performances up through the 1870's.

3538. "A musical controversy . . ." *The Musical Times* 58/896 (1.10.1917) p. 472. Reports on 550 (D.H. Blair. *The Times* (1917)).
  (d) [Henschel, George.] "The Attitude of Brahms to England" *The*

Musical Times 58/897 (1.11.1917) p. 497. notes. Reports on controversy to date; uses excerpts of 2 letters Brahms to Henschel 1878, 1887, to show that Brahms didn't dislike England. [Both letters are in 979 (G. Henschel. *Personal Recollections of Johannes Brahms*. (1907))]

3539. *Simeone, Nigel. "[Handlist for "Brahms and England"]" Goldsmiths' College, University of London, 1983.
    (a) reprint: Simeone. "Brahms and England" in *Brahms 2*. [for full citation see 5481] pp. 237–45. Description and background of the 76 items in this exhibit: Brahms's personal items, and items that show his English ties (people, editions, concert programs)

See also 3610, 3615, 3796, 3988, 5273, 5344, 5368, 5419.

Finland

See 4061.

France

3540. *Stockhem, Michel. "Armand Parent, Brahms et la France" *Revue belge de musicologie=Belgisch tijdschrift voor muziekwetenschap* 47 (1993) pp. 177–188. Studies the Belgian violinist's role in the introduction of Brahms's chamber music in Paris between 1890 and 1914, and on French critics' reception of these works. [from S109]

See also 3387, 3570, 4805, 5320.d., 5349, 5387, 5449.

Germany

Baden-Baden: 3545, 3551, 3555, 3574, 3576.
Berlin: 3546, 3553, 3569.
Breslau: 3542.
Detmold: 3554.
Göttingen: 3562.
Hamburg: see "Family History, Childhood, and Links to Hamburg" in Part II.A.
Heidelberg: 3541, 3564, 3565, 3575.
Karlsbad: 3559, 3560.

Karlsruhe: 3573.
Kiel: 3570.
Leipzig: 3550, 3563.
Meiningen: 3566, 3567.
München: 3552, 3568.
Wiesbaden: 3574.
Ziegelhausen: 3543, 3544, 3547–49, 3556–58, 3571, 3572.

3541. *B. [Friedrich Baser?] "Johannes Brahms und Anselm Feuerbach in Heidelberg" *Heidelberger neueste Nachrichten* (29.3.1941).

3542. *Bartel, Helmut. "Brahms und Breslau" *Schlesien* 32/2 (1987) pp. 106–10. mus.

3543. *Baser, Friedrich. "Brahms in Ziegelhausen" *Heidelberger Tageblatt* (6.5.1933).

3544. "[[Eine Brahms-Erinnerung]]" *Kölnische Zeitung* 1. Morgen= Ausgabe no. 948 (8.9.1908) p. [1]. Author goes to Ziegelhausen and rents the same rooms that Brahms had in 1875; reports on innkeeper's stories about Brahms's activities and his circle of friends.
(a) *reprint: *Heidelberger Tageblatt* (9.9.1908).

3545. *Brahmsgesellschaft Baden-Baden [e.V.]. [Baden-Baden: Author, 1986?] Booklet on Brahms and the Brahms-Haus. [from *The American Brahms Society Newsletter* 4/2 p. [10]]

3546. Eberle, Gottfried. "Bollwerk der musikalischen Reaktion: Berlin und Brahms" in *Verteidigung des musikalischen Fortschritts*. [for full citation see 3931] pp. 13–21. Describes Berlin's musical scene and how Brahms fit into it. Discusses his performing there (1868, 1882), his circle of friends, works played there, and what Berliners thought of him.

3547. *Eberts, Karl. "Die Komponierhöhle am Neckar. Ziegelhäuser Brahms-Erinnerungen" *Heidelberger Tageblatt* (28.5.1926).

3548. *Eggert, Walther. "Die Komponierhöhle von Ziegelhausen" *Heidelberger Fremdenblatt* (7.1955).

3549. *Fehr, Luise. "Erinnerungen an Brahms" *Heidelberger Tageblatt* (28.5.1926).

3550. *Forner, Johannes. "Johannes Brahms und seine Beziehung zur
Stadt Leipzig. Ein Beitrag zum Leipziger Konzertleben in der 2.
Hälfte des 19. Jahrhunderts" Habilitationsschrift, Musikwissen-
schaft, Karl-Marx-Universität Leipzig, 1986. 194 pp.

(a) reprint: Forner. *Johannes Brahms in Leipzig. Geschichte einer
Beziehung.* 1. Auflage. (Bilder aus Leipzigs Musikleben)
Leipzig: Edition Peters, 1987. 144 pp. ill., facsim., fig., ind.,
notes. Traces visits by Brahms (1853–96); Brahms playing in
concerts (Opp. 15, 45, 83); and Brahms works performed; includes Leipziger opinions of Brahms from the likes of Rei-
necke, Nikisch and Bülow.

(d) *Forner, Johannes. "Brahms in Leipzig: Geschichte einer
Beziehung" in *Johannes Brahms: Leben, Werk, Interpretation, Rezeption.* [for full citation see 5453] pp. 4–13.

3551. Heinen, Jeannot. "Das Brahmshaus in Baden-Lichtental" in *Johannes Brahms in Baden-Baden und Karlsruhe.* [for full citation
see 5452] pp. 10–16. ill., facsim., notes. Relates the history of the
house, what Brahms composed there (1862–77); includes comment on memorial activities in Baden-Baden, current activities in
the house. Includes postcard from Brahms to Fr. Dr. Becker,
1876.

3552. *Henzel, Christoph. *München: Münchens Musik und Musikleben
in Geschichte und Gegenwart, mit vielen Tips nicht nur für Be-
sucher.* Mit einem Vorwort von Joachim Kaiser. (Musikstädte der
Welt) Laaber: Laaber-Verlag, 1990. 131 pp.

3553. "Herrn Dr. Hans von Bülow . . ." *Neue Zeitschrift für Musik* 56/12
(Bd. 85) (20.3.1889) p. 141. Describes a Brahms sendoff from
Berlin.

(b) English translation: "Dr. Hans von Bülow was paid . . ." *Notes*
45/3 (3.1989) p. 660.

3554. "Hier wohnte Brahms . . . ." in 3451, note 33. A poem that ap-
pears on a plaque on the site of the former Hotel Stadt Frankfurt
in Detmold.

3555. Höft, Brigitte. "Clara Schumann und Johannes Brahms in Baden-
Baden" in *Johannes Brahms in Baden-Baden und Karlsruhe.* [for
full citation see 5452] pp. 17–34. ill., notes. Describes Schumann
and Brahms activities in a typical Baden-Baden season; includes

background on Baden-Baden's rise as a resort town. Focuses on Clara and her children.

3556. *Hoffmeister, Emil. "Noch einmal: Brahms in Ziegelhausen" *Volksgemeinschaft* (Heidelberg) (15.3.1936).

3557. *Hoppe, Reinhard. "Brahms-Haus in Ziegelhausen" *Volksgemeinschaft* (Heidelberg) (17.9.1938).

3558. *Hübsch, Lini. "Brahms und Ziegelhausen" *Rhein-Neckar-Zeitung* (5.9.1959).

3559. Karell, Viktor. "Brahms, Johannes . . ." in Karell. *Karlsbad von A bis Z. Ein Stadtlexikon.* München: Aufsteig-Verlag, 1971. p. 20. Reviews Brahms's links with Karlsbad, 1896-death, and his friends there; includes comments on commemorative activities in city.

3560. *Karell, Victor. *Tonkünstler in Karlsbad: von Johann Sebastian Bach bis Johannes Brahms.* Landau (Isar): Author, 1972. 56 pp. ill.

3561. Kross, Siegfried. "Brahms und das Rheinland" in *Musikalische Rheinromantik. Bericht über die Jahrestagung 1985.* (Beiträge zur rheinischen Musikgeschichte 140) Kassel: Merseburger, 1989. pp. 93–105. ill., notes. Reviews Brahms's connections with this area, from the time of his meeting the Schumanns, to his attending Clara's funeral.

3562. Küntzel, Hans. *Brahms in Göttingen. Mit Erinnerungen von Agathe Schütte, geb[oren]. von Siebold.* (Gottingensia 2) Göttingen: edition herodot, 1985. 105 pp. ill., facsim., fig., notes. Describes Brahms's activities with Grimm, Joachim and von Siebold. Includes a chronology from 1835–1909. Includes 3973.

3563. Kupsch, Joachim. *Neujahrskonzert. Ein Brahms-Roman.* 1. Auflage. Berlin: Henschelverlag, 1984. 194 pp. Fiction; takes as its premise a visit by Brahms in the late 1870's to Leipzig to perform Op. 15.

3564. Lo, Kii-Ming. "Johannes Brahms in Heidelberg" in *Musik in Heidelberg 1777–1885. Eine Ausstellung des Kurpfälzischen Museums der Stadt Heidelberg in zusammenarbeit mit den Musikwissenschaftlichen Seminar der Universität [Heidelberg].* Redaktion von Susanne Himmelheber and Barbara Böckmann. Heidelberg: Kurpfälzischen Museum der Stadt Heidelberg, [1985?]. pp. 189–206. ill., facsim., ind., notes. Discusses Brahms's visits, 1854–1875; mostly linked with Clara Schumann. Also discusses the evolution of Op. 60 and the series of letters between Brahms and Wagner regarding the Tannhauser manuscript incident.

3565. *Montang, Wilhelm. "Brahms und Heidelberg" *Rhein-Neckar-Zeitung* (4.9.1959).

3566. Müller, Herta. "Mäzene und berühmte Kapellmeister. 300 Jahre Meininger Orchestertradition" *Musik und Gesellschaft* 40/12 (12.1990) pp. 617–21. Brahms: p. 619. Discusses Brahms as a conductor of the orchestra in the 1880's.

3567. Müller, Herta. "Richard Wagner und Johannes Brahms in Meiningen" *Musik und Gesellschaft* 33/5 (5.1983) pp. 282–85. Brahms: pp. 283–85. ill., notes. Discusses Brahms's connection to Meiningen through Hans v. Bülow; also Brahms rehearsing his works with the Hofkapelle.

3568. *Münster, R[obert]. "Abseits, wer ist's? Johannes Brahms und das musikalische München" *Unser Bayern. Heimatbeilage der Bayerischen Staatszeitung* (München) 32[/6] ([5.] 1983) pp. 33–35.
    (d) *continued (?): Münster. "Endlich inthronisirt. Johannes Brahms und das musikalische München" *Unser Bayern. Heimatbeilage der Bayerischen Staatszeitung* (München) 32/6 (5.1983) pp. 45–47.

3569. Münster, Robert. "Brahms und Joachim in Berlin. Eine neuentdeckte Originalzeichnung aus dem Jahr 1892" in *De editione musices. Festschrift Gerhard Croll zum 65. Geburtstag.* Wolfgang Gratzer and Andrea Lindmayr, eds. Regensburg: Laaber-Verlag, 1992. pp. [411]–20. ill., notes. Describes the opening of the Bechsteinsaales in Berlin, 10.1892, and Brahms's involvement in the concert series; includes contemporary review/comment and background on illustrations in *Neue Berliner Musikzeitung*.

3570. Neumann, Günter. "Brahms der Norddeutsche. Versuch einer Annäherung" in *Brahms-Analysen*. [for full citation see 4888] pp. 1–11. notes. Discusses Brahms's links with Kiel, 1856–97, includes his circle and reception of his work; also includes comment on Brahms's family line, on how 5211 promoted Brahms in France and general appreciative remarks.

3571. *Rohnacher, Ilse. "Brahms hatte eine Sommerbleibe in Ziegelhausen" *Rhein-Neckar-Zeitung* no. 195 (25.8. or 29.9.; 1983) p. 4.

3572. Rohnacher, Ilse. "Brahms in Ziegelhausen" in *Musik in Heidelberg 1777–1885.* [for full citation see 3564] pp. 207–22. ill., facsim., notes. Presents a detailed look at Brahms's visit in 1875: obtaining lodgings, his activities, his circle, pieces composed here.

3573. Schulz, Ekkehard. "Brahms' Karlsruher Freundes- und Bekanntenkreis" in *Johannes Brahms in Baden-Baden und Karlsruhe.* [for full citation see 5452] pp. 35–57. ill., facsim., notes. Surveys the people he knew in Karlsruhe, 1855–96; focuses on the Ettlingers, Gustav Wendt and Julius Allgeyer.

3574. *Schwitzelgebel, Helmut. "Berühmte Musiker in Wiesbaden–Wagner und Brahms" *Nassauische Annalen* Bd. 104 (1993) pp. 189–96.

3575. Strack, Otto. "Eine kleine Geschichte um Brahms in Heidelberg" *Badische Heimat* 33/4 ([1.] 1953) pp. 352–54. Describes Brahms's visit in 1875: his circle, his activities.

3576. Weber, Nicholas Fox. "Historic Houses: Johannes Brahms. The Composer's Summer Sanctuary in Baden-Baden" *Architectural Digest* 47/7 (7.1990) pp. 58, 62, 64. ill. Describes Baden-Baden in the 19th century, Clara Schumann's prominence there and Brahms's visits there, 1863–74. Describes the house today and the history of its being saved.

See also 3522, 3646, 3718, 3743, 3744, 3754, 3772, 3779, 3808, 3814, 3830, 3848, 3851, 3853, 3884, 3906, 3975, 3976, 3987, 4000, 4004, 4028, 4029, 4061, 4542, 4617, 4660, 5414, 5415, 5419, 5452, 5457, 5461, 5468, 5474.

See also "Family History, Childhood, and Links to Hamburg" and "In Transition" in Part II.A.

Greece

See 4769, 5203.

Holland see Netherlands, The

Hungary

Budapest: 3579, 3580.

3577. *Brahms, Johannes. " "*In fliegender Eile möchte ich Ihnen sagen* . . .": *22 Briefe aus Ungarn.*" Agnes Gädor, ed. Mürzzuschlag: Österreichische Johannes Brahms-Gesellschaft, 1993. 44 pp. ill.

3578. Ebert, Wolfgang. "Brahms in Ungarn. Nach der Studie "Brahms Magyarorsagón" von Lajos Koch" Gabriella Zehetbauer, trans. [of Hungarian primary documentation] *Studien zur Musikwissenschaft* 37 (1986) pp. 103–64. ill., facsim., mus., fig., notes. A German translation of 611 (L. Koch. *A Fővárosi könyvtár évkönyve* (1932)) with commentary and substantial additions. Details Brahms's musical activities in Hungary, his circle there, and documents the influence of Hungarian music on his work.
   (a) *reprint: Ebert. *Brahms in Ungarn*. Tutzing: Hans Schneider, 1986. pp. 103–64. [62 pp. total].

3579. Emerson, Isabelle. "Brahms in Budapest. Concerts of 1867 and 1869" *The Piano Quarterly* 36/143 (Fall 1988) pp. 29–30, 32–34. notes. Relates information from contemporary reviews on Brahms's piano playing; also examines makeup of programmes (1867 with Joachim; 1869 with Stockhausen). Also includes comments about Brahms's playing from 48 (F. May. *The Life of Johannes Brahms*. (1905)) and 1180.b (E. Schumann. *Memoirs of Eugenie Schumann*. (1927)).

3580. Frank, Tibor. "Liszt, Brahms, Mahler: Music in late 19th Century Budapest" in *Hungary and European Civilization*. György Ránki, ed.; Attila Pók, assistant ed. (Indiana University Studies on Hungary 3) Budapest: Akadémiai kiadó, 1989. pp. 343–59. Brahms: pp. 347–53. ill., notes. Discusses Brahms as an influence on Budapest's musical life; reviews his visits there, performances of his music.

3581. *Horstmann, Angelika. *Die Brahms-Rezeption der Jahre 1860 bis 1880 in Ungarn*. Budapest: n.p., 1985.
   See also 3817.
   See also "Ethnic and Folksong Influences" in Part V.D.

Italy

Bologna: 3582, 3584.
Roma: 3582.

3582. Buscaroli, Piero. *Johannes Brahms a Bologna e in Romagna nel maggio 1888*. (Il Leggio) Bologna: Nuova Alfa Editoriale, 1988. 79 pp. ill., notes. Reports on the trip to these two cities: activities, people went with, people met. Also discusses Brahms's interest in Italy.

3583. Dietrich. "The various journeys . . ." *Musical Opinion and Music Trade Review* 26/301 (1.10.1902) p. 39. ill. Describes Brahms's interest in Italy.

3584. *Levi [, Hermann]. *Johannes Brahms a Bologna*. Bologna: Stabilimenti poligrafici riuniti, 1933.

3585. Seppilli, Lily Sternbach. "Johannes Brahms, l'uomo e l'amico" *Rassegna musicale curci* 42/2 (5.1989) pp. 16–20. ill. Report on 1067.a.c. (R. von der Leyen. in *Brahms-Kalender aus das Jahr 1909*. (1908)): Brahms visiting Tambosi and Trento in 1884.

See also 3703, 4769, 5317, 5476.

Netherlands, The

3586. *Leur, Tr., de, and R. Schoute. "Brahms in Nederland" *Preludium* [(Amsterdam)] [alternate title=*Concertgebouwnieuws*] (1.1983) pp. 2–10.
   (d) *"Brahms in Nederland" *Preludium* [(Amsterdam)] [alternate title=*Concertgebouwnieuws*] (5.1983) p. 13.

See also 3915.

Norway

See 4061, 5209.

Poland

See 4148.

Rumania

3587. Ebert, Wolfgang. "Brahms und Joachim in Siebenbürgen" *Studien zur Musikwissenschaft* 40 (1991) pp. 185–204. ill., facsim., notes. Describes the tour they made in 1879: destinations, programmes.

3588. *Lakatos, István. "Brahms és Joachim Kolozsváron cimen" *Utunk* 12/4 (1957) p. 38. Related to 625 (Lakatos. *Pásztortűz* (1942)).

3589. Lakatos, István. "Románia és a zeneművészet nagy mesterei" in Lakatos. *Zenetörténeti írások.* Bukarest: Kriterion könyvkiadó, 1971. pp. 67–217.
       "Brahms és Joachim": pp. 107–14. ind., notes. Traces their trip, programs, reception.

See also 3828, 4341.

Serbia

See 5128.

Slovakia

3590. *Dušinský, Gabriel. "Johannes Brahms a Bratislava" *Hudobný život* 9 (5.1983) ill. Examines the 4 recorded visits by Brahms to Bratislava. [from S102]

Sweden

See 4061.

Switzerland

General Remarks: 3594, 3597.
Thun: 3591, 3593.
Winterthur: 3596.
Zürich: 3592, 3595.

3591. *Jegerlehner, J. *Berner Kalender* (1935) pp. 73+ . Describes Brahms in Thun, 1886. [from 3597.d.ii.]

3592. Kahler, Otto-Hans. "Neues zur Erstaufführung Brahms'scher Werke in Zürich" *Schweizerische Musikzeitung. Revue musicale suisse* 123/4 (7./8.1983) pp. 234–35. Clarifies works performed 1863–67 using Billroth concert reviews; several predate known sources.

3593. Kunz, Paul, and E[rnst]. I[sler]. "Johannes Brahms in Thun" *Schweizerische Musikzeitung und Sängerblatt* 55/8 (10.7.1915) pp. 32–37. Describes time spent there, 1886–88: pieces composed there, his activities, his circle. Related to 628 (Kunz and Isler. *Rheinische Musik- und Theaterzeitung* (1915)).

3594. Mielsch, Hans-Ulrich. "Johannes Brahms" in Mielsch. *Die Schweizer Jahre berühmter Komponisten.* Zürich: Verlag Neue Zürcher Zeitung, 1992. pp. 65–82. ill., facsim., notes. Surveys all visits, 1856–95; describes his activities, pieces written during visits. Focuses on visits to Rieter-Biedermann and on Brahms's relationship with Widmann.

3595. Steiner, Adolf. "Aus dem Zürcherischen Konzertleben der zweiten Hälfte des vergangenen Jahrhunderts. I.;II., Teil." *Neujahrsblatt der Allgemeinen Musikgesellschaft in Zürich* nos. 92; 93 (1904; 1905). 42 pp.; 34 pp. Brahms et passim. Includes mentions of performances of Brahms's works and concerts that he conducted or was involved with. I. Teil covers 1855–1877; II. Teil covers 1878–1895.

3596. *Sulzer, Peter. "Johannes Brahms und Winterthur" *Landbote* (23.4.1955).

3597. Zimmermann, Werner G. "Brahms in der Schweiz. Eine Ausstellung der Präsidialabteilung der Stadt Zürich im Wohnmuseum Bärengasse, . . . 1. Mai-14. August 1983" [manuscript] [Zürich, 1983. 13 pp.] Includes an overview of Brahms and Switzerland plus specifics on Brahms's visits in 1874 and 1886–88, specifics on Brahms and various Swiss persons and a review of a Brahms concert by Widmann from 1881.

    (d) i) Zimmermann. "Brahms in der Schweiz. Betrachtungen eines Historikers" *Neue Zürcher Zeitung* no. 106 (7./8.5. 1983) pp. 67/68. facsim. Traces Brahms's links to Switzerland through works premiered there and Swiss dedicatees; includes comment on his Swiss travels and his reception.

    (d) ii) Zimmermann. *Brahms in der Schweiz. Eine Dokumentation.* Zürich: Atlantis Musikbuch, 1983. 119 pp. ill., facsim.,

notes. Discusses Brahms's connections and visits, 1856–
1895; includes much quoting of primary sources (writings,
letters, concert reviews, remembrances).

  (e) *review: ab. [A. Briner] ""Brahms in der Schweiz." Zu
      einer Dokumentation von Werner G. Zimmerman" *Neue
      Zürcher Zeitung* [(? 1983)] [1 p.].

See also 3703, 3898, 4131, 4137, 5364, 5418, 5419.

United States of America

3598. Johnson, H. Earle. "Brahms, Johannes (1833–97)" in Johnson.
      First Performances in America to 1900. Works with Orchestra.
      (Bibliographies in American Music 4) Detroit: Information Coor-
      dinators, 1979. pp. 74–90. 28 works of Brahms cited; includes de-
      tails on where, when and by whom, excerpt from review, note of
      work manuscript if there's one in US, plus note if this is the very
      first performance.

See also 4033, 4052, 4055, 4139, 4148, 4532, 5209, 5331, 5372, 5385,
      5437.

C. Brahms the Man

1. Physical/Emotional Being and Lifestyle

Brahms the bibliophile and collector: 3622, 3636, 3644, 3646, 3647.
Brahms the pianist: 3607, 3611, 3633, 3635, 3642, 3657, 3660. See also
      "Brahms's recording" below.
Brahms the teacher: 3631, 3632.
Brahms's recording: 3603, 3609, 3626, 3638, 3642, 3645.

3599. *Presto* (Chicago) 10/8 (21.12.1893) p. 12.

3600. *Ackere, Jules E. van. "Muziek, menselijk document" *Vlaan-
      deren* 28/168 (1.–2.1979) pp. 1–40. ill., facsim., mus., notes. Il-
      lustrates the motto "Music as Interpreter of Sorrow but also Joy"
      by means of biographical information and works of Brahms and 9
      other composers. [from S102]

3601. *Albini, Eugenio. "Giovanni Brahms intimo" *Musica* (Roma) 4/9
      (1910) pp. 1–2.

3602. *"Anecdotes of Famous Composers" *Presto* (Chicago) 14/571 (3.6.1897) p. 9.

3603. Berger, Jonathan, and Charles Nichols. "Brahms at the Piano: An Analysis of Data from the Brahms Cylinder" *Leonardo Music Journal* 4 (1994) pp. 23–30. mus., fig., notes. Analysis and reconstruction of what Brahms is playing (Ungarische Tänze no. 1 [McCorkle WoO 1, no. 1]) and how he plays it; includes description of technique used to do the reconstruction.

3604. Bernstein, Leonard. "Zwei Gesichter des Johannes Brahms" *Welt am Sonntag* no. 19 (8.5.1983) pp. 51, 53. Looks at images of Brahms in his 20's and 50's and describes the man; includes comment on Brahms and the Schumanns, Brahms and women, and what Brahms has to offer us today.

3605. *Brady, Stephen H. [University of Washington, 198_?].

    (d) Brady, Stephen [H.], and George S. Bozarth. "Brahms's Pianos" *The American Brahms Society Newsletter* 6/2 (Autumn 1988) pp. [1–7]. ill. Uses Brahms's correspondence and other documentary materials to reveal information on pianos Brahms played on in his life. Focuses on 1839 Conrad Graf and 1868 Johann Baptist Streicher but talks about ones used on tours, in summer residences, too.

    (d) expanded: Bozarth, George S. and Stephen H. Brady. "The Pianos of Johannes Brahms" in *Brahms and His World.* [for full citation see 5478] pp. 49–64. ill., notes.

3606. *"Brahms as a humorist" *Musical Courier* 34 (9.6.1897) p. 25.

3607. [Hancock, Virginia Lee.] "Brahms as Pianist" *The American Brahms Society Newsletter* 6/2 (Autumn 1988) pp. [7–8]. Excerpt from 48 (F. May. *Johannes Brahms.* (1905)) on hearing Brahms play in 1871, 1881–82, and what he played.

3608. *"Brahms Substitutes for Piano Player in Coffee House" *Musical Courier* 42 (27.2.1901) pp. 23–24.

3609. *[*Johannes Brahms und sein Freundeskreis.* Various performers. (Tondokumente aus dem Phonogrammarchiv der Österreichischen Akademie der Wissenschaften) Verlag der Österreichischen Akademie der Wissenschaften, 1983. PHA EP 5. Includes a recording of Brahms playing Ungarische Tänze no. 1 [McCorkle WoO 1, no. 1]].

(e) i) report: Biba, Otto. "Brahms und sein Freundeskreis" *Öster-reichische Musikzeitschrift* 40/6 (6.1985) p. 341.

(e) ii) report: Kowar, Helmut. "Johannes Brahms und sein Freun-deskreis" in *Bruckner Symposion*. [for full citation see 5434] pp. 219–24. notes. Includes short biographies on the people speaking, and describes how Brahms got on the recording as a performer.

(e) iii) report: "Mehr Originaltöne, bittschön!" *NZ-Neue Zeit-schrift für Musik* 147/3 (3.1986) p. 26. Includes comments on Brahms the pianist.

3610. "Brahms's known aversion to letter-writing . . ." *The Musical Times* 38/651 (1.5.1897) p. 306. Gives anecdote of Brahms in Hamburg, 1850's, in contact with English publisher, to show his aversion not to Englishmen or to receiving visitors, but to letter-writing.

3611. *"Brahm's (sic) Pianoforte Playing" *Musical Standard* new series 3 [vol. 15] (22.9.1900).

3612. *"Brahms' "Vendetta"" *Musical Courier* 26 (29.3.1893) p. 8.

3613. *Braun, Robert. "Brahms-Anekdoten" *Deutsche Musiker-Zeitung* (Berlin) 64/18 (6.5.1933) pp. 236–37.

3614. "The Brusqueness of Brahms" *The Etude* 35/6 (6.1917) p. 380. Relates various anecdotes to illustrate Brahms's sharp tongue; in-cludes one involving Popper where Brahms met his match.

3615. [Ellis, Horace.] "The Character of Brahms" *Music* (Chicago) [14/3] (7.1898) pp. 320–21. Transcription in English translation of Dr. Zimmermann's speech at Brahms's funeral: on Brahms's qualities.

3616. *Comini, Alessandra. "Ansichten von Brahms: Idole und Bilder" in *Johannes Brahms: Leben, Werk, Interpretation, Rezeption*. [for full citation see 5453] pp. 58–67. Related to 655 (A. Comini. *Arts Magazine* (1979)).

3617. Crofton, Ian, and Donald Fraser. "Brahms" in Crofton and Fraser. *A Dictionary of Musical Quotations*. London & Sydney: Croom Helm, 1985. pp. 24–26; also et passim. Includes 40 quotes by Brahms and about Brahms, from his times to the present. Also includes quotes of Brahms on other composers, critics, and general topics.

3618. Finck, Henry T. "Pranks on Parnassus. How Great Composers Have Seen the Humorous and Joyous Side of Life" *The Etude* 42/10 (10.1924) pp. 665–66. Brahms: p. 666. Gives examples of witty Brahms, Brahms as butt of jokes, Brahms's sharp tongue.

3619. Finscher, Ludwig. "Der Grundton der Melancholie. Zum 150. Geburtstag von Johannes Brahms" *Frankfurter allgemeine Zeitung* no. 106 (7.5.1983) [Section:] "Ereignisse und Gestalten" p. [2]. ill. Describes Brahms as a complicated, lonely person with examples from his life.

3620. Finscher, Ludwig. "Johannes Brahms" in *Johannes Brahms in Baden-Baden und Karlsruhe*. [for full citation see 5452] pp. 5–9. ill. Looks at Brahms's correspondence to see what kind of person he is, the environment he lives in; includes comment on Brahms the composer and his connection to older music (Bach, Beethoven) and ethnic music.

3621. Flotzinger, Rudolf. "Brahms als Briefschreiber" in *Bruckner Symposion*. [for full citation see 5434] pp. 95–114. fig., notes. Drawing on all published letters (from 1908–), describes their content and Brahms's writing style. Includes chronological and statistical tables.

3622. Folter, Siegrun. "Brahms, Johannes (1833–1897)" in Folter. *Private Libraries of Musicians and Musicologists. A Bibliography of Catalogs with Introduction and Notes*. (Auction Catalogues of Music 7) Buren: Frits Knuf Publishers, 1987. pp. 41–43. Cites 3 works that catalogue Brahms's library, plus secondary literature.

3623. Frisch, Walter [M.]. "Brahms Was Too a Modernist (Wagner Was the Old Fogy)" *The New York Times* 144/50,012 (26.3.1995) Section 2, pp. 33, 45. ill. Discusses how in contrast to handed down impressions, Brahms may have been more modern and forward-looking than we think, both personally and as a composer. Contrasts Brahms (Op. 45) and Wagner (*Der Meistersinger*).
   (d) expanded: Frisch. "Musical Politics Revisited. Brahms the Liberal Modernist vs. Wagner the Reactionary Conservative" *The American Brahms Society Newsletter* 13/1 (Spring 1995) pp. [1]–3. ill.

3624. Gallois, Jean. "La Musique de chambre de Brahms. Le Refuge de l'âme" *Diapason* (Paris) no. 283 (5.1983) pp. 34–36. ill. Explains

Brahms's character through the chamber music; reviews the music in chronological order.

3625. Geiringer, Karl. "Brahms The Ambivalent" *The American Brahms Society Newsletter* 1/2 (Autumn 1983) pp. [5–6]. ill. Discusses the contradictions in Brahms's person with examples taken from his life, activities, personality. Includes discussion of his father, from whom he got this trait. Also looks at music, where contradictions unite in harmonious solution.

    (a) reprint: Geiringer. "Brahms The Ambivalent" in *Brahms Studies: Analytical and Historical Perspectives*. [for full citation see 5480] pp. [1]–4. ill. omitted.

3626. Gibbs, W. Wayt. "Making Wavelets" *Scientific American* 268/6 (6.1993) pp. 137–38. Brahms's performance of Ungarische Tänze no. 1 [McCorkle WoO 1, no. 1] used as example in explanation of how adapted waveform analysis can be used to strip random noise from a recording. Source is a recording of a 1930's radio broadcast of a 78 rpm recording of the original cylinder.

    (e) report: Canby, Edward Tatnall. "Math for Music" *Audio* 77/9 (9.1993) pp. 16, 18–19. Discusses the process used; discusses the cylinder and the background of its being made. Author exhorts to have the cylinder made generally available.

        (d) Canby, Edward Tatnall. "A New Spin on Brahms" *Audio* 78/2 (2.1994) pp. 14, 16. Discusses whether the original Brahms cylinder can be found; traces all the copies that were made, and speculates that the original is in Wisconsin?

        (d) Canby, Edward Tatnall. "Boulevard of Broken Brahms" *Audio* 78/8 (8.1994) pp. 14, 16. More on what copies are available and what their respective sources are. Discusses the provenance of the cylinder and copies made off the cylinder.

        (d) Canby, Edward Tatnall. "Johannes Brahms Variation No. IV" *Audio* 79/1 (1.1995) pp. 12, 14. Reports on his search for the cylinder, possibly in Berlin? Speculates that original cylinder is in United States, points out that original cylinder had two selections, 1935 copy only has 1. Discusses who is talking at the beginning of the track.

3627. Greenblatt, Robert B. "Johannes Brahms" (Profile) *Medical Aspects of Human Sexuality* 18/12 (12.1984) pp. 173–74. ill. Discusses Brahms's fixation on his mother and how this carries over into his relationships with women and his experiences as a child; includes a survey of the women in his life. Speculates that Brahms suffered from delayed testicular maturation.

3628. Gregor-Dellin, Martin. "Brahms als geistige Lebensform" in *Brahms und seine Zeit*. (Hamburger Jahrbuch für Musikwissenschaft 7) [for full citation see 5428] pp. 223–34. Discusses the way Brahms conducted himself in life and his place in music history.

3629. *Halbedl, Evelyn Virginia. "Certain Philosophical Implications in the Life and Work of Johannes Brahms" M.A. diss., Texas State College for Women, 1943. notes.

3630. Hobbes, John Oliver, pseud. [Pearl Mary Teresa Craigie née Richards] "The Artist's Life" in Hobbes. *The Artist's Life*. London: T. Werner Laurie, 1904. pp. [1–2] 3–67. Brahms: pp. 40–47. Uses Balzac, Turner and Brahms as examples in a discussion of what is an artist and the type of life an artist leads. Gives overview of Brahms's life, mostly pre-1862; includes comment on Brahms's music.
Alternate title: "Balzac, Turner and Brahms."

3631. *Jenner, Gustav. *Johannes Brahms als Mensch, Lehrer und Künstler. Studien und Erlebnisse.* (Wollenweber-Reprint-Serie 3) Gräfelfing: Wollenweber, 1989. Reprint of 694.a. (Jenner. *Johannes Brahms* (1905)).

3632. Jenner, Gustav. "Johannes Brahms as Man, Teacher, and Artist" Susan Gillespie, trans. in *Brahms and His World*. [for full citation see 5478] pp. 185–204. notes. Excerpts translated from 694.a. (Jenner. *Johannes Brahms. . .* (1905)).

3633. Kehler, George. "Brahms, Johannes" in Kehler. *The Piano in Concert*. Metuchen, NJ and London: The Scarecrow Press, Inc., 1982. vol. 1, pp. 156–58. Lists 11 concerts where Brahms played at (dates, locations) with entire concert programme and review if available (only 1 review); includes brief biographical note and comments on Brahms as a piano player.

3634. Kerr, Caroline V. "Brahms as a Man and as a Friend. New and Intensely Interesting Human Aspects of the Great Master" *The*

Etude 35/4 (4.1917) pp. 233–34. ill. Presents anecdotes that illustrate facets of Brahms's character, sources are Clara Simrock, and 1067.a. (R. von der Leyen. *Johannes Brahms als Mensch und Freund.* (1905)).

(d) *continued: *The Etude* 36/? (1918?).

3635. *Kidd, Leonice Thompson. "Brahms" in Kidd. *They All Sat Down. Pianists in Profile.* Charleston: Charleston Press, 1986.
2nd ed.: 1989. pp. [83]–86. ill. [p. [82]], notes. Presents a series of anecdotes in chronological order to paint a personal portrait of the qualities of musicians who started out as pianists.
*also: Florence, KY: Willis Music Company, 1994.

3636. *Kinsky, Georg. "Brahms als Autographensammler" *Der Autographen-Sammler* (?) 2/2 (7.1937) [=Stargardt Auction Catalog no. 388] pp. 1–4.

3637. Kneif, Tibor. "Brahms-ein bürglicher Künstler" in *Johannes Brahms: Leben und Werk.* [for full citation see 3215] pp. 9–13. Raises the question of whether Brahms was "bourgeois." Describes the times that Brahms lived in, his lifestyle, his attitude towards composing. Also looks at the opposite point of view.

3638. Kowar, Helmut. "Zum Klavierspiel Johannes Brahms" *Brahms-Studien* Bd. 8 (1990) pp. 35–47. ill., mus., notes. Reworked from 3359.d. Presents background to Brahms's recording session, discusses music that was played (Ungarische Tänze no. 1 [McCorkle WoO 1, no. 1]).

3639. Krull, Kathleen. "The Checked Cotton Underwear of Johannes Brahms" in Krull. *Lives of the Musicians: Good Times, Bad Times (And What the Neighbours Thought).* Kathryn Hewitt, illus. San Diego, New York, London: Harcourt Brace Jovanovich, 1993. pp. 48–53. ill. anecdotal survey of Brahms's life, focuses on his habits and what he wore.

3640. *Lange-Eichbaum, Wilhelm. *Genie Irrsinn und Ruhm.* [1. Auflage] München: Verlag Ernst Reinhardt, 1928. 497 pp. notes.
*2. vermehrte Auflage: 1935. 531 pp. adds ind.
3. stark vermehrte Auflage: 1942. 607 pp. Brahms: pp. 347, 511.
4. vollständig neu bearbeitet und um über 1500 neue Quellen vermehrt von Wolfram Kurth: *Genie Irrsinn und Ruhm. Eine Pathographie des Genies.* Adds Basel to place of publication

information. 1956. 628 pp. Brahms: pp. 89, 97, 100, 157, 220, 267, 282, 501. adds fig. Brahms cited as example of various conditions.

*[5. [unveränderte] Auflage] vollständig neu bearbeitet von Wolfram Kurth: 1961.

  6. völlig umgearbeitete, um weitere 800 Quellen vermehrte Auflage: Lange-Eichbaum, Wilhelm, and Wolfram Kurth. *Genie Irrsinn und Ruhm. Genie-Mythus und Pathographie des Genies.* Ernest Reinhardt Verlag, 1967. Brahms: pp. 71, 90, 91, 98, 169, 243, 337, 622. Includes "Brahms, Johannes (1833–1897)": p. 337, which is a pathological workup.

*7. völlig neubearbeitete Auflage von Wolfgang Ritter: *Genie Irrsinn und Ruhm. Bd. 3: Die Komponisten.* 1986.

3641. Lebrecht, Norman. "Johannes Brahms (1833–1897)" in Lebrecht. *The Book of Musical Anecdotes.* London: Andre Deutsch, 1985. pp. 201–08; also et passim. notes. Presents 18 anecdotes, 1853–1896, that show Brahms in relation with various peoples, his actions and personality, Brahms discussing topics such as composing, marriage.
*also: New York: Free Press, 1985.

3642. Lechleitner, Gerda. "Der Brahms-Zylinder—Kuriosität oder musikalisches Vermächtnis" in *Bruckner Symposion.* [for full citation see 5434] pp. 225–32. ill., notes. Analyses Brahms's playing of Ungarische Tänze no. 1 [McCorkle WoO 1, no. 1] and compares it to the score and to performances of the other versions of the same piece.

3643. Mecklenburg, Günther. "Johannes Brahms. 1833–1897" in Mecklenburg. *Vom Autographensammeln. Versuch einer Darstellung seines Wesens und seiner Geschichte im deutschen Sprachgebiet.* Marburg: J.A. Stargardt, 1963. pp. 58–59. Briefly describes Brahms's manuscript collection and where the items are now; includes comment in other collectors' sections of Brahms manuscripts, plus index of manuscripts offered in 1960 contains 1 item of Brahms.

3644. Methuen-Campbell, James. "Brahms, Johannes (1833–1897)" in Methuen-Campbell. *Catalogue of Recordings by Classical Pianists. Volume 1 (Pianists born to 1872).* Chipping Norton, Oxfordshire: Disco Epsom Limited, 1984. p. 7; also et passim.

Discusses Brahms's recording of Ungarische Tänze no. 1 [Mc-
Corkle WoO 1, no. 1], also includes reference to 12 of Brahms's
contemporaries recording his work.

3645. Mikoletzky, Lorenz. "Johannes Brahms und die Politik seiner
Zeit" in *Brahms-Kongress Wien 1983*. [for full citation see 5431]
pp. 387–96. notes, appendixes. Shows that Brahms always
thought of himself as a German, not as an Austrian by looking at
his library, his circle, Op. 55; includes comment about his exposure in both Hamburg and Wien. 2 appendixes contain: 1)
Brahms's correspondence with government officials regarding the
Leopold order; and 2) a list of books on politics and history in his
library (the list excerpted from 690 (K. Hofmann. *Die Bibliothek
von Johannes Brahms.* (1974))).

3646. *Mila, Massimo. "Brahms dei ghiacciai" in Mila. *Scritti di mon-
tagna*. Anna Mila Giubertoni, ed. Torino: Einaudi, 1992. pp.
63–66.

3647. Musgrave, Michael. "The Cultural World of Brahms" in *Brahms:
Biographical, Documentary and Analytical Studies*. [for full citation see 5479] pp. 1–26. ill., ind., notes. Disproves that Brahms is
conservative and insular by taking a fresh considerdation of
Brahms's interests in other arts and his relationship to world of
ideas. Looks at who he knew, the holdings in his library, his relationships with Feuerbach, Klinger, Wagner, and Hanslick, his aesthetic outlook as a musician.

3648. *Neumayr, Anton. *Musik und Medizin. Am Beispiel der deutschen
Romantik*. (Musik und Medizin 2) [Wien:] J&V Edition Wien
[Edition Wien], 1989. 357 pp.
      2. Auflage: 1991. "Johannes Brahms": pp. 211–60. ill., facsim.,
      notes. An overview of Brahms the composer that takes into
      consideration his relations with people, his psychological
      side and physical illness in order to understand his behaviour
      and individual characteristics in creativity; includes comment
      on Brahms and Billroth and medical diagnosis of death.
      "Medizinische Steckbriefe der behandelnden Ärzte": Brahms: pp.
      330–35. ill. An overview of Brahms's physicians: biograph-
      ical information and medical studies.
      (b) *English translation by Bruce Cooper Clarke (of ? Auflage):

Neumayr. *Music & Medicine.* [vol. 1–] Bloomington: MEDI-ED Press, 1994– .

3649. *Ophüls, Gustav. "Johannes Brahms. Zu seinem 25. Todestag 3. April 1897" *Düsseldorfer Lokalzeitung* no. 13 (1.4.1922).
(a) reprinted in 3686.c. pp. 460–63. Describes Brahms's qualities and how they come out in his music.

3650. *Ostwald, Peter F. "Johannes Brahms, "Frei, aber (nicht immer) froh"" in *Johannes Brahms: Leben, Werk, Interpretation, Rezeption.* [for full citation see 5453] pp. 52–57.
(d) i) Ostwald. "Johannes Brahms, Solitary Altruist" in *Brahms and His World.* [for full citation see 5478] pp. 23–35. ill., notes. Discusses why Brahms is a solitary (but generous and responsible) person, looks at his activities, habits; includes comment about Brahms and women.
(d) ii) expanded: Ostwald, Peter. "Johannes Brahms-Music, Loneliness, and Altruism" in *Psychoanalytic Explorations in Music.* Stuart Feder, Richard L. Karmel and George H. Pollock, eds. (Applied Psychoanalysis Series. Monograph 3) Madison, CT: International Universities Press Inc., 1989. pp. 291–320. notes. Reviews life emphasizing relationships, musical development, effects of circumstances on Brahms. Uses relationship with Billroth and Clara Schumann (in later years) as examples of altruistic side.

3651. Pflicht, Stephan. *". . . fast ein Meisterwerk." Die Welt der Musik in Anekdoten. Eine heitere Musik-Soziologie.* Mainz [et al.]: Schott, 1987. 189, [1] pp. ill., ind. Brahms et passim. Presents 17 anecdotes: Brahms on other composers, Brahms's modesty, Brahms on marriage and women.

3652. Prillinger, Elfriede. "Ein Porträt des jungen Brahms" *Österreichische Musikzeitschrift* 40/6 (6.1985) pp. 307–09. ill., notes. Reports on a new portrait of Brahms being found (from late 1840's), includes background.
(b) English translation by Virginia [Lee] Hancock: Prillinger. "A Portrait of The Young Brahms" *The American Brahms Society Newsletter* 5/2 (Autumn 1987) pp. [2–3]. ill.

3652.5. *Reich, Nancy B. "His music expressed the tender feelings missing from his life" *TV Guide* 34 (17.5.1986) pp. 41+ . ill.

3653. Reik, Theodor. *The Haunting Melody. Psychoanalytic Experiences in Life and Music.* New York: Farrar, Straus and Young, 1953. viii, [2], 3–376 pp. Brahms: pp. 79–84. Recounts second-hand stories of Brahms's associations with prostitutes; author describes seeing Brahms when he was 8–9 years old. Includes psychosexual interpretation of Op. 84 no. 4.
   (b) i) *French translation: Reik. *Écrits sur la musique.* Preface de Jacqueline Rousseau-Dijjardin. (Confluents psychoanalytiques) Paris: Société d'édition les belles lettres, 1984. 267 pp.
   (b) ii) *Spanish translation: Reik. *Variaciones psicoanaliticas sobre un tema de Mahler.* (Ensayistas 131) Madrid: Taurus, 1975. 193 pp.

3653.1. "La salute di Brahams (sic)" *Rivista musicale italiana* 40/1–2 (1936) pp. 197–98. Commemorates his birth centennial by celebrating Brahms the liver of life, presents a series of anecdotes about his activities.

3653.2. Schliepe, Ernst. "Anekdoten um Brahms" *Sängerblatt. Chronique des chanteurs* [(1.6.1933)] [issued with *Schweizerische Musikzeitung und Sängerblatt. Gazette musicale Suisse* 73/11 (1.6.1933)] pp. 435–36. Presents anecdotes about Brahms and Bruch and Wolf, Brahms as an accompanist, Brahms on the theme from Op. 68, last movement, Brahms on "Bach wine".

3653.3. Schneider, Frank. "Brahms: Politisch skizziert" in *Johannes Brahms: Leben, Werk, Interpretation, Rezeption.* [for full citation see 5453] pp. 78–83. ill. Examines Brahms's political profile. [from S102]
   (d) *Schneider. "Brahms politisch skizziert" *Bulletin des Musikrates der DDR* 21/1 (1984) pp. 2–11. ill. summaries in English and French. [from S102]

3653.4. *Stearns, Ruby Godwin. "Brahms A Reluctant Concert Pianist" M.A. diss., University of Denver, 1989. v, 126 pp.

3653.5. "Titelblatt: . . ." *Musik und Bildung* 15/5 (Bd. 74) (5.1983) p. 2. ill. Sources for picture montage on issue cover.

3653.6. Tronnier, Richard. "Johannes Brahms (1833–1897)" in Tronnier. *Von Schaffen grosser Komponisten.* Stuttgart: Carl Grüninger nachf. Ernst Klett, [1927]. pp. 218–55. ind., notes. Presents a pic-

ture of Brahms as seen in his letters, especially Brahms and Vienna, his music, Brahms and the Schumanns and Joachim.

3653.7. *Tubeuf, A[ndré]. "La main de Brahms, les voix en Brahms"
Diapason (Paris) no. 390 (2.1993) pp. 37–39.

3653.8. "Unwittingly the ABS Newsletter . . ." see 3669.5.

3653.9. *Van Vechten, Carl. "The Cat in Music" *Musical Quarterly* [6]
(10.1920).
   (a) *Van Vechten. "The Cat in Music (October 1920)" *Musical
   Quarterly* 75/4 (Winter 1991) pp. 37–47. Investigates cats in
   music, includes composers' attitudes towards cats, includes
   Brahms's feelings. [from S102]

3653.95. *Wahl, Antonia Sophia. "Die Überraschung des Johannes
Brahms" *Neues Rheinland* 33/5 (1990) p. 19.

3654. "Why Brahms Never Wrote An Opera and Never Married" *Musical Courier* 35 (29.12.1897) p. 54. Report on 755 (J. Widmann.
Die Nation (Berlin) (1897)).

3655. "Why Brahms Never Wrote an Opera and Never Married" *Presto*
(Chicago) 14/614 (7.4.1898) pp. 9–10. Report on 755 (J. Widmann. *Die Nation* (Berlin) (1897)).

3656. *Witeschnik, Alexander. *Leider nicht von Brahms oder Johannes
Brahms in Geschichten und Anekdoten.* (Kleine Neff-Breviere)
n.p.: Verlagsunion Pabel-Moewig, 1988. 192 pp. ill.
*also: Wien: Paul Neff Verlag, 1988. 189 pp. adds mus.

3657. Wythe, Deborah. "The Pianos of Conrad Graf" *Early Music* 12/4
(11.1984) pp. 446–60. Brahms: Appendix 2. "Op. 2616, owned
by the Schumanns, and Brahms": pp. 458–59. A description of the
piano.

See also 3203, 3207, 3210, 3212, 3217, 3223, 3231, 3237, 3240, 3251,
3271, 3273, 3273.5, 3274, 3276, 3289, 3290, 3291, 3359, 3400,
3401, 3438, 3441, 3454, 3462, 3463, 3467, 3468, 3474, 3487, 3501,
3509, 3532, 3563, 3566, 3567, 3570, 3579, 3597, 3667, 3668, 3703,
3704, 3725, 3732, 3737, 3810, 3813, 3819, 3820, 3838, 3848, 3882,
3908, 3910, 3912, 3934, 3979, 3988, 4000, 4020, 4028, 4061, 4070,
4259, 4262, 4298, 4301, 4420, 4434, 4459, 4515, 4539, 4561.c.,
4580, 4609, 4626, 4659, 4681, 4732, 4754, 4769, 4811, 4835, 4839,

4914, 4935, 5000, 5009, 5018, 5019, 5022, 5023, 5039, 5056, 5059, 5080, 5102, 5118, 5142, 5143, 5145, 5147, 5157, 5169, 5203, 5209, 5210, 5226, 5229, 5305, 5315, 5319, 5373, 5381, 5401, 5404, 5417, 5439, 5452, 5457.

See also "Brahms and Women" and "Schumann Family" in Part III; "Politics" and "Religion" in Part VI.B.

See also I7, I8, I15 in Appendix A.

2. Visual Images and Iconography

For both the man and his music.

3658. *Baton (New York) 8/5 (3.1929) p. 16. A portrait. [from WPA Index]

3659. *Le Guide du concert 5 [3]/9 (12.1913).

3660. *L'Illustration 109/2824 (10.4.1897) p. 280. Drawing of Brahms after photograph by C. Brasch. [from S093]

3661. Beckerath, Willy von. "An Unusual Crayon Portrait of Brahms" Etude 49/12 (12.1931) p. 850. Illustration to 638 (A.M. Abell. Etude (1931)).

3662. Buettner, Stewart, and Reinhard G. Pauly. "Johannes Brahms" in Buettner and Pauly. Great Composers-Great Artists: Portraits. Portland: Amadeus Press, 1992. pp. 98–99. Brahms's portrait is the one done by J.-J.-B. Laurens: gives its background, comments on the artist's craft. Includes comment on Brahms and the Schumanns.

3663. Comuzio, Ermanno. ""Attraverso il fuoco mi son fatto strada." Le vite fiammeggianti dei musicisti sullo schermo e in televisione" Chigiana 42/nuova serie no. 22 (1990) pp. 245–87. Brahms: pp. 250–51, 255. notes. Discusses Brahms as portrayed in the 1947 movie Song of Love; includes comment on Brahms's music as used in this film.

3664. Goldhan, Wolfgang. "Johannes Brahms, Händelvariationen" in Goldhan. Musik-Ornamente von Ferdinand Eckhardt sen. Beethoven-Brahms-Bruckner-Rachmaninov-Wagner. Berlin: edition q, 1993. pp. 119–24; also p. 20. ill., notes. Eckhardt's line graphics for Op. 24, the theme and variations 2,3,6 and 7. Attempts to portray music in a visual sense.

3665. *Great Composers in Historic Photographs. 244 Portraits from the 1860s to the 1960s.* James Camner, ed. New York: Dover Publications, Inc., 1981. [8], 124, [2] pp. Brahms: pp. 16–17. Includes 2 photos, one of older Brahms (1880's–90's) and one of younger Brahms (1850's). The older Brahms photo is also reproduced on book's cover.

3666. Natkin, Robert. "Brahms" *Art in America* 76/11 (11.1988) p. 97. Depiction of artist's work.

3667. Salmen, Walter. "Johannes Brahms und die bildende Kunst" *Neue Zürcher Zeitung* no. 106 (7./8.5.1983) p. 66. ill. Brahms and art, what it tells us; includes comment on art that he owned, relations with artists, especially Klinger, photographs and paintings of Brahms.

3668. Shomette, Donald. "Variationen" [Library of Congress Music Division, 1983] 18 1/2 × 25 inches. ill. Poster for the International Brahms Festival and Conference, includes large Brahms signature and sketches of the composer at 4 stages of his life.
   (a) reproduced: *Impromptu* (Washington, DC) no. 2 (Winter 1984) p. [4].

3669. "A Triptych of Brahms" *Musical Opinion and Music Trade Review* 23/271 (1.4.1900) p. 475. ill. 3 photographs of Brahms, both profiles and head-on.

3669.5. [Hancock, Virginia Lee.] "Unwittingly the ABS Newsletter . . ." *The American Brahms Society Newsletter* 2/1 (Spring 1984) p. [9]. Reports that Brahms illustration in *Newsletter* 1/2 (Autumn 1983) p. [1] may not be of Brahms; evidence is presented for this opinion.

3670. Worbs, Hans Christoph. *Das Dampfkonzert. Musik und Musikleben des 19. Jahrhunderts in der Karikatur.* Wilhelmshaven [et al.]: Heinrichshofen's Verlag, 1982. 289 pp. Brahms: pp. 176–77. ill., ind. Includes 2 caricatures and background on each: Brahms and Hanslick, by Theodor Zasche (from *Figaro* (1890)); Brahms auf dem Weg zum "Roten Igel," by Otto Böhler.

See also 3397, 3413, 3432.5, 3450, 3604, 3652, 3653.5, 3672, 3687, 3914, 3968, 4378, 4777, 4799, 5451, 5461, 5465.d., 5469.
See also "Klinger, Max" in Part III.B.
See also I10 in Appendix A.

Part III

Brahms's Relations
to Other People

Contains materials that discuss Brahms's physical, emotional or musical
relationship with other individuals from any time, on any level.

See also 3199, 3201, 3203, 3210, 3223, 3401, 3402, 3408, 3458, 3463,
3621, 3641, 3647, 3648, 3651, 4070, 4489, 5452, 5465.
See also "Bibliography" in Part I.C.

A. Brahms and Women

Contains materials that discuss the subject in general, or in terms of specific groupings of individual women.

3671. Hofmann, Renate, and Kurt Hofmann. "Frauen um Johannes
Brahms, von einer Freundin im Adressen-Buch des Komponisten
vermerkt—eine erste Bestandsaufnahme" in *Festschrift Rudolf
Elvers zum 60. Geburtstag*. Ernst Herttrich and Hans Schneider,
eds. Tutzing: Hans Schneider, 1985. pp. 257–70. facsim., notes.
Goes through Vienna addressbook of Brahms and notes the
women included, giving background on them. First sequence is alphabetical by last name, second sequence is alphabetical by name
of place where they live. Also includes background on giver of
book (Bertha Faber geb. Porubszky) to Brahms, Op. 49/4, the
Hamburger Frauenchor. Includes brief comment on others mentioned in addition to the women.

See also 3231, 3604, 3627, 3641, 3650, 3651, 3653–55, 3945, 4100, 4609, 4782, 4842, 5102, 5148, 5210, 5373.

See also I32 in Appendix A.

B. Brahms and Particular Individuals

1. Persons Not Identified

3672. *"Brahms and His Friends" *Musical Opinion and Music Trade Review* 51/612 (9.1928) p. 1182. ill.

3673. *"Erinnerungsblätter" *Die Musik* (Berlin) 21/[9] (6.1929) preceding p. 669.

3674. *"Erinnerungsblatt" *Die Musik* (Berlin) 29 (12.1936) preceding p. 193.

3675. *Fehrle-Burger, Lili. "Eine Freundin von Brahms" *Rhein-Neckar-Zeitung* (15.9.1983).

3676. *Rohnacher, Ilse. "Ein unbekannter Brief von Johannes Brahms" *Rhein-Neckar-Zeitung* (28.10.1983).

3677. *"Schluss eines Briefes von Brahms" *Die Musik* (Berlin) 25 (10.1932) following p. 32.

3678. *Winn, Edith Lynwood. "Johannes Brahms. A Bit of Reminiscence" *Jacobs' Orchestra Monthly [and Cadenza]* 2/8 (1911) pp. 32, 65.

2. Persons Identified

This subsection is arranged alphabetically by individual family name. If more than one person is mentioned in a citation, the item is filed under the name of the first person referred to, with cross-references from the other people discussed.

See also cross-references at beginning of this part.

Abbado, Claudio (1933–)

See 3362.

Adler, Guido (1855–1941)

3679. Wessely, Othmar. "Johannes Brahms und die Denkmäler der Tonkunst in Österreich" in *Brahms-Kongress Wien 1983*. [for full citation see 5431] pp. 481–88. notes. Discusses Brahms's involvement with the Denkmäler, 1885–93, and his connection to Adler. Describes 2 letters Brahms to Adler, 3.1892 and 3.1894.

Adorno, Theodor Wiesengrund (1903–1969)

See 4945.

Ahle, Johann Rudolf (1625–1673)

See 4865.

Albert, Eugen d' (1864–1932)

See 3359.b.e., 3645, 3813.

Albinoni, Tomaso Giovanni (1671–1761)

See 5000.5.

Allgeyer, Julius (1829–1900)

See 3397, 3573, 3712, 3850.

Allmers, Hermann (1821–1902)

See 4667, 4720.

Ambros, August Wilhelm (1816–1876)

See 5030.

Ansermet, Ernest (1883–1969)

3680. *Tétaz, Numa F. *Ernest Ansermet, interprète*. (Les Musiciens) Lausanne: Payot; Tours: Van de Velde, 1983. Includes a chapter on Ansermet's strategies for interpreting the symphonies of Brahms and Beethoven. [from S102]

See also 5360.

Armond, Peter Laurencin d' [fl. 19th century]

See 5350.

Arnold, Friedrich Wilhelm (1810–1864)

See 4634.

Arrau, Claudio (1903–)

See 4075, 5164.

Auer, Leopold [von] (1845–1930)

See 3359.b.e., 4571.

Ax, Emanuel (1949–)

See 4254.

Bach, Carl Philipp Emanuel (1714–1788)

See 4250.

Bach, Johann Sebastian (1685–1750)

3681. *Johann Sebastian Bach: Zeit, Leben, Wirken*. Barbara Schwendowius and Wolfgang Dömling, eds. Kassel [et al.]: Bärenreiter, 1976. 179 pp. ill., ind., notes.
(b) *English translation: *Johann Sebastian Bach: Life, Times, Influence*. Schwendowius and Dömling, eds. New Haven: Yale University Press, 1984. 179 pp.

3682. Ochs, Siegfried. "Bach als Inspirationsquelle" in *Verteidigung des musikalischen Fortschritts*. [for full citation see 3931] p. 22. mus. Excerpt from 1100 (S. Ochs. *Geschehenes, Gesehenes*. (1922))

that talks about Bach's influence on Brahms and uses the example of Bach's BWV 150 inspiring Brahms in Op. 98.

See also 3390, 3426, 3468, 3560, 3600, 3620, 3653.2, 3813, 3951, 4105, 4124, 4126, 4167, 4211, 4258, 4285, 4303, 4311, 4351, 4398, 4414, 4470, 4526, 4614, 4616, 4814, 4816, 4829, 4884, 4889.d., 4891, 4923, 4957, 4975, 4985, 4988, 5035, 5118, 5143.d.i., 5178, 5232, 5287, 5288, 5336.

Bach, Wilhelm Friedemann (1710–1784)

See 4250, 4370.

Backhaus, Wilhelm (1884–1969)

3683. International Piano Archives at Maryland. *Catalog of the Repro- ducing Piano Roll Collection. International Piano Archives at Maryland.* (Publications of the Music Library of the University of Maryland at College Park 2) College Park: University of Mary- land, 1983. xii, [2], 281 pp. ind. 37 works performed by 17 per- formers.

See also 3355

Balzac, Honoré, de (1799–1850)

See 3630.

Barber, Samuel (1910–1981)

See 4323.

Barbirolli, John, Sir (1899–1970)

See 5360.

Bartók, Bela (1881–1945)

See 3242, 3600, 4411, 5179.

Bauer, Harold (1873–1951)

See 3683.

Baumann, Alexander (1814–1857)

See 4712.

Baumgardten & Heins [piano manufacturer] [fl. 19th century]

See 3932.

Bax, Arnold (1883–1953)

3684. *Wilson, Colin. "Brahms and Bax" *Audio* (?) (12.1972) pp. 48–49, 122.

Beaux Arts Trio (1955–)

See 3366.

Beck, Julius [fl. 19th century]

3685. "Eine Kritik von Brahms" *Neue Zeitschrift für Musik* 78/33/34 (17.8.1911) p. 496. Report on 802 (J. Beck. *Der Sammler* (1911)).

Becker, Frau Doktor [fl. 19th century]

See 3551.

Beckerath, von, Family

Kurt (1864–1926): 3687.
Rudolf (1907–1976): 3687.
Willy (1868–1938): 3686, 3687, 3688.

3686. *Beckerath, Willy von. "Willy von Beckerath—Gustav Ophüls Briefwechsel" [manuscript] Erika Ophüls, ed. 3 vols. n.d.
  (c) abridged: Beckerath, Willy von. *Willy von Beckerath—Gustav Ophüls. Briefwechsel. 1896–1926.* Erika Ophüls, ed. (Beiträge zur rheinischen Musikgeschichte 146; Edition Merseburger 1246) Kassel: [Verlag] Merseburger [Berlin], 1992. 464, [7] pp. ill., ind. Brahms et passim: discusses Brahms the composer, his music, performances of his music. 277 letters;

includes reprint of 2338 (G. Ophüls. *Zeitschrift für Musik* (1925)) and 3649.

(e) report: [Bozarth, George S.] "Frau Erika Ophüls . . ." *The American Brahms Society Newsletter* 10/1 (Spring 1992) p. 9. Announces availability of her work for study by scholars and discusses its interest to Brahms scholars. Includes locations where it can be seen.

3687. Fusner, Henry. "Brahms and the von Beckerath Family" *The American Organist* 17/5 (5.1983) pp. 47–48. ill., notes. Examines connections with family, 1874–96: Rudolf, Willy and Kurt. Devotes significant portion of article to Willy's artwork and his drawings of Brahms.

3688. *Hofmann, Renate. "'Brahms am Klavier': Zeichnung von Willy von Beckerath" in 4805.5. pp. 27–30. notes. Discusses 1896 charcoal drawing of Brahms by Beckerath. [from *The American Brahms Society Newsletter* 12/2 pp. 8–9]

See also 3661, 3884, 4830.a.

Beechman, Thomas, Sir (1879–1961)

See 5360.

Beethoven, Ludwig van (1770–1827)

3689. *"Beethoven, Brahms and Wagner" *Presto* (Chicago) 13/568 (13.5.1897) p. 12.

3690. *Brinkmann, Reinhold. "Wirkungen Beethovens in der Kammermusik" in *Beiträge zu Beethovens Kammermusik*. Sieghard Brandenburg and Helmut Loos, eds. (Veröffentlichungen des Beethovenhauses in Bonn 4/10) München: Henle, 1987. pp. 79–110. mus. Includes discussion of Beethoven's influence on Brahms in his string quartets and piano sonatas. [from S102]

3691. Comini, Alessandra. "[Beethoven Interpreted:] The Musicians' Musician. Part 2: Berlioz to Brahms" in Comini. *The Changing Image of Beethoven. A Study in Mythmaking*. New York: Rizzoli, 1987. pp. 226–314.

"Johannes Brahms": pp. 305–14. ill., notes. Summarizes Brahms's attitude to Beethoven, his holdings of Beethoveniana and cites many of the comparisons made between the two composers during Brahms's lifetime.

3692. Floros, Constantin. "Brahms—der zweite Beethoven?" in *Brahms und seine Zeit*. (Hamburger Jahrbuch für Musikwissenschaft 7) [for full citation see 5428] pp. 235–58. mus., fig., notes. Discusses Brahms's links with Beethoven: contact with the music, his opinions of, modellings on, compositional influence; also includes comment on Brahms's place relative to Beethoven.

3693. *Grasberger, Franz. "Beethoven, Brahms und Bruckner" *Musikblätter der Wiener Philharmoniker* 24 (1969/70) pp. 154–58.

3694. *Grove, George, Sir. *St. James's Gazette* (London) [13] (2.11. 1886). [from 3796]

3695. Messing, Scott. "The Vienna Beethoven Centennial Festival of 1870" *The Beethoven Newsletter* 6/3 (Winter 1991) pp. 58–63. notes. Examines the failure of Vienna's musical establishment to secure participation of leading musicians of the day in the Festival; comments on Brahms's role in the maneuvering, his thoughts on Beethoven, his musical links.

See also S060, 3267, 3390, 3426, 3469, 3523, 3620, 3718, 3762, 3780, 3813, 3871, 3951, 4105, 4126, 4140, 4167, 4225, 4230, 4255, 4264, 4265, 4289, 4292, 4302, 4311, 4312, 4330, 4351, 4354, 4376, 4398, 4456, 4463, 4514–16, 4550, 4582, 4583, 4616, 4706, 4737, 4826, 4891, 4923, 4927, 4934, 4957, 4964, 4968, 4974, 4975, 4999, 5026, 5027, 5030, 5052, 5054, 5070, 5071, 5118, 5123, 5125, 5178, 5179, 5188, 5201, 5232, 5250, 5279, 5323, 5336, 5385.

Bellini, Vincenzo (1801–1835)

3696. Deathridge, John. "Reminiscences of »Norma«" in *Das musikalische Kunstwerk. Geschichte. Ästhetik. Theorie. Festschrift Carl Dahlhaus zum 60. Geburtstag*. H[ermann]. Danuser; H[elga]. de la Motte-Haber; S[ilke]. Leopold; and N[orbert]. Miller, eds. Laaber: Laaber, 1988. pp. 223–27. Brahms: p. 224. notes. Touches on Brahms's opinion of this opera, he is grouped with Wagner.

Berg, Alban (1885–1935)

3697. *Chadwick, Nicholas. "A Survey of the Early Songs of Alban Berg" Ph.D. diss., Music, University of Oxford, 1972. 2 vols. mus., notes. Surveys all of Berg's vocal music in the period

1900–10; shows that Berg's style derives from Brahms and Schoenberg, rather than Mahler. [from S102]

(d) Chadwick. "Berg's Unpublished Songs in the Österreichische Nationalbibliothek" *Music and Letters* 52/2 (4.1971) pp. 123–40. Brahms: pp. 133–35, 139–40. mus., notes. Discusses the influence of Brahms (through Schoenberg) on Berg and uses this as a factor to propose a different dating for composition of these Berg works.

See also S060, 3475, 3523, 3526, 4213, 4411, 4873, 5370.

Bergman, Carl (1821–1876)

See 4139.

Berio, Luciano (1925–)

See 4214.

Berkeley, Lennox (1903–1989)

See 5413.

Berlioz, Hector (1803–1869)

See 3617, 4994, 5063, 5071.

Beu, Octavian [fl. 20th century]

See 4341.

Bibl, Rudolf (1832–1902)

See 3809.

Bihari, János (1764–1827)

See 4632.

Billroth, Theodor (1829–1894)

3698. *Absolon, Karel B. *The Surgeon's Surgeon. Theodor Billroth. 1829–1894.* 4 vols. Lawrence: Coronado Press, 1979–8_?.

(b) *German translation (of ? vol(s).): Absolon. *Der Grossmeister der Chirurgie, Theodor Billroth (1829–1894).* 1. deutsche Auflage. Rockville: Kabel, 1989. xii, 413, [18] pp. ill., notes.

3699. *Billroth, Theodor. *Billroth und Brahms im Briefwechsel. Mit Einleitung, Anmerkungen.* [Otto Gottlieb-Billroth, ed.] München: Urban und Schwarzenberg, 1991. viii, 528 pp. ill. Reprint of 819 (T. Billroth. (1935)).

3700. *"Johannes Brahms" in Hans Gal. *In Dur und Moll. Briefe grosser Komponisten von Orlando di Lasso bis Arnold Schönberg.* Lizensausgabe. Stuttgart, Hamburg: Deutscher Bücherbund, 1969. 558, [10] pp. Reprint of 1009.c.x (1966). Includes excerpts from 819 (J. Brahms. *Billroth und Brahms im Briefwechsel.* (1935)), 983 (J. Brahms. *Johannes Brahms im Briefwechsel mit Heinrich und Elisabet von Herzogenberg.* (1907)), 1009 (J. Brahms. *Johannes Brahms im Briefwechsel mit Joseph Joachim.* (1908)) and 1179 (C. Schumann. *Clara Schumann. Johannes Brahms. Briefe . . .* (1927)). (d) See: 3702.

3701. *"Médico y músico. Las dos facetas del Dr. Theodor Billroth" *M D en español* 12 (7.1974) pp. 125–30.

3702. *The Musician's World. Letters of the Great Composers.* Paperback edition. Hans Gal, ed. London: Thames and Hudson 1978. 462 pp. ind. Reprint of 819.c.vi (1965); includes excerpts in English translation by Daphne Woodward from 819 (J. Brahms. *Billroth und Brahms im Briefwechsel.* (1935)); 983 (J. Brahms. *Johannes Brahms im Briefwechsel mit Heinrich und Elisabet von Herzogenberg.* (1907)); 1009 (J. Brahms. *Johannes Brahms im Briefwechsel mit Joseph Joachim.* (1908)); 1179 (C. Schumann. *Clara Schumann. Johannes Brahms. Briefe . . .* (1927)). See: 3700.

3703. Nagel, Martin, Karl-Ludwig Schober, and Günther Weiß. *Theodor Billroth, Chirurg und Musiker.* Regensburg: ConBrio Verlagsgesellschaft mbH, 1994. ill., ind., notes. 9–329 pp. Brahms: pp. 134–40. ill. Discusses Brahms and Billroth in Zürich, 1865– . Also:
"Der Musiker Billroth in Wien": pp. 185–210. ill. Discusses Brahms and Billroth in Vienna, the circumstances of the Op. 51 dedication, their travels to Italy.
"Abkühlung des Verhältnisses zu Brahms—Das zerschnittene

Autograph des Brahms-Quartetts — Ein fehlgeleiteter Brief ":
pp. 239–51. facsim. Describes the change in their relationship
(cooling off) from 1887 on and why this occurred.

3704. Roses, Daniel F. "Brahms and Billroth" (The Surgeon's Library)
Surgery, Gynecology & Obstetrics 163/4 (10.1986) pp. 385–98.
ill., notes. Surveys Billroth's life, noting important events (musical, medical) and his links to Brahms, 1865–1892. Compares the
two men and their personalities, stresses the parallels in their
achievements.

   (d) condensed: Roses, Daniel F. "Brahms and Billroth" *The Amer-
      ican Brahms Society Newsletter* 5/1 (Spring 1987) pp. [1–5].
      ill. only; omits notes.

3705. Roses, Daniel F. "On The Sesquicentennial of Theodor Billroth"
The American Journal of Surgery 138/5 (11.1979) pp. 704–09.
notes. Uses excerpts of letters from 819.c.ii (J. Brahms. *Johannes
Brahms and Theodor Billroth.* (1957)) to illustrate Billroth the
man in a survey of his life.

3706. Rutledge, Robb H. "In Commemoration of Theodor Billroth on
the 150th Anniversary of His Birth [Parts I–II]" *Surgery* 86/5
(11.1979) pp. 672–93.
"Billroth II: His Personal Life, Ideas, and Musical Friendships":
   pp. 681–93. Brahms: p. 691; also et passim. ill., facsim.,
   notes. Describes their friendship with all its ups and downs,
   1865–1892; includes Brahms's comments on Billroth.

3707. *Strohl, E.L. "The Unique Friendship of Theodor Billroth and Johannes Brahms" *[Institute of Medicine of Chicago. Proceedings]*
28/8 (1971) p. 301. Reprint of 827 (E.L. Strohl. *Surgery, Gynecology & Obstetrics* (1970)).

3708. *Sunderman, F. William. "Music, Medicine and Academia" *The
College of Physicians of Philadelphia. Transactions and Studies*
27 (1969) pp. 140–48. Related to 828 (F.W. Sunderman. *American String Teacher* (1970)).

   (d) adapted from above and 829 (F. W. Sunderman. *Bulletin of the
      Medical Library Association* (1937)): Sunderman, F. Will-
      iam. *Musical Notes of A Physician. 1980–1982.* Philadelphia:
      Institute for Clinical Science Inc., 1982. [8], 255 pp.
      "Music, Medicine and Academia": pp. 11–41. Brahms: pp.
         18–41. ill., mus., notes. Discusses their friendship; also
         discusses Op. 80 and how much Billroth and how much
         Brahms is in it.

"Brahms": pp. 153–61. ill. (p. 162), mus., notes. Descriptive
analysis of Op. 51 nos. 1 and 2.
[Revised ed.]: [1992]. *Musical Notes of A Physician.* [10],
320 pp.
"Medicine, Music and Academia": pp. 7–27. Brahms:
pp. 12, 15–27.
"Johannes Brahms": pp. 147–65. mus. (also p. 146).
Adds descriptive analysis for Opp. 8, 40, 108.

3709. *Teply, I. *Bratislavske lekarske listy* 90/9 (1989) pp. 705–10. Abstract in English. [from S094]

3710. *Torre López, Enrique. *Revista médica del Hospital Central de San Luis Potosí* 4/1–4 (1986?) pp. 47–55.
(d) Torre López. "Vida musical de Theodor Billroth (1829–1894) y su amistad con Johannes Brahms: una semblanza" *Heterofonia* 19/3 (no. 94) (7.–8.–9.1986) pp. 32–45. ill., notes. Provides overview of Billroth the musician and musicologist; examines friendship with Brahms, other musical friendships; includes comment on 19th century Vienna.

See also 3592, 3648, 3650.d.ii., 3712, 4235, 5364.

Bismarck, Otto, Fürst von (1815–1898)

See 3260.

Bizet, Georges (1838–1875)

See 3748, 3951.

Bloom, Harold [fl. 20th century]

See 5119, 5120.

Böcklin, Arnold (1827–1901)

See 3838, 4887.

Böhler, Otto (?–1913)

See 3670.

Böhm, Karl (1894–)

See 3362.

Bösendorfer [piano manufacturer] (1828–)

See 4262.

Bösendorfer, Ludwig (1835–1919)

See 3741.

Boulez, Pierre (1925–)

See 4265.

Boult, Adrian, Sir (1889–1983)

See 3362, 5272, 5360.

Brahms Family

Caroline [stepmother] (1823–1902) and Johann Jakob (1806–1872): 3711.

3711. Bozarth, George S. "The Music Division . . ." *The American Brahms Society Newsletter* 3/2 (Autumn 1985) p. [10]. Reports on Library of Congress Music Division acquiring letter Brahms to his parents from Vienna, 30.11.1862, and describes content.

3712. Brahms, Johannes. *Briefe.* 1. Auflage. Mathias Hansen, ed. (Reclams Universal-Bibliothek [Kunstwissenschaften] 980) Leipzig: Verlag Philipp Reclam jun., 1983. 309, [2] pp. mus., fig., ind., notes. Portrays Brahms's life through his letters; includes life chart. 212 letters, 1853–1897, taken from 39 (M. Kalbeck. *Johannes Brahms.* 8 vols. in 4. (1903–14)), 789 (A. Orel. *Johannes Brahms und Julius Allgeyer.* (1964)), 819 (J. Brahms. *Billroth und Brahms im Briefwechsel.* (1935)), 836 (J. Brahms. *Briefwechsel.* 16 vols. (1907–22)), 837.d.i (J. Brahms. *Johannes Brahms in seiner Familie.* (1973)), 956 (J. Brahms. *Briefe der Freundschaft.* (1956)),

1079 (K. Geiringer. *Zeitschrift für Musikwissenschaft* (1933));
1179 (C. Schumann. *Clara Schumann. Johannes Brahms. Briefe*
. . . (1927)).

3713. *Brahms, Johannes. *Lettere*. Hans Gal, ed. Translated and Notes
by Laura Dallapiccola. (Contrappunti 20) Fiesole: Discanto Edizioni, 1985. viii, 193 pp. Translation of 1179.c.i. (Brahms. *Johannes Brahms Briefe*. (1979)).

3714. *[Marginalia Book of] Composers' Letters*. Jan Fielden, ed. London: Marginalia Press, 1994. ii, 193 pp. ill., facsim.

See also 3441.d.i., 3625, 3627, 5137, 5465.

Brandt, Auguste née Wolters (1822–1887)

3715. Schumann-Reye, Irmgard. "'Johannes Brahms im Leben unserer
Mutter und Großmutter" berichtet von Gertrud Reye" *Brahms-
Studien* Bd. 8 (1990) pp. 61–70. notes.
"Gertrud Reye: Johannes Brahms im Leben unserer Mutter und
Großmutter": pp. 63–69. Describes Brahms's visits to their
house, 1858–62, and includes 4 letters Brahms to Brandt,
1859; includes comment on Brahms and Bertha Porubsky
(married name Faber).

Breitkopf & Härtel [music publisher]

3716. *Breitkopf und Härtel [music publisher]. *Festbroschüre anlässlich des 275jährigen Bestehens des Buch- und Musikverlages
Breitkopf und Härtel, Wiesbaden, Leipzig, Paris: 1719–1994*. Mit
einer Betrachtung von Peter Gülke und einer Zeittafel über die
Jahre 1719 bis 1994. Wiesbaden [et al.]: Author, 1994. 50 pp.

3717. Hempel, Irene and Gunter Hempel. "Komponist und Verleger—
Drei Exempel einer wohlbekannten Aufgabe" in *Festschrift Wolfgang Rehm zum 60. Geburtstag am 3. September 1989*. Dietrich
Berke and Harald Heckmann, eds. Kassel [et al.]: Bärenreiter,
1989. pp. 274–78. Brahms: pp. 277–78. notes. Article examines
Schumann, Wagner and Brahms and their relationships with their
respective publishers. Brahms, Breitkopf und Härtel and Simrock
looked at.

3718. *Plesske, Hans-Martin. "Das Leipziger Musikverlagswesen und
seine Beziehungen zu einigen namhaften Komponisten. Ein Beitrag

zur Geschichte des Musikalienhandels im 19. und zu Beginn des 20. Jahrhunderts" Phil.F. diss., Karl-Marx-Universität Leipzig, 1974. 255 pp. Includes historical sketches of 14 publishing houses and evaluates their relationships with Brahms and 14 other composers; also looks at newly found unpublished data in Staatsarchiv Leipzig relating to Breitkopf und Härtel, Peters and Hofmeister. [from S102]

See also 3410.

Britten, Benjamin (1913–1976)

See 3600, 3951, 4810, 4816, 5404.

Brodsky Family (Adolph (1851–1929), and Anna [fl. 19th–20th centuries])

See 3421, 4004.

Browning, Robert (1812–1889)

3719. *Hobbes, John Oliver, pseud. [Pearl Mary Teresa Craigie née Richards]. Article that compares Brahms to Browning. [from 3630]

See also 5035.

Bruch, Max (1838–1920)

3720. *Nicol, K.L. "Der allbekannte Unbekannte im Auf—Bruch" *Neue Musikzeitung* 37 (12.1988) pp. 17–18.

See also 3617, 3653.2, 3822, 3951, 4578, 5091.

Bruckner, Anton (1824–1896)

3721. *Morgenpost* (Brünn) (26.7.1937). On the meeting of Brahms and Bruckner at Der Rote Igel in Vienna.
(a) reprint: see 3727.

3722. *Bachmann, Louise George. "Bruckner und Brahms" *Rundpost* (Wien) (1.7.1939).

3723. *"Brahms über Bruckner" *Deutsche Militärmusikerzeitung* [32] (8.4.1910).

3724. *Decsey, Ernst. "Wie Brahms und Bruckner sich verstanden" *Deutsche Kunst- und Musikzeitung* (Wien) 27 (1900) pp. 179–80. Excerpt from 853 (Decsey). *Grazer Tagespost* (1900)).

3725. Fellinger, Imogen. "Brahms' und Bruckners Verhältnis zu ihren Interpreten" in *Bruckner Symposion* [for full citation see 5434] pp. 81–88. mus., notes. Compares the relationships that both composers had with the orchestras they dealt with.

3726. Floros, Constantin. "Gedanken über Brahms und Bruckner" *Österreichische Musikzeitschrift* 38/7–8 (7.–8.1983) pp. 398–402. Compares and contrasts them as composers, also what they thought of each other, what their contemporaries thought of them, their place in music history.

3727. Grasberger, Renate, Erich Wolfgang Partsch, and Uwe Harten. *Bruckner-Skizziert. Ein Porträt in ausgewählten Erinnerungen und Anekdoten.* (Anton Bruckner Dokumente & Studien 8) Wien: Musikwissenschaftlicher Verlag, 1991. 290 pp. Brahms: pp. 161–71; also et passim. ill., notes. Reports their thoughts on each other's music and describes their meeting in Vienna at Der Rote Igel. Includes 3721.a.

3728. *Hallwachs, K. *Musik-Post* (Kassel) (27.10.1929). (e) report: "Brahms contra Bruckner" *Die Musik* (Berlin) 22/5 (2.1930) pp. 401–02. Presents excerpt from unpublished letter that shows that Brahms thought little of Bruckner.

3729. Heller, Friedrich C. "Der Musiker in seiner gesellschaftlichen Stellung in Wien in der zweiten Hälfte des 19. Jahrhunderts. Am Beispiel Brahms und Bruckner" in *Bruckner Symposion* [for full citation see 5434] pp. 41–47. notes. Draws on 39 (M. Kalbeck. *Johannes Brahms.* (1976)) and August Göllerich and Max Auer's *Anton Bruckner.* (Regensburg: G. Bosse, 1974) to contrast the two men as musicians, as to their financial statuses, their honors and the dignitaries who attended their respective funerals.

3730. *Hofmann, Kurt. "Bruckneriana in den Brahms-Erinnerungen von Richard Heuberger" *Mitteilungsblatt der Internationalen Bruckner-Gesellschaft* 23 (8.1983) pp. 5–10. notes. Examines Heuberger's work for his recording of Brahms's thoughts on Bruckner, to show Brahms's attitude towards Bruckner and his music. [from S102]

3731. *Karpath, Ludwig. "Antworten der Redaktion. Bruckner-Brahms (mit Brief von Ernst Ludwig Schellenberg)" *Der Merker* (Wien) 6 (1915) pp. 363–64.

3732. Maier, Elisabeth. "Brahms und Bruckner. Ihr Ausbildungsgang" in *Bruckner Symposion.* [for full citation see 5434] pp. 63–71. notes. Compares both men in regard to their livelihoods and education.

3733. *Maier, Elisabeth. "Johannes Brahms und Anton Bruckner" in 5458.5. pp. 13–[33]. ill.

3734. *Mila, Massimo. "Rinascita Bruckneriana" *L'Espresso* (Roma) 1–5(?) (1955–59)(?).
    (a) *reprint: in Mila. *Cronache musicali, 1955–1959.* (Saggi 258) Torinto: G. Einaudi, 1959.

3735. Paumgartner, Bernhard. "Brahms stand am Seitenaltar. Erinnerungen an Anton Bruckner. Zum 60. Todestag des großen Symphonikers" *Salzburger Nachrichten* 12/238 (13./14.10.1956) p. 12. [Date on page is 13.10.1956] Includes comments on Brahms and Bruckner interacting in Vienna, a Bruckner comment on Brahms as reported to author by his mother.

3736. *Wallisch, Friedrich. "Symphonie in e-Moll (von Johannes Brahms). Lebendige Stadt" *Literarischer Almanach* (?) 3 (1956) pp. 187–92. Related to 1285 (F. Wallisch. *Deutsche Rundschau* (1963)).

3737. Wessely, Othmar. "Johannes Brahms und Anton Bruckner als Interpreten" in *Bruckner Symposion.* [for full citation see 5434] pp. 73–79. notes. An overview of how they conducted their own and others' works.

3738. *Zöllner, Heinrich. "Bruckner und Brahms" *Linzer Tagblatt* (13.11.1904). Reprint (?) of 866 (H. Zoellner. *Leipziger Tagblatt* (1904)).

See also 3237, 3454, 3464, 3469, 3474, 3475, 3477, 3523, 3617, 3693, 3740, 3767, 3809, 3820, 3844, 3860, 3951, 4012, 4239, 4433, 4445, 4482, 4545, 4906, 4981, 5016, 5026, 5036.d., 5066, 5073, 5269, 5270, 5305, 5323, 5350, 5351, 5371, 5381, 5399, 5458.5.

Brüll, Ignaz (1846–1907)

See 3609.e.ii.

Budapest Quartet (1917–1967)

See 5163.

Bülow, Hans von, Freiherr (1830–1894)

3739. *Vossische Zeitung* (Berlin) (28.6.1914).
(a) reprint: Bülow, Marie v[on]. "Hans v[on]. Bülow und der
Brahmsbiograph" *Musikpädagogische Blätter* 37/19, 20 (1.,
15.;10.1914) pp. 366–67, 379–81. notes. Refutes Kalbeck's
treatment of Bülow in his Brahms biography (39), especially
vol. 4.

3740. Antonicek, Theophil. "Aus dem gemeinsamen Freundeskreis" in
Bruckner Symposion. [for full citation see 5434] pp. 115–22.
notes. Looks at Brahms's and Bruckner's circles of friends in Vienna, noting in particular those who overlap: von Bülow, Perger,
Helm, Nikisch.

3741. Antonicek, Theophil. "Aus dem Wiener Brahmskreis" in *Brahms-
Kongress Wien 1983*. [for full citation see 5431] pp. 21–43. notes.
Looks at writings and letters to see what people were saying about
Brahms, provides background information: von Bülow family to
Bösendorfer (1875–); Richter to others (1888–90); Walter to oth-
ers (1874); Epstein to others (1889, 1897); Röger-Soldat to Speyer
(1891, 1896–97); Nottebohm to others; Pohl to others; and the
Faber family to others. Includes many excerpts, most sources are
unpublished; only 1 whole letter: Epstein to Brahms, 8.12.1891.

3742. Bülow, Hans von. *Hans von Bülow: Die Briefe an Johannes
Brahms*. Hans-Joachim Hinrichsen, ed. Tutzing: Hans Schneider,
1994. 154 pp. ill., mus., ind., notes. 57 items ([1877]–1892); includes physical description of originals and an overview of the
two men's relationship.

3743. *Bülow, Marie von. *Neue freie Presse* (Wien) (7.6.1912). Refutes
Kalbeck's discussion of Brahms and Bülow in Meiningen. [from
Library of Congress Index]

3744. *"Over von Bülow, Brahms en de meininger kapel" *Kunst* (Haarlem) 4/8/9 (8./9.1923) pp. 202–12.

See also 3465, 3550, 3567, 3569, 3813, 4260, 4617.

Bull, John (1562?–1628)

See 4353.

Burleigh, Henry Thacker (1866–1949)

See 4892.

Busch, Adolf (1891–1952)

See 4571.

Busoni, Ferruccio (1866–1924)

See 4362, 4571, 5193, 5194.

Buxtehude, Dietrich (c1637–1707)

See 4616.

Byrd, William (1543–1623)

See 4772.

Candidus, Karl (1817–1872)

See 4667.

Carter, Elliott (1908–)

See 5413.

Chaikovskii, Petr Il'ich, see Tchaikovsky, Peter Ilyich

Chausson, [Amédée-]Ernest (1855–1899)

See 4750, 5110.

Chopin, Frédéric (1810–1849)

See S060, 3284, 3389, 3718, 4064, 4140, 4257, 4268, 4270, 4322, 4327,
    4363, 4377, 4428, 4874, 4957, 4973, 4974, 4988, 4997, 5005,
    5052, 5120, 5123, 5179, 5385.

Chrysander, Friedrich (1826–1901)

See 5059, 5141.

Clauss-Szarvady, Wilhelmine (1834–1907)

See 4377.

Cobb, Gerard Francis (1838–1904)

See 3535, 3539.

Collin, Heinrich Joseph von (1772–1811)

See 3839.

Concertgebouworkest

See 3355.

Conrad Graf [piano manufacturer]

See 3605, 3657.

Cooper, Grosvenor W. [fl. 20th century]

See 4406.

Copland, Aaron (1900–)

See 4354.

Corner, David Gregor (1585–1648)

See 4634.

Cosimi, Nicola [fl. 17th century?]

See 4628.

Cossel, Otto Friedrich Willibald [fl. 19th century]

See 3441.d.iii., 3446, 3447.

Couperin, François [le grand] (1668–1733)

See 4351.

Czech Quartet (1891–1933)

3745. *Kvet, J.M. *Zpametí Ceského Kvarteta*. Praha: Edice corona, 1936. 136 pp. Includes anecdotes about the Quartet's interactions with Brahms. [from S033]

Czerny, Carl (1791–1857)

See 4414.

Dahlhaus, Carl (1928–)

See 3331, 5055.

d'Albert, Eugen, see Albert, Eugen d'

Dallapiccola, Luigi (1904–1979)

See 4526.

Damrosch, Leopold (1832–1885)

See 4532.

d'Armond, Peter Laurencin, see Armond, Peter Laurencin d'

Daumer, Georg Friedrich (1800–1875)

See 3905, 4699, 5092.

Davies, Fanny (1861–1934)

3746. "Miss Fanny Davies. A Biographical Sketch" *The Musical Times*
46/748 (1.6.1905) pp. 365–70. Brahms: pp. 367, 368–69. ill. Details Davies meeting Brahms in Baden-Baden and also in Vienna.

3747. *[Davies, Fanny] "The "Olympian Johannes"" *The Musical Leader*
58/1 (2.1.1930) p. 22.

Davis, Gussie (1863–1899)

See 4892.

Debussy, Claude (1862–1918)

3748. *Vallas, Léon. "Debussy, Brahms et Carmen" *Le Guide du concert* 12/2 (10.1925) pp. 42–43.

See also 3600, 4133, 4182, 4193, 4917, 5000.5, 5095, 5178, 5179, 5385.

Deiters, Hermann (1833–1907)

See 3822.

Delius, Frederick (1862–1934)

3749. E.E.R. "Delius and Brahms" *The Delius Society Journal* no. 88
(Winter 1986) pp. 21–22. Reports on a lecture given by Dr.
Roland Gibson, where he compares and contrasts these two composers.

3750. Foss, Hubert. "The Instrumental Music of Frederick Delius"
Tempo no. 26 (Winter 1952–1953) pp. 30–37. Compares Delius
and Brahms as composers, in the context of Delius's Violin
Sonatas Nos. 1–3 and Cello Sonata.

Derenburg, Ilona née Eibenschütz (1873–1967)

3751. Raynor, Henry. "She played duets with Liszt" *The Times* (London) Late London Edition. no. 56,934 (6.5.1967) p. 7. ill. Discusses her life and musical career; includes comment on her friendship with Brahms and how she was a proponent of his late piano works.

3752. Rountree, Kathleen. "The Short-Lived Career of Ilona Eibenschütz" *American Music Teacher* 43/[5] (4./5.1994) pp. 14–17. Brahms: pp. 15–16. ill., notes. Discusses their relationship and her many premieres of his piano music.

See also 3359.b.e., 5157.

Derrida, Jacques [fl. 20th century]

See 4404.d.

Desprez, Josquin, see Josquin Desprez

Dessoff, Otto (1835–1892)

3753. Draheim, Joachim. "Johannes Brahms und Otto Dessoff" in *Johannes Brahms in Baden-Baden und Karlsruhe*. [for full citation see 5452] pp. 103–20. ill., notes. Overview of Dessoff's life; discusses Dessoff's connection to Brahms; includes comment on Dessoff as composer and conductor.

Devrient, Eduard (1801–1877)

3754. *Devrient, Eduard. *Aus seinen Tagebüchern*. 2 vols. Rolf Kabel ed. (Veröffentlichung der Deutschen Akademie der Kunste zu Berlin) Weimar: H. Bohlaus Nachf., 1964. Brahms: vol. 2. et passim. Discusses Brahms and Devrient in Karlsruhe, 1850's–1870's.

Dietrich, Albert Hermann (1829–1908)

3755. *Dietrich, Albert Hermann. *Erinnerungen an Johannes Brahms in Briefen aus seiner Jugendzeit*. [miniature book] 1. Auflage. Irene Hempel, ed. Leipzig: Deutscher Verlag für Musik, Anderson Nexo, 1989. 314 pp. ill., facsim. Reprint of 894 (A.H. Dietrich. *Erinnerungen* . . . (1898)) [from Library of Congress]

See also 3866.

D'Indy, Vincent (1851–1931)

See 4934.

Dohnányi, Ernő (1877–1960)

See 4135, 4957.

Doktor, Paul (1919–)

See 4201.

Door, Anton (1833–1919)

See 3609.e.ii.

Dougherty, Celius [Hudson] (1902–)

See 4892.

Drinker, Henry S[andwith]., Jr. (1880–1965)

See 3395.

Dukas, Paul (1865–1935)

See 3617, 5393, 5404.

Duke, John Woods (1899–)

See 4892, 5095.

Duparc, Henri (1848–1933)

See 4644, 4892.

Dupre, Rene [fl. 20th century]

3756. *Filion, Sylvain-Claude. "Between Brahms and Pink Floyd" *Canadian Composer* 2/1 (Winter 1991) p. 4.

Dvořák, Antonín (1841–1904)

3757. *Altmann, Wilhelm. "Antonin Dvořák im Verkehr mit seinem Verleger Fritz Simrock" *Die Musik* (Berlin) [10/17,18 (Bd. 40)] (9.1911) pp. 259–92, 346–53.

3758. Beckerman, Michael. "Dvořák and Brahms: A Question of Influence" *The American Brahms Society Newsletter* 4/2 (Autumn 1986) pp. [6–8]. ill. Poses the question of whether Dvořák influences Brahms, in addition to vice-versa; includes a brief look at significant details of their relationship (1877–97).
> (d) comment: [Russell, Tilden A.] "Michael Beckerman's article . . ." *The American Brahms Society Newsletter* 5/1 (Spring 1987) p. [12]. Refutes suggestion that Brahms was influenced by Dvořák in his Op. 88.

3759. Beveridge, David [R.]. "Dvořák and Brahms: A Chronicle, An Interpretation" in *Dvořák and His World*. Michael Beckerman, ed. Princeton: Princeton University Press, 1993. pp. 56–91. notes. A systematic review of their relationship (1870–97) which includes 10 letters (1877–1897) [Dvořák (7); Brahms (3)]. Looks at their physical encounters, their influences on each other, how Brahms viewed Dvořák's work. Letters are newly translated by author, this is first time they've all been together, and that they've been fully translated.
> (d) i) *Beveridge, David. "Vliv Antonína Dvořáka na Johannese Brahmse" Jitka Slavíková, trans. *Hudební rozhledy* 44/3 (4.1991) pp. 35–37.
> (d) ii) see also: 3760.

3760. Dvořák, Antonín. *Korespondence a dokumenty = Korrespondenz und Dokumente = Correspondence and Documents. Korespondence odeslaná = Abgesandte Korrespondenz = Correspondence Dispatched*. Kritické vydání = Kritische Ausgabe = A Critical Edition. 3 vols. Milan Kuna, editor-in-chief. Praha: Editio Supraphon, 1987–89. The same letters as in 3759. Provides source details and publication history for each letter.
> Svazek = Band = Volume 1. 1871–1884: Brahms: pp. 128–35, 140–43, 179–81; also et passim. ind., notes. 6 letters, 1877–79.
> Svazek = Band = Volume 2. 1885–1889: Brahms et passim. ind.
> Svazek = Band = Volume 3. 1890–1895: Brahms: pp. 339–42; also et passim. ind. 1 letter, 1894.

3761. Lehmann, Dieter. "Die Erforschung der deutsch-tschechischen musikalischen Wechselbeziehungen, ihre Methoden und ihre Aufgaben" *Deutsches Jahrbuch für Musikwissenschaft* [10] (1963) pp. 36–53. Includes discussion of Dvořáks connections with many German composers, including Brahms.

3762. Petersen, Peter. "Brahms und Dvořák" in *Brahms und seine Zeit.* (Hamburger Jahrbuch für Musikwissenschaft 7) [for full citation see 5428] pp. 125–46. mus., fig., notes. Presents analysis of both composers' works (rhythm and meter) to show their connection: Beethoven's Op. 26 scherzo with Brahms's Op. 8 scherzo with Dvořák's Op. 95 scherzo; Brahms's Op. 77 1st mvt. with Dvořák's Op. 69 1st mvt.; Brahms's Op. 83 3rd mvt. with Dvořák's Op. 104 2nd mvt.; Brahms's Op. 73 3rd mvt. with Dvořák's Op. 88 3rd mvt. Also takes a parallel look at their lives and output.

3763. *Rethinking Dvořák. Views from Five Countries.* David R. Beveridge, ed. Oxford: Clarendon Press; New York: Oxford University Press, 1996. xi, 305, [7] pp.

3764. *Šourek, Otakar. *Dvořák ve vzpomínkách a dopisech.* Praha: Topičova edice, 1941(?). 230 pp. ill., facsim., notes.
*also: Praha: Orbis, ?.
*9th edition: 1951.
(b) i) English translation by Roberta Finlayson Samsour (of ?): Šourek, Otakar. *Antonín Dvořák. Letters and Reminiscences.* Prague: Artia, 1954. 234 pp. ill., notes only.
(a) reprint with a new index by Linda Sirkus: (Da Capo Press Music Reprint Series) New York: Da Capo Press, 1985. 243 pp. adds ind. Brahms: pp. 35–44, 51–52, 70–71; also et passim. Describes their first encounters in the late 1870's, includes 7 letters (Brahms (3); Dvořák (4)), 1877–1879; includes two letters Brahms to Simrock discussing Dvořák from late 1870's. Also describes Dvořák's visits to Brahms, 1883–1897, as reported secondhand.
(b) ii) *German translation by Bedřich Eben (of ?): *Antonín Dvořák in Briefen und Erinnerungen.* Prague: Artia, [1954]. 250 pp. ill., facsim. only.

3765. *Wirth, H[elmut]. "Brahms und Dvořák—Eine Freundschaft" in 5257 pp. 33–48.
See also S060, 3237.d.i., 3533, 3617, 3813, 3877, 3951, 4162, 4163, 4179, 4225, 4593, 4808, 4934.

Ebner, Ottilie [fl. 19th century]

3766. *Lakatos, István. "Brahmsfreundin Ottilie Ebner" *Pásztortűz* 27 (1941) pp. 664–65. Report on 914 (?) (O. von Balassa. *Die Brahmsfreundin Ottilie Ebner und ihrer Kreis.* (1933)).

Eccard, Johannes (1553–1611)

See 5143.d.i.

Eckhardt, Ferdinand (1876–1952)

See 3664.

Eckstein, Friedrich [fl. 19th century]

3767. Eckstein, Friedrich. "Bruckner, Brahms und Wolf. Erinnerungen" *Die Musik* (Berlin) 24/8 (5.1932) pp. 632–33. Reprint of 916 (F. Eckstein. *Rhein-Mainische Volkszeitung* (Frankfurt a.M.) (1931)).

Eibenschütz, Ilona, see Derenburg, Ilona

Eichendorff, Joseph [Karl Benedikt] (1788–1857)

See 4745, 5057, 5089.

Eisler, Hanns (1898–1962)

3768. Szeskus, Reinhard. "Die Deutsche Sinfonie Hanns Eisler im Musikunterricht" *Musik in der Schule* 25/7/8 (1974) pp. 290–97. mus. A study of Eisler's Op. 50, traces the influence of Brahms through Schoenberg to Eisler.

Elgar, Edward, Sir (1857–1934)

3769. Dennison, Peter. "Elgar's Musical Apprenticeship" in *Elgar Studies*. Raymond Monk, ed. Foreword by Yehudi Menuhin. Afterword by Jerrold Northrop Moore. Discography by John Knowles. Brookfield, VT: Scolar Press, 1990. pp. 1–34. Brahms: pp. 8, 20–21. notes. Includes comment on Brahms's influence on Elgar and lists Brahms works that Elgar performed.

See also 4740.

Epstein, Julius (1832–1918)

See 3609.e.ii., 3741.

Eschmann, J. Carl (1826–1882)

See 3597.

Ettlinger, Anna [fl. 19th century]

3770. *Ettlinger, Anna. *Lebenserinnerungen*. Leipzig: n.p., 1920.
See also 3573, 3850.

Exener Family, see Keller, Gottfried

Faber Family (Arthur and Bertha (née Porubsky)) [fl. 19th century]

See 3398, 3671, 3715, 3741.

Fait, Emil [fl. 19th century]

See 3419.

Fantin-Latour, Henri (1836–1904)

See 3838.

Fauré, Gabriel (1845–1924)

3771. *Halbreich, Harry. "La Musique de chambre de Fauré," *Harmonie* no. 151 (10. 1979) pp. 42–51. Includes contrast of Brahms and Fauré as chamber music composers. [from S033]

See also 4377, 4688, 4816, 5035, 5331.

Fehr, Luise [fl. 19th century]

See 3549.

Felderhoff, Reinhold Karl (1865–1919)

See 5451.

Fellinger Family [fl. 19th century]

See 3950.

Ferdinand, Louis, Prince of Prussia (1772–1806)

See 4162.

Ferguson, Howard (1908–)

See 4957.

Feuerbach Family (Anselm (1829–1880); and Henriette (1812–1892))

3772. Baser, Friedrich. "Johannes Brahms und Henriette Feuerbach in
     Heidelberg" *Heidelberger Tageblatt* (30.4.1932).

See also 3541, 3647, 3813, 3838, 4887.

Fischer, Edwin (1886–1960)

See 3355.

Flatz, Franz [fl. 19th century]

See 3460.

Floyd, Carlisle (1926–)

See 4644.

Frager, Michael [Malcolm] (1935–)

See 4588.

Francescatti, Zino (1902–)

See 5176.

Franck, Cesar (1822–1890)

See 4135, 4162, 4163, 4377, 4440, 4906.

Frank, Ernst (1847–1889)

3773. Brahms, Johannes. *Johannes Brahms im Briefwechsel mit Ernst
     Frank*. Robert Münster, ed. (Johannes Brahms-Briefwechsel.

Neue Folge 19) Tutzing: Hans Schneider, 1995. 210 pp. ill., facsim., ind., notes. 83 letters, 1870–89; includes editorial commentary and a life of Frank. Includes letters from 933 (A. Einstein.
Zeitschrift für Musikwissenschaft (1922)) and information on primary sources.

Frankenstein, Alfred von (1906–)

See 4152.

Franz, Robert (1815–1892)

See 4667, 4985, 5091.

Freifrau von Heldburg, see Georg II, Herzog von Sachsen-Meiningen

Frescobaldi, Girolamo (1583–1643)

See 5413.

Freud, Sigmund (1856–1939)

See 5210.

Freund, Etelka (1879–1977)

See 3359.b.e., 5157.

Fridberg, Franz [fl. 19th century]

See 3465.

Friedberg, Carl (1872–1955)

See 3359.b.e., 3645, 5157.

Fritzsch, Ernst Wilhelm (1840–1902)

See 5369.

Fuchs, Robert (1847–1927)

3774. Mayr, Anton. *Erinnerungen an Robert Fuchs*. Graz: Universitäts-Buchhandlung Leuschner & Lubensky, 1934. 130 pp. ind., notes. Brahms: pp. 31–34, 46–48. Describes Brahms's promoting of Fuch's works in Mürzzuschlag in 1884 and Fuchs's likes and dislikes in Brahms's music.

3775. Pascall, Robert. "Robert Fuchs: Eine kritische Würdigung" in *Brahms-Kongress Wien 1983*. [for full citation see 5431] pp. 449–53. Brahms: pp. 449–50. notes. Includes comments on Fuchs's friendship with Brahms (late 1860's–), Brahms's thoughts on Fuchs, the influence of Brahms on Fuchs's music.

See also 3809, 3866.

Fürstner [music publisher] (1868–)

See 3975, 3976.

Furtwängler, Wilhelm (1886–1954)

3776. Shirakawa, Sam H. *The Devil's Music Master. The Controversial Life and Career of Wilhelm Furtwängler*. New York: Oxford University Press, 1992. xvi, [2], 3–506 pp. Brahms: pp. 458–64. ind., notes. Describes Furtwängler's thoughts on Brahms.

See also 3334, 3362, 4439, 5174, 5295, 5360, 5404.

Gabrieli, Giovanni (c1553–1612)

See 5143.

Gänsbacher, Josef (1829–1911)

See 3609.e.ii.

Gardiner, John Eliot (1943–)

See 5360.

Geiringer Family (Karl (1889–1989); Irene [first wife; fl. 20th century]; and Bernice [second wife; (1918–)])

3776.5. Bozarth, George S. "In Memoriam Karl Geiringer" *The American Brahms Society Newsletter* 7/1 (Spring 1989) pp. 4–5. ill. Obituary.

3777. *Geiringer, Karl, with Bernice Geiringer. *This I Remember. Memoirs of a Life in Music*. Santa Barbara: Fithian Press, 1993. 205 pp. ill., ind.

    (e) report: Bozarth, George S. "This We Remember" *The American Brahms Society Newsletter* 11/2 (Autumn 1993) p. 10. ill. Describes the circumstances that led to Geiringer's Brahms biography (25: *Johannes Brahms*. (1934)) and the full extent of Irene Geiringer's collaboration in this work.

Genette, Gérard (1930–)

See 4376.

Georg II, Herzog von Sachsen-Meiningen (1826–1914); and Helene Freifrau von Heldburg (1839–1923)

3778. Brahms, Johannes. *Johannes Brahms im Briefwechsel mit Herzog George II von Sachsen-Meiningen und Helene Freifrau von Heldburg*. Herta Müller and Renate Hofmann, eds. (Johannes Brahms-Briefwechsel. Neue Folge 17) Tutzing: Hans Schneider, 1991. 162 pp. ill., facsim., ind., notes. 99 letters, 1881–1897. Includes physical description.

    (e) report: [Bozarth, George S.] "Brahms Briefwechsel Continues" *The American Brahms Society Newsletter* 9/2 (Autumn 1991) p. 6.

Gernsheim, Friedrich (1839–1916)

3779. Ringer, Alexander L. "Friedrich Gernsheim (1839–1916) and the Lost Generation" *Musica Judaica* 3/1 (5741 / 1980–81) pp. [1]–12. notes. Brahms: pp. 3, 4, 6. Describes their meetings in 1853 and 1862, their friendship in Köln, 1865–1874; includes comment on how Gernsheim's Op. 32 has strong affinities to Brahms's Op. 68 and compares the two composers as symphonists.

(b) *German translation: Ringer. in Ringer. *Musik als Geschichte: Gesammelte Aufsätze.* Albrecht Riethmüller and Steven Moore Whiting, eds. (Spektrum der Musik 1) Laaber: Laaber-Verlag, 1993.

See also 3866.

Gershwin Family (George (1898–1937); and Ira (1896–1983))

See 3396, 4489.

Gibbons, Orlando (1583–1625)

See 5413.

Gieseking, Walter (1895–1956)

See 3355, 5160.d.ii.

Gilels, Emil (1916–)

3780. *Flier, Jakov. "Scedrost' hudožnika" *Sovetskaia muzyka* 10 (10. 1976) pp. 51–54. Discusses Gilel's style and his interpretations of works by Beethoven, Brahms, Tchaikovsky and Prokofiev. [from S102]

Giulini, Carlo Maria (1914–)

See 3362, 5166.

Gluck, Christoph Willibald (1714–1787)

See 4988.

Göbbels, Joseph (1897–1945)

See 5239.

Goethe, Johann Wolfgang von (1749–1832)

3781. Walker, Ernest. "Goethe and Some Composers" *The Musical Times* 73/1072 (6.1.1932) pp. 497–502. Brahms: p. 499. notes. Reviews

Brahms's setting of Goethe texts and gives personal opinions as to
their musical merits; includes comment on the text setting.

See also S060, 4777, 4833, 4835, 4842, 4843, 5149.

Goetz, Hermann (1840–1876)

3782. Hunziker, Rudolf. "Ein Brief von Hermann Goetz an Brahms"
Neues Winterthurer Tagblatt (1.12.1940). Letter dates 6.6.1870?
[from 3597.d.ii.] Related to 945 (?) (R. Hunziker. *Hermann Goetz
und Johannes Brahms*. (1940)) [from compiler]

See also 3597.

Goldmark, Carl (1830–1915)

3783. *Goldmark, Károly. [Carl Goldmark] *Emlékek életemböl*. István
Kecskeméti, trans. and ed. With a biographical chart and works
index. Budapest: Zenemukiado, 1980. 207 pp. ill. New complete
edition in Hungarian, based on 949 (C. Goldmark. *Erinnerungen*
. . . (1922)). [from 5431]

See also 3951.

Gomperz, Theodor (1832–1912)

3784. *Gomperz, Theodor. *Essays und Erinnerungen*. Stuttgart und
Leipzig: Deutsche Verlags-Anstalt, 1905. x, 249 pp.

Goossens, Eugene, Sir (1893–1962)

See 5165.

Gotthard, Johann Peter [fl. 19th century]

3785. "Brief von Brahms an J[ohann]. P[eter]. Gotthard" *Die Musik*
(Berlin) 2/15 (Bd. 8) ([5.] 1903) Beilage p. ? facsim. text: p. 248.
Letter is from 1880, Vienna, regarding Schubert Ländler [Mc-
Corkle Anhang Ia, no. 6].

See also 3460.

Gould, Glenn (1932–1982)

See 4291.

Gould, Morton (1913–)

See 5413.

Grädener, Hermann (1844–1929)

See 3609.e.ii.

Graener, Paul (1872–1944)

3786. Graener, Paul. "Besuch bei Johannes Brahms" *Brahms-Studien* Bd. 6 (1985) pp. 71–73. Describes going to Vienna to meet Brahms in early 1895. Reprint (?) of 952 (P. Graener. *Magdeburger Bühnenblätter. Spielzeit* (1936/37)).

Graf, Conrad, see Conrad Graf

Graf, Max (1873–1958)

3787. Bozarth, George S. "Encounters: Max Graf" *The American Brahms Society Newsletter* 4/2 (Autumn 1986) pp. [4–6] ill., notes. Describing Brahms in Vienna, late 1880's–90's. Excerpted from 953 (M. Graf. *Legend of a Musical City*. (1945)).

See also 5350.

Grainger, Percy (1882–1961)

3788. Clifford, Phil. *Percy Grainger Music Collection. Part 2. Grainger's Collection of Music by Other Composers.* (University of Melbourne. Grainger Museum. Catalogue 2) Parkville: Board of The Grainger Museum, University of Melbourne, 1983. viii, 435 pp. Brahms: pp. 26–29; also et passim. ind. Describes Grainger's holdings of scores (48 items), includes descriptions of editions, provenance, notes of Grainger's markings.

See also 3683.

Grieg, Edvard (1843–1907)

3789. *"Brahms and Grieg" *Presto* (Chicago) 17/734 (2.8.1900) p. 7.

3790. *Brock, H. "Grieg und Deutschland" *Studia musicologica norvegica* 19 (1993) pp. 97+ .

3791. *Kortsen, Bjarne. *Griegikon: et Edvard Grieg leksikon.* Bergen: Alma mater, 1993. 94 pp.

See also 3617, 3718, 4004, 4650, 4657, 5374.

Grimm, Julius Otto (1827–1903)

3792. *Grimm, Julius Otto. "Erinnerungen aus meinem Musikerleben" *Jahresbericht des westfälischen Provinzialvereins für Wissenschaft und Kunst* (Münster) 29 (1900/1901) pp. 151–60.

3793. Grimm, Julius Otto. *Zukunfts-Brahmanen-Polka dem lieben Johanni Kreislero juniori (pseudonymo Brahms) dediziret.* Otto Biba, ed. Tutzing: Hans Schneider, 1983. [7] pp. facsim., notes. Includes manuscript facsimile and transcription; includes background on work (Grimm's birthday gift to Brahms, 1854) and commentary.

See also 3401, 3562, 3822, 3825, 3866, 3987.

Groth, Klaus (1819–1899)

3794. *Langner, Martin-M[aximilian]. *Brahms und seine schleswig-holsteinischen Dichter.* [Brahmsgesellschaft Schleswig-Holstein e.V., sponsor] Heide: Verlag-Anstalts Boyens, 1990. 144 pp. ill., fig., notes. Covers Groth, Hebbel, von Liliencron, Storm, and Voss. [from S014]

3795. Sannemüller, Gerd. "Die Freundschaft zwischen Johannes Brahms und Klaus Groth" Landesbibliothek Kiel, n.d. Related to 960 (?) (G. Sannemüller. *Klaus-Groth-Gesellschaft. Jahresgabe* (1969)). A copy of author's Phil.F. diss., Pädagogische Hochschule, Kiel, 1969 (?) [from compiler, based on information in S102]

See also 3231, 3570, 3712, 4718.

Grove, George, Sir (1820–1900)

3796. Graves, Charles L. *The Life & Letters of Sir George Grove, C.B.* London: Macmillan and Co., Limited; New York: The Macmillan Company, 1903. xi, 484 pp. Brahms: pp. 148, 208, 259–60, 324–25; also et passim. Describes visits Grove made to Brahms in Vienna in 1866 and 1880, includes reference to 2 letters 1874 and

1887 (only 1887 transcribed); also includes Grove's thoughts on Brahms, Grove as a Brahms promoter in England.

See also 3535, 3539.

Grünfeld, Alfred (1852–1924)

See 3609.e.ii., 3645.

Händel, Georg Friedrich (1685–1759)

3797. Antcliffe, Herbert. "Handel and Brahms" in Antcliffe. *Art, Religion and Clothes.* Hague: Ten Hagen Limited, [1927]. pp. 101–07. Discusses Brahms's relation to music of the past.

3798. *Fellinger, Imogen. "Das Händel-Bild von Brahms" *Göttinger Händel-Beiträge* 3 (1989) pp. 235–57. facsim., mus. Reviews Brahms's study of Händel, including his interpretations and his editing of Händel's works [McCorkle Anhang I, nrs. 10, 11]; includes comment on Händel's influence on Brahms's music. [from S102] *Also known as *Gedenkschrift für Jens Peter Larsen 1902–1988.* Hans Joachim Marx, ed. Kassel [et al]: Bärenreiter, 1989.

3799. Siegmund-Schultze, Walther. "Händel und Brahms" *Händel-Jahrbuch* 29 (1983) pp. [75]–83. notes. Discusses Brahms's reception of Handel and works that show influences—Opp. 50, 55, but 24 in particular. Looks at their style and aesthetic, their work as choral composers.

See also 4354, 4814, 4862, 4920, 4988, 5141, 5331.

Härtel, see Breitkopf und Härtel

Hafiz [fl. 14th century]

See 4699.

Haggin, Bernhard H. (1900–)

See 5058, 5408.

Haitink, Bernard (1929–)

See 3260.

Hambourg, Mark (1879–1960)

3800. Hambourg, Mark. "Recollections of Master Musicians and Master Pianists Whom I Have Known" *The Etude* 42/10 (10.1924) pp. 663–64. Brahms: p. 663. Anecdotes of Brahms in Vienna c. 1894.

Hanslick, Eduard (1825–1904)

3801. *Grimm, Hartmut. "Zwischen Klassik und Positivismus: Zum Formbegriff Eduard Hanslicks" Phil.F. diss., Humboldt-Universität Berlin, 1982. 168, vii pp.

3802. Hanslick, Eduard. "Memories and Letters" Susan Gillespie, trans. in *Brahms and His World.* [for full citation see 5478] pp. 163–84. notes. English translation of 969.a. (E. Hanslick. "Johannes Brahms. Die letzten Tage. II." in Hanslick. *Am Ende des Jahrhunderts. [[1895–1999]].* (1899)).

3803. *Lenneberg, Hans. "The Memoirs of Eduard Hanslick" in Lenneberg. *Witnesses and Scholars: Studies in Musical Biography.* (Musicology 5) New York: Gordon and Breach, 1988.

See also 3231, 3617, 3647, 3670, 3991, 4012, 4017, 4365, 4515, 4617, 5342, 5344, 5350.

Hartmann, Emil von [fl. 19th century]

See 5350.

Haskil, Clara (1895–1960)

See 3355.

Hauer, Josef Matthias (1883–1959)

See 3475.

Haupt, Leopold [fl. 19th century]

See 3708.

Hausmann, Robert (1852–1909)

3804. Hausmann, Friedrich Bernhard. "Brahms und [Robert] Hausmann" *Brahms-Studien* Bd. 7 (1987) pp. 21–39. notes. Presents an
overview of Hausmann's life, his relationship with Brahms,
1872–1897, and his work with Brahms on Opp. 102, 111. Includes
21 letters, 1886–1895; 10 letters discuss Op. 102.

Haydn, Franz Joseph (1732–1809)

3805. *Biba, Otto. "Brahms und Haydn" *Musikblätter der Wiener Philharmoniker* 36/7 (1982) pp. 277–78.

See also 3426, 3813, 4230, 4398, 4489, 4498, 4772, 4927, 4988.

Hebbel, Friedrich (1813–1863)

See 3531, 3794, 4714.

Hegar, Friedrich (1841–1927)

See 3597, 3989.

Hegel, Georg Wilhelm Friedrich (1770–1831)

See 4841.

Heger, Robert (1886–1978)

See 5272.

Heifetz, Jascha (1901–)

See 4571.

Heimsoeth, Friedrich (1814–1877)

See 3822.

Heine, Heinrich (1797–1856)

See 5057, 5094.

Helene, Freifrau von Heldburg, see Georg II, Herzog von Sachsen-Meiningen

Hellmesberger, Joseph (1828–1893)

See 3617, 4012, 5404.

Helm, Theodor (1843–1920)

See 3740, 5350.

Henschel, George (1850–1934)

3806. Bozarth, George S. "Encounters: George Henschel" *The American Brahms Society Newsletter* 5/2 (Autumn 1987) pp. [5–9]. ill., facsim., mus. Presents excerpts from 979 (G. Henschel. *Personal Recollections of Johannes Brahms.* (1907)) with prose commentary linking the excerpts.

3807. *Henschel, Georg [George]. "Persoonlijke herinneringen aan Johannes Brahms" *Weekblad voor musiek [muziek]* 10/22–24, 28, 31 (1903). Dutch translation of 978.d (?) (G. Henschel. *Century Magazine* (1901)). [from compiler]

3808. Henschel, George. "Recollections of Famous Musicians" *The Etude* 31/5 (5.1913) pp. 317–18. ill. Excerpt from 979 (?) (G. Henschel. *Personal Recollections of Johannes Brahms.* (1907)). [from compiler] Describes meeting Brahms in 1874 in Köln, performing under him in Vienna in 1875.

See also 3538.d., 4460.d.i., 5360.

Henze, Hans Werner (1926–)

See 5124.

Herbeck, Johann (1831–1877)

3809. Biba, Otto. "Wiener Kirchenmusik im Umkreis von Johannes Brahms" *Singende Kirche* 30/2 ([6.] 1983) pp. 58–59. ill. Examines Brahms's connection to church music of his time; looks at links with Herbeck, Fuchs, Bibl, and Bruckner.

See also 3460, 3809.

Herder, Johann Gottfried (1744–1803)

3810. *Chapot, Mary Anne. "Johann Gottfried Herder and Johannes Brahms: A Study in the Relationship between German Nationalism, Folk Song, and the German Lied" M.A. diss., San Francisco State University, 1989. x, 166 pp. mus., notes.

See also 5091.

Hermann, Hugo (1844–1935)

See 4571.

Herzog von Sachsen-Meiningen, see Georg II, Herzog von Sachsen-Meiningen

Herzogenberg, von, Family (Elisabet (1847–1892); and Heinrich (1843–1900))

3811. [Brahms, Johannes. *The Herzogenberg Correspondence*. London: John Murray; New York: E.P. Dutton & Co., 1909. [= 983.b]].
   (a) reprint: Brahms, Johannes. *The Herzogenberg Correspondence*. Max Kalbeck, ed. Hannah Bryant, trans. New Introduction by Walter [M.] Frisch. (Da Capo Press Music Reprint Series) New York: Da Capo Press, 1987. xi, [5], v–xix, [1], 425 pp. mus., ind., notes. Includes note on editorial discrepancies between the original German edition and this one and an inventory of the most important errors (mainly dating).
   (c) excerpt: see 4955.
   (d) adapted from Introduction: Frisch, Walter M. "Brahms and the Herzogenbergs" *The American Brahms Society Newsletter* 4/1 (Spring 1986) pp. [1–3]. ill., facsim. Surveys their relationship; examines Brahms's comments on Herzogenberg as a composer.
   (c) excerpt: "The Criticism of Friends (From Frau Herzogenberg to Brahms)" *The Etude* 35/5 (5.1917) p. 341. Reports on her negative opinion of some of his songs.
   (e) i) report: "Brahms as Revealed by His Letters" *Musical Opinion and Music Trade Review* 32/379 (1.4.1909) p. 480. ill.
   (e) ii) report: "Brahm's Character Revealed in Letters" *Musical America* 9/18 (13.3.1909) p. 17. ill.

See also 3231, 3563, 3700, 3702, 3822, 3866, 3950, 5116.

Hess, Myra, Dame (1890–1965)

See 3683.

Heuberger, Richard (1850–1914)

3812. Grunsky, Peter. "Epigone oder gescheiterter Reformer? Richard
Heuberger in historischer Sicht" in *Brahms-Kongress Wien 1983.*
[for full citation see 5431] pp. 187–98. notes. Studies Heuberger
as a composer in Brahms's time; includes overview of life and
works, contemporary evaluation of Heuberger, and what Brahms
and Heuberger thought of each other's work.

3813. *Hughes, Holly Elaine. "Richard Heuberger's *Erinnerungen
an Johannes Brahms:* The Life, Work and Times of Johannes
Brahms as Revealed by a Contemporary" D.A., diss., Ball State
University, 1987. 155 pp. Studies 991 (R. Heuberger. *Erinnerungen an Johannes Brahms.* (1971)) for its view of the personal
Brahms, and for insights into Brahms as composer, performer and
conductor. Also examines Brahms's opinions on other composers,
artists and on musical practice of his day. [from S081]

See also 3231, 3609.e.ii., 3730.

Heyse, Paul (1830–1914)

3814. Münster, Robert. "Johannes Brahms und Paul Heyse. Zu den
Beziehungen zwischen dem Komponisten und dem Dichter" *Neue
Zürcher Zeitung* 204/164 (16./17.7.1983) pp. 43–44. notes. Discusses the poems that Brahms set, their relationship 1864–97
(very few in-person meetings, mostly liaison through Kalbeck,
Levi), Brahms's discussion with Heyse about opera libretti. Includes 1 letter Brahms to Heyse [3.1885].
    (d) expanded: Münster. "Brahms und Paul Heyse. Eine Künstler-
freundschaft" in *Land und Reich, Stamm und Nation. Probleme und Perspektiven bayerischer Geschichte: Festgabe für
Max Spindler zum 90. Geburtstag. Band III: Vom Vormärz
bis zur Gegenwart.* Andreas Kraus, ed. (Schriftenreihe zur
bayerischen Landesgeschichte 80) München: C.H. Beck'sche
Verlagsbuchhandlung, 1984. pp. 339–57. notes. Adds all the
texts of the Heyse poems that Brahms set; includes an additional letter, Brahms to Ludwig II, 10.1.1874.

(a) reprint: Münster. *Brahms-Studien* Bd. 7 (1987) pp. 51–76.

See also 3905, 4847.

Hindemith, Paul (1895–1963)

See 4200, 4211, 4370, 4719, 4891, 4992, 5393.

Hobday, Ethel née Sharpe (1872–1947)

See 3645.

Hölderlin, Johann Christian Friedrich (1770–1843)

See 4777, 4839, 4841.

Hölty, Ludwig (1748–1776)

See 5097.

Hörburger, Franz Carl [fl. 19th–20th centuries]

See 3998.

Hoffmann, E[rnst]. T[heodor]. A[madeus]. (1776–1822)

See 4515, 5027, 5185, 5449.5.

Hofmann, Kurt [fl. 20th century]

See 5429, 5435, 5436, 5441, 5448, 5459, 5473.

Hofmannsthal, Hugo von (1874–1929)

See 4253.

Hofmeister [music publisher] [fl. 19th century]

See 3718.

Holst, Gustav (1874–1934)

See 4772.

Honegger, Arthur (1892–1955)

3815. *Honegger, Arthur. *Beruf und Handwerk des Komponisten: Illusionslose Gespräche, Kritiken, Aufsätze*. 1. Auflage. Eberhardt Klemm, ed.; Oswald and Willi Reich, transs. (Universal Bibliothek. Kunstwissenschaften. 825) Leipzig: Verlag Philipp Reclam, 1980. 231 pp.

See also 3600.

Horowitz Family (Vladimir (1904–); and Wanda Toscanini (fl. 20th century))

3816. *Yale University. Music Library. *The Papers of Vladimir and Wanda Toscanini Horowitz: Yale University Music Library Archival Collection MSS 55*. Adrienne Scholtz, comp. New Haven: The Library, 1992. vii, 281 pp.

Hubay, Jenő (1858–1937)

3817. Rohr, Robert. *Unser klingendes Erbe. Beiträge zur Musikgeschichte der Deutschen und ihrer Nachbarn in und aus Südosteuropa unter besonderer Berücksichtigung der Donauschwaben. Von den Anfängen bis 1918*. Passau: Verlag Passavia, 1988. 394 pp. Brahms: p. 276; also et passim. facsim. 1 letter Hubay to Brahms, 15.1.1891.

Huber, Hans (1852–1921)

3818. "Ein Brief von Brahms an Hans Huber" *Neue Zürcher Zeitung* no. 106 (7./8.5.1983) p. 68. facsim. 1 letter Brahms to Huber, [1878?].

Indy, Vincent D', see D'Indy, Vincent

Isaac, Heinrich (c1450–1517)

See 3523, 5143.d.i.

Ives, Charles E[dward]. (1874–1954)

See 5114, 5393.

James, Henry (1843–1916)

See 4409.

Japha-Langhans, Louise (1826–1910)

See 3932.

Jean Paul [Johann Paul Friedrich Richter] (1763–1825)

See 4580.

Jenner, Gustav (1865–1920)

3819. *Henkhaus, Uwe. "Gustav Jenner—der unbekannte Brahms-schüler" *Üben & Musizieren* 7/5 (1990) p. 268.

3820. Heussner, Horst. "Der Brahmsschüler Gustav Jenner" in *Brahms-Kongress Wien 1983*. [for full citation see 5431] pp. 247–57. notes. Discusses the times that Jenner lived in and the different factions in that musical world. Discusses Jenner as a pupil of Brahms and their relationship in general, 1887– ; includes overview of Jenner's career and performances of his works.

See also 3631, 3632, 5101.d.ii.
See also I42 in Appendix A.

Jensen, Adolf (1837–1879)

3821. *Stuart, Lila. "Selected Songs from the Spanish Songbook of Adolf Jensen: a comparative study of the settings of Hugo Wolf and Johannes Brahms" D.M. diss., Performance Practice, Indiana University, 1993. 116 pp. mus., notes, discog., works list. Includes biographical information. [from S109]

Jessen, M. [fl. 19th century]

See 4820.

Joachim Family

Joachim, Amalie (1839–1898): 3826.
Joachim, Joseph (1831–1907): 3822–28.

3822. *Brandt, H. *Meister der deutschen Musik in ihren Briefen.* (Die Bücher der Rose) Ebenhausen bei München: Wilhelm Langewiesche-Brandt, 1928.

[? Auflage:] 1935. "Johannes Brahms": pp. 287–318. ill., facsim., notes. Includes reprint of 3013 (R.S. *Neue Zeitschrift für Musik* (1853)), and excerpts from 1009 (J. Brahms. *Johannes Brahms im Briefwechsel mit Joseph Joachim.* (1908)); 954 (J. Brahms. *Johannes Brahms im Briefwechsel mit J.O. Grimm.* (1908)); 1179 (C. Schumann. *Clara Schumann. Johannes Brahms. Briefe. . .* (1927)); 1122 (J. Brahms. *Johannes Brahms im Briefwechsel mit Karl Reinthaler, Max Bruch, . . . Luise Scholz.* (1908)); 1297 (J. Brahms. *Johannes Brahms Briefe an Joseph Viktor Widmann, . . . Schubring.* (1915)); 618.a. (J.V. Widmann. *Johannes Brahms in Erinnerungen.* (1898)); and 983 (J. Brahms. *Johannes Brahms im Briefwechsel mit Heinrich . . . Herzogenberg.* (1907)).

"Robert Schumann": pp. 247–84. Brahms: p. 283. ill., facsim. Excerpts 1 letter, 1854, from 1183 (R. Schumann. *Robert Schumanns Briefe.* (1904)).

(e) report (on 1928 Auflage): Roggeri, Edoardo. "Epistolario di musicisti" *Rivista musicale italiana* 35/[3] (1928) pp. 348–68. Brahms: pp. 365–66. notes.

3823. *Campbell, Margaret. *The Great Violinists.* Foreword by Ruggiero Ricci. Garden City, NY: Doubleday, 1981. xxix, 366 pp.
*also: London: Granada Publishing, 1980. ind., notes, discog.
(b) *Japanese translation by Hiroyuki Okabe: *Mei vaiorinisutotachi.* (Music Library) Tokyo: Tokyosogensha, 1983. 378 pp.

3824. *Hoggett, T.J. "Brahms" *Music Student* 1/7–8 (1908/09). Report on 1009 (J. Brahms. *Johannes Brahms im Briefwechsel mit Joseph Joachim.* (1908)).

3825. *Musikerbriefe aus Vier Jahrhunderten. "Alles endet, was entstehet".* Margot Wetzstein, ed. Mainz [et al]: Schott, 1987. 255, [1] pp. Brahms: pp. 192–99. ind., notes. Excerpts from other collections of letters relating to music. [Primary sources cited here:] From 1009 (J. Brahms. *Johannes Brahms im Briefwechsel mit Joseph Joachim.* (1908)); 954 (J. Brahms. *Johannes Brahms im Briefwechsel mit J.O. Grimm.* (1908)); 1280 (R. Wagner. *Richard*

Wagner Briefe . . . 2 Folge. Bd. XVII. (1912)); 1069 (La Mara. *Musikerbriefe aus Fünf Jahrhunderten.* ([1886])).

3826. Schonberg, Harold C. "Joseph Joachim. The Incorruptible" in Schonberg. *The Glorious Ones. Classical Music's Legendary Performers.* New York: Times Books, 1985. pp. [155]–67. Brahms: pp. 159–61, 163. notes. Discusses their friendship in the 1850's, Joachim as promoter of Brahms's music, their split over the issue of Joachim's wife.

    (a) reprint: Schonberg. *The Virtuosi: Classical Music's Legendary Performers from Paganini to Pavarotti.* 1st Vintage Books ed. New York: Vintage Books, 1988.

3827. Tovey, Donald F. "Joseph Joachim, Hungarian Concerto for Violin and Orchestra, op. 11" in *Brahms and His World.* [for full citation see 5478] pp. 151–59. Reprinted from 1372C (D.F. Tovey. *Essays in Musical Analysis. Volume III. Concertos.* (1936)). Includes discussion of Joachim's relationship with Brahms at the time of this work, as well as the origins of Brahms's Op. 15.

3828. Weisskircher, Richard. "Brahms und Joachim" *Volk und Kultur* (Bucaresti) 9 (1957) pp. 14–15.

See also 3359.b.e., 3442, 3449, 3562, 3569, 3579, 3617, 3653.6, 3695, 3700, 3702, 3866, 3881, 3950, 3957, 4325, 4342, 4426, 4460.d.i., 4571, 4575, 4577, 4630, 4864, 4867, 4855.5, 4988, 4990, 4991, 5004, 5008, 5110, 5162, 5404.

Jochum, Eugen (1902–)

See 3362.

Jonas, Oswald (1897–1978)

See 3914.

Josquin Desprez (c1440–1521)

See 4975.

Jurenák, Carl [fl. 19th century]

3829. *Grenzbote* (?) (Preßburg [=Bratislava]) (31.3.1929). Includes letter Brahms to Jurenák, 11.1879. [from 3533]

Kabalevsky, Dmitri Borisovich (1904–)

See 4884.

Kagel, Mauricio (1931–)

See 5025.

Kahn, Robert (1865–1951)

3830. Laugwitz, Burkhard. "Robert Kahn erinnert sich . . . [Parts 1,2]" *Das Orchester* (Hamburg) 34/65 (6.1986) pp. 640–48. Part 1 is an account of Kahn's life; Part 2 is Kahn's recollections of Brahms. [The recollection = 1024 (R. Kahn. *Vossische Zeitung* (Berlin) (1933)) + new postscript that tells more anecdotes about Brahms in Vienna (1887) and in Baden-Baden (1887).]
    (a) reprint: Kahn, Robert. "Erinnerungen an Brahms" *Brahms-Studien* Bd. 10 (1994) pp. 43–51. notes.
    (b) English translation by Reinhard G. Pauly: Laugwitz. "Robert Kahn and Brahms [Parts 1,2]" *The Musical Quarterly* 74/4 (1990) pp. 595–609. ill., mus., notes. Part 2 (pp. 601–09) is headed: Kahn, Robert. "Recollections of Johannes Brahms".

Kalbeck, Max (1850–1921)

3831. *Kalbeck, Max. *Neues Wiener Tagblatt* (31.12.1899). Related to 1027 (?) (M. Kalbeck. *Der Lotse* (1900; 1901)). [from compiler]

3832. Musgrave, Michael. "Brahms und Kalbeck. Eine mißverstandene Beziehung?" in *Brahms-Kongress Wien 1983*. [for full citation see 5431] pp. 397–404. notes. Looks at 3 aspects of their relationship: 1) their friendship, 1874–96, and both parties' part in the friendship; 2) Kalbeck's biography (39) and the mistakes he makes in background information for music and biography; and 3) Kalbeck's comments on Op. 90. Concludes that Kalbeck didn't know Brahms as well as he portrays.

See also 3300, 3712, 3739, 3743, 3814, 3864, 5027, 5203.

Karadzic, Vuk Stefanovic (1787–1864)

See 5128.

Karajan, Herbert von (1908–1989)

See 3260, 3362, 4048.a., 4825, 5360.

Keller, Gottfried (1819–1890)

3833. *Smidt, Irmgard. *Aus Gottfried Kellers glücklicher Zeit. Der Dichter im Briefwechsel mit Marie und Adolf Exener.* Stäfa: Th. Gut & Co. Verlag, 1981. Erweiterte Neuausgabe: 1988. Brahms: pp. 66–71. facsim. Includes 3 letters, 1874 regarding the "Kleine Hochzeitscantate" [McCorkle WoO posthum 16]; last letter has a postscript from Marie Exener.

See also 4651, 5100.

Keller, Robert (d. 1891)

3834. *Brahms, Johannes. *The Brahms-Keller Correspondence.* Edited by George S. Bozarth in collaboration with Wiltrud Martin. Lincoln and London: University of Nebraska Press, 1996. 320 pp. ill., mus., ind., notes.

(d) Bozarth, George S. "The Brahms-Keller Correspondence" *The American Brahms Society Newsletter* 14/1 (Spring 1996) pp. 6–9. facsim. only. Surveys the extant correspondence, 1877–1890, and their relationship.

See also 3406.

Kempe, Rudolf (1910–1976)

See 3362.

Kempf, Wilhelm (1895–)

See 3355, 4080.

Kindler, Hans (1892–1949)

See 4152.d.

Kipnis, Alexander (1891–1978)

3835. [Hamilton, David] "Slice of Life" *Opera News* 56/2 (8.1991) pp.
24–26. ill., discog. Brief mention of him as singer of Brahms
lieder, says Op. 121 well done.

Kirchl, Adolf (1858–1936)

See 5463.

Kirchner, Theodor (1823–1903)

3836. Kahler, Otto-Hans. "Ein Brahmszitat in Theodor Kirchners
Walzer op. 86,6" *Brahms-Studien* Bd. 8 (1990) pp. 31–33. mus.,
notes. Kirchner cites Brahms's Op. 97 no. 5 in this work; author
postulates why, and talks generally about Kirchner as a composer
for piano.

See also 3597, 3989.

Klemperer, Otto (1885–1973)

See 3362, 4155.

Klengel, Paul (1854–1935)

See 4181.

Klinger, Max (1857–1920)

3837. Bozarth, George S. "Klinger's Brahms" *The American Brahms
Society Newsletter* 4/2 (Autumn 1986) pp. [8–9]. ill., notes. Describes 2 exhibitions in Germany that show Klingers Op. XII in its
entirety; calls for new facsimile edition of entire work, including
the music.

3838. [Kiel. Kunsthalle] *Brahms-Phantasien. Johannes Brahms—Bild-
welt, Musik, Leben. 18. September bis 26. Oktober 1983. Katalog
der Kunsthalle zu Kiel der Christian-Albrechts-Universität.* Herausgegeben von Jens Christian Jensen. Bearbeitet von Ingeborg
Kähler, Annegret Friedrich und Christoph Caesar. Kiel: Kunst-

halle zu Kiel der Christian-Albrechts-Universität und Schleswig-Holsteinischer Kunstverein, [1983]. 64 pp. Brahms: pp. 16–64. ill., fig., notes. Discusses the link between Brahms the composer and Klinger's Op. XII; also includes comment on Brahms and pictorial art (who he was exposed to, his holdings), his relationships with other artists (Menzel, Böcklin, and Feuerbach); artwork inspired by him by Fantin-Latour. Item also includes 3839, 4335.

3839. Friedrich, Annegret. "Zum Promotheus-Bild in Max Klingers "Brahms-Phantasie"" in *Brahms-Phantasien*. [for full citation see 3838] pp. 11–15. ill., notes. Discusses the image of Prometheus in the 19th century as seen in von Collin and Klinger; includes comment on Brahms the musician coupled with Klinger the artist.

3840. Kersten, Ursula. [Muller-Kersten, Ursula (?)] *Max Klinger und die Musik*. 2 vols. Frankfurt am Main: Peter Lang, 1993. Vol. 1 is the text, vol. 2 is the illustrations. "Max Klinger und Johannes Brahms": vol. 1, pp. 49–112. ill. (vol. 2, pp. 26–73), ind., notes. Examines all works Klinger did inspired by Brahms (includes sketches), focuses on Klinger's Opus XII, describes it and relates it to the respective text and Brahms's music; compares it to Klinger's Opus XI, and Brahms's Opp. 45 and 121; discusses the particular works and how Brahms set the text, discusses how Brahms treats the theme of death in his songs.
"Brahms-Denkmal": vol. 1, pp. 131–36. ill. (vol. 2, pp. 82–91), notes. Provides background and description.
"Briefe von Max Klinger an Johannes Brahms": vol. 1, pp. 163–75. 9 letters, 12.1880—[early 1897]. Most are 1894–97.

3841. Klinger, Max. "Brahms Fantasies (Brahmsphantasie), 1894" in Klinger. *Graphic Works of Max Klinger*. Introduction, notes and bibliography by J. Kirk and T. Varnedoe; with Elizabeth Streicher; Foreword by Dorothea Carus; Technical Note by Elisabeth Sahling. New York: Dover Publications, Inc., 1977. pp. 88–90. ill., notes. 5 plates, with background on the cycle and the individual plates.

3842. *Max Klinger: Wege zum Gesamtkunstwerk. [4. August bis 4. November 1984.] Katalog [der Roemer- und Pelizaeus-Museum, Hildesheim] mit Beitrag von Manfred Boetzkes . . . u.e. umfassenden Klinger Dokumentation.* Mainz am Rhein: Verlag Philipp von Zabern, 1984. 297 pp. ill.

3843. Mehnert, Karl Heinz. "Max Klinger und Johannes Brahms. Begegnungen und Briefe" in *Max Klinger 1857–1920*. Dieter Gleisberg, ed. Leipzig: Edition Leipzig, 1992. pp. 56–64. ill., notes. Traces their relationship, 1885–97; discusses Brahms's interest in art/artists and Klinger's Op. XII.

3844. Nelson, Thomas K. "Klinger's Brahmsphantasie and the Cultural Politics of Absolute Music" *Art History* 19/1 (3.1996) pp. 26–43. ill., notes. Focuses on analysing "Accorde" [frontispiece of Brahmsphantasie] and its subsequent reception as a visual representation of absolute music. Also discusses Vienna's musical politics during Brahms's times, compares Brahms and Klinger in regard to philosophy, and compares "Accorde" with "Evocation."

3845. *Singer, Hans Wolfgang. "Brahmsphantasie Opus XII" in Singer. *Max Klingers Radierungen Stiche und Steindrucke. Wissenschaftliches Verzeichnis*. Luxusausgabe. Berlin: Amsler und Ruthardt, 1909.
   *also: Berlin: Amsler und Ruthardt, 1959.
   (a) i) reprint (of 1909 edition): Singer. [total pp.:] [6], ix–xviii, 148, 69 pp.
   "Brahmsphantasie Opus XII": pp. 73–88. ill. ([2nd sequence of arabic numbering:] pp. 41–50) New York: Martin Gordon, Inc., 1978. Catalogue raisonée approach, describing all extant materials for each part from sketch to exemplar.
   (a) ii) *reprint (of 1909 edition) with new English translation and added ill.: Singer. *Max Klinger: Radierungen, Stiche und Steindrucke = Etchings, Engravings and Lithographs, 1873–1903*. [with Bernd K. Estabrook and Steven Connell.] San Francisco: Alan Wofsy Fine Arts, 1991. xviii, 326, 69 pp. ill., ind.

See also 3647, 3667, 3813, 4739, 4777, 4840, 4887, 5266, 5426.

Koelle, Magdalene née Murjahn [fl. 19th century]

3846. *Koelle, Magdalene. *Erinnerungen*. Karlsruhe: n.p., 1892.

Kogan, Leonid (1924–1982)

See 5176.

Kraus, Detlef (1919–)

See 5169.

Kreisler, Fritz (1875–1962)

See 4571, 5176.

Kretschmann, Theobald (1850–1929)

3847. *Kretschmann, Theobald. "Erinnerungen eines Wiener Philharmonikers an Johannes Brahms" *Musikblätter der Wiener Philharmoniker* 47/3 (11.1992) pp. 93–95.

Kromnitzer, Josef (186_?–193_?)

See 5463.

Kubelik, Jan (1880–1940)

See 4048.a., 4571.

Kufferath, Antonie, see Speyer, Antonie

Kulmer, Maria von, Baronin [fl. 20th century]

See 3864.

Kupfer, Wilhelm (1843–?)

See 3409.

La Mara, see Lipsius, Ida Maria

Lachner, Vincenz [Vinzenz] (1811–1893)

See 4561.c.

Lamond, Frederic (1868–1948)

3848. Lamond, Frederic. "Brahms" in Lamond. *The Memoirs of Frederic Lamond*. With a Foreword by Ernest Newman. Introduction and Postscript by Irene Triesch Lamond. Glasgow: William MacLellan (sic), 1949. pp. 46–62. Describes their meeting in Meiningen (1885) and Vienna (1895–97) and hearing Brahms perform in solo recital in 1886; includes comments on playing Op. 83 with Bülow (pp. 40–41).

See also 3645.

Lanner, Josef (1801–1843)

See 3523.

Lara, Adelina de (1872–1961)

See 3359.b.e., 3645, 5157.

Larue, Jan (1918–)

See 4352.

Latour, Henri Fantin- , see Fantin-Latour, Henri

Laurens, Jean-Joseph Bonaventure (1801–1890)

See 3662.

Lehman, Liza (1862–1918)

See 5404.

Leschetizky, Theodor [Teodor Leszetycki] (1830–1915)

See 3609.e.ii.

Levi, Hermann (1839–1900)

3849. *[American Brahms Society. Brahms Archive. "Full Index to the Brahms-Hermann Levi Correspondence" Seattle: 1986(?)]

3850. *Geiringer, Karl. "Das Bilderbuch der Geschwister Ettlinger: Zur Jugendgeschichte Hermann Levis und seiner Freunde Johannes Brahms und Julius Allgeyer" *Musik in Bayern* 37 (1988) pp. 41–68. ill.

3851. Haas, Frithjof. "Johannes Brahms und Hermann Levi" in *Johannes Brahms in Baden-Baden und Karlsruhe.* [for full citation see 5452] pp. 58–82. ill., facsim., notes. Discusses their friendship, 1864–78; includes background on Levi, comments on the opera project, Opp. 45, 52, 54, Brahms and Levi in both Karlsruhe and München, the men as rival composers.

(d) Haas. *Zwischen Brahms und Wagner. Der Dirigent Hermann Levi.* Zürich und Mainz: Atlantis Musikbuch-Verlag, 1995. ind., notes.

Brahms: pp. 89–161. ill. Covers 1864–72: Levi conducting Opp. 45 and 55, their friendship and activities; Brahms's works composed during this time.

Brahms: pp. 196–214. ill., facsim. Covers 1875–78: Discusses the breakup of their friendship, Levi's interest in Wagner.

See also 3401, 3814, 3950, 4713, 5148, 5219.

Leyen, Rudolf von der [fl. 19th century]

See 3404.

Lienau, Robert Ernst (1838–1920)

3852. Lienau, Robert. *Unvergeßliche Jahre mit Johannes Brahms.* Berlin: Musikverlag Robert Lienau, 1990. 52 pp. ill. Essentially a reprint of 1068 (R. Lienau. *Erinnerungen an Johannes Brahms.* (1934)) with some minor omissions and rearrangement of material.

Ligeti, György (1923–)

See 5467.

Liliencron, Detlev von, Freiherr (1844–1909)

See 3794, 4648.d.ii.

Lindeck, Wilhelm (1833–1911)

3853. Brahms, Johannes. *Briefwechsel mit dem Mannheimer Bankprokuristen Wilhelm Lindeck 1872–1882.* Herausgegeben vom

Stadtarchiv Mannheim. Bearbeitet von Michael Martin. (Sonderveröffentlichung des Stadtarchivs Mannheim 6) Heidelberg: Heidelberger Verlagsanstalt und Druckerei GmbH, 1983. 51 pp. ill., facsim., ind., notes. 27 letters. Introduction gives letters' provenance, biography of Lindeck and how he and Brahms met; includes comment on Brahms' links with Mannheim and his reception there.
See also 4720.

Lipatti, Dinu (1917–1950)

3854. *Băargăuanu, Grigore, and Dragoş Tănăsescu. "Aspects inédits de l'activité d'interprète de Dinu Lipatti" *Muzica* 20/1 (1.1970) p. 47. Reports on the discovery of unreleased recordings, includes Lipatti playing 2 Brahms intermezzos. [from S102]
  (d) *Tănăsescu, Dragoş, and Grigore Băargăuanu. "Considérations sur l'activité d'interprète de Dinu Lipatti" *Muzica* 21/11 (11.1971) pp. 41–43. Discusses Lipatti's interpretations. [from S102]

Lipsius, Ida Maria (1837–1927)

See 3825, 3954.

Liszt, Franz (1811–1886)

3855. [Mason, William] "Brahms' (sic) First Visit to Liszt" *Music* (Chicago) [10/3] (7.1896) pp. 326–227 [326–27]. Reprints letter from Mason to ?, 5.1889, which describes Brahms's visit to Liszt.
  (d) *[Mason, William] "Short Letter from Dr. William Mason" *Music* (Chicago) 18 (8.1900) p. 396. Relates story of Brahms's first meeting with Liszt as evidence that Liszt was unfavorably impressed, initially, with Brahms's compositions. [from S050]
  (e) *report: Salter, Sumner. "Gottschalk-Brahms-Mackenzie" *Pianist and Organist* 3/6 (6.1897) p. 155. Reports on Mason's story of Brahms's first meeting with Liszt. [from S050]

3856. *Liszt, Franz. *Franz Liszt's Briefe. Bd. 8. 1823–1886. Neue Folge zu Bde. I und II.* Gesammelt und herausgegeben von La Mara [Ida Maria Lipsius]. Leipzig: Breitkopf & Härtel, 1904. Brahms: p. 394. [from C. Sutoni. "Franz Liszt's Published Correspondence:

an Annotated Bibliography" *Fontes artis musicae* 26 (1979) pp. 191–234.
(a) reprint (?): in 4012.

3857. Sorel, Nancy Caldwell. "Franz Liszt and Johannes Brahms" (First Encounters) *The Atlantic Monthly* 273/5 (5.1994) p. 109. ill. Describes their meeting in Weimar, 1853.

See also 3260, 3450, 3580, 3617, 3641, 3906, 4012, 4257, 4302, 4325, 4329, 4330, 4355, 4358, 4361–63, 4385, 4437, 4440, 4445, 4506, 4595, 4596, 4869, 4884, 4909, 4934, 5008, 5014, 5015, 5036.d., 5062, 5095, 5183, 5326, 5345, 5385.

London Symphony Orchestra (1904–)

See 4610.

Lortzing, Albert (1801–1851)

See 3718.

Louis Ferdinand, Prince of Prussia, see Ferdinand, Louis

Ludwig II, King of Bavaria (1845–1886)

See 3814.d.

Lutosławski, Witold (1913–)

See 4362.

Maazel, Lorin (1930–)

See 3362.

Mach, Ernst (1838–1916)

See 4253.

Mahler, Gustav (1860–1911)

3858. *Altmann, Wilhelm. "Urteile Gustav Mahlers über Tonsetzer und Dirigenten" *Allgemeine Musikzeitung* 57/27 (4.7.1930) pp. 720–22.

3859. Brodbeck, David [Lee]. "Mahler's Brahms" *The American Brahms Society Newsletter* 10/2 (Autumn 1992) pp. [1]–5. ill., mus. Surveys their relationship, 1890–97; reviews Mahler's comments on Brahms's music and allusions in his first 3 symphonies to Brahms.

3860. Newlin, Dika. "Mahler" in Newlin. *Bruckner Mahler Schoenberg.* New York: King's Crown Press, 1947. pp. 103–206. "Mahler, Bruckner, and Brahms": pp. [105]–110. ind., notes. Surveys the Brahms-Mahler personal and musical relationship. revised edition: New York: W.W. Norton & Company Inc., 1978. "Mahler": pp. [103]–205; "Mahler, Bruckner, and Brahms": pp. [105]–110. No changes in text.

3861. Stahmer, Klaus Hinrich. "Mahlers Frühwerk—eine Stiluntersuchung" in *Form und Idee in Gustav Mahlers Instrumentalmusik.* Klaus Hinrich Stahmer, ed. (Taschenbücher zur Musikwissenschaft 70) Wilhelmshaven: Heinrichshofen's Verlag, 1980. pp. 9–28. notes. Contrasts Mahler and Brahms as chamber music composers; includes a detailed analysis of the opening movement of Mahler's Piano Quartet (1876).

3862. Vondenhoff, Bruno, and Eleonore Vondenhoff. *Gustav Mahler Dokumentation, Sammlung Eleonore Vondenhoff. Materialien zu Leben und Werk.* (Publikationen des Instituts für Österreichische Musikdokumentation 4) Tutzing: Hans Schneider, 1978. xxii, 676 pp. Brahms: pp. 124–25. ind. 8 references to Brahms's opinions on Mahler and his works.

3863. Werba, Robert. "Mahlers Weg nach Wien" *Österreichische Musikzeitschrift* 34/10 (10.1979) pp. 486–98. On Mahler's appointment to the Hofoper in 1897, discusses Brahms's role in this.

See also 3475, 3523, 3526, 3580, 3697, 3718, 3951, 4135, 4179, 4463, 4482, 4553, 4841, 4873, 4906, 5057, 5186, 5201, 5209, 5228, 5360, 5371, 5393, 5399.

Malinin, Evgeny (1930–)

See 4294.

Mandyczewski, Eusebius (1857–1929)

3864. *Bejinariu, Mircea. "Die Erinnerungen der Baronin Maria von Kulmer an Eusebius Mandyczewski" *Studien zur Musikwis-*

senschaft 34 (1983) pp. 85–109. Reviews what she wrote about her uncle in her letters; includes details on his relationship with Brahms, Kalbeck and others. [from S102]

See also 3609.e.ii., 5404.

Marks, G.W. [pseud.]

See 4299.

Marschner, Heinz (1795–1861)

See 3718, 4553.

Martino, Donald (1931–)

See 4215.

Marteau, Henri (1874–1934)

See 4571.

Martinů, Bohuslav (1890–1959)

See 3533.

Marxsen, Eduard (1806–1887)

3865. *Jaffe, Jane. "Eduard Marxsen and Johannes Brahms" ? diss., University of Chicago, 199_?.

3866. Pascall, Robert. "Brahms und die Kleinmeister" in Brahms und seine Zeit. (Hamburger Jahrbuch für Musikwissenschaft 7) [for full citation see 5428] pp. 199–209. mus., notes. Traces Brahms's connections with lesser composers, particularly through the 1860's: Marxsen, Joachim, Fuchs, Grimm, Dietrich, Clara Schumann, Gernsheim, Herzogenberg. Looks at what Brahms thought of them, compares their style to Brahms's, looks at what makes Brahms significant and them not significant.

See also 3446, 4061, 5066.

Mason, Daniel Gregory (1873–1953)

3867. *Mason, Daniel Gregory. *Music in My Time and Other Reminiscences.* New York: The Macmillan Company, 1938.
(a) reprint: Westport, CT: Greenwood Press, Publishers, 1970. [14], 409 pp. ind. Describes what various musicians thought of Brahms; the process behind the writing of 174.a. (D.G. Mason. *From Grieg to Brahms.* (1902)); Brahms used et passim for musical examples.

Mason, William (1829–1908)

See 3855, 3867, 4139.

Mattheson, Johann (1681–1764)

See 3415.

May, Florence (1845–1915)

See 3607, 4420.

Mayer-Mahr, Moritz (1869–1947)

See 3645.

Medtner, Nicolas (1880–1951)

3868. *Surace, Ronald Dominic. "The Solo Piano Music of Nicolas Medtner" DMA diss., University of Cincinnati, 1973. ii, 76 pp. mus.

Meister, Karl Severin (1818–1881)

See 4634.

Mendelssohn, Felix (1809–1847)

See 3244, 3381.a.vii., 3718, 3881, 4226, 4255, 4269, 4381, 4440, 4445, 4710, 4761, 4774, 4826, 5005, 5062, 5188.

Menuhin, Yehudi, Sir (1916–)

See 5360.

Menzel, Adolph (1815–1905)

See 3838.

Messiaen, Olivier (1908–)

See 5413.

Meyer, Leonard B. (1918–)

See 4406.

Miller zu Aichholz, Eugen von (1845–1910)

See 3529, 3530, 5454, 5465.

Milstein, Nathan (1903–)

See 4571, 5176.

Mörike, Eduard (1804–1875)

See 4676.

Moldenhauer, Hans (1906–)

See 3417.

Monteux, Pierre (1875–1964)

See 4152.d., 5360.

Monteverdi, Claudio (1567–1643)

See 5074.

Mozart, Wolfgang Amadeus (1756–1791)

3869. Daverio, John. "From "Concertante Rondo" to "Lyric Sonata": A Commentary on Brahms's Reception of Mozart" *Brahms Studies* 1 (1994) pp. 111–38. fig., notes. Pairs Mozart and Brahms as progressives, and suggests that Mozart provided principal impetus for some of Brahms's unusual work by looking at amplified binary movements in the works of both; includes comment on how Brahms transformed Mozart's design to his needs. Includes comment on Brahms's knowledge of Mozart's music, influence of movements from Mozart's KV 576, 428 and 466 on movements from Brahms's Opp.108, 51 no. 1, and 101, respectively.

3870. Engel, Hans. "Die Meister liebten Mozart" *Mozart-Jahrbuch* (1955) pp. 170–80. Brahms: pp. 173–74. notes. As part of a survey, discusses Brahms's knowledge of Mozart's music and allusions to it in Brahms's own music.

3871. Fellinger, Imogen. "Brahms's View of Mozart" in *Brahms: Biographical, Documentary and Analytical Studies.* [for full citation see 5479] pp. 41–57. ind., notes. Examines Brahms's remarks and memoirs of his circle to show that throughout his life he applied himself consciously and extensively to Mozart and his music: exposure, study, programming, source study and research, influence.
(d) expanded: Fellinger. "Brahms und Mozart" *Brahms-Studien* Bd. 5 (1983) pp. 141–68. omits ind., adds ill., facsim.

3872. *Levy, Sharon Gail. "Developing Variation, Mozart and the Classical Style" Ph.D. diss., University of Chicago, 1991. 2 vols. mus., notes. Includes comparison with Brahms as to how they both use this technique. [from S102]

See also S060, 3426, 3523, 3600, 3813, 3951, 4067, 4213, 4241, 4398, 4498, 4518, 4583, 4616, 4630, 4874, 4892, 4923, 4927, 4946, 5000.5, 5007, 5030, 5077, 5179, 5307, 5323.

Mühlfeld, Richard (1856–1907)

3873. Sacchini, Louis. "Fräulein von Mühlfeld" *The Clarinet* 11/2 (Winter 1984) pp. 12–15. notes. Discusses Mühlfeld's life and his contribution to the clarinet field, his relationship with Brahms, 1891–97 and his role in Opp. 114, 115, 120; includes comment on

the early performances of these works (tryout to public performance), and contemporary reaction.

3874. *Seldomridge, Linda K. "The Brahms-Mühlfeld Coincidence"
M.M. diss., Ball State University, 1977. iii, 29 pp. + tape reel (65
min.). mus., notes.

3875. *Toenes, George. "Richard Muehlfeld" *Clarinet* no. 23 (Summer
1956) pp. 22–23. A brief biography; includes comment on influence on Brahms in writing of Opp. 114, 115, 120 nos. 1 and 2.
[from S033]

3876. Weston, Pamela. ""Meine Primadonna": Mühlfeld" in Weston.
Clarinet Virtuosi of the Past. London: Robert Hale, 1971. pp.
209–35. Brahms: pp. 209, 215–31. notes. Gives the story of the
relationship between Brahms and Mühlfeld (1891–97) and discusses Mühlfeld's role in the creation of Opp. 114, 115, 120.

See also 3201.d., 4095, 4461, 5072.

Murjahn, Magdalene, see Koelle, Magdalene

Nedbal, Oskar (1874–1930)

3877. *Nedbal, Oskar. "Was mir Brahms und Dvořák anvertrauten"
Neues Wiener Journal (12.4.1925).

Nielsen, Carl (1865–1931)

See 3534.

Nietzsche, Friedrich (1844–1900)

See 5344.

Nikisch, Artur (1855–1922)

3878. "Brahms and Nikisch" *The Etude* 26/2 (2.1908) p. 96. Relates anecdote of Nikisch conducting a Brahms symphony in front of Brahms,
and Brahms's approval, as justification for having conductors.

See also 3359.b.e., 3550, 3645, 3740.

Norrington, Roger (1934–)

See 4460.d.i.

Nottebohm, Gustav (1817–1882)

See 3741, 4020, 4428.d.

Oistrakh, David (1931–)

See 5176.

Ondricek, Franz (1865–1922)

See 4571.

Ophüls, Gustav (1866–1926)

3879. Ophüls, Gustav. *Erinnerungen an Johannes Brahms. Ein Beitrag aus dem Kreis seiner rheinischen Freunde.* [Neuausgabe] Mit zeitgenössischen Photographien. [Vorwort zur Neuausgabe von Erika Ophüls] Ebenhausen bei München: Langewiesche-Brandt, 1983. 45 pp. ill., mus. Reissue of 1101 (G. Ophüls. *Erinnerungen an Johannes Brahms.* (1921)).

3880. "Ein schöneres Geschenk als das Ihre aber gibt es nicht . . . Zwei Briefe aus dem Nachlaß Gustav Ophüls" *Brahms-Studien* Bd. 10 (1994) pp. 33–41. facsim. (pp. 38–41), notes. 2 letters, Ophüls to his parents in Berlin, 10.1892; Brahms to Ophüls, 12.1896.

See also 3686, 4654.

Oppitz, Gerhard [fl. 20th century]

See 5189.

Ossian [fl. 3rd century]

A literary hoax, James Macpherson (1736–1796) actual; poet. See 5205.

Otten, George Dietrich (1806–1890)

3881. Zinnow, Ingrid. "Hochgeehrte Herr!—Lieber Freund! Unveröffentlichte Briefe an Georg Dietrich Otten" *Brahms-Studien* Bd. 9 (1992) pp. 36–47. Brahms: pp. 41–45. facsim. (pp. 46–47). 4 letters, 1856–[59], + letter Otten to his sister Constanze, with background. All cited in 1103 (K. Stephenson. *Johannes Brahms und Georg Dietrich Otten*. (1972)). Article also has letters from Mendelssohn, Joachim and Clara Schumann to Otten.

Pachmann, Vladimir de (1848–1933)

See 3645.

Paderewski, Ignacy Jan (1860–1941)

See 3645, 3867, 4302.

Paganini, Nicolò (1782–1840)

See 4124, 4355, 4361, 4988.

Parent, Armand (1863–1934)

See 3540.

Parlow, Albert (1822–1888)

See 3419.

Pasatieri, Thomas (1945–)

See 4750.

Paul, Jean, see Jean Paul

Pedross [fl. 19th century]

3882. Stearns, Theodore. "Brahms and a Young Composer" *The Etude* 18/4 (4.1900) p. 137. ill. Relates anecdote of Pedross meeting

Brahms in Salzburg, Summer 1865, another example of Brahms's blunt evaluation style.

Percy, Thomas (1729–1811)

See 5091.

Perger, Richard von (1854–1911)

See 3740.

Peters, C. F. [music publisher]

See 3404, 3718.

Pfitzner, Hans (1869–1949)

3883. *Floros, C[onstantin]. "Gedanken über Brahms und Pfitzner" *Hans-Pfitzner-Gesellschaft. Mitteilungen* no. 49 (1.1988) pp. 68–73.

See also 3718, 5100.

Philadelphia Orchestra (1900–)

See 5165.

Piening, Karl Theodor (1867–1942)

3884. Reinhardt, Klaus. *Ein Meininger Musiker an der Seite von Brahms und Reger. Das Wirken des Cellisten und Dirigenten Karl Theodor Piening (1867–1942).* Dargestellt nach Dokumenten aus dem Nachlaß mit unveröffentlichten Fotos und Faksimiles. Hannover: Jan Reinhardt Verlag und Versandbuchhandlung, 1991. 147 pp. ill., ind., notes.
"Krefeld (1893–1894)": pp. [33]–34. Relates their meeting (Piening was part of Beckerath circle).
pp. 35–58: Describes their links (1894–1902), includes Piening playing Brahms's music and participating in Festivals.
Includes 3514.a.ii. and 4852.a.

Pink Floyd [fl. 20th century]

See 3756.

Pohl, Carl Ferdinand (1819–1887)

See 3741.

Popper, David (1843–1913)

See 3614.

Porubsky, Bertha, see Faber, Bertha

Poulenc, François (1899–1963)

See 3951.

Prince of Prussia, see Ferdinand, Louis

Prokofiev, Sergey (1891–1953)

See 3780, 4124, 4294, 4311.

Puccini, Giacomo (1858–1924)

See 4892.

Raabe & Plothow [music publisher]

See 3975, 3976.

Rabl, Walter (1873–1940)

3885. Strauss, John F. "Walter Rabl, the Brahms Prize, and a Quartet, Opus 1. Ghosts and Monuments in Fin de Siècle Vienna" *Chamber Music* 7/2 (Summer 1990) pp. 18–19, 30–31. ill. Discusses Rabl and his relation to Brahms.

Rachmaninoff, Sergei, see Rakhmaninov, Sergey

Raff, Joachim (1822–1882)

See 4257, 5332.

Rakhmaninov, Sergey (1873–1943)

See 4270, 4361, 4362, 4414, 5360.

Rameau, Jean-Philippe (baptized 1683–1764)

See 4270, 4351.

Ravel, Maurice (1875–1937)

3886. *La Revue musicale* (Paris) [5] (4.1925).
(a) *reprint: Ravel, Maurice. "Raveliana" in *Ravel par lui-même et ses amis*. Jacques Bonnaure, ed. Paris: Maule, 1987. pp. 61–74. Includes Ravel remarks on Brahms. [from S102]

See also 3951, 4270, 4311, 4920, 5182.

Reger, Max (1873–1916)

3887. Kross, Siegfried. "Reger in seiner Zeit" in *Max Reger in seiner Zeit. Max-Reger-Tage Bonn 1973. Ausstellung vom 13. bis 18. März 1973 vorbereitet vom Musikwissenschaftlichen Seminar der Rheinischen Friedrich-Wilhelms-Universität in zusammenarbeit mit dem Kulturamt der Stadt Bonn und dem Max-Reger-Institut Bonn. Katalog.* Siegfried Kross, ed. Bonn: Rheinische Friedrich-Wilhelms-Universität Bonn Musikwissenschaftliches Seminar, 1973. pp. 7–22. notes. Includes discussion on how Reger was influenced by Brahms's work, and Reger's thoughts on Brahms's music.

3888. Leichentritt, Hugo. "Max Reger als Kammermusik Komponist" *Neue Zeitschrift für Musik* 72/44 (Bd. 101) (25.10.1905) pp. 866–68. Studies Reger's Opp. 49–84, pointing out Brahms's influence, especially Brahms's violin sonatas on Reger's Op. 49, and Brahms's variation works on Reger's variation works.

3889. Möller, Martin. "Max Reger—ein Brahms-Epigone? Zum Klavierkonzert op. 114" in *Beiträge zur Geschichte des Konzerts*. [for full citation see 4515] pp. [343]–52. mus., ind., notes. Studies Brahms's influences on Reger and compares Brahms's Op. 15 and Reger's Op. 114 looking particularly at the formal elements, and how Reger puts on his personal stamp.

3890. *Popp, S. "Reger in der Brahmsnachfolge—Grundlagen und Grenzen einer Einordnung" *Jahrestagung der Gesellschaft für Musikforschung Marburg* (1983).

3891. Reger, Max. *Max Reger. Briefe eines deutschen Meisters. Ein Lebensbild.* Else von Hase=Koehler, ed. 6.–10. Tausend. Leipzig: v. Hase & Koehler, 1928. Brahms: pp. 54–55; also et passim. 1 letter, Brahms to Reger, 3.1897.

3892. *Reiser, Rudolf. "Max Reger. Zwischen Fortschritt und Reaktion. Zum 100. Geburtstag" *HiFi Stereophonie* 12/3 (1973) pp. 261–66.

3893. *Stein, Fritz Wilhelm. *Max Reger.* (Die groβen Meister der Musik) Potsdam: Akademische Verlagsgesellschaft Athenaion, 1939.
   (a) *reprint: Laaber: Laaber-Verlag, 1980. 159, [12] pp. ill., mus., notes.

See also 3419, 3884, 4135, 4162, 4274, 4369, 4407, 4440, 4822, 4848, 4964, 4992, 5116, 5393.

Rehbock, Alexander (1829–1914)

3894. *Leur, Tr. de. "Johannes Brahms en Alexander Rehbock (1829–1914)" *Preludium* [=*Concertgebouwnieuws*] (Amsterdam) (6.1983) pp. 23–25.

Reik, Theodor (1888–1969)

See 3653.

Reim, Edmund (1859–1928)

See 5463.

Reinecke, Carl (1824–1910)

See 3550, 3822.

Reiner, Fritz (1888–1963)

3895. Hart, Philip. *Fritz Reiner: A Biography.* Evanston: Northwestern

University Press, 1994. xii, 330 pp. ind., notes, discog. Brahms et passim and:

pp. 278–79: Reiner's recordings of Brahms's works.

p. 293: Brahms works in Reiner's repertoire.

Reinthaler, Karl (1822–1896)

See 3822.

Reményi, Eduard (1830–1898)

See 3442, 3449, 3450, 5127, 5129.

Reti, Rudolph (1885–1957)

See 4396.

Ricci, Ruggiero (1918–)

See 4571.

Richter, Hans (1843–1916)

3896. Fifield, Christopher. *True artist and true friend. A Biography of Hans Richter.* [Foreword by Sir Georg Solti] Oxford: Clarendon Press, 1993. xx, 519 pp. ill., fig., ind., notes. Brahms et passim. Includes Richter's encounters with Brahms, Richter on Brahms's music, Richter performing Brahms's music.

3897. *Schenk, Erich. "Hans Richter. Ein Dirigent zwischen Wagner und Brahms" *Musikblätter der Wiener Philharmoniker* 38 (1983) p. 74.

See also 3741.

Richter, Johann Paul Friedrich, see Jean Paul

Rieter, Ida [fl. 19th century]

3898. Sulzer, Peter. "Johannes Brahms und Ida Rieter" *Winterthurer Jahrbuch* (1974) pp. 47–53. ill. Discusses their relationship 1861–

75, including Brahms visiting in spring 1866. Includes letter Brahms to Rieter, 10.1871.

Rieter-Biedermann, Jakob Melchior (1811–1876)

3899. *Hofmann, Renate. "Vier Briefe des Verlages J. Rieter-Biedermann an Johannes Brahms" in 4805.5. ill. Letters are from 1869 (2), 1873 (1) and 1877 (1). [from *The American Brahms Society Newsletter* 12/2 pp. 8–9]

3900. *Sulzer, Peter. "Johannes Brahms und sein Winterthurer Verleger" *Landbote* (9.6.1956).

3901. Sulzer, Peter. "13 neu aufgefundene Postkarten und ein Brief von Johannes Brahms an Jakob Melchior Rieter-Biedermann" *Brahms-Studien* Bd. 6 (1985) pp. 31–60. ill., notes. Letter is 2.1873; postcards are 1873–75. Includes provenance and commentary.

See also 3409, 3410, 3594, 3597, 4830.a.

Rilke, Rainer Maria (1875–1926)

3902. *Rilke, Rainer Maria. *Letters of Rainer Maria Rilke. Vol. 2. 1910–1926.* Jane Bannard Green and M.D. Herter Norton, transs. New York: W.W. Norton & Company, Inc., 1948.

(c) excerpt: [Hancock, Virginia Lee] "Encounters: Rainer Maria Rilke" *The American Brahms Society Newsletter* 12/2 (Autumn 1994) p. 6. ill. Excerpt of letter Rilke to Ilse Sadée, 8.2.1912, where he tells about encountering Brahms in the Salzkammergut, Summer 1892 or 1893.

(d) letter also in: Rilke. *Selected Letters of Rainer Maria Rilke 1902–1926.* R.F.C. Hull, trans. London: Macmillan & Co. Ltd., 1946. pp. 205–08. Brahms: pp. 206–08. Identified as Rilke to N.N.

Rimsky-Korsakov, Nikolay Andreyevich (1844–1908)

See 4934.

Rochberg, George (1918–)

See 5117, 5121.

Röger-Soldat, Marie, see Soldat, Marie

Rorem, Ned (1923–)

See 4772.

Rosé, Arnold (1863–1946)

See 3359.b.e.

Rose, Jerome [fl. 20th century]

See 4512.

Rosenthal, Moritz (1862–1946)

3903. *Rosenthal, Moritz. *Neues Wiener Journal* (6.4.1930).

Rubinstein, Anton (1829–1894)

3904. "Rubinstein on the Playing of Brahms" *The Etude* 27/1 (1.1909) p. 71. Report on 18 (J.L. Erb. *Brahms*. (1905)) discussing Rubinstein's opinion of Brahms and his playing of Brahms's music.

See also 3617, 4298, 4616, 4994, 5324.

Rubinstein, Artur (1887–1982)

See 3683, 4030.

Rubner, Cornelius, see Rybner, [Peter Martin] Cornelius

Rudorff, Ernst (1840–1916)

See 3822.

Rückert, Friedrich (1788–1866)

3905. *Otto, Eberhard. "Dichter in Bayern und ihre Komponisten" *Musik in Bayern* 18–19 (1979) pp. 95–109. Discusses poets native to or active in Bavaria from the 19th century to the present, and the composers who set them. Daumer and Heyse are also discussed. [from S102]

Rybner, [Peter Martin] Cornelius [formerly Cornelius Rubner] (1855–1929)

3906. *The New York Times* (12.1916 (?) or early 1.1917 (?)).
(e) report: "How Brahms and Liszt Welcomed Their Friends" *The Etude* 35/1 (1.1917) p. 14. Describes meeting Brahms in Baden-Baden and contrasts Brahms's rudeness to him at this meeting with Liszt's reception on another visit made at another time.

3907. *"A Brahms-Rubner Anecdote" *Musical Observer* (New York) 2/6 (1908) p. 15.

Sachsen-Meiningen, Herzog von, see Georg II, Herzog von Sachsen-Meiningen

Sadée, Ilse [fl. 20th century]

See 3902.

Saint-Saëns, Camille (1835–1921)

See 4168, 4369.

Sapellnikoff, Vassily (1868–1941)

See 3645.

Sappho (c. 612 B.C.– ?)

See 5203.

Sarasate, Pablo de (1844–1908)

See 3951.

Scandello, Antonio (1517–1580)

See 5143.d.i.

Scarl`atti, Domenico (1685–1757)

3908. Goebels, Franzpeter. "Scarlattiana: Bermerkungen zur Scarlatti-Rezeption von Johannes Brahms" *Musica* 40/4 (7./8.1986) pp. 320–28. ill., mus., notes. Comments on Brahms's knowledge of Scarlatti, editions he owned, his editings and allusions, most notably op. 72, no. 5.

3909. *Klimovickiĭ, Abram. "Ob odnoĭ neizvestnoĭ rukopisi Bramsa" in *Pamiatniki kul'tury: novye otkrytiia pis'mennost', iskusstvo, arheologiia. Ezegodnik, 1978.* Leningrad: Nauka, 1979. pp. 211–18. facsim. Examines Brahms's attitude toward the music of Scarlatti and studies a Brahms manuscript at USSR-Lan (?) which is a copy of Scarlatti's K.394. [from S102]

3910. McKay, Elizabeth [Norman]. "Brahms and Scarlatti" *The Musical Times* 130/1760 (10.1989) pp. 586–88. facsim., notes. Discusses Brahms as a collector of Scarlatti editions, Scarlatti's influence on Brahms; includes comment on Brahms as a collector.
   (d) comment: Häfner, Klaus. "Brahms and Scarlatti" *The Musical Times* 131/1763 (1.1990) p. 10. Critical of McKay article, pointing out numerous inaccuracies (problems in translation, German to English?).
   (d) reply: McKay, Elizabeth Norman. *The Musical Times* 131/1763 (1.1990) p. 10. Acknowledges Häfner's concerns and apologizes.

3911. Sheveloff, Joel Leonard. "The Keyboard Music of Domenico Scarlatti: A Re-evaluation of the Present State of Knowledge in the Light of The Sources" Ph.D. diss., Brandeis University, 1970. 3 vols. [= xiv, 688 pp. total] mus., notes, appendixes.
   Brahms: [vol. 1] pp. 70–88. Describes 8 vols. of Scarlatti sonatas handcopied by Brahms, with comments on Brahms's notations.
   Brahms: [vol. 2] pp. 275–79. Discusses Brahms's editings of Scarlatti in light of his editing principles, and allusions to Scarlatti in Brahms's Op. 72, no. 5.

See also 4330, 4920, 5182.

Schack, Adolf Friedrich, Graf von (1815–1894)

See 4647.

Schellenberg, Ernst Ludwig [fl. 20th century]

See 3731.

Schenker, Heinrich (1868–1935)

3912. Pastille, William. "Schenker's Brahms" *The American Brahms Society Newsletter* 5/2 (Autumn 1987) pp. [1–2.] ill. Describes Brahms's significance to Schenker by reviewing Schenker's writings.

3913. *Slatin, Sonia. "The Theories of Heinrich Schenker in Perspective" Ph.D. diss., Columbia University, 1967. 742 pp.

3914. University of California. Riverside. Library. *Heinrich Schenker, Oswald Jonas, Moriz Violin. A Checklist of Manuscripts and Other Papers in the Oswald Jonas Memorial Collection.* [Prepared by Robert Lang and JoAnn Kunselman] (University of California Publications. Catalogs and Bibliographies. 10) Berkeley: University of California Press, 1994. xxvi, [2], 3–227 pp. ind. Inventory: includes comments by Schenker on Brahms, excerpted from Schenker's letters to Violin (p. 165); 2 photos of Brahms (p. 193); 6 writings on Brahms manuscripts (pp. 49, 53); photocopies of published writings (pp. 57–58, 61–62); 34 writings by others on Brahms, including Jonas's projected projects (pp. 149–52); 17 editions of Brahms's music with Schenker editings (pp. 87–89); manuscripts of Schenker studies on Op. 76 no. 7, Op. 117 no. 2 (p. 93); Jonas's holdings of Brahms editions and manuscripts in both hard copy, slides, reels (pp. 142–49, 169, 203).
  (e) announcement: "We have three communications . . ." *19th Century Music* 3/3 (3.1980) pp. 281–82. Brahms: p. 282. Reports on 10 boxes of documents relating to Brahms from the Oswald Jonas Memorial Collection.

See also 4261.d.iv., 4366, 4401, 4406, 4728, 4764, 4911, 4931, 4972.d.i.

Schlegel, Leander (1844–1913)

3915. "Johannes Brahms—Leander Schlegel" in *Brieven en opdrachten van beroemde musici: acht autografen uit een collectie van Willem Noske = Briefe und Widmungen berühmter Musiker: acht Handschriften einer Sammlung Willem Noskes = Letters and Dedications from Famous Musicians: eight autographs from the Willem Noske collections.* Inleiding en commentaar = Einleitung und Kommentar = Introduction and Commentary by Willy Lievense. Buren: Frits Knuf, 1985. pp. [57]–66. ill. (pp. 63, 65), facsim. (pp. [58, 60]). 1 letter, Brahms to Schlegel, 1.1880. Includes transliteration, background on their connection, and on Brahms and The Netherlands. Information is provided in all three languages.

Schmaler, Johann Ernst (1816–1884)

See 4708.

Schmaltz, Susanne (1838–1934)

3916. *Schmaltz, Susanne. *Enchanted Remembrances, 1838–1925.* n.p.: Evanston Pub., 1995. Contains remembrances of Brahms and Clara Schumann. [from S079]

Schmidt, Hans (1854–1923)

3917. *Hernried, R. "Der Dichter von Brahms' "Sapphischer Ode"" *Rigasche Rundschau* no. 187 (19.8.1933).

3918. Torgāns, Jānis. "Hans Schmidt, der Dichter der Sapphischen Ode—seine Bedeutung als Musiker und Mensch" Renate Hofmann, Redaktion. *Brahms-Studien* Bd. 8 (1990) pp. 71–81. Presents Schmidt's life and discusses link with Brahms; compares Schmidt's musical works to Brahms's. Includes 2 letters, 1881.

Schnabel, Artur (1882–1951)

3919. *Schnabel, Artur. [Autobiography. [Manuscript]] University of Chicago, 1945.

(d) i) Schnabel, Artur. *My Life and Music*. With an introduction by Edward Crankshaw. London: Longmans, Green & Co. Ltd., 1961. xv, [1], 223 pp. Brahms: pp. 15–18. Describes meeting Brahms in Vienna, 1896–97, being part of Brahms's circle, his thoughts on Brahms's music.

also: New York: St. Martin's Press, 1963.

(a) reprint (of London edition): Schnabel. *My Life and Music & Reflections on Music*. With a Foreword by Sir Robert Mayer and an Introduction by Edward Crankshaw. Gerrards Cross: Colin Smythe Ltd., 1970. xv, [3], 3–248 pp. ind. Brahms: pp. 15–18. *Reflections on Music* reprinted from Schnabel, Artur. *Reflections on Music = Betrachtungen über Musik*. English version by César Saerchinger. (Manchester University Lectures 31) [Manchester:] Manchester University Press, 1933. 31 pp.

(a) unabridged, slightly corrected reprint: Schnabel. *My Life and Music*. New York: Dover Publications, Inc.; Gerrards Cross: Colin Smythe Ltd., 1988. adds ill. xv, [5], 3–248 pp.

(d) ii) Saerchinger, César. *Artur Schnabel: a biography*. With a Tribute by Clifford Curzon. London: Cassell & Company Ltd., 1957. xxi, [1], 354 pp. ind., discog. Brahms: pp. 27–31; also et passim. Describes Schnabel and Brahms in Vienna, 1896–97, and performances of Brahms's music throughout Schnabel's career.

also: New York: Dodd, Mead & Company, 1957.

(a) reprint (of New York edition): Saerchinger. *Artur Schnabel. A Biography*. Westport, CT: Greenwood Press, 1973.

See also 3355, 5286.

Schnitzler Family (Robert (1825–1897); Viktor (1862–1934); Ludowika (1865–1955); and Olga Johanna (1890–1970))

3920. Knierbein, Ingrid. "''Solche Medicin lobe ich mir . . .'' Unveröffentlichte Briefe von und an Johannes Brahms aus dem Besitz der Familie Justizrat Dr. Viktor Schnitzler'' *NZ-Neue Zeitschrift für Musik* 147/3 (3.1986) pp. 4–7. ill., facsim., notes. 4 letters: Robert [father] to Brahms, 3.1882; Brahms to Viktor [son], Summer 1890 and 11.1896; and Brahms to Ludowika [Viktor's wife], 8.1890. Includes brief survey of Brahms's relationship to the family, 1857–97, and mentions Olga Johanna [Viktor's daughter, Brahms's Godchild].

Schoenberg, Arnold (1874–1951)

3921. Bailey, Walter B. "Prophetic Aspects of Musical Style in the Early Unpublished Songs of Arnold Schoenberg" *Musical Quarterly* 74/4 (1990) p. 491–520. Includes reference to Brahms's influence on Schoenberg, and notes similarities between the two composers' vocal styles.

3922. Dümling, Albrecht. "Warum Schönberg Brahms für fortschrittlich hielt" in *Verteidigung des musikalischen Fortschritts*. [for full citation see 3931] pp. 23–49. notes. Describes how Schoenberg was influenced by Brahms's romanticism and how he was alone in his opinion of Brahms. Includes comment on the "Brahms the Progressive" speech (1933).

3923. *Frisch, Walter [M.]. "Schoenberg and the Brahms Tradition 1893–1897" in Frisch. *The Early Works of Arnold Schoenberg, 1893–1908*. Berkeley: University of California, 1993.

3924. Hansen, Mathias. " "Zusammenhang im Dienste der Faßlichkeit." Anmerkungen zu einer Konstellation: Brahms-Schönberg-Webern" *Musik und Gesellschaft* 33/12 (12/1983) pp. 700–04. mus. Discusses Brahms and the [Zweite] Wiener Schule, especially his influence on it.

3925. *Kalisch, Volker. "Schönberg und Brahms oder Vom praktischen Nutzen geschichtlicher Argumente" *Das Liebhaberorchester. Zeitschrift für das Liebhabermusizieren* 33 (1989) pp. 4–9.

3926. *Meier, Urs. "Wohlklang in trostloser Zeit. Was Schönberg gegen Brahms vorzubringen hat" *Reformatio. Zeitschrift für Politik, Kirche und Kultur* 42/4 (1993) pp. 283–91.

3927. Musgrave, Michael. "Schoenberg's Brahms" in *Brahms Studies: Analytical and Historical Perspectives*. [for full citation see 5480] pp. [123]–37. mus., notes. Discusses how Schoenberg's view of Brahms relates to his theoretical outlook and examines Schoenberg's writings for their comments on Brahms. Related to

1146 (M. Musgrave. "Schoenberg and Brahms" Ph.D. diss. (1980))?

3928. [Schoenberg, Arnold] "Schönberg für Brahms" in *Verteidigung des musikalischen Fortschritts*. [for full citation see 3931] pp. 49–50. notes. Contains 11 excerpts from Schoenberg's writings on Brahms.

3929. Schuhmacher, Gerhard. "Tradition auf Schönbergs Weg zum Zwölftonkonzept" *NZ-Neue Zeitschrift für Musik* 145/3 (3.1984) pp. 4–10. ill. (cover), mus., notes. Discusses Brahms's influence on Schoenberg, looking at the "Brahms der Fortschrittliche" ["Brahms the Progressive"] article and its musical examples, plus other writings reprinted in 2493.b.ii. (A. Schönberg. *Stil und Gedanke* [=*Style and Idea* in translation] (1975)). Shows that the influence shows up most particularly in Schoenberg's Op. 16 and Pierrot Lunaire; also he uses Brahms's bass-variation technique.

3930. Straus, Joseph N. *Remaking the Past. Musical Modernism and the Influence of the Tonal Tradition*. Cambridge, MA and London: Harvard University Press, 1990. ix, [5], 207 pp. Brahms: pp. 29–34. mus., notes. Suggests that Schoenberg misreads Brahms so he can show himself as the culmination. Re-examines the analyses of Opp. 51 no. 2 and 121 no.1 in the "Brahms the Progressive" article.

3931. *Verteidigung des musikalischen Fortschritts. Brahms und Schönberg*. Albrecht Dümling, ed. Hamburg: Argument, 1990. 185 pp. ind., notes. Discusses Schoenberg's relationship to Brahms. Contains: 3546, 3682, 3922, 3928, 3976, 4028, 4094.a., 4153.d., 4155, 4914, 5046, 5398.

See also 3256, 3362, 3475, 3523, 3697, 3768, 3976, 4031, 4102, 4191, 4254, 4274, 4309, 4375, 4439, 4614, 4645, 4789, 4895, 4907, 4914, 4921, 4942, 4982, 4992, 5006, 5011, 5023, 5024, 5032, 5045, 5046, 5116, 5123, 5231, 5338, 5344, 5370, 5380, 5391, 5393, 5449.5.
See also "Op. 25" in Part IV.A.1.a.

Scholz Family (Bernard and Luise) [fl. 19th century]

See 3398, 3822.

Schopenhauer, Arthur (1788–1860)

See 5080.

Schröder, C. H. [piano manufacturer]

3932. Pilipczuk, Alexander. "Die Hamburger Pianoforte-Fabrik C.H. Schröder und Johannes Brahms" *Das Musikinstrument* 39/9 (9.1990) pp. 22–30, 32. notes. Discusses Brahms's connection to Schröder and Baumgardten & Heins, also the two firms's history; also includes comment on Louise Japha-Langhans memories of Brahms, 1844–48, and technical details on the Schröder piano.

Schubert, Franz (1797–1828)

3933. *Endler, Franz. in *Schubertiade Hohenems 1983. Programmbuch.* Gerd Nachbauer, ed. Bregenz: Vorarlberger Graphische Anstalt Russ, 1983. Discusses Schubert's influence on Brahms. [from S102]

3934. Pascall, Robert. "Brahms and Schubert" *The Musical Times* 124/1683 (5.1983) pp. 286–87, 289, 291. facsim., notes. Discusses Brahms's thoughts on Schubert, the influence of Schubert on Brahms's music; Brahms's performances of Schubert's music; Brahms's editing and arranging of Schubert's music; and Brahms's holdings of Schubert editions and manuscripts.

3935. *Sherlock, Andrea Elizabeth. "Brahms and Schubert: An Examination of Influence in the Chamber Music of Johannes Brahms" M.A. thesis, Music, University of Western Ontario, 1990. vii, 178 pp. mus., notes.

See also S060, 3267, 3292, 3426, 3523, 3600, 3718, 3785, 4105, 4117, 4167, 4230, 4269, 4289, 4292, 4298, 4323, 4364, 4365, 4376, 4429, 4457, 4550, 4616, 4633, 4667, 4670, 4672, 4684, 4688, 4706, 4710, 4761, 4774, 4892, 4909, 4923, 4974, 4975, 4982, 4988, 4990, 4998, 5001, 5027, 5057, 5078, 5079, 5088, 5104, 5123, 5179, 5201, 5232, 5331.
See also I13 in Appendix A.

Schubring, Adolf (1817–1893)

See 3822, 5345.

Schütte, Agathe, see Siebold, Agathe von

Schütz, Heinrich (1585–1672)

See 4772, 4810, 4814, 5143.d.i.

Schumann Family

Clara (1819–1896): 3936, 3937, 3940–43, 3945, 3946, 3948, 3950, 3952–59, 3962, 3965, 3966–69.
Eugenie (1851–1938): 3960, 3963.
Felix (1854–1879): 3970.
Julie (1874–1955): 3962.
Robert (1810–1856): 3937–39, 3943, 3944, 3947–49, 3951, 3952, 3956, 3957, 3961, 3964, 3966, 3968.

3936. *[American Brahms Society. Brahms Archive. "Index to the Music in Volume 1 of the Brahms-Clara Letters" Seattle: 1986(?).] Indexes 1179 (C. Schumann. *Clara Schumann. Johannes Brahms* ... (1927)).

3937. "Brahms" *The Etude and Musical World* 15/6 (6.1897) p. 158. Discusses Brahms and the Schumanns, and wonders what Brahms's fame will be.

3938. *"Brahms and Schumann: short biography" *Presto* (Chicago)13/565 (22.4.1897) p. 10.

3939. *"Brahms visits Schumann in the Asylum" in Antony Hopkins. *Music All Around Me. A Personal Choice from the Literature of Music*. London: Leslie Frewin, 1967. pp. 141–43.
    2. Impression: 1968. pp. 141–43. Letter Brahms to Clara Schumann, 1855, reprinted from 1179.d.ii.c.i (F. Bonavia. *Musicians on Music*. (1956)).

3940. Chissell, Joan. *Clara Schumann: A Dedicated Spirit. A Study of Her Life and Work*. London: Hamish Hamilton, 1983. xvi, [1], 2–232 pp. ill., ind., notes, appendixes. Brahms et passim. Includes excerpt from 1170.d.i. (B. Litzmann. *Clara Schumann. An Artist's Life*. (1913)).

3941. [Reich, Nancy B.] "Clara Schumann Centenary, 1996" *The American Brahms Society Newsletter* 13/2 (Autumn 1995) p. 4.

Presents a list of commemorative events for the centennial of her death.

3942. "Clara Schumann's Debt to Johannes Brahms" *The Etude* 34/3 (3.1916) p. 174. Shows Clara's tributes to Brahms (1854) with excerpt from 1170.d.i. (B. Litzmann. *Clara Schumann. An Artist's Life.* (1913)).

3943. *Creyghton, Germain. "Het relationeel complex Clara Wieck-Robert Schumann-Johannes Brahms" in *Psychoanalyse en muziek.* Joost Baneke, ed. (Psychoanalyse en cultuur 4) Amsterdam, Atlanta: Rodopi, 1992.

3944. *De Pillecyn, Jurgen. "Johannes Brahms en Robert Schumann. Een onderzoek naar Schumanns invloed in Brahms' pianomuziek, symfonische werken, kamermuziek en enkele koorwerken, voorafgegaan door biografische studies" Diss., Facultet letteren en wijsbegeerte, Katholieke Universiteit Leuven, 1986. 2 vols.

(d) De Pillecyn. "Schumanniaanse technieken en modellen bij Brahms" *Revue belge de Musicologie=Belgisch tijdschrift voor muziekwetenschap* 44 (1990) pp. 133–52. mus., notes. Looks at rhythmic, melodic and harmonic aspects. Relates Brahms's Opp. 76, 116–19 with Schumann's Opp. 6, 12, 15, 16, 28; Brahms's Op. 68 with Schumann's Op. 115; Brahms's Op. 90 with Schumann's Opp. 38, 97; Brahms's Op. 83 with Schumann's Opp. 20 and 54.

3945. Fröhlich, Hans J. "Freunde und Bekannte" in *Johannes Brahms: Leben und Werk.* [for full citation see 3215] pp. 51–54. Examines Brahms's circle by ethnic, professional and gender groupings; also discusses Brahms in Vienna and the qualities of his friendship.

3946. *Halberstadt-Freud, Hendrika C. "Clara Schumann: "A woman's love and life": A Psychoanalytic Interpretation" *Psychohistory Review* 23/2 (Winter 1995) pp. 143–66.

3947. Hanslick, Eduard. "Robert Schumann in Endenich (1899)" Susan Gillespie, trans. in *Schumann and His World.* R. Larry Todd, ed. Princeton: Princeton University Press, 1994. pp. 268–87. Brahms: pp. 277–84. notes. Translation of 1153.a. (E. Hanslick. "Robert Schumann in Endenich" in Hanslick. *Am Ende des Jahrhunderts [[1895–1899]].* (1899)).

3948. *Höcker, Karla. *Clara Schumann: die grosse Pianistin, ihrer Zeit, die Lebensgefährtin Robert Schumanns, die Freundin von Johannes Brahms.* (dtv 7308; dtv-Junior) München: Deutscher Taschenbuch-Verlag, 1975.
      *issue: 1978. 188 pp. ill.

3949. *Hofmann, Kurt. "Wie sah Johannes Brahms die Persönlichkeit Robert Schumanns?" in *Traditionsbeziehungen bei Schumann: Robert-Schumann-Tage, 1986.* Karl-Marx-Stadt: n.p., 1987. pp. 58–63.

3950. Hofmann, Renate. "Johannes Brahms im Spiegel der Korrespondenz Clara Schumanns" in *Brahms und seine Zeit.* (Hamburger Jahrbuch für Musikwissenschaft 7) [for full citation see 5428] pp. 45–58. notes. Discusses what she thinks of Brahms and his music, particularly during Schumann's last days and the time just after his death. Based on review of approximately 2,000 letters (mostly unpublished) at D-ddr-Zsch, of Clara to Joachim, Levi, the Herzogenbergs and Fellingers, and Antonie Speyer née Kufferath.

3951. Holmes, John L. "Johannes Brahms (1833–1897)" in Holmes. *Composers on Composers.* New York [et al.]: Greenwood Press, 1990. pp. [36]-38. ind., notes. Lists what other composers have said about Brahms and his music as well as Brahms's thoughts on other composers.

3952. Howitt, Basil. "Robert Alexander Schumann" in Howitt. *Love Lives of the Great Composers from Gesualdo to Wagner.* Toronto: Sound and Vision, 1995. pp. 165–93.
      "Enter Brahms, Exit Schumann": pp. 189–93. Discusses Brahms's first contacts with the Schumanns, and the speculation that he and Clara were lovers.

3953. "In Memoriam Clara Schumann (1819–1896)" *The American Brahms Society Newsletter* 14/1 (Spring 1996) p. [12]. Excerpt from ? Describes Clara Schumann's last months and Brahms's feelings about her death in words and music.

3954. "Johannes Brahms" in *Writings of German Composers.* Jost Hermand and James Steakley, eds. (The German Library 51) New York: Continuum, 1984. pp. 176–80. Includes 2 letters Brahms to Clara, 8.1855 and 7.1888 from 1179.d.ii (C. Schumann. *Letters of Clara Schumann and Johannes Brahms 1853–1896.* (1927)) and 1 letter Brahms to Marie [Ida Maria] Lipsius, 5.1885, translated by Michael Gilbert from 1069 (La Mara. *Musikerbriefe aus Fünf Jahrhunderten.* (1886)).

3955. *Lépront, Catherine. *Clara Schumann: la vie à quatre mains.* (Elle était une fois) Paris: R. Laffont, 1988. 283, [8] pp. ill.
(b) i) *Japanese translation by Kanako Yoshida: *Kurara Shuman: hikari ni michita shirabe.* Tokyo: Kawadeshoboshinsha, 1990. 329 pp.
(b) ii) *Korean translation: *Kullara Syuman: ne son ui insaeng.* [1.] Chopan. Soul-si: Samjin Kihoek, 1991. 282 pp. ill.

3956. Macy, Sheryl. "The First Trio. Clara Wieck Schumann, Robert Schumann, Johannes Brahms" in Macy. *Two Romantic Trios. The Story of Six Passionate People Who Changed the World of Music.* 1st ed. Portland: Allegro Publishing, 1991. pp. [9]–106 pp. Brahms: pp. 77–106. ill., fig., notes, discog. A popular retelling of their relationship, 1853–1896, emphasizing the personal side; focuses on 1853–1862 period.

3957. Melkus, Eduard. "Eine vollständige 3. Violinsonate Schumanns" *NZ [Neue Zeitschrift] für Musik* 121/6/7 (6./7.1960) pp. 190–95. A study and history of Schumann's Violin Sonata No. 3 in A minor, detailing Clara's, Joachim's and Brahms's roles in both its creative process and its suppression.

3958. Pennington, Kenneth. "Clara Schumann: Lieder Composer and Champion" *The NATS [National Association of Teachers of Singing] Journal* 47/2 (11./12.1990) pp. 5–11. Brahms: pp. 9–11. notes, discog. Surveys their relationship, 1853–1896, and includes excerpts of their letters concerning Brahms's songs.

3959. Reich, Nancy B. "Clara Schumann and Johannes Brahms" in Reich. *Clara Schumann. The Artist and the Woman.* Ithaca and London: Cornell University Press, 1985. pp. 187–207; also et passim. ill., notes. A detailed overview of their relationship on personal and musical levels.
(d) i) abridged: Reich. "Johannes Brahms and Clara Schumann" *The American Brahms Society Newsletter* 3/2 (Autumn 1985) pp. [1–4]. omits notes, adds facsim.
(d) expanded: Reich. "Clara Schumann and Johannes Brahms" in *Brahms and His World.* [for full citation see 5478] pp. 34–47. omits facsim., adds notes.

(d) ii) *Reich, Nancy B. "Clara Schumann und Johannes Brahms: Eine vielschichtige Freundschaft" in *Johannes Brahms: Leben, Werk, Interpretation, Rezeption.* [for full citation see 5453] pp. 34–41.

3960. Ryssel, Fritz Heinrich. "Johannes Brahms 1833–1897" [Section title in Table of Contents is "Eugenie Schumann spricht von Johannes Brahms, dem Freund ihrer Familie"] in Ryssel. *Aus der Nähe gesehen.* Tubingen: Rainer Wunderlich Verlag Hermann Leins, 1954. pp. 49–55. Describes Brahms at the Schumann's house, 1850's. Excerpt from 1180 (? Auflage) (E. Schumann. *Erinnerungen.* (1925)).

3961. *Schoppe, Martin. "Schumann und Brahms: Begegnung in Düsseldorf" in *Johannes Brahms: Leben, Werk, Interpretation, Rezeption.* [for full citation see 5453] pp. 26–33.

    (a) reprint: Schoppe. "Schumann und Brahms—Begegnung in Düsseldorf" *Brahms-Studien* Bd. 7 (1987) pp. 77–90. notes. Describes their first meeting in 1853, Schumann's reaction, the pieces Brahms had composed.

3962. *Schumann, Clara. *Mein liebes Julchen. Briefe.* Dietz-Rüdiger Moser, ed. München: Nymphenburger, 1990. 267 pp. ill., facsim., fig., ind., notes. Letters between Clara and her daughter Julie. [from S031]

3963. Schumann, Eugenie. "Brahms" in Schumann. *Memoirs of Eugenie Schumann.* Marie Busch, trans. London: Eulenburg Books, 1985. pp. 141–73. ill., mus. Reprint of 1180.b (London edition) (1927).

    *also: Schumann. *Memoirs.* New York: Da Capo Press Inc., [198?]. Reprint of 1180.b (London edition) (1927).

    *also: Schumann. Lawrence, MA: Music Book Society, 1991. Reprint of 1180.b (London edition) (1927).

3964. *Siegmund-Schultze, Walther. "Auf den Beziehungen Robert Schumanns und Johannes Brahms'" in *Robert-Schumann-Tage 1985.* Gunther Müller, ed. (Wissenschaftliche Arbeitstagung zu Fragen der Schumann-Forschung 10) Zwickau: Rat des Bezirkes Karl-Marx-Stadt, Abteilung Kultur, 1986.

3965. *Soccanne, Pierre. "Les Inspiratrices: Clara et Brahms" *Le Guide du concert* 19/22–24 (1933) pp. 583–85, 615–18, 647–49.

3966. Struck, Michael. "Gerüchte um den "späten" Schumann" *NZ-Neue Zeitschrift für Musik* 143/5 (15.5–15.6.1982) pp. 52–56. ill. Uses biographical and medical arguments to speak against the hypothesis that an alleged affair between Brahms and Clara is partially responsible for Robert's mental illness and the suppression of his last compositions. [from S102]

3967. Struck, Michael. "Revisionsbedürftig: Zur gedruckten Korrespondenz von Johannes Brahms und Clara Schumann. Auswirkungen irrtümlicher oder lückenhafter Überlieferung auf werkgenetische Bestimmungen (mit einem unausgewerteten Brahms-Brief zur Violinsonate op. 78)" *Die Musikforschung* 41/3 (7.–9.1988) pp. 235–41. Reports on necessary revisions in published readings of letters concerning Opp. 116–19, 34, and 115 upon consultation of Brahms-Clara Schumann correspondence at D-brd-B. Also publishes for first time letter Brahms to Clara, 2.1879, relevant to Op. 78. Includes comment on significance of revisions and completeness of letters to Brahms research.

   (c) excerpt in English translation by Ben Kohn and George [S.] Bozarth: Struck. "New Evidence on the Genesis of Brahms's G major Violin Sonata, Op. 78" *The American Brahms Society Newsletter* 9/1 (Spring 1991) pp. 5–6. facsim. Focuses on this letter and Clara's role in Op. 78 creative process. Includes translation of the letter.

3968. Tibbetts, John C. "The Lyre of Light" *Film Comment* 28/1 (1.–2.1992) pp. 66–68, 71, 73. Brahms: pp. 68, 71. In a survey of composer "biopixes," discusses *A Song of Love* (1947) which is about the Schumanns and Brahms.

3969. *Virneisel, Wilhelm. "Johannes Brahms y Clara Schumann" *Revista de musica* 2/9 (4.1929) pp. 94–100. A Spanish translation of 1179.e.vi (?) (W. Virneisel. *Musica d'oggi* (1928)).

3970. Zwol, Cornelis van. "Felix Schumann—petekind van Johannes Brahms" (Menselijk stukje muziekgeschiedenis) *Mens en melodie* 43/12 (12.1988) pp. 12–17. ill. Traces life of Felix Schumann, particularly his relationship with Brahms and Brahms's setting of some of his poems in Opp. 63 nos 5 and 6; and 86 no. 5.

See also S060, 3231, 3244, 3247, 3260, 3270, 3291, 3294, 3310, 3381.a.vii., 3397, 3398, 3401, 3407, 3414, 3419, 3431, 3453, 3537, 3555, 3561, 3564, 3576, 3600, 3604, 3617, 3628, 3650.d.ii.,

3653.6, 3657, 3662, 3663, 3695, 3700, 3702, 3712, 3717, 3718, 3822, 3825, 3866, 3881, 3916, 4040, 4082, 4105, 4129, 4133, 4140, 4161, 4163, 4167, 4257, 4264, 4269, 4272, 4285, 4298, 4317, 4322, 4325, 4349, 4355, 4363, 4364, 4377, 4398, 4407, 4430, 4440, 4445, 4515, 4517, 4539, 4549, 4553, 4577, 4582, 4590, 4670, 4671, 4678, 4684, 4688, 4706, 4717, 4739, 4745, 4759, 4761, 4774, 4824, 4835, 4864, 4866, 4879, 4881, 4900, 4906, 4909, 4923, 4935, 4947, 4970, 4973, 4974, 4992, 4994, 5005, 5009, 5015, 5020, 5027, 5029, 5046, 5052, 5054, 5057, 5077, 5078, 5080, 5091, 5104, 5105, 5115, 5118, 5137, 5187, 5188, 5209, 5212, 5231, 5232, 5234, 5249, 5305, 5317, 5319, 5331, 5333, 5341, 5344, 5366, 5367, 5385, 5404, 5457.
See also "Op. 9" in Part IV.A.2.a.

Schwarzkopf, Elisabeth (1915–)

3971. *Sanders, Alan. *Elisabeth Schwarzkopf: a career on record. Elisabeth Schwarzkopf in a discussion of her records with J[ohn].B. Steane*. Portland: Amadeus Press, 1995. 184 pp.

Scriabin, Alexander, see Skyrabin, Alexander

Shakespeare, William (baptized 1564–1616)

3972. *Draheim, Joseph. "Shakespeares Dramen in der Musik" in *William Shakespeare: Didaktisches Handbuch*. [3 vols., total] Rüdiger Ahrens, ed. (Uni-Taschenbücher 1111–1113) München: Wilhelm Fink, 1982. vol. 2, pp. [693]–727. Brahms: p. 708. ind., notes, discog.

See also 4052.

Sharpe, Ethel, see Hobday, Ethel

Shaw, [George] Bernard (1856–1950)

See 3371, 3617, 5058, 5344, 5348.5, 5354, 5404, 5408.

Shostakovich, Dmitry (1906–1975)

See 4182, 5178.

Sibelius, Jean (1865–1957)

See 4892.

Siebold, Agathe von (1835–1909)

3973. Siebold, Agathe von. "Allerlei aus meinem Leben" in 3562 pp. 89–105. Describes her friendship with Brahms in the late 1850's.

See also 3562, 3945.

Simrock Family

Friedrich August [Fritz] (1837–1901): 3974–77.
P.J. (1792–1868): 3974–76.

3974. [Bozarth, George S.] "The Brahms-Simrock Correspondence" *The American Brahms Society Newsletter* 10/2 (Autumn 1992) p. 5. notes. Reports on Library of Congress acquisition of Simrock correspondence (postcards and letters) with general comment on how originals compare with published versions in 1203 (J. Brahms. *Johannes Brahms Briefe an Fritz Simrock*. (1919)) and 1204 (J. Brahms. *Johannes Brahms Briefe an P.J. Simrock und Fritz Simrock*. (1917)).

3975. *Döll, Stefanie. "Das Berliner Musikverlagswesen in der Zeit von 1880 bis 1920" Phil.F. diss., Freie Universität Berlin, 1984. 216 pp. Examines individual components of Berlin music life, ways in which the publishers were organized. [from S102]

3976. Ehlert, Gero. "Brahms, Schönberg und ihre Berliner Verleger" in *Verteidigung des musikalischen Fortschritts*. [for full citation see 3931] pp. 111–16. notes. Focuses on Brahms and Simrock, with only a mention of other Brahms publishers (Raabe & Plothow, Fürstner); contrasts with Schoenberg's situation with Dreililien-Verlag.

3977. *Hofmann, Kurt. "Zu den Beziehungen zwischen Johannes Brahms und Fritz Simrock" in *32 Stichvorlagen von Werken Johannes Brahms* [for full citation see 3412] pp. 7–15. notes (p. 21).

See also 3397, 3398, 3409–12, 3496, 3634, 3717, 3757, 3764.b.i., 4262, 4605, 4713, 4716.

Singer, Edmund (1831–1912)

See 4571.

Sistermans, Anton (1867–1926)

See 3359.b.e., 5157.

Skyrabin, Alexander (1872–1915)

See 4289.

Smyth, Ethel (1858–1944)

3978. Hancock, Virginia [Lee]. "Encounters: Ethel Smyth" in *The American Brahms Society Newsletter* 7/2 (Autumn 1989) pp. 9–10. ill. Excerpts from 1208.d (E. Smyth. *Female Pipings in Eden.* (1933)) describing meetings with Brahms 1877–79.
    (d) continued: Hancock. *The American Brahms Society Newsletter* 8/1 (Spring 1990) pp. 6–8. ill. Describes meetings with Brahms in 1879.

3979. Smyth, Ethel. "Brahms" in Smyth. *The Memoirs of Ethel Smyth.* Abridged and Introduced by Ronald Crichton. With a List of Works by Jory Bennett. Harmondsworth: Viking, 1987. pp. 99–[108]; also et passim. notes. Describes meetings with Brahms 1877–79 with excerpts from 1208 (E. Smyth. *Impressions That Remained.* (1919)) and 1208.d (E. Smyth. *Female Pipings in Eden.* (1933)).

3980. Smyth, Ethel. "Brahms" in 4609.

See also 4609.

Soldat, Marie (1863–1955)

3981. *Deneke, Margaret. "What I Remember" [manuscript] 2 vols., n.d. Oxford, Lady Margaret Hall, Deneke Deposit.

3982. Musgrave, Michael. "Marie Soldat 1863–1955: An English Perspective" in *Beiträge zur Geschichte des Konzerts.* [for full citation see 4515] pp. [319]–30. Brahms: pp. [319]–23. ind., notes.

Relates Brahms's and Soldat's first contact and describes their relationship, 1879–97. Soldat was a proponet of Op. 77.
See also 3741.

Solomon (1902–)

See 5163.

Solti, Georg, Sir (1912–)

See 3362.

Speidel, Ludwig [fl. 19th century]

3983. *Pinter, Charlotte. "Ludwig Speidel als Musikkritiker" Phil. F.
diss., Universität Wien, 1949. 777 pp.
See also 5027.

Spengel, Julius (1853–1936)

See 3441.d.iii.

Speyer, Antonie née Kufferath [fl. 19th century]

See 3741, 3950.

Spies Family (Hermine (1857–1893); and Minna [fl. 20th century])

3984. [Spies, Minna] *Hermine Spies. Ein Gedenkbuch für ihre Freunde
von ihrer Schwester*. Leipzig: G.J. Göschen'sche Verlagshand-
lung, 1905. 317 pp. ill., notes. Revised entry for 1214. [previously
not seen]
  Groth, Klaus. "An Hermine Spies (als Sie die Rhapsodie von
    Brahms gesungen)": pp. 267–68. Poem makes tribute to
    Spies in her performing Op. 53.
  "Briefwechsel mit Johannes Brahms": pp. 293–317. 28 letters,
    1885–94, between Brahms and Spies; also 1 letter Brahms to
    Hermine's husband, 1893, and 2 letters Brahms to Minna (?),
    [1894?].

3985. *Schuppener, Ulrich. "Hermine Spies aus Löhnberg und ihre Beziehungen zu Johannes Brahms" *Nassauische Annalen* Bd. 104 (1993) pp. 197–216.

Spitta, Philipp (1841–1894)

3986. *Schilling, Ulrike. "Philipp Spitta; Leben und Wirken im Spiegel seiner Briefwechsel" Phil.F. diss., Eberhard-Karls-Universität Tübingen, 1993.

  (a) *reprint: Schilling. *Philipp Spitta; Leben und Wirken im Spiegel seiner Briefwechsel. Mit einem Inventar des Nachlasses und einer Bibliographie der gedruckten Werke.* (Bärenreiter Hochschulschriften) Kassel, New York: Bärenreiter, 1994. xii, 425 pp. ind., notes.

3987. *Wiechert, Bernd. "Philipp Spittas Studienjahre in Göttingen 1860 bis 1864: Eine biographische Skizze" *Göttinger Jahrbuch* 39 (1991) pp. 169–81. Discusses Spitta making the acquaintance of Grimm and Brahms. [from S102]

See also 3398, 3404.

Spohr, Louis (1784–1859)

See 3718, 4215.

Stanford, Charles Villiers, Sir (1852–1924)

3988. Stanford, Charles Villiers, Sir. *Pages from an Unwritten Diary.* London: Edward Arnold, 1914. xiii, 328 pp. ind. Brahms: pp. 133–36, 173–77, 200–02, 299; also et passim. Describes meeting Brahms in 1873 and hearing various Brahms works with Brahms as performer and conductor, 1880– ; Stanford performing Opp. 68 and 54 in England; includes comments on Brahms's reception in England.

See also 4135, 5404.

Steiner, Adolf (1843–1930)

3989. Fehr, Max. "Adolf Steiner. Mit unveröffentlichten Briefen von Brahms, Kirchner, Richard Strauß, Friedrich Hegar, Joseph v[on]. Widmann, zwei Illustrationen und einem Faksimile" *Neu-jahrsblatt der Allgemeinen Musikgesellschaft in Zurich* no. 119 (1931) pp. 1–27. Brahms: pp. 15–17. 2 letters, 1887 and [1895].

Stern, Isaac (1920–)

See 5176.

Stockhausen, Julius (1826–1906)

3990. *Brahms, Johannes. *Johannes Brahms im Briefwechsel mit Julius Stockhausen.* Renate Hofmann, ed. (Johannes Brahms-Briefwechsel. Neue Folge 18) Tutzing: Hans Schneider, 1993. 192 pp. ind.

See also 3534, 3579, 5157.

Storm, Theodor (1817–1888)

See 3794.

Strauss, Franz Joseph (1822–1905)

See 4000.

Strauss, Johann (1825–1899)

3991. Lange, Fritz. "Wie Johannes Brahms und Johann Strauss gute Fre-unde wurden. Allerlei Neues über das Verhältnis zwischen Sym-phoniker und Walzerkönig" *Neues Wiener Journal* 41/14,191 (25.5.1933) pp. 13–14. Describes how Hanslick brought them to-gether and provides details on their friendship.

3992. *Perger, Richard [von]. "Johannes und Johann" *Die Zeit* [Tageszeitung] (Wien) (2.6.1909).

3993. Strauss, Johann (Sohn). *Leben und Werk in Briefen und Doku-menten. Bd. II: 1864–1877.* Im Auftrag der Johann-Strauß-Gesellschaft Wien gesammelt und kommentiert von Franz Mailer. Tutzing: Hans Schneider, 1986. Brahms: pp. 261–64. Presents a letter from Strauss to ?, [11.1874] and speculates that the recipi-ent is Brahms.

3994. *Würzl, Eberhard. "Johann über Johannes—Begleubigung einer Abschrift" *Musikerziehung* 47 (12.1993) pp. 81–83.
(d) *Würzl, Eberhard. "Zum letztenmal über "Johannes und Johann"" *Musikerziehung* 48/1 (1994–95) p. 33.

3995. Würzl, Eberhard. "Johannes und Johann—Kritisches zur Beziehung zwischen Brahms und Strauß" *Musikerziehung* 41 (6.1988) pp. 207–13. Discusses Brahms and Strauss as the theme for the Wiener Musiksommer 1988, reviews their relationship and concludes that neither had any influence on the other's music.

3996. *Würzl, Eberhard. *Johann-Strauß-Studien. Aufsätze über Musik, Beiträge zur Musikpädagogik, Erinnerungen und Bekenntnisse.* Bibliographie zusammengestellt und herausgegeben von Autor. (Strauss. *Ausgewählte Schriften.*) Wien: Author, 1991. 168 leaves.

See also 3475, 3523, 3813, 3951, 4955, 4998.

Strauss, Josef (1827–1870)

See 3359.d.

Strauss, Richard (1864–1949)

3997. *Biba, Otto. "Richard Strauss und Johannes Brahms" *Musikblätter der Wiener Philharmoniker* 37 (1982/83) pp. 195–97.

3998. *Hörburger, Felix. "Über einige Briefe von Richard Strauss an Franz Carl Hörburger" in *Gedenkschrift Hermann Beck.* Hermann Dechant and Wolfgang Sieber, eds. Laaber: Laaber-Verlag, 1982. pp. 201–08. Presents quotes from Strauss's letters to his uncle, 1885–91, where he reports on his activities and on contemporary musical life; includes impressions, meetings with Brahms. [from S102]

3999. *Strauss, Richard. "An Johannes Brahms" in Strauss. *Betrachtungen und Erinnerungen.* 1. Auflage. [for full citation see 4000.a.] 2. Auflage: 1957. pp. 275–76. 1 letter Strauss to Brahms, 1884.
(a) reprint: in Strauss. *Der Strom der Töne trug mich fort. Die Welt um Richard Strauss in Briefen.* In Zusammenarbeit mit Franz und Alice Strauss herausgegeben von Franz Grasberger. Tutzing: Hans Schneider, 1967. pp. 21–22.

4000. Strauss, Richard. *Dokumente. Aufsätze, Aufzeichnungen, Vor-worte, Reden, Briefe.* 1. Auflage. Ernst Krause, ed. (Reclams Universal-Bibliothek. Kunstwissenschaften 830) Leipzig: Ver-lag Philipp Reclam jun., 1980. ind., notes.
"Brahms": pp. 45–46. Comments on Opp. 90 and 98, excerpted from letters to Strauss's father (1884), Ludwig Thuille (1884) and Franz Wüllner (1885).
"Erinnerungen an Hans von Bülow": pp. 239–46. Brahms: pp. 242–46. Recounts meeting Brahms at Bülow's (1892?); conducting Brahms works in Meiningen, 1885; Brahms's comments on his *Sinfonie* and Brahms as a conductor. This is reprinted from 1232 (R. Strauss. *Neue freie Presse* (Wien) (1909)).
(a) *reprint (of "Erinnerungen . . . Bülow" only): Strauss. "Aus meinen Jugend- und Lehrjahren" in Strauss. *Betra-chtungen und Erinnerungen.* Willi Schuh, ed. Zürich: Atlantis-Verlag, 1949.
2. Auflage: 1957. pp. 247–58. Brahms: pp. 249–52.

See also 3256, 3718, 3989, 4135, 4719, 4750, 4751, 5088, 5371, 5393, 5399.

Stravinsky, Igor (1882–1971)

See 3951, 4370, 4921, 5074, 5344.

Streicher, Johann Baptist (1796–1871)

See 3336, 3605, 4262.

Suk, Joseph (1874–1935)

See 3533.

Szalitz, Paula [fl. 19th–20th centuries]

4001. "- When Brahms first saw little Paula Szalitz . . ." *The Etude and Musical World* 14/6 (6.1896) p. 139. Anecdote about Brahms telling Szalitz a story and her sitting down at a piano and express-ing what she had understood and heard, as an illustration of the importance of practising piano.

Szarvady, Wilhelmine, see Clauss-Szarvady, Wilhelmine

Szell, George [Georg] (1897–1970)

See 3362.

Szeryng, Henryk (1918–)

See 3260.

Tausig, Carl (1841–1871)

See 4012.

Tchaikovsky, Peter Ilyich [Chaikovskĭ, Petr Il'ich] (1840–1893)

4002. *Musikalisches Wochenblatt* (1894).
    (e) i) *report: "Peter Tschaikowsky meets Johannes Brahms in Leipsic" *Musical Courier* 29 (19.9.1894) pp. 7–8.
    (e) ii) *report: Tschaikowski[, Peter]. "Criticism of Brahms" *Presto* (Chicago) 11/51 (18.10.1894) p. 9.
    (e) iii) *report: "Tschaikowski and Brahms" *Musical News* (London) 7 (18.7.1894) p. 140.

4003. *Biba, Otto. "Tschaikowsky über Brahms oder: Brauchen wir ein neues Brahms-Bild?" *Musikblätter der Wiener Philharmoniker* 18 [38] (1983/84) pp. 169–72.

4004. Brodsky, A[nna]. *Recollections of A Russian Home . . . (A Musician's Experiences)*. Manchester, London: Sherratt & Hughes, 1904. pp. 155–62. An account of a midday dinner at the home of Adolph Brodsky in Leipzig, 1.1888, with Tchaikovsky, Grieg, and Brahms in attendance.
    2nd ed.: 1914. *Recollections of A Russian Home. A Musician's Experiences*. Brahms: pp. 159–66.
    (d) *worked into (from 1904 ed.) : 48 (F. May. *Johannes Brahms.* (1905)).
    (c) excerpt: [Hancock, Virginia Lee] "Encounters: Tchaikovsky, Grieg, and Brahms" *The American Brahms Society Newsletter* 11/2 (Autumn 1993) pp. 7–8.

4005. Tchaikovsky, P[eter]. I[lyich]. "A Pen Picture of Brahms" *Etude* 31/7 (7.1913) p. 472. Reports on Tchaikovsky's description of Brahms and his reactions to Brahms's music.

See also 3231, 3293, 3426, 3617, 3780, 3951, 4486, 4587, 4841, 4943, 4968, 4980, 5063, 5070, 5228, 5404.

Telemann, Georg Philipp (1681–1767)

See 3426.

Thomas, Theodore (1835–1905)

4006. [Hancock, Virginia Lee] "Encounters: Theodore Thomas" *The American Brahms Society Newsletter* 8/2 (Autumn 1990) p. 9. Excerpt from 1244 (R.F. Thomas. *Memoirs of Theodore Thomas.* (1911)): anecdote and 1 letter Brahms to Thomas, 1.8.[9.] 1892.

See also 4139, 4532.

Thuille, Ludwig (1861–1907)

See 4000.

Tieck, [Johann] Ludwig (1773–1853)

See 4701–03.

Tiessen, Heinz (1887–1971)

4007. *Für Heinz Tiessen 1887–1971. Aufsätze, Analysen, Briefe, Erinnerungen, Dokumente, Werkverzeichnis, Bibliographie.* Manfred Schlösser, ed. (Schriftenreihe der Akademie der Künste 13) Berlin: Akademie der Künste, 1979. Includes Tiessen's thoughts on Brahms. [from S102]

Toscanini, Arturo (1867–1957)

See 3362, 5360.

Tovey, Donald Francis, Sir (1875–1940)

See 4159, 4571, 5354.

Truxa, Celestine [fl. 19th century]

See 3462.

Turgenev, Ivan (1818–1883)

4008. *Waddington, Patrick. "Some Gleanings on Turgenev and His International Connections, with Notes on Pauline Viardot and her Family" *New Zealand Slavonic Journal* [7] (1983) pp. 175–205. "Turgenev and Brahms": pp. 182–83.

See also 5148.

Turner, J[oseph]. M[allord]. W[illiam]. (1775–1851)

See 3630.

Uhland, Ludwig (1787–1862)

See 4667.

Vaughan Williams, Ralph (1872–1958)

See 5053.

Verdi, Giuseppe (1813–1901)

4009. *Mistretta, Giorgia. "Fuori dall'ansia: Brahms e Verdi sull acqua" *Mondo economico* (Milano) 49/31 (30.7.1994) p. 74.

See also 4644, 4955.

Vetter Family (Ferdinand and Ellen) [fl. 19th century]

See 3404, 3822.

Viardot, Pauline (1821–1910)

See 4008.

Violin, Moriz (1879–1956)

See 3914.

Viotti, Giovanni Battista (1755–1824)

4010. *McVeigh, Simon. "Brahms's Favourite Concerto" *The Strad*
105/1248 (4.1994) pp. 343–44, 346–47. ill., mus. Discusses
Brahms's enthusiasm for Viotti's Violin Concerto no. 2. [from
S092]

See also 4630, 5007.

Vogelweide, Walter von der, see Walther von der Vogelweide

von der Leyen, Rudolf, see Leyen, Rudolf von der

Voss, Johann Heinrich (1751–1826)

See 3794.

Wagner, Cosima (1837–1930)

See 3289.

Wagner, Richard (1813–1883)

4011. ab. [A. Briner] "Johannes Brahms und Richard Wagner. Konturen
eines Doppeljubiläums" *Neue Zürcher Zeitung* no. 106 (7./8.1983)
p. 65. Compares them as composers.

4012. Biba, Otto. "Brahms, Wagner und Parteiungen in Wien. Texte und
Beobachtungen" *Musica* 37/1 (1./2.1983) pp. 18–22. notes. Takes
excerpts from contemporary writings, letters, diaries, 1853–88,
to show how Vienna was divided into "camps" for Brahms and
Wagner. Letters include Liszt to Brahms, 4.1882; Tausig to
Brahms, no date; and Hellmesberger to Brahms, 10.1876. Includes comments on Hanslick and Bruckner.
   (d) *Biba, Otto. "Beobachtungen zum Wirken von Johannes
      Brahms in Wien" in *Johannes Brahms: Leben, Werk, Inter-
      pretation, Rezeption.* [for full citation see 5453] pp. 42–51.

4013. *Grey, Thomas S. *Wagner's Musical Prose: Texts and Contexts.*
(New Perspectives in Music History and Criticism) Cambridge,
New York: Cambridge University Press, 1995. xix, 397 pp. mus.,
ind., notes.

4014. Grimm, Hartmut. "Brahms in der ästhetischen Diskussion des 19. Jahrhunderts" *Musik und Gesellschaft* 33/5 (5.1983) pp. 270–76. ill., notes. Discusses Brahms and Wagner as the two poles in 19th century music, and how this came about.

4015. Istel, Edgar. "Wagner und Brahms" *Neue Zeitschrift für Musik* 80/21 (22.5.1913) pp. 302–05. Related to 1267 (E. Istel. *Münchner neueste Nachrichten* (1909)).

4016. Korn, Peter Jona. "Brahms—der beste Wagnerianer. Über die Toleranz des Konservativen" *Brahms-Studien* Bd. 6 (1985) pp. 61–64. Discusses Brahms as the contrast to Wagner, the "New German School of Music" episode and Brahms and tradition.

4017. Kropfinger, Klaus. "Wagner und Brahms" *Musica* 37/1 (1./2. 1983) pp. 11–17. ill., notes. Discusses the two schools and Hanslick's role; what the composers thought of each other. Compares both as composers and sees them both as leading into the 20th century.

4018. *Mila, Massimo. *Brahms e Wagner*. Alberto Batisti, ed. (Einaudi tascabili 200) Torino: Einaudi, [1994]. xix, 443 pp.

4019. Newman, Ernest. "The Putzmacherin Letters" in Newman. *The Life of Richard Wagner. Vol. 3: 1859–1866*. New York: Alfred A. Knopf, 1941. pp. 567–69. [4 vols. in total, 1933–46] Reports on the role that Brahms is alleged to have played in their publication.
also: London [et al.]: Cassell and Company Limited, 1933–47. [for all 4 vols.]
(a) reprint (of New York edition): Paperback ed. Cambridge [et al.]: Cambridge University Press, 1976.

4020. w. [Wittmann, Hugo] "Stammtischabende. (Erinnerungen an Johannes Brahms.)" *Neue freie Presse* (Wien) no. 15,704 (10.5. 1908) Morgenblatt pp. [1]–3 [across page bottoms]. Describes Brahms the man including reference to the Putzmacherin letters and Brahms's role in disseminating them; also looks at Brahms and Nottebohm, Brahms and Wagner, Brahms and opera.

4021. Wagner, Richard. [*Briefe*]
(b) English translation by Stewart Spencer and Barry Millington: Wagner. *Selected Letters of Richard Wagner*. Spencer and Millington, eds. With original texts of passages omitted

from existing printed editions. London & Melbourne: J.M.
Dent & Sons Ltd., 1987. Brahms: pp. 848–49. 2 letters,
Wagner to Brahms, 6.1875, *Rheingold* manuscript incident.
German source is 1280 (Wagner. *Richard Wagners Briefe
. . . 2. Folge. Bd. XVII. An Freunde und Zeitgenossen.*
(1909)).

   (c) Wagner, Richard. *Briefe 1830–1883.* 1. Auflage. Werner Otto,
ed. [Translations from French done by Egon Wiszniewsky]
Berlin: Henschelverlag Kunst und Gesellschaft, 1986. 511,
[1] pp. ind. Brahms: pp. 387–88. 2 letters, Wagner to Brahms,
6.1875, *Rheingold* manuscript incident.

4022. Wirth, Helmut. "Richard Wagner und Johannes Brahms" in *Brahms
und seine Zeit.* (Hamburger Jahrbuch für Musikwissenschaft 7)
[for full citation see 5428] pp. 147–57. mus., notes. Discusses
their many links: Brahms no opera, Wagner, no symphony; Wagner's Faust overture contrasted to Brahms's Op. 81; discusses allusions in Brahms's music to Wagner; and Wagner's comments
on Brahms's music.

See also 3231, 3260, 3289, 3564, 3567, 3574, 3617, 3623, 3647, 3689,
3695, 3696, 3717, 3718, 3813, 3820, 3825, 3832, 3844, 3851,
3897, 3951, 4028, 4349, 4582, 4590, 4595, 4596, 4617, 4648,
4699, 5009, 5020, 5054, 5067, 5068, 5073, 5124, 5147, 5305,
5344, 5345, 5363, 5366, 5370, 5373, 5377, 5404.

Walter, Bruno (1876–1962)

See 4825.

Walter, Gustav (1834–1910)

See 3359.b.e., 3362, 3741, 5157.

Walther von der Vogelweide (c1170–c1230)

See 3523.

Walton, William (1902–1983)

See 4470.

Weber, Carl Maria von (1786–1826)

4023. Henderson, Donald G., and Alice H. Henderson. *Carl Maria von Weber. A Guide to Research.* (Garland Composer Resource Manuals 24; Garland Reference Library of the Humanities 1006) New York & London: Garland Publishing Inc., 1990. xxii, [2], 385 pp. ind. Contains 4 references that relate to Weber and Brahms: as composers for solo piano, for clarinet; as romanticists.

See also 3718, 4988.

Webern, Anton (1883–1945)

See 3475, 3523, 3526, 3924, 4193, 5370.

Webster, James (1942–)

See 4982.

Weigl, Karl (1881–1949)

See 4032.

Weingartner, Felix (1863–1942)

See 3617, 5061, 5360.

Weiss, Josef (1864–?)

See 3645.

Wendt, Gustav (1827–1912?)

4024. *Neumann, Martin. "Die Freundschaft zwischen Gustav Wendt und Johannes Brahms" in *Bismarck-Gymnasium Karlsruhe Festschrift.* [Ulrich Staffhorst, ed.] Karlsruhe: Fördergemeinschaft des Bismarck-Gymnasiums, 1986. pp. 332–43.

See also 3201.d., 3573, 5057.d., 5203.

Wesendonck, Mathilde (1828–1902)

See 3231.

Weyermann Family [fl. 19th century]

See 3514.a.ii.

Weyr, Rudolph [von] (1847–1914)

See 5426.

White, Elise Fellows [fl. 19th–20th centuries]

4025. *White, Elise Fellows. "How I Met Brahms" *Musical Observer* (New York) 5 (1911) p. 14.

Whiting, Arthur Battelle (1861–1936)

See 3687.

Widmann, Josef Viktor (1842–1911)

4026. Teller, Charlotte. "European Gleanings" *Music* (Chicago) [13/6] (4.1898) pp. 787–90. Brahms: pp. 787–88. Report on 1302 (J.V. Widmann. *Deutsche Rundschau* (1897)).

See also 3231, 3582, 3594, 3597, 3822, 3989.

Wolf, Hugo (1860–1903)

4027. *Fleischer, Hugo. "Der Brahmsgegner Hugo Wolf" *Der Merker* 9 (15.12.1918) pp. 847–56.

See also 3237.d.i., 3475, 3523, 3526, 3617, 3653.2, 3767, 3821, 3951, 4040, 4617, 4667, 4676, 4678, 4699, 4737, 4981, 5078, 5082, 5100, 5101.d.ii., 5201, 5340, 5344, 5359, 5363, 5404, 5406.

Wolf, Louise [fl. 19th century]

4028. Wolf, Louise. "Begegnung mit Brahms" in *Verteidigung des musikalischen Fortschritts*. [for full citation see 3931] pp. 109–10. Describes meeting Brahms in Berlin in the 1890's: physical description and thoughts on Wagner. From her "Tagebuchaufzeichnungen."

Wolff, Leonhard (1848–1934)

4029. *Kross, Siegfried. "Leonhard Wolff: Städtischer und Universitätsmusikdirektor in Bonn" *Bonner Geschichtsblätter* 37 (1988) pp. 153–73. ill. Presents Wolff's biography, includes his connections with Brahms. [from S102]

Wolters, Auguste, see Brandt, Auguste

Wooge, Emma (1857–1935)

4030. Hofmann, Kurt. "Brahms' Hamburger Aufenthalt im April 1882 in den Erinnerungen der Sängerin Emma Wooge" *Brahms-Studien* Bd. 7 (1987) pp. 41–50. notes. Describes meeting Brahms in Hamburg, 4.1882; includes "Emma Wooges Erinnerung an Johannes Brahms": pp. 46–49. Also relates Wooge's memories of Artur Rubinstein.

Wüllner, Franz (1832–1902)

See 4000.

Ysaÿe, Eugen (1858–1931)

See 4571, 5110.

Zasche, Theodor [fl. 19th century]

See 3670.

Zemlinsky, Alexander von (1871–1942)

4031. Clayton, Alfred. "Brahms und [von] Zemlinsky" in *Brahms-Kongress Wien 1983*. [for full citation see 5431] pp. 81–93. mus., notes. Discusses von Zemlinsky's connections to Brahms circle and his acquaintance with Brahms, 1895– . Also looks at von Zemlinsky as link between Brahms and Schoenberg, influences of Brahms on von Zemlinsky's music, and examines von Zemlinsky's Op. 3.

4032. Zemlinsky, Alexander [von], and Karl Weigl. "Brahms and the
Newer Generation: Personal Reminiscences" Walter [M.] Frisch,
trans. in *Brahms and His World*. [for full citation see 5478] pp.
205–07. notes. Translation of 1320 (A. von Zemlinsky and K.
Weigl. *Musikblätter des Anbruch* (1922)).

See also 3475, 5116.

Zuccalmaglio, Anton Wilhelm Florentin von (1803–1869)

See 4659.

Part IV

Works

Contains historical background and analytical discussion for the works. To facilitate the grouping of references, this part is organized according to instrumental genres. Within each section, provision has been made for subsections to deal with general remarks (when more than one work is discussed in a citation), or to focus on individual opus numbers. The following chart shows the principal genres used and their relation to each other:

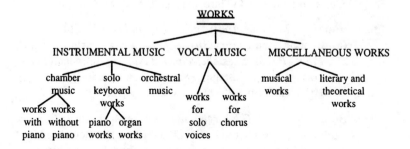

For example, an article on one of the string quartets would be located in IV.A.1.b., "Chamber, Music—Works without Piano—Specific Works" under the respective opus number. An article on all the piano and string quartets would be located in IV.A.1., "Chamber Music—General". An article on one of the string quartets and a piano sonata would be located in IV.A, "Instrumental Music—General". An article on all the chamber music, two of the symphonies, and the *Triumphlied* would file in IV, "Works—General."

217

Citations at the "General" level within each genre are for the most part cross-referenced to particular opus numbers at the "Specific" level. Only when the citation is a broad overview of Brahms's works is cross-referencing not provided.

Entry numbers with decimals provide the entry numbers of other entries of interest. These decimal entries apply to the entire section at whose end they appear, and not only to the entry above.

Identification for works without opus number is given in accordance with Margit L. McCorkle, *Johannes Brahms: Thematisch-Bibliographisches Werkverzeichnis*. Herausgegeben nach gemeinsamen Vorarbeiten mit Donald M. McCorkle† (München: G. Henle Verlag, 1984).

An index to the works discussed in this part is included in the indexes at the end of this volume. It includes access by opus number; by title, for those works without opus number; and by name of composer, for those works by other composers that Brahms edited or arranged.

4033. *Music Review Monthly*. 1– (2.1987–). Indexes and reprints reviews of classical music concerts from 11 major newspapers, including *The New York Times, The Los Angeles Times, Boston Globe, Washington Post.*

4034. *Musical Standard* 3 [Third series] (20.5.1865) p. 368.

4035. *Andrade, Mário de. *Diário de S[ão]. Paulo* (1933–35).
    (a) *reprint: Andrade. *Música e jornalismo: Diário de S[ão]. Paulo. Pesquisa, estabelecimento do texto*. Introduction and notes by Paulo Castagna. (Mariodeandradiando 3) São Paulo: HUCITEC: Edusp, 1993. xxx, 327 pp.

4036. Beadle, Jeremy J. *The Virgin Guide to Classical Music*. London: Virgin Books, 1993. [6] vii–viii, [2] 3–312 pp. ind. Book is divided by genre, citations include short overviews and discographies.
    Brahms: pp. 61–64. Symphonic works, focusing on Op. 68, 10 items.
    Brahms: pp. 114–17. All concertos, 17 items.
    Brahms: pp. 234–35. Chamber and solo piano music. Focus is on chamber music. 11 items.
    Brahms: pp. 262–64. Lieder, Opp. 45, 53, 54, 82. 5 items.
    Brahms: p. 269. 6 items in the "Your Ideal Starter Kit in 100 CD Purchases" list.

4037. Bozarth, George S. "Paths Not Taken: The "Lost" Works of Jo-

hannes Brahms" *The Music Review* 50/3/4 (8./11.1989) pp. 185–
205. mus., notes. An accounting of pieces that never made it to publication (tracked through primary and secondary sources); includes
appendix of extant sketches of unfinished works held at A-Wgm.
(d) related to: 5449.5.

4038. Candé, Roland de. "Johannes Brahms. 1833–1897" in Candé. *Les
Chefs-d'œuvre de la musique. [Vol.] 2. De Rossini à Berg. An-
thologie.* Paris: Seuil, 1992. pp. 77–100. ill., facsim., notes.,
discog. Background information, descriptive analysis and suggested listening for 18 works.

4039. *Chwialkowski, Jerzy. *The Da Capo Catalog of Classical Music
Compositions.* New York: Da Capo Press, 1996. 1412 pp.

4040. Colles, H[enry]. C[ope]. *Symphony and Drama, 1850–1900.* (The
Oxford History of Music 7) London: Humphrey Milford, Oxford
University Press, 1934. xi, [1], 504 pp.
"1853": pp. [16]–37. Brahms: pp. 22–37. notes. Discusses
Brahms's first meeting with Schumann, the "Neue Bahnen"
article, Brahms's piano works.
"Brahms and Chamber Music": pp. [38]–72. mus., notes. A
chronological survey with descriptive analysis.
"Symphony in Vienna": pp. [165]–213. Brahms: pp. 182–213.
mus., notes. Surveys the symphonies, with descriptive analysis.
"Song. I. Brahms": pp. [354]–81. mus., notes. A chronological
survey with descriptive notes; includes comment on Brahms
as a song composer and Brahms's setting of text.
"Song. II. Wolf and Others": pp. [382]–414. Brahms: pp. 386–92.
mus. Contrasts Brahms and Wolf as song composers by comparing their settings of Goethe's "Phänomen" (Brahms Op.
61 no. 3; Wolf *Gedichte von J.W. Goethe* no. 32).
"Choral Music": pp. [415]–44. Brahms: pp. 418–32. mus., notes.
Surveys large choral works only.
(a) *reprint: [Revised ed.] New York: Cooper Square, 1973.
(d) later edition: see 4059.

4041. Daniels, David. "Brahms, Johannes, 1833–1897" in Daniels. *Orchestral Music. A Source Book.* Metuchen, NJ: The Scarecrow
Press, Inc., 1972. pp. 42–44. Provides instrumentation, timing and
edition information for 19 orchestral and choral works.
2nd ed.: *Orchestral Music. A Handbook.* Metuchen and London:
1982. pp. 66–68. Adds 1 work.

4042. Dietel, Gerhard. *Musikgeschichte in Daten*. München: Deutscher Taschenbuch Verlag GmbH & Co. K.G.; Kassel: Bärenreiter-Verlag Karl Vötterle GmbH & Co. KG, 1994. 1026 pp. ind. Brahms: pp. 652–722 et passim; also et passim the entire book. Book is arranged chronologically, under date of composition provides short descriptive comments on 30+ works.

4043. Downes, Edward, see 4468.

4044. *Ehlert, Louis. "Brahms" *Musical Items* 2 (2.–9.1885) pp. 1–2; 2–3; 1–2; 1; 1–2; 1–2; 4; 2. Excerpts of 1336.a.b (L. Ehlert. *From the Tone World.* (?)).

4045. *Federlein, Gottlieb. "Commentaries on Some of Brahms' Music" *Musical Review* [=*The Musical Review* (Chicago)] 3 (2.1893) pp. 224–26.

4046. Feil, Arnold. *Metzler Musik Chronik vom frühen Mittelalter bis zur Gegenwart*. Stuttgart und Weimar: J.B. Metzler, 1993. xxiv, 836 pp. Brahms: pp. 593–644 et passim. Book is arranged chronologically, under date of composition excerpts of writings on each work's character are given; discusses 13+ works.

4047. Holoman, D. Kern. "Johannes Brahms" in Holoman. *Evenings with the Orchestra. A Norton Companion for Concertgoers*. New York, London: W.W. Norton & Company, 1992. pp. [140]–58. ill., notes. Descriptive analysis and background particulars (includes instrumentation and duration) for 9 works; includes short introduction on life, overview of output, and comment on Brahms as a composer.

4048. *Kaiser, Joachim. *Süddeutsche Zeitung* (München) (1962–1977).
(a) reprinted: Kaiser. "Anton Bruckner. César Franck. Johannes Brahms" in Kaiser. *Erlebte Musik von Bach bis Strawinsky*. Hamburg: Hoffmann und Campe, 1977. pp. 405–31.
"Johannes Brahms": pp. 413–31. Includes performance reviews, work interpretations or analyses of Opp. 15, 34, 45, 77, 83, the symphonies with Karajan and Kubelik, the chamber music style. [Not all pieces are reprints, some pieces are original to monograph.]

4049. Keith, Alan. "Johannes Brahms (1833–1897)" in Keith. *Your Hundred Best Tunes*. London: J.M. Dent & Sons Ltd., 1975. pp.

40–43. Author chooses Opp. 45, 49 no. 4, 53, 56b, 83, Ungarische Tänze [McCorkle WoO 1]; provides brief background on works, also brief overview of life.

4050. Kern, Ernst. "Johannes Brahms und die Orgel" in *Zur Orgelmusik im 19. Jahrhundert. Tagungsbericht 3. Orgelsymposion Innsbruck 9–11.10.1981.* Walter Salmen, ed. (Innsbrucker Beiträge zur Musikwissenschaft 9; Verlags-Nr. 3904) Innsbruck: Musikverlag Helbing, 1983. pp. 127–31. notes. An overview of all organ works and works with organ accompaniment. Includes comments on the chorales used in Op. 122.

(a) reprint: Kern. *Gottesdienst und Kirchenmusik* no. 1 (1./2.1984) pp. 2–8.

4051. Kirby, F.E. *Music in the Romantic Period. An Anthology with Commentary.* New York: Schirmer Books, 1986. xi, [3], 986 pp. Brahms: pp. 543–629. mus. (full scores), notes. Analysis of Opp. 47 no. 3, 56a, 85 no. 5, 111, 116 no. 6, 118 no. 3.

4052. Kupferberg, Herbert. *The Book of Classical Music Lists.* New York: Facts on File Publications, 1985. xii, 240 pp. Brahms et passim. ind. Most information focuses on various aspects of works, including place in American symphonic repertoire; also includes information on Brahms the man.

revised ed.: New York: Penguin Books, 1988. xii, 244 pp.

4053. McKinney, Timothy R. "Beyond the 'Rain-Drop' Motif: Motivic and Thematic Relationships in Brahms's Opera 59 and 78" *The Music Review* 52/2 (5.1991) pp. 108–22. mus., notes. Goes beyond use of the same motif and rhythm in both works to show other relationships between them.

4054. McLeish, Kenneth, and Valerie McLeish. "Brahms, Johannes (1833–97)." in McLeish and McLeish. *Listeners' Guide to Classical Music. An Introduction to the Great Classical Composers and Their Works.* Harlow: Longman, 1986. pp. 35–40. ind. An overview of works, by genre with descriptive remarks; includes comments on Brahms the composer and his style, also on life 1833–69. Includes comparative remarks to other composers' music and suggestions for further listening from other composers' works. 1st American ed.: *The Listener's Guide to Classical Music. An Introduction to the Great Classical Composers and Their*

Works. New York [et al.]: G.K. Hall, Maxwell Macmillan International, 1992.

4055.   *Morton, Arthur, and Herbert Morton. *Morton Evening Concerts, 1954–1971: The Lawrence Morton Years; Composers and Works Played, Conductors and Performing Artists.* Los Angeles: Lawrence Morton Fund, 1993. xii, 112 pp.

4056.   Musgrave, Michael. *The Music of Brahms.* (Companions to the Great Composers) London, Boston and Henley: Routledge & Kegan Paul, 1985. [12], 329 pp. ill., mus., fig., ind., notes. A chronological discussion, focusing on discussion by genre within 1855–90 time frame; also includes comment on Brahms and folk music, Brahms and early music.
        also: *Oxford: Clarendon Press, 1994.
              paperback ed.: 1994. series omitted.

4057.   *Northcott, Bayan. "Young Man's Fancy" *Independent* (London) (24.10.1992) p. 29. Assesses work of the young Brahms. [from S092]

4058.   Reddick, William, see 4489.5.

4059.   *Romanticism (1830–1890).* Gerald Abraham, ed. (The New Oxford History of Music 9) Oxford, New York: Oxford University Press, 1990. xx, 935 pp. mus., ind., notes. Overview of works with descriptive analysis.
        Pascall, Robert. "VIII. Major Instrumental Forms: 1850–1890": pp. 534–658. Brahms: pp. 542–45, 550–55, 593–600, 628–35.
        Orrey, Leslie. "IX. Solo Song (a) Germany": pp. 659–83. Brahms: pp. 672–77.
        Abraham, Gerald. "X. Choral Music": pp. 793–830. Brahms: pp. 810–13.
        (b) *Italian translation by Franco Sgrignoli: *Il romanticismo, 1830–1890.* ([The New Oxford History of Music in Italian.] Storia della musica 9) Milano: Feltrinelli; Garzanti, 1991. 1003, [24] pp. ill.
        (d) *earlier edition: see 4040.

4060.   *Sargenti, G. "Passato e futuro nell'opera di Brahms" *I Quaderni della civica scuola di musica* (1983).

4061.   *Thalmann, Joachim. "Untersuchungen zum Frühwerk von Johannes Brahms. Harmonische Archaismen und die Bedingungen ihrer Entstehung" Phil.F. diss., Universität-Gesamthochschule Paderborn, 1987.

(a) reprint: *Untersuchungen zum Frühwerk . . . und die Bedingungen ihrer Entstehung.* (Detmold-Paderborner Beiträge
zur Musikwissenschaft. 2[; Bärenreiter-Hochschulschriften])
Kassel [et al.]: Bärenreiter, 1989. 218 pp. mus., notes. Uses
harmonic and form analysis to show that Brahms used Scan-
dinavian folksong in his early works. Includes analysis of
Opp. 4 and 7 no. 6, as well as discussion of Hamburg musical life 1838–53 and of Brahms's interest in music history.

(d) *Thalmann. "Studien zu Brahms' frühesten Komponisten.
Sein Interesse an alter Musik und dessen Niederschlag in
seinem Frühwerk" in *Festschrift Arno Forchert zum 60.
Geburtstag zum 29. Dezember 1985.* Gerhard Allroggen and
Detlef Altenburg, eds. Kassel: Bärenreiter, 1986. Establishes
that Brahms couldn't have been influenced by early music as
result of exposure in Hamburg; features present in his work
are result of early compositional style. [from S102]

4062. Tovey, Donald Francis. *Concertos and Choral Works.* (Tovey.
Essays in Musical Analysis [2]) Oxford, New York: Oxford University Press, 1989. Reprint of 1372 (D.F. Tovey. *Essays . . . Vol.
2.* (1981)) with an index. Includes publisher's note that was only
in vol. 1 of 1372.

4063. Tovey, Donald Francis. *Essays in Musical Analysis.* See 4062,
4087, 4507.5.

4063.3. See also 3211, 3225, 3235, 3277, 3282, 3298, 3338, 3357, 3377,
3380–82, 3400, 3401, 3408, 3426, 3428, 3432, 3432.5, 3433,
3435, 3441.d.i., 3468, 3523, 3653.6, 3686, 3895, 3896, 3919.d.ii.,
4596, 4909, 4988, 5035, 5146, 5184, 5369.

4063.7. See also I19, I47 in Appendix A.

A. Instrumental Music

4064. *Augustini, Folke Eckhard. "Die Klavieretüde im 19. Jahrhundert. Studien zu ihrer Entwicklung und Bedeutung" Phil.F. diss.,
Universität zu Köln, [1986?].

(a) reprint: Augustini, Folke [Eckhard]. *Die Klavieretüde im 19.
Jahrhundert. Studien zu ihrer Entwicklung und Bedeutung.*
Duisburg: Gilles & Francke, 1986. xii, 548 pp.

"Die Etüde in der zweiten Jahrhunderthälfte: Brahms und die Klavierpädagogen": pp. 223–60. Brahms: pp. 242–48. mus., notes. Compares Chopin's Op. 25 no. 2 with Brahms's "Klavierstudie" on same [no. 1 in McCorkle Anhang Ia, no. 1].

"Sonderformen der Etüde": pp. 329–45. mus., notes. Brahms: pp. 340–45. Analysis of Op. 35.

"Ein Übungswerk als Individualdokument": pp. 346–50. mus., notes. Points out parallels between Opp. 15 and 83 and the 51 Übungen [McCorkle WoO 6].

(d) *Augustini, Folke [Eckhard]. "Die neue Schule der Geläufigkeit: zur Klavieretüde des 19. Jahrhunderts" *Concerto* 3/2 (1986) pp. 50–58.

4065. Berger, Melvin. "Johannes Brahms" in Berger. *Guide to Sonatas: Music for One or Two Instruments.* 1st Anchor Books ed. New York [et al.]: Doubleday, 1991. pp. 68–77. discog. Background and descriptive analysis for the sonatas for cello, clarinet, piano and violin.

4066. Bookspan, Martin, see 4459.5.

4067. Bozarth, George S. ""Leider nicht von Johannes Brahms"" *The American Brahms Society Newsletter* 3/1 (Spring 1985) pp. [3–4]. Reviews the cadenza for Mozart's K466 (McCorkle Anhang IV no. 4) and the cello arrangement of Op. 78 and concludes that they are not by Brahms.

4068. Brahms, Johannes. *Johannes Brahms Autographs: Facsimiles of Eight Manuscripts in the Library of Congress.* Introduction by James Webster; Notes about the Manuscripts by George S. Bozarth. (Music in Facsimile 1) New York and London: Garland Publishing Inc., 1983. xxvi, 286 pp. Opp. 18, 34, 39 (piano 2 hand and 2 hand easy versions), 40, 87, 118 no. 1, 119 no. 1; discusses what they show about Brahms as a composer, also detailed notes on manuscripts' physical characteristics.

4069. Bussi, Francesco. *La musica strumentale di Johannes Brahms. Guida alla lettura e all'ascolto.* Roma: Nuova ERI [Edizioni Radiotelevisione Italiana], 1989. 438 pp. ill., facsim., ind., notes. A consideration of the works by genre, with background and descriptive analysis; includes a chronology.

4070. Dubal, David. "Johannes Brahms 1833–1897—Germany" in Dubal. *The Art of the Piano. Its Performers, Literature, and Recordings.*

New York [et al.]: Summit Books, 1989. pp. 299–303. discog. Overview of solo piano works and piano concertos with background and descriptive comments; also short entry on Brahms as pianist on p. 53 and et passim references regarding other performers and how they play him. *2nd ed.: San Diego, New York and London: Harcourt Brace and Company, Harvest Books, 1995.

4071. Fallows-Hammond, Patricia. "Johannes Brahms" in Fallows-Hammond. *Three Hundred Years at the Keyboard. A Piano Sourcebook from Bach to the Moderns. Historical Background, Composers, Styles, Compositions, National Schools.* Berkeley: Ross Books, 1984. pp. [160]–72. ill., mus., ind., notes. Overview with short comments, in chronological order, of works for solo piano and the piano concertos. pp. 170–72 is music for Op. 10 no. 1; works list includes all solo/duo/duet piano work, cadenzas, McCorkle WoO's, etc.

4072. *Gieseler, Walter. "Das virtuose Klavier bei Brahms" *Üben & Musizieren* 4/4 (1987) pp. 264–72.

4073. *Gordon, Stewart. *A History of Keyboard Literature. Music for the Piano and Its Forerunners.* New York, London: Schirmer, Prentice Hall International, 1996. viii, 566 pp. mus., ind., notes.

4074. Hanslick, Eduard. "Brahms's Newest Instrumental Compositions (1889)" Susan Gillespie, trans. in *Brahms and His World.* [for full citation see 5478] pp. 145–50. mus., notes. Translated out of 1378.a. (E. Hanslick. *Musikalisches und Litterarisches.* (1889)); reviews Opp. 99, 100, 102, and 108.

4075. Harden, Ingo. "Schumann und Brahms" in Harden. *Claudio Arrau. Ein Interpretationporträit.* [book + cassette] (Musik im Ullstein Buch) Frankfurt/Main-Berlin-Wien: Verlag Ullstein GmbH, [1983]. pp. 94–100. Brahms: pp. 99–100. ind., discog. Describes how Arrau plays Brahms's solo piano and piano concerto works.

4076. Heim, Norman M. *Clarinet Literature in Outline.* Hyattsville, MD: Norcat Music Press, 1984. ii, 86 pp. Brahms: pp. 27–29. Opp. 114, 115, 120 nos. 1 and 2: gives number of movements and their tempi designation; includes comment on technique, editions.

4077. *Hinson, Maurice. *Guide to the Pianist's Repertoire*. Bloomington: Indiana University Press, 1973. xlv, 831 pp.
*[updated] issue: 1975. xlv, 832 pp. ind., notes. Page 832 is an ad-
dendum covering 1973–75. [from S031]
2nd, revised and enlarged ed.: 1987. xxxiii, 856 pp. "Johannes
Brahms (1833–1897) Germany": pp. 130–38. notes only.
Comments on editions and suggestions for performance for
42 items (single editions and collections).
*[paperback ed. (of 2nd ed.):] 1st Midland Book ed. 1994.
(d) *Hinson. *Guide to the Pianist's Repertoire. Supplement.*
Bloomington: Indiana University Press, 1979. xxxiii, 413 pp.
ind., notes.

4078. Kramer, A. Walter. "The Piano Music of Brahms" *Musical America* 16/14 (10.8.1912) p. 27. ill. Surveys the solo piano and piano
concerto works; includes comments on Brahms as composer for
both genres.

4079. Kramer, Jonathan D., see 4479.5.

4080. Kraus, Detlef. *Johannes Brahms als Klavierkomponist. Wege und
Hinweise zu seiner Klaviermusik.* Wilhelmshaven: Edition Heinrichshofen, 1986. 121 pp. mus., notes. A series of essays based on
descriptive commentaries delivered in the context of Brahms
recitals in various countries. Includes analyses of Opp. 2; 10 no.
3; Op. 5, 2nd movement [reprint of 1612 (D. Kraus. *Brahms-
Studien* (1979)]; and 35 [reprint of 1647 (D. Kraus. *Brahms-
Studien* (1981)]; an overall general survey as well as surveys of
individual forms (variations, concertos, etc.); and remarks on the
piano's role in the chamber music, the relation of the piano music
to the vocal music, and performance practice. Includes reminiscences of Wilhelm Kempff performing Brahms.
(b) English translation by Lillian Lim: *Johannes Brahms. Composer for the Piano.* (Paperbacks on Musicology 9) Wilhelmshaven: Florian Noetzel Verlag »Heinrichshofen-
Books«, 1988. 118 pp. Wilhelm Kempff reminiscences and
sources for essays are not included.
(d) i) *Kraus. in *EPTA [European Piano Teachers Association.
Sektion des Bundesrepublik Deutschland.] Kongress [(4th:
1983: Hamburg, West Germany). Dokumentation 1983.*
Saarbrucken: EPTA, 1983.] Role of piano in the chamber music. [from German ed.]

(d) ii) *Kraus. *Hamburg Kulturell* [14] (1983).

(d) iii) *Kraus. *Musica Nova* (?) (Tokyo) (1983).

(d) iv) *Kraus. *Üben & Musizieren* no. 5 (1984). Reminiscences of Wilhelm Kempff. [from German ed.]

(d) v) see: 4357.

4081. *Lister, Laurie-Jeanne. "Formal and Developmental Procedures in the Independent Variations of Johannes Brahms" M.A. diss., Music, University of Victoria, 1985. xii, 124 pp. on 138 leaves. mus., notes.

4082. Mathews, W.S.B. "The Pianoforte and Piano Music in the XIX. Century" (Music in the 19th Century. Third Paper) *Music* (Chicago) 17/5 (3.1900) pp. [459]–82.
"Brahms and Later Writers": pp. 478–82. Discusses Brahms as continuing Schumann's line, looks at Opp. 15, 24, 35, 83 as examples of his best work.

4083. *Matthews, Denis. *Brahms Piano Music*. (BBC Music Guides) London: Ariel, 1986. 76 pp. mus., ind. Reprint of 1404.d.ii. (D. Matthews. (1978)).
(b) *French translation by Alain and Marie-Stella Paris (of ? edition): Matthews. *La Musique pour piano de Brahms: essai*. (Serie "musique") Arles: Actes Sud, 1994. 114 pp. mus.

4084. Newman, William S. "Brahms and Others in Austria from About 1850 to 1885" in Newman. *The Sonata Since Beethoven*. 3rd ed. New York, London: W.W. Norton & Company, 1983. pp. 319–52.
"Brahms: Output, Resources, and Chronology": pp. 321–48. facsim., mus., fig., ind., notes. Provides historical background and commentary on the piano sonatas and ensemble sonatas: Opp. 1, 2, 5, 34bis, 38, 78, 99, 100, 108, 120 nos. 1 and 2, and the destroyed sonata for violin and piano [McCorkle Anhang IIa nr. 8]

4085. Schubring, Adolf. "Five Early Works by Brahms" Walter [M.] Frisch, trans. and ed. in *Brahms and His World* [for full citation see 5478] pp. 103–22. mus., notes. Excerpts in English translation from 1332 (DAS. *Neue Zeitschrift für Musik* (1862)): Introduction and Opp. 1, 2, 5, 8, 15.

4086. *Thiele, Siegfried. "Grösse und Grenze des Klavierklangs: Betrachtungen zu Orchester- und Klavierfassung der Haydn-Variationen von Johannes Brahms" in *Johannes Brahms: Leben, Werk,*

Interpretation, Rezeption. [for full citation see 5453] pp. 98–99. Discusses the possibilities and limitations of the piano's sound with observations on Opp. 56a and 56b. [from S102]

4087. *Tovey, Donald Francis. *Essays in Musical Analysis. [Vol. 3?] Chamber Music.* Oxford, New York: Oxford University Press, 1989. Reprint of 1372 (D.F. Tovey. *Essays . . . Analysis* (1981)) with an index (?). [from compiler]
(a) *reprint: (Music Book Index) Temecula: Reprint Services Corporation, 1993.

4088. *Wier, Albert E.[, and Vera Brodsky.] *The Piano: Its History, Makers, Players and Music.* London [et al.]: Longmans, Green and Co., 1940.
issue: 1941. viii, [2], 467 pp. notes, discog. (pp. 421–22, 444).
Wier. "[Part II—The Development of Piano Music.] Chapter III. The Romantic and Early Modern Composers": pp. 122–73. Brahms: pp. 156–61. Discusses Brahms as a composer for piano, surveys the works for piano including the concertos.
Wier. "Part VI—The Piano in Ensemble Music. [Chapters I–III.]": pp. 314–37. Brahms: pp. 317, 322, 325–31. Descriptive comments for Opp. 8, 25, 26, 34, 38, 60, 78, 87, 99, 100, 101, 108.
Brodsky. "Part VII—The Art of Two-Piano Playing. [Chapters II, III]": pp. 338–74. Brahms: pp. 351, 357. Surveys and lists the works in this genre.

4089. *Zenger, Max. *Entstehung und Entwicklung der Instrumentalmusik. Vol. 2: Von Beethoven bis inklusive Johannes Brahms.* (Musikalisches Magazin 13) Langensalza: H. Beyer & Söhne, 1906.

4089.5. See also 3412, 3433, 3436, 3653.4, 3683, 3780, 3871, 4059, 4951, 4958, 4971, 4978, 5014, 5020, 5040, 5042, 5151.

1. Chamber Music

4090. Benedict, Emil v[on]. "The Chamber Music of Johannes Brahms" *The American Music Lover* 5/1 (5.1939) pp. 2–7. An overview, includes critical comments on recordings.

4091. Berger, Melvin. "Johannes Brahms" in Berger. *Guide to Chamber Music.* 1st ed. New York: Dodd, Mead & Company, 1985. pp.

85–112. discog. Background and descriptive analysis for Opp. 8, 18, 25, 26, 34, 36, 40, 51 nos. 1 and 2, 60, 67, 87, 88, 101, 111, 114, 115; includes brief look at life.
*also: New York: Anchor Books, 1989.

4092. Brahms, Johannes. *The Brahms Arrangements for Piano Four Hands of His String Quartets.* Edited and with a New Introduction by Ellwood Derr. New York: Dover Publications Inc., 1985. x, 145 pp. Unabridged republication of the 1874 Simrock editions; includes notes on performing and editorial remarks.
(d) Derr's remarks related to: 5449.5.

4093. *Carpenter, Tethys L. "Analytical Studies in the Chamber Music of Brahms" Ph.D. diss., Oxford University, 1982.

4094. *Dahlhaus, Carl. "1848–1870" in Dahlhaus. *Die Musik des 19. Jahrhunderts.* (Neues Handbuch der Musikwissenschaft 6) Wiesbaden: Akademische Verlagsgesellschaft Athenaion; Laaber: Laaber-Verlag Dr. Henning Müller-Buscher, 1980.
"Brahms und die Tradition der Kammermusik": pp. 210–16. ill., mus., fig., notes. [from 3331] This is related to 2362.a. (C. Dahlhaus. *Brahms-Studien* (1974)). [from compiler]
(a) reprint (of 2362.a.): Dahlhaus. "Brahms und die Idee der Kammermusik" in *Verteidigung des musikalischen Fortschritts.* [for full citation see 3931] pp. 57–68.
(b) English translation by J. Bradford Robinson: Dahlhaus. "1848–1870" in Dahlhaus. *Nineteenth-Century Music.* (California Studies in 19th Century Music 5) Berkeley, Los Angeles: University of California Press, 1989. pp. 192–262.
"Brahms and the Chamber Music Tradition": pp. 252–62. Discusses the background of the chamber music tradition in Germany and Austria during Brahms's times. Examines "developing variation" as used by Brahms with analysis of Opp. 3 no. 1, 25, 116 no. 3 and poses question of whether this technique was recognized by his contemporaries for what it is.
*Paper ed.: 1989?
(a) reprint (from cloth edition): Dahlhaus, Carl. "Brahms and the Chamber Music Tradition" *The American Brahms Society Newsletter* 7/2 (Autumn 1989) pp. [1]–5. ill., mus.

4095. *Fay, James Spencer. "The Clarinet and Its Use as a Solo Instrument in the Chamber Music of Johannes Brahms" D.M.A.,

Performance, Peabody Conservatory, 1991. xii, 191 pp. mus., fig., notes. Discusses Opp. 114, 115, 120 nos. 1 and 2. Background and analysis of works, includes discussion of manuscripts, editions and first performances. Includes discussion on Brahms and Muhlfeld. [from Internet site]

(c) excerpt: Fay. "Brahms' Clarinet Works: Manuscripts, Editions and First Performances" *The Clarinet* 19/4 (7./8.1992) pp. 20–23. ill., notes. Relates works' history and includes descriptions of both manuscripts and editions.

4096. Fladt, Hartmut. "Die Kammermusik bis zum Klavierquartett op. 60" in *Johannes Brahms: Leben und Werk.* [for full citation see 3215] pp. 181–82. A survey of the works up to Op. 60.

(d) continued: Stahmer, Klaus Hinrich. "Der eigenwillige Traditionalist—Das kammermusikalische Spätwerk von Johannes Brahms" in *Johannes Brahms: Leben und Werk.* [for full citation see 3215] pp. 183–85. Continues the survey to Op. 120.

4097. Forsyth, Ella Marie. *Building A Chamber Music Music Collection. A Descriptive Guide to Published Scores.* Metuchen, NJ & London: The Scarecrow Press, Inc., 1979. xix, [1], 191 pp. ind., notes. Brahms: pp. 2–4, 12–13, 27, 31–32, 41–42, 67–68, 91–93, 103–04, 107, 120, 123–24. Provides descriptive performance comments on each work; includes comment on editions. Essential collection indicated.

4098. Gleason, Harold. "Johannes Brahms (1833–1897)" in Gleason. *Chamber Music from Haydn to Ravel.* (Music Literature Outlines. Series V) Rochester, NY: Levis Music Stores, 1955. pp. 72–81. notes, discog. Includes Opp. 18, 34, 36, 51 nos. 1 and 2, 67, 88, 111, 115: movement-by-movement analysis and notes on editions; includes general overview of all chamber music and of life.

2nd ed.: Gleason, and Warren Becker. *Chamber Music From Haydn to Bartok.* Bloomington: Frangipani Press, 1980. Brahms: pp. 64–71. notes only.

4099. [Hanslick, Eduard] "Hanslick on Brahms's Chamber Music with Clarinet" John Daverio, trans. *The American Brahms Society Newsletter* 13/1 (Spring 1995) pp. 5–7. ill., notes. Review of Opp.

114, 115, 120. Excerpt in English translation from 2947 (E. Hanslick. *Fünf Jahre Musik*. 3. aufl. (1896)).

4100. Headington, Christopher. "The German Romantics" in Headington. *The Listener's Guide to Chamber Music*. (The Listener's Guide) New York: Facts on File Inc., 1982. pp. 59–78. "Johannes Brahms": pp. 73–78. ill., ind., discog. Descriptive comments on the works and on suggested recordings; includes comments on Brahms and women, Brahms's life up to the mid 1850's, Brahms and Classical composers.

4101. *Kaplan, David Leon. "The Clarinet Works of Brahms" M.Mus. diss., Oberlin College, 1950. 316 pp. ill., mus., notes.

4102. *Kempski-Racoszyna-Gander, Irina von. "J[ohannes]. Brahms' Kammermusik: Untersuchung zum historischen Kontext von Früh- und Spätwerk" Phil.F. diss., Albert-Ludwigs-Universität Freiburg i. Br., 1986. 193 pp. mus. Looks at the early and late chamber works to clarify Brahms's view of himself as a musician; includes comment on Brahms's significance as seen in contemporary journalism, Schoenberg's view of Brahms, and Brahms the traditionalist. [from S102]

4103. *Keys, Ivor. *Brahms Chamber Music*. (BBC Music Guides) London: Ariel, 1986. 64 pp. mus., ind. Reprint of 1432 (I. Keys. (1974)). [from compiler]

4104. *Kilburn, N. "The Chamber Music of Johannes Brahms" *Musical Observer* (New York) 4/1,2,4,5 (1910).

4105. Latham, Peter. "Johannes Brahms (1833–1897)" in *Chamber Music*. Alec Robertson, ed. (Pelican Books A372) Harmondsworth: Penguin Books, 1957. pp. [191]–201. mus., ind., notes. General discussion with selected examples; includes comment on Brahms as a chamber music composer and his influences from Beethoven, Schubert, Schumann, and Bach.
*issues: 1960, 1963, 1967, 1970.

4106. MH [Mathias Hansen]. "Johannes Brahms" in *Kammermusik*. *[Vol. 1.] A–G*. Ingeborg Allihn, ed. (Konzertbuch) Leipzig: VEB Deutscher Verlag für Musik, 1988. pp. 319–47. mus. Overview of works, with comment on their place in his output;

includes information on ensemble size, tempi, duration, also brief movement-by-movement analyses.

4107. *Page, Athol. *Playing String Quartets.* New York: Longmans, Green (David McKay), 1964.
also: London: Longmans, 1964. "The Romantics": pp. [86]–94. "Brahms [[1833–1897]]": pp. 89–92, 119 (timings). Discusses technique, interpretation for Opp. 18, 34, 36, 51 nos. 1 and 2, 67, 88, 111, 135 [115]; Opp. 25, 26, 60 added in timings.
*also: Boston: B. Humphries, 1964.
*issue: 1965.
(a) *reprint (of New York ed.): Brookline, MA: Branden Publ., 1965.

4108. *Puckett, Carol Elizabeth. "An Analysis of Three Chamber Works of Brahms" M.Mus. diss., Oberlin College, 1952. ii, 94; i, 39 pp. ill., mus. (2nd paging), notes.

4109. Pulver, Jeffrey. "Chamber Music by Brahms in the Breitkopf Edition" *The Strad* 64/520 (8.1933) pp. 144, 146. Descriptive comments on the 13 works in that edition, focuses on Opp. 18, 87, 101.

4110. Rangel-Ribeiro, Victor, and Robert Markel. *Chamber Music. An International Guide to Works and Their Instrumentation.* New York, Oxford: Facts on File, 1993. xiv, [2], 271 pp. Brahms: pp. 62–63. 24 items: besides instrumentation, other data given is when composed, key, publisher (but no durations).

4111. *Reinhardt, Lauriejean. "The Chamber Works of Johannes Brahms: a study in classic and romantic synthesis" Honors paper, Houghton College, 1981. vii, 113 pp. mus., notes.

4112. Schwadron, A[braham]. A. "Romanticism and the Clarinet" (Woodwind Clinic) *The Instrumentalist* 20/8 (March 1966) pp. 80–86. Brahms: pp. 84–86. notes. Survey by genre of use of the clarinet in Romantic period, includes descriptive comments on Brahms's works and Brahms as composer for clarinet.
(a) reprint: Schwadron, Abraham A. in *Woodwind Anthology. A Compendium of Articles from The Instrumentalist on the Woodwind Instruments.* Evanston, IL: The Instrumentalist, 1972. pp. 321–24. Brahms: p. 324.
also: Schwadron, Abraham A. in *Woodwind Anthology. A Compendium of Woodwind Articles from The Instrumen-*

talist. vol. 2. Northfield, IL: The Instrumentalist Publishing Company, 1992. pp. 119–22. Brahms: p. 122.

4113. Tovey, Donald Francis, see 4087.

4114. Ulrich, Homer. "Brahms and the Decline of Romanticism" in Ulrich. *Chamber Music. The Growth & Practice of an Intimate Art.* New York: Columbia University Press, 1948. pp. [317]–53. "Brahms": pp. 319–35. mus., notes, discog. Overview and descriptive analysis; includes comment on stylistic characteristics.
2nd ed.: *Chamber Music.* New York & London: 1966. "Brahms and the Decline . . .": pp. [299]–338.
"Brahms": pp. 301–18. ind., notes only.
(d) "freely adapted": Ulrich. "Brahms and Chamber Music" *The American Music Teacher* 32/5 (4./5.1983) pp. 10–11. mus. General observations on quantity written, compositional features.

4115. *Vaught, Raymond. *Notes for Chamber Music.* Honolulu: Honolulu Chamber Music Series, 1995. v, 126 pp.

4116. *Wagar, Pauline. "The Chamber Music of Brahms" M.Mus. diss., Oberlin College, 1934. 3, 108, ii pp. ill., mus., notes.

4117. Webster, James. "Schubert's Sonata Form and Brahms's First Maturity" in *Nineteenth-Century Music.* (The Garland Library of the History of Western Music 9) New York: Garland Publishing Inc., 1985. pp. 252–89. mus., fig., notes. Literal reprint of 1444 (J. Webster. *19th Century Music* (1978–79)) with addendum.
(d) "Unfortunate errors . . ." *19th Century Music* 3/3 (3.1980) pp. 282–83. Lists corrections in music examples for original publication of 1444 (J. Webster. *19th Century Music* (1978–79)).

4117.3. See also 3288, 3371, 3372, 3540, 3624, 3771, 3788, 3861, 3935, 3944, 4036, 4037, 4040, 4048.a., 4098, 4505, 4876, 4883, 4933, 4949, 4966, 5060.

4117.7. See also I37 in Appendix A.

a. Works with Piano

General

4118. *Baker, Susan Diane. "Some Aspects of Brahms's Compositional Style as Reflected in Two Chamber Works" B.A. Honors thesis,

Queens College (Charlotte, NC), n.d. iii, 114, [54] pp. mus. Discusses Opp. 8 and 87. [from S031]

4119. *Bialyĭ, I. *Iz istoriĭ fortepiannogo trio; genezis i stanovlenie zhanra*. [From The History of Piano Trios: Genesis and Establishment of a Genre] Moskva: Muzyka, 1989. 94 pp. [from S123]

4120. *Blumberg, Jane W. "The Piano Trios of Johannes Brahms" M.A. diss., San Francisco State University, 1985. 181 pp. mus., notes.

4121. *Bondurjanskiĭ, Aleksandr. "Dialekticheskoe edinstvo klassicistskogo i romanticheskogo istokov stilja Bramsa: Na pimere sonatnoĭ formy v fortepiannyh trio" [Dialectical Unity of Classic and Romantic Sources of Brahms's Style: With Special Reference to Sonata Form in the Piano Trios] in *Muzykal'no-ispolnitel'skoe iskusstvo: Problemy stilja i interpretacii*. Vladimir Grigor'ev, ed. Moskva: Gosudarstvennaĭa konservatoriĭa imeni P.I. Chaikovskogo, 1989. pp. 32–45. [from S102]

4122. *"Brahms's cello compositions" *The Strad* 107/1248 (1.10.1996) pp. 1048+ .

4123. *Carr, Beth Ann. "A Comparative Analysis of Johannes Brahms' Violoncello Sonatas Opus 34 [38] in E minor and Opus 99 in F major" M.M. diss., Ball State University, 1989. 15 pp. + 1 cassette (55 min.) mus., notes.

4124. *Davenport, Mark J. "Style Characteristics in Selected Solo Violin Compositions of Bach, Brahms, Prokofiev and Paganini" M.M. diss., Ball State University, 1980. 35 pp. + 1 tape reel (52 min.) mus., notes.

4125. *Donoghue, Celia. "The Duo Sonatas of Johannes Brahms: An Historical and Analytical Study" M.Litt. diss., Trinity College, Dublin, 1987.

4126. *Eppstein, Hans. "Duo och dialog. Om ett struktur- och stilproblem i kammarmusiken" *Svensk Tidskrift för Musikforskning* 54 (1972) pp. 53–75. summary in German. mus. Stylistic analysis of duo sonatas with examples taken from the violin sonatas of Bach, Beethoven and Brahms. [from S102]

4127. Hinson, Maurice. "Johannes Brahms" in Hinson. *The Piano in Chamber Ensemble. An Annotated Guide*. Bloomington and Lon-

don: Indiana University Press, 1978. pp. 22, 99, 130–31, 237, 305–06, 347, 370, 419, 466. ind., notes. Provides information on editions and comments on style and interpretation.
*Paperback ed.: Bloomington and Indianapolis: Indiana University Press, 1996.

4128. *Hu, Pei Yi. "A Comparative Analysis of Brahms' Two (sic) Violin Sonatas: the First, Op. 78 in G major and the Third, Op. 108 in D minor" M.M. diss., Ball State University, 1990. 14, [2] pp. + 1 cassette (39 min.) notes.

4129. Hughes, Walden. "The Brahms Piano Chamber Music" *Clavier* 32/8 (10.1993) pp. 15–19. ill., facsim., mus., notes. Compares the versions of Op. 8, gives descriptive comments on Opp. 25, 26, 34, 40, 60, 87, 101, 114; also contemporary reaction to these works, particularly Clara Schumann's.

4130. Loft, Abram. "The Brahms Sonatas" in Loft. *Violin and Keyboard: The Duo Repertoire. Volume II. From Beethoven to the Present.* New York: Grossman Publishers, 1973. pp. 109–38. mus., ind., notes. Provides background, descriptive analysis, especially performance suggestions for Opp. 78, 100, 108, and FAE Sonate [see McCorkle WoO posthum 2].
(a) reprint: Portland: Amadeus Press, 1991.

4131. *Notley, Margaret Anne. "Brahms's Chamber-Music Summer of 1886: A Study of Opera 99, 100, 101, and 108" Ph.D. diss., Yale University, 1992. 302 pp. Assesses the importance of these pieces within Brahms's output and their significance to his audience. Extensive formal and stylistic analysis and extensive look at the autographs; includes comment on Brahms in Thun. [from S081]
(d) Notley, Margaret [Anne]. "Brahms's Cello Sonata in F Major and Its Genesis: A Study in Half-Step Relations" in *Brahms Studies* 1 (1994) pp. 139–60. notes.

4132. *Palmer, Fred E. "A Biographical Study of Composers and An Analysis of Their Works Performed in Recital" M.A. diss., San Jose State College, 1959. 1 vol. notes. Includes discussion of Opp. 78, 100, 108. [from S031]

4133. *Shand, David A. "The Sonata for Violin and Piano from Schumann to Debussy (1851–1917)" Ph.D. diss., Boston University, 1948. xxviii, 403 pp.

4134. Smallman, Basil. "The German Romantics" in Smallman. *The Piano Trio: Its History, Technique, and Repertoire.* Oxford: Clarendon Press, 1990. pp. 97–130. Brahms: pp. 117–29. mus., ind., notes. [total pp.=vii, [2], 230 pp.] Focuses on Opp. 8, 87, 101, with mention of Opp. 40, 114. Places the works within Brahms's life and output, includes a comparison of both versions of Op. 8, and a comparison of Op. 87 to Op. 101.
    *also: New York: Oxford University Press, 1990.
    *Paperback ed. (of ?): 1992. [total pp.=240 pp.]

4135. *Smallman, Basil. *The Piano Quartet and Quintet. Style, Structure and Scoring.* Oxford: Clarendon Press, 1994.
    also: New York: Oxford University Press, 1994. "The Ascendancy of Brahms": pp. 84–112. mus., ind., notes. Parallel stylistic analysis of Opp. 25 and 26; Op. 60 analysed alone; the piano quartets are also compared to Mahler's Piano Quartet in A minor and Richard Strauss's Op. 13. Includes stylistic comparison of Op. 34 to Franck's M.7. Includes comment on Brahms's influence as seen in Reger, Dohnányi and Stanford.
    *Paperback ed. (of New York ed.): Oxford University Press, 1996.

4136. *Threlfall, Sheila Marzolf. "Unity and Variety in the Piano Quartets of Johannes Brahms" D.M.A. diss., Piano Performance, University of Cincinnati, 1981. 173 pp. mus., ind., notes. Presents background information and formal analysis for each movement and discusses certain characteristic unifying and varying devices of each work as a whole; includes a brief survey of piano quartet literature from Mozart to the 20th century, putting Brahms's works in a historical context. [from S102]

4137. *Weiss-Aigner, Günter. "Die Thuner Instrumentalwerke: Thematische Kristallisationsfelder im Schaffen von Johannes Brahms" *Augsburger Jahrbuch für Musikwissenschaft* 2 (1985) pp. 113–251. facsim., mus. Examines melodic figures in Opp. 99–101, 108 and the similarities in their construction. [from S102]

4138. *Zelinsky, Sherman. "A Brief Historical Survey of the Piano Trio Through Brahms" M.S. diss., Boston University, 1951. iii, 56, 53 pp.

4138.5. See also 3366, 3373, 3374, 4080, 4173, 5038, 5161, 5222, 5367.d.i.a.

Specific

Op. 8 Piano Trio no. 1 in B major

4139. Bozarth, George S. "Brahms's B Major Trio: An American Première" *The American Brahms Society Newsletter* 8/1 (Spring
1990) pp. [1]–4. ill., notes. Provides background on this event, especially William Mason's involvement. Includes reprints of contemporary reviews; includes comment on the revised (1890's)
version of this work.

   (d) letter to editor: "ABS member Lon Levy . . ." *The American
   Brahms Society Newsletter* 8/2 (Autumn 1990) p. 10. Sug-
   gests 1443 (D.F. Tovey. *Cobbett's Cyclopedic Survey of
   Chamber Music.* (1929)) as another source that discusses
   Op. 8.

4140. *Cone, Edward T. "Twelfth Night" Hermann Danuser, trans.
Musiktheorie 1/1 (1986) pp. 41–59. Proposes a new method of
analysis and applies it to Beethoven's Op. 95, Chopin's Op. 32 no.
1, Schumann's Op. 17 and Brahms's Op. 8. [from S102]

4141. *Gardenal da Silva, Fabio Roberto. "Brahms' Piano Trio Op. 8,
in B Major: a comparison between the early (1854) and late (1860)
(sic) versions" Ph.D. diss., New York University, 1992. 160 pp.
Work is discussed in the context of Brahms's times. Versions
compared in terms of compositional techniques and stylistic differences; includes performance guide. [from S081]

4142. *Greenwood, J.E.P. "Brahms's Trio Op. 8: The Two Versions of
the First Movement" diss., University of London, Goldsmiths
College, 1983.

4143. *Horan, Catherine Anne. "A Survey of the Piano Trio from 1800
through 1860" Ph.D. diss., Northwestern University, 1983. 2 vols.
mus., notes, discog. Vol. 1 contains analyses of 20 trios, a contemporary definition of the trio and a short history; vol. 2 is a thematic catalogue of the studied works. [from S081]

4144. *Küchler, Stephan. "Das Klaviertrio in H-Dur, op. 8 von Johannes
Brahms. Ein Vergleich der beiden Fassungen" in *Professor
Rudolf Stephan zum 3. April 1985 in seinen Schülern.* Berlin: n.p.,
1985 (?).

4145. *Leonard, Thomas George. "An Interpretive Analysis of the Piano Trio in B major, No. 1, Op. 8 by Johannes Brahms" M.M. diss., California State University, Fullerton, 1988. iii, 253 pp. mus., notes.

4146. *Mayerovitch, Robert. "Brahms's Stylistic Evolution: A Comparison of the 1854 and 1891 Versions of the B-major Piano Trio, Op. 8" D.Mus. diss., Indiana University, 1986. viii, 306 pp. mus., notes.

4147. Meurs, Norbert. "Das verstellte Frühwerk. Zum H-dur Trio op. 8 von Johannes Brahms" *Musica* 37/1 (1./2.1983) pp. 34–39. notes. A comparison of the two versions, to show how the early version is reflected in the later one.

4148. Struck, Michael. "Noch einmal Brahms's B major Trio: Where was the Original Version First Performed?" Virginia [Lee] Hancock, trans. *The American Brahms Society Newsletter* 9/2 (Autumn 1991) pp. 8–9. ill., notes. Presents documentation to prove that first performance of Op. 8, first version, was in Europe (Danzig), not in North America (New York).

4149. *Trismen, Donald A. "A Comparative Analysis of the Original and Revised Versions of the Trio in B major, Opus 8, of Brahms" M.M. diss., University of Rochester, 1952. vi, 100 pp. ill., mus., notes.

4150. *Wyner, David. "An Analytic Comparison of the First Movements of Brahms's Opus 8 Trio in B major (1854 and 1889 (sic) versions)" M.A. diss., Music, Queens College (New York), 1969. 79 pp. mus.

4151. *Zaunschirm, Franz. "Der frühe und der späte Brahms. Eine Fallstudie anhand der autographen Korrekturen und gedruckten Fassungen zum Trio Nr. 1 für Klavier, Violine und Violoncello opus 8" Phil.F. diss., Universität Hamburg, 1987.
   (a) reprint: *Der frühe und der späte Brahms. Eine Fallstudie anhand der autographen Korrekturen und gedruckten Fassungen zum Trio Nr. 1 für Klavier, Violine und Violoncello opus 8.* (Schriftenreihe zur Musik 26) Hamburg: Verlag der Musikalienhandlung Karl Dieter Wagner, 1988. 260 pp. mus., fig., notes. Very detailed analysis of compositional techniques in both versions, utilizes all extant sources, including print sources.

See also 3267, 3294, 3378, 3381.a.v., 3598, 3708.d., 3762, 4042, 4085, 4088, 4091, 4097, 4106, 4114, 4118, 4119, 4120, 4121, 4127, 4134, 4138, 4890, 4926, 4931, 4944, 5002, 5058, 5118, 5176, 5232, 5345, 5367.

Op. 25 Piano Quartet no. 1 in G minor

4152. [Schoenberg, Arnold] *Arnold Schoenberg Letters.* Selected and Edited by Erwin Stein. Translated from the original German by Eithne Wilkins and Ernst Kaiser. London: Faber and Faber, 1964. 309 pp. Brahms: pp. 207–08. ind., notes. Letter Schoenberg to v[on]. Frankenstein, 3.1939, on his orchestral arrangement of Op. 25. Letter in original English only.
also: New York: St. Martin's Press, 1965.
also: Paperback ed. London, Boston: Faber and Faber, 1974.
*issue: 1987.
(a) i) *reprint (of letter from New York edition): Schoenberg, Arnold. [Paperback ed.] Berkeley: University of California Press, 1987.
(a) ii) reprint (of letter from Faber 1964 edition): "March 18, 1939— Los Angeles. Letter to Alfred V. (sic) Frankenstein, San Francisco Chronicle" in *Arnold Schoenberg Self-Portrait. A Collection of Articles Program Notes and Letters by the Composer About His Own Works.* Nuria Schoenberg Nono, ed. Pacific Palisades: Belmont Music Publishers, 1988. p. 95. ind. only.
(b) German translation (of letter): *Arnold Schoenberg ausgewählte Briefe.* [titlepage=*Arnold Schoenberg Briefe.*] Erwin Stein, ed. Mainz: B. Schott's Söhne, 1958. 309, [1] pp. Brahms: pp. 223–24. German translation only.
(d) *Arnold Schönberg 1874–1951: Lebensgeschichte in Begegnungen.* Nuria Nono-Schoenberg, ed. Buchgestaltung von Catherine Lorenz, Realisation von Nuria Nono-Schoenberg und Anita Luginbuehl. [Klagenfurt:] Ritter Klagenfurt, 1992. 467 pp. adds mus.:
Brahms: p. 356. Reproductions of this letter and letters between Schoenberg and Monteux and Kindler (1 each, 1939) concerning performing the arrangement.
Brahms: p. 452. German translation of letter.
Brahms also et passim.

4153. *Hansen, Mathias. "Arnold Schönbergs Instrumentierung des Klavierquartetts g-Moll opus 25 von Johannes Brahms" in *Johannes Brahms: Leben, Werk, Interpretation, Rezeption*. [for full citation see 5453] pp. 90–97.
(d) Hansen. "'Ich wollte einmal alles hören'. Arnold Schönbergs Orchesterfassung des Klavierquartetts op. 25 von Johannes Brahms" in *Verteidigung des musikalischen Fortschritts*. [for full citation see 3931] pp. 69–74. Discusses the background to the project.

4154. *Lueck, H. "Eine imaginäre Sinfonie: Arnold Schoenbergs Brahms-Bearbeitung auf Schallplatten" *Dissonanz=Dissonance* (Zürich) no. 11 (2.1987) pp. 22–25.

4155. "Otto Klemperer: "Man mag das Originalquartett gar nicht mehr hören . . ." Aus den Gesprächen mit Peter Heyworth" in *Verteidigung des musikalischen Fortschritts*. [for full citation see 3931] pp. 75–76. Klemperer speaks of Schoenberg working on the Op. 25 arrangement and his asking Klemperer to premiere.

4156. Shoaf, R. Wayne. *The Schoenberg Discography*. (Fallen Leaf Reference Books in Music [5]) Berkeley: Fallen Leaf Press, 1986. Brahms: pp. 108–09. 21 references to performances, by 7 different groups, of Op. 25 arranged for orchestra; includes timings and all formats available.

4157. *Vannatta, Paul Edward. "A Comparative Study of Schoenberg's Orchestration of Brahms' Piano Quartet, Op. 25" M.A. diss., Ohio State University, 1986. ix, 93 pp. notes.

4157.5. See also 3362, 3381.a.iii., 3578, 4042, 4087, 4088, 4091, 4094, 4097, 4100, 4106, 4114, 4127, 4129, 4135, 4136, 4160, 4371, 4479.5, 4889, 4929, 4931, 4944, 4971, 5002, 5127, 5153, 5332, 5396, 5449.5.

Op. 26 Piano Quartet no. 2 in A major

4158. *Johannes Brahms Klavierquartett Nr. 2 A-Dur op. 26*. Autograph. [text by Kurt Hofmann] (Patrimonia 53) Kiel: KulturStiftung der Länder, 1993. 27 pp. ill., facsim. Presents compositional history, discusses the autograph manuscript at Brahms-Institut and the work's reception. [from S114]

4159. *Tovey, Donald Francis. *Thematic Epitome of Pianoforte Quartet in E minor by D.F. Tovey, and of Pianoforte Quartet in A major, Op. 26, by Brahms.* London: Joseph Williams, Limited, 1901. 18 pp. mus. Reprinted in 1372 (D.F. Tovey. *Essays in Musical Analysis.* (1944)). [from S031] *issue: 1949.

4160. *Wolff, Christoph. "Von der Quellenkritik zur musikalischen Analyse. Beobachtungen am Klavierquartett A-Dur op. 26 von Johannes Brahms" in *Brahms-Analysen.* [for full citation see 4888] pp. 150–65. facsim., fig., notes. Discusses Op. 26 in relation to the other two piano quartets. Reviews compositional background and focuses on sketch at US-Wc and the edition in the Serkin Deposit (US-CA) in comparison with the D-brd-Hs manuscript and its corrections.

4160.5. See also 3381.a.iii., 3405, 3410, 3578, 4087, 4088, 4091, 4097, 4106, 4114, 4127, 4129, 4135, 4136, 4910, 4929, 4944, 4971, 4982, 5127, 5153, 5332.

Op. 34 Piano Quintet in F minor

4161. *Del Gobbo, George. "The Piano Quintets of Schumann and Brahms: a comparative analysis" M.A. diss., Catholic University of America, 1976. 207 pp. mus., notes. [Schumann's Piano Quintet is his Op. 44]

4162. *Garcia, Ana Lucia Altino. "Brahms's Opus 34 and the 19th-century Piano Quintet" D.M.A. diss., Boston University, 1992. 223 pp. Analysis of Op. 34 is the focus, includes a comparison of the piano quintet and the string quintet version, including a hypothetical reconstruction of the string quintet. Also compares this work to Schumann's Op. 44, Prince Louis Ferdinand of Prussia's Op. 1, Dvořák's Op. 81, Franck's M. 7 and Reger's Op. 64. [from S081]

4163. *Koo, Jae-Hyang. "A Study of Four Representative Piano Quintets by Major Composers of the Nineteenth Century: Schumann, Brahms, Dvorak and Franck" D.M.A. diss., University of Cincinnati, 1993. 97 or 101 pp. mus. Stylistic analysis examining compositional techniques. [from S081] [Schumann's Op. 44, Dvořák's Op. 81, and Franck's M. 7]

4164. *Nakagawa, Eri. "A Study of the Piano Quintet in F minor, Op. 34 by Johannes Brahms" M.M. diss., Ball State University, 1987. 16 pp. notes.

4165. *Raney, Lynn Longford. "The Evolution of Brahm's Opus 34" Honors Paper, Music, Mount Holyoke College, 1986. 40 pp. mus., notes.

4165.5. See also 3276, 3378, 3381.a.iii., 3967, 4038, 4048.a., 4068, 4084, 4088, 4091, 4097, 4098, 4100, 4106, 4114, 4127, 4129, 4135, 4284, 4299, 4910, 4926, 4931, 4944, 5127, 5153, 5162, 5316, 5332, 5396.

Op. 38 Violoncello Sonata no. 1 in E minor

4166. Cohen, Robert. "The First Truly Romantic . . ." *The Strad* 103/1223 (3.1992) pp. 224–26. ill., mus. Discusses how to play the first movement.

4167. Derr, Ellwood. "Brahms' Op. 38: Ein Beitrag zur Kunst der Komposition mit entlehnten Stoffen" in *Brahms-Kongress Wien 1983.* [for full citation see 5431] pp. 95–124. mus., fig., notes. An analysis shows that Brahms borrowed from Bach's BWV 1080, Schumann's Op. 92, Beethoven's Op. 2 no. 3, and Schubert's piano pieces; discusses his intent and his interest in earlier musical forms.

4168. *Ringenberg, Paul D. "A Comparative Analysis of Johannes Brahm's Sonata Op. 38 and Camille Saint-Saens's Concerto no. 1 Opus 33" M.M. diss., Ball State University, 1979. 17 pp. + 1 tape reel (49 min.) notes.

4168.5. See also S060, 3363, 3381.a.vi., 3750, 3840, 4042, 4065, 4084, 4088, 4097, 4100, 4106, 4114, 4122, 4123, 4125, 4127, 4898, 4926, 4982, 5232, 5396.

Op. 40 Horn Trio

4169. *Bentley, Nelson. "Brahms Horn Trio" in Bentley. *Snoqualmie Falls Apocalypse.* (A Confluence Chapbook) Lewiston, ID: Confluence Press, 1981. Reflections upon hearing Op. 40. [from S114]
    (a) *Bentley. in Bentley. *Collected Shorter Poems.* Seattle: Bellowing Ark Press, 1988. pp. 110–11.

4170. *Chromy, Jo-Anne. "A Study of the Horn in Nineteen-Century Chamber Music for Horn, Violin and Piano and Its Applications to the Brahms Horn Trio Op. 40" M.M. diss., Bowling Green State University, 1983. iv, 97 pp. mus., notes.

4171. *King, John Robert. "The Technique of Writing for the French Horn as Illustrated in the Trio Opus 40 by Johannes Brahms" M.M. diss., University of Rochester, 1946. iv, 48 pp. ill., mus., notes.

4172. *Leslie, Kent L. "On The Interpretation of the Horn Part of the Trio in E-flat Major, Opus 40, by Johannes Brahms" M.M. diss., Ball State University, 1983. ii, 35 pp. + 1 cassette (31 min.).

4173. *MacDougall, Susan A. "The Developmental Style of Johannes Brahms as seen in Representative Chamber Works with Piano" M.M. diss., Ball State University, 1980. ii, 46 pp. + 1 tape reel (62 min.) mus., notes.

4174. *Pease, Edmund. "Performing the Brahms Horn Trio" *The Horn Call* 4/1 (Autumn 1973) pp. 44–51.

4175. *S.B. [Selmar Bagge] *Allgemeine musikalische Zeitung* 2 (1867) pp. 15–17, 24–25.

4176. *Van Norman, Clarendon Ess, Jr. "The French Horn: Its Use and Development in Musical Literature" Ed.D. diss., Columbia University, 1965. 74 pp. A historical look at the use of the horn, with a detailed look at Op. 40. [from S033]

4177. Zarzo, Vincente. "Brahms Horn Trio, Op. 40: A Brief Account" *Historic Brass Society Newsletter* no. 4 (Summer 1992) p. 27. Presents work's background and history of performances and descriptive comments on the music; includes comment on the later arrangements that replaced the horn with stringed instruments.

4177.5. See also S060, 3352, 3378, 3381.a.v., 3692, 3708.d., 4042, 4068, 4091, 4097, 4100, 4106, 4114, 4127, 4129, 4134, 4797, 4931, 4959, 5058, 5137, 5232, 5396.

Op. 60 Piano Quartet no. 3 in C minor

4178. *Smitherman, James T. "Of Variations and Themes: A Study of the First Movement of Brahms's Piano Quartet in C minor, Opus 60" M.M. diss., Louisiana State University, Baton Rouge, 1992. iv, 80 pp. ill., mus., notes.

4179. Stahmer, Klaus Hinrich. "Drei Klavierquartette aus den Jahren 1875/76. Brahms, Mahler und Dvořák im vergleich" in *Brahms und seine Zeit.* (Hamburger Jahrbuch für Musikwissenschaft 7) [for full citation see 5428]. pp. 113–23. mus., notes. Compares the first movements of Op. 60, Mahler's Piano Quartet in A minor, and Dvořák's Op. 23 for thematic and harmonic features—focus is on the Mahler.

4180. *Tovey, Donald Francis. *Brahms's Third Pianoforte Quartet: An Essay in Musical Analysis.* London: Joseph Williams, Ltd., 1901. 15 pp. mus. Reprinted in 1372 (D.F. Tovey. *Essays in Musical Analysis.* (1944)). [from S031]
*issue: 1949.

4180.5. See also 3381.a.iii., 3564, 3578, 4087, 4088, 4091, 4097, 4106, 4114, 4127, 4129, 4136, 4160, 4935, 4950, 4956, 4972.d.i., 5153, 5188, 5232.

Op. 78 Violin Sonata no. 1 in G major

4181. [Bozarth, George S.] " 'Leider nicht von Johannes Brahms' " *The Strad* 99/1174 (2.1988) pp. 146–50. ill., mus., notes. Discusses the history of the cello arrangement and examines it, concluding that it isn't up to Brahms's skill and standards; also compares the editions with original work.
(d) letter to editor: Starker, Janos. " 'Gott Sei Dank' " *The Strad* 99/1180 (8.1988) p. 611. Reacts to Bozarth's comments on his edition of arrangement and suggests that beauty of work is paramount over who authored it.

4182. *Polendo, Sylvia Elena. "A Brief Analysis of Debussy's Violin Sonata [(1917)], Brahms' Violin Sonata, Op. 78, and Shostakovich's Eighth String Quartet, Op. 110" M.A. diss., University of Texas at El Paso, 1986. 108 pp. mus., notes.

4183. *Poveshchenko, Galina. in *Aktual'nye problemy muzykal'noĭ pedagogiki i ispolnitel'stva: Mezhvuzovskiĭ sbornik.* Gennadiĭ Nizovskiĭ, ed. Vladivostok: Dal'nevostochni Universitet, 1984. Item discusses teaching and performance issues in Op. 78. [from S102]

4183.5. See also S060, 3294, 3337, 3340, 3356, 3363, 3381.a.vi., 3383, 3410, 3750, 3758, 3888, 3964, 4053, 4065, 4067, 4084, 4088, 4097, 4100, 4106, 4114, 4125–28, 4130, 4132, 4133, 4894, 4895, 4960, 4979, 5058, 5162, 5176, 5177, 5188.d.d., 5396.

Op. 87 Piano Trio no. 2 in C major

4184. *Gilling, Graeme. "An Analytical Study of Johannes Brahms's Piano Trio No. 2 in C Major Op. 87" M.Mus. diss., University of Western Australia, 1985. ii, 69 pp. + 2 cassettes.

4184.5. See also 3378, 3381.a.v., 3578, 4068, 4088, 4091, 4097, 4106, 4109, 4114, 4118–21, 4127, 4129, 4134, 4138, 4871, 4931, 4944, 5176.

Op. 99, Violoncello Sonata no. 2 in F major

4185. *ck. *Neue Berliner Musikzeitung* [41] (31.3.1887). Review. [from 4131.d.]

4186. *Helm, Theodor. *Deutsche Zeitung* (Wien) [Morning edition] (27.11.1886) Review. [from 4131.d.]

4187. *h.p., dr. [Hans Paumgartner] *Wiener Abendpost* [= Supplement to *Wiener Zeitung*] (30.11.1886). Review. [from 4131.d.]

4188. *m.s. *Pester Lloyd* (Budapest) (23.12.1886) Review. [from 4131.d.]

4188.5. See also S060, 3363, 3381.a.vi., 3750, 4065, 4074, 4084, 4088, 4097, 4100, 4106, 4114, 4122, 4123, 4125, 4127, 4131, 4137, 4913.d., 4931, 4972.d.ii.

Op. 100 Violin Sonata no. 2 in A major

4189. *Case, Evan L. "Johannes Brahms: A Study of the Sonata in A Major for Violin and Piano" M.A. diss., Kent State University, 1969. 30 pp. mus.

4190. *Stellfeld, Bent. "J[ohannes]. Brahms: Sonate no. 2 für Pianoforte und Violine" in *Otte ekkoer af musikforskning i Århus*. Århus: Musikvidenskabelight Institut, 1988. pp. 173–201.

4190.5. See also S060, 3337, 3340, 3356, 3363, 3381.a.vi., 3578, 3750, 3888, 4065, 4074, 4084, 4088, 4097, 4100, 4106, 4114, 4125–27, 4130–33, 4137, 4894, 4977, 5176, 5188.d.

Op. 101 Piano Trio no. 3 in C minor

4191. *Carpenter, T[ethys].L. "Brahms: Progressive or Regressive? An Analysis of the Piano Trio Op. 101 in C minor from other

Schoenbergian Perspectives" diss., University of London, Goldsmiths College, 1983.

4192. Sachs, Klaus-Jürgen. "Zur Konzeption des Ersten (sic) Satzes aus dem Klaviertrio c-moll op. 101" in *Brahms-Analysen*. [for full citation see 4888] pp. 134–49. mus., fig., notes. Detailed analysis to show how this movement was conceived; its motifs are basis for all of this work.

4192.5. See also 3378, 3381.a.v., 3869, 4088, 4091, 4097, 4106, 4109, 4114, 4119–21, 4127, 4129, 4131, 4134, 4137, 4138, 4871, 4944, 5176.

Op. 108 Violin Sonata no. 3 in D minor

4193. *Halen, Thalia. "A Study of Three Compositions for Violin and Piano" M.A. diss., Central Missouri State College, 1969. 82 pp. ill., notes. Studies Op. 108, Webern's Op. 7 and Debussy's Sonata [(1917)]. [from S031]

4194. *Klopac, Rok. "Brahms's Violin Sonata no. 3" *The Strad* 104/1244 (12.1993) pp. 1176–77, 1179. mus., notes.

4195. *Watkins, Marlene Jeanette. "The Pianist and the Brahms Violin Sonata Op. 108 in D minor" M.M. diss., University of Natal, 1989. 120 pp. mus., notes, discog. Discusses how pianists should approach this work. [from S102]

4195.5. See also S060, 3337, 3340, 3356, 3363, 3381.a.vi., 3569, 3598, 3708.d., 3750, 3869, 3888, 4065, 4074, 4084, 4088, 4097, 4100, 4106, 4114, 4125–28, 4130, 4130–33, 4137, 4871, 4890, 4894, 4944, 4955, 4972.d.i., 5176.

Op. 114 Clarinet Trio

4196. *Cady, Calvin B. *Music Review* (Chicago) 1 (8.1892) pp. 210–11. Review. [from WPA Index]

4197. *Goode, Helen Margaret. "Performance Practice Issues in Johannes Brahms's Trio for Clarinet, Cello, and Piano, Op. 114" M.F.A. diss., University of California, Los Angeles, 1993. viii, 66 pp. ill., notes.

4198. Grassi, Andrea Massimo. "Varianti d'autore e varianti di trasmissione nel Trio op. 114 di Johannes Brahms. Osservazioni sui testimoni manoscritti e a stampa" in *La critica del testo musicale. Metodi e problemi della filologia musicale.* Maria Caraci Vela, ed. (Studi e testi musicali. Nuova serie 4) Lucca: Libreria musicale italiana, 1995. pp. [325]–357. mus., facsim., notes. A detailed comparison of all sources, includes listing of differences; also comment on all manuscript and edition sources.

4199. *Konrad, Ulrich. "Ökonomie und dennoch Reichtum: zur Formbildung im ersten Satz des Trios für Klavier, Klarinette und Violoncello a-Moll, op. 114 von Johannes Brahms" in *Festschrift Emil Platen zum sechzigsten Geburtstag.* Martella Gutiérrez-Denhoff, ed. (Collegium musicologicum) Bonn: Universität [Bonn], 1986. pp. 153–74. fig. Analyses motif and theme and contrasts work's form with traditional sonata form. [from S102]

4199.3. See also 3378, 3381.a.v., 3873–76, 4023, 4046, 4076, 4091, 4095, 4097, 4099–4101, 4106, 4112, 4114, 4127, 4129, 4134, 4898, 4944, 5072, 5076, 5155.

4199.7. See also I17, I18 in Appendix A.

Op. 120 Two Clarinet (or Viola) Sonatas: No. 1 in F minor and No. 2 in E flat major

4200. *Aoki, Kenneth Tadashi. "A Brief History of the Sonata with an Analysis and Comparison of a Brahms' and Hindemith's Clarinet Sonata [(1939)]" M.Ed. diss., Central Washington State College, 1968. 52 pp. mus.

4201. *Davidson, Kevin. "Paul Doktor and the Brahms Viola Sonatas: a critical edition with commentary" D.M.A. diss., Juilliard School, 1990. 2 vols. Volume 1 is the critical remarks, volume 2 is Doktor's copies of edition parts with emendations, and the "critical edition" based on them. [from S031]

4202. *Deal, Deborah Jean. "Brahms's Sonata in F minor for Clarinet" M.Mus. diss., Bowling Green State University, 1975. 57 pp. mus. (pp. 32–57)

4203. *Dobree, Georgina. "Breaking The Mold—Reflections On the Opus 120 Sonatas By Brahms" *The Clarinet* 23/4 (1.7.1996) pp. 38+ .

4204. Fan, Paula. "The Unashamed, Unabashed Clarinetist's Accompanist and the Brahms Sonatas" *The Clarinet* 9/4; 10/1 (Summer

1982; Fall 1982) pp. 22–25; 26–27. mus. Presents suggestions on how to perform.

4205. *Fernandez, Rosemary Ruiz. "A Discussion of Interpretative Suggestions of the Brahms Clarinet Sonata in F minor, Opus 120 No. 1" M.M. diss., California State University, Fullerton, 1988. v, 57 pp. ill., notes.

4206. Giuranna, Bruno, with Ross Charnock. "Brahms' 'Viola' Sonata in E flat" *The Strad* 104/1238 (6.1993) pp. 552–53, 555, 557. ill., mus. A discussion about playing this arrangement of Op. 120 no. 2; includes comments on the different available editions and on the arranging method.

4207. *Guthrie, E. Ward. "Analysis" M.Mus.Ed. diss., Oberlin College, 1970. 2 vols. mus. (vol. 2), notes (vol. 1). Discusses Op. 120 no. 1 among other clarinet works. [from S031]

4208. *Heim, Norman. *The Clarinet Sonata in Outline*. Hyattsville, MD: Norcat Music Press, 1995. iv, 207 pp. ind.

4209. Jack, Adrian. "This Month's CD" *BBC Music Magazine* 3/2 (10. 1994) pp. 7–8. ill., discog. Background, descriptive analysis and movement timings.

4210. *John, Christine W. "A Style Analysis and Solutions to Performance Problems of the Viola Transcription of Johannes Brahm's Sonata for Clarinet and Piano in F minor" M.M. diss., Ball State University, 1983. iii, 37 pp. + 1 cassette (78 min.).

4211. *Loewi, Karen H. "The Compositional Treatment of the Viola as a Solo Instrument in Selected Repertoire of Three Composers: Bach, Brahms, and Hindemith" M.A. diss., California State University, Long Beach, 1986. v, 57 pp. + 1 cassette (60 min.). mus., notes.

4212. *Loomis, James E. "The Brahms Clarinet Sonatas" M.M.E. diss., Music, Southern Illinois University, 1961. 41 pp. notes.

4213. *McClure, Ross Roger. "Motivic and Thematic Material in Three Works by Mozart, Brahms, and Berg" M.A. diss., Western State College of Colorado, 1971. iv, 16 pp. + 1 tape reel (67 min.). mus., notes. Includes discussion of Op. 120 no. 1. [from S031]

Works 249

4214. Marks, Anthony. "BBC PO/Berio" *The Musical Times* 129/1740 (1.1988) pp. 33–34. Comments on Berio's orchestration of Op. 120 no. 1, in the context of a performance review.

4215. *Nordstrom, Erland Nihls. "Mechanical Improvements as a Function of Selected Works for the Clarinet from 1815 to 1982" Ph.D. diss., New York University, 1986. iv, 192 pp. ill., mus., notes. Relates performance practices to mechanical improvement and technical capability. Examples are Spohr's Opp. 26 no. 1 and 57 no. 3; Brahms's Op. 120 nos. 1 and 2; and Donald Martino's "A set (1954)." [from S102]

4216. *O'Hair, Dawn Lynn. "Musical analysis in relation to performance and Sonata in F minor, op. 120, no. 1 by Johannes Brahms" B.M. diss., Music (Honors), Butler University, 1996. 53, [13] pp. mus., notes.

4217. *Parks, Caroline. "The Brahms E Flat Clarinet Sonata, Op. 120, no. 2; an analytic study" M.A. diss., Kent State University, 1970. iv, 32 pp. mus., notes.

4218. *Selby, Nancy W. "Sonata #1, Opus 120, in F minor, for Viola and Piano by Johannes Brahms: a comparative study of editions" M.M. diss., Ball State University, 1988. 28 pp. + 1 cassette (66 min.). mus., notes.

4219. Severin, Christopher. "The Piano and Its Role in the Clarinet Repertoire" *The Clarinet* 8/1 (Fall 1980) pp. 54–55. Presents practical solutions to problems of balance, rhythm, and pedalling in Op. 120 no. 1.

4220. Simon, Karem Joseph. "Historical and Performance Perspectives of Clarinet Material Performed in a Thesis Recital" D.M.A. diss., Music, University of British Columbia, 1985. [1], ii–vii, [1], 28, [1] pp. "Johannes Brahms' Sonata in E-flat Major, Op. 120, No. 2": pp. 17–24. notes. A descriptive analysis; includes background on the work. Focus is on structural features and how to interpret them.

4221. *Tuthill, Burnet C. "Sonatas for Clarinet and Piano: Annotated Listings" *Journal of Research in Music Education* 20 (Fall 1972) pp. 308–28.

4221.3. See also S060, 3363, 3381.a.vi., 3873–76, 4023, 4046, 4065,

4076, 4084, 4095, 4097, 4099–4101, 4106, 4112, 4114, 4125, 4127, 4871, 4931, 4950, 5005, 5072, 5076, 5155, 5176, 5189.

4221.6. See also I17, I18 in Appendix A.

Scherzo from the F.A.E. Violin Sonata [McCorkle WoO posthum 2]

4221.9. See 3383, 3957, 3961, 4106, 4130, 5190.

Piano Trio in A major [McCorkle Anhang IV, nr. 5]

4222. *Brahms, trio in là maggiore—1853" *La Rassegna musicale* 11 (10.1938) p. 392.

4222.3. See also 3217.

Violin Sonata in A minor [McCorkle Anhang IIa, nr. 8]

4222.7. See 4084.

b. Works without Piano

General

4223. Chafetz, Lester. *The Ill Tempered String Quartet. A Vademecum for the Amateur Musician.* Jefferson, NC and London: McFarland & Company, Inc., Publishers, 1989. xii, 168 pp. ind.
  "Johannes Brahms (1833–1897)": pp. 88–89. Lists the repertoire with its level of difficulty.
  "Johannes Brahms": pp. 103–04. Outlines the technical challenges of the quartets and their rewards.

4224. Christensen, James. "Brahms (1833–1897)" in Christensen. *Chamber Music: Notes for Players.* Plantation, FL: Distinctive Publishing Corp., 1992. pp. 41–45. notes. Places the quartets in Brahms's life and provides descriptive comments on each, movement-by-movement; includes summary of Brahms's life and level of skill needed to play.

4225. Griffiths, Paul. "Adagio 1871–1913" in Griffiths. *The String Quartet.* New York: Thames and Hudson, 1983. pp. 126–68. Brahms: pp. 127–31. mus., fig. (p. 235), ind. Descriptive analysis

of the quartets; includes comments on Brahms the composer and
Brahms and Dvořák.

4226. Kohlhase, Hans. "Brahms und Mendelssohn. Strukturelle Paralle-
len in der Kammermusik für Streicher" in *Brahms und seine Zeit*.
(Hamburger Jahrbuch für Musikwissenschaft 7) [for full citation
see 5428] pp. 59–85. mus., notes. Discusses the two composers'
similiarities, Brahms's opinion of Mendelssohn and his knowledge of Mendelssohn's music; includes analytical comparision of
Mendelssohn's Opp. 11–13 with Brahms's Opp. 88, 111.

4227. Loft, Abram. *Ensemble! A Rehearsal Guide to Thirty Great
Works of Chamber Music.* Reinhard G. Pauly, General Ed. Portland: Amadeus Press, 1992.
"Brahms. Sextet No. 2 in G, Op. 36": pp. [206]–15. ill., notes.
"Brahms. Quartet in C minor, Op. 51, no. 1": pp. [216]–39. ill.,
notes. Provides descriptive and technical comments for both
works, movement-by-movement.

4228. *Murphy, Meta Frances. "The String Quartets of Brahms: an
analysis" M.Mus. diss., University of Oklahoma, 1962. ix, 343 pp.
mus., notes.

4229. Ruf, Wolfgang. "Die zwei Sextette von Brahms. Eine analytische
Studie" in *Brahms-Analysen*. [for full citation see 4888] pp.
121–33. mus., notes. A comparative analysis of Opp. 18 and 36.

4230. *Velten, Joan Elizabeth. "Texture in String Quartet Writing from
Haydn to Brahms" M.M. diss., Indiana University, 1963. 181 pp.
mus.

4230.3. See also 3373, 3411, 5367.d.i.a.

Specific

Op. 18 String Sextet no. 1 in B flat major

4230.7. See 3296, 3569, 3598, 4038, 4068, 4091, 4097, 4098, 4100,
4106, 4109, 4114, 4229, 4931, 5345.

Op. 36 String Sextet no. 2 in G major

4231. *[Grädener, Carl G.P. (?)] *Theater und Musik* (Wien) (1.1867).
(a) reprint: Grädener, Carl G.P. "Johannes Brahms und sein

Sextett" in Grädener. *Gesammelte Aufsätze über Kunst, vorzugsweise Musik. [Bd.] X. Anhang.* Hamburg: Verlag von Hugo Pohle, 1872. pp. 142–47. Presents a positive evaluation of Brahms the composer.

4231.5. See also 3276, 3378, 3405, 3578, 4091, 4097, 4098, 4106, 4114, 4227, 4229, 4926, 4935, 4947, 4970, 5030, 5188.d.

Op. 51 Two String Quartets: No. 1 in C in minor and No. 2 in A minor

4232. Forte, Allen. "Motivic Design and Structural Levels in the First Movement of Brahms's String Quartet in C minor" *The Musical Quarterly* 69/4 (Fall 1983) pp. 471–502. mus., fig., notes. Analysis based on Schenkerian principles, focusing on motif for Op. 51 no. 1.
(a) reprint: Forte. in *Brahms 2.* [for full citation see 5481] pp. 165–96.
(e) review: see 5481.e.

4233. Krummacher, Friedhelm. "Reception and Analysis: On the Brahms Quartets, Op. 51, Nos. 1 and 2" *19th Century Music* 18/1 (Summer 1994) pp. 24–45. mus., notes. An analysis of these works according to criteria of their times. Looks at people's reactions, print reviews.

4234. Musgrave, Michael, and Robert Pascall. "The String Quartets Op. 51 No. 1 in C minor and No. 2 in A minor: a preface" in *Brahms 2.* [for full citation see 5481] pp. 137–43. notes. Brief review of their background, their place in Brahms's output and their critical reception.

4235. Sunderman, F. William. "Brahms" in Sunderman. *Musical Program Notes. String Quartets for Performing Arts Society of Philadelphia, Inc., 1980–81 Series.* Philadelphia: Institute for Clinical Science, Inc., 1981. pp. 39–43. mus., notes. Provides background on Brahms and Billroth and descriptive comments on Op. 51 no. 1.

4236. Whittall, Arnold. "Two of a Kind? Brahms's Op. 51 Finales" in *Brahms 2.* [for full citation see 5481] pp. 145–64. mus., notes. An analysis to show how Brahms deals with minor mode.

4237. *Yang, Benjamin Hoh. "A Study of the Relationship Between Motive and Structure in Brahms's Op. 51 String Quartets" Ph.D. diss., University of North Texas, 1989. 260 pp. Investigates how Brahms distributes main motivic material to all 4 voices, while at the same time highlighting each voice. Includes background on both numbers in Op. 51, and assesses their position in Brahms's career. [from S081]

4237.3. See also 3578, 3690, 3692, 3703, 3708.d., 3869, 3930, 4091, 4092, 4097, 4098, 4100, 4106, 4114, 4223–25, 4227, 4228, 4230, 4871, 4889, 4894, 4929, 4944, 4956, 4972.d., 5030, 5058, 5153, 5396.

Op. 67 String Quartet no. 3 in B flat minor

4237.7. See 3405, 3690, 4091, 4092, 4098, 4100, 4106, 4114, 4223–25, 4228, 4230, 4971, 5153, 5163.

Op. 88 String Quintet No. 1 in F major

4238. *Brahms, Johannes. *Quintett, op. 88, F-Dur*. Faksimile-Ausgabe. Baden-Baden: Brahmsgesellschaft Baden-Baden, 1994. 45 pp. Facsimile of the manuscript they own.
   (d) Hoppe, Werner. "Zum Autograph des Streichquintetts Nr. 1 F-Dur op. 88 von Johannes Brahms" *Brahms-Studien* Bd. 10 (1994) pp. 53–55. facsim. Provides provenance and description for Brahmsgesellschaft Baden-Baden manuscript.

4239. Seidel, Wilhelm. "Das Streichquintett in F-Dur im Œuvre von Anton Bruckner und Johannes Brahms" in *Bruckner Symposion.* [for full citation see 5434] pp. 183–89. notes. A followup to 1535 (H.F. Redlich. *Music and Letters* (1955)); compares the works relative to their place in each composer's chamber works, and in each composer's total output.

4239.5. See also 3378, 3692, 3758, 4038, 4091, 4097, 4098, 4106, 4114, 4226, 4898, 4926, 4934, 4935, 4947, 5037.

Op. 111 String Quintet No. 2 in G major

4240. *McBride, Robert. "An Analysis of the First Movement of Brahm's String Quintet in G major, Op. 111" M.M. diss., Louisiana State University, Baton Rouge, 1992. v, 117 pp. mus.

4240.5. See also 3578, 3804, 4038, 4051, 4091, 4097, 4098, 4106, 4226, 4899, 4955, 4970, 5162.

Op. 115 Clarinet Quintet

4241. *Andrieux, Françoise. "Le quintette avec clarinette de Mozart: Un modele?" *Ostinato: Revue internationale d'etudes musicales* no. 1–2 (1993) pp. 113–26. mus. Compares Mozart's clarinet quintet K581 with Brahms's Op.115.
issue title: "Mozart" [from S109]

4242. *Gray, Edwin John. "Analytical Approaches to Brahms, using the Clarinet Quintet Op. 115 as a Case Study" M.A. diss., Music Theory and Analysis, University of Ulster, 1990.

4243. *Hofmann, Kurt. *Zur Entstehung und frühen Rezeption des Klarinettenquintetts.* Lübeck: Brahms-Institut, [1991?].

4244. *Holzworth, Janet L. "Quintet for Clarinet and String Quartet in B minor, Op. 115" M.A. diss., Kent State University, 1972. iv, 40 pp. mus.

4245. *Osseck, William Frederick. "Brahms' Clarinetquintet" M.M. diss., University of Rochester, 1942. iii, 34 pp. ill., mus., notes.

4246. Pociej, Bohdan. "Kwintet h-moll" (Proby utrwalenia) *Ruch muzyczny* 29/17 (18.8.1985) pp. 6–7 [across page bottoms]. Discusses the qualities of the work, of Brahms's music as a whole; includes placing the work in Brahms's last creative period.

4247. *Salvetti, Guido. "Brahms: Quintette avec clarinette op. 115" *Analyse musicale* 21 (11.1990) pp. 45–54. summary in English. Analysis of formal structure of each movement, with emphasis on motivic structural relations and cyclic unity. [from S102]

4248. *Woodward, James Eugene. "An Analysis of Brahms' Quintet for Clarinet and Strings, Opus 115" M.A. diss., University of Rochester, 1966. vii, 124 pp. ill., mus., fig., notes.

4249. Zwicky, Jan. "Five Poems" *The Malahat Review* no. 105 (12.1993) p. 5–10.
"Brahms' Clarinet Quintet in B Minor, Op. 115": p. 9. Poet's impression of this work.

4249.2. See also S060, 3276, 3363, 3569, 3578, 3873–76, 3967, 4023, 4046, 4076, 4091, 4095, 4097–4101, 4106, 4112, 4114,

4830.a., 4880, 4882, 4889, 4890, 4947, 5072, 5076, 5127, 5396, 5430.

4249.4. See also I17, I18 in Appendix A.

Quintet in F minor for Strings [earlier version of Op. 34]

4249.6. See 4162, 4165.

c. Brahms's Editing and Arranging of Other Composers' Chamber Music

General

4249.8. See 4988.

Specific

Bach, Carl Philipp Emanuel

4250. Mauser, Siegfried. "Brahms und die vorklassische Instrumental-musik" in *Brahms-Kongress Wien 1983*. [for full citation see 5431] pp. 367–78. mus., notes. Examines Brahms's editing in Mc-Corkle Anhang VI, nos. 1–3; includes comments on the editions and writings he was studying at the time he was doing this work.

Schumann

4250.5. See 3975, 3976.

2. Solo Keyboard Music

a. Piano Works

General

4251. **Musical News* (London) (27.5.1911) pp. 517–18. A report on 1391 (E. Howard-Jones. *Proceedings of the Musical Association* (1910–11)). [from WPA index]

4252. *Allen, William Duncan. "[Johannes Brahms] his work for the pianoforte . . ." Mus.M. diss., Oberlin College, 1936. 137, [3] pp. ill., mus., notes.

4253. Angerer, Manfred. "Das Leben und die Formen. Die Musikanschauung des Wiener Fin de Siècle und Brahms" in *Brahms-Kongress Wien 1983*. [for full citation see 5431] pp. 9–19. notes. Discusses the characteristics of Fin de Siècle as seen in Viennese literary and philosophical circles, particularly Mach and von Hofmannsthal, and then looks at Brahms's works to see if it's reflected. Concludes that it's reflected somewhat in Opp. 116–19.

4254. *Ax, Emanuel. "Master Class: Emanuel Ax on Brahms and Schoenberg" *Piano Today* 15/3 (1.5.1995) pp. 66+ .

4255. Bauer, Harold. "Preparing for the Study of Beethoven, Brahms and Mendelssohn" (The Spirit of the Masters) *The Etude* 37/5 (5.1918) pp. 301–02. Brahms: p. 302. mus. Discusses Brahms as a composer for the piano.

4256. *Beggs, Hugh Harlan. "The Pianoforte Music of Johannes Brahms" M.M. diss., University of Rochester, 1936. 4, 163, [3] pp. mus., notes.

4257. Berger, Francesco. "A Quintet" *Monthly Musical Record* 54/646 (1.10.1924) pp. 293–95. Reviews Chopin, Brahms, Schumann, Liszt and Raff in their role as piano composers; includes comment on Brahms and Liszt and author's personal opinions of Brahms's piano music.

4258. *Bortolussi, Anne. "Possible Influences of Bach on the Harmonic and Contrapuntal Language of Brahms's Klavierstücke Op. (sic) 116–119" M.Mus. diss., University of Melbourne, 1991. v, 75 pp. mus., notes.

4259. *Brahms Piano Music" *Musical Courier* 35 (7.,21.,28; 7; and 4.8.;1897) pp. 19–21, 18–19, 18–19, 18–19. Excerpt from 1598 (?) (J.S. Shedlock. *The Pianoforte Sonata*. (1895)).

4260. Brower, Harriette. "Brahms's Piano Works Viewed Through von Bülow's Spectacles" *Musical America* 16/19 (14.9.1912) p. 20. Relates Bülow's suggestions for interpreting Opp. 1, 2, 4, 5, 10, 76, 79; includes comment on Brahms as a piano player.
(d) continued: Brower. "More About Brahms's Piano Music" *Mu-*

sical America 16/20 (21.9.1912) p. 14. Suggestions for interpreting Opp. 9, 24, 116, 117.

4261. *Cadwallader, Allen Clayton. "Multileveled Motivic Repetition in Selected Intermezzi for Piano of Johannes Brahms" Ph.D. diss., University of Rochester, Eastman School of Music, 1983. 238 pp. Demonstrates how a unique motif operates at various levels in Opp. 76 no. 7, 116 no. 4, 117 nos. 2 and 3, 118 no. 2, and 119 nos. 1 and 2 and shows motif's effect on harmonic and formal aspects of works. [from S081]

    (d) i) Cadwallader, Allen [Clayton]. "Echoes and Recollections: Brahms's Op. 76, No. 6" (Analysis Symposium: Brahms's Op. 76, no. 6) *Theory and Practice* 13 (1988) pp. [65]–78. fig., notes. Notes motivic resemblances between Opp. 76 no. 6 and 118 no. 2 and how such resemblances are part of a composer's compositional language.

    (d) ii) Cadwallader, Allen [Clayton]. "Foreground Motivic Ambiguity: Its Clarification at Middleground Levels in Selected Late Piano Pieces of Johannes Brahms" *Music Analysis* 7/1 (3.1988) pp. 59–91. fig., notes. Traces the consequences of a particular motivic process, explores its ambiguities and its effects. Examples are: Opp. 117 no. 2, 118 no. 2, and 119 no. 2.

    (d) iii) Cadwallader, Allen [Clayton]. "Motivic Unity and Integration of Structural Levels in Brahms's B Minor Intermezzo, Op. 119, No. 1" *Theory and Practice* 8/2 (12.1983) pp. [5]–24. mus., fig., notes. Illustrates effects of motif on formal and harmonic structure.

    (d) iv) Cadwallader, Allen [Clayton]. "Schenker's Unpublished Graphic Analysis of Brahms's Intermezzo Op. 117, No. 2: Tonal Structure and Concealed Motivic Repetition" *Music Theory Spectrum* 6 (1984) pp. [1]–13. mus., fig., notes. Demonstrates how Schenker's analysis (US-NYp sketch) illuminates the motif and describes how its repetitions unify the piece. Looks at piece's "A" and "B" sections only.

    (d) v) see: 4395.

4262. Cai, Camilla. "Brahms' Short, Late Piano Pieces—Opus Numbers 116–119: A Source Study, an Analysis and Performance Practice" Ph.D. diss., Musicology, Boston University, 1986. xvi, [1]–545 pp. mus., fig., notes, appendixes. A study of extant sources to partially reconstruct Brahms's compositional process, with special emphasis on publication stages. (Also includes discussion of Opp. 76 and 79 in publication stages section.) Includes discussion of pianos that Brahms would have used and his interest in music of the past. Appendix includes textual critical remarks.

(d) i) Cai. "Brahms, Johannes (1833–1897)" in *The Encyclopedia of Keyboard Instruments. Volume 1. The Piano.* Robert and Margaret W. Palmieri, eds. (Garland Reference Library of the Humanities 1131) New York & London: Garland, 1994. pp. 51–54. notes. Discusses the pianos Brahms used and had, their construction and features and how that is reflected in the music composed for them; includes comments on Brahms performing on these pianos.

(d) ii) Cai. "Brahms's Pianos and the Performance of His Late Piano Works" *PPR [-] Performance Practice Review* 2/1 (Spring 1989) pp. 58–72. mus., notes. Focuses on the types of pianos (Streicher, Bösendorfer) from Brahms's times to gain insight into performance practice for the piano works.

(d) iii) Cai. "Was Brahms A Reliable Editor? Changes Made in Opuses 116, 117, 118, and 119" *Acta musicologica* 61/[1] ([1.–4.]1989) pp. 83–101. facsim., mus., fig., notes. Reconsiders Brahms's reputation as a careful editor in light of new evidence from sources—sketches through to "Handexemplar". Traces compositional process, pointing out variants, discrepancies and how these affect our understanding of these pieces.

(e) report: in 4648.e.

4263. *Carter, Mary Constance. "The Piano Works in Smaller Forms by Johannes Brahms—A Style-Critical Study" M.A. diss., University of North Carolina at Chapel Hill, 1953. iv, 204 pp. mus., notes.

4264. *Cummings, Craig Campney. "Large-Scale Coherence in Selected Nineteenth-Century Piano Variations" Ph.D. diss., Indiana University, 1991. xviii, 413 pp. ill., mus. Analytical study of Beethoven's Op. 109, 3rd movement, Schumann's Op. 13 and Brahms's Opp. 9 and 24. Schumann and Brahms are looked at together. [from S081]

4265. *Da Beethoven a Boulez: il pianoforte in ventidue saggi.* Paolo Petazzi, ed.. Milano: Longanesi, in conjunction with [Associ-

azione musicale Umberto Micheli] Concorso pianistico internazionale Umberto Micheli, 1994. 248 pp.

4266. Dale, Kathleen. *Nineteenth Century Piano Music. A Handbook for Pianists.* With a Preface by Dame Myra Hess. London [et al.]: Geoffrey Cumberlege, Oxford University Press, 1954. [4], 320 pp. ind. Brahms: pp. 84–89, 114–18, 152–53, 160–62, 221–24, 293–94. Descriptive analysis to assist in performance. Discusses Opp. 1, 5, 9, 10, 21, 23, 24, 35, 39, 76, 79, 116–19, McCorkle WoO 1.

4267. *Demby, Marian. "The Character Pieces of Johannes Brahms for Pianoforte" M.M. diss., University of Michigan, 1962. 141 pp. notes.

4268. *Dobrowolski, Janusz. "Innowacje Chopinowskie w miniaturach fortepianowych Brahmsa" [Chopin Innovations in the Piano Miniatures of Brahms] *Muzyka fortepianowa IV.* Janusz Kras-sowski, ed. (Prace specjalne 25) Gdańsk: Państwowa Wyzsża Szkoła Muzyczna, 1981. pp. 93–106. summary in English. [from S102]

4269. *Donat, M. "Crosscurrents: Schubert, Schumann, Mendelssohn, Brahms" in *The Book of The Piano.* Dominic Gill, ed. Ithaca, N.Y. : Cornell University Press, 1981. ind., notes, discog.

4270. *Doulis, Barbara. "An Analysis of Selected Piano Works: an his-torical, analytical and pedagogical discussion of piano works by Rameau, Chopin, Brahms, Rachmaninoff and Ravel" M.M. diss., Music, Virginia Commonwealth University, 1982. iii, 51 pp. mus.

4271. *Faulkner, Lynn Fetzer. "Continuity in Johannes Brahms's Late Piano Works" D.M.A. diss., University of Alabama, 1994. vi, 67 pp. mus. Examines Brahms's methods for achieving continuity in Opp. 76, 79, 116–119. [from S081]

4272. Floros, Constantin. "Studien zur Brahms's Klaviermusik" *Brahms-Studien* Bd. 5 (1983) pp. 25–63. mus., fig., notes. Discusses what kind of composer Brahms is and examines the artistic relationship between Schumann and Brahms with analyses of Opp. 9, 76, 116–19.
   (d) Schubert, Giselher. *NZ-Neue Zeitschrift für Musik* 144/12 (15.12.1983–15.1.1984) pp. 48–49. Review of *Brahms-Studien* Bd. 5.

(d) letter to the editor: Floros, Constantin. "Giselher
    Schuberts zornige Auslassung . . ." *NZ-Neue*
    Zeitschrift für Musik 145/3 (15.3.–15.4.1984) p. 2.
    Rebuts Schubert and defends his article.

4273. Floros, Constantin. "Die Werke für Klavier" in *Johannes Brahms:*
      Leben und Werk. [for full citation see 3215] pp. 120–23. mus. Pre-
      sents an overview of the works; includes comment on Brahms as
      a composer of piano music.

4274. Frisch, Walter [M.]. "Brahms: From Classical to Modern" in
      Nineteenth-Century Piano Music. R. Larry Todd, ed. (Studies in
      Musical Genres and Repertories) New York: Schirmer Books;
      Toronto: Collier Macmillan Canada; New York [et al.]: Maxwell
      Macmillan International, 1990. pp. 316–54. facsim., mus., fig.,
      notes. A chronological survey with analysis of solo piano works
      to trace the classical/romantic and romantic/modern threads in
      Brahms's piano works. Includes comment on Brahms's influence,
      particularly on Schoenberg and Reger.
      *Paper edition: New York: Schirmer Books, 1994 (?).
      (d) adapted: Frisch. "Brahms's Late Piano Works: Explorations in
          Musical Space" *The American Brahms Society Newsletter*
          9/2 (Autumn 1991) pp. [1]–4. ill., facsim., mus. only. Ana-
          lytical study of Opp. 116–119.

4275. *Galston, Gottfried. *Johannes Brahms*. (Studienbuch. V. Abend)
      [2. Auflage] München: Otto Halbreiter, 1926. 38 pp. Excerpt from
      1562 (G. Galston. *Studienbuch*. (1910)). Performance suggestions
      for Opp. 24, 35, 39, 79, and 119. [from 3914]

4276. *Germane, Sydney L. "Analytical Study of the First Movements
      of the Three Piano Sonatas of Johannes Brahms" M.A. diss., Mu-
      sic, Brigham Young University, 1981. ix, 85 pp. ill., notes.

4277. *Giannini, Antoinette Frances. "Variation Forms in Piano Music
      from Brahms to the Present" M.A. diss., Boston University, 1948.
      xi, 157 pp.

4278. Glennon, James. "Brahms, Johannes (1833–1897) Germany" in
      Glennon. *Making Friends with Piano Music. The History and An-*
      alytical Notes on over a Hundred Piano Compositions with Short
      Notes on the Composers. Adelaide: Rigby Limited, 1967. pp.
      17–20. Historical and analytical notes for the layman on Opp. 1,

2, 5, 10, 24, 35, 39, 116–19. Includes a list of all piano works, including concertos.

4279. *Grandy, Phyllis. "An Analytical Study of the Piano Works of Johannes Brahms" M.F.A. diss., University of Georgia, 1952. v, 49 pp. ill., mus., notes.

4280. Hahn, A. *Neue Berliner Musikzeitung* 11/27 (1.7.1857) p. 210. Reviews Op. 5, second movement [separate publication from whole] and Op. 10.

4281. *Hancock, Lorraine Wood. "Musicological Study of the Compositions Performed on a Recital" [M.A. (?) diss.,] San Jose State College, 1962. 1 vol.

4282. *Hauschka, Thomas. "Stilkritische Untersuchungen zur Thema und Form in den späten Klavierwerken von Johannes Brahms" Phil.F. diss., Musikwissenschaft, Universität Salzburg, 1986. 313 pp. mus., notes.

4283. *Henke, Jamie Lynn. "Circle Series in the Keyboard Works of Johannes Brahms: Structure and Function" Ph.D. diss., University of Wisconsin-Madison, 1989. 289 pp. Looks at specific functions of this harmonic progression; includes comment on Brahms's influence on compositional process. [from S081]

4284. Hinson, Maurice. "Johannes Brahms (1833–1897) Germany" in Hinson. *Music for More than One Piano: an annotated guide.* Bloomington: Indiana University Press, 1983. pp. 22–23. notes. In dictionary format. Includes comment on playability as well as pianistic features. Works included are Opp. 34b, 56b and Brahms's arrangements of Opp. 90, 98 and 5 waltzes out of Op. 39.

4285. Horne, William. "Brahms's Düsseldorf Suite Study and His Intermezzo, Opus 116, No. 2" *The Musical Quarterly* 73/2 (1989) pp. 249–83. mus., notes. Uses manuscripts and source documents (mid-1854 to end 1855) to pinpoint creative process of these works, watches for influences from earlier music and proposes possible relation between suite and Op. 116 no. 2. Suite = McCorkle WoO posthum's 3–5.

4286. *Imberty, Michel. *Entendre la musique; sémantique psychologique de la musique.* (Psychismes) Paris: Dunod, 1979. 236 pp. notes. Attempts an analysis of musical perception, Brahms's intermezzos are included in the examples. [from S102]

4287. Jervis, Perlee V. "The Pedagogic Value of Brahms" *The Etude* 22/10 (10.1904) p. 419. Discusses the value of the late piano works for teaching.

4288. Jonás, Alberto. "The Proper Understanding of the Style of Several Master Composers" *The Etude* 37/3,4 (3.,4.;1919) pp. 143–44, 208. "Johannes Brahms": p. 208. Discusses how to play the piano music.

4289. Kämper, Dietrich. "Brahms" in Kämper. *Die Klaviersonate nach Beethoven. Von Schubert bis Skrjabin.* (Grundzüge 69) Darmstadt: Wissenschaftliche Buchgesellschaft, 1987. pp. 151–70. mus., ind., notes. Analyses Opp. 1, 2, and 5; places Brahms in his time.

4290. *Kirby, F.E. *A Short History of Keyboard Music.* New York: Free Press, 1966. xviii, 534 pp. mus., ind., notes.
       *also: New York: Schirmer Books; London: Collier Macmillan, 1966.
       (d) "rewritten, expanded and updated": Kirby. "Liszt and Brahms and Their Age" in Kirby. *Music for Piano. A Short History.* Foreword by Maurice Hinson. Reinhard G. Pauly, General Ed. Portland: Amadeus Press, 1995. pp. 205–44. Brahms: pp. 227–43. Work now includes discussion of piano duet and 2 piano 4 hands music; organ music is dropped. Overview of Brahms's sonatas, variations and "character pieces", focusing on style; also comments on other piano works and compares Brahms and Liszt as composers.

4291. Kraus, Detlef. "De mortuis nihil nisi bene" *Brahms-Studien* Bd. 9 (1992) pp. 23–28. Remarks on Glenn Gould's playing of Brahms: Opp. 10, 79, 117 and individual pieces from Opp. 76, 116, 118–19.
       (d) i) *Kraus. [*European Piano Teachers Association. [Piano] Bulletin*]
       (d) ii) *Kraus. [*Glenn Gould Society. Bulletin (?)*]

4292. Kraus, Detlef. "Wiener Einflüsse auf die Klaviermusik von Brahms" in *Brahms-Kongress Wien 1983.* [for full citation see 5431] pp. 291–99. mus., notes. Looks at Viennese influences (rhythms, editing of Schubert piano works [McCorkle Anhang Ia nr. 6]) in all works for piano or that have piano in them (Opp. 52

and 65 in particular); also looks at works written prior to 1862 that have these influences. Includes comment on influence of Beethoven's WoO 57 on Op. 52 no. 17.

(a) reprint: Kraus. *Brahms-Studien* Bd. 10 (1994) pp. 23–32.

4293. *Kullak, Adolf. "Der Führer durch die neueste Claviermusik." *Neue Berliner Musikzeitung* [15]/35 (28.8.1861) p. 276.

4294. *Kulova, Elizaveta. "V klasse professora Evgenija Malinina: Rabota nad proizvedenijami Bramsa i Prokof'eva" in *Ispolnitel'i muzykal'noe proizvedenie*. Mihail Ovchinnikov, ed. Moskva: Gosudarstvennaîa konservatoriîa imeni P.I. Chaikvskogo, 1989. pp. 117–27. Describes a master class where Brahms is played. [from S102]

4295. *Large, Josephine. *Music Review* (Chicago) 3 (10.1893). Review of Opp. 116 and 117. [from WPA index]

4296. *Liebling, Emil. "The Piano Compositions of Brahms Considered in Their Practical Relation to Music Teaching" *Musician* (Philadelphia) [8] (3.1903) p. 102.

4297. Lubin, Ernest. "Brahms" in Lubin. *The Piano Duet. A Guide for Pianists*. New York: Grossman Publishers, 1970. pp. [95]–105, 190. facsim., mus., ind. Descriptive comments on Opp. 23, 39, 52a, 65a, WoO 1 and McCorkle Anhang Ia nr. 6. Page 190 is a brief overview of 2 piano 4 hand works.

4297.5. McGraw, Cameron. "Brahms, Johannes (1833–1897)" in McGraw. *Piano Duet Repertoire: Music Originally Written for One Piano, Four Hands*. Bloomington: Indiana University Press, 1981. pp. 39–40. 6 works, includes bibliography of publishers.

4298. Molsen, Uli. *Die Geschichte des Klavierspiels in historischen Zitaten von den Anfängen des Hammerklaviers bis Brahms*. Foreword by Nicholas Harnoncourt. Balingen-Endingen: Musik-Verlag Uli Molsen, 1982. 192 pp. Brahms: pp. 171–79. mus. Excerpts from contemporaries on Brahms's piano music and how he played; also includes Brahms's comments on piano music of other composers and on piano playing.

4299. Nelson, Allison. "The Piano Ensemble Works of Brahms" *The American Music Teacher* 36/1 (9./10.1986) pp. 30–31, 40. fig., notes. A popular appreciation of Brahms's works, includes original works as well as his arrangements of his own and others' works; includes comment about his work as G.W. Marks.

4300. *Pittson, Suzanne L. "Developmental Techniques in the Late Piano Pieces of Johannes Brahms: Opp. 116–119" M.A. diss., San Francisco State University, 1985. x, 138 pp. mus., notes.

4301. Rattalino, Piero. *Piano Recital. L'Evoluzione del gusto musicale attraverso la storia del programma da concerto.* (I Libri di Bron) Napoli: Flavio Pagano Editore, 1992. 205, [2] pp. Includes references to Brahms's works as presented on concert programs by various artists; includes reference to Brahms as a solo pianist.

4302. Rattalino, Piero. *La sonata romantica e altri saggi sulla letteratura del pianoforte.* 1st ed. (La Cultura 28) Milano: Il Saggiatore, 1985. 387 pp. ind. Brahms et passim, also:
pp. 119–21: Compares Paderewski's Op. 11 to Brahms's Op. 24.
pp. 181–85: Traces the Brahmsian tradition in composers after him.
"Le Sonate de Liszt e di Brahms": pp. 173–80. Brahms: pp. 173–79. Descriptive analytical remarks on Opp. 1, 2, and 5 show Brahms as a follower of Beethoven.

4303. *Robert, Walter. *From Bach to Brahms: a musician's journey through keyboard literature.* Bloomington: Tichenor Publishing, 1994. ix, 149 pp. ill., mus.

4304. *Schilb, Virginia Clough. "A Study of the Piano Style of Johannes Brahms" M.A. diss., University of Missouri, 1970. 110 pp. ill., notes.

4305. *Schneideman, Barbara. "The Gesture: A Study of Thematic Structure in the Late Piano Works of Johannes Brahms: A Thesis . . ." M.A. diss., University of California, San Diego, 1978. vi, 87 pp. ill., mus., notes.

4305.5. *Shaviner, Mark. "Tembro-koloristicheskie svojstva fortepiannoĭ faktury Iogannesa Bramsa" Ph.D. diss., Music Theory, Gosudarstvennaîa konservatoriîa Leningrad, 1987.
(d) i) *Shaviner. "Nekotorye osobennosti faktury fortepiannyh proizvedenii I[ogannesa]. Bramsa" [The Peculiarities of Texture in the Piano Works of Brahms] in *Problemy muzykal'noi faktury.* A. Stepanov, ed. (Trudy GMPI 59) Moskva:

Muzykal'no-Pedagogicheskiĭ Inst. imeni Gnesinyh, Moskva, 1982. [from S102]

(d) ii) *summary: 1987. 20 pp. mus., notes. Discusses timbre and color in the texture of the piano music; includes comments on their relationship to formal structure and to the orchestral works' texture. [from S102]

4306. Siki, Béla. "Johannes Brahms" in Siki. *Piano Repertoire. A Guide to Interpretation and Performance.* New York: Schirmer Books; London: Collier Macmillan Publishers, 1981. pp. 263–88. mus., notes. Tips for performance and comments on style for Opp. 76 no. 1, 79 no. 1, 116 no. 3, 117 no. 2, 118 nos. 2 and 3.

4307. *Smith, Stephen J[ames]. "The Interpretation of Rhythmic Irregularities in the Piano Music of Brahms" M.Mus., diss., Performance, Royal Northern College of Music, 1989. vii, 171 pp. Examines the music to understand rhythmic interpretation issues. [from *Music Matters* no. 25 (Summer 1990) p. 13]

4308. *Sorokina, E. *Fortepiannyĭ duet: istorīĩa zhanra.* Moskva: Muzyka, 1988. 316, [8] pp. ill., notes.

4309. Steuermann, Edward. "Brahms's Piano Music" in Steuermann. *The Not Quite Innocent Bystander. Writings of Edward Steuermann.* Clara Steuermann, David Porter, and Gunther Schuller, eds. Richard Cantwell and Charles Messner, transs. Lincoln, NE and London: University of Nebraska Press, 1989. pp. [159]–64. notes. Examines the line that goes from Brahms to Schoenberg; includes comments on qualities of the Romantic period.

4310. Shaviner, Mark, see 4305.5.

4311. *Taylor, Marilyn Gail. "A Discussion of Five Piano Works by Bach, Beethoven, Brahms, Prokofiev and Ravel" M.Mus. diss., University of Texas at San Antonio, 1988. 91 pp. notes.

4312. Tubeuf, André. "Le Piano de Brahms. Être Beethoven ou rien" *Diapason* (Paris) no. 283 (5.1983) pp. 32–34. ill. Looks at Brahms in the shadow of Beethoven, also how he wrote for piano and how performers play him at the piano from his times to the present.

4313. *Turney, Margaret Teresa. "Variation Principles in Selected Piano Works of Johannes Brahms" M.M. diss., Indiana University, 1970. 125 pp. mus.

4314. *Urquhart, Dan Murdock. "Variations for Solo Piano by Johannes
       Brahms, Op. 9, Op. 21, Op. 24; A Structural Analysis" M.A. diss.,
       University of Rochester, 1966. iii, 82 pp. mus., fig., notes.

4315. *The Vienna Urtext [=Wiener Urtext] Guide to Piano Literature.
       Written by the Editors of The Vienna Urtext [=Wiener Urtext]
       Edition. Compiled and Introduced by Maurice Hinson. (Edition
       EA 763) Valley Forge, PA: European American Music Corpora-
       tion, 1995. 240 pp. ill., ind., notes.

4316. *Wennerstrom, Mary H. "Harmonic Structures and Tonal Rela-
       tionships in Brahms' Piano Works, Op. 76–Op. 119" M.M. diss.,
       Indiana University, 1963. v, 88 pp. mus., notes.

4317. *Wierman, Cheryl Jean. "Schumann's Influence on Brahms'
       Early Piano Music" M.A. diss., Ohio State University, 1981. 101
       pp. notes.

4318. *Williams, Jo Ann Stanfield. "Piano Works of Brahms: Compo-
       sitional Techniques" M.A., Music, California State College, Long
       Beach, 1971. iii, 20 pp. + 2 phonorecords (60 min.). notes.

4319. Wolff, Konrad. "Brahms" in Wolff. Masters of the Keyboard. In-
       dividual Style Elements in the Piano Music of Bach, Haydn,
       Mozart, Beethoven, Schubert, Chopin and Brahms. Enlarged Edi-
       tion. Bloomington and Indianapolis: Indiana University Press,
       1990. pp. 249–87. mus., notes. Looks at melody, harmony,
       rhythm, meter and how written for the piano (no overall compar-
       ison provided). First edition of this work to have a Brahms entry.
       Includes comments on Brahms's interest in music of the past.

4320. *Wolters, Klaus. "Johannes Brahms (1833–1897)" in Wolters.
       Handbuch der Klavierliteratur. Klaviermusik zu zwei Händen.
       Zürich: Atlantis Handbuch, 1967.
       2., revidierte und erweiterte Auflage: 1977. pp. 379–88. notes.
       Comments on Brahms's place in piano music, includes de-
       scriptive comments and a list of editions. Includes reference
       to all solo piano and arranged for piano works, all piano con-
       certo cadenzas.

4320.3. See also 3284, 3355, 3371–74, 3378, 3427, 3683, 3788, 3854,
       3944, 4023, 4036, 4037, 4040, 4046, 4070, 4071, 4075, 4078,
       4080, 4083, 4088, 4418, 4604, 4870, 4874, 4876, 4884, 4910,
       4917, 4920, 4946, 4948, 4949, 4957, 4968, 4973, 4974, 4997,

5000, 5001, 5038, 5122, 5126, 5164, 5169, 5178, 5179, 5182, 5221, 5227, 5385, 5396.

4320.7.   See also I19, I34 in Appendix A.

Specific

Op. 1 Piano Sonata no. 1 in C major

4321.   Einstein, Alfred. "Opus I" *The Musical Quarterly* 20/4 (10.1934) pp. 367–83.
"Johannes Brahms": pp. 379–80. Looks at composers' Op. 1's to see what is typical or characteristic of that composer; includes comment on Brahms and the "Neue Bahnen" article and on the early pieces that never made it to print.

4322.   *Jacobson, Allan S. "A Study of Rondo in C Minor, Op. 1 by Frederic Chopin; Abegg Variations Op. 1, by Robert Schumann; Sonata in C Major Op. 1, by Johannes Brahms" D.M.A. diss., University of Wisconsin-Madison, 1982. 84 or vi, 73 pp. mus., notes.

4323.   *Roberts, Alice Parker. "A Comparative Analysis of the First Movements of Sonata in B-flat major, op. post. [D. 960] by Franz Schubert; Sonata in C major, Op. 1 by Johannes Brahms; and Sonata in E-flat minor, Op. 26 by Samuel Barber" [diss. (?)] Georgia Southern University, 1971. 30 pp.

4324.   *Szklarska, Kamilla F. "The Sonata in C major op. 1 by Johannes Brahms: a performance analysis" M.M. diss., Bowling Green State University, 1994. 38 pp. mus., notes.

4324.3.   See also S060, 3690, 3961, 4042, 4065, 4084, 4085, 4088, 4260, 4266, 4274, 4276, 4278, 4289, 4302, 4317, 4890, 4929, 5091, 5125, 5185, 5188.d., 5232, 5345, 5367.

Op. 2 Piano Sonata no. 2 in F sharp minor

4324.7.   See S060, 3690, 3961, 4042, 4065, 4080, 4084, 4085, 4088, 4260, 4274, 4276, 4278, 4289, 4302, 4317, 4929, 5164, 5185, 5188.d., 5345, 5367.

Op. 4 Scherzo for Piano in E flat minor

4325.   Brahms, Johannes. *Scherzo es-Moll op. 4. Faksimile des Autographs.* Margot Wetzstein, ed. Hamburg: J. Schuberth & Co.,

1987. [2, 8 [=facsimile], 1] + 15–19 pp. notes. Includes manuscript description and discussion of Brahms in the 1850's with Schumann, Liszt, and Joachim.

4326. Lee, E. Markham. "The Student Interpreter" *Musical Opinion and Music Trade Review* 56/672 (9.1933) pp. 1020–21. mus. Suggestions on how to play.

4327. *Marley, Judith L. "The Nineteenth-Century of the Scherzo: Selected Scherzi for the Piano written by Chopin and by Brahms" M.A. diss., Music, Kent State University, 1988. xiv, 170 pp. ill., mus.

4327.5. See also 3961, 4061, 4260, 4274, 4317, 5120, 5125, 5157, 5345, 5367.

Op. 5 Piano Sonata no. 3 in F minor

4328. *Etcheverry, Juan Martin. "Structural Analysis of Johannes Brahms' Piano Sonata op. 5, no. 3 in F minor" M.M. diss., Ball State University, 1988. 21, [1] pp. + 1 cassette (86 min.) mus., notes.

4329. Schläder, Jürgen. "Zur Funktion der Variantentechnik in den Klaviersonaten f-Moll von Johannes Brahms und h-Moll von Franz Liszt" in *Brahms und seine Zeit.* (Hamburger Jahrbuch für Musikwissenschaft 7) [for full citation see 5428] pp. 171–97. mus., fig., notes. Looks at the parallels between Op. 5 and Liszt's R. 21 in background, and motivic and harmonic particulars.

4329.5. See also S060, 3690, 3961, 4042, 4065, 4080, 4084, 4085, 4088, 4260, 4266, 4274, 4276, 4278, 4280, 4289, 4302, 4317, 4407, 4890, 4929, 4931, 5185, 5188.d., 5232, 5345, 5367.

Op. 9 Variations for Piano on a Theme by Robert Schumann

4330. *Ashe, Mary Lai. "An Analysis of Six Piano Pieces by Scarlatti, Beethoven, Brahms and Liszt" M.Mus. diss., University of Texas at San Antonio, 1985. i, 35 pp. notes.

4331. Danuser, Hermann. "Aspekte einer Hommage-Komposition. Zu Brahms' Schumann-Variationen op. 9" in *Brahms-Analysen.* [for full citation see 4888] pp. 91–106. mus., fig., notes. Focuses on an analysis that centres on the theme's handling; includes comment on the work's background, Brahms and Schumann.

4332. *Hegwood, Michele Byrd. "An Analysis of Variants Affecting Structural Changes in the Variations on a Theme by Schumann, Op. 9, by Johannes Brahms" Master's Thesis, Kansas State University, 1974. 28 pp.

4333. Hinson, Maurice. "Varying Schumann's Theme" *Clavier* 25/10 (12.1986) pp. 9–12. ill., mus. Discusses Clara Schumann's Op. 20 and Brahms's Op. 9, both of these works being variations on the theme from Robert Schumann's Op. 99 no. 4.; includes descriptive analysis and background.

4334. *Kenyon, Paul S. "Compositional Techniques in Brahms' Variations on a Theme of Schumann" M.M. diss., Bowling Green State University, 1985. 72 pp. mus., notes.

4335. Klassen, Janina. ""Recht Brahms, ernst und humoristisch." Noch ein paar Bemerkungen zu Clara Schumann und Johannes Brahms" in *Brahms-Phantasien*. [for full citation see 3838] pp. 7–10. mus., fig., notes. Looks at the motivic link between Brahms's Op. 9 and Clara's Op. 20, and presents background on Brahms coming in contact with the Schumanns and his relationship with Clara. Both of these works are variations on the theme from Robert Schumann's Op. 99 no. 4.

4336. *Lai, Li-chin. "Variations on a Theme by Robert Schumann Op. 20 by Clara Schumann: An Analytical and Interpretative Study" D.M.A. diss., Music, Temple University, 1992. xi, 111 pp. ill., mus., notes. Compares this piece to Brahms's Op. 9. Both of these works are variations on the theme from Robert Schumann's Op. 99 no. 4. [from S081]

4337. Neighbour, Oliver. "Brahms and Schumann: Two Opus Nines and Beyond" *19th Century Music* 7/3 (3.4.1984) pp. 266–70. mus., notes. Discusses the influence of Schumann on Brahms's Op. 9, particularly Schumann's Op. 9 and its compositional techniques.

4338. *Smith, Stephen James. "Eloquence, reference, and significance in Clara Schumann's Opus 20 and Johannes Brahms' Opus 9" D.M.A. diss., University of British Columbia, 1994. facsim., mus., notes. iii, 92 leaves + 4 cassettes. Both of these works are variations on the theme from Robert Schumann's Op. 99 no. 4. [from S109]

4338.5. See also S060, 3578, 4260.d., 4264, 4266, 4272, 4274, 4277, 4314, 4317, 4910, 4970, 5003, 5188.d., 5345, 5367.

Op. 10 Ballades for Piano

4339. *Chen, Wen-Sun. "Performance Problems in Johannes Brahms's Ballades, Op. 10" M.F.A. diss., University of California, Los Angeles, 1989. iii, 24 pp. mus., notes, discog.

4340. *Kărklisijski, Tomi. "Za hudožestvenata logika (struktura—vreme —văzprijatie) v Baladite op. 10 ot Johanes Brahms" [On Artistic Logic (Structure—Time—Perception) in Op. 10] *Bălgarsko muzikoznanie* 16/4 (10.12.1992) pp. 45–78. mus., fig., notes. [from S102]

4340.5. See also S060, 4042, 4080, 4088, 4260, 4266, 4274, 4280, 4291, 4317, 4591, 4955, 4956, 4960, 5091, 5064, 5188.d., 5345, 5367.

Op. 21 Variations for Piano: No. 1, on an Original Theme; and No. 2, on a Hungarian Song

4341. *Ferenc, László. "Brahms Variationen über ein ungarisches Lied, op. 21 nr. 2—jének témája: Újabb Széljegyzetek egy 1930-as levélrészletre" *Magyar zene* 26/4 (12.1985) pp. 363–77. mus. Cites remarks from a 1930's letter by Octavian Beu that state that the theme is a Rumanian song, not Hungarian. [from S102]
(d) *Francisc, László [Ferenc, László]. "Brahms: "variaţiuni pe melodia trei păstori se întîlniră"?" *Studii de muzicologie* (Bucaresti) 18 (1984) pp. 219–239. Suggests a source for the theme for Op. 21 no. 2. [from compilor]

4342. Struck, Michael. "Dialog über die Variation-präzisiert. Joseph Joachims "Variationen über ein irisches Elfenlied" [for piano, published in 1989] und Johannes Brahms' Variationenpaar op. 21 im Licht der gemeinsamen gattungstheoretischen Diskussion" in *Musikkulturgeschichte. Festschrift für Constantin Floros zum 60. Geburtstag.* Peter Petersen, ed. Wiesbaden: Breitkopf & Härtel, 1990. pp. 105–54. mus., notes. Discusses variation technique as seen in Brahms-Joachim contrapuntal exercises exchange in 1850's and looks at Joachim's work in light of Brahms's understanding of variation technique and Joachim's "homage" to Brahms.

4342.3. See also S060, 3578 (no. 2 only), 4266, 4274, 4314, 5003, 5127 (no. 2 only).

Op. 23 Variations for Piano 4 hands on a Theme by Robert Schumann

4342.7. See 3578, 4266, 4274, 4297, 4299, 4308, 5127, 5162.

Op. 24 Variations and Fugue for Piano on a Theme by Händel

4343. *Anselmi, Enrico. "Appunti per un'analisi delle variazioni e fuga su un tema di Haendel, op. 24 di Brahms" in Anselmi. *Aspetti del pianismo ottocenteso.* (Athena) Palermo: Italo-Latino-Americana Palma, 1981.

4344. *Barela, Margaret Mary. "A Study of Variations and a Fugue on a Theme by Handel by Johannes Brahms" [diss. ?] University of New Mexico, 1969.

4345. *Chapin, Sarah S. "Extracting an unfamiliar theme from its variations" *Psychomusicology* 2/1 (Spring 1982) pp. 48–50. Op. 24 used in test to see if subjects could identify original theme from hearing only its variations. [from S108]

4346. *Fisher, Suzanne Aleta. "Research in Music Theory: the Falsificationist Methods of a Scientific Programs (sic); based on a Study of Johannes Brahms' Opus 24, Variationen und Fuge über ein Thema von Handel involving the Development of a Model and the Use of Graphical Techniques for the Analysis of Compositions" M.A. diss., Ohio State University, 1973.

4347. *Frye, Louise. "Baroque and Romantic Stylistic Qualities in Brahm's (sic) Variations and Fugue on a Theme of Handel, Op. 24" M.M.diss., California State University, Fullerton, 1984. ii, 84 pp. mus., notes.

4348. *Grant, Richard C. "Brahms' Variations and Fugue on a Theme by Handel, Op. 24: A Study of the Technique of Harmonic Variation" M.A. diss., Central Washington State College, 1970. 62, [16] pp. mus.

4349. Kaiser, Joachim. "Der Reichtum einer Aria. Statt eines Gedenkartikels zum 150. Geburtstag von Johannes Brahms: Hinweis auf die Verlaufsform seiner Händel-Variationen" *Süddeutsche Zeitung* (München) 39/105 (7./8.5.1983) p. 138. Analysis, includes work's background and reactions to it of Clara Schumann and Wagner.

4350. *Noah, Betty Lynn. "A Characterization of Brahms' Variations and Fugue on a Theme by Handel" diss., University of Texas at Austin, 1966.

4351. Schuhmacher, Gerhard. "Historische Dimensionen in den Händel-Variationen Op. 24 von Johannes Brahms" in *Alte Musik als ästhetische Gegenwart. Bach Händel Schütz. Bericht über den internationalen musikwissenschaftlichen Kongreß Stuttgart 1985.* Dietrich Berke and Dorothee Hanemann, eds. Kassel [et al.]: Bärenreiter, 1987. vol. 2, pp. 72–77. mus (pp. 76–77), notes. Reviews Op. 24's background and examines its historical roots as seen in Bach's BWV 988 and Beethoven's Opp. 35 and 120, and works of Couperin and Rameau.

4352. *Sharon, Robert Barry. "A Performance Guide to the Variations and Fugue on a Theme by Handel for Piano, Opus 24 by Johannes Brahms" Ph.D. diss., New York University, 1981. v, 279 pp. mus., notes. Includes a "Larue-ian" analysis of the variations (following J. LaRue. *Guidelines for Style Analysis.* (1970)); also discusses role of the variation form in Brahms's music. [from S081]

4353. *Swickard, Alice Jayne. "A Comparison of the Keyboard Variation Music of John Bull and Johannes Brahms" M.S. diss., Eastern Illinois University, 1959. [iii,] 85 pp. mus., notes. Compares Op. 24 with John Bull's "The King's Hunt."

4354. *Worman, Regina Marydent. "The Effects and Roles of Unity and Contrast as Implemented by Composer and Performer of Four Different Periods with Special Emphasis on a Variation Set Representative of Handel, Beethoven, Brahms and Copland" D.M.A. diss., University of Alabama, 1993. ix, 151 pp. mus., notes. These components are examined and illustrated by example from Händel's No. 148, Beethoven's WoO 80, Brahms's Op. 24 and Copland's *Piano Variations* (1930).

4354.5. See also S060, 3410, 3578, 3664, 3799, 4038, 4042, 4082, 4087,

4260.d., 4264, 4266, 4274, 4275, 4277, 4278, 4302, 4314, 4931, 5003, 5127, 5313, 5396.

Op. 34bis Sonata in F minor for Two Pianos.

See "Op. 34 Piano Quintet in F minor" in Part IV.A.1.a. *"Specific"* and 4084.

Op. 35 Studies for Piano. Variations on a Theme by Paganini

4355. Berger, Francesco. "Paganini. As Treated by Schumann, Brahms and Liszt" *Monthly Musical Record* 44/525 (1.9.1914) pp. 243–44. Compares their treatments and concludes that Schumann's is the best. Other composers' works are Schumann's Opp. 3 and 10 and Liszt's R. 3b.
(a) reprint: "Paganini" *Musical Courier* 70/7 (Whole no. 1821) (17.2.1915) p. 48.

4356. *Kolakowski, Lawrence. "An Historical and Theoretical Study of Keyboard Variation Technique as Reflected in the Variations on a Theme by Paganini, Opus 35, by Johannes Brahms" M.M. diss., California State University, Fullerton, 1979. ii, 72 pp. mus., notes.

4357. Kraus, Detlef. "Brahms' Paganini Variations: A Special Case?" *Clavier* 22/10 (12.1983) pp. 17–19. ill., mus. A translation and condensation of 1647 (D. Kraus. *Brahms-Studien* (1981)).
(d) i) *Kraus. *Piano Music* (Seoul) (1984). (?)
(d) ii) Kraus. "Die Paganini-Variationen von Johannes Brahms— ein Sonderfall" *Piano-Jahrbuch* Bd. 3 (1983) pp. 85–88, 90.
(d) iii) see: 4080.

4358. *Liao, Chi-Kun. "The Treatments of Paganini's A minor Caprice by Brahms and Liszt" M.M. diss., Music, Southern Illinois University at Carbondale, 1984. vi, 52 pp. mus., notes. Works discussed are Op. 35 and Liszt's R. 3b.

4359. Meyer, Martin. "Virtuosität und Tiefsinn. Brahms' "Paganini-Variationen" im interpretatorischen Vergleich" *FonoForum* [28]/10 (10.1983) pp. 20–26. ill., mus., discog. Analysis and review of its interpreters.

4360. Schädler, Stefan. "Technik und Verfahren in den Studien für Pianoforte: Variationen über ein Thema von Paganini op. 35 von Johannes Brahms" in *Aimez-vous Brahms "the progressive"?* [for full citation see 4872] pp. [3]–23. mus., fig., notes. Analysis that shows Brahms's development of the variation form.

4361. *Scott, Lois Margaret. "A Comparative Study of the Variations on a Theme of Paganini by Paganini, Liszt, Brahms, and Rachmaninoff" M.M. diss., University of Rochester, Eastman School of Music, 1950. v, 143 pp. mus., notes. Works discussed are Paganini's Op. 1 no. 24, Liszt's R. 3b, Brahms's Op. 35 and Rachmaninoff's Op. 43. [from compiler]

4362. *Tse, Benita Wan-Kuen. "Piano Variations Inspired by Paganini's Twenty-Fourth Caprice from Op. 1" D.M.A. diss., Performance Practice, University of Cincinnati, 1992. 154 pp. mus., notes. Analyses 5 composers' variations: Brahms's Op. 35, Liszt's R. 3b, Rachmaninov's Op. 43, Busoni's piano transcription of Liszt's R. 3b, and Lutosławski's *Wariacje na temat Paganiniego*. Discusses their individual styles and approaches to transcription. [from S102]

4363. *Upper, Henry August. "The Concert Etudes of Chopin, Schumann, Liszt and Brahms" M.M. diss., Southern Methodist University, 1960. v, 93 pp. ill., mus. Other composers' works are Chopin's Opp. 10 and 25, Schumann's Op. 13, Liszt's R.3b and R. 5. [from compiler]

4363.5. See also S060, 4042, 4064, 4080, 4082, 4087, 4088, 4266, 4274, 4275, 4278, 4292.

Op. 39 Waltzes for Piano

4364. Brodbeck, David [Lee]. "Primo Schubert, Secondo Schumann: Brahms's Four-Hand Waltzes, Op. 39" *The Journal of Musicology* 7/1 (Winter 1989) pp. 58–80. facsim., mus., notes. Traces the influence of Schubert and Schumann on Op. 39 through harmonic and form analysis; includes comparison of Op. 39 to the waltz at that time.

4365. McCorkle, Margit L. "Die "Hanslick"-Walzer, opus 39" [with assistance of Wiltrud Martin] in *Brahms-Kongress Wien 1983*. [for full citation see 5431] pp. 379–86. Discusses background and Schubert influence. Examines Brahms's affinity to piano 4-hand works and his arrangements of his own works, with Op. 39 and its various versions as an example.

4366. Narmour, Eugene. *Beyond Schenkerism. The Need for Alternatives in Music Analysis.* Chicago and London: The University of Chicago Press, 1977. xi, [1], 238 pp. Brahms: pp. 7–11. fig., ind., notes. Argues that Schenker's work doesn't apply anymore, uses Op. 39 no. 1 as example.

4367. Rodriguez, Santiago. "Brahms' Waltzes, Op. 39" *Keyboard Classics* 10/3 (5./6.1990) pp. 40–41. ill., mus. (pp. 36–38). Suggestions on how to play Op. 39, nos. 1–4.

4367.3. See also 3336, 3405, 3578, 4042, 4069, 4266, 4274, 4275, 4278, 4284, 4292, 4297, 4299, 4308, 4429, 4880, 4931, 4965, 4998, 5176.

Op. 52a Waltzes for Piano 4 hands after the Liebeslieder Op. 52

4367.7. See 4297, 4299, 4308.

Op. 56b Variations for 2 Pianos on a Theme by Joseph Haydn

4368. *Brahms, Johannes. *Variationen für zwei Klaviere über ein Thema von Joseph Haydn Opus 56b. Faksimile-Ausgabe nach dem Originalmanuskript im Besitz der Musiksammlung der Wiener Stadt- und Landesbibliothek.* Ernst Hilmar, ed. (Schriftenreihe zur Musik 1) Tutzing: Hans Schneider, 1989 or 1991. 17, [20] pp. ill.

4369. *Edwards, Karin Redekopp. "A Comparison of Selected Duo-Piano Variations" D.Mus. diss., Indiana University, 1982. vi, 94 pp. mus., notes. Compares Saint-Saëns's Op. 35, Brahms's Op. 56b and Reger's Opp. 86 and 132a (?). [from S057]

4370. *Smith, Donald King. "Two Piano Literature: A Comparative Study of Its Textures" diss., University of Southern California, 1964. 182 pp. mus., notes. Compares W.F. Bach's F.10, Brahms's Op. 56b, Hindemith's *Sonate für 2 Klavieren* (1942) and Stravinsky's *Concerto for 2 Pianos.* [from S031]

4370.3. See also 4049, 4086, 4284, 4297, 4299, 4989, 5160, 5162.

4370.6. See also I20, I30 in Appendix A.

Op. 65a Waltzes for Piano 4 hands [after the New Liebeslieder Waltzes Op. 65]

4370.9. See 3417, 4297, 4299, 4308.

Op. 76 Eight Piano Pieces

4371. Atlas, Raphael. "Enharmonic Trompe-l'oreille: Reprise and the Disguised Seam in Nineteenth-Century Music" *In Theory Only* 10/6 (5.1988) pp. 47–51. mus., fig., notes, appendixes. Uses Op. 76 no. 4 to illustrate how reprise via enharmonic means is adapted to different contexts; examples are also taken from Opp. 25 and 68. Appendixes contain further examples.

4372. Berry, Wallace. "First Case: Brahms, Intermezzo in B-flat, Op. 76, No. 4" in Berry. *Musical Structure and Performance*. New Haven and London: Yale University Press, 1989. pp. 45–82. mus., fig., notes. Uses this work to show how questions relating to performance practice can be answered by examining a work's formal and structural elements.

4373. Bozarth, George S. "At the J.A. Stargardt auction . . ." *The American Brahms Society Newsletter* 7/1 (Spring 1989) p. 8. Reports on sale of manuscripts for Op. 76 nos. 5–8.

4374. Cahn, Peter. "Johannes Brahms: Intermezzo B-dur op. 76, Nr. 4" *Musica* 42/1 (1./2.1988) pp. 47–51. mus., fig., notes. An analysis to show how the analytical and poetic sides of a piece work together.

4375. Carpenter, Patricia. "A Problem in Organic Form: Schoenberg's Tonal Body" (Analysis Symposium: Brahms's Op. 76, No. 6) *Theory and Practice* 13 (1988) pp. [31]–63. Brahms: pp. 39–63. mus., fig., notes. Uses Op. 76 no. 6 as an example for elucidating Schoenberg's concept of musical form.

4376. *Code, David Loberg. "Narrative Strategies in Tonal Compositions" Ph.D. diss., Music, University of Maryland, College Park, 1990. 340 pp. Analyses Op. 76 no. 1 using the theories of Gérard Genette on narrative structures in music; includes analysis of Beethoven's Op. 70 no. 1 and Schubert's D.957, no.13 and D.911, no.14. [from S102]

4377. Eigeldinger, Jean-Jacques. "Note sur des autographes musicaux inconnus. Schumann-Brahms-Chopin-Franck-Fauré" *Revue de musicologie* 70/1 (1984) pp. 107–11. Brahms: p. 110. facsim (p. 115), notes. Presents a description and provenance for Op. 76 manuscript; includes comment on Wilhelmine Clauss-Szarvady's and Brahms's relationship.

4378. *Faxon, Alicia Craig. *Women Artists News* 15 (Winter 1991) pp. 7–8. ill. ("Improvisation, opus 76 #2, Brahms") [from S090]

4379. *Holm, Bill. "Brahms' Capriccio in C Major, Opus 76, No. 8" in Holm. *Brahms' Capriccio in C Major, Opus 76, No. 8*. (Minnesota Miniatures 1) Browerville, MN: Oxhead Press, 1990. (a) reprint: in Holm. *The Dead Get By With Everything. Poems.* Minneapolis: Milkwood Editions, 1991. pp. 90–91. Poem describes the memories that playing this piece evokes for the poet.

4380. *Kirkpatrick, Diane. "Brahms' Poetic Character Pieces—Eight Clavierstücke, Opus 76" M.Mus. diss., Bowling Green University, 1977. 73 pp. mus.

4381. Konold, Wulf. "Mendelssohn und Brahms. Beispiele schöpferischer Rezeption im Lichte der Klaviermusik" in *Brahms-Analysen*. [for full citation see 4888] pp. 81–90. mus., notes. Discusses the influence of Mendelssohn in Brahms's music, analyses Op. 76 no. 4 versus Mendelssohn's Op. 67 no. 3.

4382. *Pelusi, Mario Joseph. "Contemplating a Brahms Intermezzo: Toward a Comprehensive Analytical Method for the Explication and Interpretation of "Prescriptive Music Structures,"" Ph.D. diss., Princeton University, 1982. 149 pp. Op. 76 no. 7 is used as example for presenting a method of analysis that places emphasis on all events in a work of music. [from S102]

4383. *Trucks, Amanda Louise. "The Metric Complex in Johannes Brahms's Klavierstücke, Op. 76" Ph.D. diss., University of Rochester, 1992. xv, 254 pp. mus., notes.

4383.5. See also 3407, 3578, 3914, 3944, 4260–63, 4266, 4271, 4272, 4274, 4291, 4292, 4306, 4316, 4880, 4931, 4935, 5041, 5117, 5121, 5157, 5160.d.ii.

Op. 79 Two Rhapsodies for Piano

4384. *The Musical Times* 21/452 (1.10.1880) p. 513. Review.

4385. *Collins, Paulette. "Franz Liszt's *Die Trauer Gondel* I and II [R. 81] and Johannes Brahms's Rhapsodie Op. 79 no. 2: Extended Tonality and Structural Integration" M.M. diss., University of London, King's College, 1987.

4385.5. See also S060, 3578, 3758, 4088, 4260, 4262, 4263, 4266, 4271, 4274, 4275, 4291, 4306, 4316, 4931, 4959, 5002, 5030, 5157.

Op. 116 Seven Fantasies for Piano

4386. Cone, Edward T. "Attacking A Brahms Puzzle" *The Musical Times* 136/1824 (2.1995) pp. 72–77. ill., mus., fig., notes. Looks at harmonic shape and thematic design to counter the ambiguities of Op. 116 no. 4.

4387. Dunsby, Jonathan. "The Multi-Piece in Brahms: Fantasien Op. 116" in *Brahms: Biographical, Documentary and Analytical Studies*. [for full citation see 5479] pp. 167–89. mus., fig., ind., notes. Looks at the degree of unity within Op. 116 as evidence of Brahms's attempts to link works.

4388. Kraus, Detlef. "Brahms' op. 116: das Unikum der sieben Fantasien" *Brahms-Studien* Bd. 8 (1990) pp. 49–60. mus., notes. Discusses the use of the Czech folk motif "Ach, není tu není-beginning"; includes general comments on the piano fantasy form.

4389. Rink, John. "Playing in Time: Rhythm, Metre and Tempo in Brahms's Fantasien Op. 116" in *The Practice of Performance. Studies in Musical Interpretation*. John Rink, ed. Cambridge [et al.]: Cambridge University Press, 1995. pp. 254–82. mus., fig., ind., notes. Uses performances by the author and on recordings, to analyse this work.

4389.5. See also S060, 3363, 3569, 3751, 3944, 3967, 4038, 4042, 4051, 4094, 4253, 4258, 4260.d., 4261–63, 4266, 4271, 4272, 4274, 4278, 4282, 4285, 4287, 4291, 4295, 4300, 4305, 4306, 4316, 4877, 4916, 4925, 4935, 4960, 5030, 5157, 5160, 5162, 5388.

Op. 117 Three Intermezzi for Piano

4390. *Correo musical sud-americano* 1 (1915) pp. 6–7.

4391. Budde, Elmar. "Johannes Brahms' Intermezzo op. 117, Nr. 2" in *Analysen. Beiträge zu einer Problemgeschichte des Komponierens. Festschrift für Hans Heinrich Eggebrecht zum 65. Geburtstag*. Werner Breig, Reinhold Brinkmann and Elmar Budde, eds. (Beihefte zum Archiv für Musikwissenschaft 23) Stuttgart: Franz Steiner Verlag Wiesbaden, 1984. pp. [324]–337.

fig., ind., notes. Examines overall form, and then to show depth of piece author reviews harmonic and "orchestral" colour.

4392. *Craner, Paul. "Musical space as musical idea in Brahms' Op. 117 no. 2" M.F.A. diss., Mills College, 1994. 70 pp. mus.

4393. *Dasseleer, Pascal. "Pour une approche du jugement de beaute aux confins de l'ontologie et de l'analyse musicale: Application a l'Intermezzo op. 117 no 1 de Johannes Brahms" *Revue des archeologues et historiens d'art de Louvain* 26 (1993) pp. 73–128. mus. The first section of Brahms's intermezzo is analyzed and reconstructed in terms of beauty-judgment criteria. This piece's organizational coherence and resistance are ascertained through falsification attempts; the piece is subjected to perfection evaluations. [from S109]

4394. *Davie, Cedric Thorpe. *Musical Structure and Design.* (The Student's Music Library) London: Dennis Dobson, 1953. 2. impression: 1960. Brahms: pp. 46–48. notes. A measure-by-measure analysis of Op. 117 no. 3. *also: 1965. (a) *reprint (of 1953 edition): New York: Dover Publications, 1966.

4395. *Virtanen, Timo. "Johannes Brahms: Intermezzo Es-duuri op. 117 nr 1—Nakokulmia motiivianalyysiin" *Savellys ja musiikinteoria* no. 2 (1993) pp. 20–35. mus., notes. Brahms's intermezzo op. 117, no. 1, is analyzed using Allen Cadwallader's multileveled motivic repetition analysis method [see 4261], which is based on Schenker's analytic practice. [from S109]

4396. *Waller, Mary Louise. "Three Intermezzi, Opus 117, by Johannes Brahms: an Analysis according to the Theories prescribed in Rudolph Reti's *The Thematic Process in Music*" M.M. diss., Florida State University, 1985. iv, 138 pp. mus., notes. [Imprint for Reti's book is: New York: Macmillan, 1951]

4397. Zabrack, Harold. "Musical Timing: a view of implicit music reality as it affects musical flow in Brahms' Intermezzo op. 117 No. 1 in E flat major" *Journal of the American Liszt Society* 16 (12.1984) pp. 89–97. mus. (pp. 95–97), notes. Stylistic analysis of Op. 117 no. 1.

4397.5. See also S060, 3363, 3569, 3751, 3810, 3914, 3944, 3967, 4038, 4042, 4253, 4258, 4260.d., 4261–63, 4266, 4271, 4274, 4278,

4282, 4287, 4291, 4292, 4295, 4300, 4305, 4306, 4316, 4877,
4908, 4916, 4931, 4960, 4980, 5091, 5157, 5160, 5188.d.

Op. 118 Six Piano Pieces

4398. Kelterborn, Rudolf. "Johannes Brahms: Intermezzo op. 118 Nr. 2
(A-Dur)" in Kelterborn. *Analyse und Interpretation. Eine Einführung anhand von Klavierkompositionen: Bach, Haydn,
Mozart, Beethoven, Schumann, Brahms, Schönberg, Bartók*. Herausgegeben von der Musik-Akademie der Stadt Basel. (Musikre-
flexionen 4) Winterthur: Amadeus Verlag, 1993. pp. 54–67. mus.,
fig. Analyses form, motif and harmony as an aid to performance.
See 4398.b. for comment on bibliographical history.
   (b) *Japanese translation by Fumiku Takeuchi: Tokyo: SINFO-
NIA INC., 1990. Work was originally prepared in German,
then translated into Japanese. 4398 is a reworking of the original German text.

4399. *Lamb, Marvin Lee. *The Expansion of the "Ur motive" in the Intermezzo in A Major, op. 118, no. 2, of Johannes Brahms: a Public Lecture Given as Part of the Johannes Brahms Festival, 1978*.
[Nashville:] School of Music, George Peabody College for Teachers, 1978. 27, [2] pp. notes.

4400. Miller, Patrick. "Tonal Structure and Formal Design in Johannes
Brahms's Opus 118, No. 6" in *Music From the Middle Ages
Through the Twentieth Century. Essays in Honor of Gwynn
McPeek*. Carmelo P. Comberiati and Matthew C. Steel, eds. (Mu-
sicology: A Book Series. 7) New York [et al.]: Gordon and
Breach, 1988. pp. 213–34. facsim., mus., fig., ind. Analytical
study, includes comments by other writers on this piece.

4401. *Modena, Elena. "Analisi schenkeriana e libertà compositiva: Al-
cune particolarità strutturali dell'intermezzo op. 118, n. 1 di
J[ohannes]. Brahms" *Analisi: Rivista di teoria e pedagogia musi-
cale* 2/5 (5.1991) pp. 23–31. mus. summary in English. Uses
Schenkerian analysis to understand the structural idiosyncrasies in
Op. 118 no. 1. [from S102]

4402. *Narmour, Eugene. "On the Relationship of Analytical Theory to
Performance and Interpretation" in *Explorations in Music, the Arts
and Ideas: Essays in Honor of Leonard B. Meyer*. Eugene Narmour

and Ruth A. Solie, eds. (Festschrift Series 7) Stuyvesant, NY: Pendragon, 1988. pp. 317–40. Op. 118 no. 1 used as an example in an analysis of music interpretation that combines the composers' and the listeners' points of view. Includes an evaluation and ranking of recorded performances of the work. [from S102]

4403. *Ro, Kyung-Ah. "Performance Practices in Brahms's Piano Pieces, Op. 118" M.F.A. diss., University of California, Los Angeles, 1993. ix, 41 pp. ill., notes.

4404. Snarrenberg, Robert. "The Play of Différance: Brahms's Intermezzo Op. 118, No. 2" *In Theory Only* 10/3 (10.1987) pp. 1–25. mus., fig., notes. Describes focusing on the intertwined contexts of the beginning and ending of this piece throughout the work and how the former transforms to the latter.
(d) Samuels, Robert. "Derrida and Snarrenberg" *In Theory Only* 11/1–2 (5.1989) pp. 45–58. notes. Examines the legitimacy of Snarrenberg's application (author believes it isn't successful) and reviews the concept of différance in both Derrida and Snarrenberg.

4404.5. See also S060, 3363, 3569, 3751, 3944, 3967, 4038, 4042, 4051, 4068, 4088, 4253, 4258, 4261–63, 4266, 4271, 4272, 4274, 4278, 4282, 4287, 4291, 4300, 4305, 4306, 4316, 4877, 4880, 4882, 4896, 4916, 4931, 5120.e., 5157, 5160, 5188.d.

Op. 119 Four Piano Pieces

4405. Braus, Ira [Lincoln]. "An Unwritten Metrical Modulation in Brahms's Intermezzo in E Minor, Op. 119, No. 2" *Brahms Studies* 1 (1994) pp. 161–69. mus., fig., notes. Uses analysis and notational clues to understand the metrical proportions between the A and B sections of this piece, with its implications for performance.

4406. *Ferencz, George Joséph. "Application of the Analytical Techniques of Heinrich Schenker and Grosvenor W. Cooper/Leonard B. Meyer" M.A. diss., Kent State University, 1979. iii, 75 pp. ill., mus., notes. Op. 119 nos. 2 and 4 are among the examples. [from S031]

4407. Goebels, Franzpeter. "Adagio h-moll. Bemerkungen zum Intermezzo h-moll op. 119, Nr. 1 von Johannes Brahms" *Musica* 37/3 (5./6.1983) pp. 230–31. mus., notes. Shows how Brahms emulates Clara Schumann's Op. 3 in the theme, also examines allusions

Brahms makes to his Op. 5 and Reger's allusions to the theme in
his Op. 53 no. 2.

4408. *Hozdic, Rosemary, Sister. "The Innovative Piano Techniques of
Johannes Brahms as Exhibited by the Rhapsody, Op. 119, No. 4"
Master's diss., Kent State University, 1974. iv, 37 pp. mus.

4409. Jordan, Roland, and Emma Kafalenos. "The Double Trajectory:
Ambiguity in Brahms and Henry James" *19th Century Music* 13/2
(Fall 1989) pp. 129–44. mus., fig., notes. Discusses how certain
works elicit a recognition of the significant characteristics they
share, and examines Brahms's Op. 119 no. 1 and James's "Owen
Wingrave" on their ambiguous character.
(d) Kramer, Lawrence. "Dangerous Liaisons: The Literary Text in
Musical Criticism" *19th Century Music* 13/2 (Fall 1989) pp.
159–67. notes. Uses 4409 as a test case to weigh the prospects
of a musical/literary criticism methodology—its purpose,
what it would look like.

4410. *Lyon, Elizabeth Kohlenberger. "Rhythmic complexities in the
Opus 119 short piano works of Johannes Brahms" M.M. diss.,
California State University, Fullerton, 1995. xii, 132 pp. notes.

4411. Mainka, Jürgen. "Permutation bei Brahms" *Beiträge zur Musikwissenschaft* 28/2 (1986) pp. 145–46. mus. Examines Op. 119 no.
2 for its implications for composers who followed Brahms. Concludes that Brahms's technique anticipates Bartók more than it
does Berg.

4412. *Refsdal, Arnfinn. "Brahms' Klaverstykker: Opus 119" Ph.D.
diss., Universitetet i Oslo, 1979.

4413. *Stewart, Jimmy Dan. "The Evaluation of Musical Elements that
Influence Grouping in Opus 119 of Johannes Brahms" M.Mus.
diss., University of Oklahoma, 1985. 2 vols. mus.

4413.1. See also S060, 3363, 3384, 3569, 3751, 3944, 3967, 4042, 4068,
4088, 4253, 4258, 4261–63, 4266, 4271, 4272, 4274, 4275, 4278,
4282, 4287, 4291, 4292, 4300, 4305, 4316, 4830.a., 4877, 4890,
4894, 4931, 4959, 5157, 5160, 5235.

Gavottes for Piano in A minor and A major [McCorkle WoO 3]

4413.3. See 4285, 4947.

Gigue for Piano in A minor [McCorkle WoO 4, no. 1]

4413.5. See 4285.

Gigue for Piano in B minor [McCorkle WoO 4, no. 2]

4413.7. See 3383, 4285.

Sarabandes for Piano in A minor and B minor [McCorkle WoO 5]

4413.9. See 3383, 4285, 4947.

Five Studies for Piano after Chopin, Weber, and Bach
[McCorkle Anhang Ia, nr. 1]

4414. *Carruthers, Glen Blaine. "Bach and The Piano: Editions, Arrangements, and Transcriptions from Czerny to Rachmaninov" Ph.D.
diss., University of Victoria (School of Music), 1987. notes, mus.
vi, 251 pp. on 259 leaves. Isolates a number of conventions in Bach
interpretation in the 19th century, and explains Romantic interest
for rewriting Brahms when transferring his work to the piano. [from
S102]

4415. *Feder, Georg. "Bachs Werke in ihren Bearbeitungen 1750–
1950" Phil.F. diss., Christian-Albrechts Universität zu Kiel, 1955.
387 pp.
(d) 2447 (G. Feder. in *Bach-Interpretationen*. (1969)).
   (b) *English translation by Egbert M. Ennulat: Feder. "History of the Arrangements of Bach's Chaconne" in *The
   Bach Chaconne for Solo Violin. A Collection of Views*.
   Jon F. Eiche, ed. Athens, GA: American String Teachers
   Association, 1985. pp. 41–61. mus.

4416. *Wilson, Geoffrey. *The Pianoforte‑Etude*. [Sydney?:] The Author, 1990. 169 pp.

4416.5. See also 3374, 4064, 5120.e.

Exercises for Piano [McCorkle WoO 6]

4417. *Music Review* (Chicago) 4 (11.1894) p. 66. Review.

4418. *McLendon, Maxine Anne. "The 51 Piano Exercises of Brahms and Their Relation to His Piano Works" M.Mus. diss., Baylor University, 1952. iii, 110 pp. mus., notes. Includes the Schirmer edition of this work.

4419. *Novikova, Raisa. "Fortepiannyi ispolnitel'skii stil' i pedagogika Bramsa" Ph.D. diss., Music Performance, Gosudarstvennaia Konservatoriia, Vilnius, 1983.
    (d) *summary: 20 pp. Examines interaction of Brahms's style as composer and performer by analyzing this work. Also looks at pianistic texture in all his works. [from S102]

4420. Purswell, Joan. "Johannes Brahms: Pianist and Pedagogue" *The American Music Teacher* 33/5 (4.–5.1984) pp. 14, 16. notes. Presents the background to this work with suggestions for practicing. Also discusses Brahms as a pianist with contemporary descriptions, and Brahms as teacher, focusing on Brahms and Florence May.

4420.5. See also 4064, 4262.d.ii.

Hungarian Dances [McCorkle WoO 1]

4421. *Allgemeine musikalische Zeitung* 4/14 (7.4.1869) pp. 108–09. Reviews Hefts 1 and 2.

4422. *The Musical Times* 21/452 (1.10.1880) p. 511. mus. Reviews all 4 Hefts.

4423. *Bereczky, János. "Brahms hét magyar témájának forrása" in *Zenetudományi dolgozatok* (1990–91) pp. 75–88. mus. summary in German. Describes previously unknown sources for 7 of the themes from the Ungarische Tänze; comparison of these sources with what Brahms wrote, shows he used printed sources rather than what he remembered hearing, when he was composing this work. [from S102]

4424. *Brahm's Hungarian Dances" *Musical Courier* 35 (8.9.1897) p. 19.

4425. *Ehlert, Louis. "Claviermusik zu vier Händen" *Neue Berliner Musikzeitung* [22]/6 (5.2.1868) p. 44.

4426. "The Interpretation of Hungarian Music. How to Play the Brahms-

Joachim Hungarian Dance (No. 2) in D-minor" *Musical Courier*
74/15 (Whole no. 1933) (12.4.1917) p. 39.

4427. *Roberts Bell, Carol Ann. "A Performance Analysis of Selected
Dances from the "Hungarian Dances" of Johannes Brahms and
the "Slavonic Dances" of Antonin Dvorak for one-piano, four
hands" D.M.A. diss., University of Oklahoma, 1990. Detailed
analysis pointing out stylistic traits and performance problems; includes general comments on basic music elements and ethnic
viewpoints. Dvořák's Dances are his Opp. 46 and 72.

4427.3. See also 3267, 3358, 3359, 3374, 3378, 3578, 3598, 3603, 3609,
3626, 3638, 3642, 3645, 3653.7, 4041, 4042, 4049, 4088, 4266,
4274, 4297, 4308, 4478, 4489.5, 5127, 5129, 5157, 5162, 5167.

**b. Brahms's Editing and Arranging of Other Composers' Piano
Music**

General

4427.7. See 4988.

Specific

Chopin

4428. *Leibnitz, Thomas. "Johannes Brahms und der Historismus: Seine
Tätigkeit als Herausgeber unter besonderer Berücksichtigung der
Chopin-Gesamtausgabe. Dargestellt an Beständen der Sammlung
Hoboken" Forschungsauftrag des Bundesministeriums für Wissenschaft und Forschung. Wien, 1982. Manuscript, Österreichische Nationalbibliothek [Instituts für Österreichische Musik-
dokumentation].

(d) Leibnitz. "Johannes Brahms als Musikphilologe" in *Brahms-
Kongress Wien 1983.* [for full citation see 5431] pp. 351–59.
facsim., notes. Discusses Brahms as editor of Chopin's
Gesamtausgabe [McCorkle Anhang VI, nr. 5] and how he
handled textual questions; also examines his relationship
with Gustav Nottebohm. Includes comment on Brahms's interest in philology and older music.

Scarlatti, Domenico

4428.5. See 3908.

Schubert

4429. Brodbeck, David Lee. "Brahms as Editor and Composer: His Two Editions of Ländler by Schubert and His First Two Cycles of Waltzes, Opera 39 and 52" Ph.D. diss., University of Pennsylvania, 1984. 314 pp. Discusses how Brahms as editor and musicologist affects Brahms the artist; Brahms as a perpetuator of Schubert, Schubert's inspiration for Brahms, specifically relating D.790 [McCorkle Anhang VI, nr. 11] to Op. 39, and Schubert's D.366 and D.814 [together = McCorkle Anhang Ia, nr. 6] to Op. 52.

    (d) adapted: Brodbeck, David [Lee]. "Brahms's Edition of Twenty Schubert Ländler: An Essay in Criticism" in *Brahms Studies: Analytical and Historical Perspectives.* [for full citation see 5480] pp. [229]–50. mus., fig., notes. Studies Brahms's work as editor on Schubert's D.366 and D.814 [together = McCorkle Anhang Ia, nr. 6]: his decisions on grouping them all together, on the ordering. Decisions appear to have been strongly influenced by his own compositional and aesthetic preferences.

4429.3. See also 3785, 3934, 4292, 4297.

Schumann, Clara

4429.7. See 3414.

Schumann, Robert

4430. Roesner, Linda Correll. "Brahms's Editions of Schumann" in *Brahms Studies: Analytical and Historical Perspectives.* [for full citation see 5480] pp. [251]–282. facsim., mus., fig., notes, appendix. Focuses primarily on the mid-1860's to early 1870's when Brahms edited unpublished Schumann piano works [McCorkle Anhang VI, nrs. 14, 15] and the Schumann *Gesamtausgabe* [McCorkle Anhang VI, nr. 17]. Uses the editions and 1179 (C. Schumann. *Clara Schumann. Johannes Brahms . . .* (1927)) to follow the editorial process and trace the background for decisions that were made. Also studies a later period of editing (1878–81). Includes 2 unpublished letters Brahms to Clara (both from 5.1881); appendix includes unpublished portions of letters from 1179 (C. Schumann. *Clara Schumann. Johannes Brahms.* . . . (1927)) for #363 and 377 (both from 1878), #390 (1879); as well as a portion of an unpublished letter from 11.1880. Letters are transcribed in original German, with English translation.

4430.5. See also 3414.

c. Organ Works

General

4431. Beechey, Gwilym. "The Organ Music of Brahms" *The American Organist* 17/5 (5.1983) pp. 43–46. ill., mus., notes. Survey of all works, focusing on analysis of counterpoint and chorale bases.
   (d) revised and shortened: Beechey. "Brahms' Organ Music" *Musical Opinion* 107/1281 (7.1984) pp. 309–13. notes only.

4432. Bertram, Hans Georg, see 4445.5.

4433. Biba, Otto. "Brahms, Bruckner und die Orgel" in *Bruckner Symposion.* [for full citation see 5434] pp. 191–96. notes. Compares the two composers' interest in the organ and how they wrote for it.

4434. Biba, Otto. "Orgel und Orgelspiel in Leben und Schaffen von Johannes Brahms" *Ars organi* 31/4 (12.1983) pp. 215–21. facsim., notes. Surveys the organ works and describes their background; includes comment on Brahms as an organist.

4435. Bozarth, George S. "Brahms's Organ Music" [Program for Concert 'The Organ Music of Johannes Brahms,' Carole Terry, Organ. Feb. 20, 1987. St. Alphonsus Church, Seattle, WA.] Presented by the University of Washington School of Music. [American Brahms Society.] Brahms Archive. pp. [4–10.] A survey of all works, includes chorale texts. Includes comment on sources not previously consulted and on the creative process for these works.
   (d) Bozarth, George S. "Brahms's Organ Works: A New Critical Edition" *The American Organist* 22/6 (6.1988) pp. 50–59. mus., notes. An account of the history of the sources and how

this new edition (J. Brahms. *Werke für Orgel.* George S. Bozarth, ed. München: G. Henle Verlag, 1988) supercedes previous work. For each piece sources (both extant and missing), background and critical remarks are given. This item is an expansion of the editorial report in the edition.

4436. "Brahms's Organ Works" *Musical Opinion and Music Trade Review* 56/669 (6.1933) p. 804. Overview of all works.

4437. *Brooks, G. "Building a Repertoire: Brahms and Liszt" *Organists Review* 68/273 (1984) pp. 34–36.

4438. *Damp, George Edward. "The Organ Works of Johannes Brahms; a Manifestation of Musical Craft Employed in the Service of Beauty and Expression" [Ithaca, NY:] 1964. 34 pp. mus.

4439. Dorfmüller, Joachim. "Orgelmuziek aan de periferie. Over de renaissance van barokke vorm- en genreconcepten bij Johannes Brahms" *Adem* 19/1 (1.–2.1983) pp. 10–14. ill., notes. abstracts in French and English on p. 14. An overview of the organ works, noting in particular Brahms's style as seen in Op. 122. Also reports on people's comments on Op. 122, on Brahms's interest in early music and on Brahms in general (Furtwängler, Schoenberg).
    (d) *Dorfmüller, J[oachim]. ""Orgelmusik ved periferien". Om den barokke form- og idéforståelses renæssance hos Johannes Brahms" *Dansk Kirkemusiker-Tidende* 79/5 (1983) pp. 5–9.

4440. *Kucharski, Lech. "Fuga organowa w epoce romantyzmu" *Zeszyty naukowe: Akademia muzyczna im. St. Moniuszki* 26 (1987) pp. 65–106. mus. summary in English. An analysis of 30 organ fugues by Mendelssohn, Brahms, Liszt, Franck, Schumann and Reger. [from S102]

4441. *Little, William A. "Brahms and the Organ: Redivivus: Some Thoughts and Conjectures" in *The Organist as Scholar: Essays in Memory of Russell Saunders.* Kerala J. Snyder, ed. (Festschrift Series 12) Stuyvesant, NY: Pendragon Press, 1994. pp. 273–97. notes.

4442. *Lukas, Viktor. *Reclams Orgelmusikführer.* Stuttgart: Philipp Reclam Jun., 1963.
    *2., neubearbeitete und erweiterte Auflage: 1967.
    3., neubearbeitete und erweiterte Auflage: 1975. (Universal-

Works   289

Bibliothek Nr. 8880–87) "Johannes Brahms": pp. 147–49.
mus. Brief descriptive analyses for all works.
5., revidierte und erweiterte Auflage: 1986. (Universal-Bibliothek
Nr. 8880) "Johannes Brahms": pp. 214–16. adds notes.
(b) English translation by Anne Wyburd (from the 5. Auflage):
Lukas. *A Guide to Organ Music*. With Addenda by Lee Garrett . . . Reinhard G. Pauly, General Ed. Portland: Amadeus
Press, 1989. "Johannes Brahms": pp. 124–25. mus., notes.

4443. Pascall, Robert. "Brahms' Orgelwerke" Monika Lichtenfeld,
trans. in *Johannes Brahms: Leben und Werk* [for full citation see
3215] pp. 123–24. mus. Overview of all works, focusing on Op.
122. Includes comment on Brahms as a composer for the organ,
his techniques, and his use of counterpoint.

4444. *Schroeder, H. "Die Orgelkompositionen von Johannes Brahms"
Musica sacra 103 (1983) pp. 196–201.

4445. *Vogt, Klaus. "Ideologiegeschichtliche Aspekte zum Verhältnis
zwischen Orgel und Komponist im 19. Jahrhundert" in *Orgel und
Ideologie: Orgelschrifttum des Barock*. Murrhardt: Musikwissenschaftliche Verlags-Gesellschaft, 1984. pp. 117–32. Investigates the ways in which the organ was a musical medium of
the 19th century and what connotations were associated with it.
Pays particular attention to works of Brahms, Schumann,
Mendelssohn, Bruckner and Liszt. [from S102]

4445.3. See also 3381.a.vii., 3383, 4037, 4050, 5062, 5170.

Specific

See also "Op. 27 The 13th Psalm for 3 part Women's Choir" in Part
IV.B.2. *"Specific."*

Op. 122 [posthumous] Eleven Chorale Preludes for Organ

4445.5. *Bertram, Hans Georg. "Zu dem Choralvorspiel "O wie selig
seid Ihr doch, Ihr frommen" (op. 122, 6) von Johannes Brahms"
Württembergische Blätter für Kirchenmusik 52/5 (1985) pp.
154–55.

4446. *Brahms, Johannes [transcribed by Gerald Heierman]. "A Transcription of Brahm's Eleven Chorale Preludes for Clarinet Choir"

D.M.A. diss., University of Rochester, 1970. iii, 64, 84 pp. mus. (last segment of paging is for the score), notes.

4447. Gehring, Philip. "Discussion of Three Pieces on the CAGO Repertoire List for 1992–93" *The American Organist* 25/10 (10.1991) pp. 90–92. Brahms: pp. 90–91. mus., notes. Includes comments on form, chorale text, aspects of performance practice, registration.

4448. May, Stephen M. "Tempo in Brahms' Op. 122" *The Diapason* 82/3 (Whole no. 976) (3.1991) pp. 12–14. notes. Attempts to establish a convention regarding tempi for the individual pieces by looking historically at the chorale tune convention in the 17th–19th centuries. Also examines organ notation, and speculates that these works were not ready for publication.

4449. Owen, Barbara. "Brahms's "Eleven": Classical Organ Works in a Romantic Age" *Journal of Church Music* 25/9 (11.1983) pp. 5–9. ill. (issue cover), facsim., fig., notes. Contends that these works are not romantic and looks at their character and style, and Brahms's life and how all this points to a conservative, classical framework. Also conjectures that the organ at the Maximiliankirche in Düsseldorf, Germany, is a probable representative of the type of organ that Brahms was writing for.

4450. *Rees, John Walter. "Analysis" M.Mus.Ed. diss., Oberlin College, 1972. 2 vols. mus. (vol. 2), notes (vol. 1). Op. 122 nos. 9 and 10 are among works analysed. [from S031]

4451. Reinhard, Karen. "A Rigorous Analysis of the Brahms Chorale Preludes 2–7 for Organ, Opus 122" D.Music diss., Organ Performance, Northwestern University, 1986. iv, 70 pp. mus., fig., notes. Purpose of analysis is to determine the technical means that Brahms uses in interpreting the chorale texts or portraying their general substance. Includes complete German text and English translation of all chorale texts, and comments on Brahms's attitude towards religion.

4452. *Shaw, John Abbott. "The Eleven Chorales Op. 122 Johannes Brahms" M.A. diss., Music, University of Victoria, 1990. viii, 156, [2] pp. mus., notes.

4452.3. See also S060, 3383, 4042, 4050, 4439, 4443, 5005, 5192–94.

Chorale Prelude and Fugue for Organ on "O Traurigkeit, o Herzeleid" [McCorkle WoO 7]

4452.6. See 4864, 4924.

4452.9. See "Organ Works—General" in Part IV.A.2.c.

Fugue for Organ in A flat minor [McCorkle WoO 8]

4453. Hartmann, Günter. "Zur Orgelfuge in as-Moll von Johannes Brahms" *Brahms-Studien* Bd. 7 (1987) pp. 9–19. mus., fig., notes. Surveys previous writings on this piece and then conducts a structural analysis on the Bach motif and its permutations which is the basis for this piece.

4454. *Sampson, Edward Allen. "Fugue in As-Moll" D.M.A. diss., Music, Stanford University, 1971. 21, [2, 4] pp. mus., notes.

4454.1. See 4864, 4924.

4454.3. See also "Organ Works—General" in Part IV.A.2.c.

Prelude and Fugue for Organ in A minor [McCorkle WoO posthum 9]

4454.5. See 3383, 4864, 4924.

4454.6. See "Organ Works—General" in Part IV.A.2.c.

Prelude and Fugue for Organ in G minor [McCorkle WoO posthum 10]

4454.7. See 3383, 4924.

4454.9. See "Organ Works—General" in Part IV.A.2.c.

3. Orchestral Music

a. Orchestral Works

General

4455. *L'Avant-scène opera operette musique,* see 5484.

4456. *Andrieux, Françoise. "Le Thème dans les formes sonate des symphonies de Brahms" *Analyse musicale* 13 (10.1988) pp. 58–68. mus. summary in English. Looks at Brahms's approach to the concept of theme, relative to the work of Beethoven. [from S102]

4457. *Bartlett, Dale L. "Effect of Repeated Listenings on Structural Discrimination and Affective Response" *Journal of Research in Music Education* 21/4 (Winter 1973) pp. 302–17. notes. Symphonic works of Brahms and Schubert are used in a study among non-musical people to investigate relationships between discrimination of musical structure and affective response. No relationship was found. [from S102]

4458. *Beller-McKenna, Daniel. "Reconsidering the Identity of an Orchestral Sketch by Brahms" *The Journal of Musicology: JM* 13/4 (1995) pp. 508+ .

4459. Berger, Melvin. "Johannes Brahms" in Berger. *The Anchor Guide to Orchestral Masterpieces.* First Anchor Books ed. New York [et al.]: Anchor Books, 1995. pp. [54]–69. discog. (p. 342). Background, descriptive analysis and comment on place in repertoire provided for Opp. 15, 56a, 68, 73, 77, 80, 81, 83, 90, 98, 102; includes introduction to Brahms's life that covers up to the 1850's and comments on Brahms the man and composer.

4459.5. *Bookspan, Martin. (Basic Repertoire Series) *Stereo Review* (1960–68).

    d) expanded and updated: Bookspan. "Johannes Brahms" in Bookspan. *101 Masterpieces of Music and Their Composers.* Garden City, NY: Doubleday & Company, Inc., 1968. pp. [87]–113. ind., discog (pp. 471–72). Overview of life and works, background and descriptive comments on Opp. 15, 68, 73, 77, 83, 90, 98, 102; includes comments on recommended recordings.

        revised and updated: Dolphin Books edition. (A Dolphin Reference Book) 1973. pp. [85]–111. Discography is absorbed into the prose text.

4460. [Brahms, Johannes. *Variations on a Theme by Joseph Haydn, Op. 56a; Symphony no. 1 in C minor, Op. 68.* London Classical Players; Roger Norrington, conductor. (EMI Classics; Reflexe) EMI, 1991. CDC 7 54286 2. 1 compact disc. Program notes by Roger

Norrington in English with German and French translations (27 pp.) in container. [from S031]]

(d) i) ["Brahms's First Symphony"] *The American Brahms Society Newsletter* 11/1 (Spring 1993) pp. [1]–7. ill.

Norrington, Roger. "Performing Brahms's Symphonies with Period Instruments" [George [S.] Bozarth, ed.] pp. [1]–3. Discusses whether it is a valid exercise to perform in period. Explains differences in size and sitting of orchestra; tells how he relied on comments from Joachim and Henschel and other contemporary information sources. Adapted from commentary accompanying the recording.

Knapp, Raymond. "A Review of Norrington's Brahms" [George [S.] Bozarth, ed.] pp. 4–7. Examines the pros and cons of Norrington's approach (tempi, balance, dynamics). Also narrows in on features of the music itself, and Norrington's approach to these features.

(d) ii) Norrington, Roger. "Aimez-vous Brahms?" *Gramophone* 69/821 (10.1991) pp. 67–68. Describes the challenges in preparing for this recording. Discusses whether accuracy is important considering how relatively recently these works were composed. Includes comment on playing techniques and styles of that day, and some background on Op. 68.

(e) i) review: *Gramophone* 69/821 (10.1991) p. 75.

(e) ii) report: Stearns, David Patrick. "Back to the Future" *Opera News* 56/7 (21.12.1991) pp. 16–18. Also discusses Norrington's preparations for recording Brahms's Op. 45.

4460.5. *"Brahms: symphonies and piano concertos" *American Record Guide* 52/3 (5.–6.1989) pp. 8+ . ill.

4461. *The Cambridge Companion to the Clarinet.* Colin Lawson, ed. (Cambridge Companions to Music) Cambridge, New York: Cambridge University Press, 1995. xiv, [3] 2–240 pp. ill., ind., notes. Brahms et passim. Discusses history of recordings of Brahms works; also tips and suggestions for performing Opp. 68, 83, 90, 98, and material on Brahms and Mühlfeld.

4462. Chasins, Abram. "Brahms in D minor and B flat" in Chasins. *Speaking of Pianists.* 3rd ed. with a New Preface. (Da Capo Paperback) New York: Da Capo Press, 1981. pp. 240–45. ind. New edition of 1784. Recollects performances of Opp. 15 and 83.

4463. *Chion, Michel. *La Symphonie à l'époque romantique: de Beethoven à Mahler.* (Collection les chemins de la musique) Paris: Fayard, 1994. 256 pp. ind., notes.

4464. Chissell, Joan. "The Symphonic Concerto: Schumann, Brahms and Dvořák" in *A Companion to the Concerto.* Robert Layton, ed. London: Christopher Helm, 1988. pp. 152–76. "Brahms": pp. 159–68. ind., notes, discog. Looks at where the concertos lie in Brahms's life, provides descriptive comments and analysis.
   *also: New York: Schirmer Books, 1989.

4465. Christen, Norbert. "Die Konzerte" in *Johannes Brahms: Leben und Werk.* [for full citation see 3215] pp. 133–34. Presents the background to each work, and comments on their composition.

4466. *Cuyler, Louise. *The Symphony.* 2nd ed. (Detroit Monographs in Musicology/Studies in Music 16) Warren, MI: Harmonie Park Press, 1995. New edition of 1786.

4467. Del Mar, Norman. *Orchestral Variations. Confusion and Error in the Orchestral Repertoire.* London: Eulenburg Books, 1981. xvi, 240 pp. Brahms: pp. xiv, xv, 67–72. Intent of work is to point out confusions, omissions, errors between editions of the same work or different reprints of a single edition. A comparative survey of changes in Op. 16 edition between original and revised versions of score is presented; includes comment on Op. 77. Related to 1789 (N. Del Mar. *The Score* (1957; 1958)).

4468. Downes, Edward. "Johannes Brahms" in Downes. *The New York Philharmonic Guide to the Symphony.* New York: Walker and Company, 1976. pp. 174–204. mus. Descriptive analysis with some background for Opp. 11, 15, 16, 56a, 68, 73, 77, 80, 81, 83, 90, 98, 102.
   also: Downes. *Guide to Symphonic Music.* New York: Walker and Company, 1981.
   *paperback edition: 1981.

4469. Ellman, Donald. "The Symphony in Nineteenth-Century Germany" in *A Companion to the Symphony.* Robert Layton, ed. London [et al.]: Simon & Schuster, 1993. pp. [124]–54. Brahms: pp. 147–54. mus., ind., notes, discog. (p. 461). Descriptive comments on all 4 symphonies; includes examination of forms.

4470. Erlebach, Rupert. "Style in Pianoforte Concerto Writing" *Music & Letters* 17/2 (4.1936) pp. 131–39. Brahms: pp. 137, 138. Follows differences of style in composing this genre from Bach through Walton.

4471. *Farlow, Betsy C[lifford]., see 4906.

4472. *Finscher, L[udwig]. "La lotta con la tradizione: Johannes Brahms" in *Il mondo della sinfonia*. Milano: n.p., 1972.

4473. *Frisch, Walter [M.]. *Brahms, the four symphonies*. (Monuments of western music) New York: London: Schirmer Books; Prentice Hall International, 1996. xiv, 226 pp. mus., ind., notes.

4474. Hinson, Maurice. "Johannes Brahms" in Hinson. *Music for Piano and Orchestra. An Annotated Guide*. Bloomington: Indiana University Press, 1981. pp. 46–47. ind., notes. Descriptive analysis and performance comments for Opp. 15 and 83.
   Enlarged Edition, 1st Midland ed. "with supplement containing over 200 new entries": Bloomington and Indianapolis, 1993. "Johannes Brahms (1833–1897)": pp. 46–47, 323. Also includes information on editions.

4475. Ho, Allan Benedict. "The Late-Romantic Piano Concerto Finale: A Stylistic and Structural Analysis" Ph.D. diss., University of Kentucky, 1985. xii, 496, [5] pp.
   "Brahms: Concerto No. 1": pp. 56–60; also pp. 360–62. mus., fig. (pp. 361–62), notes, discog. Traces the revision of Op. 15's finale through 836 (Brahms *Briefwechsel*) and 1179 (C. Schumann. *Clara Schumann. Johannes Brahms. Briefe . . .* (1927)); includes tabular analysis of Opp. 15 and 83.
   (d) see: 3353.

4476. Hopkins, Antony. *Talking About Concertos. An Analytical Study of a Number of Well-known Concertos from Mozart to the Present Day*. Belmont, CA: Wadsworth Publishing Company Inc., 1964. 148 pp. Brahms: pp. 85–111. mus., ind., notes. Background and descriptive analysis for Opp. 15 and 77.
   (a) *reprint (?): as part of Hopkins. *Talking About Music: Symphonies, Concertos, and Sonatas*. Illustrated by J. Barkwith. London: Pan Books, 1977. 462 pp. ill., mus., ind., notes. Includes 4562. [from compiler]
   (d) Hopkins. "Brahms 1833–97" in *The Concertgoer's Companion*.

Volume 1: Bach to Haydn. London: J.M. Dent & Sons Ltd., 1984. pp. [123]–65. mus., notes. Descriptive comments on Opp. 15, 68, 73, 77, 83, 90, 98; includes comment on Brahms the man.

also: London & Melbourne: J.M. Dent & Sons Ltd., 1984. [new edition:] Hopkins. *The Dent Concertgoer's Companion.* [1993] total pp.: [12, 1] 2–651 pp. Reprints vols. 1 and 2 of *The Concertgoer's Companion.* in one volume. *paperback ed.: 1995. total pp.: 672 pp.

4477. *Horton, John. *La Musique d'orchestre de Brahms: symphonies, concerts, ouvertures.* Helene Le Moal, trans. La Calade: Actes Sud, 1989. 92 pp. mus. Translation of 1807 (J. Horton. *Brahms Orchestral Music.* (1968)).

4478. "Johannes Brahms" in *Lexikon Orchestermusik Romantik. [Vol. 1.] A-H.* Wulf Konold, ed. mit Beitragen von . . . (Serie Musik Piper·Schott 8226) Mainz: Schott; München: Piper, 1989. pp. 74–113. mus., notes. Begins with a short overview of Brahms up to 1862, his place in music history, his output as a composer. Entries for works have specifics on when written, first performed, the 1st edition, arrangements, orchestration and timing; includes movement-by-movement descriptive analysis.

AB [Alfred Beujean]: pp. 74–81, 89–93. Discusses Opp. 11, 56a, 68, 73.

KD [Klaus Döge]: pp. 81–88. Discusses Opp. 90, 98.

WK [Wulf Konold]: pp. 94–96, 101–13. Discusses Opp. 15, 16, 77, 83, 102. GE [Gottfried Eberle]: pp. 96–97. Discusses Op. 80.

BR [?]: pp. 98–101. Discusses Op. 81 and McCorkle WoO 1 (nos. 1, 3, 10) arranged for orchestra.

4479. *Knapp, Raymond. "Brahms and the Problem of the Symphony: Romantic Image, Generic Conception, and Compositional Challenge" Ph.D. diss., Musicology, Duke University, 1987. 619 pp. A careful study of the symphonies to ascertain compositional problems and how Brahms circumvented them. Examines related orchestral works, the literature and relevant manuscripts from A-Wgm, A-Wn, A-Wst, US-NYpm. Includes comments on importance of symphonic form to Brahms, his orchestrations, and an appendix with over 120 contemporary reviews of his orchestral music. [from S081]

4479.5. Kramer, Jonathan D. "Johannes Brahms" in Kramer. *Listen to the*

Music. A Self-Guided Tour Through the Orchestral Repertoire. New York: Schirmer Books; London: Collier Macmillan Publishers, 1988. pp. 137–71. notes. Provides background and descriptive analysis; adapted from program notes written by the author for Cincinnati Symphony Orchestra concerts, 1980–89.

4480. Kretzschmar, Hermann. "The Brahms Symphonies" Susan Gillespie, trans. in *Brahms and His World*. [for full citation see 5478] pp. 123–43. mus., notes. Translated from 1353 (H. Kretzschmar. *Führer durch den Concertsaal*. (1887)).

4481. Kross, Siegfried. "Johannes Brahms—Der Sinfoniker" *Brahms-Studien* Bd. 5 (1983) pp. 65–89. mus., notes. Surveys Brahms's life from 1853–97 focusing and discussing Brahms as a composer of symphony-scale works (Op. 15 and the symphonies). Descriptive analysis with some background, also reaction to each work from contemporaries.

(b) English translation: Kross. "Brahms the Symphonist" in *Brahms: Biographical, Documentary and Analytical Studies*. [for full citation see 5479] pp. 125–45. adds ind.

4482. *Litzenburg, Deborah Ann. "The Sonata-Allegro Form in the Late Romantic Period as Exemplified in Selected Symphonies of Brahms, Bruckner and Mahler" M.A. diss., Music, University of Pennsylvania, 1961. 74 pp. mus., fig., notes.

4483. *Magruder, Richard J. "The Brahms Symphonies" *Disques* (Philadelphia) 1/8 (10.1930) pp. 294–98.

4484. Mordden, Ethan. "Johannes Brahms 1833–1897" in Mordden. *A Guide to Orchestral Music. The Handbook for Non-Musicians*. New York, Oxford: Oxford University Press, 1980. pp. 221–32. ind. Descriptive comments for 11, 15, 16, 56a, 68, 73, 77, 80, 81, 83, 90, 98, 102.

*Paperback ed.: 1986. (Oxford Paperback Reference) adds mus.

4485. Nelson, Wendell. "The romantic concerto" in Nelson. *The Concerto*. (The Brown Music Horizons Series) Dubuque: Wm. C. Brown Company Publishers, 1969. pp. 49–87.

"Brahms": pp. 66–76. ind., notes. Descriptive analysis for Opp. 15, 77, 83, 102; mostly on the first two works.

4486. *Nemirovskaîa, I[zabella]. "O printsipe simfonicheskogo kontrdeystviîa" *Sovetskaia muzyka* [47]/8 (8.1983) pp. 105–07. notes.

Examines the symphonies of Brahms and Tschaikovsky, pointing out similarities in the development of dramatic conflict. [from S102]

4487. Pistone, Danièle. *La Symphonie dans l'Europe du XIXe siècle (histoire et langage)*. (Musique-Musicologie 3) Paris: Librairie Honoré Champion, 1977. Brahms: pp. [58]–61; also et passim. fig. (pp. 58–59), ind., notes. total paging: 189 pp. Presents information on symphonies in chart format, also some descriptive comments. Symphonies used as examples in discussion of form and structure (pp. 143–49) and in discussion of thematic development and tonality (pp. 156–61).

2ième édition, revue et augmentée: (Musique-Musicologie MM3) 1984. total paging: 189 pp.

4488. Pociej, Bohdan. "Symfonia romantyczna ([Part] 3)" in Pociej. "Symfonia ([Part] 7)" (Historia muzyki. Formy ([Part] 73)) *Ruch muzyczny* 31/5 (1.3.1987) pp. [13–16].

"Brahms": pp. [13–14]. ill. Descriptive comments with details on background, first performances, instrumentation, also includes comments on the works as they show the classical and romantic music.

4489. Rattalino, Piero. "Johannes Brahms" in Rattalino. *Il concerto per pianoforte e orchestra. Da Haydn a Gershwin.* (Guide alla musica) [Firenze:] Ricordi/Giunti, 1988. pp. 235–42. Discusses Opp. 15 and 83, mostly on latter; reviews background of works and who of Brahms's contemporaries played them. Also pp. 69–71, 95–97 includes discussion of Brahms in an overview of the development of the concerto form.

4489.5. *Reddick, William. *The Standard Musical Repertoire with Accurate Timings.* New York: Doubleday & Company, Inc., 1947.

(a) reprint: New York: Greenwood Press, 1969. [4], 5–192 pp. Brahms: pp. 36–41. Timings for Opp. 11, 56a, symphonies, and McCorkle WoO 1 nos. in orchestral arrangement: goes movement-by-movement and has different conductors' versions of individual works.

4490. *Reidy, John. "Counterpoint in the Symphonies of Brahms" Ph.D. diss., Musicology, Trinity College, [198–?].

4491. *Rickenbacher, K.A. "Brahms et la symphonie" *Diapason* (Paris) no. 390 (2.1993) pp. 32–37.

4492. Rienäcker, Gerd. "Nachdenken über Brahms' Sinfonien" *Musik und Gesellschaft* 33/5 (5.1983) pp. 263–69. ill., facsim., notes. Thoughts on various movements from the symphonies, looking at form, motif, and theme.

4493. *Roeder, Michael Thomas. *A History of the Concerto*. Portland: Amadeus Press, 1994. 480 pp. ind., notes.

4494. *Rossini, Paolo. "La componente liederistica nella musica sinfonica" in *I Lieder di Johannes Brahms*. [for full citation see 4677] pp. 141–67.

4495. *Roth, William Gardner. "An Analysis of the More Signal Values of Expression in the Symphonies of Brahms" M.A. diss., University of Minnesota, 1945. ill., mus., notes.

4496. *Salmenhaara, Erkki. *Löytöretkiä musiikkiin; valittuja kirjoituksia 1960–1990*. Helsinki: Gaudeamus 1991. 390 pp. [Contains selections from original materials collected in 1827 (?) (E. Salmenhaara. *Tutkielmia brahmsin sinfonioista*. (1979))] [from compiler]

4497. Sanborn, [John] Pitts. *Brahms and Some of His Works*. [New York:] The Philharmonic-Symphony Society of New York, 1940. 32 pp. ill., mus. Background and descriptive analysis for Opp. 15, 56a, 68, 73, 77, 80, 81, 83, 98, 102.

4498. *Schipperges, Thomas. "Die kammermusikalische Serenade zwischen Beethoven und Dohnanyi/Reger" Phil.F. diss., Ruprecht-Karls-Universität Heidelberg, 1988.
(a) reprint: Schipperges. "Johannes Brahms" in Schipperges. *Serenaden zwischen Beethoven und Reger. Beiträge zur Geschichte der Gattung*. (Europäische Hochschulschriften =Publications universitaires Européennes=European University Studies. Reihe=Série=Series 36. Musikwissenschaft =Musicologie=Musicology 39) Frankfurt am Main [et al.]: Peter Lang, 1989. pp. [170]–236. mus., fig., notes. Discusses Opp. 11 and 16. Mostly analysis but also includes background, compares each to the other, and looks at their links to older music: Haydn (Op. 11) and Mozart (Op. 16).

4499. *Schneider-Kohnz, Brigitte. "Motiv und Thema in den Orchesterwerken von Johannes Brahms" Phil.F. diss., Universität des Saarlandes, 1982. v, 209 pp.

4500. Seedorf, Thomas. "Brahms' 1. Symphonie. Komponieren als Auseinandersetzung mit der Geschichte" *Musik und Bildung* 15/5 (Bd. 74) (5.1983) pp. 10–14. übersicht: p. 2. mus., fig., notes. Discusses the "trial runs" before Brahms completed the first symphony: Opp. 11, 15, 16.

4501. *Sollertinskii, Ivan Ivanovich. *Chetvertaîa simfoniîa Bramsa.* (Putevoditel po kontsertam) [Leningrad:] Leningradskaîa Filarmonika, 1935. 22 pp. ill., mus.

4502. Stedman, Preston. "Johannes Brahms (1833–1897)" in Stedman. *The Symphony.* 2nd ed. Englewood Cliffs, NJ: Prentice Hall, 1992. pp. 140–58. ill., mus., ind., notes. New edition of 1840. Discusses Brahms's symphonic style, indepth analysis of Op. 68 and survey of other works; includes comment on Brahms's contribution to the symphonic form.

4503. Steinbeck, Susanne. *Die Ouvertüre in der Zeit von Beethoven bis Wagner. Probleme und Lösungen.* (Freiburger Schriften zur Musikwissenschaft 3) München: Musikverlag Emil Katzbichler, 1973. 170 pp. mus., notes.
    Brahms: pp. 108–11. Analyses Op. 81 relevant to shortened sonata form.
    Brahms: pp. 139–42. Compares Op. 80 and 81 to the traditional sonata-form overture.

4504. Steinberg, Michael [P.]. "Johannes Brahms" in Steinberg. *The Symphony. A Listener's Guide.* New York, Oxford: Oxford University Press, 1995. pp. [67]–91. mus., notes. Provides descriptive comments and details on background, tempi, instrumentation. Revised and rewritten from Boston Symphony Orchestra. *Program Book Notes* (1976–79).

4505. Stellfeld, Bent. "Kontrapunktik og dens funktion i Brahms's orkesterværker" *Dansk Årbog for Musikforskning* 14 (1983) pp. [115–32]. mus., fig., notes. Analytical discussion with examples drawn from the works, includes references to the chamber music, and Op. 45.

4506. *Stengel, Theophil. "Die Entwicklung des Klavierkonzerts von Liszt bis zur Gegenwart" Phil.F. diss., Ruprecht-Karls-Universität Heidelberg, 1931. 146 pp.
    (a) reprint: Stengel. "Brahms und seine Nachfolger" in Stengel.

Die Entwicklung des Klavierkonzerts von Liszt bis zur Gegenwart. Heidelberg: Neuenheimer Musikhaus Reiher & Kurth, 1931. pp. 99–109. mus., ind., notes. Discusses Brahms as a proponent of absolute music, presents background and descriptive comments on Opp. 15 and 83, discusses Brahms's followers and their piano concertos.

4507. *Stevens, H[enry]. C[harles]. *Brahms: Symphonies.* (Decca Music Guides Series 3) n.p.: Cassell, 1952. 31 pp. ill.

4507.5. *Tovey, Donald Francis. *Symphonies and Other Orchestral Works.* (D.F. Tovey. *Essays in Musical Analysis* [1]) Oxford, New York: Oxford University Press, 1989. Reprint of 1372 (D.F. Tovey. *Essays . . . Vol. 1.* (1981)) with an index.

4508. *Tsareva, E[katerina]. "O simfonicheskoy kontseptsii" *Sovetskaia muzyka* [47]/8 (8.1983) pp. 98–105. ill., notes. Views Brahms's symphonies as a revival of the classical symphony. [from S102]

4509. Ulrich, Homer. "Johannes Brahms" in Ulrich. *Symphonic Music: Its Evolution Since the Renaissance.* New York: Columbia University Press, 1952. pp. [201]–19. mus., ind., notes. Most of the article is descriptive comments and background on the symphonies; includes comments on other symphonic works, including concertos, also on Brahms as a classical composer.

4510. *Wannamaker, Mary Ruth. "A Study of the Two Piano Concertos of Brahms with Emphasis on Expressive Content" M.A. diss., University of Minnesota, 1949. 193 pp. ill., notes.

4511. *Wells, Eleanor Ruth. "The Symphonies of Brahms" M.A. diss., Claremont Colleges, 1943. 19 pp. notes.

4512. Zilberkant, Edward. "The Piano Concerti of Johannes Brahms" M.M. diss., Bowling Green State University, 1989. viii, 52 pp. mus., notes. Accompanied by a video of interview-lesson on Op. 15 by Jerome Rose + audiocassette of both concerti performed by the author. [from S031]

4512.3. See also 3335, 3371, 3372, 3374, 3437, 3788, 3944, 4036, 4037, 4305.5, 4806, 4839, 4866, 4883, 4906, 4919, 4943, 5016, 5050, 5063, 5067, 5068, 5071, 5073, 5076, 5209, 5360, 5367.d.i.a., 5372.

4512.6. See also I35, I36 in Appendix A.

Specific

Op. 11 Serenade no. 1 in D major for Orchestra

4512.9. See 3352, 3358, 3378, 3477, 3598, 3692, 3840, 4041, 4042, 4468, 4477, 4478, 4484, 4489.5, 4498, 4500, 4509, 5112, 5158, 5181, 5345.

Op. 15 Piano Concerto no. 1 in D minor

4513. Badura-Skoda, Paul. "Fehler-Fehler! Einige Anmerkungen zu weitverbreiteten Fehlern in klassischen Notenausgaben" *Österreichische Musikzeitschrift* 42/2–3 (2.–3.1987) pp. 92–98. Brahms: pp. 93–95. facsim., mus. Comments on 2 places in the soloist's part in Op. 15, 3rd movement, where the edition needs to be rechecked against the manuscript.

4514. Böttinger, Peter. "Jahre der Krise, Krise der Form. Beobachtungen am 1. Satz des Klavierkonzertes op. 15 von Johannes Brahms" in *Aimez-vous Brahms "the progressive"*? [for full citation see 4872] pp. [41]–68. mus., fig., notes. Discusses this work as a reflection of Brahms's world; includes comment on Beethoven's influence in the work, also the contrapuntal and polyphonic techniques employed, and the role of form.

4515. Bozarth, George S. "Brahms's First Piano Concerto op. 15: Genesis and Meaning" in *Beiträge zur Geschichte des Konzerts. Festschrift Siegfried Kross zum 60. Geburtstag.* Reinmar Emans and Matthias Wendt, eds. Bonn: Gudrun Schröder Verlag, 1990. pp. [211]–47. facsim., mus., ind., notes. Reviews the documentary evidence associated with Op. 15 to better understand its conception and creation and to see if new avenues of inquiry are suggested. Links to Beethoven, E.T.A. Hofmann explored.

4516. Collier, Michael. "The Rondo Movements of Beethoven's Concerto No. 3 in C minor, Op. 37 and Brahms's Concerto No. 1 in D minor, Op. 15: A Comparative Analysis" *Theory and Practice* 3/1 (1978) pp. [5]–15. mus., fig., notes. Examines parallels between the two, looks at Beethoven's influence on Brahms.

4517. *Hildebrandt, Dieter. *Pianoforte oder der Roman des Klavier im 19. Jahrhundert.* München, Wien: Carl Hanser Verlag, 1985. 4. Auflage: 1986. "Vier Jahre im eigenen Labyrinth (Brahms)":

pp. [263]–80. ill., ind. covers 1853–56, reviews the background to Op. 15 and its evolution from piano sonata to concerto; also discusses Brahms meeting the Schumanns, Brahms and Clara Schumann.

(b) English translation by Harriet Goodman (of ? Auflage): Hildebrandt. "Four Years in His Own Labyrinth: Brahms" in Hildebrandt. *Pianoforte. A Social History of the Piano.* Introduction by Anthony Burgess. New York: George Braziller, 1988. pp. 128–36. ill. omitted, notes added.
*also: London: Hutchinson, 1988.

4518. *Johnson, Janet. "Brahm's Mozart: Sources of Classicism in the First Movement of Op. 15" M.A. diss., Music, University of California, Los Angeles, 1979. vi, 102 pp. mus., notes. Attempts to build a case for the form of the 1st movement of Op. 15 having been modeled on the 1st movement of Mozart's K466. [from 4515]

4519. *Musikgedeutet und gewertet: Dokumente zur Rezeptionsgeschichte von Musik.* Werner Klüppelholz and Hermann J. Busch, eds. Kassel: Deutscher Taschenbuch; Bärenreiter, 1983. ind., notes. Includes a study of the reception of Op. 15. [from S102]

4520. *Torgan, Janis. [Jānis Torgāns] "Fortepiannie koncerty Bramsa v svete évoljucii dannogo žanra v pervoi polovine XIX veka" Ph.D. diss., Piano, Institut iskusstvoznanîa, fol'klora i etnografii akademii nauk USSR, Kiev, 1978.
(d) *summary: 24 pp. Analyses imagery and style in the piano concertos; includes an historical survey. [from S102]

4521. *Underwood, Marianne. "Brahms Piano Concerto no. 1 in D minor: An Analysis" M.A. diss., Music Theory and Analysis, University of Ulster, 1990.

4521.3. See also 3251, 3267, 3287, 3353, 3358, 3363, 3368, 3378, 3381.a.i., 3477, 3550, 3563, 3578, 3598, 3692, 3827, 3889, 4036, 4038, 4041, 4042, 4046, 4048.a., 4062, 4064, 4070, 4071, 4075, 4078, 4080, 4082, 4085, 4088, 4459, 4459.5, 4460.5, 4462, 4464, 4465, 4468, 4470, 4474–78, 4479.5, 4481, 4484, 4485, 4489, 4493, 4497, 4500, 4506, 4509, 4510, 4512, 4520, 4866, 4903, 4929, 5002, 5007, 5037, 5038, 5048, 5112, 5125, 5127, 5158, 5160, 5164, 5188.d., 5232, 5345, 5396.

4521.7. See also I19 in Appendix A.

Op. 16 Serenade no. 2 in A major for Orchestra

4522. *Bowden, David. "Brahms' Serenade in A major, opus 16: origins, unity, and musical time" D.Mus. diss., Indiana University, 1992. xviii , 273 pp. mus., notes.

4522.5. See also 3411, 3477, 3598, 3692, 3840, 4041, 4042, 4467, 4468, 4477, 4478, 4484, 4498, 4500, 4509, 5037, 5064, 5112, 5158, 5345.

Op. 56a Variations for Orchestra on a Theme by Joseph Haydn

4523. *Brahms, Johannes [arranged by Bruce A. Morlock]. "A Band Transcription of Brahms' Variations on a Theme by Haydn" M.Mus. diss., Northern Illinois University, 1982. 72 pp.

4524. Haggin, B[ernard]. H. *Music for the Man Who Enjoys 'Hamlet'*. 1st ed. New York: Alfred A. Knopf, 1944. [4], 128, [1], ii pp. Brahms: pp. 25–34. mus., ind., discog. (p. 125). An aural analysis of Op. 56a emphasizing the orchestral textures and colours, and attention to theme and its reworkings. Includes details on where to find sections described on specific recordings.
*issue: 1945.
*also: London: D. Dobson, 1947.
*[2nd. revised ed.:] New York: Vintage Books, 1960.
*also: New York: Horizon, 1983.

4525. *Kabo, Linda. "A Study of Variation Technique in Brahm's Variations on a Theme by Joseph Hayden (sic), Op. 56a" M.A. diss., Music, Queens College (New York), 1972. [26] pp. + 10 charts.

4526. Magrill, Samuel Morse. "The Principle of Variation: A Study in the Selection of Differences with Examples from Dallapiccola, J.S. Bach and Brahms" D.M.A. diss., University of Illinois at Urbana-Champaign, 1983. x, 243 pp. mus., fig., notes. A comparative analysis of Bach's BWV 1004, Brahms's Op. 56a, and Dallapiccola's *Quarderno musicale di Annalibera* (1952).

4527. *Rice, James A. "A score and rehearsal analysis of the Variations on a Theme of Haydn by Johannes Brahms" M.A. diss., University of Washington, 1995. v, 61 pp. mus., notes.

4528. *Ross, Elaine M. "Analysis of Johannes Brahms' "Variations on

a Theme by Haydn"" M.M. diss., Music Theory, Michigan State
University, 1990. vi, 94 pp. ill., mus., notes.

4529. Stein, Leon. *Structure and Style. The Study and Analysis of Musical Forms.* Evanston, IL: Summy-Birchard Company, 1962. xix,
[3], 3–266 pp. Brahms: pp. 96–98. Discusses the variation treatments/procedures seen in Op. 56a.

4529.3. See also S060, 3267, 3358, 3381.a.ii., 3410, 3477, 3598, 3840,
4041, 4042, 4047, 4051, 4086, 4459, 4460, 4468, 4477, 4478,
4479.5, 4484, 4489.5, 4497, 4509, 4880, 4931, 4989, 5112, 5158,
5174, 5175.

4529.7. See also I20, I30 in Appendix A.

Op. 68 Symphony no. 1 in C minor

4530. *Le Guide du concert* 10/3 (10.1923) pp. 43–44.

4531. *Musical America* 57 (?) (11.1937 (?)) p. 10.

4532. *The World. A Journal for Men and Women* [no. 181] (23.12.
1877).
(a) reprint: "Music in New York" *Dwight's Journal of Music* 37/20
(Whole no. 958) (5.1.1878) p. 160. Critics' remarks on the
American premiere of Op. 68 (by Leopold Damrosch) and a
performance of Op. 68 a week later (by Theodore Thomas): assessment of the work and comparison of the two performances.
(a) reprint: "Brahms in America. First Hearings" *The American Brahms Society Newsletter* 10/2 (Autumn 1992) pp.
7–8. ill.
(d) see: 4537.

4533. *Berry, Wallace. "Brahms, Symphony No. 1 in C minor, Op. 68,
First Movement (Un poco sostenuto); Introduction" in Berry.
Structural Functions in Music. Englewood Cliffs, NJ: Prentice-Hall, 1976.
(a) reprint with corrections by the author: New York: Dover Publications, Inc., 1987. pp. 266–80. mus., fig., ind., notes. Detailed analysis of the first 37 measures of first movement; considers textual features as pertaining to structure.

4534. Brahms, Johannes. *Symphony No. 1 in C Minor, Op. 68. The Autograph Score.* With an Introduction by Margit L. McCorkle,

Vancouver, Canada. (The Pierpont Morgan Library Music Manuscript Reprint Series) New York: The Pierpont Morgan Library in association with Dover Publications, Inc., 1986. ix, [1], 94 pp. notes. Facsimile of US-NYpm manuscript (movements 2–4 only); introduction presents provenance of the manuscript, background on the work, detailed information on prepublication performances and a detailed description and collation of the manscript.

4535. *Carozzo, Mario. "Le due versioni del secondo movimento della sinfonia n. 1 op. 68 di Johannes Brahms: un problema storiografico o analitico?" *Analisi: rivista di teoria e pedagogia musicale* 5/13 (1994) pp. 16–28.

4536. Christinat, Lukas. "Brahms Symphony No. 1, 4th Movement" (Orchestral Excerpt Clinic) *The Horn Call* 21/2 (4.1991) p. 89. mus., notes. Discusses how to play the horn solo, looks at its derivation from an alphorn melody.

4537. *Damrosch, Walter. *My Musical Life*. New York: Charles Scribner's Sons, 1923. viii, [2] 376 pp.
*issues: 1924, 1936, 1930.
*new edition: 1930 (?). viii, 390 pp.
*issues: 1935, 1940.
also: London: George Allen & Unwin Ltd., 1924. vii, [2], 376 pp.
(a) reprint (of New York 1923 edition): Westport, CT: Greenwood Press, 1972.
(c) excerpt (from New York 1930 issue or edition (?)): "Brahms in America" *The American Brahms Society Newsletter* 11/2 (Autumn 1993) p. 6. ill. Reprints sections that provide further details on the competition between Leopold Damrosch and Theodore Thomas to mount Op. 68 in the United States; also comments on the temperaments and conducting styles of the two men.

4538. *DAS [Adolph Schubring]. "Die Sinfonie von Johannes Brahms" *Echo. Berliner Musik-Zeitung* [27]/48 (22.11.1877) pp. 505–07.

4539. *Fink, Robert. "Desire, Repression & Brahms's First Symphony" *Repercussions* (Emeryville, CA) 2/1 (Spring 1993) p. 75.

4540. Friedel, Lance. "Tempo Relations in the Finale of Brahms's First Symphony" *Journal of the Conductors' Guild* 23/3&4 (Summer & Fall 1991) pp. 96–100. facsim., mus., notes. Examines the section where tempo changes from Adagio to Piu Andante to see if there is a mathematical relationship between the tempos, examines timpani part, looks at manuscripts and editions for background.

4541. Fuchs, Ingrid. "Zeitgenössische Aufführungen der ersten Symphonie Op. 68 von Johannes Brahms in Wien. Studien zur Wiener Brahms-Rezeption" in *Brahms-Kongress Wien 1983*. [for full citation see 5431] pp. 167–86. notes, appendix (pp. 489–515). Examines 80+ critiques in 58 different newspapers (dailies, weeklies) and music magazines for 6 performances of Op. 68 in Vienna, 1876–1897. Appendix contains transcripts of reviews. Looks at background of work, especially comments that describe the alterings that were done in the work.

4542. Haas, Frithjof. "Die Uraufführung der ersten Sinfonie von Johannes Brahms in Karlsruhe" in *Johannes Brahms in Baden-Baden und Karlsruhe* [for full citation see 5452] pp. 121–32. ill., facsim., mus., fig., notes. Describes the performance and the reaction in Karlsruhe. Points out differences between this version and final version in 2nd and 3rd movements and follows through to conclusion of creative process, 1 year later.
(d) Haas. "Die Erstfassung des langsamen Satzes der ersten Sinfonie von Johannes Brahms" *Die Musikforschung* 36/4 (10.–12.1983) pp. 200–11. mus. (pp. 205–11, plus in text), notes only. Presents the history of this version and how it compares with the 1877 edition.

4543. "In Case of Brahms, Exit Here . . ." *The American Brahms Society Newsletter* 13/2 (August 1995) p. [12]. Reprints excerpt of a concert review of Op. 68 from *Boston Daily Advertiser* (29.12. 1883).

4544. Knapp, Raymond. "Brahms's Revisions Revisited" *The Musical Times* 129/1749 (11.1988) pp. 584–88. mus., fig., notes. Speculates on the compositional process behind the 2nd movement, including description of an earlier version of the movement from which the first performing version was derived. Charts its transformation all the way to the 1877 edition; also looks at the weight and balance of the whole work.

4545. Kross, Siegfried. "Brahms und Bruckner. Über Zusammenhänge von Themenstruktur und Form" in *Bruckner Symposion* [for full

2

8 rt IV

citation see 5434] pp. 173–81. fig., notes. Compares Op. 68 and Bruckner's Symphony no. 5 to precisely define the typology of the symphonic works of both composers. [from S102]

4546. *Lambert, Lee. "Brahms, Johannes" in Lambert. *Basic Library of the World's Greatest Music. Master Volume.* Fort Lauderdale: Basic Library of the World's Greatest Music, [1995?].
*also: Textbook.
*also: Workbook.
*also: "Brahms' Symphony No. 1 in C Minor" [video] (Nature, Art and Music Series. X) [video + program lesson booklet].

4547. Leuba, [Julian] Christopher. "Johannes Brahms Symphony No. 1" (Orchestral Excerpt Clinic) *The Horn Call* 24/1 (11.1993) pp. 31–32. mus., fig. Performance suggestions for passages from the 2nd, 1st and 4th movements.

4548. Leuba, Julian Christopher. "Leuba's Loonie Tunes" *The Horn Call* 16/1 (10.1985) p. 87. Suggestions on how to get the right rhythmic stress in 4th movement solo by using a mneumonic device.

4549. Musgrave, Michael. "Brahms's First Symphony: Thematic Coherence and Its Secret Origins" *Music Analysis* 2/2 (7.1983) pp. 117–33. mus., notes. Examines how the work's evolution extended to thematic process; reviews work's background and unity between movements. Includes comment on Brahms and Clara Schumann and symbolism relating to them in the work.

4550. Musgrave, Michael. "Die erste Symphonie von Johannes Brahms: Stilistische und strukturelle Synthese" in *Probleme der symphonischen Tradition im 19. Jahrhundert. Report of the Internationales Musikwissenschaftliches Colloquium Bonn.* Siegfried Kross and Marie Luise Maintz, eds. Tutzing: Schneider, 1990. pp. 537–44. The lengthy evolution of Op. 68 is viewed in light of influence of Beethoven (on 1st movement) and Schubert (on 4th movement).

4551. *Pascall, Robert. *Brahms's First Symphony Andante—the Initial Performing Version: Commentary and Realisation.* (Papers in Musicology 2) [Nottingham:] Department of Music, University of Nottingham, 1992. 19, 26 pp. mus. [the 26 pp.], notes.

4552. Plattensteiner, Richard. "Vereint" in Plattensteiner. *Musikalische*

Gedichte. Dresden-Leipzig: Heinrich Minden-Verlag, 1927. p.
49. Poet is inspired by the finale of Op. 68.

4553. Ringer, Alexander L. ""Ende gut Alles gut." Bemerkungen zu
zwei Finalsätzen von Johannes Brahms und Gustav Mahler" in
Neue Musik und Tradition. [for full citation see 4626] pp.
[297]–309. mus., notes. Looks at quotations of and allusions to
other composers' music in the last movement of Op. 68 (Schumann
and Marschner) and in Mahler's Symphony No. 7 (Wagner).

4554. Robinson, Harold. "Brahms' First Symphony" (Different Strokes)
International Society of Bassists 17/2 (Winter/Spring 1991) pp.
38–40, 43–44, 47. mus. Discusses how to play 4 passages from
movements 1, 2 and 4.

4555. Rudel, Anthony J[ason]. "Brahms: Symphony No. 1 in C minor,
Op. 68" in Rudel. *Classical Music Top 40*. [Preface by Billy Joel]
[A Fireside Book edition] New York [et al.]: Simon & Schuster,
1995. pp. 91–97. Descriptive comments linked to timings of spe-
cific recordings, also includes suggestions for further listening in
Brahms works.

4556. *Scruggs, Anderson M. "First Symphony: Johannes Brahms" [be-
fore 1951].
(a) reprint: in Scruggs. *What Shall the Heart Remember*. (S. Price
Gilbert Contemporary Poetry Series) Athens, GA: University
of Georgia Press, 1951. p. 26. Poem; what Op. 68 evokes in
the poet.

4557. *[Brahms, Johannes.] *Symphonic Score Guide. Brahms: Symphony no. 1 in C minor* ... Olga Samaroff Stokowski, ed. Philadelphia: Elkan-Vogel Co. Inc., 1942. 6, 166 pp.

4558. "Symphonies of Johannes Brahms" *The Metronome* 23/11
(11.1907) p. 16. Descriptive analysis of Op. 68; includes comments on Brahms the composer, especially his classical roots.

4558.3. See also 3250, 3251, 3260, 3267, 3276, 3287, 3358, 3363, 3368,
3378, 3379, 3411, 3598, 3653.2, 3779, 3832, 3840, 3944, 3988,
4036, 4038, 4040–42, 4046, 4047, 4048.a., 4371, 4455, 4456,
4459–61, 4466, 4468, 4469, 4473, 4476.d., 4477–81, 4483, 4484,
4487, 4488, 4489.5, 4490, 4491, 4495, 4497, 4502, 4504, 4507,
4509, 4511, 4594, 4596, 4879, 4889.d., 4906, 4929, 4931, 4944,

4955, 4956, 4966, 4979, 4981, 4989, 5022, 5028, 5037, 5048, 5066, 5077, 5112, 5158, 5160, 5174, 5181, 5232, 5326, 5396.

4558.7. See also I40 in Appendix A.

Op. 73 Symphony no. 2 in D major

4559. *[The Editor] *Gramophone* [2/14] (11.1924). Observations on recent recordings of Op. 73 and speculation on the role of the magazine in getting the work recorded. [from (e)]
(e) report: Sanders, Alan. "Hindsight November" *Gramophone* 72/858 (11.1994) p. 272. "1924".

4560. *"Brahms' New Symphony" *Musical Record* (Boston) [no. 2?] (11.1878(?)) p. 83.

4561. Brinkmann, Reinhold. *Johannes Brahms. Die zweite Symphonie: Späte Idylle.* (Musik-Konzepte 70) München: edition text + kritik, 1990. 123 pp. mus., fig., notes. Background and analysis for this work; addresses the question of whether this work is really idyllic.
(b) English translation by Peter Palmer: Brinkmann. *Late Idyll: The Second Symphony of Johannes Brahms.* Cambridge, London: Harvard University Press, 1995. ix, [6] 2–241 pp. adds ind. "Slightly expanded and revised."
(e) report: Botstein, Leon. "Embracing the Gift of Life" *TLS. The Times Literary Supplement* no. 4842 (19.1.1996) pp. 20–21. Also discusses vol. 1 of 5498.
(c) Brinkmann, Reinhold. "Die "heitre Sinfonie" und der "schwer melancholische Mensch": Johannes Brahms antwortet Vincenz Lachner" *Archiv für Musikwissenschaft* 46/4 ([10.–12.] 1989) pp. 292–306. notes. Looks at three letters between the two men (2, Lachner to Brahms, 8.1879; 1, Brahms to Lachner, 8.1879) where Brahms discusses how to interpret the first movement of Op. 73.

4562. Hopkins, Antony. *Talking About Symphonies. An Analytical Study of a Number of Well-known Symphonies from Haydn to the Present Day.* London, Melbourne, Toronto: Heinemann, 1961. 157 pp. Brahms: pp. 108–25. mus., ind. Descriptive analysis of Op. 73. *issue: 1967.

*also: London: Mercury Books, 1964.
(a) *reprint (?): in 4476.a.
(d) see: 4476.d.

4563. *Lee, Morris Franklin. "A Research Design of the Brahms Symphony No. 2" M.M. diss., University of Utah, 1965. iii, 68 pp. mus., notes.

4564. Schachter, Carl. "The First Movement of Brahms's Second Symphony: the Opening Theme and Its Consequences" *Music Analysis* 2/1 (3.1983) pp. 55–68. fig., notes. Describes how motivic contents and character of opening theme influence the structure and form of the 1st movement's exposition.
(d) related to: 5449.5.

4565. Steinbeck, Wolfram. "Liedthematik und symphonischer Prozeβ. Zum ersten Satz der 2. Symphonie" in *Brahms-Analysen*. [for full citation see 4888] pp. 166–82. mus., notes. Analyses how Brahms takes the 1st movement motif and incorporates it into symphonic form by using 'developing variation.'

4566. *Tovey, Donald Francis. "La seconda sinfonia in re maggiore op. 73 di Brahms" in Ian Bent and William Drabkin. *Analisi musicale*. Italian edition. Claudio Annibaldi, ed.; Claudio Annibaldi and Francesca Vacca, transs. Torino: EDT, 1990. pp. 158–71. This is a translation of material in 1372A (D.F. Tovey. *Essays in Musical Analysis*. vol. 1. (1935)) (?).

4566.5. See also S060, 3251, 3287, 3294, 3358, 3363, 3368, 3378, 3379, 3578, 3598, 3762, 3840, 4038, 4040–42, 4046, 4047, 4048.a., 4455, 4456, 4459, 4459.5, 4460.5, 4466, 4468, 4469, 4473, 4476.d., 4477–81, 4483, 4484, 4487, 4488, 4489.5, 4490, 4491, 4495, 4497, 4502, 4504, 4507, 4509, 4511, 4593, 4594, 4596, 4890, 4906, 4931, 4954, 4964, 4966, 4971, 4979, 4980, 5022, 5028, 5066, 5077, 5112, 5158, 5160, 5174, 5181, 5232, 5235, 5326, 5396.

Op. 77 Violin Concerto in D major

4567. Auer, Leopold. "The Three Master-Concertos of Violin Literature" in Auer. *Violin Master Works and Their Interpretation*. With a Foreword by Frederick H. Martens . . . New York [et al.]: Carl Fischer, Inc., 1925. pp. 93–104. Brahms: pp. 101–03. Suggestions for performance and some descriptive analysis.

(a) reprint: (Encore Music Editions) Westport, CT: Hyperion Press, Inc., 1979.

4568. *Bachmann, Alberto. "The Concerto in D major by Johannes Brahms, Op. 77 (1833–1897)" in Bachmann. *An Encyclopedia of the Violin.* Introduction by Eugene Ysaÿe. Frederick H. Martens, trans. Albert E. Wier, ed. New York, London: D. Appleton-Century Company, 1925.
   issue: 1937. pp. 246–55. ill., mus. total pp.: xiv, [2], 470 pp. Presents analysis with some performance suggestions.
   (a) *reprint (of 1937 edition): Preface to the Da Capo Edition by Stuart Canin. New York: Da Capo Press, 1966.
   (a) *paperback reprint: 1975.
   issue: 1986. mus. only. total pp.: [5], p. vi, [6], xi–xiv, [2], 470 pp.

4569. Barbier, Pierre-E. "Le Concerto pour violon et orchestre de Brahms" (Le Point sur) *Diapason* (Paris) no. 283 (5.1983) pp. 38–39. discog. A comparative discography for Op. 77, includes descriptive analysis and some history of the work.

4570. *Beadle, J[eremy J.] "The Collector's Choice: Brahms's Violin Concerto" *Classic CD* no. 33 (2.1993) pp. 26–30.

4571. [Brahms, Johannes. *Ruggiero Ricci plays Brahms violin concerto* [Op. 77]. Ruggiero Ricci, violin; Sinfonia of London; Norman Del Mar, conductor. Biddulph Recordings, 1991. LAW 002. 1 compact disc. Recorded with the 1st movement cadenza by Ferruccio Busoni; also includes 15 alternate cadenzas by various violinists and composers, from Brahms's time through the 1930's. Biographical and program notes by Wayne Kiley ([12] p.) in container. [from S031]]
   (e) i) report: see 4570.
   (e) ii) report: Bozarth, George S. "[On Record:] Cadenza by . . ." *The American Brahms Society Newsletter* 10/1 (Spring 1992) p. 7. Focuses on evaluating the various cadenzas.
   (e) iii) report: see 4573.
   (e) iv) report: Foreman, Lewis. "Cadenzas: A Survey" *Gramophone* 70/833 (10.1992) pp. 33–34. ill. Reviews Op. 77 and the many different cadenzas written for it; examines the Joachim tradition. Discusses the issue of cadenzas for con-

certos being "inserted" by a different composer, with a look at McCorkle WoO posthum 12.

(e) v) report: Inglis, Anna. "16 Kadenzen zur Auswahl. Ruggiero Ricci und Brahms' Violinkonzert auf CD" *Das Orchester* (Hamburg) 40/5 (1992) p. 621.

4572. *Caroli, Angelo. *Brahms opera 77 : doppia morte in agguato.* Torino : D.Piazza, 1995. 236 pp. Novel. [from S031]

4573. Denton, David. "A Brahms tour de force" *The Strad* 103/1232 (12.1992) pp. 1205–06, 1208. ill. Compares recordings by 15 soloists.

4574. Lancastrian. "Arthur Catterall and the Brahms Concerto" *The Strad* 21/247 (11.1910) pp. 256–57. Letter to editor, very negative impressions of Op. 77.

(d) i) letter to the editor: Woof, Rowsby. "The Brahms Concerto" *The Strad* 21/248 (12.1910) p. 272. Rebuts Lancastrian's opinion with glowing comments of the work.

(d) continued: 4574.d.ii.

(d) ii) letter to the editor: S.O. ""Lancastrian" and the Brahms Violin Concerto" *The Strad* 21/250 (2.1911) pp. 365–66. Suggests Lancastrian should look at piece differently, try it with different soloists, etc.

(d) letter to the editor: Lancastrian. "The Brahms Violin Concerto. On Musical Criticism, and Personal" *The Strad* 21/252 (4.1911) pp. 446–48. Rebuffs both previous correspondents, sees Brahms as an intellectual composer only.

4575. Schwarz, Boris. "Joseph Joachim and the Genesis of Brahms's Violin Concerto" *The Musical Quarterly* 69/4 (Fall 1983) pp. 503–26. facsim., mus., notes. Traces the creative process behind Op. 77 through their friendship, especially Joachim's influence on the solo violin part. Examines US-Wc manuscript and other manuscripts, too.

(d) related to: 5449.5.

4576. Swalin, Benjamin F. "The Brahms Violin Concerto. A Stylistic Criticism" *Papers [read at the Annual Meeting] of the American Musicological Society* (1936) pp. [65]–77. mus., notes. Reprint of 1947 (B.F. Swalin. *Music Teachers National Association.* (1936)).

4577. *Wederquist, Marsha Jones. "The Brahms, Schumann and

Joachim Violin Concerti: An Analysis of Relationships" M.A. diss., University of Wyoming, 1961. 131 pp. mus., notes.

4578. *Weiss-Aigner, Günter. "Ohne Bruch-Konzert kein Brahms" *Neue Musikzeitung* 38 (6.–7.1989) p. 11.

4578.5. See also 3260, 3278, 3287, 3345, 3358, 3363, 3381.a.i., 3410, 3578, 3598, 3762, 3982, 4010, 4036, 4038, 4041, 4042, 4046, 4048.a., 4062, 4068, 4459, 4459.5, 4464, 4465, 4467, 4468, 4476–78, 4479.5, 4484, 4485, 4493, 4497, 4931, 4954, 4979, 5007, 5038, 5110, 5112, 5125, 5158, 5162, 5174, 5176, 5396.

Op. 80 Academic Festival Overture

4579. *Beck, Robert L. "Transcribing for the High School Band, the Brahms "Academic Festival Overture", Opus 80" diss., University of South Dakota, 1954. 16 pp. mus.

4580. Daverio, John. "Brahms's Academic Festival Overture and the Comic Modes" *The American Brahms Society Newsletter* 12/1 (Spring 1994) pp. [1]–3. ill. Uses Jean Paul's anatomy of comic modes to assist in defining the comic side of Brahms. Uses student tunes as guide through the work.

4580.5. See also 3358, 3381.a.ii., 3598, 3708.d., 3840, 4041, 4047, 4459, 4468, 4477, 4478, 4484, 4497, 4503, 4509, 5064, 5112, 5158, 5188.d., 5232.

Op. 81 Tragic Overture

4581. Spies, Claudio. " 'Form' and the Tragic Overture: An Adjuration" in *Brahms Studies: Analytical and Historical Perspectives.* [for full citation see 5480] pp. [391]–98. mus. Since this piece doesn't fit standard "sonata form," examines musical materials, their use, their linkages, and compositional decisions to understand the piece's design.

4582. Webster, James. "Brahms's Tragic Overture: the form of tragedy" in *Brahms: Biographical, Documentary and Analytical Studies.* [for full citation see 5479] pp. 99–124. mus., fig., ind., notes, appendix (pp. 122–24). Discusses the first thematic group, especially the opening motto, and then the form as a whole with some attention to Brahms's other orchestral music and his instrumental traditions. Assesses certain musical aspects in which the work can be said to be tragic and compares it to Beethoven's Op. 62, Schumann's Op. 115 and Wagner's *Faust Overture*. Appendix cites thematic materials in Op. 81.

4582.5. See also 3358, 3381.a.ii., 3598, 3840, 4022, 4041, 4043, 4459, 4468, 4477, 4478, 4479.5, 4484, 4497, 4503, 4509, 4759, 4944, 4955, 5064, 5112, 5149, 5158, 5160, 5175, 5188.d., 5232.

Op. 83 Piano Concerto no. 2 in B flat major

4583. Benary, Peter. "Die Anfänge dreier Klavierkonzerte: zur Individualisierung von Form und Gattung" *Musica* 40/1 (1./2.1986) pp. 22–26. Brahms: pp. 25–26. mus. Compares Op. 83 to Mozart's K271 and Beethoven's Op. 58 to show personal style and approaches to form and the play of the solo piano and orchestra in the works.

4584. Kraeft, Norman. "To A Young Pianist" [Author, n.d.]. Poem on not taking Op. 83 lightly into one's repertoire and how one must prepare, work hard and then take it on.

4585. Mahlert, Ulrich. *Johannes Brahms. Klavierkonzert B-dur Op. 83.* (Meisterwerke der Musik. Werkmonographien zur Musikgeschichte 63) München: Wilhelm Fink Verlag, 1994. mus., fig., notes. Presents background and analysis for this work; includes a review of contemporary opinions on the work and a list of editions.

4586. *Stokes, Charles Frank. "Analysis of Piano Concerto II, Opus 83, of Johannes Brahms" B.Mus. diss., Oberlin College, 1969. 2 vols. in 1.

4587. W.S.B.M. [W.S.B. Mathews] "Editorial Bric-A-Brac" *Music* (Chicago) 15/1 (11.1898) pp. 65–80. Brahms: pp. 73–74. Compares Op. 83 to Tschaikovsky's Op. 23.

4588. Whiteway, Doug. "Concerto renewed. Pianist goes to original Brahms score" *Winnipeg Free Press* 113/65 (15.2.1985) p. 19. ill. Reports on how pianist Malcolm Frager examined the D-brd-Hst manuscript for Brahms's intentions, as part of his study of this work.

4588.3.   See also 3251, 3260, 3276, 3287, 3294, 3353, 3358, 3363, 3368,
3378, 3381.a.i., 3550, 3578, 3598, 3762, 3848, 3944, 4036, 4038,
4041, 4046, 4047, 4048.a., 4049, 4062, 4064, 4068, 4070, 4071,
4075, 4078, 4080, 4082, 4088, 4459, 4459.5, 4460.5–62, 4464,
4465, 4468, 4470, 4474, 4475, 4476.d., 4477, 4478, 4479.5, 4484,
4485, 4489, 4493, 4497, 4506, 4509, 4510, 4512, 4520, 4960,
5007, 5038, 5064, 5112, 5118, 5125, 5158, 5160, 5163, 5164,
5174, 5181, 5396.

4588.7.   See also I19 in Appendix A.

Op. 90 Symphony no. 3 in F major

4589.   *Dominant* (New York) 21/3 (1913) pp. 17–18.

4590.   Bailey, Robert. "Musical Language and Structure in the Third Symphony" in *Brahms Studies: Analytical and Historical Perspectives.*
[for full citation see 5480] pp. [405]–21. mus., fig., notes. Sees allusion to the works of Wagner and Schumann in Op. 90, and looks at
its form and musical language in the context of these two composers.

4591.   Barra, Donald. *The Dynamic Performance. A Performer's Guide
to Musical Expression and Interpretation.* With a Foreword by
Yehudi Menuhin. Englewood Cliffs, NJ: Prentice-Hall Inc., 1983.
viii, 181 pp. Brahms: pp. 152–57; also et passim. Uses the 4th
movement as an example of how aspects of a work give it dramatic shape; also mentions other aspects of Opp. 10 no. 3, 90 and
98 et passim.

4592.   Benary, Peter. "Wagnis und Scheitern. Zu Brahms' dritter Sinfonie" *Neue Zürcher Zeitung* no. 106 (7./8.5.1983) pp. 65–66.
notes. Studies the symphony's ending and why it's like that, includes comment on work's background and reception.

4593.   Beveridge, David [R.]. "Echoes of Dvořák in the Third Symphony
of Brahms" *Musik des Ostens* 11 (1989) pp. [221]–30. mus., notes.
Examines common features (borrowings?) in Brahm's Op. 90 that
are seen in Dvořák's Op. 76. Also looks at when Dvořák wrote his
work and where that fits in with Brahms's work on Op. 90. Speculates that if Dvořák's Op. 60 is indebted to Brahms's Op. 73, then
Brahms returns the favour in his Op. 90?

4594.   *Boaz, Joy Christine. "The Symphonic Style of Johannes Brahms:

with particular Emphasis on the Third Symphony" B.M. diss., Butler University, 1981. [23 pp.] ill., mus.

4595. Brodbeck, David [Lee]. "Brahms, the Third Symphony, and the New German School" in *Brahms and His World*. [for full citation see 5478] pp. 65–80. mus., notes, appendixes. Points out links between Op. 90 and Wagner's Tannhauser and Liszt's R. 456. Is Brahms taking on and beating the School at their own game? Appendixes contain the Manifesto against the School, and its parody.

4596. Brown, A. Peter. "Brahms' Third Symphony and the New German School" *The Journal of Musicology* 2/4 (Fall 1983) pp. 434–52. mus., fig., notes. Uses Op. 90 to argue that Brahms as a composer was not antipodal to Liszt and Wagner, he is in the centre. Provides examples of Brahms's work with extra-musical allusions and suggests that Op. 90 contains same. Compares Op. 90 to other symphonies for common factors, reviews contemporaries' interpretation of Op. 90 and Brahms's relations with Wagner and Liszt.

4597. *Eichhorn, Andreas. "Melancholie und das Monumentale: Zur Krise des symphonischen Finaldenkens im 19. Jahrhundert" *Musica* 46/1 (1.–2.1992) pp. 9–12. Discusses Brahms's concept of a symphony finale with Op. 90 as example. [from S102]

4598. *Gilbert, Christopher Michael. "The Role of Development in Symphonic Form" Honors paper, Music Department, Macalester College, n.d. 42 pp. ill., notes. Op. 90 is one of the examples used. [from S031]

4599. Hanslick, Eduard. "The still unpublished Third Symphony . . ." in *Words on Music*. Collected by Robin Ray. London: Methuen, 1984. pp. 73–76. Reprinted from 2470.b. (E. Hanslick. *Music Criticisms, 1846–99*. (1963)).

4600. *Harder, Paul O. "The Orchestral Style of Brahms as based upon an Analysis of the Third Symphony" M.M. diss., University of Rochester, 1945. 2, ii–iv, 111 pp. ill., mus., notes.

4601. *Hoffman, Richard Mark. "Melodic, Harmonic and Formal Unity in Johannes Brahms' Symphony no. 3 in F major, Opus 90" Master of Church Music diss., Southern Baptist Theological Seminary, 1986. v, 79 pp. mus., notes.

4602. Karl, Gregory. "The Temporal Life of the Musical Persona: Implications for Narrative and Dramatic Interpretation" *Music Research Forum* 6 (1991) pp. 42–72. Brahms: pp. 60–67. mus., notes. Op. 90 used as an example to show how "flashback" in a musical work invokes the sense of time passing.

4603. McClary, Susan. "Narrative Agendas in "Absolute" Music: Identity and Difference in Brahms's Third Symphony" in *Musicology and Difference. Gender and Sexuality in Music Scholarship.* Ruth A. Solie, ed. Berkeley [et al.]: University of California Press, 1993. pp. 326–44. notes. Analytical study focusing on 1st movement; looks at "masculine" 1st theme and "feminine" 2nd theme. Includes comment on how contemporaries tried to describe this work in programmatic terms.

4604. *Moore, Hilarie Clark. "The Structural Role of Orchestration in Brahms's Music: A Study of the 'Third Symphony'" Ph.D. diss., Yale University, 1991. 365 pp. Analyses structural role in articulating form and voicing, compares the piano arrangement to the orchestral version, studies the role of orchestration in defining form, and analyses the 4th movement exposition. [from S081]

4605. Pascall, Robert. "The Publication of Brahms's Third Symphony: A Crisis in Dissemination" in *Brahms Studies: Analytical and Historical Perspectives.* [for full citation see 5480] pp. [283]–94. ill., facsim., fig., notes. Presents a detailed account of the publication process for Op. 90, traces the history of it through the correspondence, manuscripts and early editions. Studies a massive sample of characteristic errors and looks at some of the processes used to correct them.

4606. *Ravizza, Victor. "Brahms' Dritte: Eine Abschiedssinfonie?" *Neue Zürcher Zeitung* 47 (2.1989) pp. 67–68. facsim. A hermeneutically-oriented analysis of Op. 90; looks at how the theme comes out of the closing figure of the work. [from S102]

4607. *Van der Stucken, Frank. *Musical Items* 1 (10.1884) pp. 1–5.

4608. *Weger, Roy J. "A Symphonic Band Adaptation of Symphony No. 3 (Opus 90) Andante Movement, (Originally for Orchestra) by Johannes Brahms" M.A. diss., Music, Colorado State College of Education, 1949. xvi, 34 pp. notes.

4609. *Words on Music: From Addison to Barzun.* Jack Sullivan, ed. Athens, OH: Ohio University Press, 1990. xvii, [4] 4–438 pp. notes. Hanslick, Eduard. "The Brahms "Eroica"": pp. [241]–44. Performance review of Op. 90, reprinted from 2470.b. (E. Hanslick. *Music Criticisms, 1846–99.* (1950)). Smyth, Ethel. "Memories of Great Composers": pp. [396]–405. "Brahms": pp. 398–405. From 1879– , with lots of anecdotes about Brahms and women. Reprinted from 1208 (E. Smyth. *Impressions That Remained.* (1919)).

4609.5. See also 3251, 3276, 3287, 3345, 3358, 3363, 3368, 3378, 3379, 3598, 3758, 3832, 3944, 4000, 4038, 4040, 4041, 4046, 4047, 4048.a., 4284, 4455, 4456, 4459, 4459.5, 4460.5, 4461, 4466, 4468, 4469, 4473, 4476.d., 4477–81, 4483, 4484, 4487, 4488, 4489.5, 4490, 4491, 4495, 4502, 4504, 4507, 4509, 4511, 4880, 4906, 4910, 4913.d., 4931, 4934, 4944, 4966, 4972.d.i., 5002, 5022, 5028, 5066, 5077, 5112, 5114, 5158, 5162, 5174, 5175, 5232, 5326, 5396.

Op. 98 Symphony no. 4 in E minor

4610. Cole, Tabitha. "Orchestra sues DFSD over Hellmans track" *Campaign (London)* (17.2.1995) p. 4. ill. Reports that members of London Symphony Orchestra are suing over the use, without their consent, of parts of their recording of Op. 98 in commercials for Hellmans mayonnaise.

4611. *Day, Tim. *Flute Talk* (?) (11.1986).
(a) reprint: Day, Tim. "Brahms and Beethoven. Brahms' Symphony No. 4 and Beethoven's "Leonore" Overture No. 3. A Performance Guide" in *Woodwind Anthology. A Compendium of Woodwind Articles from The Instrumentalist.* Northfield, IL: The Instrumentalist Publishing Company, 1992. vol. 1, pp. 398–401. Brahms: pp. 400–01. Presents performance suggestions for the solo in the 4th movement, bars 93–105.

4612. *Farah, Wanda Therese. "The Varied Thing: A Study of Continuity in the Variations of Brahms' Fourth Symphony" M.Mus. diss., University of Texas at Austin, 1978. iv, 173 pp. ill., mus.

4613. *Grove, George, Sir. *St. James's Gazette* (London) [12] (10.5.

1886). Letter to the editor on Op. 98, 4th movement, particularly
the use of the chaconne. [from 3796]

4614. *Hekkers, William. "Johannes Brahms: Symphonie n 4 en mi
mineur, op. 98" *Analyse musicale* 23 (4.1991) pp. 51–63. mus.
summaries in French and English. A reading of the 1st movement
(examines interval of a third) and the 4th movement (the chaconne's links to Bach's BWV 150 and 1004; also examines
Schoenberg's comments on Brahms in context). [from S102]

4615. *Joo, Arpad. "Brahms's Fourth Symphony, Fourth Movement: A
Conductor's Preparation" M.M. diss., Indiana University, 1972.
63 pp. ill., mus.

4616. Knapp, Raymond. "The Finale of Brahms's Fourth Symphony:
The Tale of the Subject" *19th Century Music* 13/1 (Summer 1989)
pp. 3–17. mus., fig., notes. Discusses the compositional history
and Brahms's intent in this movement; examines how the subject
is derived from Bach's BWV 150, and its expressed relationship
to the rest of the work. Suggests that Bach is not the source, and
puts forward the opinion that Buxtehude BuxWV160 is more relevant musically. Includes comment on other possible models from
Beethoven, Mozart, Rubinstein and Schubert.

4617. Lesle, Lutz. "Reicher Gedankenschatz oder todmüde Phantasie?
Brahms' Vierte im Zerrspiegel zeitgenössischer Kritik" *Das Orchester* (Hamburg) 33/11 (11.1985) pp. 1040–44. facsim., notes.
Examines criticisms from the time of Op. 98's first performances
through 1885. Includes comment on opinions of Wolf and Hanslick; also Brahms and the Wagner school.
  (d) Lesle, Lutz. ""Wie vom heiligem Weh benagt," Brahms'
  Vierte im Meinungsstreit und die geteilte Liebe Hanslick-
  Brahms" *Das Orchester* (Hamburg) 41/6 (1993) pp. 676–79.
  ill., mus., notes. Discusses initial negative reception of work
  and Bülow's playing it at Meiningen. Includes analysis and
  survey of comments by contemporary critics.

4618. Litterick, Louise. "Brahms the Indecisive: Notes on the First
Movement of the Fourth Symphony" in *Brahms 2*. [for full citation see 5481] pp. 223–35. mus., facsim., fig., notes. Studies the
alternative opening that's crossed out in the CH-Zz manuscript,
for insight into Op. 98 and Brahms the composer.
  (e) review: see 5481.e.

4619. Mäckelmann, Michael. *Johannes Brahms. IV. Symphonie E-moll op. 98.* (Meisterwerke der Musik 56) München: Wilhelm Fink Verlag, 1991. 84, [2] pp. mus., notes. Presents the history of the work, detailed movement-by-movement analysis, excerpts from contemporary opinions; includes comment on Brahms the progressive composer, Brahms and symphonic form.

4620. *Martin, James Michael. "A Comparison of Interpretations of Viennese Symphonies by Selected Composers based upon Recordings" D.M.A. diss., University of Cincinnati, 1976. iv, 165 pp. + 2 cassettes (120 min. each cassette) mus., notes. 4th movement of Op. 98 is one of the works discussed. [from S031]

4621. *Moore, Ruth Marie. "The Chaconne and Passacaglia: A Study of These Forms with Emphasis on the Finale of Brahms' Fourth Symphony" M.A. diss., University of Rochester, 1960. v, 98 pp. ill., mus., notes.

4622. Osmond-Smith, David. "The Retreat from Dynamism: A Study of Brahms's Fourth Symphony" in *Brahms: Biographical, Documentary and Analytical Studies.* [for full citation see 5479] pp. 147–65. mus., fig., ind., notes. Analytical study showing how the chains of thirds are a common element unifying structure and tonality.

4623. Pascall, Robert. "Genre and the Finale of Brahms's Fourth Symphony" *Music Analysis* 8/3 (10.1989) pp. 233–45. mus., fig., notes. Explains general categories of generic difference and development and then takes the 4th movement of Op. 98 as an example of how generic considerations enhance an analysis project.

4624. Plattensteiner, Richard. "Brahms, IV. Symphonie" in Plattensteiner. *Neue musikalische Gedichte.* Dresden=Leipzig: Heinrich Minden Verlag, 1928. pp. 42–43. Poem of impressions, especially of movements 2–4.

4625. *Richter, Christoph. "J[ohannes]. Brahms: IV. Sinfonie e-Moll" in *Werkanalyse in Beispielen.* Siegmund Helms and Helmuth Hopf, eds. (Bosse-Musik-Paperback 27) Regensburg: Bosse, 1986. pp. 192–218.

4626. Weber, Horst. "Melancholia: Versuch über Brahms' Vierte" in *Neue Musik und Tradition: Festschrift Rudolf Stephan zum 65.*

Geburtstag. Josef Kuckertz, Helga de la Motte-Haber, Christian Martin Schmidt, and Wilhelm Seidel, eds. Laaber: Laaber Verlag, 1990. pp. 281–95. mus. Analysis of the thirds in the 1st theme of the 1st movement to show Brahms as a melancholic, waiting for death.

4627. Wolf, Hugo. "Brahms's Symphony No. 4 (1886)" in *Writings of German Composers.* [for full citation see 3954] pp. 196–98. Reprint from 3048.d. (H. Wolf. *The Music Criticism of Hugo Wolf.* (1979)).

4627.5. See also S060, 3251, 3267, 3287, 3358, 3363, 3378, 3379, 3598, 3682, 3736, 3848, 4000, 4038, 4040–42, 4046, 4047, 4048.a., 4284, 4455, 4456, 4459, 4459.5, 4460.5, 4461, 4466, 4468, 4469, 4473, 4476.d., 4477–81, 4483, 4484, 4487, 4488, 4489.5, 4490, 4491, 4495, 4497, 4502, 4504, 4507, 4509, 4511, 4591, 4594, 4596, 4822, 4880, 4895, 4899, 4906, 4928, 4931, 4935, 4944, 4955, 4966, 4972.d.ii., 4989, 5022, 5028, 5048, 5064, 5066, 5077, 5112, 5114, 5158, 5165, 5174, 5203, 5232, 5326, 5396.

Op. 102 Concerto in A minor for Violin and Violoncello [Double Concerto]

4628. *Beach, Thelma. "The Form of the Brahms Double Concerto" M.M. diss., University of Rochester, 1941. 3, ii–iv, 53, 5 pp. mus., notes. Last 5 pages is the Andante and Vivace from Nicola Cosimi's Op. 1 Sonata XII, edited by the author. [from S031]

4629. [Denton, David] "Brahms's Double Concerto" *The Strad* 105/ 1256 (12.1994) pp. 1258–59, 1261–63. ill. Surveys the 20 available recordings and makes some listening suggestions.

4630. Hartmann, Günter. "Vorbereitende Untersuchungen zur Analyse von Brahms' Doppelkonzert a-moll op. 102" in *Beiträge zur Geschichte des Konzerts.* [for full citation see 4515] pp. [273]–93. mus., fig., ind., notes. Analyses Op. 102 in relation to Joachim's Op. 11, Viotti's No. 22 and Mozart's K466; focuses on 1st movement, bars 1–57.

4631. *Parente, A. "Difficoltà di Brahms (riascoltando il Doppio Concerto per violino, cello e orchestra)" *Cultura e scuola* [1]/5 (9.–11.1962) p. 169.

4631.1. See also 3287, 3358, 3363, 3378, 3381.a.i., 3598, 3758, 3804,

4036, 4041, 4046, 4047, 4062, 4068, 4074, 4459, 4459.5, 4464, 4465, 4468, 4477, 4478, 4479.5, 4484, 4485, 4493, 4497, 4509, 4882, 5007, 5112, 5127, 5158, 5162, 5176, 5207, 5396.

Symphony no. 5 [speculated]

4631.2. See 5209.

Concerto for Violoncello [speculated]

4631.3. See 5209.

b. Cadenzas Composed by Brahms for Other Composers' Concertos

General

4631.4. See 4320.

Specific

Beethoven

4631.5. See 4571.e.iv.

Mozart

4631.7. See 3383, 4067.

c. Brahms's Editing and Arranging of Other Composers' Orchestral Music

General

4631.8. See 4988.

Specific

Bach, Carl Philipp Emanuel

4631.9. See 3422, 4250.

Bihari, János (1764–1827) [attributed]

4632. *Gowen, Bradford. "Music for Performance" *Piano & keyboard: the bimonthly piano quarterly* no. 172 (1.1995) pp. 55+ . There's some brand-new Brahms, and Bradford Gowen has played it. (Brahms, Johannes. *Racoczi-Marsch: fur Klavier* = for piano = pour piano. Michael Topel, ed. (BA 6557) Kassel; New York: Barenreiter, 1995) [McCorkle Anhang III, nr. 10] [from S087]

Joachim

4632.5. See 4990.

Schubert

4633. Neubacher, Jürgen. "Zur Interpretationsgeschichte der Andante-Einleitung aus Schuberts großer C-Dur-Sinfonie (D. 944)" *NZ-Neue Zeitschrift für Musik* 150/3 (3.1989) pp. 15–21. Brahms: pp. 16–17. notes. Brings to readers' attention an error at beginning of 1st movement in time signature; traces the error back. Looks at Brahms as an editor of Schubert [McCorkle Anhang VI, nr. 13] and how it influenced his own work.
    (d) letter to the editor: Dechant, Herman. *NZ-Neue Zeitschrift für Musik* 150/7/8 (7./8.1989) pp. 2–4. Includes response from Neubacher. Dechant defends Brahms's actions, Neubacher disagrees with them.

d. Cadenzas Composed by Others for Brahms Concertos

4633.3. See 4571.

B. Vocal Music

4633.5. *Bell, A. Craig. *Brahms—The Vocal Music*. Madison, NJ: Fairleigh Dickinson University Press; London: Associated University Presses, 1996. 262 pp. mus., ind., notes.

4634. Bozarth, George S. "Johannes Brahms und die Liedersammlungen von David Gregor Corner, Karl Severin Meister und Friedrich

Wilhelm Arnold" Wiltrud Martin, trans. *Die Musikforschung* 36/4 (10.–12.1983) pp. 177–99. mus., fig., notes. Collections of these three people serve as sources for texts and melodies, especially for McCorkle WoO 33. Article is a study of these collections, starting with descriptions of them and extensive comments on Brahms's markings in them. Includes corrections to 2566 (S. Kross. *Die Musikforschung* 11 (1958)) and 2570 (W. Morik. *Johannes Brahms und sein Verhältnis zum deutschen Volkslied.* (1965)); further inquiry into sources for McCorkle WoO 33 no. 29 and "In Stiller Nacht"; links to Opp. 74 no. 2 and 91 no. 2; and study of the arrangements from Corner in McCorkle WoO 34.

(d) Bozarth. "Johannes Brahms und die Geistlichen Lieder aus David Gregor Corners Groß-Catolischem Gesangbuch von 1631" Wiltrud Martin, trans. in *Brahms-Kongress Wien 1983.* [for full citation see 5431] pp. 67–80. facsim., mus., fig., notes. Describes the Gesangbuch manuscript, discusses the history of Opp. 74 no. 2 and 91 no. 2. Studies how Brahms altered "Komm Mainz" melody for McCorkle WoO 34 no. 4.

4635. Burnsworth, Charles C. *Choral Music for Women's Voices: An Annotated Bibliography of Recommended Works.* Metuchen: The Scarecrow Press, Inc., 1968. iv, 5–180 pp. Brahms: pp. 64–69. ind. Includes particulars such as number of parts, range, publisher, level of difficulty, type of accompaniment; also includes comment on style. 14 items, includes Opp. 52, 65 and 66.

4636. Dunlap, Kay, and Barbara Winchester. "Brahms, Johannes (1833–1897)" in Dunlap and Winchester. *Vocal Chamber Music. A Performer's Guide.* (Garland Reference Library of the Humanities 465) New York & London: Garland Publishing, Inc., 1985. pp. 19–21. ind. Provides details on ensemble required, editions and text authors for Opp. 20, 28, 31, 52, 61, 64–66, 75, 91–92, 103, 112, and McCorkle WoO posthum 16.

4637. Kross, Siegfried, see 4761.5.

4638. *Van Ackere, Jules. [Ackere, Jules E. van] *De vocale muziek van Brahms.* Wolvertem: Libri Musicae, 1992. 104 pp. ill.

4638.5. See also 3412, 3433, 4080, 5126.

1. Works for Solo Voices

General

4639. *Alsleben, Julius. "Geschichte des deutschen Liedes" *Allgemeine deutsche Musik-Zeitung* 1 (1874) pp. 259+ .

4640. Atlas, Raphael. "Text and Musical Gesture in Brahms's Vocal Duets and Quartets with Piano" *The Journal of Musicology* 10/2 (Spring 1992) pp. 231–60. mus., fig., notes. Studies how musical setting of a text complements a vocal line and how formal or tonal idiosyncrasies can be accounted for in this way. Analyses Opp. 31 no. 2, 61 no. 1, 66 no. 1, 75 no. 4, 112 no. 4. Includes comments on Brahms as musical dramatist.

4641. *Beaufils, Marcel. *Le Lied romantique allemand.* Paris: Gallimard, 1956.
        *2ième édition: 1956. (Pour la musique 2) 322 pp. discog.
        *another edition: 1982: (Les Essais 221) 346 pp.

4642. *Berry, Corre. "The Secular Dialogue Duet: 1600–1900" *Musical Review* 40/4 (11.1979) pp. 272–84. notes. Works by Brahms used as examples in this discussion of how dialogue text is set to music. [from S102]
        (d) Berry. "Brahms, Johannes (1833–1897)" in Berry. *Vocal Chamber Duets. An Annotated Bibliography.* n.p.: National Association of Teachers of Singing, Inc., 1981. pp. 8–10. ind. Provides details on vocal range, tempi, timing, voicing, text author, key, level of difficulty and brief explanation of text for Opp. 20, 28, 61, 66, 75.

4643. Black, Leo. "Brahms's Songs" *The Musical Times* 134[133]/1794 (8.1992) pp. 395–96. An appreciation of the solo songs, highlighting those that are special to the author over his life to date; includes comment on texts set.

4644. *Blair, Wallace Edwin. "A Discussion of My Graduate Voice Recital: Works by Handel, Brahms, Duparc, Floyd, and Verdi" M.M. diss., University of Texas at El Paso, 1987. 40 pp. notes.

4645. Bortolotto, Mario. *Introduzione al Lied romantico.* 1. edizione. (PBR [=Piccola Biblioteca Ricordi] / 19) Milan: G. Ricordi & C., 1962. 203, [1] pp. ind. Discusses stylistic development of the Ger-

man lied in the 19th century; includes a brief historical and aesthetic introductory section. Brahms cited in overview, also has
own paging (pp. 140–49) where he's discussed as song composer
and setter of text, and general impressions of his lieder are given.
Includes comment on Brahms and religion and Brahms's work
leading through to Schoenberg.

"versione riveduta e ampliata": (Piccola Biblioteca Adelphi 165)
Milano: Adelphi Edizioni, 1984. 206 pp. Brahms: pp. 144–
54. ind. omitted. No change in text.

4646. Bos, Coenraad v[on]. *The Well-Tempered Accompanist. As Told
to Ashley Pettis.* [With a Foreword by Helen Traubel] Bryn Mawr,
PA: Theodore Presser, Co., 1949. [[x, 162, 1]] pp. Brahms: pp.
[[43,47, 113–16]]. mus., discog. Talks about performing Op. 121
at premiere and subsequently; also comments on playing Brahms,
with Op. 19 no. 4 and Op. 105 no. 4 as examples.

4647. Brahms, Johannes. *Johannes Brahms: Three Lieder on Poems of
Adolf Friedrich von Schack. A Facsimile of the Autograph Manuscripts of "Abenddämmerung," Op. 49 No. 5, "Herbstgefühl,"
Op. 48 No. 7, and "Serenade," Op. 58 No. 8 in the Collection of
the Library of Congress.* [Preface by Donald L. Leavitt. With Introduction by George S. Bozarth] Washington, DC: The Library
of Congress, 1983. [2, 7, 4, 4 pp.] facsim., notes. Introduction discusses manuscript provenance, background on the works and discusses variants between the manuscripts and the 1st editions. Also
includes the original texts for all 3 poems in both original German
and English translation, and comments on changes that Brahms
made in the texts for these settings.

4648. *Braus, Ira Lincoln. "Textual Rhetoric and Harmonic Anomaly in
Selected Lieder of Johannes Brahms" Ph.D. diss., Harvard University, 1988. 225 pp. mus., notes. Analyses 12 songs from the
viewpoint of how text is set to music.

(d) i) Braus, Ira [Lincoln]. "Brahms's Liebe und Frühling II, Op.
3, No. 3: A New Path to the Artwork of the Future?" *19th
Century Music* 10/2 (Fall 1986) pp. 135–56. adds fig. Shows
that Brahms's early Lied composition may have been influenced by Wagner's mid-century writings on the relationship
of word to tone. Presents internal analytical and historical
evidence for the hypothesis that Op. 3 no. 3 leads on to

Wagner's *Tristan und Isolde.* Includes an analysis that focuses on parallels between poetic and musical rhetoric, with
special attention to the harmonic consequences of these parallels.

(d) ii) based on Chapter 6: Braus, Ira [Lincoln]. "Poetic-Musical
Rhetoric in Brahms's Auf dem Kirchhofe, Op. 105, No. 4"
Theory and Practice 13 (1988) pp. 15–30. adds fig.

(d) iii) expanded from Chapter 6: Braus, Ira [Lincoln]. ""Skep-
tische Beweglichkeit" Die Rhetorik von Wort und Ton in So
stehn wir, ich und meine Weide op. 32/8" Peter Jost and Anne
Schneider, transs. in *Brahms als Liedkomponist.* [for full citation see 5083] pp. [156]–72. omits mus.; adds fig., ind.

(e) report: "Three Dissertations in Progress" *The American
Brahms Society Newsletter* 3/1 (Spring 1985) pp. [8–9]. Includes reports on 4262 and 4987.

4649. *Di Marco, Giuseppina. "Il pianoforte nei Lieder di Brahms—a)
La funzione pianistica" in *I Lieder di Johannes Brahms.* [for full
citation see 4677] pp. 233–56.

4650. Douty, Nicholas. "Interpretation of Modern Songs: exemplified
by some Songs of Brahms and Grieg" *The Etude* 25/6 (6.1907) p.
402. ill., facsim. (p. 541), mus. (p. 400). Examines the close relationship of poem to music in songs. Examples from Brahms's
songs include individual songs from Opp. 32, 49 (+ facsim.), 94
and McCorkle WoO posthum 31.

4651. Dümling, Albrecht. "Ehre statt Ehe. Zu den Gottfried Keller-
Vertonungen von Brahms" *Dissonanz* (Gümligen) no. 7 (1986)
pp. 10–17.

4652. Elson, James. "A Brief Survey of the Brahms Lieder" *The NATS
[National Association of Teachers of Singing] Bulletin* 40/1
(9./10.1983) pp. 18–23. notes. Surveys Brahms's songs in chronological order of composition, with comment on individual opuses;
includes comment on Brahms as a song composer and his setting
of texts.

4653. Espina, Noni. "Johannes Brahms, 1833–1897 (German)" in Espina. *Repertoire for the Solo Voice. A Fully Annotated Guide to
Works for the Solo Voice published in Modern Editions and covering Material from the 13th Century to the Present.* With a Fore-

word by Berton Coffin. Metuchen: The Scarecrow Press, Inc., 1977. vol. 1, pp. 507–24; vol. 2, pp. 1214–19. A guide to performing songs; annotations focus on singer requirements, plus some comment on piano playing and text sources. Volume 1 entries separate song cycles [Opp. 33, 103, 121] from individual songs; volume 2 entries are et passim for arrangements of folk songs.

4654. Fellinger, Imogen. "Cyclic Tendencies in Brahms's Song Collections" in *Brahms Studies: Analytical and Historical Perspectives.* [for full citation see 5480] pp. [379]–88. notes. Examines correspondence and manuscripts to understand Brahms's process in assembling and ordering his songs in their "sets." Also looks at Brahms's thoughts on this and contemporary performance practice. No analysis by key is done. Includes comments on Brahms and Ophüls, 1896.

4655. *Finck, Henry T. *Evening Post* (?.1912).
(e) report: "The House of Music" in "Reflections by the Editor [W.J. Baltzell(?)]" *The Musical Courier* 65/4 (Whole no. 1687) (24.7.1912) p. 24. Finck is critical of Brahms's lieder.

4656. Finscher, Ludwig. "Lieder für verschiedene Vokalensembles" in *Johannes Brahms: Leben und Werk* [for full citation see 3215] pp. 153–54. Examines Brahms as a composer: the vocal duets, quartets, McCorkle WoO 33, nos. 43–49 [=Heft 7].

4657. *Foster, B. "Grieg and the European Song Tradition" *Studia musicologica norvegica* 19 (1983) pp. 128+.

4658. **German Lieder in the Nineteenth Century.* Rufus E. Hallmark, ed. (Studies in Musical Genres and Repertories) New York, London: Schirmer Books, Prentice Hall International, 1996. xviii, 346 pp. mus., ind., notes.

4659. Gorrell, Lorraine. "Johannes Brahms" in *The Nineteenth-Century German Lied.* Portland: Amadeus Press, 1993. pp. 257–81. ill., mus., ind., notes. Focuses on Brahms's choices of texts and how he set them; also Brahms and folksong, Brahms and Zuccalmaglio, influence of older music on songs, Brahms the man. Examples include Opp. 33, 121, McCorkle WoO posthum 31 and McCorkle WoO 33.

Part IV

4660. *Grüner, Wulfhard von. "Das deutsche Lied des 19. Jahrhunderts und seine Rezeption in der D.D.R." Phil.F. diss., Martin-Luther Universität, Halle-Wittenberg, 1975. 248 pp. Traces the lied's development, outlining its characteristics and reviewing its prerequisites; also studies present day reception of lied in the DDR [former East Germany]. [from S102]

4661. *Guide de la mélodie et du lied. Sous la direction de Brigitte François-Sappey et Gilles Cantagrel. Avec la collaboration de Marie-Claire Beltrandi-Patier et al. (Collection Les Indispensables de la musique) Paris: Fayard, 1994. 916 pp. ill., ind.

4662. Gut, Serge. Aspects du lied romantique allemand. (Série musique) [Arles:] Actes Sud, 1994. 248, [17] pp. fig., ind., notes.
"Brahms (1833–1897). Une superbe onctuosité mélodique": pp. 146–[62]. Divides Brahms's work into 2 periods, 1851–68 and 1868–86; presents overview and descriptive comments within each period, also ties in with events in life. Also examines Brahms and folkmusic in both songs in opuses and folksong settings. Presents detailed analysis of Opp. 63 no. 8, 84 no. 4 and 105 no. 2. Also pp. 71–72 presents Op. 86, no. 2 as an example of varied strophe form.

4663. H.D. [Hermann Deiters] Allgemeine musikalische Zeitung 4/14 (7.4.1869) pp. 106–08. mus. Review of Opp. 46–49.

4664. *Hussey, William Gregory. "Modified Strophic Form in Four Songs of Johannes Brahms" M.M. diss., University of Texas at Austin, 1992. vi, 100 pp. mus., notes.

4665. *Ingraham, Mary I[sabel]. "Brahms and the Folk Ideal: His Poets and His Art Song" M.A. diss., Musicology, University of Victoria, 1987. viii, 188, [2] pp. mus., notes.

4666. *Johnson, Diane E. "The Vocal Quartets with Piano Accompaniment of Johannes Brahms: Their Significance in the Development of the Genre" D.M.A. diss., Claremont Graduate School, 1990. vi, 109 pp. mus., notes.

4667. Jost, Peter. "Brahms und das Deutsche Lied des 19. Jahrhunderts" in Brahms als Liedkomponist. [for full citation see 5083] pp. [9]–37. mus., fig., ind., notes. Places Brahms in the lieder line of Schubert — Wolf; traces his development as a song composer and text setter with analyses of Opp. 7 no. 6, 58 no. 5, and Op. 92 no. 2. Compares Brahms's work to Robert Franz's, with Franz's Op. 13 no. 3 as example.

4668. *Kim, Mi-Young. "Das Ideal der Einfachheit im Lied von der Berliner Liederschule bis zu Brahms" Phil.F. diss., Universität zu Köln, 1995.

(a) *reprint: Kim. *Das Ideal der Einfachheit im Leid (sic) von der Berliner Liederschule bis zu Brahms.* (Kölner Beiträge zur Musikforschung 192) Kassel: Gustav Bosse Verlag, 1995. 214 pp. mus., notes.

4669. Kolb, G. Roberts. "The Vocal Quartets of Brahms (ops. (sic) 31, 64, and 92). A Textual Encounter" in *Five Centuries of Choral Music. Essays in Honor of Howard Swan.* Gordon Paine, ed. (Festschrift Series 6) Stuyvesant, NY: Pendragon Press, 1988. pp. 323–55. mus., notes. Examines how Brahms responded to texts set in these works.

4670. Krause, Emil. "Geschichtliche Mittheilungen über die Entwick-lung des einstimmigen Liedes am Clavier und dessen Abarten" *Neue Zeitschrift für Musik* 57/21–24, 26 (Bd. 86) (21., 28.;5.; and 4.,11.,25.;6.;1890) pp. 237–39, 249–51, 261–64, 273–75, 315–17. Brahms: pp. 274–75. Brahms seen in the line from Schubert and Schumann; includes comment on his style.

4671. *Kretzschmar, Hermann. "Das deutsche Lied seit Robert Schu-mann" *Die Grenzboten* [40 (1881)].

(a) *reprint: Kretzschmar. "Das deutsche Lied seit Robert Schu-mann (1881)" in Kretzschmar. *Gesammelte Aufsätze über Musik und Anderes aus den Grenzboten.* (Kretzschmars Gesammelte Aufsätze über Musik 1) Leipzig: Breitkopf & Härtel, 1910.

4672. Krones, Hartmut. "Der Einfluss Franz Schuberts auf das Lied-schaffen von Johannes Brahms" in *Brahms-Kongress Wien 1983.* [for full citation see 5431] pp. 309–24. mus., notes. Compares Op. 3 no. 1 to Schubert's D. 118; also looks at both composers' han-dling of text.

4673. Kross, Siegfried. "Johannes Brahms" in Kross. *Geschichte des Deutschen Liedes.* (WB-Forum 41) Darmstadt: Wissenschaftliche Buchgesellschaft, 1989. pp. 144–50. Discusses Brahms as a composer of song, his thoughts on composing songs, Brahms as a setter of text. Uses Op. 3 no.1 as an example of his work.

4674. *Kross, Siegfried. "Johannes Brahms als Liedkomponist" in *Herbstliche Musiktage Urach '83*. Stadtverwaltung Bad Urach, ed. Bad Urach: n.p., 1983. pp. 13–27.

4675. Lee, E. Markham. "The Student-Interpreter" *Musical Opinion and Music Trade Review* 56/671 (8.1933) pp. 932–33. mus. Suggestions on how to perform Opp. 59 no. 1, 71 no. 5, 85 no. 6, 107 no. 3, McCorkle WoO 33 no. 43.

4676. *Leuwer, Ruth Pirkel. "Mörike-Lyrik in ihren Vertonungen: Ein Beitrag zur Interpretation" Phil.F. diss., Rheinische Friedrich-Wilhelms-Universität Bonn, 1953. Critiques settings of Mörike's poems by various composers, including Brahms: Opp. 19 no. 5, 59 no. 5, 61 no. 1. [from S071]

4677. *I Lieder di Johannes Brahms*. Guido Salvetti, ed. [Sponsored by the Istituto musicale pareggiato "A. Tonelli" and the Conservatorio di musica Giuseppe Verdi (Milano)] (Quaderni di Musica/Realtà 12) Milano: Edizioni Unicopli, [1986]. 384 pp. ind., notes. Contains: 4494, 4649, 4685, 4687, 4724, 4881, 4961, 4962, 4969, 5085, 5129, 5131, 5154.
"Festival internazionale di musica vocale da camera. Carpi—Settembre/Ottobre 1985."

4678. Lowe, George. "The Songs of Brahms" *Musical Opinion and Music Trade Review* 33/391 (1.4.1910) pp. 480–81. ill. Discusses Brahms as a song composer with many individual songs cited as examples, in particular Opp. 33 and 121. Includes comparison of Brahms to Schumann and Wolf.

4679. Moore, Gerald. *Singer and Accompanist. The Performance of Fifty Songs*. New York: The Macmillan Company, 1954. xi, [1], 232 pp. ind., discog. (after each song). Brahms: pp. 11–32. mus. Explains how to sing and play with some analysis: Opp. 43 no. 1, 63 no. 5, 84 no. 4, 86 no. 2.
*also: London: Methuen, 1953.
[new edition:] London: Hamish Hamilton, 1982. x, 235 pp. discog. now at end of volume.
(a) reprint (of London 1953 edition): Westport, CT: Greenwood Press, 1973.

4680. *"New Lieder" *Economist* 331/7857 (2.4.1994) p. 81.

4681. Niecks, Fr[ederick]. "Johannes Brahms" (Modern Song Writers IV) *The Musical Times* 27/[521] (1.7.1886) pp. 387–91. notes. Contains an overview of the songs and looks at Brahms the song composer; also includes an overview of his life (mostly pre-1862) and works, and comment on Brahms the man.

4682. Ord, Alan J. *Songs for Bass Voice. An Annotated Guide to Works for Bass Voice.* Metuchen & London: The Scarecrow Press, Inc., 1994. x, 217 pp. Includes 19 Brahms songs with comments on difficulty, range, and performance suggestions. Also includes songs that have been transposed down.

4683. Osborne, Charles. *The Concert Song Companion. A Guide to The Classical Repertoire.* London: Victor Gollancz Ltd., 1974. [1–9,] 10–285 pp. Brahms: pp. 79–93. ind., notes. A survey of opuses with descriptive remarks and performance suggestions for individual songs.

4684. *Panagl, Oswald. "Trost und Schrecken der Kunst im romanischen Lied" *Polyaisthesis* 4/2 (1989) pp. 146–56. notes. summary in English. Analyses 10 examples from the songs of Schubert, Schumann and Brahms to show conflict between the semantic and the musical. [from S102]

4685. *Pieri, Donatella. "[Il pianoforte nei Lieder di Brahms]—b) Strutture pianistiche autonome" in *I Lieder di Johannes Brahms.* [for full citation see 4677] pp. 257–79.

(d) *appendix: "Annotazioni su "Die schöne Magelone" di Guido Salvetti su materiali di Romano Superchi" in *I Lieder di Johannes Brahms.* [for full citation see 4677] pp. 294–305.

4686. *Preciado, Dionisio. "Los cantos folklóricos: ¿Lo auténtico contra lo bello? Un nuevo concepto de música folklórica" *Revista de folklore* 75 (1987) pp. 75–80. Surveys folklore theories, including the folkmusic concepts of Brahms. [from S102]

4687. *Rondelli, Claudia. "[Il pianoforte nei Lieder di Brahms]—c) Figuralismi e descrittivismi nella parte pianistica" in *I Lieder di Johannes Brahms.* [for full citation see 4677] pp. 280–94.

4688. *Ruiz Conde, José Manuel. "El Lied romántico" *Temporadas de la música* 8/1 (1989) pp. 49–55. Surveys the lieder of Schubert, Schumann, Brahms and Fauré. [from S102]

4689. *Sams, Eric. *Les lieder de Brahms*. Myriam Tchamitchian-Fauré, trans. La Calade: Actes Suds, 1989. 98 pp. mus. Translation of 2090 (E. Sams. *Brahms Songs*. (1972)). [from compiler]

4690. Schumann, Elisabeth. "A Spirit Merged in Nature's" in Schumann. *German Song*. (The World of Music) New York: Chanticleer Press Inc., 1948. pp. 34–41. ill., facsim. Presents an overview of Brahms as a song composer, looks at influences of ethnic music. Also pp. 69–70, Op. 84 no. 4 is used as an example to illustrate general principles of lieder singing.
also: London: Max Parrish & Co. Limited, 1948.
(a) reprint (of New York edition): Westport, CT: Greenwood Press, 1979.

4691. Schwab, Heinrich W. "Brahms' Kompositionen für zwei Singstimmen mit Pianofortebegleitung" in *Brahms-Analysen*. [for full citation see 4888] pp. 60–80. ill., mus., notes. Studies Opp. 20, 28, 61, 66 and 75; examines Brahms's work in the context of his times's norm and how the voice parts are composed.

4692. *Sheil, Richard F. "Brahms Liebeslieder Walzer" M.M. diss., University of Rochester, 1946. iii, 38 pp. ill., mus., notes.

4693. *Stark, Lucien. *A Guide to the Solo Songs of Johannes Brahms*. Bloomington: Indiana University Press, 1995. x, 374 pp. ill., mus., ind., notes. Analyses in detail 200+ solo songs by Brahms; includes translation of the texts. [from publisher information]

4694. *Tubeuf, André. *Le lied allemand: poètes et paysages*. Paris: Editions F. Bourin, 1993. 537 pp. ill., ind.

4695. *Wagner, Monica. "A Comparison of the Lieder by Johannes Brahms between the Solo Songs dedicated to Men and Those dedicated to Women" M.M. diss., University of Oregon, 1993. vi, 77 pp. notes. Examines Opp. 7, 121 for the men; Opp. 3, 6 for the women. [from compiler]

4696. Walker, Ernest. "Brahms's Songs" *Monthly Musical Record* 59/700 (1.4.1929) p. 100. notes. Review of 2052.b. (M. Friedländler. *Brahms's Lieder*. (1928)).

4697. Whitton, Kenneth. *Lieder: an Introduction to German Song*. Foreword by Dietrich Fischer-Dieskau. London: Julia MacRae, 1984. xii, 203 pp. ind., notes.

Brahms: pp. 62–67. mus. General comments on Brahms as a song composer and features of his songs, with examples given.

Brahms: pp. 145–52. mus., notes. Background and performance suggestions for Opp. 43 no. 2, 84 no. 4, 86 no. 2; includes texts in original and English translation.

*also: New York: Franklin Watts, 1984.

4697.3.   See also 3200, 3278, 3365, 3371, 3372, 3374, 3400, 3411, 3429, 3781, 3810, 3811.c., 3821, 3835, 3905, 3921, 3958, 3971, 4036, 4037, 4040, 4046, 4059, 4873, 4876, 4881, 4892, 4922, 4961, 4962, 4969, 5012–14, 5037, 5040, 5042, 5095, 5108, 5115, 5131, 5138, 5139, 5154, 5157, 5180, 5188.d., 5197, 5201, 5235, 5331, 5368.

4697.7.   See also I22 in Appendix A.

Specific

Op. 3 Six Songs for Tenor or Soprano

4698.   *Niederrheinische Musik-Zeitung* 2 *Literaturblatt* no. 3 (25.3. 1854) p. 11.

4698.2.   See also S060, 3406, 3961, 4094, 4672, 4673, 4683, 4695, 5081, 5084, 5089, 5090, 5102, 5104, 5107, 5185, 5195, 5198, 5200, 5345, 5367.

Op. 6 Six Songs for Tenor or Soprano

4698.3.   See 3814, 3961, 4683, 4695, 5089, 5090, 5185, 5198, 5345, 5367.

Op. 7 Six Songs for Solo Voice

4698.4.   See 3961, 4061, 4667, 4683, 4695, 5089, 5102, 5185, 5200, 5202, 5345, 5367.

Op. 14 Eight Songs and Romances for Solo Voice

4698.5.   See 3810, 4683, 5090, 5091, 5345.

Op. 19 Five Poems for Solo Voice

4698.6.   See 3413, 4646, 4676, 4683, 5082, 5084, 5090, 5097, 5168, 5195, 5198, 5200.

Op. 20 Three Duets for Soprano and Alto

4698.7. See 3810, 4636, 4642.d., 4691.

Op. 28 Four Duets for Alto and Baritone

4698.8. See 4636, 4642.d., 4691, 5162.

Op. 31 Three Quartets for 4 Solo Voices (SATB)

4698.9. See 4292, 4636, 4640, 4666, 4669, 5162, 5396.

Op. 32 Nine Songs for Solo Voice

4699. *Seedorf, Thomas. "Hafis und die "Westöstliche Literatur" des 19. Jahrhunderts: Zur literarisch-musikalischen Vorgeschichte von Hugo Wolfs Divan-Vertonungen" in *Glasba in poezija: 130 letnica rojstva Huga Wolfa.* [Report of the Slovenski Glasbeni Dnevi.] Primož Kuret and Julijan Strajnar, eds. Ljubljana: Festival Ljubljana, 1990. pp. 176–84. summary in Slovene. Discusses influence of Daumer's edition of Hafis poems on work of Brahms, Wolf and Wagner. Discusses Brahms's Op. 32 no. 9 and Wolf's *Gedichte von Johann Wolfgang von Goethe* no. 35.

4699.5. See also 3375, 3413, 4648, 4650, 4682, 4683, 4699, 4830.a., 4880, 4931, 5084, 5088, 5090, 5092, 5093, 5101, 5168, 5195, 5198, 5200, 5202.

Op. 33 Magelone Romances for Solo Voice

4700. *Cottle, William Andrew. "A History and Analysis of Johannes Brahms' "Die Schone (*sic*) Magelone"" M.A. diss., Eastern New Mexico University, 1964. v, 39, 3 pp. notes.

4701. Daverio, John. "Brahms's Magelone Romanzen and the "Romantic Imperative"" *The Journal of Musicology* 7/3 (Summer 1989) pp. 343–65. fig., notes. Article ends at p. 360, pp. 361–65 is an appendix: "A Connecting Narrative for Brahms's Magelone Romanzen, Opus 33." Attempts to explain Brahms's concept behind Op. 33 by defining it as a musical reaction to the literary form of Tieck's "Magelone." Brahms combines elements of song cycle and romantic opera just like Tieck's work is a combination of a lyric cycle and a novel. Operatic and dramatic qualities ofBrahms's setting pointed out; examines Brahms's own thoughts on the setting.

4702. *Giribaldi, Emilia. *Una scena per la fantasia: Die Schone Magelone di Ludwig Tiek e Johannes Brahms*. (Musica e letteratura 3) Alessandria : Edizioni dell'Orso, 1996. 128 pp. notes, discog.

4703. Jost, Peter. "Brahms und die romantische Ironie. Zu den "Romanzen aus L. Tieck's Magelone" op. 33" *Archiv für Musikwissenschaft* 47/1 (1990) pp. 27–61. mus., notes. After discussion of romantic irony in general, looks at this quality in the poems themselves and analyses Brahms's setting of ironic passages throughout the cycle. Concludes that Brahms did not identify with Tieck's irony as it is not reflected in his setting. Includes background on Op. 33.

4704. *Kawakami, A. *Gunma Daigaku Kyōiku Gakubu kiyō. Geijutsu gijutsu hen [Gunma [Gumma] University. Faculty of Education. Annual Report. Art, Technology, Health and Physical Education and Science of Human Living Series]* 25 (1989) p. 71. Analyses the rhythmic structure of Brahms's Op. 33. [from S087]

4705. *Pociej, Bohdan. "Johannes Brahms: Die schöne Magelone, cykl pieśni op. 33 do słow L. Tiecka (1861–1862)" in *Cykle pieśni ery romantycznej 1816–1914. Interpretacje*. Mieczysław Tomaszewski, ed. (Muzyka i liryka 1) Kraków: Akademia muzyczna, 1989. pp. 73–82.

4706. *Skaar, David Wayne. "A Comprehensive Study of The German Song Cycle: Beethoven, Schubert, Schumann and Brahms" diss., Mankato State University, 1970. 31 pp. notes.

4707. *Van Sickle, Marilyn Redinger. "A Study of the Song Cycle Romances from Magelone by Johannes Brahms" M.M. diss., University of Rochester, 1949. v, 64 pp. ill., mus., notes.

4707.5. See also S060, 3300, 3301, 4659, 4678, 4683, 4685.d., 4879, 4899, 5087, 5090, 5200, 5201, 5232.

Op. 43 Four Songs for Solo Voice

4708. Mětšk, Juro. "Einige Anmerkungen zur Textvorlage des Brahms-Liedes "Von ewiger Liebe", op. 43, Nr. 1" *Beiträge zur*

Musikwissenschaft 26/1 (1984) pp. 55–58. notes. Refutes 2129's
(W. Barlmeyer. *Melos/NZ für Musik* (1978)) claim that text for
Op. 43 no. 1 is by Leopold Haupt, suggests it's by Johann Ernst
Schmaler.
(d)*Mĕtšk. "K Brahmsawemu serbskemu spĕwej" *Rozhlad* 30/3
(?) (1980?) pp. 159–60.

4709.   Schmidt, Christian Martin. "Überlegungen zur Liedanalyse bei
Brahms' "Die Mainacht" op. 43, 2" in *Brahms-Analysen*. [for full
citation see 4888] pp. 47–59. mus. (pp. 56–59), notes. A detailed
formal analysis of the music noting links between sections, etc.
No attempt to analyse the musical setting of the text.

4709.3. See also 3375, 3810, 4679, 4682, 4683, 4697, 5084, 5090, 5097,
5101, 5102, 5104, 5168, 5195, 5198, 5200.

Op. 46 Four Songs for Solo Voice

4709.7. See 3300, 3404, 3417, 3422, 4663, 4682, 4683, 5084, 5090,
5097, 5195, 5198, 5200, 5316.

Op. 47 Five Songs for Solo Voice

4710.   *Thym, Jürgen, and Ann Clark Fehn. "Sonnet Structure and the
German Lied: Shackles or Spurs?" *JALS: The Journal of the American Liszt Society* 32 (7.–12.1992) pp. 3–15. Compares three settings of Goethe's "Die Liebende schriebt" by Mendelssohn (Op. 86
no. 3), Brahms (Op. 47 no. 5), and Schubert (D. 673) to demonstrate
productivity of literary sonnet form in a musical setting. [from S102]

4710.3. See also 3300, 4051, 4663, 4682, 4683, 5084, 5087, 5090, 5168,
5195, 5198, 5200.

Op. 48 Seven Songs for Solo Voice

4710.7. See 3300, 4061, 4647, 4663, 4683, 4931, 5090, 5093, 5198, 5200.

Op. 49 Five Songs for Solo Voice

4711.   *Musical Courier* 86/17 (Whole no. 2246) (26.4.1923 (?)) p. 33.
Discusses Op. 49 no. 4. [from WPA Index]

4712. Kahler, Otto-Hans. "Brahms' Wiegenlied und die Gebirgs-Bleamln des Alexander Baumann" *Brahms-Studien* Bd. 6 (1985) pp. 65–70. ill., notes. Suggests that the accompaniment for Op. 49 no. 4 comes from a ländler collected by Alexander Baumann in Heft 2, no. 1 of his *Gebirgs-Bleamln*. Background on Baumann and his ethnic work presented.

4712.5. See also 3300, 3671, 3814, 3840, 4049, 4647, 4650, 4663, 4683, 4960, 5084, 5090, 5097, 5168, 5195, 5198, 5200, 5202.

Op. 52 Liebeslieder Waltzes for Piano 4 hands and Solo Voices (SATB)

4713. Brodbeck, David [Lee]. "Compatibility, Coherence and Closure in Brahms's Liebeslieder Waltzes" in *Explorations in Music, The Arts, and Ideas: Essays in Honor of Leonard B. Meyer.* [for full citation see 4402] pp. 411–37. mus., fig., ind., notes. Shows that this work is more than just "fluff" but as tightly constructed as the major works. Examines background, manuscripts to show how Brahms carefully chose the final sequence and the groupings of songs. Includes review of correspondence Brahms-Levi and Brahms-Simrock.

4713.3. See also 3365, 3578, 3851, 4041, 4292, 4429, 4635, 4636, 4666, 4692, 4880, 4965, 4998, 5162, 5368, 5396.

Op. 57 Eight Songs for Solo Voice

4713.7. See S060, 3300, 4683, 4880, 4982, 5090, 5092, 5195.

Op. 58 Eight Songs for Solo Voice

4714. Bozarth, George S. "Synthesizing Word and Tone: Brahms's Setting of Hebbel's 'Vorüber'" in *Brahms: Biographical, Documentary and Analytical Studies.* [for full citation see 5479] pp. 77–98. facsim., mus., ind., notes, appendix. Studies the compositional history of the word-tone synthesis achieved in this song by Brahms. Looks at why Brahms chose to set this poem to music and examines in detail the 3 extant versions of the song: 2 sketches at A-Wgm and a manuscript at US-Wc. Appendix, pp. 97–98: "The Various Versions of Hebbel's 'Vorüber'", which lists the sources for this poem and shows the variants in different sources for Stanza 2.

(d) i) corrections: see 3400.d.i.e. ii) related to: 5449.5.

4714.5.   See also 3300, 4647, 4667, 4683, 5202.

Op. 59 Eight Songs for Solo Voice

4715.   *Scott, Lora Kinsinger. "A Study of Brahms' Songs, Opus 59" M.A. diss., Western Carolina University, 1986. vi, 44 pp. + 1 cassette (65 min.) mus., notes.

4715.5.   See also 3794, 4053, 4675, 4676, 4683, 4716, 4960, 5082, 5084, 5088.5, 5090, 5168, 5195, 5200.

Op. 61 Four Duets for Soprano and Alto

4716.   Bozarth, George S. "Brahms's Duets for Soprano and Alto, op. 61: A Study in Chronology and Compositional Process" *Studia musicologica* 25 (1983) pp. [191]–210. mus., notes, appendix. Uses information from new or previously ignored musical and documentary sources to posit composition dates for Op. 61 and to detail the long compositional history of its no. 1. Appendix examines Op. 59 no. 5 for its parallel in setting to Op. 61 no. 1. Alternate title for periodical is: *Studia musicologica academiae scientiarum hungaricae.*
(d) corrections: see 3400.d.i.e.

4716.5.   See also 3406, 4636, 4640, 4642.d., 4676, 4691, 5162.

Op. 63 Nine Songs for Solo Voice

4717.   Biba, Otto. "Brahms, Johannes" in *Beiträge zur musikalischen Quellenkunde. Katalog der Sammlung Hans P. Wertitsch in der Musiksammlung der Österreichischen Nationalbibliothek.* Günter Brosche, ed. (Publikationen des Instituts für Österreichische Musikdokumentation 15) Tutzing: Hans Schneider, 1989. pp. 33–35. facsim. Entry is for autograph of Op. 63 no. 5. Provides background on the work and the text's author (Felix Schumann), manuscript description and provenance.

4718.   Bruckmann, Annett. ""O wüßt ich doch den Weg zurück . . ." Ein Beitrag zum Brahmsschen Liedschaffen" *Brahms-Studien* Bd. 9 (1992) pp. 49–73. mus. (pp. 68–69), fig., notes. Analyses Brahms's setting of the text; includes comment on Brahms's thoughts about setting text and about Brahms and Groth.

4718.2. See also 3794, 3970, 4662, 4679, 4683, 5084, 5090, 5168, 5195, 5198, 5200.

Op. 64 Three Quartets for Solo Voices (SATB)

4718.4. See 3578, 4636, 4666, 4669, 5162, 5396.

Op. 65 New Liebeslieder Waltzes for 4 Solo Voices (SATB) and Piano 4 hands

4718.6. See 3365, 3398, 3404, 3578, 4292, 4635, 4636, 4666, 4692, 4836, 4931, 4965, 4998, 5162.

Op. 66 Five Duets for Soprano and Alto

4718.8. See 3794, 4635, 4636, 4640, 4642.d., 4691.

Op. 69 Nine Songs for Solo Voice

4719. King, David. "Brahms, Hindemith, and Salome" *Ars musica Denver* 1/1 (Fall 1988) pp. [31]–39. mus., notes. Compares Op. 69 no. 8 to Hindemith's *Herodiade* (1944) in regards to setting of text (Brahms set Keller text; Hindemith set Mellarmé text); includes comment on interest in Salome in 19th century, and Strauss's opera.

4719.2. See also 3409, 4683, 5081, 5082, 5090, 5100, 5202.

Op. 70 Four Songs for Solo Voice

4719.3. See 4683, 5100.

Op. 71 Five Songs for Solo Voice

4719.4. See 4675, 4683, 5084, 5090, 5094, 5097, 5195, 5198, 5200.

Op. 72 Five Songs for Solo Voice

4719.5. See 3407, 3840, 3908, 3911, 4683, 5090, 5195.

Op. 75 Ballads and Romances for 2 Solo Voices

4719.7. See 3810, 4636, 4640, 4642.d., 4691, 4960, 5081, 5084, 5090, 5091, 5396.

Op. 84 Five Romances and Songs for 1 or 2 Solo Voices

4719.8. See 3375, 3653, 4662, 4679, 4683, 4690, 4697, 5081, 5084, 5087, 5090, 5168, 5195, 5198, 5200, 5396.

Op. 85 Six Songs for Solo Voice

4719.9. See 4051, 4675, 4683, 5084, 5090, 5094, 5101, 5195, 5200, 5202.

Op. 86 Six Songs for Low Voice

4720. Brahms, Johannes. *Feldeinsamkeit. Opus 86 Nr. 2. "Ich ruhe still im hohen grünen Gras". Faksimile nach dem in Privatbesitz befind-lichen Autograph.* ["Geleitwort" by Ernst Herttrich] München: G. Henle Verlag, 1983. [2, 4 [=facsim.], 1, 3 pp.] mus. "Geleitwort" is 3 pages at end, includes English translation ("Accompanying Note"). Provides background on the song, and on Allmers the poet and his reaction to the setting. Provides background on the manu-script and its dedicatee Wilhelm Lindeck, includes some textual comparison comments.

4720.5. See also 3375, 3840, 3970, 4662, 4679, 4682, 4683, 4697, 4928, 5084, 5090, 5093, 5100, 5157, 5168, 5195, 5198, 5200.

Op. 91 Two Songs for Contralto and Viola

4721. *Swartz, Melinda. "Johannes Brahms—Two Songs for Contralto and Viola, Opus 91: A Poetic and Musical Analysis" M.Mus. diss., Bowling Green State University, 1975. 120 pp. mus.

4721.3. See also S060, 3375, 3405, 4634, 4636, 4683, 5198.

4721.7. See also I42 in Appendix A.

Op. 92 Four Quartets for 4 Solo Voices (SATB)

4722. *Pickett, Kyle William. "Brahms' Quartette, Op. 92: A Perfor-mance Study" M.A. diss., California State University, Chico, 1994. vii, 50 pp.

4722.3. See also 4636, 4666, 4667, 4669, 5396.

Op. 94 Five Songs for Low Voice

4722.6. See 3840, 3917, 3918, 4650, 4682, 4683, 5084, 5090, 5101, 5157, 5168, 5195, 5198, 5200.

Op. 95 Seven Songs for Solo Voice

4722.9. See 3814, 4683, 5088.5, 5090, 5092, 5101, 5195, 5200.

Op. 96 Four Songs for Solo Voice

4723. Von Troschke, Michael. "Johannes Brahms' Lied op. 96 Nr. 1 Der Tod, das ist die kühle Nacht" *Brahms-Studien* Bd. 8 (1990) pp. 83–93. mus. (pp. 92–93), notes. Analyses Brahms's setting of the text.

4723.3. See also 3375, 3840, 4683, 4880, 4931, 5084, 5090, 5092, 5094, 5101, 5168, 5195, 5198, 5200, 5202.

Op. 97 Six Songs for Solo Voice

4723.7. See 3794, 3836, 3840, 4682, 4683, 5090, 5168, 5195, 5200.

Op. 103 Zigeunerlieder

4724. *Borghetto, Gabriella. "Gli "Zigeunerlieder" e la loro fonte ungherese" in *I Lieder di Johannes Brahms*. [for full citation see 4677] pp. 117–40.

4725. *Davis, Timothy Barker. "Zigeunerlieder, Opus 103 by Johannes Brahms: A Comparative Analysis of the Choral Work and the Arrangement by the Composer for Solo Voice and its Performance Implications" M.M. diss., Bowling Green State University, 1982. iii, 33 pp. notes.

4726. *Pfingsten, Rodger Kenneth. "Romanticism as Exemplified by the Gipsy-Song Cycle" M.A. diss., Music, San Jose State University, 1981. ix, 55 pp. mus., notes. Discusses Brahms's Op. 103 and Dvořák's Op. 55. [from S031]

4726.5. Teat, Sue Ellen. "Delight for the Solo Singer: Brahms' Gypsy Songs" *The American Music Teacher* 33/2 (11./12.1983) pp. 24–25. notes. Descriptive comments, background and performance suggestions for Op. 103 nos. 1–7, 11 as arranged for solo voice and piano.

4727. See also S060, 3578, 3758, 4636, 4683, 5090, 5127, 5200, 5396.

Op. 105 Five Songs for Low Voice

4728. Siegel, Hedi, and Arthur Maisel. "Heinrich Schenker Graphic Analysis of Brahms's Auf dem Kirchhofe, Op. 105, No. 4 as prepared for publication by William J. Mitchell and Felix Salzer" *Theory and Practice* 13 (1988) pp. 1–14. fig. (pp. 6–9), notes. Siegel provides the background on the analysis ("Introduction": pp. [1]–5) and Maisel discusses the work ("A Commentary": pp. 10–14).

4728.3. See also 3375, 3487, 3794, 4646, 4648, 4662, 4682, 4683, 4822, 4880, 4908, 4931, 4960, 5084, 5090, 5093, 5168, 5195, 5198, 5200.

Op. 106 Five Songs for Solo Voice

4728.7. See 3375, 4683, 5084, 5090, 5195, 5198, 5200.

Op. 107 Five Songs for Solo Voice

4729. *Jasińska, Danuta. "Johannes Brahms: Mädchenlied, pieśń op. 107 nr 5 do słów P[aul]. Heyse (1886)" in *Forma i ekspresja w liryce wokalnej 1808–1909: Interpretacje*. Mieczysław Tomaszewski, ed. (Muzyka i liryka 2) Kraków: Akademia muzyczna, 1989. pp. 119–38. summary in German. How to interpret this song. [from S102]

4729.3. See also 3814, 4675, 4683, 4931, 5084, 5090, 5105, 5168, 5195, 5198, 5200, 5388.

Op. 112 Six Quartets for Solo Voices (SATB)

4729.7. See 3578, 4636, 4640, 4666, 5396.

Op. 121 Four Serious Songs for Bass

4730. *[Browman, David] "A-level history and analysis" *Music Teacher* 75/8 (1.8.1996) pp. 23+ . [from S092]

4731. *Bockholdt, Rudolf. "Anwesenheit und Abwesenheit von Musikgeschichte in den Vier ernsten Gesängen von Johannes Brahms" in *Glasba in poezija*. [for full citation see 4699] pp. 167–75. mus. summary in Slovene. Wonders whether Op. 121 is really lieder, as set text is prose, not verse. Analyses texts and their possible influence on the overall form of the settings and the musical character of the songs. [from S102]

4732. Decarsin, François. "J. Brahms (1833–1897), Quatre Chants sérieux, op. 120 (sic), 1896, . . ." (Actualités) *Revue d'esthétique* nouvelle série no. 7 (1984) pp. 187–88. mus. Discusses how Brahms reflects on death in Op. 121 and the work's cyclic unity.

4733. *Greene, David B[eckwith], Jr. "Music, Text and Meaning in Religious Music" Ph.D. diss., Yale University, 1967. 267 pp. notes. Brahms's Op. 121 no. 4 is one of the examples. [from S031]

4734. *Hirschfeld, Robert. "Vier ernste Gesänge von Johannes Brahms" *Neue musikalische Presse* [=*Internationale Musik- und Instrumenten-Zeitung*] [5] (25.11.1896) pp. 2–3.

4735. *Iams, Kathryn E. "Brahms' Vier ernste Gesange: A Study of Textual and Musical Content" M.Mus. diss., Bowling Green State University, 1973. 65 pp.

4736. *Lewin, Alison Williams. "The Four Serious Songs of Johannes Brahms: A Textural and Structural Analysis" M.A. diss., University of Pittsburgh, 1983. 45 pp. mus., notes.

4737. *Moore, Mark Alexander. "A Comparative Analysis of the Origin and Culmination of Nineteenth Century Lieder as seen in Ludwig von Beethoven's "Sechs Lieder von Gellert", Op. 48, Johannes Brahms's "Vier ernste Gesänge", and Selected Songs from Hugo Wolf's "Spanisches Liederbuch"" D.M.A. diss., Southwestern Baptist Theological Seminary, 1990. 180 pp. Purpose is to show that Brahms and Wolf are the culmination of the lied form, where Beethoven sets the standard. Also discusses each composer's religious philosophy and associations.

4738. *Preissinger, Cornelia. "Die vier ernsten Gesänge op. 121: vokale und instrumentale Gestaltungsprinzipien im Werk von Johannes Brahms" Phil.F. diss., Ludwig-Maximilians-Universität München, 1993.
   (a) *reprint: Preissinger. *Die vier ernsten Gesänge op. 121: vokale und instrumentale Gestaltungsprinzipien im Werk von Johannes Brahms.* (Europäische Hochschulschriften=Publications universitaires européennes=European University

Studies. Reihe=Série=Series 36. Musikwissenschaft=
Musicologie=Musicology 115) Frankfurt a.M., New York:
P. Lang, 1994. 244 pp. mus., notes.

4739. Simpson, Anne. "Some Thoughts on Brahms' Four Serious Songs"
The American Music Teacher 33/2 (11./12.1983) pp. 20–21, 23.
notes. Background and descriptive comments; includes comment on
Brahms and Klinger, and Brahms and Clara Schumann.

4740. Skouenborg, Ulrik. "Elgar's Enigma: the solution" *Music Review*
43/3–4 (8.–11.1982) pp. 161–68. mus. Op. 121 no. 4 and Elgar's
Op. 36 have text in common; author speculates that Brahms's
work is Elgar's unplayed theme and points out musical connections between these two items.

4741. *Smith, Wilbur Michael. "An Analysis of Brahms' "Denn es
gehet dem Menschen . . ." from Vier ernste Gesänge" M.A. diss.,
University of Redlands, 1969. 69 pp. ill., mus., notes. Song is no.
1 in the cycle.

4742. *Stefan, Paul. *Die Stunde* (Wien) (1937). Article is based on
Coenraad von Bos's remembrances of premiering Op. 121, see
4646.

4743. Whittall, Arnold. "The Vier ernste Gesänge Op. 121: enrichment
and uniformity" in *Brahms: Biographical, Documentary and Analytical Studies*. [for full citation see 5479] pp. 191–207. mus.,
fig., ind., notes. Analytical study pointing out Brahms's use of developing variation in this song and his method of achieving unity.

4744. Zacher, Gerd. "Komponierte Formanten" in *Aimez-vous Brahms
"the progressive"?* [for full citation see 4872] pp. [69]–75. fig.,
mus. For Op. 121 no. 4 examines settings of particular words
throughout the song.

4744.5. See also S060, 3267, 3365, 3375, 3487, 3835, 3840, 3930, 3958,
4038, 4646, 4659, 4678, 4682, 4683, 4695, 4796, 4822, 4910,
4928, 5080, 5084, 5090, 5195, 5200, 5201.

Mondnacht [McCorkle WoO 21]

4745. *Jasińska, Danuta. "Mondnacht Eichendorffa w pieśniach Schu-
manna i Brahmsa" in *Wiersz i jego piesniowe interpretacje: Za-*

gadnienie tekstów wielokrotnie umuzycznianych—Studia porów-
nawcze. Mieczysław Tomaszweski, ed. (Muzyka i liryka 3)
Kraków: Akademia muzyczna, 1991. pp. 137–42. summary in
German. Compares Brahms's setting of text with that of Schumann in his Op. 39 no. 5. [from S102]

4745.3.   See also 3975, 3976, 4683, 5057, 5089, 5090, 5105, 5198.

Brautlied [McCorkle Anhang IIa, nr. 29]

4745.7.   See 3814.

Children's Folksongs for Solo Voice (1858) [McCorkle WoO
posthum 31]

4746.   *Suppan, Wolfgang. "Zwischen Volkstümlichkeit und Kunst-
anspruch: Geschichte, Struktur und Ästhetik der "Heidenröslein"-
Melodien" Musicologica austriaca 8 (1988) pp. 83–122. mus.,
notes. Surveys all settings of this melody, includes a thematic catalog with melodic incipits. Brahms's is McCorkle WoO posthum
31 no. 6. [from S102]

4746.5.   See also 4650, 4659, 5195, 5198.

Forty-nine German Folksongs for Solo Voice and 4 part Choir
with Soloist (1894) [McCorkle WoO 33]

4747.   Cogan, Robert, and Pozzi Escot. "Johannes Brahms: "Wach' Auf,
Mein Hort," from German Folk Songs" in Cogan and Escot. Sonic
Design. The Nature of Sound and Music. Englewood Cliffs, NJ:
Prentice-Hall Inc., 1976. pp. 148–57. mus., fig. Discusses har-
mony, harmonic progression and voice leading using McCorkle
WoO 33 no. 13 as example.

4747.2.   See also 3365, 4634, 4659, 4675, 4682, 4683, 4686, 5192.

Du bist wie eine Blume [McCorkle Anhang IIa, nr. 12*]

4747.4.   See 5057.

Kleine Hochzeitskantate [McCorkle WoO posthum 16]

4747.6.   See 3398, 3833, 4636, 5108.

Müllerin, Die [McCorkle Anhang III, nr. 13]

4747.8. See 3399.

Ophelia Songs [McCorkle WoO posthum 22]

4748. "Brahms and His Songs" *Musical Opinion and Music Trade Review* 58/696 (9.1935) p. 1007. Reports on the first edition, presents their background and includes comment on Brahms and the theatre.

4749. "New Brahms "Find"" *Musical Courier* 109 (1.12.1934) p. 16. Report on Ophelia Lieder. [from compiler]

4750. *Odom, Susan Gale Johnson. "Four Musical Settings of Ophelia" D.M.A. diss., University of North Texas, 1991. v, 115 pp. ill., notes. A detailed analysis of [Brahms's] McCorkle posthum WoO 22, Richard Strauss's Op. 67 no. 1, Chausson's Op. 28 no. 3 and Pasatieri's *Ophelia's Lament*. Looks at techniques used by these composers in setting Shakespeare and for being dramatic. [from S102]

4751. *Preissinger, Cornelia. "Die Ophelia-Lieder von Richard Strauss und Johannes Brahms" *Richard-Strauss-Blätter* no. 29 (1993) pp. 53–67. mus. summary in English. Compares Strauss's Op. 67 with [Brahms's] McCorkle WoO posthum 22 [from S109]

Regenlied [McCorkle WoO posthum 23]

4751.5. See 3383, 3794.

2. Works for Chorus

General

4752. *Alexander, David Charles. "An Analysis of the A cappella Motets of Johannes Brahms" M.M. diss., California State University, Fullerton, 1983. 108 pp. ill., mus., notes.

4753. Berger, Melvin. "Johannes Brahms" in Berger. *Guide to Choral Masterpieces. A Listener's Guide.* 1st Anchor Books edition. New

York: Anchor Books, 1993. pp. [80]–91. discog. (p. 360). Presents
background, timings, and texts in German and English for Opp.
45, 53, 54.

4754. Beuerle, Hans Michael. "Brahms' Verhältnis zum Chor und zur
Chorwerk" *Brahms-Studien* Bd. 5 (1983) pp. 91–115. mus., notes.
Reworked section from 2187 (H.M. Beuerle. "Untersuchungen
zum historischen Stellenwert der a-cappella-Kompositionen von
J. Brahms" (1976?)).

    (d) Beuerle. *Johannes Brahms. Untersuchungen zu den A-cap-
pella-Kompositionen. Ein Beitrag zur Geschichte der Chormusik.* Hamburg: Verlag der Musikalienhandlung Karl Dieter
Wagner, 1987. 433 pp. mus., fig., ind., notes. Places Brahms's
works in the history of choral a cappella music; also includes
analysis. This work is a reworked version of 2187 (H.M.
Beuerle. "Untersuchungen zum historischen Stellenwert der
a-cappella-Kompositionen von J. Brahms" (1976?)).

4755. Biba, Otto. "Johannes Brahms in der Kirchenmusik" *Singende
Kirche* 30/3 ([9.] 1983) pp. 102–03. ill. A review of the sacred
works, including the rediscovered Missa canonica [McCorkle
WoO postum 18].

4756. "Brahms's Kyrie [McCorkle WoO posthum 17] and Missa canonica [McCorkle WoO posthum 18]:", see 4854.5.

4757. Bredenbach, Ingo, see 4855.5.

4758. Carlson, Stanley A. *Music for Male Chorus.* Staples, MN: Associated Male Choruses of America, 1985. 69 pp. ind. 30 references
for Brahms items (original and arranged works). Listings are
arranged alphabetically by English language title of work.

4759. Daverio, John. "Brahms and Schumann's Dramatic Choral Music. Giving Musical Shape to "Deeply Intellectual Poetry"" *The
American Brahms Society Newsletter* 14/1 (Spring 1996) pp.
[1]–4. ill., mus., notes. Demonstrates a very strong affinity between Brahms's and Schumann's dramatically inclined choral
music; looks at Brahms works that reflect Schumann: Op. 45
seen as a continuation of a Schumann work; discusses connections between Schumann's Op. 139 and Brahms's Op. 50; Schumann's *Szenen aus Goethes Faust* and Brahms's Opp. 81
and 89.

350 Part IV

4760. *Finney, Theodore M. "The Oratorio and Cantata Market: Britain, Germany, America c.1830—c.1910" in *Choral Music: A Symposium*. Arthur Jacobs, ed. Harmondsworth: Penguin Books, 1963. also: Baltimore: Penguin Books, 1963. "The Oratorio and Cantata Market: Britain, Germany, America c.1830—c.1910": pp. [217]–30. "Brahms" pp. 224–28. mus., ind., notes., discog. A brief look at Brahms's place in the history of choral music; takes a more in-depth look at his style as seen in Op. 45.

4761. *Konecki, Konnie Jo. "Study of the Choral Works written for Women's Choruses by Schubert, Mendelssohn, Schumann, and Brahms" M.M. diss., Southern Methodist University, 1961. v, 89 pp. ill., mus. Works by Brahms include Opp. 12, 17, 27, 37, 44. [from compiler]

4761.5. Kross, Siegfried. "The Choral Music of Johannes Brahms" [Adapted from German text by Alfred Mann] *American Choral Review* 25/4 (10.1983) pp. 3–30. [entire issue] mus., fig., ind., notes. Biography of Brahms written from point of view of the development of his choral style; includes details of works' background and reception. Shows goal of Brahms's work is to be a synthesis of romanticism and strict polyphonic traditions. Includes a chronological list of the works [list is actually in order by opus number, showing date of composition].

4762. Kross, Siegfried. "Kleinere Chorwerke" in *Johannes Brahms: Leben und Werk*. [for full citation see 3215] pp. 160–62. mus. Surveys Brahms as a composer of this genre.

4763. Laster, James. *Catalogue of Choral Music Arranged in Biblical Order*. Metuchen & London: The Scarecrow Press, Inc., 1983. vii, [1, 3] 4–261 pp. ind. 22 references for Brahms items. Information provided includes Biblical reference, number of performers, publication data.

4764. *Locke, Benjamin Ross. "Performance and Structural Levels: A Conductor's Analysis of Brahms's Op. 74, No. 2, 'O Heiland, Reiss die Himmel auf' and Op. 29, No. 2, 'Schaffe in Mir, Gott, ein rein Herz'" D.M.A. diss., University of Wisconsin-Madison, 1985. 240 pp. Uses Schenkerian analysis to aid in performance preparation. [from S081]
(d) Locke, Benjamin [Ross]. "Melodic Unity in Brahms's Schaffe

in Mir, Gott, ein rein Herz" *The Choral Journal* 27/9 (4.1987) pp. 5–7. mus., fig. Shows that Brahms uses melodic fragments from bars 1–27 to create a bond between all 3 movements; also shows his techniques to disguise the borrowings.

4765. *Martin, Paul David. "Analyses of the Seven (sic) A cappella Motets of Johannes Brahms" M.M. diss., Indiana University, 1970. viii, 110 pp. ill., mus., notes.

4766. *Mueller, Paul F. "Brahms Rhapsodie, Op. 53, and Schicksalslied, Op. 54: A Conductor's Analysis" D.M. diss., Indiana University, 1990. vi, 134 pp. ill., mus., notes.

4767. *Myrvik, Norman Clifford. "The Expressive Technique Employed in the Choral Works of Johannes Brahms" M.A. diss., University of Minnesota, 1941. viii, 136 pp. ill., mus., notes.

4768. Pahlen, Kurt. "Johannes Brahms 1833–1897" in Pahlen. *Oratorien der Welt. Oratorium, Messe, Requiem, Te Deum, Stabat Mater und große Kantate.* Dr. Werner Pfister and Rosemarie König, eds. Zürich: SV International/Schweizer Verlagshaus, 1985. pp. 64–74. mus. Discusses Opp. 45, 53–55, 82, 89 with background and descriptive analysis. Also includes particulars such as text, date composed and first performed, ensemble required, original title and language. Includes sketch of life and comment on characteristics of music.

(b) English translation by Judith Schaefer: Pahlen. "Johannes Brahms 1833–1897" in Pahlen. *The World of the Oratorio: Oratorio, Mass, Requiem, Te Deum, Stabat Mater and Large Cantatas.* With the collaboration of Dr. Werner Pfister and Rosemarie König. Additional material for the English language edition by Thurston Dox. Reinhard G. Pauly, General Ed. Portland: Amadeus Press, 1990. pp. 73–82. adds notes.

4769. Papanikolaou, Eftychia. "Brahms's Reception of Greek Antiquity with Emphasis on The Gesang der Parzen" M.Mus. diss., Boston University, 1995. x, [1] 2–145 pp. notes., appendix. Studies how Brahms expressed the changing trends towards Greek art in his music. Looks at Opp. 54 and 82 as well as 89; presents works' background, examines the texts and how they are set. Includes comment on Brahms's knowledge of Greece. The appendix continues the texts in original and English language translation.

4770. Petersen, Peter. "Werke für Chor und Orchester" in *Johannes Brahms: Leben und Werk.* [for full citation see 3215] pp. 170–72. Reviews background of each work and the setting of their text.

4771. Sharp, Avery T. "Brahms, Johannes" in Sharp. *Choral Music Reviews Index, 1983–1985.* (Garland Reference Library of the Humanities 674) New York & London: Garland Publishing, Inc., 1986. p. 222. 13 entries for Brahms items. Body of work is arranged alphabetically by title. Total pp.: [6] vii–x, [2] 3–260 pp.

    (d) Sharp. in Sharp. *Choral Music Reviews Index II, 1986–1988.* (Garland Reference Library of the Humanities 962) New York & London: Garland Publishing, Inc., 1990. p. 283. 7 entries for Brahms items. Total pp.: [6] vii–xi [3] 3–397 pp.

4772. *Sheppard, Cynthia C. "A Conductor's Analysis of Selected Works by William Byrd, Heinrich Schutz, Alessandro Scarlatti, Michael Haydn, Johannes Brahms, Gustav Holst and Ned Rorem" M.M. diss., Southwestern Baptist Theological Seminary, 1985. ix, 157 pp. ill., mus., notes.

4773. *Smith, Gregory Eugene. "A Study of the Unaccompanied Vocal Canons of Johannes Brahms" A.M. diss., Washington University, 1971. 73 pp. ill., mus., notes.

4774. *Sopeña Ibáñez, Federico. *Ciclo "El Lied coral romántico".* Madrid: Fundación Juan March, 1987. 88 pp. Includes choral works of Schumann, Brahms, Schubert and Mendelssohn. Based on program notes. [from S102]

4775. *Stevenson, Robert. *Notes on Choral Masterworks.* (Pro/AM General Music Series GMS-4) White Plains, NY: Pro/AM Music Resources, Inc., 1985.

4776. *Ulrich, Homer. *A Survey of Choral Music.* New York: Harcourt Brace Jovanovich, [1973]. ix, 245 pp. ill., notes.

4777. *Vinay, Gianfranco. "Johannes Brahms, Max Klinger e l'angoscia di Prometeo" in *Musica senza aggettivi: Studi per Fedele D'Amico.* 2 vols. Agostino Ziino, ed. (Quaderni della Rivista italiana di musicologia 25) Firenze: Olschki, 1991. vol. 1, pp. 365–74. ill. Investigates whether Brahms's text settings accurately reflect the tone of the text. Op. 54 is compared with text source (Hölderlin's *Hyperion*) for its interpretation of Prometheus and then with Klinger illustration in his *Brahms-Phantasie* (1894) Part 2, which was inspired by Op. 54. Op. 89 is compared with text source (Goethe's *Iphigenie auf Tauris*). Brahms's setting often conveys more hope than original text conveys. [from S102]

4778. Wienandt, Elwyn A. *Choral Music of the Church*. New York: The Free Press; London: Collier-Macmillan Limited, 1965. xi, [5], 494 pp. Brahms: pp. 332–33, 369–72. mus., ind., notes. Discusses Brahms's contribution to the motet form, focuses on Op. 45 in relation to the history of the oratorio. Includes comment on Brahms's contribution to sacred choral music, and his relationship to other religious composers of the 19th century.

4779. *Williams, Nettie Jean. "Complicating Factors in the Motets of Johannes Brahms Created by the Harmonic Rhythm in Conjunction with the Use of Contiguous Modes Resulting in Problems of Tempo and Intonation" D.M.A. diss., University of Oklahoma, 1987. 157 pp. An aid to performing Opp. 29, 74, 110 with detailed analysis of selected areas and quotes from Brahms's contemporaries attesting to the aural difficulty of this music. [from S081]

4780. *Williamson, Richard Anthony. "Linear and Motivic Connections in Two Brahms Motets" M.A. diss., University of Rochester, 1986. iii, 135 pp. mus., notes.

4781. Young, Percy M. "The Nineteenth Century II" in Young. *The Choral Tradition. An Historical and Analytical Survey from the Sixteenth Century to the Present Day*. London: Hutchinson & Co., 1962. pp. 236–70.
"Germany and Austria: The Works of Brahms and Bruckner": pp. 239–48. Brahms: pp. 241–46. ind., notes. Describes changes in Brahms's style in the choral works, includes an analysis of Op. 45 and comment on its reception.
Revised edition: *The Choral Tradition*. New York, London: W.W. Norton & Company, 1981.

4781.2. See also 3318, 3361, 3371, 3372, 3395, 3411, 3799, 3944, 4037, 4040, 4059, 4866, 4994, 5014, 5135, 5143, 5144, 5152, 5227, 5230, 5282, 5367.d.i.a.

4781.4. See also I31 in Appendix A.

Specific

Op. 12 Ave Maria for Women's Choir

4781.6.   See 4050, 4635, 4755, 4761, 4924, 5143, 5345.

Op. 13 Begräbnisgesang for Choir and Wind Instruments

4781.8.   See 4755, 4924, 4931, 4956, 5143, 5345.

Op. 17 Four Songs for Women's Choir, 2 Horns and Harp

4782.   Anderson, Julia S., and Jane B. Weidensaul. "Notes on the Four
Songs for Women's Chorus, Two Horns, and Harp (Op. 17) by Johannes Brahms" *The American Harp Journal* 9/2 (Winter 1983)
pp. 32, 36–37. ill., notes. Based on 2221 (J.S. Anderson. "Music
for Women's Chorus and Harp . . ." (1977)), abridged and sup-
plemented by Weidensaul. Reviews Brahms works for women's
chorus, particularly in the late 1850's, early 1862. Comments on
the texts set and the instrumentation.

4783.   *Breden, Mary Catherine. "Analyses and Rehearsal Guide for Selected Treble Choral Literature" D.M.A. diss., Arizona State University, 1983. 2 vols. mus., notes.
(d)   Breden, Mary [Catherine]. "Classic Beauty and Romantic
Flair in Brahms' Vier Gesänge für Frauenchor, Zwei Hörner
und Harfe" *Choral Journal* 31/5 (12.1990) pp. 35–43. mus.,
fig., notes. Analysis and background of the work, as an aid
in rehearsal. Includes examination of text-music links, and
Brahms's style as a classical romantic.

4783.3.   See also 3352, 3365, 3407, 3414, 3810, 4635, 4761, 5091, 5205,
5345.

Op. 22 Marienlieder for Mixed A Cappella Choir

4783.7.   See 3365, 4754, 4755, 4924, 5143.

Op. 27 The 13th Psalm for 3 part Women's Choir

4784.   Walters, Kevin. "AGO Colleague Examination Repertoire. Interpretive Notes for C2 and C3" *The American Organist* 24/7 (7.1990) pp. 41–42. Brahms: p. 41. Discusses the organ part for this work: tempi, registration, manuals.

4784.5. See also 4050, 4755, 4761, 4924, 5143.

Op. 29 Two Motets for 5 part A Cappella Choir

4785. Blume, Jürgen. "Johannes Brahms: Schaffe in mir, Gott, ein rein Herz (Op. 29, Nr. 2)" (Im Konzertsaal gehört) *NZ-Neue Zeitschrift für Musik* 146/5 (5.1985) pp. 34–36. mus., notes. Presents work's background and an analysis of Brahms's composing techniques.

4785.2. See also 4042, 4752, 4754, 4755.

Op. 30 Geistliches Lied for 4 part Choir

4785.3. See 4050, 4755, 4765, 4924.

Op. 37 Three Geistliche Chöre for A Cappella Women's Choir

4785.4. See 4635, 4754, 4755, 4761, 4864, 4924, 5143.

Op. 41 Five Songs for Men's Choir

4785.6. See 3407, 4061, 4754, 4758.

Op. 42 Three Songs for 6 part A Cappella Choir

4785.7. See 3810, 4754, 5091, 5205.

Op. 44 Twelve Songs and Romances for 4 part A Cappella Women's Choir

4785.8. See 3814, 4635, 4754, 4761, 4931, 5105.

Op. 45 Ein Deutsches Requiem

4786. *Musical Standard* new series [1, vol.] 4 (29.3.1873) pp. 192–93. Review. [from WPA Index]

4787. *Adamski, Ursula. Phil.F. diss., Westfälische Wilhelms-Universität Münster, 1991.

(d) Adamski-Störmer, Ursula. *"Requiem aeternam": Tod und Trauer im 19. Jahrhundert im Spiegel einer musikalischen Gattung.* (Europäische Hochschulschriften=Publications universitaires européennes=European University Studies. Reihe=Série=Series 36. Musikwissenschaft=Musicologie=Musicology 66) Frankfurt am Main [et al.]: Peter Lang, 1991. 354 pp. ill., mus., works list. Traces the history of the genre, relates it to shifts in the relationship between society and the church and society's attitude to death and mourning. [from S102]

4788. *Ambros, A.W. "Das Requiem seit hundert Jahren und das Requiem von Franz Lachner" *Echo. Berliner Musik-Zeitung* [22]/24 (12.6.1872) pp. 260–61.

4789. *Ben-Chorin, Schalom. *Ich lege meine Hand auf meinen Mund. Meditation zu Johannes Brahms 'Ein Deutsches Requiem' (Ausschnitte) und Arnold Schönberg 'Ein Überlebender aus Warschau'.* Vorwort von Urs Meier. Zürich: Theologischer Verlag, 1992. 36 pp.

4790. Blain, T. "The Collector's Choice: Brahms's German Requiem" *Classic CD* no. 37 (6.1993) pp. 32–36.

4791. Boughton, Rutland. "The Masterpiece of Brahms" *Musical Opinion and Music Trade Review* 25/292 (1.1.1902) pp. 279–80. Descriptive comments on Op. 45.

4792. [Brahms, Johannes. *Ein deutsches Requiem = A German Requiem = Un Requiem allemand = Un requiem tedesco. Op. 45.* Charlotte Margiono, soprano; Rodney Gilfrey, baritone; Monteverdi Choir; Orchestre Revolutionnaire et Romantique; John Eliot Gardiner, conductor. (Digital Classics D115329) Philips, 1991. [Philips] 432 140–2. 1 compact disc. Program notes in English and text with English translation (11 pp.) inserted in container. [from S031]]

(d) i) [Gardiner, John Eliot] "Brahms and The "Human" Requiem" *Gramophone* 68/815 (4.1991) pp. 1809–10. Gardiner discusses his approach to recording Op. 45 with period instruments.

(d) ii) Vernier, David. "Organic Gardiner" *CD Review* 8/1 (9.1991) pp. 48, 55. ill. Gardiner discusses the recording and the problems of trying to breathe new life into the classics.

(e) i) review: *CD Review* 8/1 (9.1991) p. 56.

(e) ii) review: *Gramophone* 68/815 (4.1991) p. 1881.

(e) iii) review: Hancock, Virginia [Lee]. "Brahms in Better Balance" *Historical Performance. The Journal of Early Music America* 5/1 (Spring 1992) pp. 37–39. notes. Includes comments on conductor-composer relationships, and advises that Gardiñer acknowledges consulting 4793.

  (d) condensed: Hancock. "On Record: An "Historic" Performance of the Brahms Requiem?" *The American Brahms Society Newsletter* 10/1 (Spring 1992) pp. 4–7. adds new notes.

4793. *Brahms, Johannes. *A German Requiem. Op. 45. Piano vocal score.* 150th Anniversary edition. Translation from the German Bible with paraphrase, adaptation, and prosodic underlay by Lara Hoggard. Chapel Hill: Hinshaw Music, 1984. [8], 92, xv pp. notes.
*[published with revisions:] 1986. [6], 92, xv pp.
*3rd edition: 1989. [6], 92, xviii pp.

  (d) *Brahms. *A German Requiem=Ein deutsches Requiem. Op. 45. Full Score.* 1989. 206, xiii pp.

    (e) report: Weinert, William. "A New Edition of Ein deutsches Requiem: Implications for Future Research and Performance" *Choral Journal* 31/10 (5.1991) pp. 35–39, 42–43. facsim., mus., notes. A detailed comparison between standard editions and this new edition. Changes in dynamics, articulation and tempo, and in choral and orchestral markings are analysed; examines basis for these changes. Is this editing or interpreting?

  (e) *review (of 1984 edition): Janower, David. *The Choral Journal* 25/3 (11.1984) pp. 37–39.

    (a) reprint: Janower. "Recent Scores" *American Choral Review* 31/1 (Winter 1989) pp. 40–42.

4794. *Brahms, Johannes, Ein deutsches Requiem, Stichvorlage des Klavierauszuges, see* 4805.5.

4795. *"The Brahms "Requiem"" *Music News* 27 (7.3.1935) p. 2.

4796. Döbertin, Winfried. "Johannes Brahms' Deutsches Requiem als religiöses Kunstwerk" *Brahms-Studien* Bd. 8 (1990) pp. 9–30. notes. Looks at Brahms's text from a religious-philosophical point of view and tries to ground Brahms's feelings about religion and his links to the Bible; also looks at other religious works, like Op. 121.

4797. *Dolan, Marian E. "Brahms' Requiem Op. 45: A Reexamination in Light of New Manuscript Evidence to the Horn Trio Op. 40" M.A. diss., Music, Boston University, 1980. vii, 119 pp. ill., facsim., mus., notes.

4798. *Ehrlich, H[einrich]. *Neue Berliner Musikzeitung* [23]/46 (17.11. 1869) pp. 373–75.

4799. Hague. Gemeentemuseum. "Ein Deutsches Requiem. After Brahms" in Hague. Gemeentemuseum. *Tom Phillips. Works. Texts. To 1974*. Stuttgart [et al.]: edition hansjörg mayer, 1975. pp. 159–71. Black and white reproduction of this art work with technical information.

    (d) Phillips, Tom. "Ein Deutsches Requiem. After Brahms" in Phillips. *Works and Texts*. With an Introduction by Huston Paschal. London, New York: Thames and Hudson, 1992. pp. 54–57. ill. Colour reproduction of work, with background; includes English and German versions of texts.

4800. Heffernan, Charles W. "Standard Works for Chorus: Ein deutsches Requiem. "How lovely is thy dwelling place"" *Music Educators Journal* 70/4 (12.1983) pp. 26–31. ill., fig., mus. Suggestions for learning this movement (4th movement), aimed at study by a youth choir. Includes background of work and comments on whole work.

4801. Herford, Julius. "[The Choral Conductor's Preparation of the Musical Score:] Brahms: Ein Deutsches Requiem Opus 45 (1868): First Movement" in *Choral Conducting. A Symposium*. Harold A. Decker and Julius Herford, eds. Englewood Cliffs, NJ: Prentice-Hall Inc., 1973. pp. 214–24. mus., fig., notes. An indepth analysis with many figures, focuses on motivic development.

4802. *Hinds, Marguerite June. "Johannes Brahms' Ein deutsches Requiem: A Study of Its Style and Place in History with a Detailed Musical Analysis of "Denn Alles Fleisch" (Movement Two), and "Den Wir haben" (Movement Six)" M.M. diss., Music, University of Houston, 1972. v, 127 pp. ill., mus.

4803. Holley, Margaret. "Brahms' Requiem" *The Southern Review* 27/3 (7.1991) pp. 700–01. Poem. Impressions of this work.

Works 359

4804. *Horn, E. "Johannes Brahms—Ein deutsches Requiem" *Musica sacra* 103 (1983) pp. 215–26, 303–14, 393–99.

4805. Imbert, Hugues. "Le Requiem Allemand de Johannès Brahms" *Le Guide musical* 37/13 (29.3.1891) pp. 99–101. notes. Descriptive analysis, relates to "Neue Bahnen" and compares to work of other composers; includes comment on its performance history in France.
(a) *reprint?: in 2259 (H. Imbert. *Portraits et études* . . . (1894)).

4805.5. *Johannes Brahms, Ein deutsches Requiem, Stichvorlage des Klavierauszuges.* (Patrimonia 80) Kiel: KulturStiftung der Länder, 1994. 36 pp. ill. Includes 3688, 3899 and 4823.

4806. Krummacher, Friedhelm. "Symphonie und Motette: Überlegungen zum "Deutschen Requiem"" in *Brahms-Analysen.* [for full citation see 4888] pp. 183–200. mus., fig., notes. An analysis to show work's links to symphonic form; includes discussion of work's place within Brahms's œuvre and its links with the traditional requiem form and contemporary oratorio music.

4807. Lissauer, Ernst. "Trost des "Deutschen Requiems"" in Lissauer. *Der inwendige Weg. Neue Gedichte.* 1. und 2. Tausend. Jena: Eugen Diederichs, 1920. p. 53. A poem in which the author, in sorrow, is comforted by Op. 45. Poem is in "Finsternisse" [section title]; "Dunkel" [subsection title].

4808. *Lundin, Eric Paul. "Performance Considerations for Brahms' Ein Deutsches Requiem, Op. 45 and Dvorak's Requiem Op. 89" B.A. diss., Eckerd College, 1984. 74 pp. ill., mus.

4809. Meiser, Martin. "Johannes Brahms' Theologie im Deutschen Requiem und die Erwartungshaltung der Hörer" *Gottesdienst und Kirchenmusik* no. 5 (9./10.1986) pp. 145–46. notes. A theological analysis that concludes that Brahms is insensitive to the Requiem text.

4810. *Mies, P[aul]. "Trauermusiken von Heinrich Schütz bis Benjamin Britten" *Musica sacra* 93 (1973) pp. 206–14.

4811. Minear, Paul S. "Johannes Brahms. A German Requiem" in Minear. *Death Set To Music. Masterworks by Bach, Brahms, Penderecki, Bernstein.* Atlanta: John Knox Press, 1987. pp. [59]–83. Concentrates on studying Brahms's interpretation of the biblical

citations in the work, his setting of the texts and how they inter-
relate; includes comment on Brahms and religion, and includes
the text in original and English translation.

4812. *Musgrave, Michael. *Brahms: A German Requiem.* (Cambridge
Music Handbooks) New York: Cambridge University Press,
1996. 120 pp. A detailed study that examines its history and reception, analyzes its textual and musical structure, and discusses
performing traditions from Brahms's times to the present. [from
publisher's catalogue]
*also: paperback ed.: 1996.

4813. *Niggli, A[rnold]. "Zum 50jährigen Jubiläum des "Deutschen Requiems" von Johannes Brahms" *Schweizerische Musikzeitung
[und Sängerblatt]* 56/23 (1916).

4814. Nowak, Adolf. ""Ein deutsches Requiem" im Traditionszusam-
menhang" in *Brahms-Analysen.* [for full citation see 4814] pp.
201–09. mus., notes. Examines the Trauermusik tradition of Bach
(BWV 106), Händel and Schütz (Op. 7) and looks to see what
Brahms's connection to that tradition is. Includes comment on the
setting of the biblical text.

4815. Pintér, Éva. "Seligpreisung der Leidtragenden. Johannes Brahms:
Ein deutsches Requiem" *FonoForum* [28]/8 (8.1983) pp. 68–72.
ill., discog. Analysis of the work and its interpretations on records.

4816. Reeth, Michel van. "Gelovite opgang naar God. Didactische luis-
teroefening voor het hoger secundair" *Adem* 19/3 (5.–6.1983) pp.
144–54, 157 [last page is abstract in English and French]. mus.,
notes. Op. 45 included in a lesson plan on listening to religious
musical works dealing with or commemorating death: Bach's
BWV 106, Fauré's Op. 48 and Britten's Op. 66 are the others. Includes comment on orchestration, texts, structure, place of work
in respective composer's overall oeuvre.

4817. Reynolds [Reynolds, David]. "Overview: Choral Masterpieces"
American Record Guide 56/5 (9./10.1993) pp. 78–84. Brahms: p.
79. Gives 1 recommended recording with an overview of others.

4818. *Robbins, Russell Allen. "A Conductor's Study of Ein deutsches
Requiem by Johannes Brahms" B.M. thesis, Music (Honors),
Mississippi College, 1993. 42 pp. notes.

4819. *Rosenthaler, Wolfgang. "Die Harmonik im Schaffen von Johannes Brahms aufgezeigt am Deutschen Requiem" M.A. diss., Composition, Hochschule für Musik und darstellende Kunst, Wien, 1982. 52 pp. mus., notes. Analyses harmonic principles; includes history of requiem composition. [from S102]

4820. Russell, Tilden A. "Brahms and Wer nur den lieben Gott lässt walten: A New Contribution" The American Brahms Society Newsletter 6/2 (Autumn 1988) pp. [8–9]. mus. Suggests that maybe Brahms free composed the theme of the 2nd movement, rather than borrowing it from a chorale; makes analogy with Jessen's Op. 6 no. 1 and contemporary feelings on linking chorale and funeral music.

4821. *Steane, John [B.]. "Brahms: A German Requiem" in Choral Music on Record. Alan Blyth, ed. Cambridge: Cambridge University Press, 1991. discog.

4822. Stockmann, Bernhard. "Brahms— Reger oder Von der Legitimation des religiösen Liberalismus" in Brahms und seine Zeit. (Hamburger Jahrbuch für Musikwissenschaft 7) [for full citation see 5428] pp. 211–22. notes. Discusses contemporary reaction to Op. 45; and its relationship to Opp. 55, 109, 98 (4th movement only), 105 no. 4, 121. Compares to Reger's Opp. 27, 144b for what they are both saying in their music.

4823. *Struck, Michael. "Ein deutsches Requiem—handlich gemacht. Der Klavierauszug und seine Stichvorlage" in 4805.5. pp. 4–12. facsim., notes.

4824. *Topp, Morten. "Motiv, Wort und die deutsch-evangelischen Kernlieder im Deutschen Requiem von Johannes Brahms" Musik & forskning 17 (1991–92) pp. 7–52. mus. summary in Danish. Looks at quotations from German Lutheran chorales in Op. 45 in their musical context, and suggests a possible hidden dedication of Op. 45 to Schumann. [from S102]

4825. *Topp, Morten. ""Selig sind, die da Leid tragen": Om metronomtal og spilletider før og nu i 1. sats af Johannes Brahms' Ein deutsches Requiem" Musik & forskning 15 (1989–90) pp. 69–78. ill., mus., fig. summary in German. Compares playing times by conductors Walter and von Karajan to metronome markings on autograph manuscript to see if claim of being too slow can be justified. [from S102]

4826. Van der Linde, Bernard S. "'Himmelswonn' und Freud". Ein Thementyp der Klassik und der Romantik" in *De ratione in musica. Festschrift Erich Schenk zum 5. May 1972.* Theophil Antonicek, Rudolf Flotzingef and Othmar Wessely, eds. Kassel: Bärenreiter, 1975. pp. 187–201. Identified a motif that is allied to text references to heavenly rapture and puts forward examples from Op. 45, Beethoven's Op. 123, Mendelssohn's Op. 70 to support this interpretation. [from S102]

4827. Warburton, A[nnie]. O. "Set Works for O Level, G.C.E. Brahms and Dvorak" *Music Teacher and Piano Student* 46/2 (2.1967) pp. 13, 31, 39. Brahms: p. 31. Descriptive and analytical commentary for the 6th movement.

4828. Warburton, A[nnie]. O. "Set Works for O Level, G.C.E. Schumann and Brahms" *Music Teacher and Piano Student* 46/11 (11.1967) pp. 10, 23. Brahms: p. 23. Descriptive and analytical commentary for the 3rd movement.

4829. *Woelflin, Sandra Louise. "A Symbolic Analysis and Comparison of Johannes Brahms' Ein deutsches Requiem and Johann Sebastian Bach's Mattaus-Passion [BWV 244]" M.M. diss., Roosevelt University, 1978. 59 pp.

4830. Zeileis, Friedrich Georg. "Ein deutsches Requiem von Johannes Brahms. Bemerkungen zur Quellenlage des Klavierauszuges" in *Festschrift Rudolf Elvers zum 60. Geburtstag.* Ernst Herttrich and Hans Schneider, eds. Tutzing: Hans Schneider, 1985. pp. 535–40. notes. German translation of 2305 (F.G. Zeileis. *Music and Letters* (1979)).

(a) reprint: in Zeileis. *Katalog einer Musik-Sammlung.* Gallspach [Austria]: The Author, 1992. 240 pp. Brahms: pp. 47–59. facsim. (p. 212), notes. Includes descriptions and background for manuscripts for Opp. 32 no. 6, Op. 45 arranged for piano 2 hand, Op. 115 Stichvorlage and Op. 119 nos. 2 and 3; transcriptions of 3 letters Rieter-Biedermann to Brahms, 1869 (2), 1873 (1), and 1 letter Rieter-Biedermann's son to Brahms, 1877 (1) [see 3899]. Text for Op. 45 includes the reprint; text for Op. 119 is reprinted from 1697 (J. Brahms. *Intermezzi Opus 119 Nr. 2 und 3. . . .* (1975)). Also includes information on Willy v. Beckerath's "Kohlezeichnung" of Brahms from 1896 [see 3688].

(d) see: 4823.

4830.5. See also 3267, 3276, 3278, 3287, 3358, 3360, 3363, 3365, 3381.a.iv., 3410, 3550, 3598, 3623, 3832, 3840, 3851, 4036, 4038, 4041, 4042, 4046, 4047, 4048.a., 4049, 4050, 4062, 4460.e.ii., 4505, 4753, 4759, 4760, 4768, 4770, 4778, 4781, 4852, 4866, 4885, 4931, 5048, 5080, 5112, 5158, 5174, 5210, 5212, 5333.

Op. 50 Rinaldo, A Cantata

4831. *Ingraham, Mary [Isabel]. "Brahms's Rinaldo Op. 50: A Structural and Contextual Study" Ph.D. diss., University of Nottingham, 1994.

4832. McCormick, Sherman Lindsay. "A Comparative Study and Piano Transcription of the Original Manuscript of Brahms's Cantata Rinaldo, Opus 50" M.A. diss., Music, Washington State University, 1967. 165 pp. notes. Orchestral accompaniment transcribed for two pianos. [from S031]

4832.5. See also 3365, 3404, 3417, 3598, 3781, 3799, 4041, 4759, 4770, 4879, 5112, 5463.

Op. 53 Alto Rhapsody

4833. "Analysis Symposium: Brahms, Alto Rhapsody" *Journal of Music Theory* 27/2 (Fall 1983) pp. 223–71. p. 224 is the work's text in German and English (translation by Allen Forte); pp. 225–38 is Op. 53 in piano 2-hand version.
     Berry, Wallace. "Text and Music in the Alto Rhapsody": pp. 239–53. mus., fig., notes. Study explores Brahms's treatment of Goethe's forms, and identifies by illustration various techniques by which he depends and illuminates certain of the significant implications of the text.
     Forte, Allen. "Motive and Rhythmic Contour in the Alto Rhapsody"" pp. 255–71. mus., fig. Studies the harmonic and melodic motifs and their rhythmic contours. Interprets the relations among motifs and discusses some of their extraordinary manifestations in foreground and middleground of the tonal structure.
     (a) reprint (of Forte): Forte. in *Approaches to Tonal Analysis*. (The

Garland Library of the History of Western Music 14) New
York: Garland Publishing Inc., 1985. pp. 23–39. adds notes.
(d) related to: 5449.5.

4834. Brahms, Johannes. *Alto Rhapsody Opus 53*. Introduction by Walter [M.] Frisch. New York: New York Public Library. Astor,
Lenox and Tilden Foundations, 1983. 76 pp. facsim., mus., notes.
Facsimile of US-NYpl autograph manuscript (pp. 31–76). Introduction describes the role of Op. 53 in Brahms's personal life and
output, delineates the work's structure and the significance of this
manuscript and the sketches at A-Wgm.

4835. Garlington, Aubrey S., Jr. "Harzreise als Herzreise: Brahms's
Alto Rhapsody" *The Musical Quarterly* 69/4 (Fall 1983) pp.
527–42. mus., notes. Compares the personal situations of Goethe
when he wrote "Harzreise im Winter" and Brahms at time of composing Op. 53, to see if there are parallels, and examines music
(looks only at sections where text is set) to see if it reflects this.
(d) related to: 5449.5.

4836. Stegemann, Michael. "Johannes Brahms: Rhapsodie für eine Alt-
stimme, Männerchor und Orchester op. 53" (Im Konzertsaal
gehört) *NZ-Neue Zeitschrift für Musik* 144/4 (15.4–15.5.1983) pp.
23–25. mus., notes. Background of work and descriptive analysis;
also looks at its connection with Op. 65's "Zum Schluß" and at
Brahms as an interpreter of text.

4836.5. See also 3365, 3381.c., 3598, 3781, 3984, 4036, 4038, 4041,
4049, 4062, 4753, 4766, 4768, 4770, 4931, 4956, 5112, 5396.

Op. 54 Schicksalslied

4837. *Musical Standard* new series [1, vol.] 7 (22.8.1874) p. 114. Review. [from WPA Index]

4838. *Musical World* (London) 52 (4.4.1874) p. 208. Review. [from
WPA Index]

4839. Daverio, John. "The "Wechsel der Töne" in Brahms's Schicksalslied" *Journal of the American Musicological Society* 46/1
(Spring 1993) pp. 84–113. mus., fig., notes. Looks at work's musical meaning and the apparent contradiction of the poem's message in the instrumental postlude; includes study of the poem and
Brahms's setting of it. Brahms's work is considered in light of

Hölderlin's own poetic theory to show his adherence to the spirit of poet's work, and work is further interpreted as reflecting Brahms's personal experience before the symphonic works of the 1870's and 1880's.

4840. Jung-Kaiser, Ute. "Brahms' Schicksalslied op. 54 in der Interpretation Max Klingers" in *Quaestiones in musica*. Friedhelm Brusniak and Horst Leuchtmann, eds. Tutzing: Hans Schneider Verlag, 1989. pp. 271–89. ill., notes. Presents the history of the work and the problem with the ending; analyses how Klinger viewed the work.

4841. Luhring, Alan A. "Dialectical Thought in Nineteenth-Century Music as Exhibited in Brahms's Setting of Hölderlin's Schicksalslied" *The Choral Journal* 25/8 (4.1985) pp. 5–13. mus., fig., notes. An analysis of Op. 54 to look at Brahms's setting of the poem and see if setting supports text's meanings. Also includes background on the poem, and considers Mahler's Symphony no. 8 and Tchaikovsky's *Romeo and Juliet Fantasy Overture* in the same light.

4842. Massey, Irving. "Brahms's Deconstruction of A Text by Goethe: Of Honesty in Music" in Massey. *Find You The Virtue: Ethics, Imagery and Desire in Literature*. Fairfax, VA: The George Mason University Press, 1987. pp. 161–79. mus., notes. Discusses Brahms's unmasking of the text for what it is, a sexual tragedy, and the problems of accommodating Eros to Art.
(d) comment: Garlington, Aubrey S., [Jr.]. "Reflections on "Find You The Virtue"" *The American Brahms Society Newsletter* 6/1 (Spring 1988) pp. [2–4]. Review of the article that becomes a discussion on the validity of music research by nonmusicians.

4843. See also 3358, 3365, 3381.c., 3598, 3840, 3851, 3988, 4036, 4041, 4062, 4753, 4766, 4768–70, 4777, 4956, 5090, 5112.

Op. 55 Triumphlied

4844. *Musical Standard* new series [1, vol.] 6 (13.6.1874) pp. 386–87. Review. [from WPA Index]

4845. *Busch, Helene. *Allgemeine [deutsche] Musikzeitung* 1 (4.11.(?) 1874) pp. 315–17, 323–35. Review. [from WPA Index]

4846. Häfner, Klaus. "Das "Triumphlied" op. 55, eine vergessene Komposition von Johannes Brahms. Anmerkungen zur Rezeptionsgeschichte des Werkes" in *Johannes Brahms in Baden-Baden und Karlsruhe*. [for full citation see 5452] pp. 83–102. ill., notes. A detailed look at the history of this work and its first performance. Includes comments on style, and reviews critical comments from time of its composition through contemporary performances up to the present day.

4846.5. See also S060, 3598, 3646, 3799, 3851.d., 4050, 4768, 4770, 4822, 5112, 5232.

Op. 62 Seven Songs for Mixed Choir

4847. Geiger, Joachim. "J[ohannes]. Brahms: "Waldesnacht" op. 62, Nr 3" *[Praxis Musikerzeihung] Musik & Bildung* 22/2 (Bd. 81) (2.1990) pp. 90–95. ill., mus., fig., notes. As an aid to choirs doing this work, presents analysis of the text (by Paul Heyse), the music and a guide to interpretation.

4847.5. See also 3814, 4754, 4931, 5143.d.i.

Op. 74 Two Motets for Mixed A Cappella Choir

4848. Fässler, Urs. "Rebellion und Resignation. Brahms' und Regers musikalische Auseinandersetzung mit dem Tod" *Brahms-Studien* Bd. 9 (1992) pp. 9–21. mus. Contrasts the setting of Op. 74 no. 1 with Reger's Op. 110 no. 3.

4848.5. See also 4042, 4634, 4752, 4754, 4755, 4764, 4765, 4778–80, 4860, 4864, 5080, 5143, 5396.

Op. 82 Nänie

4849. *Nelson, Eric. "Johannes Brahms' Nanie, op. 82: An Analysis of Structure and Meaning" D.M. diss., Indiana University, 1990. v, 108 pp. ill., mus., notes.

4850. *Sabol, John M. "Nanie, 82 opus of Johannes Brahms: A Conductor's Study utilizing Principles of Herford Analysis and Palmer Analysis" M.M. diss., Bowling Green State University, 1984. notes.

4850.3. See also 3365, 3381.c., 3598, 4036, 4041, 4768–70, 4928, 5112.

Op. 89 Gesang der Parzen

4850.5. *Mauro, Rosemarie P. "The Gesang der Parzen of Goethe and Brahms: A Study in Synthesis and Interpretation" M.A. diss., University of Washington, 1986. v, 149 pp. ill., mus., notes.

4850.6. See 3365, 3381.c., 3686.c., 3781, 4759, 4768–70, 4777, 5112.

Op. 93a Six Songs and Romances for 4 part A Cappella Mixed Choir

4850.9. See 4754, 4929, 5088.5.

Op. 103, see "Op. 103" in Part IV.B.1. *"Specific"*

4851. Teat, Sue Ellen, see 4726.5.

Op. 104 Five Songs for Mixed A Cappella Choir

4851.1. Beuerle, Hans Michael. "Johannes Brahms, Nachtwache Nr. 1 op. 104/1" in *Chormusik und Analyse. Beiträge zur Formanalyse und Interpretation mehrstimmiger Vokalmusik*. Heinrich Poos, ed. 2 vols. (Schott Musikwissenschaft) Mainz [et al.]: Schott, 1983. Bd. 1: pp. 235–56. mus., fig., notes. Examines Brahms's setting of the text.
Bd. 2: pp. 111–14. mus. for Op. 104 no. 1.

4851.3. See also 4754, 4931, 5388.

Op. 109 Fest- und Gedenksprüche for 8 part A Cappella Choir

4158.6. See 3598, 4042, 4754, 4778, 4822, 5080, 5143.

Op. 110 Three Motets

4158.9. See 3598, 4042, 4752, 4754, 4755, 4765, 4778–90, 5080, 5143.

Op. 113 Thirteen Canons for Women's Choir

4852. *Piening, Karl [Theodor]. "Brahms schreibt einen Kanon" in *125 Jahre Philharmonischer Chor Bremen 1815–1940*. [Bremen: n.p., 1940]

(a) i) reprint: in 3884. pp. 133–35. facsim. Provides background
on this work, which is an earlier version of Op. 113, no. 7.
(a) ii) reprint: in 4853.

4853. Reinhardt, Klaus. "Der Brahms-Kanon "Wenn die Klänge nah'n
und fliehen" op. 113, 7 und seine Urgassung (Albumblatt aus dem
Nachlaβ des Cellisten Karl Theodor Piening)" *Die Musikforschung*
43/2 (4.–6.1990) pp. 142–45. facsim., notes. A reprint of 4852 with
more on music's evolution into version in Op. 113 and analysis of
the canon itself.
See also 3403, 3413, 3598, 4754, 4773, 5203.
Kyrie and Missa canonica [McCorkle WoO posthums 17 and 18,
respectively. Published together as the *Messe für vier- bis
sechsstimmigen gemischten Chor und Continuo (Orgel).*
(Wien: Doblinger, 1984)].

4854. Biba, Otto. "Johannes Brahms. Messe für Chor und Orgel" *Württembergische Blätter für Kirchenmusik* 50/6 (11.–12.1983) pp.
206–07. Reports on the works' background and the manuscript's
provenance. Includes general comments on the work's style and
notes on the work's first performances (in 1983) and its first edition. [Based on author's remarks in 1st edition? (J. Brahms. *Messe
für vier- bis sechsstimmigen gemischten Chor und Continuo
(Orgel).* (Wien: Doblinger, 1984)]

4854.5. "Brahms's Kyrie [McCorkle WoO posthum 17] and Missa
canonica [McCorkle WoO posthum 18]: Two Discussions of the
Mass Movements and Their Publication" *The American Brahms
Society Newsletter* 3/1 (Spring 1985) pp. [5–7]. facsim. Daniel R.
Melamed: p. [5] and Virginia [Lee] Hancock: pp. [5–7]. Reports
on publication of J. Brahms. *Messe für vier- bis sechsstimmigen
gemischten Chor und Continuo (Orgel).* (Wien: Doblinger,
1984).
(a) reprint: Melamed, Daniel R. and Virginia [Lee] Hancock.
"Brahms's Kyrie [McCorkle WoO posthum 17] and Missa
canonica [McCorkle WoO posthum 18]. Two Discussions of
the Mass Movements and Their Publication" *The Choral
Journal* 28/9 (4.1988) pp. 11, 14.

4855. *"Brahms-Uraufführung in Wien: Missa canonica. Deutsche Erstaufführung im Altenberger Dom—Ein interessantes Werk"
Musica sacra 104 (1984) pp. 53–55.

4855.5. Bredenbach, Ingo. "Missa canonica [McCorkle WoO posthum 18] and Kyrie g-moll [McCorkle WoO posthum 17] von Johannes Brahms. Ein Beitrag zur Kanontechnik im Chorwerk von Johannes Brahms" *Musik und Kirche* 58/2,3 (3/4., 5/6.;1988) pp. 84–92, 135–45. mus., fig., notes. Presents background to both works, particularly the Joachim-Brahms exchange of counterpoint in the 1850's. Analyses the individual movements and comments on Brahms as a composer and his ability for self-criticism and to be criticized by his friends. Also talks about research on Brahms and the canon and some of the lacunae.

4856. Geiringer, Karl. *Notes* 43/4 (6.1987) pp. 932–33. In a review of the 1st edition (J. Brahms. *Messe für vier- bis sechsstimmigen gemischten Chor und Continuo (Orgel)*. (Wien: Doblinger, 1984)), relates the work's background and information and provenance for the manuscript.

4857. Kramer, Gerhard. "Im familiären Rahmen . . ." *Österreichische Musikzeitschrift* 38/12 (12.1983) p. 716. Descriptive comments on the Missa canonica.

4858. *Lesle, L[utz]. "Unmittelbare Klangerfahrung statt Analyse: neue Musik in der Kirche als Programm der Kasseler Musiktage 1986" *Neue Musikzeitung* 35 (12.1986) p. 48.

4859. M.St. [Michael Stegemann] "Vom Recht des Vergessenwerdens—Zur deutschen Erstaufführung von Brahms' "Missa canonica"" *NZ-Neue Zeitschrift für Musik* 144/12 (5.12.1983–15.1. 1984) Argues that there is no moral justification for resurrecting a work that Brahms chose to suppress.
(d) response: see 3303.

4860. Pascall, Robert. "Brahms's Missa canonica and Its Recomposition in His Motet 'Warum' Op. 74 No. 1" in *Brahms 2*. [for full citation see 5481] pp. 111–36. mus., facsim., fig., notes. Background of the Missa canonica and analysis, focusing on the contrapuntal aspects of the music. It's clear that the Kyrie was never part of this work. Presents background of Op. 74 no. 1, discusses text, and shows correspondence in detail, of mass parts with motet sections and how it was done.

4861. Waters, Edward N. "The Music Collection of the Heineman
Foundation" *Notes* Second series 7/2 (3.1950) pp. 181–216.
Brahms: pp. 187–88. facsim. (pp. [199–200]) Presents a history
of the Benedictus section of the Missa canonica, manuscript at
US-NYpm.

4861.15. See also 3303, 3406, 4754, 4755, 4757 (WoO posthum 17
only), 4864.

Dein Herzlein mild [McCorkle WoO posthum 19]

4861.2. See 3814, 4754.

Fourteen German Folksongs for 4 part Choir (1864) [McCorkle
WoO 34]

4861.25. See 4061, 4634, 4754.

Twelve German Folksongs for 4 part Mixed Choir (1926/27)
[McCorkle WoO posthum 35]

4861.3. See 4754.

Eight German Folksongs for 3 and 4 part Women's Choir (1938)
[McCorkle WoO posthum 36]

4861.35. See 4634, 4754.

Sixteen German Folksongs for 3 and 4 part Women's Choir
(1964) [McCorkle WoO posthum 37]

4861.4. See 4754.

Twenty German Folksongs for 3 and 4 part Women's Choir
(1968) [McCorkle WoO posthum 38]

4861.45. See 4754.

Grausam erweiset sich Amor [McCorkle WoO posthum 24]

4861.5. See 4754, 4773, 4924.

Mir lächelt kein Frühling [McCorkle WoO 25]

4861.55. See 4754, 4773, 4924.

O wie sanft [McCorkle WoO posthum 26]

4861.6. See 4754, 4924.

Spruch [McCorkle WoO posthum 27]

4861.65. See 3403, 3422, 4924.

Töne lindernder Klang [McCorkle WoO 28]

4861.7. See 4754, 4773, 4924.

Wann? [McCorkle WoO posthum 29]

4861.75. See 3397, 4754, 4773, 4924.

Zu Rauch muß werden [McCorkle WoO posthum 30]

4861.8. See 4754, 4773, 4924.

3. Brahms's Editing and Arranging of Other Composers' Vocal Music

General

4861.85. See 4988.

Specific

Ahle

4861.9. See 4865.

Bach, Johann Sebastian

4861.95. See 4985.

Händel

4862. Federhofer, Hellmut. "Georg Friedrich Händels Oratorium "Saul" in der Bearbeitung von Johannes Brahms" in *Brahms-Kongress Wien 1983*. [for full citation see 5431] pp. 125–38. mus., facsim., notes. McCorkle Anhang Ib, nr. 26: a detailed examination of Brahms's editings (articulation, dynamics, bass line, note alteration); includes comment on Brahms's connection to older music, his understanding of it, his playing of Händel.

4863. *Serwer, Howard. "Brahms and the Three Editions of Handel's (sic) Chamber Duets and Trios" *Händel-Jahrbuch* 39 (1993) pp. 134–60. Discusses McCorkle Anhang Ia, Nrs. 10 and 11. [from compiler]

4863.3. See also 3798, 5449.5.

Mozart

4863.5. See 3871.

Schubert

4863.7. See 4990.

C. Miscellaneous Works

1. Musical Works

Contains materials on music fragments and exercises.

4864. Brodbeck, David [Lee]. "The Brahms-Joachim Counterpoint Exchange; or, Robert, Clara, and "the Best Harmony between Jos[eph]. and Joh[annes]."" *Brahms Studies* 1 (1994) pp. 30–80. facsim., mus., fig., notes. Traces the exchange from its proposal through its activities to its conclusion (2.1856–10.1861). 12 items exchanged in total: Brahms (4), Joachim (8); looks at Brahms's works that "use" these items, also proposes that Brahms's relationship with Clara at this time can be traced through the use of these materials, as seen in Op. 30 and Mc-Corkle WoO 7–9.

4865. Geiringer, Karl. "Es ist genug, so nimm Herr meinen Geist: 300 years in the History of a Protestant Funeral Song" in *The Commonwealth of Music. In Honor of Curt Sachs*. Gustave Reese and Rose Brandel, eds. New York: The Free Press; London: Collier-Macmillan Limited, 1965. pp. 283–92. mus., notes. Brahms: p. 288. Comments on his use of Ahle's setting [McCorkle Anhang Va, nr. 4, (26)] in performance and discusses Brahms the amateur musicologist showing the link between Ahle's setting and Bach's chorale.

4866. Reynolds, Christopher. "A Choral Symphony by Brahms?" *19th Century Music* 9/1 (Summer 1985) pp. 3–25. mus., fig., notes. Focuses on the motifs of a few early and interrelated compositions, relates probable extra-musical allusions to the development of the 1854 Sonata-Symphony [McCorkle Anhang IIa, nr. 2]. Looks at this work as leading to Opp. 15 and 45. Comments on Brahms's allusions to Robert and Clara Schumann, and on why he didn't finish the 4th movement.

4867. Vetter, Isolde. "Johannes Brahms und Joseph Joachim in der Schule der alten Musik" in *Alte Musik als ästhetische Gegenwart. Bach Händel Schütz. Bericht über den internationalen musikwissenschaftlichen Kongreß Stuttgart 1985*. Dietrich Berke and Dorothee Hanemann, eds. Kassel [et al.]: Bärenreiter, 1987. Bd. 1, pp. 460–76. facsim. Examines the counterpoint exercises exchange between Joachim and Brahms, 1856–60; studies Joachim's extant, noting Brahms's reactions as recorded in 1009 (J. Brahms. *Johannes Brahms im Briefwechsel mit Joseph Joachim*. (1908)).

4867.5. See also 4342, 4855.5, 4988, 5037.

2. Literary and Theoretical Works

Deutsche Sprichworte [A-Wst. Handschriftensammlung. Catalog no. Ia 79.561]

4868. [Brahms, Johannes.] "Johannes Brahms's Collection of Deutsche Sprichworte (German Proverbs)" George S. Bozarth, ed. and

trans. *Brahms Studies* 1 (1994) pp. 1–29. notes. A transcription
with interlinear English translation of a commonplace notebook
of proverbs that Brahms copied from other sources. Includes an
introduction on this practice and background on sources.

Oktaven und Quinten [McCorkle Anhang Va, nr. 6]

4869. Laudon, Robert T. "The Debate about Consecutive Fifths: A Context for Brahms's Manuscript 'Oktaven und Quinten'" *Music and
Letters* 73/1 (2.1992) pp. 48–61. mus., notes. Discusses reasons
why Brahms made this collection and suggests that one reason relates to the direction of German music at the time. Includes comment about the "New German School" and Brahms, and how the
collection portrays the Brahms Manifesto.

4869.3. See also 5449.5.

Part V

Brahms the Musician

A. General Analytical Studies

Contains materials that attempt to understand Brahms's music by studying its components, such as harmony, rhythm, melody, and form. General descriptive literature on overall musical style is also included here. Analyses of individual works can be located either through this section's cross-references, or through Part IV's.

Chromaticism: 4946, 4974.
Counterpoint: 4889, 4891, 4898, 4924, 4926, 4977.
Dynamics: 4877.
Form: 4870, 4882, 4883, 4890, 4894, 4899, 4902, 4909, 4911, 4913, 4915, 4919, 4927, 4929, 4933, 4934, 4936, 4943, 4944, 4949, 4953, 4955, 4958, 4961, 4968–72, 4975, 4978, 4983.
Harmony: 4871, 4876, 4880, 4895, 4896, 4903, 4913, 4922, 4934, 4936, 4956, 4972, 4982, 4983.
Melody: 4878, 4885, 4889, 4993, 4906–08, 4916, 4928, 4929, 4936, 4946, 4955, 4966, 4967, 4974.
Rhythm: 4886, 4889, 4910, 4948, 4950, 4951, 4964, 4980.
Style: 4874, 4879, 4892, 4897, 4901, 4918, 4941, 4952, 4963.

4869.5. *L'Avant-scène opera operette musique* no. 53 (1983).

4870. *Abbott, William Walter, Jr. "Certain Aspects of the Sonata-Allegro Form in Piano Sonatas of the 18th and 19th Centuries" Ph.D. diss., Indiana University, 1956. 336 or 357 pp. fig.

4871. *Adrian, John Stanley. "Development Sections That Begin with the Tonic" Ph.D. diss., University of Rochester, Eastman School of Music, 1987. 2 vols. Examines the movements of some 50 sonatas and considers how to interpret such a phenomenon. Examples from Brahms include: Opp. 51 no. 1 (4th movement), 87 (1st movement), 101 (1st movement), 108 (1st movement), 120 no. 2 (1st movement). [from S081]

(d) Adrian, Jack [John Stanley Adrian]. "The Ternary-Sonata Form" *Journal of Music Theory* 34/1 (Spring 1990) pp. 57–80. ill. (p. 56), fig., notes. Analysis of the specific situation where the work's tonic key is present at the beginning of all 3 sections in movements in sonata form.

4872. *Aimez-vous Brahms "the progressive"?* Heinz-Klaus Metzger and Rainer Riehn, eds. (Musik-Konzepte 65) München: edition text + kritik, 1989. 85, [7] pp. ill. Contains: 4360, 4514, 4744, 4916, 4950.

4873. *Allen, Lois Petersen. "A Critical Analysis of Songs of Brahms, Mahler and Berg" M.A. diss., Claremont Graduate School, 1962. 44 pp. ill., mus., notes.

4874. *Atherton, John Robert. "An Analysis of Styles and Techniques in Piano Compositions of Mozart, Chopin and Brahms" M.A. diss., Eastern New Mexico University, 1951. i, [21] pp. mus., notes.

4875. Atlas, Raphael, see 4640.

4876. Azzaroni, Loris. "Elusività dei processi cadenzali in Brahms: il ruolo della sottodominante" *Rivista italiana di musicologia* 24/1 (1989) pp. 74–94. mus., fig., notes. Analysis of a specific harmonic progression, uses examples from the songs, solo piano and chamber music works.

4877. Baud, Jean-Marc. "Con molta espressione" *Schweizerische Musikzeitung. Revue musicale suisse* 123/3 (5./6.1983) pp. 141–48. includes abstract. An analysis of Opp. 116–19 to understand "espressivo" and how Brahms ties together elements from tempi, dynamics and articulation to achieve it.

4878. Becker, Heinz. "Das volkstümliche Idiom in Brahmsens Kammermusik" in *Brahms und seine Zeit.* (Hamburger Jahrbuch für Musikwissenschaft 7) [for full citation see 5428] pp. 87–99. mus.

Studies Brahms's use of a particular musical note pattern, also
looks at other musical genres.

4879. Bellman, Jonathan. "Aus alten Märchen: The Chivalric Style of
Schumann and Brahms" *The Journal of Musicology* 13/1 (Winter
1995) pp. 117–35. mus., fig., notes. Stylistic analysis, looking at
music where the intent is to evoke a particular period of time.
Brahms examples are Opp. 33 and 50; Schumann examples come
from his Opp. 39 and 48. Also discusses links between Schumann
and Brahms: Schumann's Op. 48 no. 5 with Brahms's Op. 33;
Schumann's Op. 98a no. 2 with Brahms's Op. 68, 1st movement
(is latter perhaps Brahms's homage to Schumann).

4880. Benjamin, Thomas, Michael Horvit and Robert Nelson. *Music for
Analysis. Examples from the Common Practice Period and the
Twentieth Century.* Boston [et al.]: Houghton Mifflin Company,
1978. xxi, [4], 3–356 pp. ind., appendixes. Presents examples to
illustrate standard harmonic usage and idiomatic procedure. Book
is organized in terms of harmonic groupings. Brahms works included (excerpt unless otherwise indicated) are from: Opp. 32, 39,
52 no. 4 (entire), 56a, 57, 76, 90, 96, 98, 105, 115, 118. English
translations of texts from song excerpts in Appendix B.
*2nd edition: Belmont: Wadsworth Pub. Co., 1984. xxi, 418 pp.
*also: Boston: Houghton Mifflin, 1984.
*issue (of Boston ed.): xxi, 356 pp.
*3rd edition: Belmont, 1992. xxi, 418 pp.
*4th edition: 1996. xix, 448 pp. adds notes.

4881. *Benzi, Manlio. "Le asimmetrie fraseologiche nel Lieder di
Brahms" in *I Lieder di Johannes Brahms.* [for full citation see
4677] pp. 216–32.

4882. Berry, Wallace. *Form in Music: an examination of traditional
techniques of musical structure and their application in historical
and contemporary styles.* Englewood Cliffs: Prentice-Hall, Inc.,
1966. [16], 472 pp. ind.
"Brahms, Ballade in G minor, Op. 118, No. 3, measures 1–40":
pp. 76–77. mus., notes. Analyses this piece as example of
simple ternary form.
"Brahms, Quintet in B minor, Op. 115, for clarinet and string
quartet, final movement": pp. 329–35. mus., fig. Analyses
this movement as example of variation form.

2nd ed.: 1986. *Form in Music: an examination of traditional techniques of musical form and their applications in historical and contemporary styles.* xx, 439 pp.

[Op. 118/3:] pp. 64–65. notes omitted

"Brahms, Concerto in A minor for violin, cello and orchestra, Op. 102, second movement": pp. 245–54. mus., fig., notes. Analyses this movement in terms of functions of soloists and orchestra.

[Op. 115, final movement:] pp. 311–17.

4883. Beveridge, David [R.]. "Non-Traditional Functions of the Development Section in Sonata Forms by Brahms" *The Music Review* 51/1 (2.1990) pp. 25–35. mus., notes. Shows that Brahms is not a strict classicist, but has a romantic side that comes out in the relaxing of tension in development sections. Identifies 4 techniques, examples are from orchestral and chamber music.

4884. *Blanton, Jane. "Analytical Program Notes" M.A. diss., Appalachian State University[, (North Carolina)], 1975. 23 pp. mus., notes., discog. Discusses piano works of Bach, Liszt and Kabalevsky and Brahms. [from S031]

4885. Borchardt, Georg. "Ein Viertonmotiv als melodische Komponente in Werken von Brahms" in *Brahms und seine Zeit.* (Hamburger Jahrbuch für Musikwissenschaft 7) [for full citation see 5428] pp. 101–12. notes. Studies Brahms's works and others for this motif and its variants; Op. 45 is a major example. Also notes motif in the chorale "Wer nur den lieben Gott läßt Walten" and this chorale's significance for Brahms and through it a link to Schumann.

4886. *Boretz, Benjamin Aaron. "Meta-Variations: Studies in the Foundations of Musical Thought (with) 'Group Variations I.' [original composition]" Ph.D. diss., Princeton University, 1970. 120 pp. Relates to 2356 (B.A. Boretz. *Perspectives of New Music* (1972–73)).

4887. Botstein, Leon. "Brahms and Nineteenth-Century Painting" *19th Century Music* 14/2 (Fall 1990) pp. 154–68. ill., notes. Presents a close scrutiny of 19th century music, Brahms in particular, within the context of the visual arts; purpose is to look at art to understand Brahms's music. Compares Brahms to Feuerbach, Böcklin and Klinger, also looks at his links to each artist. Includes comment on Vienna's state during Brahms's time and art's status during those contemporary times.

4888. *Brahms-Analysen. Referate der Kieler Tagung 1983.* Friedhelm Krummacher and Wolfram Steinbeck, eds. (Kieler Schriften zur Musikwissenschaft 28) Kassel, Basel, London: Bärenreiter, 1984. viii, 209 pp. Contains: 3570, 4160, 4192, 4229, 4331, 4381, 4565, 4691, 4709, 4806, 4814, 4890, 4956, 5020.

4889. *Breslauer, Peter Seth. "Motivic and Rhythmic Contrapuntal Structure in the Chamber Music of Johannes Brahms" Ph.D. diss., Yale University, 1984. v, [1]–181 pp. mus., fig., notes. Reviews analytical approaches to Brahms's music and presents an approach for analyzing motivic structure that combines theme-melody relationships with contrapuntal texture. Works used to demonstrate application of concept include: Opp. 25, 51 nos. 1 and 2, and the 2nd movement of Op. 115. [from S081]

(d) Breslauer, Peter [Seth]. "Diminutional Rhythm and Melodic Structure" *Journal of Music Theory* 32/1 (Spring 1988) pp. 1–21. Brahms: pp. 11–18. mus., notes. Examines melodic diminution, also shows that Brahms's melodic style shows features similar to Bach's. Examples come from Op. 68, 3rd movement; and Op. 51 no. 2, 4th movement.

4890. Brinkmann, Reinhold. "Anhand von Reprisen" in *Brahms-Analysen.* [for full citation see 4888] pp. 107–20. mus., fig., notes. Examines how Brahms handles reprise, with studies of the recapitulations of the first movements of Opp. 1, 5, 8 (1892 version), 73, 108, 115 and Op. 119 no. 3. Also looks at Op. 73, first movement to see how "developing variation" relates to reprise.

4891. *Brockmeier, Suzanne W. "A Comparison of Contrapuntal Techniques as Exemplified in Selected Fugues of Johann Sebastian Bach, Ludwig van Beethoven, Johannes Brahms and Paul Hindemith" M.S. diss., California State University, Fullerton, 1976. iii, 124 pp. ill., notes.

4892. *Buckner, Ellen Jane Poch. "A Study of Styles and Techniques in Selected Vocal Compositions of Mozart, Schubert, Brahms, Puccini, Duparc, Burleigh, Sibelius, Davis, Duke and Dougherty" M.A. diss., Eastern New Mexico University, 1956. iii, 25 pp. notes.

4893. *Callis, Sarah. "Thematic Structure in Selected Works of Johannes Brahms 1878–84" Ph.D. diss., University of Nottingham, 1994.

4894. Cone, Edward T. "Brahms: Songs With Words And Songs Without Words" *Intégral* (Rochester, NY) 1 (1987) pp. [31]–56. mus., notes. Suggests an "inner voice" approach to analyzing passages of Brahms that appear structurally or expressively unclear. Examples come from Op. 119 no. 2; and the slow movements of the violin sonatas and Op. 51 no. 2.

4895. Cone, Edward T. "Harmonic Congruence in Brahms" in *Brahms Studies: Analytical and Historical Perspectives*. [for full citation see 5480] pp. [165]–88. mus., fig., notes. Harmonic congruence is the use of same musical material both vertically and horizontally; explores ways it's used in Brahms's music. Examples come from songs, chamber and piano music, symphonies; in particular, Opp. 78, 98, 114. Poses question as to why Schoenberg didn't recognize this technique in Brahms.

4896. Cone, Edward T. "Three Ways of Reading A Detective Story—or a Brahms Intermezzo" in *Approaches to Tonal Analysis* (The Garland Library of the History of Western Music 14) New York: Garland Publishing Inc., 1985. pp. 2–22. mus., notes. A reprint of 2360 (E.T. Cone. *Georgia Review* (1977)).
also reprinted in: Cone. in *Music: A View from Delft. Selected Essays*. Robert P. Morgan, ed. Chicago and London: University of Chicago Press, 1989. pp. 77–93. adds fig., ind.

4897. *Cope, David H., see 5000.5.

4898. *Cosgrove, Audrey O'Boyle. "Brahms's fugal sonata finales" D.M.A. diss., Louisiana State University, Baton Rouge, 1995. vii, 63 pp. mus.

4899. Daverio, John. "Brahms and the Romantic Imperative" in Daverio. *Nineteenth-Century Music and the German Romantic Ideology*. New York: Schirmer Books; Toronto: Maxwell Macmillan Canada; New York [et al.]: Maxwell Macmillan International, 1993. pp. 127–54. mus., fig., notes. Studies Brahms's breaking away from classical musical form to create new structures; examples come from Opp. 33, 98, and 111.

4900. *Demierre, Bernard. *Décalques et empreintes: Autour de R[obert]. Schumann et J[ohannes]. Brahms.* (La Revue musicale) Paris: Revue musicale, 1991. 64 pp.

4901. *"Dr. Ernest Walker's Lecture on Brahms" *Musical Courier* 39 (15.11.1899) p. 26. Reports on lecture given to the Musical Association. See 2437 (E. Walker. *Proceedings of the Musical Association* (1898–99)).

4902. *Draber, Christopher T. "Approaches to the Recapitulation in the Later Works of Brahms: A Survey and Five Case-Studies" B.Mus. (Hons.) diss., University of Melbourne, 1987.

4903. Dubiel, Joseph. "Contradictory Criteria in a Work of Brahms" *Brahms Studies* 1 (1994) pp. 81–110. mus., fig., notes. Harmonic analysis of the first 25–30 bars of the 1st movement of Op. 15; looks at sections with clear tonic orientation versus unclear orientation and how this relates to the rest of the movement.

4904. Dunsby, Jonathan and Arnold Whittall. *Music Analysis in Theory and Practice.* London and Boston: Faber Music, 1988. [7], 4–250 pp. ind., notes. Brahms et passim. A general introduction to the current state of analysis and its techniques; Brahms works used as examples, relates analysts' opinions of Brahms.

4905. "*Emotionality in Brahms' Music" *Musical Courier* 27 (29.11. 1893) pp. 7–8.

4906. *Farlow, Betsy Clifford. "Thematic Unity in Selected Non-Programmatic Symphonies of the 19th Century" Ph.D. diss., University of North Carolina at Chapel Hill, 1969. v, 171 pp. mus., notes. Analyses 24 symphonies from Schumann, Brahms, Franck, Bruckner and Mahler, looking at cyclical ideas and their appearances in the works. Includes comments relative to individual compositional style, cyclical unity, thematic material. [from S102]

4907. *Federhofer, Hellmut. "Motivtechnik von Johannes Brahms und Arnold Schönbergs Dodekaphonie" *Mitteilungen der Kommission für Musikforschung [Österreichische Akademie der Wissenschaften. Kommission für Musikforschung. Mitteilungen]* (Wien) no. 41 (1989).

4908. Fowler, Andrew Judson. "Multilevel Motivic Projection as a Compositional Process in Tonal Music" Ph.D. diss., University of

Texas at Austin, 1984. x, 228, [1] pp. Brahms: pp. 80–88, 91, 133–36. mus., notes. An analysis that examines the many different levels where motivic unity can occur in a piece. Brahms examples are: Opp. 105 no. 1 and 117 no. 2.

4909. Frisch, Walter [M.]. *Brahms and the Principle of Developing Variation.* (California Studies in 19th-Century Music 2) Berkeley [et al.]: University of California Press, 1984. xv, [1], 217 pp. mus., fig., ind., notes. Reworked version of 2372 (W. Frisch. "Brahms's Sonata Structures and the Principle of Developing Variation" (1981)). Traces this principle through 18 of Brahms's works. The works are considered in relationship to each other, plus to works by Beethoven, Schubert, Schumann and Liszt.
 (d) Frisch. "How Brahms Shaped His Material" *The New York Times* 133/46,057 (27.5.1984) Section 2, p. 18.
 (d) Frisch. "Brahms's Developing Variation. Continuity and Innovation in a Musical Tradition" *The American Brahms Society Newsletter* 2/2 (Autumn 1984) pp. [1–2]. ill.

4910. Frisch, Walter [M.]. "The Shifting Bar Line: Metrical Displacement in Brahms" in *Brahms Studies: Analytical and Historical Perspectives.* [for full citation see 5480] pp. [139]–63. facsim., mus., notes. Characterizes Brahms's displacement techniques and explains where and why he employs them. Looks at where he might have encountered elsewhere, and examines their function in his music. Examples come from: Opp. 1, 9, 26, 34, 34bis, 90, 121.

4911. *Galand, Joel. "Rondo-Form Problems in Eighteenth- and Nineteenth-Century Instrumental Music, with Reference to the Application of Schenker's Form Theory to Historical Criticism" Ph.D. diss., Music, Yale University, 1990. xi, 358 pp. ill., mus., fig., notes. alternate title: "Heinrich Schenker's Theory of Form and Its Application to Historical Criticism, with Special Reference to Rondo-Form Problems in Eighteenth and Nineteenth-Century Instrumental Music."

4912. *Gieseler, Walter. *Musik im Kopf: Gesammelte Aufsätze.* (Perspektiven zur Musikpädagogik und Musikwissenschaft 20) Regensburg: G. Bosse, 1993. 268 pp.

4913. *Graybill, Roger Carper. "Brahms's Three-Key Expositions: Their Place Within the Classical Tradition" Ph.D. diss., Yale University, 1983. 383 pp. Determines the ways that Brahms's use of 3 keys departs from the classical tradition; a detailed analysis. [from S081]

(d) Graybill, Roger [Carper]. "Harmonic Circularity in Brahms's F Major Cello Sonata: An Alternative to Schenker's Reading in "Free Composition"" *Music Theory Spectrum* 10 (1988) pp. 43–55. mus., fig., notes. Analyses the tonal plan of the 1st movement, also looks at Op. 90.

4914. Heister, Hanns-Werner. "Angst und "absolute" Musik. Schönberg, Brahms and Andere" in *Verteidigung des musikalischen Fortschritts*. [for full citation see 3931] pp. 77–86. notes. Discusses the significance of autobiographical references in composers' works and writings.

4915. *Henderson, W. J. *The Aeolian Quarterly* 1 (1898) pp. 23–26. [Related to 2380 (W.J. Henderson. *New York Times Sunday Magazine Supplement* (1897))?]

4916. Hübler, Klaus K. "Die Kunst, ohne Einfälle zu komponieren. Dargestellt am Johannes Brahms' späten Intermezzi" in *Aimez-vous Brahms "the progressive"?* [for full citation see 4872] pp. [24]–40. mus., fig. Examines intervals as composition tools, particularly in regard to motivic development. Examples are from Opp. 116–18.

4917. *Imberty, Michel. "Perceptual Structure of Musical Style" *Bulletin de psychologie* 30/14–16 (1976–77) pp. 781–91. Piano works of Brahms and Debussy used in a study to examine subjects' perception of changes in a musical work. [from S108]

4918. *"Johannes Brahms' Style" *Musical Courier* 32 (12.2.1896) pp. 20–21.

4919. *Johnson, Fredric. "An Analysis of Climax in Some Symphonic Movements of Brahms" M.A. diss., Music, Wayne State University, 1965. vi, 72 pp. ill., notes.

4920. *Johnson, Gerald Darwin. "A Critical Analysis of Selected Piano Compositions of Scarlatti, Handel, Brahms and Ravel" M.A. diss., Eastern New Mexico University, 1966. x, 73, 2 pp. mus., notes.

4921. *Kates, David James. "Modernist Tendencies in Brahms, Schoenberg, and Stravinsky: A Study of Three Representative

Works" M.M. diss., Sam Houston State University, 1990. 77 pp. notes.

4922. *Keyser, Jeanette James. "A Harmonic Analysis of Eighteen Songs of Brahms" M.M. diss., University of Mississippi, 1971. v, 51 pp. notes.

4923. *Kiefer, Bruno. *Música alemã: dois estudos.* (Cuadernos do Rio Grande, Sec. cão 4: Estudos de arte, no. 6 no. 1) [Porto Alegre:] Instituto Estadual do Livro, Divisao de Cultura, 1958. 64 pp. *2nd edition revised: *Música alemão: Estudos sobre Bach, Mozart, Beethoven, Schubert, Schumann e Brahms.* (Coleccão Luís Cosme 16) Porto Alegre: Movimento, 1985. 77 pp.

4924. Kings, Janet Heitman. "Contrapuntal Techniques in the Early Organ and Choral Works of Johannes Brahms" D. Music diss., Church Music, Northwestern University, 1986. [ii], 72 pp. mus., notes. Thoroughly explores Brahms's techniques, includes a brief description of all these works and discusses their influence on Brahms's later organ and choral works. Includes comment on Brahms's interest in counterpoint.

4925. *Kinzler, Hartmuth. "Webern kam aus Wien nach Darmstadt ohne sein Gewand . . . Bemerkungen zu Opus 27/1" in *Geisteswissenschaften öffentlich.* (Schriftenreihe des Fachbereichs 3:10) Osnabrück: Universität Osnabrück, 1988. pp. 139–73. mus. Discusses ways of listening to traditional music versus serial music. Compares what one needs to know about music to understand traditional music, with what is needed to understand the "A" section of Op. 116, no. 5. [from S102]

4926. Kirkendale, Warren. *Fuge und Fugato in der Kammermusik des Rokoko und der Klassik.* Mit einem Nachwort von Jens Peter Larsen. Tutzing: Hans Schneider, 1966. 379 pp. ind.
"[Anhang III.] Fugen und Fugatosätze in der Kammermusik bis 1882 (Brahms)": pp. 323–27. Brahms: pp. 326. Lists Brahms's works (5) that have this type of movement.
"[Anhang IV.] Formübersicht der Fugen und Fugatos in der Kammermusik von Haydn bis Brahms": pp. 329–35. Brahms et passim. fig. A series of charts showing where in the movement it occurs.
(b) Revised and expanded second edition translated from the Ger-

man edition by Margaret Bent and the Author: Kirkendale. *Fugue and Fugato in Rococo and Classical Chamber Music.* Durham: Duke University Press, 1979. xxvii, 383 pp. "[Appendix III:] Formal Survey of Fugues and Fugatos in Chamber Music from Haydn to Brahms": pp. 325–331. fig. Brahms et passim. This is the material from Anhang IV in the German edition.

4927. *Knight, Wanda Louise Vernon. "Compositional Techniques in Symphonic Transitions; (as found in Selected Works of Haydn, Mozart, Beethoven, and Brahms)" M.Mus. diss., University of Oklahoma, 1971. iii, 44 pp.

4928. Kross, Siegfried. "Die Terzenkette bei Brahms und ihre Konnotationen" in *Die Sprache der Musik. Festschrift Klaus Wolfgang Niemöller zum 60. Geburtstag am 21. Juli 1989.* Im Namen aller Kollegen des Musikwissenschaftlichen Instituts der Universität zu Köln unter Mitarbeit von Bram Gätjen und Manuel Gervink. Jobst Peter Fricke, ed. (Kölner Beiträge zur Musikforschung 165) Regensburg: Gustav Bosse Verlag, 1989. pp. 335–45. mus., notes. Looks at the use of the interval of a third in the melodic line of Brahms's works and whether its use can be linked to programmaticism. Main examples are Opp. 82, 86 no. 2, 98, 121.

4929. *Kross, Siegfried. "Themenstruktur und Formprozess bei Brahms" in *Johannes Brahms: Leben, Werk, Interpretation, Rezeption.* [for full citation see 5453] pp. 100–10. ill., mus. Starting with Op. 5, Brahms increasingly invested his themes with intervallic or contrapuntal characteristics, these structural elements were meant to legitimate the development of his forms. They cause his formal construction to depend on whatever thematic material is being employed. [from S102]

(b) English translation: Kross. "Thematic Structure and Formal Processes in Brahms's Sonata Movements" in *Brahms Studies: Analytical and Historical Perspectives.* [for full citation see 5480] pp. [423]–43. mus., fig., notes. Examples come from Opp. 1, 2, 5, 15, 25, 26, 51 no. 1, 68, 93a no. 2.

4930. *Lach, Robert. "Das Ethos bei Brahms" *Der Auftakt* 2/4 [(1922)] pp. 103–05. [Related to 2395 (R. Lach. *N. Simrock Jahrbuch* (1930–34)? [from compiler]])

4931. Laskowski, Larry. "Brahms" in Laskowski. *Heinrich Schenker. An Annotated Index to His Analyses of Musical Works.* ([Pendragon Press] Series IV. Annotated Reference Tools in Music. No. 1) New York: Pendragon Press, 1978. pp. 70–80. Indexes Schenker's discussion of 35 Brahms instrumental and vocal works in his writings.

4932. *Lederer, Felix Heinrich. "Johannes Brahms e il suo tempo" *La Rassegna musicale* 6 (5.,6.;1933) pp. 148–51.

4933. *Leones, Kathleen Baird. "An Analysis of the Scherzi and Intermezzi in the Chamber Works of Johannes Brahms" M.A. diss., California State University, San Francisco, 1973. xiii, 307 pp. ill., notes.

4934. Longyear, Rey M., and Kate R. Covington. "Tonic Major, Mediant Major: A Variant Tonal Relationship in 19th-Century Sonata Form" *Studies in Music from The University of Western Ontario* 10 (1985) pp. 105–39. Brahms: pp. 117–26. fig., notes. Investigates this tonal relationship in the works of Beethoven, Brahms, Dvořák, D'Indy, Liszt and Rimsky-Korsakov. Brahms's examples are in Opp. 88 and 90. Analysis of Op. 88 is entire, Op. 90 is 1st movement only. Compares strategies of all composers overall, but Brahms and Dvořák compared in particular.

4935. Mahrt, William Peter. "Brahms and Reminiscence. A Special Use of Classic Conventions" in *Convention in Eighteenth- and Nineteenth-Century Music. Essays in Honor of Leonard G. Ratner.* Wye J. Allanbrook, Janet M. Levy and William P[eter]. Mahrt, eds. (Festschrift Series 10) Stuyvesant, NY: Pendragon Press, 1992. pp. 75–112. mus., fig., notes. Examines Brahms reusing of music in a work in new places and in a new light, looks at the techniques he uses to do this. Looks at those reminiscences that have personal connections.

(d) summary: Mahrt, William [Peter]. "Brahms's Reminiscences" *The American Brahms Society Newsletter* 11/2 (Autumn 1993) pp. [1]–4. ill., mus. Focuses on reminiscence as an aesthetic experience, and the traces of personal reminiscences that Brahms leaves in his music, particularly in relation to the Schumanns.

4936. *Matthes, Sandra Lee. "Some Harmonic, Melodic, and Structural

Aspects of the Brahms" M.M. diss., University of Tennessee, Knoxville, 1975. ix, 56 pp. ill., fig.

4937. *Mies, Paul. "Der Charakter der Tonart" Untersuchung, Universität zu Köln, 1948.

4938. *Morgan, Phillip. "Devices in the Intermezzi by Brahms" M.M. diss., University of Rochester, 1949. iv, 101 pp. ill., mus., notes.

4939. *Moutsopoulos, Evangelos. E aisthetike tou Gioxannes Mprams. Athens: Kardamitsas, 1986. 270 pp. notes, works list. Analyses Brahms's musical experience from a transcendental perspective. [from S102]

4940. *Mrevlov, Aleksandr. "Pozdnii period tvorčestva Bramsa" Ph.D. diss., History, Gosudarstvennaia Konservatoriia, Leningrad, 1982. (d) *summary: 13 pp. Discusses the difficulties in defining Brahms's late period. [from S102]

4941. *Murrill, Herbert. "The Style of Brahms" Music Teacher 10/12 (12.1931) pp. 679–80.

4942. *Neff, Severine. "Schoenberg and Analysis. Reworking A Coda of Brahms" International Journal of Musicology 3 (1994) pp. 187–202.

4943. *Nemirovskaia, Izabella. "Značenie bytovyh žanrov v muzykal'noi dramaturgii simfonii čajkovskogo i Bramsa" Ph.D. diss., Musicology, VNII Iskusstvoznaniia Ministerstva Kul'tury SSSR, Moskva, 1984.
(d) *summary: 24 pp. Discusses the significance of conventional genre in the musical and dramatic structure of symphonies by Tchaikovsky and Brahms. [from S102]

4944. *Nivans, David Brian. "Brahms and the Binary Sonata: A Structuralist Interpretation" Ph.D. diss, University of California, Los Angeles, 1992. 278 pp. Examines movements in all of Brahms's works that are in this form, focusing on its most important and characteristic features. Suggests alternatives for interpretation. [from S081]

4945. *Paddison, Max. Adorno's Aesthetics of Music. Cambridge, New York: Cambridge University Press, 1993. xii, 378 pp. mus., notes, ind.

4946. *Parnella, Carl V. "Chromaticism in Selected Variation Works for Solo Piano of Mozart and Brahms" M.M. diss., Indiana University, 1980. iii, 133 pp. notes.

4947. Pascall, Robert. "Die Erste in Wien aufgeführte Musik von Brahms und deren Nachklang im Brahms'schen Schaffen" in *Brahms-Kongress Wien 1983.* [for full citation see 5431] pp. 439–48. fig. (pp. 444–48). Traces links between McCorkle WoO posthum 5 Nr. 1 and McCorkle WoO 3 (both first played by Clara Schumann in Vienna in 1856) and later works: Opp. 36, 88, and 115.

4948. *Perkins, Marion Louise. "Changing Concepts of Rhythm in The Romantic Era: A Study of Rhythmic Structure, Theory and Performance Practices Related to Piano Literature" Ph.D. diss., University of Southern California, 1961. 306 pp.

4949. *Peters, Penelope. "Retransitions in the Non-Orchestral Sonata Forms of Brahms" M.A. diss., University of Rochester, 1985. x, 109 pp. mus., notes.

4950. Pfisterer, Manfred. "Eingriffe in die Syntax. Zum Verfahren der metrisch-rhythmischen Variation bei Johannes Brahms" in *Aimez-vous Brahms "the progressive"?* [for full citation see 4872] pp. [76]–85. mus., notes. Using examples from Opp. 60 and 120 no. 1, examines how altering meter affects musical syntax. Concludes that Brahms is progressive.

4951. *Plyn, Franz Hermann Wolfgang. "Die Hemiole in der Instrumentalmusik von Johannes Brahms" Phil.F. diss., Rheinische Friedrich-Wilhelms-Universität Bonn, 1984. 377 pp. mus., notes.

4952. Pociej, Bohdan. "Brahms" (Proby utrwalenia) *Ruch muzyczny* 27/15 (24.7.1983) pp. 8–9 [across page tops]. Describes the qualities of Brahms's music; includes comment on Brahms as a romantic composer.

4953. *Podolsky, Saul Bernard [Sewall Bennett Potter]. "The Theme and Variations from Brahms to the Present" M.A. diss., Boston University, 1951. v, 103 pp.

4954. Rahm, John. "D-Light Reflecting: The Nature of Comparison" in *Brahms Studies: Analytical and Historical Perspectives.* [for full citation see 5480] pp. [399]–404. fig., notes. Discusses the influence of musical events upon each other, between similar pieces; uses Opp. 73 and 77 as example.

4955. Ratner, Leonard G. *Romantic Music. Sound and Syntax.* New York: Schirmer Books; Toronto: Maxwell Macmillan Canada; New York [et al.]: Maxwell Macmillan International, 1992. xix, [1], 348 pp. mus., fig., ind., notes. Brahms et passim, also:
Brahms: pp. 6–7. Excerpts from 3811.a. on tone colour in Brahms's music: Opp. 98, 108, 111.
Brahms: pp. 60, 62–63. Op. 68 used to demonstrate the contrast between classical music orchestral scoring and romantic music orchestral scoring.
Brahms: pp. 156–59. Op. 10 no. 4 used to demonstrate how sound produces symmetry; Brahms is contrasted to Verdi and Johann Strauss.
Brahms: pp. 217–25: analysis of the melodic and scoring features of the introduction to the first movement of Op. 68 shows that it is one long period with digressions.
Brahms: pp. 280–84. Analysis of Op. 81 to show as a work in sonata form, also looks at orchestration skills as seen in this piece.

4956. Ravizza, Victor. "Brahms' Musik in tonarten-charakteristischer Sicht" in *Brahms-Analysen* [for full citation see 4888] pp. 33–46. notes. Examines those pieces written in C minor and the contemporary reaction to them; includes comments on the historical reception of this key, and looks at their structure to find out if there is any significance there.

4957. *Roberts, Ferrell. "A Critical Analysis of Selected Piano Compositions of Bach, Beethoven, Brahms, Chopin, Dohnanyi (sic) and Ferguson" M.A. diss., Eastern New Mexico University, 1970. vii, 68 pp. ill., notes.

4958. *Rohn, Matthias. "Die Coda bei Johannes Brahms" Phil.F. diss., Rheinische Friedrich-Wilhelms-Universität Bonn, 1985.
(a) reprint: Rohn. *Die Coda bei Johannes Brahms.* (Schriftenreihe zur Musik 25) Hamburg: Verlag der Musikalienhandlung Karl Dieter Wagner, 1986. [2], iii, [1], 225 pp. mus., notes. A detailed analysis of all the codas in his works to understand Brahms as a coda composer.

4959. Rosen, Charles. "Brahms the Subversive" in *Brahms Studies: Analytical and Historical Perspectives.* [for full citation see 5480] pp. [105]–19. mus., notes. Observes how Brahms deals with traditional techniques/elements of music and how he manipulates and dislocates like no composer did before. Major examples come from Opp. 40, 79 no. 2, 119 no. 3.

4960. Rummenhöller, Peter. ""Wie Melodien zieht es mir leise durch den Sinn" Liedhaftes im Instrumentalwerk von Johannes Brahms" *Musica* 46/1 (1./2.1992) pp. 4–8. mus., notes. Studies Brahms as romantic composer by looking at melodic lines in his instrumental works that allude to or link to the songs: Op. 105 no. 2 = Op. 83, 2nd movement; Op. 49 no. 4 = Op. 117 no. 1; Op. 75 no. 1 = Op. 10 no. 1; Op. 105 no. 4 = Op. 116 no. 2; Op. 59 no. 3 = Op. 78, 3rd movement.

4961. *Salvetti, Guido. "Il problema formale nel Lied brahmsiano" in *I Lieder di Johannes Brahms.* [for full citation see 4677] pp. 183–92.

4962. *Salvetti, Guido. "Proposta di una semiografia analitica per i Lieder di Brahms: portata e limiti" in *I Lieder di Johannes Brahms.* [for full citation see 4677] pp. 309–12.
  (d) *Di Fronzo, Luigi, Donatella Gulli and Guido Salvetti. "Spiegazione e discussione della simbologia utilizzata nelle schede" in *I Lieder di Johannes Brahms.* [for full citation see 4677] pp. 313–18.
  (d) *"Schede analitiche" L[uigi]. Di Fronzo, D[onatella]. Gulli and G[uido]. Salvetti, eds. in *I Lieder di Johannes Brahms* [for full citation see 4677] pp. 319–52.

4963. Schenker, Heinrich. "Johannes Brahms" William Pastille, trans. [Editorial comments by George S. Bozarth?] *The American Brahms Society Newsletter* 9/1 (Spring 1991) pp. [1]–3. ill. English translation of 2425 (H. Schenker. *Die Zukunft* (1897)).

4964. Schmidt, Christian Martin. "Von Zeitarten tonaler Musik" *Archiv für Musikwissenschaft* 42/4 ([9.–12.]1985) pp. 287–99. Brahms: pp. 296–99. Discusses the concept of "composed tempo", Op. 73 is used as an example. Brahms seen to be developing this concept from Beethoven, also links with Reger.

4965. Schönherr, Max. "Walzer und Walzer, zwei Pluralia im Sinne von

Kunst-, Konzert-, Symphonischer Walzer und Tanzwalzer" in *Brahms-Kongress Wien 1983.* [for full citation see 5431] pp. 455–69. mus., notes. Compares waltzes composed for dancing with waltzes composed to be heard in concerthall: Opp. 39, 52, and 65 used as examples.

4966. Schubert, Giselher. "Themes and Double Themes: The Problem of the Symphonic in Brahms" *19th Century Music* 18/1 (Summer 1994) pp. 10–23. mus., notes. Isolates this feature and traces its evolution through Brahms's works; it's seen as a kind of dialectic operating between the principles of symphonic and chamber music. Relationship of thematic structure and formal process in movements in sonata form and the genre-specific qualities of that form. Considers if these forms in the symphonies differ from those in the chamber music?

4967. *Scott, Ann Besser. "Thematic Transmutation in the Music of Brahms: A Matter of Musical Alchemy" *The Journal of Musicological Research* 15/3 (1995) p. 177+ . Periodical also known as *Music & Man.*

4968. *Simmons, Wray Ligon. "A Study of History, Form, and Technical Problems of Selected Piano Compositions of Beethoven, Brahms, and Tschaikowsky (sic)" M.A. diss., Eastern New Mexico University, 1956. 28 pp. notes.

4969. *Simonini, Simona. "Le tecniche della variazione nei Lieder di Brahms" in *I Lieder di Johannes Brahms.* [for full citation see 4677] pp. 193–215.

4970. Sisman, Elaine R. "Brahms and the Variation Canon" *19th Century Music* 14/2 (Fall 1990) pp. 132–53. mus., fig., notes. Suggests that Brahms tried to reconcile older and newer variation models in his works and shows how he did this. Focuses on Op. 9 and contrasts Opp. 36 and 111; also compares Brahms to Schumann in this regard. (d) related to: 5449.5.

4971. Sisman, Elaine R. "Brahms's Slow Movements: Reinventing the 'Closed' Forms" in *Brahms Studies: Analytical and Historical Perspectives.* [for full citation see 5480] pp. [79]–103. mus., fig., notes. Shows how Brahms was able to overcome this classical form and open it up; surveys across instrumental works. Focuses on Op. 25, but also features 26, 67 and 73; includes comment on creative process as seen in manuscript sources.

4972. *Smith, Peter Howard. "Formal Ambiguity and Large-Scale Tonal Structure in Brahms's Sonata-Form Recapitulations" Ph.D. diss., Yale University, 1992. 271 pp.

(d) i) Smith, Peter H[oward]. "Brahms and Schenker: A Mutual Response to Sonata Form" *Music Theory Spectrum* 16/1 (Spring 1994) pp. [77]–103. mus., fig., notes. Discusses how sonata form can be derived from a single "Ursatz" and how Brahms achieved this. Examples come from Opp. 51 no. 1, 60, 90, 108.

(d) ii) Smith, Peter H[oward]. "Liquidation, Augmentation and Brahms's Recapitulatory Overlaps" *19th Century Music* 17/3 (Spring 1994) pp. 237–61. mus., fig., notes. Examines Brahms's technique in blurring the beginning of recapitulation, with examples from Opp. 51 no. 1, 98 and 99.

4973. *Snider, Mervin Shirley. "Vertical Sonorities in the Piano Styles of Schumann, Chopin and Brahms" M.A. diss., University of Rochester, 1939. vi, 2, 124, 74, 13 pp. ill., mus.

4974. *Sterling, Eugene Allen. "A Study of Chromatic Elements in Selected Piano Works of Beethoven, Schubert, Schumann, Chopin and Brahms" *Bulletin of the Council for Research in Music Education* 17 (1969) pp. 41–52. Related to 1600 (E.A. Sterling. "A Study . . . Brahms" (1966)).

4975. *Swain, Joseph Peter. "Limits of Musical Structure" Ph.D. diss., Harvard University, 1983. 238 pp. Brahms works are among those (Josquin, Bach, Beethoven, Schubert) that are used as samples for applying author's applications regarding how length of time shapes a final work. [from S102]

4976. *Walker, Alan. *A Study in Musical Analysis.* New York: Free Press of Glencoe, 1963 (?).
*also: London: Barrie and Rockliff, 1962. 160 pp. ill., notes.

4977. *Weber, Horst. "Kalkul und Sinnbild: Eine Kurz-Geschichte des Kanons" *Die Musikforschung* 46/4 (1993) pp. 355–70. Brahms's Op. 100 used as an example. [from S109]

4978. Webster, James. "The General and the Particular in Brahms's Later Sonata Forms" in *Brahms Studies: Analytical and Historical Perspectives.* [for full citation see 5480] pp. [49]–78. mus., fig., notes, appendix. Examines sonata form first movements from

21 works, from Opp. 51–115. Looks at internal proportions, cor-
relations, compares to earlier and later works. Looks at Brahms as
a composer and compares his work to that of the Classical period.

4979. Weiβ-Aigner, Günter. "Die instrumentalen Zyklen der drei Kärtner Schaffenssommer von Johannes Brahms. Thematisch-figurale
Affinitäten im kompositorischen Entwicklungsstrom" *Augsburger
Jahrbuch für Musikwissenschaft* 1 (1984) pp. 73–124. mus., fig.,
notes. Analyses thematic material from Opp. 73, 77 and 78 to
show the links between these works, and links to other works too.

4980. Williams, C[harles]. F. Abdy. *The Rhythm of Modern Music*. London: Macmillan & Co. Limited, 1909. xvii, 321 pp. ind. Treats
rhythm as an aesthetic element rather than a compositional element.
"[Chapter IX.] Brahms, Symphony in D, Op. 73 – Tschaikowsky,
Symphony Pathétique, Op. 74": pp. 210–255. Rhythmic
analysis.
Brahms: pp. 191–209, [210]–36. Rhythmic analyses for Opp. 73
and 119 [117] no. 4.

4981. *Winkler, Gerhard J. "Anton Bruckner—ein Neudeutscher?
Gedanken zum Verhältnis zwischen Symphonie und symphonischer Dichtung" in *Bruckner, Wagner und die Neudeutschen in
Österreich*. Othmar Wessely, ed. Linz: Linzer Verlagsgesellschaft,
1986. pp. 149–62. mus., notes. Compares Wolf's *Penthesilea*,
Bruckner's Symphony No. 3 and Brahms's Op. 68. Shows that terminology is not adequate for classifying such works. [from S102]

4982. Wintle, Christopher. "The 'Sceptred Pall': Brahms's Progressive
Harmony" in *Brahms 2*. [for full citation see 5481] pp. 197–222.
mus., fig., notes. Looks at the question of how Brahms can be considered 'progressive' when examples used are drawn from classical precedent. Looks at Schoenberg's and Webster's discussions
of Brahms. Uses the example of Neapolitan relations and how
Brahms adapted/manipulated as compared to Schubert. Examples
used are from Opp. 26, 38 and 57.
(e) review: see 5481.e.

4983. *Zimmerman, Alex H. "Tonality of the sonata allegro form in certain representative classical and romantic symphonies" Ph.D.
diss., Columbia University, 1949. iv, [156] leaves. ill.

See also 3216, 3217, 3249–51, 3258, 3273, 3278, 3288, 3434, 3466,
3498, 3762, 3799, 3866, 3869, 3872, 3888, 3913, 3921, 3944,
4048.a., 4051, 4053, 4054, 4061, 4081, 4093–95, 4105, 4108,
4111, 4114, 4118, 4121, 4123–28, 4131, 4135–37, 4140, 4141,
4143, 4146, 4149–51, 4161–63, 4168, 4173, 4179, 4182, 4184,
4191, 4192, 4199, 4200, 4207, 4210, 4213, 4217, 4226, 4228,
4229, 4232, 4233, 4236, 4237, 4240, 4242, 4246–48, 4258,
4261, 4264, 4270, 4276–78, 4282, 4283, 4289, 4300, 4305,
4305.5, 4306, 4307, 4309, 4313, 4314, 4316, 4319, 4322, 4323,
4328–32, 4336, 4340, 4343, 4345–49, 4352, 4354, 4356, 4360,
4362, 4364, 4366, 4371, 4372, 4374–76, 4382, 4383, 4385,
4386–89, 4391–94, 4396–4402, 4404–06, 4409, 4410, 4413,
4419, 4427, 4430, 4439, 4443, 4450, 4451, 4453, 4456, 4457,
4469–71, 4475, 4482, 4487, 4489, 4490, 4492, 4494, 4498,
4499, 4502, 4503, 4505, 4508, 4514, 4516, 4520–22, 4525,
4526, 4528, 4533, 4535, 4540, 4545, 4549, 4564, 4565,
4581–83, 4585, 4586, 4590, 4591, 4594, 4598, 4600–04, 4606,
4612, 4614, 4617–19, 4621–23, 4625, 4626, 4628, 4630, 4648,
4662, 4664, 4670, 4700, 4701, 4703, 4704, 4709, 4713, 4721,
4728, 4732, 4735, 4736, 4741, 4743, 4747, 4752, 4760, 4761.5,
4764, 4765, 4767, 4768, 4779, 4780, 4783, 4785, 4793.d.e.,
4801, 4802, 4806, 4812, 4816, 4819, 4827–29, 4831, 4833,
4834, 4843, 4846, 4847, 4849, 4851.1, 4853, 4854, 4855.5,
4860, 5115, 5122, 5180, 5191, 5225, 5230, 5311, 5315, 5317,
5332, 5396.
See also "Composing", "Instrumentation", "Musical Mottos and Motifs",
"Texts and Text Setting" in Part V.B.

B. The Techniques

Contains materials which examine Brahms's own thoughts on and his application of various compositional methods; his compositional background,
use of the techniques in his own music, and in that of other composers.

1. Arranging

4984. *Ash, Rodney Philip. "Technique of Piano Transcribing, 1800–
1954" D.M.A. diss., University of Rochester, 1955. 3 vols. mus.,
fig., notes.

4985. Debryn, Carmen. "Kolorit und Struktur. Bachs Concerto "O ewiges Feuer" (BWV 34) in Brahms' Bearbeitung" in *Beiträge zur Geschichte des Konzerts*. [for full citation see 4515] pp. [249]–271. facsim., mus., fig., ind., notes. Presents the background on McCorkle Anhang Ib, Nr. 5 and describes sources. Compares Brahms's arrangement to Bach's original and also to Franz's arrangement of the same work. Includes comment on Brahms's links to Bach's vocal works in general.

4986. *Draheim, Joachim. ""... für das Pianoforte gesetzt". Die zweihändigen Klavierbearbeitungen von Johannes Brahms" *Üben & Musizieren* 5/2 (1988) pp. 106–14.

4987. *Goertzen, Valerie Woodring. "The Piano Transcriptions of Johannes Brahms" Ph.D. diss., Musicology, University of Illinois at Urbana-Champaign, 1987. x, 396 pp. mus., notes.
(e) report: see 4648.e.

4988. Hinson, Maurice. "Johannes Brahms (1833–1897) Germany" in Hinson. *The Pianist's Guide to Transcriptions, Arrangements, and Paraphrases*. Bloomington and Indianapolis: Indiana University Press, 1990. pp. 29–33. 32 items, Brahms arranging Brahms and others arranging Brahms, from all genres: into piano 2 hand, piano 4 hand, 2 piano 4 hand, etc. Includes comments on how to play, how arrangement was done. Also includes reference to 10 composers whose work Brahms arranged.

4989. *Loos, Helmut. "Zur Klavierübertragung von Werken für und mit Orchester des 19. und 20. Jahrhunderts" Phil.F. diss., Rheinische Friedrich-Wilhelms-Universität Bonn, 1980.
(a) reprint: Loos. "[IV.] Johannes Brahms" in Loos. *Zur Klavierübertragung von Werken für und mit Orchester des 19. und 20. Jahrhunderts*. (Schriften zur Musik 25) München-Salzburg: Musikverlag Emil Katzbichler, 1983. pp. 56–64. mus. (pp. 140–60), notes. Discusses Brahms as an arranger for piano and his technique. Compares Op. 56b to Op. 56a; compares Opp. 68 and 98 arrangements to originals.

4990. Roberge, Marc-André. "From Orchestra to Piano: Major Composers as Authors of Piano Reductions of Other Composers' Works" *Notes* 49/3 (3.1993) pp. 925–36. notes. Brahms: p. 931. 4 items included in list: arrangements of works by Joachim (3) and Schubert (1).

See also 3296, 3352, 3362, 3374, 3381.5, 3383, 3410, 3419, 3424, 3427,
    3642, 3834, 3840, 3934, 3975, 3976, 4067, 4086, 4088, 4092,
    4177, 4181, 4201, 4206, 4210, 4211, 4218, 4284, 4299, 4320,
    4365, 4426, 4446, 4478, 4523, 4579, 4604, 4608, 4632, 4725,
    4726.5, 4757, 4823, 4830, 3832, 5449.5.
See also "Op. 25" in Part IV.A.1.a.

2. Composing

Brahms the Progressive: 4996, 5006, 5011, 5021, 5023, 5032, 5045,
5046.

4991. Abell, Arthur M[aynard]. *Talks With Great Composers.* New
    York: Philosophical Library, 1987. Brahms: pp. 1–81. ill. "Paper-
    bound Reprint" of 2453 (A.M. Abell. *Talks With Great Com-
    posers.* (1955)).
    another reprint (of 1955 edition): "A Citadel Press Book". Secau-
    cus: Carol Publishing Group, 1994.

4992. *Adorno, Theodor W. "Brahms aktuell" in Adorno. *Adorno-
    Noten. Mit Beiträge von Theodor W. Adorno.* Rolf Tiedemann, ed.
    ([Katalog der Edition Wewerka] 15) Berlin: Galerie Wewerka-
    Edition, 1984. pp. 34–39.
    (a) reprint: in Adorno. *Musikalische Schriften V.* 1. Auflage. Rolf
        Tiedemann and Klaus Schultz, eds. (Theodor W. Adorno.
        Gesammelte Schriften. Bd. 18) Frankfurt am Main: Suhrkamp
        Verlag, 1984. pp. [200]–203. Places Brahms as a composer in
        his times, mostly on who he was influenced by (Schumann), but
        also on who he influenced (Reger, Schoenberg, Hindemith).

4993. *Becker, H[einz]. "Johannes Brahms nützte die Form für Phan-
    tasie. Anmerkungen zum 150. Geburtstag des Komponisten aus
    Hamburg" *Neue Musikzeitung* 32/2 (1983) pp. 1, 11.

4994. "Brahms as a Choral Composer" *Musical Courier* 43/10 (Whole
    no. 1119) (4.9.1901) p. 20. Compares Brahms to Berlioz, Schu-
    mann and Rubinstein and concludes that Brahms is the best.

4995. *Brahms, Composer" *Musical Courier* 22 (15.4.1891) pp. 364–65.

4996. [Schoenberg, Arnold] "Brahms the Progressive" in *Nineteenth-
    Century Music* (The Garland Library of the History of Western

Music 9) New York: Garland Publishing Inc., 1985. pp. 132–75. mus. Reprint of 2493.a. (in A. Schoenberg. *Style and Idea.* (1975)).

4997. *Brehm, Roberta. "The Pianistic Textures of Chopin and Brahms" M.A. diss., Kent State University, 1965. iii, 491 pp. mus.

4998. Brodbeck, David [Lee]. "The Waltzes of Brahms" *The American Brahms Society Newsletter* 4/2 (Autumn 1986) pp. [1–3]. ill., facsim. Examines Brahms as a composer of waltzes, notes influences of Schubert and Strauss, notes techniques Brahms used. Focuses on Opp. 39, 52 and 65.

4999. Brolinson, Per-Erik. "Johannes Brahms—den tidlöse traditionalisten" *Musikrevy* 38/5 (1983) pp. 217–18, 220. ill. (issue cover), mus. Sees Brahms following on in Beethoven's line; includes comment on Brahms's "developing variation" technique.

5000. Cleve, John S., van. "Johannes Brahms" *The Etude* 11/1 (1.1893) p. 12. Discusses the nature of Brahms's genius as a composer; includes comment on the piano works, and on Brahms as a piano player.

5000.5. *Cope, David H. "A computer model of music composition" in *Machine models of music.* Cambridge, MA: Massachusetts Institute of Technology, 1993. p. 403–25. ill., facsim., music. To understand algorithmic composition in various styles, EMI Project (Experiments in Music Intelligence) focuses on the stylistic replication of individual composers. Generated styles to date include Albinoni, Mozart, Brahms, and Debussy. Compositional style is defined largely as adjustments to inherited material. [from S109]

5001. *Cravens, Arline E[lizabeth]. "The Influence of Romantic Thought in the Evolution of Nineteenth-Century Piano Composition from Schubert to Brahms" M.M. diss., Music, Southern Illinois University at Carbondale, 1992. iii, 117 pp. notes.

5002. Dahlhaus, Carl. "Zur Problemgeschichte des Komponierens" in Dahlhaus. *Zwischen Romantik und Moderne. Vier Studien zur Musikgeschichte des späteren 19. Jahrhunderts.* (Berliner musikwissenschaftliche Arbeiten 7) München: Musikverlag Emil Katzbichler, 1974. pp. 40–73. mus., notes. Discusses Brahms's compositional technique, with examples from Opp. 8, 15, 25, 79 and 90.

(b) English translation by Mary Whittall in collaboration with Arnold Whittall: Dahlhaus. "Issues in Composition" in Dahlhaus. *Between Romanticism and Modernism. Four Studies in the Music of the Later Nineteenth Century.* Mary Whittall, [overall] trans. Includes the Nietzsche Fragment, "On Music and Words," translated by Walter Kaufmann. (California Studies in 19th Century Music [1]) Berkeley [et al.]: University of California Press, 1980. pp. 40–78. adds fig., ind.

(e) report: see 5055.

5003. *Davis, Wanda Mae. "Brahms' Place among the Composers of the Keyboard Variation (1550–1900)" M.A., Music, California State University, Sacramento, 1966. 206 pp.

5004. *Duchesneau, Louise. "The Voice of the Muse: A Study of the Role of Inspiration in Musical Composition" Phil.F. diss., Musikwissenschaft, Universität Hamburg, 1986.

(a) reprint: Duchesneau. "Inspiration from ABOVE" in Duchesneau. *The Voice of the Muse: A Study of the Role of Inspiration in Musical Composition.* (European University studies=Europäische Hochschulschriften=Publications universitaires européennes. Series=Reihe=Série 36. Musicology=Musikwissenschaft=Musicologie 19) Frankfurt am Main [et al.]: Peter Lang, 1986. pp. 56–[83].

"Brahms and the "Überbewußtsein"": pp. 59–64. notes. Reports on Brahms's thoughts on inspiration as recorded by Abell in 2453 (A.M. Abell. *Talks With Great Composers.* (1955) [see 4991])

5005. Einstein, Alfred. "Opus ultimum" *Musikrevy* 46/6 (1991) pp. 285–92.

"Mendelssohn, Schumann, Chopin, Brahms": p. [290] mus. Thoughts on Brahms as a composer, Opp. 120 and 122 no. 3/11 are the examples.

5006. Federhofer, Hellmut. "Johannes Brahms—Arnold Schönberg und der Fortschritt" *Studien zur Musikwissenschaft* 34 (1983) pp. 111–30. mus., fig., notes. Reviews how Schoenberg saw Brahms as the continuation to the present; goes over all of the Brahms music examples that Schoenberg uses in 2493 (A. Schoenberg. *Style and Idea.* (1950) [see 5045]).

5007. Fellinger, Imogen. "Brahms und die Gattung des Instrumentalkonzerts" in *Beiträge zur Geschichte des Konzerts.* [for full citation see 4515] pp. [201]–09. ind., notes. Discusses Brahms's connection to the concerto genre and its significance for him. Includes an overview of concertos by other composers that he knew and played, in particular Mozart's piano concertos and Viotti's G. 97; studies each of his concertos for formal, instrumental/soloist elements.

5008. Fellinger, Imogen. "Brahms und die neudeutsche Schule" in *Brahms und seine Zeit*. (Hamburger Jahrbuch für Musikwissenschaft 7) [for full citation see 5428] pp. 159–69. notes. Reviews the time period 1853–60 and Brahms's position vis à vis the "New German School."

5009. Fellinger, Imogen. "Brahms' Persönlichkeit als Komponist" in *Brahms-Wochen '83 der Freien und Hansestadt Hamburg 7.–29. Mai*. Hamburg: Kulturbehörde, 1983. pp. 7–14.
   (a) *reprint: Fellinger. in *Brahms-Zyklus-Orchesterkonzerte*. Gütersloh: n.p., 1983. pp. 10–13.
   (b) English translation: Fellinger. "Brahms's 'Way': A Composer's Self-View" in *Brahms 2*. [for full citation see 5481] pp. 49–58. notes. Examines how Brahms viewed himself as a composer—his outlook on music, his position on his contemporaries, his position on his own works—and how he viewed the concept of a "school" of composition. Includes comparative remarks against Schumann and Wagner, and traces Brahms's path of instruction through the 1850's.

5010. Fellinger, Imogen, see 5088.5.

5011. Finscher, Ludwig. "Arnold Schönberg's Brahms-Vortrag" in *Neue Musik und Tradition. Festschrift Rudolf Stephan zum 65. Geburtstag*. Josef Kuckertz, Helga de la Motte-Haber, Christian Martin Schmidt and Wilhelm Seidel, eds. Laaber: Laaber-Verlag, 1990. pp. 485–500. notes. Reviews one of the drafts of Schoenberg's speech within the context of the whole project.
   (d) see: 5032.

5012. Finscher, Ludwig. "Lieder für eine Singstimme und Klavier" in *Johannes Brahms: Leben und Werk* [for full citation see 3215] pp. 139–40, 143. Discusses Brahms and his texts, Brahms and folksong, how he set what he decided to set and how his work developed over the years.

5013. Fischer-Dieskau, Dietrich. "Brahms" in Fischer-Dieskau. *Töne sprechen, Worte klingen. Zur Geschichte und Interpretation des Gesangs.* [Stuttgart:] Deutsche Verlags-Anstalt; [München: R.] Piper, [1985]. pp. 108–13. ind., notes. Discusses Brahms as a composer of song and the way he sets text; includes comments on how the performer should approach Brahms's works.

5014. Fischer-Dieskau, Dietrich. "Zum Segen des Werkes opferte er sein Glück. Johannes Brahms und seine Lieder" *Die Welt* Hamburg-Ausgabe no. 106 (7./8.5.1983) Geistige Welt (7.5.1983) p. [I]. Discusses Brahms as a composer of song with selected examples, roughly chronological in approach. Includes comments on Brahms's interest in older music, the relationship of the songs to his choral and instrumental works, and Brahms and the "New German School."

5015. Floros, Constantin. "Kunstanschauung und Stil" in *Johannes Brahms: Leben und Werk.* [for full citation see 3215] pp. 89–92. Discusses Brahms's style, Brahms and romanticism and being in Schumann's shadow, his creative process and his position vis à vis the "New German School."

5016. Floros, Constantin. "Zur Gegensätzlichkeit der Symphonik Brahms' und Bruckners" in *Bruckner Symposion.* [for full citation see 5434] pp. 145–53. fig., notes. Contrasts their approaches to symphonic writing; compares use of tonality, slow movements, style.

5017. Goulding, Phil G. "Johannes Brahms (1833–1897). Number 6" in Goulding. *Classical Music. The 50 Greatest Composers and Their 1,000 Greatest Works.* New York: Fawcett Columbine, 1992. pp. 168–79. ill., ind., discog. (p. 588). also et passim. Focuses on Brahms the composer and his place in the 19th century. Also includes a selection of his critics' comments and an overview of his life, focusing on pre-1862. Includes suggestions for further listening.

5018. Gregor-Dellin, Martin. "Brahms und die Normalität" in Gregor-Dellin. *Was ist Größe? Sieben Deutsche und ein deutsches Problem.* München, Zürich: Piper, 1985. pp. 197–216. Compares Brahms the man and Brahms the composer; both seem serene, no turmoil in either.

(a) *reprint: in Gregor-Dellin. *Musik und Welt: 5 Essays*. 1. Auflage. Berlin: Henschel, 1988.

5019. Gülke, Peter. "Brahms. Ein Mosaik" in Gülke. *Brahms. Bruckner. Zwei Studien*. Kassel, Basel: Bärenreiter, 1989. pp. [13–72]. notes. Discusses how Brahms the musician impacts on Brahms the person; looks for traits of his personality in his music.

5020. Gülke, Peter. "Sagen und Schweigen bei Brahms" in *Brahms-Analysen*. [for full citation see 4888] pp. 12–32. notes. A collection of descriptive comments excerpted from the literature that discuss Brahms the composer and his techniques, relevant to the instrumental works. Includes comments on Brahms and the Schumanns, and Brahms and Wagner.

5021. Hansen, Mathias. "'Reife Menschen denken Komplex". Brahms' Bedeutung für die Musik des 20. Jahrhunderts" *Musik und Gesellschaft* 33/5 (5.1983) pp. 277–81. ill., facsim., notes. Discusses Brahms as a foundation for 20th century advances in composition, also comments on his dual romantic-classical nature.

5022. Hanslick, Eduard. *Hanslick's Music Criticisms*. Henry Pleasants [III] ed. and trans. New York: Dover Publications Inc., 1988. An "unabridged and slightly corrected republication" of 2470.b. (E. Hanslick. *Music Criticisms 1846–99*. (1963)).
"Brahms [[1862]]": pp. 82–86. notes. Describes Brahms the composer and pianist.
Brahms: pp. 125–28, 157–59, 210–13, 243–45. Reviews of the symphonies.

5023. Hiebert, Elfrieda F. "The Janus Figure of Brahms: A Future Built Upon the Past" *Journal of the American Liszt Society* 16 (12.1984) pp. 72–88. mus., notes. Studies the duality of Brahms as a composer: his musical inheritance and the techniques from that, and the new interpretations he makes to that.

5024. *Jacobsen, Bernard. "Über das Missverständnis der Komponisten des 20. Jahrhunderts gegenüber der Kompositionstechnik Johannes Brahms'" *Johannes Brahms: Leben, Werk, Interpretation, Rezeption*. [for full citation see 5453] pp. 84–89. ill. Discusses how 20th century composers, including Schoenberg, misunderstood Brahms's technique. Examines Brahms's modest influence in the area of rhythm. [from S102]

5025. *Kagel, M[auricio]. "Die mißbrauchte Empfindsamkeit. Zum 150. Geburtstag des Komponisten" [*Musikhochschule Köln. Journal. Nachrichten—Berichte—Meinungen*] 2/1 (1983).

(d) condensed: [Kagel, Mauricio] "Die mißbrauchte Empfindsamkeit. "Die Tradition bin ich" / Mauricio Kagel über sich, die Moderne und Brahms / Zum hundertfünfzigsten Geburtstag des Komponisten" *Frankfurter allgemeine Zeitung* no. 105 (6.5.1983) p. 25. ill. Discusses Brahms's place as a composer in music history, Brahms the Progressive; includes comment on Brahms's impact on Kagel, Kagel's feelings about Brahms over time. Includes comments on Brahms and folkmusic.

5026. Kirsch, Winfried. "Das Scherzo bei Brahms und Bruckner" in *Bruckner Symposion.* [for full citation see 5434] pp. 155–72. fig., notes. Compares and analyses the different approaches these two composers took in developing the scherzo beyond the Beethovian model.

5027. Kross, Siegfried. "Brahms' künstlerische Identität" in *Brahms-Kongress Wien 1983.* [for full citation see 5431] pp. 325–49. notes. Comments that Brahms's portrayal as a composer by Kalbeck is flawed, and suggests it needs to be reviewed. Comments on Brahms and E.T.A. Hoffmann, Brahms and Schubert, and looks at Ludwig Speidel's writings on Brahms for correct attitude. Also suggests that Brahms comes out of the Beethoven line, rather than from Schumann.

(d) related to: 5449.5.

5028. Kunze, Stefan. "Johannes Brahms oder: Das schwere Werk der Symphonie" in *Johannes Brahms: Leben und Werk.* [for full citation see 3215] pp. 111–13. Surveys Brahms as a symphonic composer.

5029. Leibowitz, René. "Schumann et Brahms et les paradoxes du reve romantique" in Leibowitz. *L'evolution de la musique de Bach à Schœnberg.* Paris: Correa, 1951. pp. [125]–140. Compares the two men as composers and concludes that Brahms is a classicist in romantic guise; finds them both lacking, but finds Brahms to be better than Schumann.

(b) Spanish translation: Leibowitz. "Schumann y Brahms y las paradojas del sueño romàntico" in Leibowitz. *La evolucion de la musica de Bach a Schonberg.* Prólogo de Leonardo

Acosta. Cuidad de la Habana: Editorial Arte y Literatura, 1980. pp. [85]–93.

5030. Lewin, David. "Brahms, His Past, and Modes of Music Theory" in *Brahms Studies: Analytical and Historical Perspectives*. [for full citation see 5480] pp. [13]–27. mus., notes, appendix. Shows how Brahms uses models from older music in his own: Beethoven and Mozart in Op. 51 no. 1; cantus firmus technique in Opp. 36 and 79; mensuration in Op. 116 no. 5.

5031. *"Logical Development" *Music Review* (Chicago) 2 (11.1892) pp. 82–84.

5032. McGeary, Thomas. "Schoenberg's Brahms Lecture of 1933" *Journal of the Arnold Schoenberg Institute* 15/2 (11.1992) pp. [5]–99. facsim., mus., notes, appendixes. A study and transcript of the actual lecture: the background, how the lecture was developed into 2493 (in A. Schoenberg. *Style and Idea*. (1950)). Most of the article is the transcript, which is presented in German and English translation in a facing-page format. Appendixes include descriptions of the 7 surviving typescripts of the lecture, and a comparison of the musical examples that Schoenberg cites in both the lecture and in 2493.
Periodical issue has title: "Schoenberg's Brahms Lecture."
(d) see: 5046.

5033. [Mencken, Henry Louis] "Mencken on Brahms. Brahms (1833–1897)" *The American Brahms Society Newsletter* 3/2 (Autumn 1985) pp. [5–6]. ill., mus. Reprint of 2481.a.iii. (in H.L. Mencken. *A Mencken Chrestomathy*. (1949)).

5034. *Mila, Massimo. "Brahms, uomo moderno" in *46° Maggio musicale fiorentino*. Firenze: Teatro comunale di Firenze, 1983. pp. 137–41.

5035. *Mismas, James. "An Historical and Compositional Prespective (sic) on Various Works by Bach, Brahms, Faure (sic) and Browning as Performed in Recital" M.Mus. diss., University of Akron, 1980. v, 40 pp. notes.

5036. *Musiker über Musik. Aus Briefen, Tagebüchern und Aufzeichnungen*. Josef Rufer, ed. Darmstadt: Verlag Stichnote GmbH Darmstadt, 1956. 320 pp. ill., mus., notes.

(d) "eine leicht veränderte und erweiterte Fassung": *Bekenntnisse und Erkenntnisse. Komponisten über ihr Werk.* Josef Rufer, ed. Frankfurt am Main: Propyläen, 1979. "Johannes Brahms (1833–1897)": pp. 96–[102]. in "Zwei Antagonisten": pp. 88–[102]. Bruckner is the other "antagonist." Relates Brahms's thoughts on composing, also traces Brahms's attempts to write an opera; also pp. 88–90 for the "New German School" incident.

5037. Pascall, Robert. "Brahms und die Gattung der Symphonie" Monika Lichtenfeld, trans. in *Johannes Brahms: Leben und Werk.* [for full citation see 3215] pp. 113–14. mus. Discusses Brahms and his difficulties in composing in symphonic form, including discussion of Andante from Op. 68 and possible 5th and 6th symphonies. Also looks at the precursors of the symphony in Opp. 11 and 16 and melodic links to other genres (songs, Op. 88).

5038. Plantinga, Leon. "Crosscurrents in the Late Century" in Plantinga. *Romantic Music. A History of Musical Style in Nineteenth-Century Europe.* (The Norton Introduction to Music History) New York, London: W.W. Norton & Company, 1984. pp. [405]–61. "Brahms": pp. 411–34. ill., facsim., mus., notes. A chronological overview of Brahms the composer with analysis of examples from selected works—Op. 77 is the focus. Includes comments on Brahms the classic and romantic composer.

5039. Ralph, Robert. "The Music and Philosophy of Brahms" *Musical Opinion and Music Trade Review* 36/423 (12.1912) pp. 171–72. Discusses Brahms as a composer of "philosophical music", detached from reality. Sees this as a reflection of Brahms the man.

5040. Rummenhöller, Peter. ""Liedhaftes" in Werk von Johannes Brahms" in *Brahms als Liedkomponist.* [for full citation see 5083] pp. [38]–46. mus., ind., notes. Takes examples from the songs of folk idiom, and finds similarities in the instrumental music. Uses this to prove that Brahms has a romantic side.

5041. Salzer, Felix, and Carl Schachter. "Brahms: Intermezzo Op. 76, no. 4" in Salzer and Schachter. *Counterpoint in Composition. The Study of Voice Leading.* (McGraw-Hill Series in Music) New York [et al.]: McGraw-Hill Book Company, 1969. pp. 458–61. mus. (also et passim), fig., ind. This piece used as example of prolonged counterpoint.

5042. Sannemüller, Gerd. "Johannes Brahms und das Lied" *Neue Zürcher Zeitung* no. 106 (7./8.5.1983) p. 67. ill. Discusses Brahms as a composer of song, the characteristics; also looks at song-like elements in the instrumental works.

5043. *Savinio, Alberto. "Brahms" in Savinio. *Scatola sonora*. Introduzione di Fausto Torrefranca. [(Le voci)?] Milano: G. Ricordi e C., 1955. 371 or xxiii, 375 pp. ill.
   *[Nuova ed. aggiornata:] Introduzione di Luigi Rognoni. (Einaudi letteratura 53) Torino: G. Einaudi, 1977. xii, 479 pp. notes.
   *also: [1988.] (Saggi 714) xxiv, 468 pp..
   (b) *French translation by Rene de Ceccatty: Savinio. *La boîte a musique*. (De l'Italieto) [Paris:] Fayard, 1989. 483 pp.

5044. Schmidt, Christian Martin. *Johannes Brahms und seine Zeit*. (Große Komponisten und ihre Zeit) [Laaber:] Laaber-Verlag, 1983. 272 pp. ill., facsim., mus., fig., ind., notes. Discusses Brahms the composer, in particular Brahms's connections with folk music and music prior to the Romantic period; Brahms's work in various musical forms with examples from all works. Also comments on Brahms's contemporary reception, Brahms and the political scene of his day. Life of Brahms presented in a timeline format.
   (b) *Italian translation by Angela Bozzo: Schmidt, Christian [Martin]. *Brahms*. Torino: EDT, 1990.
   (c) *excerpt: Schmidt. "Hie Johannes Brahms—hie Richard Wagner" *General-Anzeiger* (Bonn) (7./8.5.1983) p. 21.
   (d) related (?): see 3224.

5045. Schoenberg, Arnold. "Brahms the Progressive" in Schoenberg. *Style and Idea. Selected Writings of Arnold Schoenberg*. Leonard Stein, ed.; Leo Black, trans. Berkeley, Los Angeles: University of California Press, 1985. pp. 398–441. mus., notes. Reprint of 2493.a. (Schoenberg. *Style and Idea*. (New York, 1975)).
   *1st paperback ed. with revisions: London: Faber & Faber, 1984.

5046. Schönberg, Arnold. "Vortrag, zu halten in Frankfurt am Main am 12.II.1933" in *Verteidigung des musikalischen Fortschritts*. [for full citation see 3931] pp. 162–72. facsim. (pp. 162–69). Transcription of manuscript, with facsimile on facing page. Includes Schoenberg's comments and remarks at end of article.
   (d) see: 5032.

5047. Sennett, Richard. "The Art of Memory" *The Atlantic* 254/3 (9.1984) pp. 118–20. Discusses how Brahms's memories of his early days (up to 1853) are reflected in his music. Includes comments on Brahms the innovative composer and surveys available recordings.

5048. Siegmund-Schultze, Walther. "Johannes Brahms—Stationen seines Schaffens. Zum 150. Geburtstag des Komponisten" *Musik und Gesellschaft* 33/5 (5.1983) pp. 257–63. ill., facsim. Looks at Brahms's output as a composer and the forms he wrote in. Concludes that Brahms writes in 10 year cycles with highlight works being Opp. 15, 45, 68, 98.

5049. *Smith, Jane Stuart, and Betty Carlson. *The Gift of Music: Great Composers and Their Influence.* 3rd ed. Wheaton, IL: Crossway Books, 1995. 317 pp.

5050. Sorel, Albert. "Discours a l'Institut [de Cinq Académies]" in Sorel. *Nouveaux essais d'histoire et de critique* . . . Paris: E. Plon [Librairie Plon], 1898. pp. [145]–57. Brahms: pp. 151–52. Describes Brahms as a composer and his style, emphasizes that Brahms is a symphonist over all.

5051. *Steinberg, Michael P. "Old Brahms a Modernist? In More Ways Than One" *The New York Times* (29.9.1996) Section PG, p. 31. ill. Discusses how Brahms grappled with the issues of a century ago through his music.

5052. Šeda, Jaroslav. "Zamyšlení nad dílem Johannesa Brahmse" *Hudební rozhledy* 36/7 ([7.] 1983) pp. 332–35. Discusses Brahms the composer and the character of his music. Surveys his work by genre, includes comparison with Beethoven, Chopin and Schumann.

5053. *Vaughan Williams, Ralph. "Some Thoughts on Brahms" *Music Student* 2/8 (1910) pp. 116–20.

5054. Will, I. "L'Art de Johannes Brahms" *Le Guide musical* 38/44 (30.10.1892) pp. [295]–97. Discusses Brahms the composer and reviews and describes output to date. Also looks at links to Schumann, Beethoven and Wagner, and reports on contemporary opinions.

5055. Wintle, Christopher. "[Review Article:] Issues in Dahlhaus" *Music Analysis* 1/3 (10.1982) pp. 341–55. Brahms: pp. 353–54.

notes. Comments on Dahlhaus's remarks concerning Brahms in 5002.b.

5056. York, W. Wynn. "Posthumous Interview" *Music Educators Journal* 47/2 (11.–12.1960) pp. 84–85. Fictional report on contacting Brahms beyond the grave, and what he has to say about being a composer.

5057. Youens, Susan. "Schubert, Mahler and the Weight of the Past: 'Lieder eines fahrenden Gesellen' and 'Winterreise'" *Music & Letters* 67/3 (7.1986) pp. 256–68. Brahms: pp. 257, 267–68. notes. Discusses how Schubert's stature as a composer of songs inhibited those who followed. Examines how Brahms coped with the setting of texts previously done by Schumann and Schubert: Schumann's Op. 39 no. 5 compared to McCorkle WoO 21; Schumann's Op. 39 no. 1 with Op. 3 no. 5 (texts by Eichendorff). Also discusses songs composed in youth that were subsequently destroyed [McCorkle Anhang IIa, Nr. 12*] (texts by Eichendorff and Heine).

(d) Hafner, Klaus [Klaus Häfner]. "Brahms and Schubert" *Music & Letters* 68/2 (4.1987) p. 210. Corrects Youens on which Schubert setting Brahms is talking about in letter to Wendt, 1887, that she quotes in article.

5058. Youngren, William. "Brahms as Modernist" *The Atlantic* 256/1 (7.1985) pp. 90–92. ill., notes. Contrasts today's view of Brahms as romantic composer with his contemporaries' view - e.g., G.B. Shaw, B.H. Haggin—that he is a difficult composer. Uses examples from chamber music to explore Brahms's creative side and show his progressive nature: Opp. 8, 40, 51 no. 1, 78. Calls for re-evaluation of Brahms's position; includes suggestions for further reading and listening.

(d) [adapted by George S. Bozarth from above and 5408:] Youngren. "The Modernist Brahms" *The American Brahms Society Newsletter* 10/1 (Spring 1992) pp. [1]–3. notes omitted.

See 3203, 3207, 3210, 3215, 3217, 3225, 3235, 3249, 3256, 3273.5, 3276, 3279, 3289, 3301, 3341, 3362, 3363, 3459, 3463, 3464, 3617, 3620, 3623, 3637, 3641, 3647, 3648, 3686.c., 3726, 3729, 3749, 3750, 3771, 3779, 3813, 3815, 3827, 3838, 3839, 3844, 3861, 3866, 3871, 3888, 3912, 3922, 3924, 3928–30, 3944, 4011, 4016, 4017, 4040, 4047, 4054, 4056, 4067, 4068, 4078, 4088, 4102, 4105, 4112, 4114,

4118, 4137, 4141, 4151, 4163, 4191, 4211, 4225, 4230, 4236, 4255, 4257, 4261.d.i., 4262, 4263, 4271–73, 4283, 4304, 4312, 4318, 4334, 4342, 4354, 4356, 4358, 4362, 4387, 4408, 4419, 4429, 4433, 4443, 4445, 4451, 4459, 4479, 4481, 4494, 4515, 4524, 4553, 4558, 4565, 4581, 4583, 4597, 4600, 4603, 4616, 4618, 4645, 4649, 4652, 4654, 4656, 4666, 4667, 4669, 4673, 4674, 4678, 4681, 4685, 4687, 4690, 4691, 4697, 4701, 4713, 4714, 4757, 4762, 4785, 4820, 4848, 4864, 4687, 4881, 4914, 4916, 4940, 4950, 4959, 4960, 4970, 4973, 4978, 5066, 5118, 5131, 5141, 5143, 5145–47, 5149, 5158, 5166, 5169, 5233, 5305, 5307, 5311, 5314, 5317, 5321, 5324, 5329, 5338, 5348, 5352, 5353, 5360, 5362, 5380, 5396, 5401, 5404, 5405, 5440, 5449.5, 5467.

See also Part II.B.; and "Creative Process", "Musical Mottos and Motifs", "Texts and Text Setting" in Part V.B.

See also I15, I30, I41, I42 in Appendix A.

3. Editing

5059. Hinson, Maurice. "Brahms as Editor" *Journal of the American Liszt Society* 14 (12.1983) pp. 30–42. notes, works list (pp. 37–42). Provides background on Brahms's strong literary and scholarly interests so we may better understand Brahms as an editor. Discusses his editing techniques and how he felt about editing; includes comment on Brahms and Chrysander.

See also 3679, 3834, 3908, 3909, 3911, 3914, 3934, 4201, 4250, 4262, 4315, 4428–30, 4633, 4793.d.e., 4862, 5142, 5145.

See also "Brahms's Editing and Arranging . . ." subsections in Part IV; and "Music Prior to the Classical Period" in Part VI.A.

4. Instrumentation

5060. *Bishop, Paul Joseph. "The Viola in Brahms' Chamber Music" M.M. diss., University of Rochester, 1947. vi, 73 pp. mus., notes.

5061. Bozarth, George S. [comp. and ed.] "Brahms, A Master of Instrumentation" *The American Brahms Society Newsletter* 12/1 (Spring 1994) pp. 6–10. ill., notes. Reprint of 2519.b.i. (F. Weingartner. *New Music and Church Music Review* (1905)); in addition, includes Weingartner's comments on Brahms's music and reminiscences of meeting Brahms (1895–96).

5062. *Busch, Hermann J. "Die Orgeln Mendelssohns, Liszts und Brahms'" in *Proceedings of the Goteborg International Organ Academy 1994.* Hans Davidsson and Sverker Jullander, eds. (Skrifter fran Musikvetenskapliga avdelningen, Goteborgs universitet 39) Goteborg : [Goteborg University, Department of Musicology] 1995.

5063. *Findlay, Gavin. "The Symphonic Use of the Tuba by Berlioz, Brahms and Tchaikowsky" B.Mus. diss., University of Tasmania, 1985.

5064. FitzGibbon, H. Macaulay. "The Use of the Piccolo by The Great Composers" *Musical Opinion and Music Trade Review* 36/421, 423 (10.,12.;1912) pp. 12–13, 173–74. Brahms: p. 174. Short look at the five Brahms works that have piccolo: Opp. 16, 80, 81, 83, and 98.

5065. *Francis, George. "Horn Notes" *Monthly Musical Record* 62 (1932) pp. 105–06.

5066. Fuchs, Ingrid. "Aspekte der Instrumentation der Symphonien Brahms' und Bruckners" in *Bruckner Symposion.* [for full citation see 5434] pp. 133–44. notes. A detailed analysis that contrasts the two composers' approaches, and their formal study.

5067. *Greenberg, Stanley Samuel. "A Comparison of the Uses of the String Section of the Orchestra as Evidenced in Selected Works by Brahms and Wagner" M.M. diss., University of Rochester, 1958. [vi], 51, [27] pp. ill., mus., notes.

5068. *Harizal, Susan May. "The Use of the Hand and Valve Horns in the Orchestral Works of Johannes Brahms and Richard Wagner" M.M. diss., Ohio University, 1974. ix, 95 pp. fig.

5069. [Jenner, Gustav] "Individuality and Instrumentation" F.L., trans. *The Etude* 25/9 (9.1907) p. 580. notes. Excerpt from 694.a. (G. Jenner. *Johannes Brahms als Mensch . . .* (1905)); discusses Brahms as an orchestrator.

5070. *Leatherwood, Peggy. "A Comparison of Orchestration Techniques from Representative Works of Beethoven, Brahms and

Tchaikovsky" Undergraduate thesis, Maryville College, 1975. ii, 39 pp. mus., notes.

5071. *Lee, James D. "A Comparative Study of the Symphonic Trombone Scoring of Beethoven, Brahms and Berlioz" M.A. diss., Kent State University, 1974. v, 46 pp. mus., fig.

5072. *Manning, Leanne. "Brahms and the Clarinet: The Instrument He Knew and Wrote For" B.Mus. (Hons.) diss., University of Queensland, 1987.

5073. *Paul, Ernst. "Das Horn des Wiener Klangstils" *Österreichische Musikzeitschrift* 24/12 (12.1969) pp. 698–702. Discusses this particular type of hornplaying, realized most fully in its use in orchestral works of Bruckner, Brahms and the Viennese compositions of Wagner. [from S102]

5074. *Pryor, Thomas Rexford, Jr. "The Trumpet: Its Development and Literature from Monteverdi to Stravinsky" M.M. diss., Theory, Syracuse University, 1961. iii, 119 pp. mus., notes.

5075. *Thompson, Mark. "Brahms and the Light" *The Horn Call* 9/1 (10.1978) pp. 71–72. summaries in French and German. [from S047]

5076. *Wooters, Berthel Howard. "A Study of Brahms' Treatment of the Clarinet in His Chamber Music and in his Orchestral Works" M.M. Ed. diss., Music, Southern Illinois University, 1964. 59 pp. notes.

See also 3305, 3437, 3464, 4041, 4047, 4086, 4110, 4153, 4157, 4214, 4305.5, 4370, 4391, 4419, 4449, 4460.d., 4478, 4479, 4504, 4524, 4540, 4604, 4782, 4816, 4832, 4882, 4955, 4985, 4997, 5020, 5166.
See also "Op. 40" in Part IV.A.1.a.

5. Musical Mottos and Motifs

5077. *"Johannes Brahms und Robert Schumann . . . " *Neue musikalische Presse* [9]/19 (1900).
   (a) reprint: in Sievers, Heinrich. "Der artige Zufall" in Sievers. *Scurrilia in musica. Ergetzliches aus allerlei Journalen.* Tutzing: Hans Schneider, 1988. p. 82. Notes that the cycle of

keys for the Brahms and Schumann symphonies matches the theme of the fugue in the last movement of Mozart's KV 551.

See also 3832, 4053, 4137, 4192, 4199, 4213, 4232, 4237, 4247, 4261, 4329, 4387, 4399, 4407, 4453, 4549, 4565, 4582, 4764.d., 4801, 4826, 4833, 4916, 4972.d., 4979, 5137.

See also "Allusions" in Part V.D.

6. Texts and Text Settings

Includes materials that discuss the texts Brahms used in his vocal works.

5078. Baum, Günther. "Wort und Ton im romantischen Kunstlied" *Das Musikleben* 3/5 (5.1950) pp. 136–40. Brahms: pp. 138–39. General overview of Brahms's attitude toward poetry and what effects this attitude had on the text-music relationship of his songs. Other composers surveyed are Schubert, Schumann and Wolf.

5079. Bell, A. Craig. "An Aspect of Brahms's Lieder" *The Music Review* 52/3 (8.1991) pp. 190–94. mus. Related to 2034 (A.C. Bell. *The Lieder of Brahms.* (1979)) (?) Asks why composers set particular texts and what sorts of texts they are. Looks at the forms in which Brahms casts songs, with examples from his works. Includes comments on Brahms's links to Schubert.

5080. Beller-McKenna, Daniel. "Brahms, the Bible and Post-Romanticism: Cultural Issues in Johannes Brahms's Later Settings of Biblical Texts, 1877–1896" Ph.D. diss., Harvard University, 1994. ix, 257 or 268 pp. ill., facsim., notes. Looks at what Brahms set after 1877 in Opp. 74 no. 1; 109; 110 no. 1; and 121; examines it from a variety of viewpoints in order to determine the ways in which Brahms's approach to the Bible sheds light on his religious, philosophical and artistic attitudes. Analysis relevant to the cultural issues of the time is done—Op. 121 to Schopenhauer; Op. 110 no. 1 to the political scene. Includes study of his pocket notebook (see also 3400), examination of Schumann's influence on Brahms with Op. 45 as example.

(d) i) Beller-McKenna. "Brahms on Schopenhauer: The Vier ernste Gesänge, Op. 121, and Late Nineteenth-Century Pessimism" *Brahms Studies* 1 (1994) pp. 170–90.

(d) ii) Beller-McKenna. "Brahms, the Bible and Robert Schumann" *The American Brahms Society Newsletter* 13/2 (Autumn 1995)

pp. [1]–4. ill. only. Examines where the idea comes from that
Brahms is familiar with the Bible; reviews Brahms's own comments on the Bible and comments made about his biblical settings. Includes discussion of a Schumann influence in Op. 45.

(d) iii) *Beller-McKenna. "The Great Warum!: Job, Christ, and
Bach in a Brahms Motet" *19th Century Music* 19/3 (1996) p.
231+.

5081. Benecke, Heike. "Mutter-Tochter-Dialoge" in *Brahms als Liedkomponist*. [for full citation see 5083] pp. [137]–55. mus., fig.,
ind., notes. Looks at songs that are in format of a dialogue: Opp.
3 no. 1, 69 no. 9, 75 no. 2, 84 nos. 1–3. Studies their position in
Brahms's total output, their text-music relationships.

5082. Boylan, Paul Charles. "The Lieder of Hugo Wolf: Zenith of the German Art Song" Ph.D diss., Music, University of Michigan, 1968.
vii, [1], 402 pp.

"Brahms and Wolf": pp. 322–52. mus., fig. Settings of same text by
both composers are compared: Op. 59 no. 5 with Wolf's
Gedichte von Eduard Mörike no. 14; Op. 69 no. 8 with *Alte
Weisen* no. 4; Op. 19 no. 5 with *Gedichte . . . Mörike* no. 11.

5083. *Brahms als Liedkomponist: Studien zum Verhältnis von Text und
Vertonung*. Peter Jost, ed. Stuttgart: Franz Steiner Verlag, 1992.
ill., facsim. (on cover), ind. Contains: 4648.d.iii., 4667, 5010,
5040, 5081, 5092–94, 5097, 5102, 5203.

5084. Coffin, Berton, Ralph Errolle, Werner Singer, and Pierre Delattre.
*Phonetic Readings of Songs and Arias. Authentic Pronunciation
of 413 Italian, German and French Lyrics from "The Singer's
Repertoire" in International Phonetic Alphabet Transcription.*
[(The Singer's Repertoire 6)] Boulder, CO: Pruett Press, Inc.,
1964. viii, 361 pp. ind.

Singer, Werner, and Berton Coffin. "Phonetic Transcription of
German Songs and Arias": pp. 85–251. Brahms: pp. 97–124.
36 items. German original text interlined with phonetic transcription. Songs are arranged alphabetically by song title or
first line incipit when untitled.

2nd ed.: *Phonetic Readings of Songs and Arias*. 2nd ed., with revised German Transcriptions. Metuchen, NJ & London:
Scarecrow Press, 1982. xvi, 384 pp. ind. Singer and Coffin:
pp. 85–274. Brahms: pp. 99–129.

(d) see: 5195.

5085. *Di Fronzo, Luigi, with Moreno Covili. "Musiche diverse per texte uguali: Brahms a confronto con i liederisti dell'Ottocento" in *I Lieder di Johannes Brahms*. [for full citation see 4677] pp. 62–94.

5086. *Douliez, Paul, and Hermann Engelhard, eds. *Das Buch der Lieder und Arien: Ein Texthandbuch für Rundfunkhörer und Schallplattenfreunde*. München: Winkler, 1968. 861 pp. Contains original texts for vocal works currently available on recordings. [from S102]

5087. Dürr, Walther. *Das deutsche Sololied im 19. Jahrhundert. Untersuchungen zu Sprache und Musik*. (Taschenbücher zur Musikwissenschaft 97) Wilhelmshaven: Heinrichshofen's Verlag, 1984. ind. "Das Strophenlied": pp. 37–101. Brahms: pp. 93–102. mus., notes. Studies text and musical declamation and musical structure, Op. 84 no. 4 is example. "Das durchkomponierte Lied": pp. 103–79. Brahms: pp. 157–62. mus., notes. Studies poetry leading musical function, Op. 47 no. 5 is example. "Liederzyklen": pp. 245–311. Brahms: pp. 304–11. notes. Discusses whether Op. 33 was really supposed to be a cycle; looks at its background.

5088. Fehn, Ann C[lark]., and Jürgen Thym. "Repetition as Structure in the German Lied: The Ghazal" *Comparative Literature* 41/1 (Winter 1989) pp. 33–52. Brahms: pp. 44–51. mus., notes. Studies settings of this poetic structure by Schubert, Brahms and Richard Strauss. Brahms works studied are Opp. 32 nos. 4 and 9 and his work is compared to Schubert's—D. 741, 756a and 778.

5088.5. Fellinger, Imogen. "Doppelvertonungen" in *Brahms als Liedkomponist*. [for full citation see 5083] pp. [212]–22. mus., ind., notes. Surveys and compares those texts that are set in more than one version. Main examples are Op. 93a no. 2 and Op. 95 no. 1; and Op. 59 nos. 3 and 4.

5089. Finscher, Ludwig. "Brahms's Early Songs: Poetry versus Music" in *Brahms Studies: Analytical and Historical Perspectives*. [for full citation see 5480] pp. [331]–344. notes. Views early songs (Opp. 3, 6, 7, WoO 21) in light of Brahms's principles of poem selection and compositional procedures. Contrasts his work with Eichendorff poems with the texts he set by other poets.

5090. *Fischer-Dieskau, Dietrich. *Texte deutscher Lieder. Ein Handbuch*. München: Deutscher Taschenbuch Verlag, 1968.

3. Auflage: 1975. 36. bis 41. Tausend. [2], 7–474, [1] pp. Brahms et passim. 104 items: 103 solo songs and Op. 54; arranged alphabetically by German title.

(b) English translation by George Bird and Richard Stokes: Fischer-Dieskau. *The Fischer-Dieskau Book of Lieder.* 1st American ed. New York: Alfred A. Knopf, 1977. 435, [4] pp. ind. Arranged alphabetically by their title in English translation.

5091. Fiske, Roger. "Burns Lieder and Other Matters. Schumann— Franz—Brahms—Bruch" in Fiske. *Scotland in Music. A European Enthusiasm.* Cambridge [et al.]: Cambridge University Press, 1983. pp. 156–86. Brahms: pp. 170–74. mus., ind., notes. Related to 2532 (R. Fiske. *Musical Times* (1968)) (?) Surveys settings of Scots texts, Brahms used Herder's translations of Percy's *Reliques.* Includes songs from Opp. 14, 17, 42, and 75; also instrumental works with poetic inscriptions: Opp. 1, 10, and 117. Speculates that some of the instrumental items were conceived as songs first.

5092. Gerstmeier, August. "Brahms und Daumer" in *Brahms als Liedkomponist.* [for full citation see 5083] pp. [116]–136. mus., fig., ind., notes. Looks at Brahms's settings and how they reflect textual phrasing. Daumer seen as a translator of folk poetry, concludes that text-music relationship is strongest in folksong settings in Opp. 32, 57, 95 and 96.

5093. Goldberg, Clemens. "Vergänglichkeit als ästhetische Kategorie und Erlebnis in Liedern von Johannes Brahms" in *Brahms als Liedkomponist.* [for full citation see 5083] pp. [190]–211. mus., fig., ind., notes. Analyses the setting of text with this theme in Brahms's songs: Opp. 32 no. 1, 48 no. 7, 86 no. 4, 105 no. 4.

5094. Horne, William. "Brahms' Heine-Lieder" Peter Jost and Anne Schneider, transs. in *Brahms als Liedkomponist.* [for full citation see 5083] pp. [93]–115. mus., fig., ind., notes. An analytical study to point out the interaction between the text's history and structure and the musical setting. Also comments on Brahms's settings versus other composers' settings. Examines songs from Opp. 71, 85 and 96.

5095. *Hudock, Janet Marie. "An Analysis of the Lyrics and Their Relationship to the Music in Selected Songs by Debussy, Liszt, Brahms and Duke: an Interpretative Study" M.A. diss., Ball State University, 1981. mus., notes. ii, 46 pp. + 1 tape reel (48 min.).

5096. Magner, Candace A. *Phonetic Readings of Brahms Lieder*. Metuchen, NJ and London: The Scarecrow Press Inc., 1987. xii, 412 pp. ind., appendixes. Original text is interlined with phonetic transcription, using International Phonetic Alphabet. Folksong settings are in a separate sequence.

5097. Mahlert, Ulrich. "Die Hölty-Vertonungen von Brahms im Kontext der jeweiligen Liederhefte" in *Brahms als Liedkomponist*. [for full citation see 5083] pp. [65]–92. mus., fig., ind., notes. Examines the setting and background of each song, also examines them in the context of their cycle and compares to others' settings: songs from Opp. 19, 43, 46, 49 and 71.

5098. Meiser, Martin. "Brahms und die Bibel" *Musik und Kirche* 53/5,6 (9./10.,11./12.;1983) pp. 245–50, 292–98. notes. Discusses Brahms's settings, the types of texts set, their content. Includes comment on Brahms and religion.

5099. Ophüls, Gustav. *Brahms-Texte. Sämtliche von Johannes Brahms vertonten und bearbeiteten Texte*. Die Sammlung von Gustav Ophüls, vervollständigt und neu herausgegeben von Kristian Wachinger. Mit drei Zeichnungen von Willy von Beckerath. Ebenhausen bei München: Langewiesche-Brandt, 1983. 397, [3] pp. A reworking of 2540 (G. Ophüls. *Brahms-Texte*. (1898)) with approximately 3 dozen texts added; newly set. Songs and poetic inscriptions from instrumental pieces, arranged by their order in 3424 (M.L. McCorkle. *Johannes Brahms. Thematisch-bibliographisches Werkverzeichnis*. (1984)). Details provided include when written, information on original text source/ author, comment on Brahms changes/omissions to text as set.

5100. *Osthoff, W. "Pfitzner in der aktuellen Musikliteratur: Gottfried Kellers Humor bei Brahms, Hugo Wolf und Pfitzner" *[Hans-Pfitzner-Gesellschaft. Mitteilungen]* no. 44 (3.1983) pp. 46–51. Brahms songs are Opp. 69 no. 8, 70 no. 4, 86 no. 1, McCorkle WoO 16. [from compiler]

5101. Platt, Heather Anne. "Text-Music Relationships in The Lieder of Johannes Brahms" Ph.D. diss., Musicology, City University of New York, 1992. 490 pp. A reassessment of these relationships in 18 songs, selected for their tonal structure. [from S081]
(d) i) Platt, Heather [Anne]. "Dramatic Turning Points in Brahms

Lieder" *Indiana Theory Review* 15/1 (Spring 1994) pp. [69]–104. mus., notes. Takes the concept of "high points" in text setting, and incorporates with Schenkerian analysis to show that these points can be at deep structural (as well as foreground) levels. Examples are Opp. 43 no. 1 and 95 no. 5.

(d) ii) Platt, Heather [Anne]. "Jenner Versus Wolf: The Critical Reception of Brahms's Songs" *The Journal of Musicology* 13/3 (Summer 1995) pp. 377–403. mus., notes, appendix. Evaluates the two 19th-century streams of thought regarding Brahms's text-music synthesis; shows that Jenner, not Wolf, offers most comprehensive methodology for an historically based critique of these works. Jenner's sense comes from being a composition student of Brahms, author describes songwriting techniques of Brahms as described by Jenner (see 694.a. (G. Jenner. *Johannes Brahms als Mensch, Lehrer und Künstler.* (1905))) and corroborated by comments by Brahms's friends. Validity is tested by an analysis of Op. 94 no. 1.

(d) iii) Platt, Heather [Anne]. "Unrequited Love and Unrealized Dominants" *Integral* 7 (1993) pp. [119]–48. mus., fig., notes. Examines a particular harmonic structure for its programmatic interpretations. Analyses Opp. 32 no. 6, 85 no. 6, 94 no. 5, 96 no. 3.

5102. Sick, Thomas. ""Unsere Liebe muß ewig bestehn!" Liebestreue in Brahms' Liedschaffen" in *Brahms als Liedkomponst.* [for full citation see 5083] pp. [173]–89. mus., ind., notes. Examines how Brahms composes the confirmation of true love in Opp. 3 no. 1, 7 no. 1 and 43 no. 1. Provides background on text sources; includes comment on Brahms and women.

5103. *Snyder, Lawrence D. *German Poetry in Song. An Index of Lieder.* (Fallen Leaf Reference Books in Music 30) Berkeley: Fallen Leaf Press, 1995. xviii, 730 pp. ind. Arranged by poet's last name; includes particulars on date of composition, work number, translators. [from publisher information]
    *Supplement: Snyder. *Index of Composers' Titles: Supplement to German Poetry in Song. An Index of Lieder.* Berkeley: Fallen Leaf Press, 1995. 197 pp.

5104. Stein, Deborah, and Robert Spillman. "Comparisons with Brahms Lieder" in Stein and Spillman. *Poetry into Song. Performance and*

Analysis of Lieder. Foreword by Elly Ameling with Max Deen Larsen. Oxford and New York: Oxford University Press, 1996. pp. 221–26. fig. Compares settings of same texts from technical as well as performance points of view: Brahms's Op. 3 no. 5 with Schumann's Op. 39 no. 8; Brahms's Op. 43 no.2 with Schubert's D. 194. Also et passim, mus. (scores for songs from Opp. 3, 43, 63, 84, 105–06).

5105. *Winkler, Priscilla L. "An Analytical Comparison of Styles of Schumann and Brahms in Their Settings of "In der Fremde","Mondnacht","Die Spinnerin", and "Fruhlingslust" (sic)" M.M. diss., Music, Southern Illinois University, n.d. 77 pp. notes. Compares Schumann's Opp. 39 nos. 5 and 1, 125 no. 5 and 107 no. 4 with Brahms's WoO 21, Opp. 3 no. 5, 44 no. 7, and 107 no. 5, respectively. [from compilor]

See also 3821, 3840, 3921, 3953, 4040, 4634, 4640, 4642, 4643, 4645, 4647, 4648, 4650, 4652, 4654, 4659, 4665, 4667, 4672, 4673, 4676, 4684, 4690, 4694, 4699, 4703, 4708, 4710, 4714, 4716, 4718–21, 4723, 4731, 4733, 4735, 4736, 4744–46, 4750, 4759, 4769, 4777, 4782, 4783, 4809, 4811, 4812, 4814, 4816, 4826, 4833, 4835, 4836, 4839, 4841–42, 4848, 4850.5, 4851.1, 4881, 5012, 5013, 5057, 5108, 5115, 5180, 5185, 5188.d., 5232, 5449.5.

See also individual poets in Part III.B.2.; "Text Translations" in Part VI.A.; and "Brahms and Literature" and "Religion" in Part VI.B.

C. Musical Evolution

Contains materials which examine the various stages of the compositional process.

5106. *Bahle, Julius. *Der musikalische Schaffensprozess. Psychologie der schöpferischen Erlebnis- und Antreibsformen.* Leipzig: S. Hirzel, 1936. xv, 253 pp.
*[2. verbesserte Auflage:] (Schöpferisches Menschentum 1) Konstanz: P. Christiani, 1947. xi or xv, 203 pp.

5107. *Bastien, James William. "Some Aspects of Brahms' Revisions" M.M. diss., Southern Methodist University, 1958. iv, 36 pp. ill., mus.

5108. Bozarth, George S. "Musikalische und dokumentarische Quellen der Lieder von Johannes Brahms: Zeugnisse des Kompositions-prozesses" Monika Lichtenfeld, trans. in *Johannes Brahms: Leben und Werk.* [for full citation see 3215] pp. 144–45. mus., notes. Survey and discussion, examines not only musical change, but also change in text setting.

5109. *[Hofmann, Kurt.] "Zur Bedeutung der Stichvorlagen und Ab-schriften von Werken von Johannes Brahms" in *32 Stichvorlagen von Werken Johannes Brahms* [for full citation see 3412]. pp. 16–21, facsim., notes.

5110. *Howard, Jeffrey. "Composition by Collaboration" *The Strad* 105/1255 (11.1994) pp. 1088–89, 1091, 1093. ill., mus., notes. Examines interaction of violinist and composer, using Ysaÿe's editing of Chausson's Op. 25 and Joachim's revisions of Brahms's Op. 77. [from S092]

5111. McCorkle, Margit L. "Filling the Gaps in Brahms Research" *Musical Times* 124/1683 (5.1983) pp. 284–86. ill., notes. Assesses the situation with respect to extant versus missing manuscripts to see what remains of the evidence of Brahms's compositional process. Includes brief summary of manuscript examples that have aided in tracing evolution of Brahms's music.
(d) related to: 5449.5.

5112. McCorkle, Margit L. "The Role of Trial Performances for Brahms's Orchestral and Large Choral Works: Sources and Cir-cumstances" *Brahms Studies: Analytical and Historical Perspec-tives.* [for full citation see 5480] pp. [295]–328. fig., notes. Exam-ines manuscript sources, correspondence and publication history to see how Brahms used prepublication performances to finish off his works. Examines individual works in turn, then generalizes on common characteristics and usefulness of sources.

5113. Pascall, Robert. "Brahms and the Definitive Text" in *Brahms: Bi-ographical, Documentary and Analytical Studies.* [for full citation see 5479] pp. 59–75. facsim., mus., ind., notes. Challenges the as-sumption that musical texts for Brahms's works are definitively es-tablished; looks at publication process and the potential for change within that process. Includes a detailed look at Handexemplare.

See also 3301, 3401, 3410–12, 3420, 3804, 3873–76, 3967, 4037, 4131, 4141, 4146, 4147, 4149, 4151, 4160, 4162, 4165, 4192, 4198, 4243,

4262, 4285, 4342, 4365, 4435, 4448, 4458, 4475, 4479, 4500, 4515,
4517, 4534, 4535, 4541, 4542, 4544, 4549, 4550, 4551, 4575, 4593,
4618, 4654, 4713, 4714, 4716, 4793.d.e., 4797, 4823, 4834, 4853,
4860, 4910, 4971, 5143.d.iv., 5449.5.
See also "Composing" in Part V.B.

D. Musical Influences

1. Allusions

Contains materials that point out similarities in musical text between
Brahms's works and those of his predecessors, contemporaries or suc-
cessors.

5114. Charles, Sydney Robinson. "The Use of Borrowed Material in
Ives' Second Symphony" *The Music Review* 28/2 (5.1967) pp.
[102]–11. Brahms: pp. 104–06, 109–10. mus., notes. Notes that
material from Opp. 90 and 68 is cited in the 2nd and 3rd movements, respectively, of this work [Kirkpatrick no. 11]; also goes
into the background of why this was done.

5115. Felber, Rudolf. "Schumann's Place in German Song" Arthur
Mendel, trans. *The Musical Quarterly* 26/3 (7.1940) pp. 340–54.
Brahms: pp. 352–53. mus. Shows how Brahms exhibits many
points of similarity with Schumann in regard to melody, rhythm
and text setting.

5116. Frisch, Walter [M.]. "The "Brahms Fog": On Tracing Brahmsian
Influences" *The American Brahms Society Newsletter* 7/1 (Spring
1989) pp. [1]–3. ill., mus. An appreciation of Brahms's influence;
focuses on Zemlinsky, Herzogenberg, Reger and Schoenberg.
    (d) expanded: Frisch. "The "Brahms Fog": On Analyzing
    Brahmsian Influences at the Fin de Siècle" in *Brahms and His
    World*. [for full citation see 5478] pp. 81–99. mus., notes.

5117. Horn, Daniel Paul. "Carnival Music. An Introduction to the Piano
Music of George Rochberg" *Clavier* 27/9 (11.1988) pp. 17–21.
Brahms: p. 20. mus. Notes quotation from Op. 76 no. 6 in the
"Sfumato" movement of Rochberg's piece.

5118. *Hull, Kenneth Ross. "Brahms the Allusive: Extra-Compositional
Reference in the Instrumental Music of Johannes Brahms" Ph.D.

diss., Musicology, Princeton University, 1989. 291 pp. Examines purposeful allusive references. Reviews the relationship of Brahms's music to music of the past, and his own opinions on thematic resemblances in his music. Puts forward a criteria for allusion. Analyses Op. 98 for allusions to Beethoven's Op. 67 and Schumann's Op. 42 no. 6 as well as Bach's BWV 150; Op. 8 revised version studied as an example of public and private allusion; Op. 83 also studied. [from S081]

5119. *Hussey, William Gregory. "Compositional Modeling and Quotation in the Works of Johannes Brahms: An Application of Harold Bloom's Theory of Influence to Music." [Ph.D. diss.{?},] University of Texas at Austin, 1996.

5120. Korsyn, Kevin. "Towards A New Poetics of Musical Influence" *Music Analysis* 10/1–2 (3.–7.1991) pp. 3–72. mus., fig., notes. Presents a theory of intertextuality in music, proposing a model for mapping influence derived from work of Harold Bloom. Chopin's Op. 31 and Brahms's Op. 4 are put forward as examples of application.

   (e) review: Taruskin, Richard. *Journal of the American Musicological Society* 46/1 (Spring 1993) pp. [114]–38. Brahms: pp. 118, 120–23. notes. Discusses Brahms's knowledge of Chopin's music and reacts to Korsyn's proposition.

5121. *Lyman, Kent Marvin. "George Rochberg's Carnival music, suite for solo piano: An aesthetic compositional and performance perspective" D.M. diss., Indiana University, 1993. 90 pp. mus., fig., notes. [from S109]

5122. *Niemann, Walter. "Johannes Brahms und die neuere Klaviermusik" *Die Musik* 12/1 (Bd. 45) (10.1912) pp. 38–45. A brief survey of 50 European composers, grouped geographically, whose piano music, in Niemann's opinion, bears the unmistakable traces of Brahms's influence. Also comments on Brahms's piano music style and his style in general. [from 5116]

5123. Pascall, Robert. "Musikalische Einflüsse auf Brahms" Manfred Angerer, trans. *Österreichische Musikzeitschrift* 38/4–5 (4.–5. 1983) pp. 228–35. notes. Divides Brahms's life into three periods and studies each period to see how he was influenced (Beethoven, Schubert, Baroque forms, folk music) and in what works it comes out. Also comments on composers influenced by Brahms, especially Schoenberg.

5124. *Petersen, Peter. "" . . . eine Form und ein Name: Tristan": Strukturelle und semantische Untersuchungen an Hans Werner Henzes *Préludes für Klavier, Tonbänder und Orchester"* in *Verbalisierung und Sinngehalt: Über semantische Tendenzen im Denken in und über Musik Heute.* Otto Kolleritsch, ed. (Studien zur Wertungsforschung 21) Wien: Universal, 1989. pp. 148–76. notes. A discussion of this work as an example of representing extramusical meaning in music. The work incorporates copious allusions and quotations from the music of Brahms and Wagner. [from S102]

5125. Rosen, Charles. "Influence: Plagiarism and Inspiration" in *On Criticizing Music. Five Philosophical Perspectives.* Kingsley Price, ed. (The Alvin and Fanny Blaustein Thalheimer Lectures. 1978–79) Baltimore and London: The Johns Hopkins University Press, 1981. pp. 16–37. Brahms: pp. 24–37. mus., notes. The original of 2553 (C. Rosen. *19th Century Music* (1980)); discusses allusions to Beethoven and Chopin in Brahms works.

See also 3690, 3758, 3759, 3779, 3836, 3859, 3870, 3908, 4022, 4167, 4268, 4342, 4364, 4407, 4549, 4553, 4590, 4593, 4595, 4596, 4630, 4759, 4866, 4960, 4998, 5137, 5232.
See also "Musical Mottos and Motifs" in Part V.B.

2. Ethnic and Folksong Influences

Hungarian folkmusic: 5127, 5129, 5132, 5134.

5126. *Babcock, Lisa Gay. "The Use of Folksong in the Piano and Vocal Music of Johannes Brahms" M.A. diss., California State University, Long Beach, 1984. iv, 45 pp. mus., notes.

5127. Bellman, Jonathan. "Brahms" in Bellman. *The Style Hongrois in the Music of Western Europe.* Boston: Northeastern University Press, 1993. pp. 201–13; also et passim. mus., ind., notes, discog. (pp. 223–24). Discusses Brahms's exposure to Hungarian folkmusic, and examines his works for its influences.

5128. *Bojić, Vera. *Vukovo nasledje u evropskoj muzici: Nova gradja o recepciji srpskin narodnih pasame u Evropi.* 2 vols. Beograd:

Srpska Akademija Nauka i Umetnosti; München: Singer, 1987. ill., mus. Studies composers' use of the Serbian folk poetry collections of Vuk Stefanović Karadžić. [from S102]

5129. *Di Fronzo, Luigi. "Elementi per una grammatica zigana" in *I Lieder di Johannes Brahms*. [for full citation see 4677] pp. 95–116. Includes: "Un problema spinoso all'intern della 'tematica' magiara: la contesa Brahms-Reményi e l'origine delle Danze Ungheresi [McCorkle WoO 1]": pp. 112–16.

5130. Fellinger, Imogen. "Brahms' beabsichtigte Streitschrift gegen Erk-Böhmes "Deutscher Liederhort"'" in *Brahms-Kongress Wien 1983*. [for full citation see 5431] pp. 139–53. facsim., notes. Describes Brahms's campaign against this work (Ludwig Erk. *Deutscher Liederhort, Auswahl der vorzüglicheren deutschen Volkslieder, nach Wort und Weise aus der Vorzeit und Gegenwart gesammelt und erläutert. Nach Erks handschriftlichem Nachlasse und auf Grunt eigener Sammlung.* Neubearbeitet und fortgesetzt von Franz M. Böhme. 3 vols. Leipzig: Breitkopf & Härtel, 1893–94) Looks at his copy of it and his markings in it. Includes comment on Brahms's philosophy regarding folk music and "art" music.

5131. *Gulli, Donatella. "Il mito del canto popolare nella produzione liederistica di Brahms" in *I Lieder di Johannes Brahms* [for full citation see 4677] pp. 21–61.

5132. *Handrigan, Nancy Cheryl Eileen. "On the "Hungarian" in works of Brahms : a critical study" M.A. diss., Music, McMaster University, 1995. vi, 133 pp. mus., notes.

5133. Hemsen, Eduard. "Johannes Brahms und die Volksmusik" *Das deutsche Volkslied* 13/1–3 (1.–3.1911) pp. [1]–3, [17]–20, [37]–39. notes. A report and reaction to 2563 (R. Hohenemser. *Die Musik* (Berlin) (1903)), particularly to the comments regarding what is authentic folksong, what is "composed."

5134. *Lakatos, István. *Magyaros elemek Brahms zenéjében.* (Erdélyi tudományos füzetek 73) Cluj: Erdélyi Múzeum-Egylet Kiadása, n.d. 11 pp. Original item for 2567 (I. Lakatos. *A Zene* (1938–39)). (a) *reprint: Lakatos. *Erdélyi Múzeum* 45 (new series 6) (1940) pp. 32–40.

5135. *Larkin, Edward Alexander. "An Examination of the Influence of Folksong Elements on Selected Partsong Compositions of Johannes Brahms" M.M. diss., Music, Southern Methodist University, 1971. vi, 64 pp. notes.

5136. *Morsch, Anna. "Johannes Brahms und das Volkslied" *Gesangspädagogische Blätter* 2 (1906) pp. 47–49.

5137. Mosley, David L. "Brahms and Dort in den Weiden" *The Horn Call* 22/2 (4.1992) pp. 21–24. mus., notes. Shows how this folksong quotation in Op. 40, third movement, alludes to both the death of Brahms's mother and his relationship to the Schumanns. Includes comment on Clara ciphers.

5138. Smeed, J.W. "The Importance of Folksongs" in Smeed. *German Song and Its Poetry 1740–1900*. London, New York, Sydney: Croom Helm Ltd., 1987. pp. 156–72. Brahms: pp. 156–58. Brahms is used as an example of a composer who arranges existing folksong melodies.

5139. Szeskus, Reinhard. "Johannes Brahms und das Volkslied" *Musik in der Schule* 34/12 (1983) pp. 403–07. mus. Discusses Brahms's use of folksong as basis for lieder; article has proletariat approach.

See also 3523, 3578, 3620, 3810, 4056, 4061, 4341, 4388, 4536, 4580, 4632, 4659, 4662, 4665, 4686, 4712, 4719, 4724, 4726, 4868, 4878, 5012, 5025, 5040, 5044, 5088, 5091, 5092, 5123, 5143.d.iv., 5205, 5232.
See also "Ungarische Tänze" in Part IV.A.2.a.
See also I22 in Appendix A.

Part VI

Miscellaneous Subjects

A. Directly Related to Musical Works

1. Music Prior to the Classical Period

Contains materials on Brahms's exposure to, study of, and involvement with early music.

5140. *Ennis, M.W. "The Influence of Pre-Classical Music in Selected Works of Johannes Brahms" M.Phil. diss., Musicology, Cambridge, 1986.

5141. *Federhofer, Hellmut. *Musicologica austriaca* Bd. 8 (1988).
   (a) reprint: Federhofer. "Zur Generalbaβpraxis im 19. Jahrhundert" *Musik und Kirche* 60/1 (1./2.1990) pp. 1–10. Brahms: pp. 9–10. mus., notes. Compares figured basses by Brahms and Chrysander for Händel's *Saul*, no. 64. Concludes that Brahms's is more composed, while Chrysander's follows understood practice.

5142. Geiringer, Karl. "Brahms as a Musicologist" *The Musical Quarterly* 69/4 (Fall 1983) pp. 463–70. notes. Traces Brahms's attraction to the history of music and his contemporary musicologists. Reviews his collections of early music (editions and manuscripts), his editings of other composers' works, his performances of early music.

5143. Hancock, Virginia [Lee]. *Brahms's Choral Compositions and His Library of Early Music*. (Studies in Musicology 76) Ann Arbor:

UMI Research Press, 1983. mus., ind., notes, appendixes. A revised version of 2200 (V.L. Hancock. "Brahms and His Library of
Early Music . . ." (1977)).

(d) i) Hancock, Virginia [Lee]. "Brahms and Early Music: Evidence From His Library and His Choral Compositions" in
Brahms Studies: Analytical and Historical Perspectives. [for
full citation see 5480] pp. [29]–48. mus., notes. Uses the evidence of his personal holdings and his study of early music
to provide documentary evidence of relationships between
Brahms's music and that of his predecessors. Examines Op.
13's relationship with Bach's BWV 4, Op. 110 no. 1 to
Schütz's Op. 5, and assesses Op. 62 no. 3–5 in terms of Renaissance compositional practice.

(d) ii) Hancock, Virginia [Lee]. "Brahms' Studium alter Musik
und ihr Einfluβ auf seine Chorwerke" Monika Lichtenfeld,
trans. in *Johannes Brahms: Leben und Werk* [for full citation
see 3215] p. 163. Surveys the early music he knew, studied,
performed, the editions he held, and the characteristics that
can be found in his own music.

(d) iii) Hancock, Virginia [Lee]. "Brahms's Early Music Studies
and His Sacred Choral Music" *The American Organist* 17/5
(5.1983) pp. 40–43. ill., notes. Describes his bonds with music from the Renaissance and Baroque periods: his study and
performance, materials held in his library. Looks at small sacred choral works and Op. 45 and points out links to earlier
music.

(d) iv) Hancock, Virginia [Lee]. "Brahms's Links with German
Renaissance Music: A Discussion of Selected Choral Works"
in *Brahms 2.* [for full citation see 5481] pp. 95–110. facsim.,
mus., fig., notes. Traces development of his interest in this
music through holdings in his personal library and by its effects on choral compositions written pre-1864. Focuses on
Opp. 22, 74 no. 2 and folksong settings.

(d) v) Hancock, Virginia [Lee]. "Brahms's Performances of Early
Choral Music" *19th Century Music* 8/2 (Fall 1984) pp.
125–41. ill., facsim., mus., fig., notes. A chronological survey
of Brahms's career as a choral conductor, focusing on his
work with Renaissance and Baroque choral music. Examines
what was performed and why, also looks at his score markings and annotations; based on A-Wgm sources.

(d) Hancock, Virginia [Lee]. "Brahms' Aufführungen früher Chormusik in Wien" Brigitte Gross, trans. in *Brahms-Kongress Wien 1983*. [for full citation see 5431] pp. 199–228. facsim., notes, Includes appendix that lists early music that Brahms performed or studied over his lifetime.

(d) vi) Hancock, Virginia L[ee]. "The Growth of Brahms's Interest in Early Choral Music, and Its Effect on His Own Choral Compositions" in *Brahms: Biographical, Documentary and Analytical Studies*. [for full citation see 5479] pp. 27–40. mus., ind., notes. Reviews Brahms's life and creative career and his love for and involvement with Renaissance and Baroque music, also looks for relationships between his choral works and early music.

5144. *Li, Wai Chun. "The Influence of Early Music on The Choral Music of Brahms" M.A. diss., Music, University of Houston, 1991. x, 82 pp. mus., notes.

5145. Musgrave, Michael. "Brahms the Progressive: Another View" *Musical Times* 124/1683 (5.1983) pp. 291–94. ill., notes. Puts forward that Brahms's study and performance of early music reveals another progressive side to him. Discusses works performed and edited.

5146. *Sperber, Gloria Pihl. "Older Device and Procedure in the Works of Johannes Brahms" M.A. diss., San Francisco State College, 1968. xiv, 241 pp. ill., mus., notes.

5147. Wolff, Christoph. "Brahms, Wagner, and the Problem of Historicism in Nineteenth-Century Music: An Essay" in *Brahms Studies: Analytical and Historical Perspectives*. [for full citation see 5480] pp. [7]–11. notes. Examines the antiquarian interests of both Brahms and Wagner within the context of their time.

See also 3237, 3468, 3620, 4056, 4061, 4167, 4250, 4262, 4285, 4319, 4347, 4351, 4428.d., 4439, 4448, 4621, 4659, 4761.5, 4814, 4848, 4862, 4864, 4865, 4867, 4947, 4970, 5014, 5023, 5030, 5044, 5123, 5235, 5305, 5314.
See also individual composers in Part III.B.2.; "Arranging" and "Editing" in Part V.B.
See also I31 in Appendix A.

2. Opera

Contains materials on Brahms's attempts to write opera.

5148. Brody, Elaine. "Operas in Search of Brahms" *Opera Quarterly* 3/4 (Winter 1985/86) pp. 24–37. notes. Begins with discussion of Turgenev's libretto and the link between the two men; also looks at what Brahms wanted in a libretto, what kind of opera interested him. Includes comment on Brahms and Levi, and a parallel is suggested between Brahms's inability to write a opera and his failure with women.

5149. Wirth, Helmut. "Oper und Drama in ihrer Bedeutung für Johannes Brahms" *Brahms-Studien* Bd. 5 (1983) pp. 117–39. notes. An analysis of why Brahms never composed an opera and wonders if it was wrong type of libretti, or was it because Brahms was more comfortable writing "absolute" music? Speculates that the work that became Op. 81 was actually intended as a musical number for a work based on Goethe's Faust. Volume's index gives title as "Oper und Drama im Leben von Johannes Brahms."

See also 3617, 3647, 3654, 3655, 3696, 3814, 3851, 3871, 4108, 4020, 4022, 4640, 4701, 5036.d.

3. Performance Practice

Contains materials that suggest how to conduct or perform Brahms's music.

5150. *Musical Standard,* see 5318.5.

5151. "Aphorisms of Von Bülow on the Playing of the Music of Brahms" *The Etude* 29/5 (5.1911) p. 304. ill. Bülow's comments on playing the piano music; taken from ?

5152. *Belan, William [Wells]. "Tempo Rubato in the Nineteenth Century" in *Choral Essays: a tribute to Roger Wagner.* William Wells Belan, ed. (Festschriften) San Carlos, CA: Thomas House Publications, 1993. ind., notes.

5153. Blum, David. *The Art of Quartet Playing. The Guarneri Quartet in Conversation with David Blum.* 1st ed. New York: Alfred A. Knopf, 1986. xiii, [5], 3–247 pp. Brahms et passim. mus. (et passim), ind., discog. (p. 234). Describes how to play Opp. 34, 51, 67 and the piano quartets (largest reference is for Op. 67).

5154. *Borghetto, Gabriella. "Annotazioni sugli interpreti liederistici brahmsiani e su Brahms interprete" in *I Lieder di Johannes Brahms*. [for full citation see 4677] pp. 168–79.

5155. Bozarth, George S. "The Authentic Brahms" *The American Brahms Society Newsletter* 8/2 (Autumn 1990) pp. 7–8. ill. Reports on a recording (Amon Ra Records, CD-SAR 37) containing Opp. 114 and 120 nos. 1 and 2, where period instruments are used by the performers.

5156. Bozarth, George S. "Robert Winter's . . . " in Bozarth. "News and Comment" *The American Brahms Society Newsletter* 3/2 (Autumn 1985) p. [10]. Reacts to the single listing of a Brahms recording in Winter's 1984 discography of recordings using period instruments (R. Winter. *19th Century Music* (1984) pp. 251–65), by calling for more to be done.

5157. Crutchfield, Will. "Brahms, by Those Who Knew Him" *Opus* 2/5 (8.1986) pp. 12–21, 60. ill. (also on cover), mus. Studies Brahms's recording of McCorkle WoO 1 no. 1, recordings by his contemporaries and associates of same, in order to get an idea of how to play this work. Also reviews contemporaries' recordings of other Brahms solo piano music, and songs.
(e) report: see 3359.b.e.

5158. Del Mar, Norman. *Conducting Brahms*. Oxford: Clarendon Press, 1993. [6], 226 pp. facsim., mus., ind. Describes how to conduct the symphonies, Opp. 80, 81, 56a, the concertos, serenades, and Op. 45. Also comments on Brahms the composer, and textual variants between edition and manuscript.
also: New York: Oxford University Press, 1993.

5159. *Dunsby, Jonathan. *Performing Music: Shared Concerns*. Oxford: Clarendon Press; New York: Oxford University Press, 1995. vii, 104 pp. mus., ind., notes.

5160. Epstein, David. "Brahms and the Mechanisms of Motion: The Composition of Performance" in *Brahms Studies: Analytical and Historical Perspectives*. [for full citation see 5480] pp. [191]–226. mus., fig., notes. Studies music of Brahms to see how he built in the manner and quality of motion a work should have in performance. Examples come from Opp. 15, 68, and 73; also Op. 119 no. 2 manuscript [privately owned, see 1697 (J. Brahms. *Intermezzi Opus 119 Nr. 2 und 3. Faksimile* . . . (1975))] examined for clues.

    (d) i) abridged by Virginia [Lee] Hancock: Epstein. *The American Brahms Society Newsletter* 8/2 (Autumn 1990) pp. [1]–6. ill., mus. only.

        (b) German translation by Lillian Camphausen: Epstein. "Brahms und die Mechanismen der Bewegung: die Komposition der Aufführung" *Brahms-Studien* Bd. 10 (1994) pp. 9–21. mus. only.

    (d) ii) Epstein. *Shaping Time. Music, the Brain and Performance.* New York: Schirmer Books; London [et al.]: Prentice Hall International, 1995. xvi, [4], 3–598 pp. ind., notes.

        Brahms: pp. 82–88. mus. Using Op. 73, 2nd movement as example, studies motion as written into the music.

        Brahms: pp. 258–85. fig., mus. Examines Brahms's use of proportional tempo, with examples from the late piano music, orchestral works. Relates to 1385 (D. Epstein. *Beyond Orpheus.* (1979)).

        Brahms: pp. 405–15. fig., mus. Analyses Walter Gieseking playing Op. 76 no. 4 in an attempt to study how one deals with ambiguities and phrasing with rubato.

5161. *Finson, Jon William. "The Performance Practice of Four String Quartets Active in the First Twenty-Five Years of the Twentieth Century as Documented on Direct-Cut Macrogroove Discs" M.A. diss., University of Wisconsin-Madison, 1975. 105 pp. + 2 reel tapes.

    (d) Finson, Jon W[illiam]. "Performing Practice in the Late Nineteenth Century, with Special Reference to the Music of Brahms" *Musical Quarterly* 70/4 (Fall 1984) pp. 457–75. mus., notes. Studies instrument playing practice as documented in writings, and on recordings. Based on above and a lecture given before a historically accurate concert of Brahms's music, Smithsonian Institution, March 21, 1983.

5162. Fuller-Maitland, J.A. *The Consort of Music. A Study of Interpretation and Ensemble.* Oxford: Clarendon Press, 1915. [4], 244 pp. ind. Comments on how to perform Brahms's works et passim. Significant entries are for Opp. 34, 52, 56b, 78, 90, 115. Includes comment on Joachim and Brahms working together on Opp. 102 and 111, and Joachim playing Brahms's music.

5163. Hamilton, David. *The Listener's Guide to Great Instrumentalists.* (The Listener's Guide Series) New York: Facts on File, Inc., 1982. Brahms: pp. 56–58, 91–92 and 125–26. ind. An appreciation of special qualities and special aspects of performance: Solomon playing Op. 83, Szigeti playing Op. 77 and the Budapest Quartet playing Op. 67.

5164. Horowitz, Joseph. "Brahms, Chopin, Beethoven" in Horowitz. *Conversations with Arrau.* [Discography by T.W. Scragg] New York: Alfred A. Knopf, 1982. pp. 150–72. mus., ind., discog. (p. 297), appendixes. Brahms: pp. 150–56. Interpretative guidelines for Opp. 2, 15, 10 no. 4. Includes sample programs in Appendix A. Also:
"Listening to Brahms": pp. 173–78. Examines how Arrau's playing has changed over the years; example is Op. 15 as heard in 4 recordings, 1947–77.

5165. "How Should Brahms Be Played?" *Musical Courier* 98 (21.3. 1929) p. 34. Compares 9 New York papers' reports of a Carnegie Hall performance of Op. 98 by the Philadelphia Orchestra conducted by Eugene Goossens. They're all so different to one another, that one wouldn't know they were talking about the same concert.

5166. Jacobson, Bernard. "Carlo Maria Giulini on Brahms" in Jacobson. *Conductors on Conducting.* Frenchtown, NJ: Columbia Publishing Company, Inc., 1979. pp. [209]–27. ill., ind., discog. Observations on performing Brahms: score markings, balance, tradition, tempi, orchestration.

5167. *Lechleitner, Gerda. "Agogik: Aufführungspraxis im Spiegel der Zeit" *Studien zur Musikwissenschaft* 36 (1985) pp. 309–18. Analyses recordings of 6 orchestras, 1930–80, for their treatment of the first theme in McCorkle WoO 1 no. 1. Earlier performances are faster and freer than later ones. [from S102]

5168. Lehmann, Lotte. *More Than Singing: The Interpretation of Songs.* Frances Holden, trans. New York: Dover Publications Inc., 1985. 192 pp. Reprint of 2074 (L. Lehmann. *More Than Singing . . .* (1945)). Includes performance suggestions for songs from Opp. 19, 32, 43, 47, 49, 59, 63, 84, 86, 94, 96, 97, 105, 107.

5169. Montparker, Carol. "Two Gentlemen from Hamburg: Johannes Brahms and Detlef Kraus" *Clavier* 22/10 (12.1983) pp. 14–16. ill. An interview with Kraus, touching on Brahms's reception, how both he and Brahms are from Hamburg area, how Kraus interprets Brahms's piano music, and Brahms as a composer for piano.

5170. *Oortmerssen, Jacques van. "Johannes Brahms and the 19th-century performance practice in a historical perspective" in *Proceedings of the Goteborg International Organ Academy 1994.* [for full citation see 5062] [from S109]

5171. *Pascall, Robert. *Playing Brahms: A Study in 19th Century Performance Practice.* (Papers in Musicology 1) Nottingham: Department of Music, University of Nottingham, 1990 or 1991. 23 pp.

5172. *Performance Practice. [Vol. 2.] Music After 1600.* Howard Mayer Brown and Stanley Sadie, eds. (The New Grove Handbooks in Music) Houndmills and London: The Macmillan Press, 1989.
    issue: 1990. xi, [2], 3–533 pp. mus., ind., notes. Brahms et passim.
    *1st American ed.: New York: W.W. Norton & Company, Ltd., 1990.

5173. Philip, Robert. *Early Recordings and Musical Style. Changing Tastes in Instrumental Performance, 1900–1950.* Cambridge: Cambridge University Press, 1992. x, 274 pp. mus., fig., notes, discog. Brahms et passim.

5174. Pirie, Peter. "Brahms and Schumann" in Pirie. *Furtwängler and the Art of Conducting.* London: Duckworth, 1980. pp. 77–87. Brahms: pp. 77–86. ind., discog. Analyses the way Furtwängler played Brahms, compares his multiple recordings of works in the symphonies and Opp. 45, 56a, 77 and 83.

5175. Prausnitz, Frederik. *Score and Podium. A Complete Guide to Conducting.* New York, London: W.W. Norton & Company, 1983. x, [2], 530 pp. Brahms: pp. 63–81, 224–30, 235–43, 265–71. mus., ind., notes. Examples from Brahms's works to bring out conducting points: Opp. 56a, 81, and 90.

5176. Roth, Henry. *Great Violinists in Performance. Critical Evaluations of Over 100 Twentieth-Century Virtuosi.* Los Angeles: Panjandrum Books, 1987. xii, [2], 266 pp. Critical comments based on recordings: Op. 77 and other orchestral and chamber works performed by 6 different soloists.

5177. *Sheffet, Alice M[iller]. "Pedaling in the Duo Sonatas for Piano and Strings of Johannes Brahms" Ph.D. diss., New York University, 1987. 367 pp. ill., mus., notes. Formulates guidelines for pedalling; includes feedback from pianists on suggested guidelines. [from S081]

5178. *Sweeney, Valentine Wheeler. "Performance Problems in Selected Piano Compositions of Bach, Beethoven, Brahms, Debussy, and Shostakovich" M.A. diss., Eastern New Mexico University, 1957. vii, 68 pp. mus., notes.

5179. *Tollefson, Arthur. "Solving Interpretive Dilemmas" *Clavier* 17/2 (2.1978) pp. 17–40. mus. Examines the piano works of Mozart, Beethoven, Schubert, Chopin, Brahms, Debussy and Bartók for their features and their performance requirements. [from S102]

5180. *Tracy, Deborah Lorena. "An Interpretive Analysis of the Accompaniments of Four Selected Songs by Johannes Brahms" M.A. diss., California State University, Fullerton, 1982. 58 pp. mus. (pp. 38–58), notes.

5181. Tuckwell, Barry. "Composers and the Horn" in Tuckwell. *Horn.* [Preface by Yehudi Menuhin] (Yehudi Menuhin Music Guides) New York: Schirmer Books, 1983. pp. 59–118.
"Brahms": 104–08. mus., facsim., ind. also et passim. Presents examples from Opp. 11, 68, 73 and 83 with performance suggestions.

5182. *Wisdom, Karol Gambrell. "Preparing for Piano Performance: A Pedagogical Approach: Lecture Document" M.M. diss., University of Texas at El Paso, 1990. 51 pp. mus., notes. Deals with works by Scarlatti, Ravel, Brahms. [from S031]

5183. *Wright, Farnsworth. "Piano Technic of Brahms and Liszt Adequate in Playing Modern Music" *Musical America* 46 (?) (30.6. 1927 (?)) p. 10.

See also 3305, 3334, 3336, 3362, 3374, 3375, 3437, 3683, 3725, 3737, 3776, 3780, 3798, 3813, 3854, 3878, 3904, 4041, 4047, 4058, 4070, 4075–77, 4080, 4086, 4092, 4097, 4106, 4107, 4127, 4130,

4141, 4145, 4166, 4172, 4183, 4195, 4197, 4204–06, 4209, 4210,
4215, 4216, 4219, 4220, 4223, 4224, 4227, 4254, 4262, 4266,
4275, 4284, 4287, 4288, 4291, 4294, 4306, 4307, 4312, 4319,
4324, 4326, 4339, 4352, 4354, 4359, 4367, 4372, 4389, 4398,
4402, 4403, 4405, 4419, 4426, 4428, 4448, 4460.d. and e., 4461,
4474, 4478, 4489.5, 4504, 4510, 4512, 4527, 4532, 4536, 4540,
4547, 4548, 4554, 4555, 4561.c., 4567, 4568, 4571, 4573, 4588,
4591, 4611, 4615, 4620, 4631, 4647, 4650, 4653, 4654, 4675,
4679, 4682, 4685, 4687, 4690, 4697, 4705, 4722, 4725, 4726.5,
4729, 4753, 4766, 4772, 4779, 4783, 4784, 4792, 4793.d.e., 4800,
4801, 4808, 4812, 4815, 4818, 4825, 4846, 4847, 4850, 4850.5,
4851.1, 4877, 4964, 4988, 5013, 5104.

See also Part II.C. for discussions of Brahms's own interpretations of his
works.

4. Program Music

Contains materials that attempt to trace symbolic or programmatic elements in Brahms's music.

5184. Berkowitz, Freda Pastor. *Popular Titles and Subtitles of Musical
       Compositions.* New York: The Scarecrow Press, Inc., 1962. 182
       pp. ind. 9 references to Brahms's works, indexed by both opus no.
       and by a work's popular title. Book is arranged alphabetically by
       work title.
       2nd ed.: Metuchen. 1975. viii, 209 pp. 20 references to Brahms's
       works.

5185. Bozarth, George S. "Brahms's Lieder ohne Worte: The 'Poetic'
       Andantes of the Piano Sonatas" in *Brahms Studies: Analytical and
       Historical Perspectives.* [for full citation see 5480] pp. [345]–78.
       mus., fig., notes. Explores the relationship between word and tone
       in the andantes of Opp. 1, 2, and 5. Looks at their relationship with
       vocal counterparts from the same period and examines them with
       a programmatic perspective.

5186. *Gisbon, Michaél. "La figuration de la nature dans la musique:
       Brahms et Mahler" *Revue d'esthétique* [nouvelle série] 4 (1982).
       issue title: *Musique présente.* [from S102]

5187. Niecks, Frederick. *Programme Music in the Last Four Centuries.* *A Contribution to the History of Musical Expression.* London: Novello and Company Limited; New York: The H.W. Gray Co., [1906]. xi, [1], 548 pp. Brahms: pp. 447–57. Proposes that Brahms is a composer of program music. Looks at his link with the Schumanns, titles of his music, the influence of his environment on what he wrote, and cites writings of Kalbeck and Deiters.

5188. *Parmer, Dillon [Ravindra Rudolph]. "The Sufferings of Young Brahms: Instances of Allusion" *The Journal of Graduate Research* 1/1 (7.1989) pp. 49–57. Discusses allusions to other composers' works and their significance for understanding narrative in Brahms's Op. 60. The works are Beethoven's Op. 67, Mendelssohn's Op. 66, and Schumann's Op. 44. [from author]

(d) *incorporated into: Parmer, Dillon Ravindra Rudolph. "Brahms the Programmatic? A Critical Assessment" Ph.D. diss., University of Rochester, Eastman School of Music, 1995. 299 pp. Examines programmatic implications in Brahms music; explores how titles and mottos provided by Brahms impinge on understanding the music, shows that works that allude to song embody an oblique literary association, and discusses works that Brahms allowed to circulate privately as program music. Works discussed are: Opp. 1, 2, 5, 8–10, 15, 29, 36, 60, 80–81, 100, 117, 118 nos. 3 and 6. [from S081 and author]

(d) *revised version of Chapter 4: Parmer, Dillon [Ravindra Rudolph]. "Brahms, Song Quotation, and Secret Programs" *19th Century Music* 19/2 (Fall 1995) pp. 161–90. mus., notes. Discusses programmatic significance of song allusion in Opp. 1, 5, 8, 78. [from author]

See also 3832, 4486, 4582, 4596, 4603, 4826, 4829, 4866, 4914, 4928, 4943, 5101, 5102, 5203, 5232.

5. Settings of Brahms's Music

Contains materials that discuss other composers' settings of Brahms's works.

5189. *Süddeutsche Zeitung* (München) [(?.10. or 11.?.1993)].

(a) reprint: Lewinski, Wolf-Eberhard von. "Eine Brahms-"Urauf-führung". Neue Orchestrierung der zweiten Klarinetten-Sonate" *Das Orchester* (Hamburg) 41/11 (1993) p. 1217. Reports on an arrangement of Op. 120 no. 2 for clarinet and orchestra by Gerhard Oppitz.

5190. *Bohnet, Andra Anne Cook. "The Transcription as a Supplement to Nineteenth Century Repertoire" Ph.D. diss., Texas Tech University, 1985. 185 pp. Proposes a transcription of the F.A.E.-Sonate [see McCorkle WoO posthum 2] for flute and piano in order to expand flute/piano combination repertoire from the 19th century. [from S081]

5191. Duxbury, Janell R. *Rockin' The Classics and Classicizin' The Rock. A Selectively Annotated Discography.* (Discographies 14) Westport, CT; London: Greenwood Press, 1985. xix, [4], 4–188 pp. ind. 8 items in rockin' the classics section; 1 item in classicizin' the rock section (music done in the style of Brahms); 3 items in rock influence on classical section ("Greatest Hits" packaging).
First Supplement: (Discographies 43) New York [et al.]: 1991. xxii, [3], 4–168 pp. 8 items in rockin' the classics section.

5192. Hancock, Virginia [Lee]. "The exploitation of Brahms's music . . ." *The American Brahms Society Newsletter* 8/2 (Autumn 1990) p. 10. Reports on new editions of choral works that are arrangements that Brahms would never have contemplated: Op. 122 no. 8 for 4 mixed voices; McCorkle WoO 33 no. 24 for mixed voices with a sacred text.

5193. Jones, Sherri. "A Final Tribute to Brahms" in Jones. "Ferruccio Busoni and the Chorale Prelude" D.M.A. diss., Piano, University of Illinois at Urbana-Champaign, 1989. pp. 79–85. mus., notes. Studies Busoni's transcriptions for solo piano of 6 of Brahms's Op. 122 [see 5194 for edition citation]. Includes background to transcription, a comparison to the original and comments on how transcription is done. Also includes Busoni's opinions on Brahms, and influence of Brahms on Busoni.

5194. *Scialla, Carmen. "A Study of Ferruccio Busoni's Transcriptions of Six Organ Chorale Preludes by Johannes Brahms" D.M.A. diss., Louisiana State University and Agricultural and Mechanical

College, 1992. 76 pp. Looks at the devices which Busoni used to achieve an organ effect while attempting to remedy problems in transcribing Brahms in J. Brahms. *6 Choral-Vorspiele für Orgel, Op. 122.* (Leipzig: N. Simrock, 1902).

See also 3424, 4067, 4446, 4757, 4763.
See also "Arranging" in Part V.B.

6. Text Translations

Contains materials that contain translations of texts from Brahms's vocal works, and/or discuss text translations of Brahms's vocal works.

5195. Coffin, Berton, Werner Singer, and Pierre Delattre. *Word-by-Word Translations of Songs and Arias. Part 1—German and French. A Companion to The Singer's Repertoire.* [German translations by Werner Singer] New York: The Scarecrow Press, Inc., 1966. vii, [1], 620 pp. ind. Brahms: pp. 46–100. 42 songs. German original text interlined with English translation. Songs are arranged alphabetically by first word of first line.

5196. "Johannes Brahms" in *Lieder. Testi originali e traduzioni.* Vanna Massarotti Piazza, ed. Italian translations by Claudio Groff. [3rd ed.?] Milano: Garzanti, 1989. pp. 199–219.

5197. *Mikhaylov, Ivan. "O tsiklichnosti, pesennykh tekstakh i perevodakh" *Sovetskaia muzyka* [54]/10 (10.1990) pp. 43–46. notes.

5198. Miller, Philip L[ieson]. *The Ring of Words. An Anthology of Song Texts.* The Original Texts Selected and Translated, with an Introduction by . . . Garden City: Doubleday & Company Inc., 1963. xx, 200 pp. ind. 32 items. Texts are grouped by their original language, then alphabetically by poet (brief poet biography) within language. Includes comments on word changes in the setting and comparative setters if any. Original text faces English translation across the page.
*also: (Anchor Books A428) Anchor Books, 1966. xxviii, 518 pp.
(a) reprint (of 1966 edition): [Paperback ed.] (The Norton Library) New York: W.W. Norton & Company Inc., 1973.

5199. *Minchin, Leslie T. *Brahms Songs: some texts.* London: Author, 1977. 10 pp.

5200. Phillips, Lois. "Johannes Brahms (1833–1897)" in Phillips. *Lieder Line By Line and Word for Word*. London: Duckworth, 1979. pp. 204–45. 59 items. Arranged chronologically by date of setting. English translation is interlined with German original text on left of page; prose summary is provided on right of page. *also: New York: Charles Scribner's Sons, 1980.

5201. *Sing Them in English!* [piano-vocal score] 2 vols. Frederic Kirchberger, trans. Metuchen, NJ: Scarecrow Press, 1993. ind. Songs by German speaking composers with English words provided. Vol. 1 is song cycles from Beethoven to Mahler; vol. 2 contains one hundred selected songs by Schubert, Brahms and Wolf. [from S011]

5202. "Song Translations" *Music and Letters* 3/4 (10.1922) pp. 410–14. "Brahms": pp. 413–14. Translations from Op. 7 by L.C.; from Opp. 32, 49, 58, 69, 85 and 96 by R.; from Op. 58 by F.S.

See also 4647, 4693, 4697, 4753, 4769, 4799.d., 4811, 4880, 5090.b., 5104.
See also I16 in Appendix A.

B. Indirectly Related to Musical Works

1. Brahms and Literature

Contains materials that discuss the relationship between Brahms and the literary movements of his time.

5203. Draheim, Joachim. "Die Welt der Antike in den Liedern von Johannes Brahms" in *Brahms als Liedkomponist*. [for full citation see 5083] pp. [47]–64. facsim., mus., ind., notes. Examines Brahms's circle for people who work in Classical Greek and Latin field; looks at his library to see what titles it contained. Looks at Op. 94 no. 4 in context of its time, and for influences on other songs. Also reviews Kalbeck's Classical Greek allusions in Op. 98, 4th movement; Op. 113 no. 6; and Brahms's friendship with Wendt.

5204. *Kramer, Lawrence. *Music and Poetry: the Nineteenth Century and After*. (California Studies in 19th Century Music 3) Berkeley: University of California Press, 1984. xiii, 251 pp. ill., notes.

5205. *Wessel, Matthias. "Die Ossian-Dichtung in der musikalischen Komponisten" diss., Hochschule für Musik und Theater Hannover, 1992.

    (a) *reprint: Wessel. *Die Ossian-Dichtung in der musikalischen Komponisten.* (Publikationen der Hochschule für Musik und Theater Hannover 6) Laaber: Laaber-Verlag, 1994. ix, 273 pp. ill., mus., ind., notes.

See also 3720, 3839, 4409, 4515, 4665, 4668, 4699, 4701, 4868, 5059, 5188.

See also "Texts and Text Setting" in Part V.B.; and "Romanticism" in Part VI.B.

2. Brahms in Fiction

5206. *Brattinga, Teije. *Twadde fan Brahms.* Ljouwert: Utjowerij N. Miedema & Co., 1967. 88 pp.

5207. Braun, Lilian Jackson. *The Cat Who Played Brahms.* Jove edition. [(Jove Mystery)] New York: Jove Books, 1987. 185 pp. A precocious Siamese cat who, among other feats, figures out how to play a cassette player that has an audiocassette of Op. 102 in it. This incident is very incidental to the story.

    *also: New York: Berkley Publishing Group, 1987. *paperback edition: 1987. 245 pp.

    *Special Sales ed.: Jove/Berkley, 1995. 245 pp.

    (a) i) *reprint: Large print ed. South Yarmouth, MA: Curley, 1990. 267 pp.

    (a) ii) *reprint: in Braun. *Three Complete Novels.* New York: Putnam, 1993. total pp.: 513 pp.

    *also: 1st American Edition. 1993. total pp.: 605 pp.

    (a) iii) *reprint: (Lilian Jackson Braun. Jim Qwilleran feline whodunnit) London: Headline, 1996. 215 pp.

5208. *Charnas, Suzy McKee. "Listening to Brahms" *Omni Magazine* (1986 or 1987?).

    (a) i) *reprint: Charnas. *Listening to Brahms.* (Short Story Paperback Series 19) Eugene, OR: Pulphouse, 1991. 46 pp.

    (a) ii) *reprint: Charnas. in *Omni Best Science Fiction One.* Ellen Datlow, ed. Greensboro, NC: Omni Books, 1992.

5209. Dane, Jeffrey. "If Brahms had lived. . . . A Conjectural Obituary"
       The Musical Times 131/1769 (7.1990) pp. 358–60. Speculates
       what might have been if Brahms had lived another 15 years.

5210. Malzberg, Barry N. "Johann Sebastian Brahms" in *Universe 15.*
       Terry Carr, ed. Garden City: Doubleday & Company, Inc., 1985.
       pp. [122]–28. Story revolves around Brahms having a session
       with Freud, with much on Brahms's relations with women. In end,
       it's not clear who "Brahms" really is. Includes references by Freud
       to Op. 45.
       *also: New York: Tom Doherty Associates Inc., 1985.
       *issue: 1987.

5211. Sagan, Françoise [Françoise Quoirez]. *Aimez-vous Brahms . . ro-
       man.* Paris: [Rene] Julliard, 1959. [4], 11–186, [1] pp. The hero-
       ine decides her love life has become stale and it's time for a
       change. She becomes involved with a new man, they attend a con-
       cert where Brahms is played, but she comes to realize that she
       must go back to her first paramour.
       *paperback edition: (Livre de poche 1096) 1988. 179 pp.
       (a) *reprint (of ?): in Sagan. *Oeuvres.* (Bouquins) Paris: R. Laf-
            font, 1993.
       (b) i) English translation by Peter Wiles (of [1959] ed.): *Aimez-
            vous Brahms . .* London: John Murray, 1960. 128 pp.
            *also: Harmondsworth, 1960.
            also: 1st ed. New York: E.P. Dutton & Co., Inc., 1960. 127 pp.
       (b) ii) *German translation by Helga Treichl (of [1959] ed.):
            Berlin: Ullstein, 1959. 172 pp.
            *Sonderausgabe (of ?): *Lieben Sie Brahms . . . Roman.* Olten
            [et al.]: Fackelverlag, 1962. 174, [1] pp.
            *issue: 1966.
            *Lizenzausgabe (of ?): (Moewig; 2138: Roman) [Rastatt:]
            Moewig, 1981. 142 pp.
       (b) iii) *Italian translation by Maria Heller (of [1959] ed.): Sagan.
            Le piace Brahms? Romanzo. (Letteratura moderna) [Milano:]
            Bompiani e C., 1959. [2], 209, [4] pp.
       (b) iv) *Italian translation (of ?): Sagan. *Le piace Brahms?* (I Ro-
            manzi d'armore di Grazia) Milan: Arnoldo Mondadori, 1983.
       (b) v) *Japanese translation by Tomiko Asabuki (of [1959] ed.):
            Sagan. *Buramusu wa osuki.* (Shicho bunko 1480) Tokyo:
            Shinchosha, 1961. 163 pp.

(b) vi) *Portuguese translation (of [1959] ed.): Sagan. *Le gusta Brahms . . .?* (El Hipocampo) Buenos Aires: Plaza & Janes, 1960. 134 pp.

(b) vii) *Romanian translation by Cella Serghi and Catinca Ralea (of ?): Sagan. *Vă place Brahms?* (Colecţia Meridiane 156) Bucureşti: Editura Univers, 1971. 119 or 120 pp.

(b) viii) *Russian translation (of ?): Sagan. *Liubite li vy Bramsa?* Tel-Aviv: Or-Press, 1975. 67 pp.

(b) ix) *Russian translation (of ?): Sagan. "Liubite li vy Bramsa?" in Sagan. *Povesti.* (Biblioteka liubovnogo romana) [Sankt-Peterburg:] Bibliopolis, 1992.

(b) x) *Russian translation (of ?): Sagan. "Liubite li vy Bramsa?" in Sagan. *Zdravstvui grust': povesti.* Moskva: Avtor, 1992.

(b) xi) *Russian translation (of ?): Sagan. "Liubite li vy Bramsa?" in Sagan. *Nemnogo solntsa v kholodnoĭ vode: romany.* Kaliningrad: Kaliningradsko knizhnoe izdatelstvo, 1993.

5212. Sennett, Richard. *An Evening of Brahms.* 1st ed. New York: Alfred A. Knopf, 1984. [16], 7–220, [1] pp. The untimely death of his wife shocks the hero, a musician, into recognizing his detachment from the music he plays. A performance of Op. 45 is the catharsis. Parallels are also drawn between the hero's situation and Brahms's situation with the Schumann family.

See also 3208, 3563, 4572, 5056.

3. Brahms in Poetry

Contains reference to poems on Brahms and music.

5213. *D'Annunzio, Gabriele. "Sopra un "Adagio" [[di Johannes Brahms]]" in D'Annunzio. *Poema paradisiaco. Odi navali (1891–1893).* (Poesie di Gabriele D'Annunzio) Milano: Fratelli Treves, 1893.

*3.–32. migliaio: 1896–1928.

(a) i) *reprint (of ?): in D'Annunzio. [*Tutte le opere di Gabriele D'Annunzio*] 49 vols. Verona: Officina Bodoni, 1927–36.

(a) ii) *reprint (of ?): in D'Annunzio. *L'Orto e la prora.* Verona: Instituto Nazionale, 1930. p. 38. Poem is cast in the musical form "ABA". [from S114]

(a) iii) *reprint (of ?): in D'Annunzio. *L'Orto e la prora: Poema*

paradisiaco. Odi navali. L'Armato d'Italia. (D'Annunzio.
Opere complete 4) [Roma:] Vittoriale degli italiana, 1941.
*issue: 1942.
(a) iv) *reprint (of ?): in D'Annunzio. *Versi d'amore e di gloria—
I.* (D'Annunzio. *Tutte le opere di Gabriele D'Annunzio.*
Egidio Bianchetti, ed. [I Classici contemporanei italiani; 1])
Milano: Arnoldo Mondadori Editore, 1950. pp. 641–42.
(a) v) *reprint (of ?): in D'Annunzio. *Poema paradisiaco. Odi no-
vali. L'Armata d'Italia.* (D'Annunzio. *Edizione nazionale
delle opere di Gabriele D'Annunzio* 4) Milano: Arnoldo
Mondadori Editore S.p.A., 198–?
(b) *French translation by G[eorges]. Hérelle (of ?): in D'Annunzio. *Poésies 1878–1893.* Paris: Calman-Lévy, [1912].
*3éme ed.: 1912.

5214. *Davidson, Michael. "Brahms" in Davidson. *The Prose of Fact.*
Berkeley: The Figures, 1980.
(a) reprint: Davidson. in *In The American Tree.* Ron Silliman, ed.
Orono, ME: The National Poetry Foundation, 1986. p. 200.
Discusses Brahms's place in music history.

5215. Ettlinger, Anna. "Humoristisches Gedicht zum Geburtstag von
Johannes Brahms 1873" in *Johannes Brahms in Baden-Baden
und Karlsruhe.* [for full citation see 5452] pp. 163–65. Poem lauds
the occasion of Brahms's 40th birthday.

5216. *Fine, Carol Gabrielson. "McKinnon and I and Brahms" in *The
Charter Oak Poets.* Hartford, CT: Charter Oak Cultural Center,
1992.

5217. *Giles, Eric. *Brahms.* Walton-on-Thames, Surrey: Outposts, 1983.
23 pp.

5218. *Goldstein, David. *Musical Limericks.* Provincetown: Bookshop
Editions, 1986.

5219. Hancock, Virginia [Lee]. "In addition to poems about Brahms . . ."
The American Brahms Society Newsletter 7/2 (Autumn 1989) p.
[12]. Transcribes a poem from 600 (W. Reiss. *Badisches Tagblatt*
(1968)) written by Brahms and Levi in 1864.
(b) English translation by Elisabeth Bertol-Raffin: in 5224.d.

5220. *Harber, Randall H. "An Evening of Brahms" *The South Carolina
Review* 25/2 (Spring 1993) p. 97.

5221. Harris, Max[well Henley]. "Brahms Intermezzo. Lyrics" in Harris. *The Gift of Blood*. Adelaide: Jindyworobak Club, [1940]. "Brahms Intermezzo": p. 23; "Intermezzo by Brahms": p. 27. The music evokes images of romantic medieval times (castles, maidens, swords) for the poet.

5222. Kraeft, Norman. "His Gift" [manuscript] n.d. Describes his father's efforts to teach him the piano and how father studied Brahms's chamber works; poet expresses regrets that he didn't persevere with piano so he could share his father's joy.

5223. Kraeft, Norman. "Johannes Brahms" *The American Brahms Society Newsletter* 9/2 (Autumn 1991) p. [12]. A tribute to Brahms.

5224. Quigley, Thomas. "Poetic Tributes to Brahms" *The American Brahms Society Newsletter* 7/2 (Autumn 1989) pp. 6–8. ill. A survey of poetry written about Brahms, examines types of poems written, and when. Includes an annotated checklist (p. 8) of 21 poems.
(d) [Hancock, Virginia Lee.] "Poetic Tributes Revisited" *The American Brahms Society Newsletter* 8/2 (Autumn 1990) p. 10. Reports that 7 more poems have been brought to attention of Newsletter; provides citations and annotations. Includes 5219.b.

5225. Quinn, Doris Kerns. "Rambunctious Brahms" *The Christian Science Monitor* 77/146 (20.6.1986) p. 35. Poet describes the thunderous nature of Brahms's music, and how it almost makes one forget that there is a gentle, pastoral side to Brahms.
(a) reprint: Quinn. *The American Brahms Society Newsletter* 10/2 (Autumn 1992) p. 8.

5226. *Tibbetts, Frederick. "Brahms's Tin Soldiers" *Gettysburg Review* 9 (Winter 1996) pp. 151–52.

See also 3247, 3290, 3506, 3984, 4169, 4249, 4379, 4552, 4556, 4584, 4624, 4803, 4807.

4. Classicism

Contains materials that discuss Brahms as a proponent of the classical ethic.

5227. Einstein, Alfred. "Brahms, A Posthumous Musician" in Einstein.

Music In The Romantic Era. New York: W.W. Norton & Company, Inc., 1947. pp. 149–54. ill. (p. 117). Notes that Brahms's ties with classical music make him out of place in his time; he should have been born earlier. Also et passim references in sections dealing with choral and piano works.

    (b) *Italian translation by Adele Bartalini: Einstein. "Brahms, musicista postumo" in Einstein. *La musica nel periodo romantico.* (Biblioteca sansoniana musicale 3) Firenze: G.C. Sansoni, 1952.

5228. Piccardi, Carlo. "Realtà e virtualità del decadentismo" *Studi musicali* 14/2 (1985) pp. [263]–350. Brahms: pp. 269, 275–78, 339. Brahms, as "old school," is used as contrast to Mahler and Tchaikovsky.

See also 3625, 3844, 3869, 3872, 4016, 4100, 4102, 4111, 4121, 4274, 4449, 4466, 4488, 4508, 4509, 4558, 4783, 4883, 4887, 4899, 4955, 4978, 5021, 5023, 5029, 5038, 5052, 5377, 5386.
See also "Romanticism" in Part VI.B.

5. Politics

See 3646, 3653.3, 5044, 5080.

6. Religion

Contains materials that discuss Brahms's attitudes towards religious tenets and texts.

5229. *Geyer, Alan F. "The Grace of Brahms" in Geyer. *Brahms, Jesus and Other Matters of the Soul : ten sermons, 1993–1996.* n.p., 1996.

See also 3267, 3623.d., 3647, 3809, 4451, 4645, 4733, 4737, 4763, 4778, 4789, 4796, 4809, 4811, 4824, 5080, 5098, 5305.

7. Romanticism

Contains materials that discuss Brahms as a proponent of the 19th-Century romantic ethic.

5230. Behrmann, Martin. "Die A-cappella-Kompositionen von Johannes Brahms und das Problem des Romantischen" *Musica* 43/3 (5./6.1989) pp. 222–29. mus., notes. Analyses these works to see what they have to offer in terms of romanticisim: dynamics, use of contrast, form.

5231. Floros, Constantin. "Brahms—ein Januskopf" *NZ-Neue Zeitschrift für Musik* 144/4 (15.4.–15.5.;1983) pp. 4–7. ill. (also on issue cover), notes. Discusses Brahms as having both classical and romantic tendencies. Includes comment on Schumann's aesthetic as seen in Brahms's work and on Brahms's influence on Schoenberg.

5232. Geck, Martin. *Von Beethoven bis Mahler. Die Musik des deutschen Idealismus.* Stutttgart, Weimar: Verlag J.B. Metzler, 1993. x, 476 pp.
"Im Zeichen deutscher Innerlichkeit: Schubert-Schumann-Brahms": pp. 100–211. Brahms: pp. 105–08, 117–25, 136, 154–77, 194–98, 207–08. ill., mus., ind., notes. Discusses Brahms in the shadow of Beethoven, his symphonic works (including early version of Op. 15). Includes comment on traits that make Brahms a romantic (folksong and programmatic references in the works, Op. 33 as example of romantic lied, Op. 55 example of nationalistic tendencies) and allusions to Bach, Beethoven and Schubert in Op. 38.

5233. László, Ferenc. "Brahms maradandósága. 150 éve született Johannes Brahms" *Muzsika* [26]/7 (7.1983) pp. 3–6. ill. Discusses the romantic and classical aspects of Brahms the composer.

5234. *Ross, Alex. "A softer, gentler romanticism from Schumann and Brahms" *The New York Times* 142 (11.7.1993) p. H25. ill.

5235. Rummenhöller, Peter. "Johannes Brahms und die Romantik" in Rummenhöller. *Romantik in der Musik. Analysen, Portraits, Reflexionen.* München: Deutscher Taschenbuch Verlag; Kassel [et al.]: Bärenreiter-Verlag, 1989. pp. 203–[212]. mus., notes. Discusses the connection of Brahms and his music (songs, Opp. 119 no. 1, 73) to romanticism. Concludes that Brahms is not a romantic composer.

See also 3561, 3617, 3625, 3628, 4023, 4111, 4112, 4121, 4274, 4309,

4347, 4449, 4463, 4466, 4488, 4701, 4726, 4761.5, 4783, 4883, 4887, 4899, 4952, 4955, 4960, 5001, 5015, 5021, 5023, 5029, 5038, 5040, 5052, 5221, 5285, 5315, 5386.

See also "E.T.A. Hofmann" in Part III.B.2.; and "Classicism" in Part VI.B.

8. Science

See 3459.

Part VII

Brahms's Perpetuation

A. Brahms Festivals

Contains materials that report on commemorative festivals and conferences/congresses with Brahms as their theme; includes proposed, as well as actually held events.

1. Unidentified Locations, General Remarks and Collective Reports

5236. Bozarth, George S. "Brahms Societies in Baden-Baden, Hamburg and Japan" *The American Brahms Society Newsletter* 7/1 (Spring 1989) pp. 6–7. Reports on Baden-Baden 12th biennial Brahmstage (May 1989); includes announcement of 1990 Brahms Competition and spring activities of Johannes-Brahms-Gesellschaft Internationale Vereinigung, and report of Japan Brahms Society's 1988 activities.

5237. "Brahms Festivals and Concerts" *The American Brahms Society Newsletter* 1/2 (Autumn 1983) p. [3]. An overview of North American programs.

5238. "Brahms fever: . . ." *19th Century Music* 7/2 (Fall 1983) pp. 179–82. Reports on festivals in Indianapolis (report by ?) and Washington, DC (report by Walter [M.] Frisch).

5239. C.N.B. "Dr. Göbbels über das Verbot der Brahms-Feier" *Neues Wiener Journal* 41/14,171 (5.5.1933) p. 3. Reports on Göbbels forbidding official celebration of the Brahms centennial because Brahms's grandfather is allegedly Jewish.

5239.5. Hancock, Virginia [Lee]. "Concerts and Festivals" *The American Brahms Society Newsletter* 12/2 (August 1994) p. [12]. Reports on three festivals: two that are past (Italy, USA), and one to come (USA).

5240. [Hancock, Virginia Lee.] "In addition to the international festivals . . ." *The American Brahms Society Newsletter* 2/1 (Spring 1984) pp. [9–10]. Briefly summarizes local Brahms celebrations in Nashville (TN) and Winnipeg (MN, Canada).

5241. Saerchinger, César, and Local Correspondents [A.S., L.K., H.U.]. "Festivals all over Germany honor memory of Brahms at Twenty-Fifth Anniversary of His Death" *Musical Courier* 85/1 (Whole no. 2204) (6.7.1922) pp. 5, 16. ill., facsim. (p. 17). Reports on concert activities in Hamburg, Bremen, Baden-Baden, Essen and the Rhineland.

See also 3299, 3302.d., 5315, 5348, 5423.

2. Particular Locations

This section is arranged alphabetically by city.

Annandale-on-Hudson (NY)

5242. Frisch, Walter [M.]. ""Rediscovering Brahms." Brahms Festival at Bard College" *The American Brahms Society Newsletter* 8/1 (Spring 1990) p. 6. Reports on programme.

Assisi

See 5476.

Baden-Baden

5243. *Bergengruen, J. "Brahms—mit individueller Note" *Concerto* 2 (6.–7.1985) p. 5.

5244. Bozarth, George S. "The Brahmsgesellschaft Baden-Baden e. V. . . . " *The American Brahms Society Newsletter* 3/1 (Spring 1985) p. [12]. Reports on upcoming 10th Brahms-Tage.

5245. Bozarth, George S. "From 28 April to 5 May . . ." *The American Brahms Society Newsletter* 6/1 (Spring 1988) p. [9]. Reports on the activities of the 1987 Brahms-Tage.

5246. "Brahms News" *The American Brahms Society Newsletter* 11/2 (Autumn 1993) p. 7. "Brahmstage Baden-Baden": p. 7. Reports on the 1993 festival programme.

5247. Jung, Helge. "Baden-Baden: Symposium der Brahms-Gesellschaft" *Musik und Gesellschaft* 40/8–9 (8./9.1990) pp. 453–54. Presents an overview of the activities but asks what this program had to do with Brahms. Encourages a more focused program in the future.

5248. Kolneder, Walter. "The Progressive, fortwirkend. Das 1. Baden-Badener Brahms-Symposion" *NZ-Neue Zeitschrift für Musik* 147/7/8 (7./8. 1986) p. 76. Reports on the event.

See also 5236, 5241, 5423, 5452.

Berlin

See 5423.

Bonn

5249. Adaïewsky, E. "La Fête de Schumann-Brahms (Schumann-Brahms-Fest) à Bonn, le 3, 4 et 5 Mai 1910" *Revista musicale italiana* 17/[2] (1910) pp. [450]–56. Article is in French. Reports on the program and the perfomers, and the public's attitude towards the music of these two composers.

5250. *"Beethoven-Brahms Chamber Music Festival at Bonn" *Musical Courier* 34 (16.6.1897) pp. 5–6.

See also 3941.

Boston

5251. "Brahms in Boston" *The American Brahms Society Newsletter* 12/1 (Spring 1994) p. [12]. Reports on the "Emmanuel Music" concert series.

5252. "Brahms in Boston, 1997. A Call for Papers" *The American Brahms Society Newsletter* 13/2 (Autumn 1995) p. 4. Presents details on this forthcoming event.

Bremen

See 5241.

Buenos Aires

5253. *Cemino, R. "Festival Brahms '86" *Monsalvat* no. 141 (9.1986) p. 44.

Buffalo (NY)

5254. Townsend, Helen G. "Buffalo observes Brahms Centennial; Election by Guild" *The Diapason* (Chicago) 24/7 (1.6.1933) p. 28. Reports on a performance of Op. 45 in the Episcopal church, in commemoration of the Brahms centennial.

5255. Townsend, Helen G. "Events in Buffalo; Mrs. Wallace Gives the Brahms Requiem" *The Diapason* (Chicago) 24/6 (1.5.1933) p. 9. Reports on a performance of Op. 45 in the Presbyterian church, in commemoration of the Brahms centennial.

Calgary

See 5440.

Chicago

See 5437.

Detroit

5255.5. [Carr, Bruce, comp. and ed.] *International Brahms Festival [Program Book. April 10–26, 1980/Detroit, Michigan.* Detroit:] Detroit Symphony Orchestra, [1980.] Program Notes by Robert Holmes, with additions by Bruce Carr. [100 pp.] ill., facsim. Includes 3253, all concert programmes, International Brahms Congress (April 10–12) programme, texts in German and English for all vocal works performed and Op. 122 chorales, information about other associated events.

See also 5435.

Essen

See 5241.

Florence (Italy)

See 5425.

Forte dei Marmi (Italy)

See 5239.5

Gütersloh

5255.8. *Brahms-Zyklus-Orchesterkonzerte.* Gütersloh: n.p., 1983. Contains 5009.a.

Hague

See I11 in Appendix A.

Hamburg

5256. Bozarth, George S. "The International Brahms Society . . ." *The American Brahms Society Newsletter* 6/1 (Spring 1988) p. [9]. Reports on the 3rd Brahms Competition (1987) and its winners.

5257. *Brahms-Wochen '83 der Freien und Hansestadt Hamburg 7.–29. Mai.* Hamburg: Kulturbehörde, 1983. Includes: 3765, 5009.

5257.5. Pascall, Robert. "Brahms Conferences 1983" *The American Brahms Society Newsletter* 2/2 (Autumn 1984) pp. [2–3]. "Brahms-Symposion, Hamburg". Describes papers given. (d) see: 5428.

5258. *[Musikfest Hamburg, 18.8–9.9.1991.] *Programmbuch Johannes Brahms, Antonin Dvořák.* Mit Beiträge von Wolfgang Ruf. Susanne Litzel and Frank Gottschalk, eds. Hamburg: Philharmonie, 1991. 101 pp. ill.

5259. Sannemüller, Gerd. "Brahms-Wochen '83" *Ruch muzyczny* 27/18 (4.9.1983) p. 16. Reports on activities.

See also 5236, 5241, 5423.
See also I39 in Appendix A.

Heidelberg

5260. H.L. "Heidelberg celebrates sixth Brahms Festival" *Musical Courier* 92/25 (Whole no. 2411) (24.6.1926) p. 7. ill. Reports on programme.

Helsingborg

5261. Sjöqvist, Gunnar. "Helsingborgs Brahms-Bravader" *Musikrevy* 47/7–8 ([7.–8.] 1992) p. 292. Reports on activities.

Indianapolis

5262. "Romantic Festival XVI: "Brahms and His Vienna" in Indianapolis" *The American Brahms Society Newsletter* 1/1 (Spring 1983) p. [2]. Event announcement, includes projected programme.

See also 5238.

Juist (Germany)

5263. Bozarth, George S. "Last July [1987] a Brahms-Woche . . ." *The American Brahms Society Newsletter* 6/1 (Spring 1988) p. [10]. Reports on this festival.

Kassel

5264. Schuhmacher, Gerard. "Konstellationen und Kristallisationen" *Musik und Kirche* 57/1 (1./2.1987) p. 41. Reports on Kasseler Musiktage; Brahms and Schoenberg were themes for programme.

See also 4858.

Kiel

5265. Ehlert, Gero. "Brahms-Symposion in Kiel vom 6. bis 8. Oktober 1983" *Die Musikforschung* 37/3 (7.–9.1984) pp. 222–23. Reports on papers given.

See also 5425.

Leipzig

5266. Allihn, Ingeborg. "Gewandhaus-Festtage 1983" *Bulletin des Musikrates der DDR* 21/1 (1984) pp. 12–19. ill. summaries in English and French. Report; includes description of the Brahms Symposium and the exhibition of prints from Klinger's *Brahms-Phantasie*. [from S102]

5267. Hofmann, Renate. "Brahms-Symposium im Leipziger Gewandhaus" *Österreichische Musikzeitschrift* 39/1 (1.1984) pp. 24–25. Reports on speakers and proceedings.

5268. Siegmund-Schultze, Ute. "Zu Gast bei Brahminen. III. Gewandhaus-Symposium" *Musik und Gesellschaft* 33/12 (12.1983) pp. 714–15. Report and critique of the Symposium.

See also 5425, 5453.

Lexington (KY)

See 5239.5.

Linz

5269. Litschauer, Walburga. "Ein Symposium über Brahms und Bruckner in Linz" *Österreichische Musikzeitschrift* 38/11 (11.1983) pp. 641–42. Reports on what was discussed.

5270. *Zamazal, Franz. "Symphonische Konkurrenten. Eindrücke vom 5. Bruckner-Symposion in Linz, das im Zeichen der "feindlichen Brüder" Brahms und Bruckner stand" *Linz aktiv* 89 (1983) pp. 4–5. Report on symposium. [from S102]

See also 5434.

London (England)

5271. Saerchinger, César. "London performances commence celebration of Brahms centenary" *Musical Courier* 106/9 (Whole no.

2760) (4.3.1933) p. 7. Report on performances that turns to discussion of quality of performances versus number of performances; includes comment on Brahms's place in music history.

5272. Salzer, Egon Michael. "London feiert Brahms. Gespräch mit Professor Robert Heger und Dr. Adrian Boult" *Neues Wiener Journal* 41/14,182 (16.5.1933) p. 11. Reports on this Brahms programme.

5273. Simeone, Nigel. "The London Brahms Conference 1983" *Brio* 21/1 (Spring/Summer 1984) pp. 15–17. Reports on presentations, recitals and the exhibition.

5274. "Young Brahms on the South Bank" *Musical Opinion* 115/1378 (10.1992) p. 384. ill. Announcement of forthcoming series with performers expected; includes some background on Brahms and his work prior to 1863.

See also 3539, 5438, 5462, 5481.

Lübeck

5275. *Brahms-Festival Lübeck 1992: 25. April–3. Mai. [*Program.*] Lübeck: Musikhochschule Lübeck, 1992. 81 pp.

5276. *Brahms-Festival Lübeck 1993: 17.–25. April. [*Program.*] Lübeck: Musikhochschule Lübeck, 1993. 114 pp.

Meiningen

5277. *Lee, Vernon. *Pall Mall Gazette* (?.?.1899).
   (a) reprint: Lee. "The Brahms-Feast at Meiningen" *Musical Record* (Boston) no. 455 (1.12.1899) pp. 543–45. Reports on the unveiling of the monument and the programme surrounding the occasion.

See also 3401, 3884.

München-Gladbach

See 5241.

Mürzzuschlag

See 3527.d.

Nashville

See 4399, 5240.

New York

5278. A.W.K. [A. Walter Kramer] "New York's First Brahms Festival" *Musical America* 15/21 (30.3.1912) p. 1. Reports on programme.

5279. *"Beethoven-Brahms Festival in New York" *Musical Courier* 76 (24.1.1918) pp. 5, 12.

5280. "Brahms Chamber Cycle Opened in New York" *Musical America* 52/5 (10.3.1932) p. 42. ill. Reports on the programming and the background to this cycle.

5281. "The festivalizing of Brahms" *The Musical Courier* 64/14 (Whole no. 1671) (3.4.1912) pp. 21–23. ill. Reports on the festival.

5282. Mauro, Rose. "Brahms in New York" *The American Brahms Society Newsletter* 13/1 (Spring 1995) p. 3. Reports on a symposium held on Brahms's choral works, held as part of the series "A Philharmonic Celebration: Brahms's Choral Music."

5283. *Simpson, Sallie. "The Brahms Festival" *Music* (Boston) 1/18 (1912) pp. 4–5.

See also I13 in Appendix A.

Pomona

5284. Bozarth, George S. "We learn with regret . . ." *The American Brahms Society Newsletter* 3/1 (Spring 1985) p. [12]. Reports that Southern California Brahms Festival is terminated.

Poznaniu

5285. Gwizdalanka, Danuta. "Brahms—inny romantyzm" *Ruch muzyczny* 24/23 (16.11.1980) pp. 14–15. Reports on the music programme.

Santa Barbara

See 5239.5.

Stockholm

5286. *O.R., Dr. "Artur Schnabel the star of Stockholm's Brahms festival" *Musical Courier* (Whole no. 2177) (29.12.1921) p. 38. ill. Reports on programme and reviews Schnabel.

Stuttgart

5287. Baruch, Gerth-Wolfgang. "Bach und Brahms fünfte Sommerakademie in Stuttgart" *Musica* 37/6 (11./12.1983) p. 534. Reports on the programme.

5288. Baruch, Gerth-Wolfgang. "Bach und Brahms von früh bis spät. Helmuth Rillings Sommerakademie in Stuttgart" *NZ-Neue Zeitschrift für Musik* 44/11 (5.11–5.12.1983) p. 31. Reports on programme; includes comments on Bach and Brahms.

Thun

See 5418.

Tokyo

See 5423.

Toronto, Canada

See I11 in Appendix A.

Washington, D.C.

5289. *Bozarth, George S. "International Brahms Conference Papers" Seattle, WA: 1983. Abstracts only. [from 3302.d.i.]
(d) see: 5480.

5290. "International Festival and Conference. Washington, D.C., May 1983" *The American Brahms Society Newsletter* 1/1 (Spring 1983) p. [6]. ill. Describes the various events.

5291. "LC is site of Brahms sesquicentenary International Festival and Conference" *Library of Congress Information Bulletin* 42/15

(11.4.1983) pp. 123–24. Provides general information and programme.

5292. "Library Plans Six-Day Celebration Observing Brahms Sesquicentenary" *Library of Congress Information Bulletin* 42/17 (25.4.1983) pp. 139–40. Describes upcoming event; includes details on manuscripts that will be displayed.

5293. Mueller, Rena. "International Festival and Conference on the Occasion of the Sesquicentenary of the Birth of Johannes Brahms. Washington, D.C. 3–8 May, 1983" *The Journal of Musicology* 2/4 (Fall 1983) pp. 456–58. This report focuses on the Conference. Reports on papers given, with some critical reaction. Includes comment on state of Brahms research.

See also 5238, 5438, 5458, 5462, 5480.

Wien

5294. Bechert, Paul. "Vienna celebrates Brahms' anniversary in Official as well as Private Events" *Musical Courier* 84/21 (Whole no. 2198) (25.5.1922) pp. 8, 46. ill. Reports on programme and events.

5295. Eder, Gabriele Johanna. "Johannes Brahms-Fest (16. bis 21. Mai 1933)" in Eder. *Wiener Musikfeste zwischen 1918 und 1938. Ein Beitrag zur Vergangenheitsbewältigung* (Veröffentlichungen zur Zeitgeschichte 6) Wien-Salzburg: Geyer Edition, 1991. pp. 324–38. notes. Discusses all aspects from planning through to programme; includes comments on climate of times and contemporary reaction and Furtwängler's role in event.

5296. Funk, Addie. "Brahms Prominent in Vienna Music" *Musical America* 14/2 (20.5.1911) p. 13. ill. Comments on programming that recognizes 78th anniversary of Brahms's birth.

5297. Gruber, Gerold W[olfgang]. "Brahms-Kongress: Wien, 10.–15. November 1983" *Musikerziehung* 37/[3] (2.1984) pp. 137–38. Reports on sessions.

5298. Gürtelschmied, Walter. "Brahms-Festmenü im Wiener Musikverein" *Österreichische Musikzeitschrift* 38/7–8 (7.–8.1983) pp. 427–28. Reports on music performed.

5299. Klein, Rudolf. "Wiener Brahms-Kongress. Mosaiksteinchen zum Gesamtbild" *Österreichische Musikzeitschrift* 39/1 (1.1984) pp. 23–24. Reports on speakers and sessions.

5300. *Pisk, Paul A. "Het Weensche Brahms Feest" *[De] Muziek* (Amsterdam) 7 (6.1933) pp. 405–06.

5301. Rapoport, Anatol. "German and Austrian nations unite to honor Brahms' Memory" *Musical Courier* 106/23 (Whole no. 2774) (10.6.1933) p. 5. Reports on programs and comments on works performed.

5302. W. "Eröffnung des Brahms-Festes. Festversammlung im grossen Musikvereinssaal" *Neues Wiener Journal* 41/14,183 (17.5.1933) p. 7. Reports on the Festival's opening programme.

See also 3995, 5398, 5423, 5425, 5431.

Wiesbaden

5303. [Baltzell, W.J. ?] "Reflections By The Editor" *The Musical Courier* 64/26 (Whole no. 1683) (26.6.1912) pp. 21–22. "Brahms Fest". Reports on 2nd Deutsche Brahms-Gesellschaft Brahms-Fest.

Winnipeg

See 5240.

B. Commemorative Pieces

Contains materials written to observe either an anniversary of Brahms's birth or of his death. The comments are very general, invariably celebratory in nature, sometimes overwhelming in their adulation.

1907 (10th anniversary of death): 5304.
1933 (100th anniversary of birth): 5310, 5311.
1937 (40th anniversary of death): 5308.
1958 (125th anniversary of birth): 5307.
1983 (150th anniversary of birth): 5305, 5313, 5313.5, 5315, 5316, 5316.5.

5304. *Svensk musiktidning* 27 (1907) pp. 65–67.

5305. Bach, Hans Elmar. "Ich lasse die Welt laufen, wie Sie läuft. Zum 150. Geburtstag von Johannes Brahms am 7. Mai 1983" *Lied & Chor* 75/5 (5.1983) pp. 98–99. ill. Discusses Brahms's links to sacred texts and religion; his ties to Schumann, Bruckner and Wagner. Includes comment on his links to music of the past and future, Brahms and Vienna, Brahms the man.

5306. *Haubiel, Charles. "Johannes Brahms" *The Clef* (6.1916) pp. 5–7.

5307. *Jarnach, Philipp. in *Johannes Brahms, geboren am 7. Mai 1833 in Hamburg. Festwoche anlässlich seines 125. Geburtstages, veranstaltet von der Freien und Hansestadt Hamburg. Programm.* Geschäftsstelle der Johannes-Brahms-Festwoche 1958 in Hamburg, ed. [Verantwortlich für den Inhalt: K[enneth]. W[alter]. Bartlett, ed.] Hamburg: Geschäftsstelle der Johannes-Brahms-Festwoche, 1958.
(b) English translation by Jan Emerson: Jarnach. "Brahms in his Century and in the Present" *Sonus* 9/2 (1989) pp. 1–7. notes. Discusses Brahms the composer and the differing assessments of him over time. Points out parallels between Mozart's and Brahms's lives.

5308. *Lakatos, István. "Brahms negyven éve halott" *Keleti Újság* (15.4.1937).

5309. *Lakatos, István. "Johannes Brahms" *Igazság* (12.5.1963).

5310. *Mantelli, Giacomo Alberto. "Introduzione a Brahms" *La Rassegna musicale* 6 (5.,6. (?);1933) pp. 141–47.

5311. Mason, Daniel Gregory. "The Centenary of Brahms, 1833–1933" *The Etude Music Magazine* 51/8 (8.1933) pp. 505–06. ill., notes. Discusses the most essential qualities of Brahms's music and why they have been so long misunderstood and undervalued. Includes a brief look at Brahms the composer.

5312. *Mayer, Hans. "Brahms und die Nachwelt" in *Festschrift zur Einweihungsfeier eines Denkmals für den in Hamburg geborenen Komponisten vor dem Gebäude der Musikhalle.* n.p., 1981.
(a) i) reprint: Mayer. "Ein Denkmal für Johannes Brahms" *Brahms-Studien* Bd. 5 (1983) pp. 9–24.
(a) ii) reprint: Mayer. "Ein Denkmal für Johannes Brahms" in Mayer. *Ein Denkmal für Johannes Brahms. Versuche über*

Musik und Literatur. 1. Auflage. (Bibliothek Suhrkamp 812) Frankfurt am Main: Suhrkamp Verlag, 1983. pp. 68–[89]. Discusses Brahms's worth to music and his place in music history. Includes comments on Brahms's relationships with his contemporaries.

5313. "Pianisten, Musik—Professionelle . . ." *Süddeutsche Zeitung* (München) 39/105 (7./8.5.1983) p. 138. ill. An appreciation of Brahms's worth and in particular, Op. 24. Includes survey of the life pre-1853.

5313.5. *Rich, Alan. "Listening Again to the least of the "3 B's."" *House & Garden* 155 (6.1983) pp. 178+ . ill.

5314. *Schenker, Heinrich. "Ein Gruβ an Johannes Brahms zu seinem 60. Geburtstag, 7. Mai 1893" *Die Zukunft* Bd. 3 (1893) p. 279.
(a) reprint: Schenker. in Schenker. *Heinrich Schenker als Essayist und Kritiker.* [for full citation see 5388] pp. 43–44. notes. Includes comment on Brahms's ability to take from music of the past and carry it through to the future.

5315. Schonberg, Harold C. "Low-Key Celebration for a Master" *New York Times Magazine* (24.4.1983) pp. [81–82, 84,] 85, [86–87,] 90. ill. Discusses Brahms as a romantic composer, and a conservative person. Includes comments on Brahms's style, Brahms the man and his place in music history. Also describes events that are taking place.

5316. Siegmund-Schultze, Walther. "Johannes Brahms in seiner Bedeutung für unsere Zeit. Gedanken zum 150. Geburtstag des Komponisten" *Musik in der Schule* 34/4 (1983) pp. 124–29. ill. Places Brahms in his time, compares to his predecessors. Includes analysis of Opp. 34 and 46 no. 3.

5316.5. *"Still Brahms after all these years" *Vogue* 173 (5.1983) pp. 70+ .

5317. Untersteiner, Alfredo. "In morte di Giovanni Brahms" *Gazzetta musicale di Milano* 52/15 (15.4.1897) pp. 221–22. Discusses Brahms the composer, Brahms's links with Schumann, Brahms's style and the Italian view of Brahms.

See also 3604, 3646, 3653.1, 4035, 5025.

C. Evaluation

Contains materials that assess Brahms's position in music history, discuss the reception accorded him by other composers and the general public, or describe the honors he received during his lifetime.

Programming patterns: 5323, 5331, 5368, 5369, 5372, 5385.

Stature in 1850's: 5341, 5345, 5366, 5367, 5385.
Stature in 1860's: 5319, 5364, 5367.
Stature in 1870's: 5332, 5367.d., 5396.
Stature in 1880's: 5326, 5333, 5367.d., 5396, 5405.
Stature in 1890's: 5318.8, 5325, 5327, 5328, 5330, 5334, 5339, 5351, 5361, 5365, 5371, 5381, 5388, 5396, 5402, 5405.
Stature in 1900's: 5318, 5318.5, 5378, 5388, 5396, 5405.
Stature in 1910's: 5324, 5337, 5362, 5382, 5396, 5405.
Stature in 1920's: 5321, 5374, 5396, 5405.
Stature in 1930's: 5336, 5356, 5357, 5375, 5396, 5398, 5400, 5403, 5405, 5407.
Stature in 1940's: 5353, 5355, 5399.
Stature in 1950's: 5346, 5352.
Stature in 1980's: 5329, 5335, 5338, 5383, 5401, 5408.
Stature in 1990's: 5380.

5318. *Musical News* (London) 32 (22.6.1907) p. 611. Report on 2951? (H.A. Harding. *Proceedings of the Musical Association* (1906–07)) [from compilor]

5318.5. *Musical Standard* new series 3 [vol. 17] (7.12.1901) p. 353.

5318.8. *Presto* (Chicago) 10/29 (18.5.1893) p. 11.

5319. *Recensionen und Mittheilungen über Theater und Musik* (Wien) [8 or 9 (1862 or 1863)].
(b) English translation: "Johann (sic) Brahms" *Dwight's Journal of Music* 22/23 (Whole no. 570) (7.3.1863) pp. 389–90. Reviews Brahms to date, noting Schumann's "Neue Bahnen" and Brahms's links to Schumann. Includes comment on public's reaction to him in Vienna, and Brahms as a piano player.

5320. *La Revue et gazette musicale de Paris.*
(d) *Ellis, Katharine. Music Criticism in Nineteenth-Century*

France. Cambridge, New York: Cambridge University Press, 1995. xiii, 301 pp. ind., notes.

5321. Anti, An. "Brahms" *Musical Courier* 89/5 (Whole no. 2312) (31.7.1924) pp. 7, 33. ill. Comments that Brahms's music is all craft, no inspiration.
(d) Weller, S.M. "In defense of Brahms" *Musical Courier* 89/7 (Whole no. 2314) (14.8.1924) p. 10. Rebuts "An Anti."

5322. **The Attentive Listener. Three Centuries of Music Criticism.* Harry Haskell, ed. Princeton: Princeton University Press, 1996. xvii, 398 pp. ind., notes.

5323. Blaukopf, Herta, and Kurt Blaukopf. "B wie Brahms" in Blaukopf. *Die Wiener Philharmoniker. Wesen, Werden, Wirkin eines grossen Orchesters.* Wien, Hamburg: Paul Zsolnay Verlag Gesellschaft mbH, 1986. pp. 220–222. ill. Discusses how Brahms's works were slow to become part of the orchestral repertoire (not until 1883).
"wesentlich erweiterte und verbesserte Neuausgabe": Blaukopf, Herta, and Kurt Blaukopf. in Blaukopf. *Die Wiener Philharmoniker.* (Welt des Orchesters—Orchester der Welt) Wien: Löckner Verlag, 1992. pp. 224–26. adds fig. (p. 223). Figure is a tabulation of number of performances of works of Brahms, Beethoven, Bruckner, and Mozart in time period 1842–1974.

5324. "Brahms" *Musical Courier* 61/11 (Whole no. 1590) (14.9.1910) pp. 22–23. Contrasts Rubinstein and Brahms; looks at Brahms's childhood for insight into his music.

5325. *"Brahms and Brahmsism" *Musical Courier* 29 (24.10.1894) p. 8.

5326. "Brahms e Liszt giudicati dalla critica tedesca" *Gazzetta musicale di Milano* 40/10 (8.3.1885) p. 94.
"Giovanni Brahms": p. 94. Focuses on the symphonies.

5327. *"Brahms haters" *Musical Courier* 39 (1.11.1899) p. 27.

5328. *"The Brahms Question" *Musical Courier* 30 (3.4.1895) p. 21.

5329. Burkholder, J. Peter. "Brahms and Twentieth-Century Classical Music" *19th Century Music* 8/1 (Summer 1984) pp. 75–83. notes. Redefines modernism in music and begins the movement with Brahms. Discusses Brahms's importance for the music of the last 100 years.

5330. *Cady, Calvin B. "Brahms criticism" *Musical Courier* 25 (31.8.1892) pp. 5–6.

5331. Dalton, John Truman. "An Analysis of Programming Patterns of Undergraduate Solo Vocal Recitals as Found in Selected Educational Institutions for the Academic Years 1964–65 through 1974–75" Ph.D. diss., Music Education, Indiana University, 1980. xii, 230 pp. notes, works list. Analyses which works are included, what voice types are singing them, which languages are being sung, which musical periods and genres. Brahms is in a group of 5 composers (with Schumann, Schubert, Fauré, and Händel) that account for 25% of the repertory. [from S102]

5332. Dancla, Ch[arles]. "Brahms" in Dancla. *Miscellanées musicales. Un peu de tout, à tort et à travers, au courant de la plume. Opinions, Réflexions, Appréciations d'un Musicien sans parti pris. Mendelssohn, Schumann, Brahms, Raff, Rubenstein, Wagner; Quelques mots sur les derniers Quatuors de Beethoven.* Paris: Colombier, 1876. pp. 8–13. Discusses Brahms's and Raff's style in tandem, also Brahms's Opp. 25, 26, and 34. Calls both composers mediocre.

5333. E. "Brahms" *L'Art musical* 19/9 (26.2.1880) p. 67. On an occasion of a performance of Op. 45, reviews Schumann's opinion of Brahms to see if Brahms fulfills it. Not so, to date, but Op. 45 does fulfill it. Includes French translation by Adolphe Julien of excerpt of 3013 (R.S. *Neue Zeitschrift für Musik* (1853)).

5334. "Edouard Hanslick's criticism of Brahms' works" *Musical Courier* 24 (23.3.1892) p. 5. Report on 2944 (?) (E. Hanslick. *Aus dem Tagebuche eines Musikers.* (1892)) [from compilor]

5335. *Endler, F[ranz]. "Erst "Maienkind", dann "einschichtiger Herr"—Johannes Brahms, nicht nur als Patriarch gesehen" *Die Presse* (Wien) (7./8.5.1983) Spectrum pp. iii–iv.

5336. Ewen, David. "Bach, Beethoven, Brahms and Bovines" *Musical Courier* 108/19 (Whole no. 2822) (12.5.1934) p. 6. Speculates that cows would not appreciate Brahms's music—author is reacting to article that notes that the type of music that cows listen to can affect their milk production.

5337. Farwell, Arthur. "A Word About Brahms" *Musical America*

15/12 (27.1.1912) p. 17. Discusses the history of the controversy over Brahms's worth. Suggests avenues we can pursue to learn why he is important.

5338. Fellinger, Imogen. "Brahms' Bedeutung in heutiger Zeit" *Brahms-Studien* Bd. 6 (1985) pp. 9–30. mus., notes. Discusses Brahms's place in the musical scene of his time and contrasts it with current views of him. Includes comment on Brahms as seen by Schoenberg.

5339. *Finck, Harry G. *Evening Post* (New York) (10.(?)1896).

5340. Fleischer, Hugo. "Der Brahmsgegner Hugo Wolf" *Der Merker* (Wien) 9/24 (15.12.1918) pp. 847–56. Reviews Wolf's opinion of Brahms, as seen in his criticisms, and its background.

5341. Floros, Constantin. "Brahms—der "Messias" und "Apostel". Zur Rezeptionsgeschichte des Artikels "Neue Bahnen"" *Die Musik-forschung* 36/1 (1.–3.1983) pp. 24–29. notes. Reviews the background of the writing of "Neue Bahnen" and how it was received at the time; also looks at Brahms's actions that reflect the article. (d) Kross, Siegfried. "In *Mf* Jahrgang . . ." *Die Musikforschung* 36/4 (10.–12.1983) p. 222. Advises that he feels that Floros is plagiarizing his work.

5342. Floros, Constantin. "Das Brahms-Bild Eduard Hanslicks" in *Brahms-Kongress Wien 1983*. [for full citation see 5431] pp. 155–66. notes. Examines Hanslick's opinions of Brahms to see if they were a true impression; also reviews the two men's relationship, 1855–97. Discusses what Brahms thought about Hanslick's understanding of his music; Hanslick's favourite Brahms works; works that Hanslick initially didn't like then came around to.

5343. Floros, Constantin. "Über Brahms' Stellung in seiner Zeit" in *Brahms und seine Zeit*. (Hamburger Jahrbuch für Musikwissenschaft 7) [for full citation see 5428] pp. 9–19. notes. Reviews what his contemporaries thought of him, in contrast to how he is viewed now. Includes aesthetic point of view.

5344. Frisch, Walter M. "Brahms and His Critics" *The American Brahms Society Newsletter* 3/1 (Spring 1985) pp. [1–3]. ill. Traces the history of Brahms's fluctuating reputation among musical commentators: Schumann, Hanslick, Wolf, Wagner, Nietzsche,

Shaw, Stravinsky and Schoenberg. Includes comment on the reception of Brahms's music in England.

5345. Frisch, Walter [M.]. "Brahms and Schubring: Musical Criticism and Politics at Mid-Century" *19th Century Music* 7/3 (3.4.1984) pp. 271–81. notes. A close examination of 1332 (DAS. *Neue Zeitschrift für Musik* (1862)); concludes it is basically sympathetic but reserved in tone. Also examines it from the point of view of the highly politicized German musical scene (New German School) of its time.

5346. Furtwängler, Wilhelm. "Brahms" in Furtwängler. *Furtwängler on Music. Essays and Addresses.* Ronald Taylor, ed. and trans. Aldershot, Hants, England: Scolar Press, 1991. pp. 97–104. ind., notes. Translation of 2931.a.iii. (W. Furtwängler. *Ton und Wort.* (1954)).
*also: Brookfield, VT: Gower Publishing Company, 1991.

5347. *Gay, Peter. *Freud, gli ebrei e altri tedeschi: dominatori e vittime nella cultura modernista.* (Saggitari Laterza 39) Roma, Bari: Laterza, 1990. xix, 257 pp. ind., notes. Translation of 2932.a. (P.Gay. *Freud, Jews and Other Germans.* (1978)).

5348. Geiringer, Karl. "Brahms in His Time and Ours" *The Triangle of Mu Phi Epsilon* 78/2 (Winter 1983–84) pp. 6–10. ill. Describes the honours accepted and not accepted by Brahms, and the relationship between Brahms and 20th century composers. Includes an overview of current research and sesquicentenary activities.

5348.5. *Geng, Veronica. "Settling an old score" *The New Yorker* 61 (17.6.1985) pp. 36+ . An appreciation of G.B. Shaw; includes comment on Shaw's criticisms of Brahms. [from S084]

5349. Goubault, Christian. *Le Critique musicale dans la presse française de 1870 à 1914.* Genève-Paris: Editions Slatkine, 1984. 535 pp. Brahms: pp. 435–37 and et passim. ind., notes. Discusses what French music critics say about Brahms.

5350. Gruber, Gerold Wolfgang. "Brahms und Bruckner in der zeitgenössischen Wiener Musikkritik" in *Bruckner Symposion.* [for full citation see 5434] pp. 201–18. notes. Compares amount and type of criticism for both composers in Viennese art or music journals. Critics discussed include Hanslick, d'Armond, Helm, von

Hartmann and Graf. Concludes that Bruckner gets more coverage because Brahms is better known.

5351. H[ugo].W[olf]. "Bruckner, Brahms und die Kritik" *Wiener Sonn- und Montagszeitung* (19.10.1896).

5352. Haggin, B[ernard]. H. "Brahms" in Haggin. *The Listener's Musical Companion.* New Brunswick, NJ: Rutgers University Press, 1956. pp. 125–27. ind., discog. (p. 233). Describes how his opinion of Brahms has changed over time (from negative to positive) and how it was the nature of the music that lead to the change.

"New and expanded version": *The New Listener's Companion and Record Guide.* New York: Horizon Press, 1967. pp. 125–27. discog. now on pp. 258–59.

[8th ed.?] New edition: *The Listener's Musical Companion.* Compiled and edited by Thomas Hathaway. New York, Oxford: Oxford University Press, 1991. pp. 108–11. adds notes, discog. now on pp. 400–01. "This edition incorporates supplementary remarks and outside remarks in the text." Contains references to more music examples, discography revamped to include current good recordings that are likely to remain available.

*Paperback ed.: 1991.

5353. Haggin, B[ernard]. H. "From the beginning . . ." *The Nation* 155/11 (12.9.1942) pp. 113–14. Defends his unfavourable opinion of Brahms by saying it's based on his study of the composer, not personal prejudice.
(a) reprint: in 5356.

5354. Haggin, B[ernard]. H. "In his *New Republic* . . ." *The Nation* 160/13 (31.3.1945) p. 371. Reacting to review of 1372F (D.F. Tovey. *Chamber Music.* (1944)), where reviewer says it's Tovey's stand that Brahms is great that makes him great. Also discusses Shaw's opinions of Brahms.
(a) reprint: in 5356.

5355. *Haggin, Bernard H. *Music & Ballet, 1973–1983.* New York: Horizon Press, 1984. 282 pp.

5356. Haggin, B[ernard]. H. *Music in the Nation.* New York: William Sloane Associates, Inc., 1949. ix, [2], 376 pp. Reprints 5353 (pp. 113–14) and 5354 (pp. 223–25).

5357. *Hamel, Fred. *Deutsche allgemeine Zeitung* (Berlin) (?.5.1933). (c) excerpt: in 5398.

5358. *Hanslick, Eduard. *Aus dem Tagebuch eines Rezensenten. Gesammelte Musikkritiken.* Reinhard Ermen and Peter Wapnewski, comps. Kassel: Bärenreiter, 1989. 363 pp. notes. Excerpts from 2943–48, 2950 (?). [from compilor]

5359. Höslinger, Clemens. "Hugo Wolfs Brahms-Kritiken. Versuch einer Interpretation" in *Brahms-Kongress Wien 1983.* [for full citation see 5431] pp. 259–68. notes. Looks at Wolf as critic and suggests that we cannot get a true impression of his opinion of Brahms because of the uncertainty as to what was published, versus not published. Includes a reprint of a manuscript of Wolf Brahms-criticism for *Wiener Salonblatt* (9.1.1887) which was never published.

5360. Holmes, John L. "Johannes Brahms (1833–1897)" in Holmes. *Conductors on Composers.* Westport, CT; London: Greenwood Press, 1993. pp. 48–52. notes. Comments on Brahms from 15 conductors: Brahms as a composer, his orchestral works, his tempi, some descriptions of meetings.

5361. "Johannes Brahms" *The American Brahms Society Newsletter* 6/1 (Spring 1988) pp. [1–2]. ill. Reprint of 2966 ("Johannes Brahms" *The Outlook* (1894)).

5362. "Johannes Brahms" (The Etude Gallery of Musical Celebrities) *The Etude* 28/8 (8.1910) pp. 513–14. ill. Discusses Brahms's place in music history; includes comments on his music.

5363. Johnson, Carl. "Hugo Wolf as Music Critic" *The NATS [=National Association of Teachers of Singing, Inc.] Bulletin* 38/5 (5./6.1982) pp. 12–15. notes. Surveys his activity as a critic and his stance in the Wagner-Brahms controversy. Reports on his criticisms of various Brahms works.

5364. Kahler, Otto-Hans. *Theodor Billroth as Musical Critic. (A Documentation).* K.B.A. [Karel B. Absolon] trans. 1st English Limited Numbered ed. Rockville, MD: Kabel Publishers, 1988. 85, [31] pp. ill., notes. An evaluation of Billroth's published music critiques in the *Neue Zürcher Zeitung.* Feuilleton section (1860–1867); also reports on his essays that relate to music and discusses critiques probably Billroth-authored, and critiques certainly not Billroth-authored. Includes some comments on Brahms and Billroth and their relationship.

5365. [Kelley, Edgar Stillman. "Why Brahms fails to Inspire Us. An Apology" *Looker-On* 3/2 (8.1896) pp. 89–101. [= 2479]]
(d) i) *"Brahms not a great composer" *Looker-On* 3/[4] (10.1896) pp. 336+. Related to 2479? [from compilor]
(d) ii) [W.S.B.M.] "Editorial Bric-a-Brac" *Music* (Chicago) [11/1] (11.1896) pp. 72–83. Brahms: pp. 72–74. Includes rebuttal of 2479.
(d) iii) Russell, Louis Arthur. "Mr. Brahms again" *Music* (Chicago) [11/1] (11.1896) pp. 62–71. Shows where Kelley has failed to prove his argument.

5366. Kirchmeyer, Helmut. *Robert Schumanns Düsseldorfer Brahms-Aufsatz "Neue Bahnen" und die Ausbreitung der Wagnerschen Opern bis 1856. Psychogramm eines "letzten" Artikels.* (Abhandlungen der Sächsischen Akademie der Wissenschaften zu Leipzig, Philologisch-historische Klasse Bd. 73, 6) Berlin: Akademie Verlag, 1993. 95 pp. notes. Discusses Schumann's role as a "prophet" and his power to do so. Examines how "Neue Bahnen" leads to the split in German music of Brahms versus Wagner.

5367. *Klauke, Angelika. [becomes Angelika Horstmann] "Anfänge des Brahms-Bildes in den musikalischen Fachzeitschriften von der Begegnung mit Schumann bis zur mittleren Periode, dargestellt an Opus 1 bis 10" Magisterarbeit, Georg-August-Universität zu Göttingen, 1979.
(d) i) *Horstmann, Angelika. [formerly Angelika Klauke] "Untersuchungen zur Brahms-Rezeption der Jahre 1860 bis 1880" Phil.F. diss., Musicology, Georg-August-Universität zu Göttingen, 1984.
(a) reprint: Horstmann. *Untersuchungen zur Brahms-Rezeption der Jahre 1860 bis 1880.* (Schriftenreihe zur Musik 24) Hamburg: Verlag der Musikalienhandlung Karl Dieter Wagner, 1986. v, [1], 445 pp. mus., fig., ind., notes, appendixes. Examines reviews of the editions and concert reviews in the German language daily presses and music periodicals. Includes comments on the quality of writing and the critics' understanding of music in their time.

Book is arranged by genre, within that by opus number, with a general summary at the end of each section. Also includes background on the critics. Appendixes include tables that show appearances of Brahms's works, arranged by genre, and within that chronologically.

(d) ii) Horstmann, Angelika. "Die Rezeption der Werke op. 1 bis 10 von Johannes Brahms zwischen 1853 und 1860" in *Brahms und seine Zeit*. (Hamburger Jahrbuch für Musikwissenschaft 7) [for full citation see 5428] pp. 33–44. mus., notes. Comments on critics' reaction to Schumann's "Neue Bahnen" article, then examines reviews of Opp. 1–10 in that shadow. The study examines 6 periodicals; the reviews are grouped by the title of the periodical they are in.

5368. Klein, Herman [Hermann]. "The Singing of Brahms" (The Gramophone and the Singer) *The Gramophone* no. 118 (3.1933) pp. 385–86. Comments on slow interest in Brahms's music and how performances of Op. 52 lead people to investigate the other works. Includes comment on English singers' feelings about Brahms songs.

(a) reprint: in Klein, Herman [Hermann]. in *Herman Klein and the Gramophone: being series of essays on . . . and other writings from The Gramophone by Herman Klein*. Edited and with a Biographical Sketch by William R. Moran. Reinhard G. Pauly, General ed. Portland: Amadeus Press, 1990. pp. 369–70.

5369. Kross, Siegfried. "The Establishment of a Brahms Repertoire 1890–1902" in *Brahms 2*. [for full citation see 5481] pp. 21–[38]. fig., notes. Examines *Musikalisches Wochenblatt* as a means of tracing the establishment of Brahms's music in the repertoire in Germany and elsewhere. Examination also illustrated the kinds of difficulties which attend the compilation of reliable statistics for such a study. Survey is done by genre.

5370. Kross, Siegfried. "Kontinuität und Diskontinuität im heutigen Brahms-Bild" *Österreichische Musikzeitschrift* 38/4–5 (4.–5. 1983) pp. 218–227. ill., notes. Traces the view of Brahms from his times to now, points out what has influenced it and how it isn't stable. Includes comments on his contemporary proponents, the Zweite Wiener Schule's opinions of Brahms, Brahms versus Wagner.

5371. *McColl, Sandra. *Music Criticism in Vienna, 1896–1897. Critically Moving Forms.* (Oxford Monographs on Music) Oxford: Clarendon Press; New York: Oxford University Press, 1996. xiv, 246 pp. ill., ind., notes. A study of the work of 24 music critics. [from publisher information]

5372. Mark, Desmond. *Zur Bestandaufnahme des Wiener Orchesterrepertoires. Ein soziographischer Versuch nach der Methode von John H. Mueller.* 1. Auflage. (UE Report) Wien: Universal Edition, 1979. 67 pp. fig., notes. Includes analyses of the repertoires of the Wiener Philharmoniker and the Wiener Symphonie from their inception to the present. Trends are also shown graphically and compared with repertoire analyses of leading American orchestras.

5373. Marsh, Robert. "Two Sides of a Grumpy Genius" *The Vancouver Sun* 96/67 (20.1.1983) p. C9. ill. Reviews Brahms's standing as a composer from the late 1890's to the present day. Includes comment on Brahms the man, his attitude towards women, and Brahms and Wagner.

5374. *Mason, Daniel Gregory. "A Postscript "From Grieg to Brahms"" *New Music [Review] and Church Music Review* 26 (7.–9.1927) pp. 258–60, 297–99, 333–36. Reprint of 2988 (from D.G. Mason. *From Grieg to Brahms.* (1927)). [from compilor]

5375. *Mayer, Ludwig K. *Völkischer Beobachter* (?.5.1933). (c) excerpt: in 5398.

5376. *Meurs, Norbert. "Aspekte der Brahms-Rezeption" Phil.F. diss., Freie Universität Berlin, n.d. (?)

5377. Müller, Gerhard. "Brahms im Widerstreit der Kritik" in *Johannes Brahms: Leben, Werk, Interpretation, Rezeption.* [for full citation see 5453] pp. 68–77. ill. Remarks that contemporary critical debate (Wagner versus Brahms) largely established Brahms's reputation; Brahms seen as traditionalist, classical composer.

5378. *Mueller, Kurt. "Is Brahms becoming popular?" *The Symphony* (Atlanta) 1/3–4 (1906) p. 39.

5379. *Musik—gedeutet und bewertet. Texte zur musikalische Rezeptionsgeschichte.* Hermann J. Busch and Werner Klüppelholz, eds. Original-Ausgabe. (dtv-Dokumente 2937) München: Deutscher

Taschenbuch-Verlag; Kassel [et al.]: Bärenreiter, 1983. 313 pp. notes.

5380. Northcott, Bayan. "Once and Future Master" *The Independent* (London) [6] (30.3.1991) p. 29. ill. Studies and surveys Brahms's changing reputation in light of new surge of interest, in the guise of a report on 5480; includes comment on Brahms the minimalist and Brahms the modernist.

5381. Notley, Margaret [Anne]. "Brahms as Liberal: Genre, Style and Politics in Late Nineteenth-Century Vienna" *19th Century Music* 17/2 (Fall 1993) pp. 107–23. notes. Studies Brahms's political personality in the background of his time. Includes comment on the Brahms-Bruckner "camps" and contemporary views of Brahms.

5382. *Oehmler, Leo. "The Art of Johannes Brahms as Compared to That of His Predecessors" *Musical Observer* (New York) 5/5 (1911) pp. 4–5.

5383. "Posthumous Platinum" [Cartoon caption] *The New Yorker* 64/18 (20.6.1988) p. 71. Cartoon shows Brahms's headstone being giving a platinum disk by executives from the recording industry, with media taking photographs of the event.

5384. [R.S. [Robert Schumann] "Neue Bahnen" *Neue Zeitschrift für Musik* Bd. 39/18 (28.10.1853) pp. 185–86. [= 3013]]
(a) i) reprint: R.S. "Neue Bahnen" in Schumann, Robert. *Gesammelte Schriften über Musik und Musiker*. 3. Auflage. 2 Bde. Leipzig: Georg Wigands Verlag, 1875. Bd. 2, pp. 374–75. notes.
also: in Schumann, Robert. *Gesammelte Schriften über Musik und Musiker*. Heinrich Simon, ed. [3 Bde. in 1] Leipzig: Philipp Reclam jun., [1888]. ind. Bd. III, pp. 175–77. adds more notes.
(a) ii) reprint (of ?): Schumann, Robert. "Neue Bahnen" in Schumann. *Schriften über Musik und Musiker*. Josef Häusler, comp. and ed. (Universal-Bibliothek 2472[[3]]) Stuttgart: Philipp Reclam Jun., 1982. pp. 210–12. ind.
(b) i)*English translation by Henry Pleasants [III] (of ?): R.S. "New Paths (1853)" in Schumann, Robert. *The Musical World of Robert Schumann. A Selection From His Own Writings*. Translated, Edited and Annotated By Henry Pleasants

[III]. New York: St. Martin's Press, 1965. American edition of 3013.b.i. (London: Victor Gollancz Ltd., 1965)

(b) ii) English translation by Henry Pleasants [III] (of ?): R.S. "New Paths (1853)" in Schumann, Robert. *Schumann on Music. A Selection from the Writings.* Translated, edited and annotated by Henry Pleasants [III]. New York: Dover Publications, Inc., 1988. "A slightly corrected republication" of 3013.b.i. (R. Schumann. *The Musical World of Robert Schumann.* (1965)) notes, ind.

(b) iii) *English translation by Fanny Raymond Ritter (of ?): in Schumann, Robert. *Music and Musicians.* 1st series. (?) New York: Edward Schuberth, 1877.

*also: London: William Reeves, 1877.

(b) iv) English translation by Henry Pleasants [III] (of ?): Schumann, Robert. "New Paths (1853)". in *Writings of German Composers.* [for full citation see 3954] pp. 141–42. Reprinted from 3013.b.i. (R. Schumann. *The Musical World of Robert Schumann.* (1965))

(b) v) *English translation by Paul Rosenfeld (of German 1914 Auflage): Schumann, Robert. "New Roads [[1853]]" in reprint of 3013.a.i.b. (R. Schumann. *On Music and Musicians.* (New York, 1946)) as First California paperback ed. Berkeley, Los Angeles: University of California Press, 1983.

(b) vi) *French translation by Henri de Curzon (of ?): in Schumann, Robert. *Écrits sur la musique et les musiciens.* 2 vols. Paris: Fischbacher, 1894–98.

(b) vii) *Swedish translation (of ?): Schumann, Robert. *Musik-Kultur* 4 (1929) pp. 97–98.

(c) i) excerpt (of ?): R.S. "Er heißt Johannes Brahms . . ." *Süddeutsche Zeitung* (München) 39/105 (7./8.1983) p. 16.

(c) ii) excerpt in French translation by Adolph Julien (of ?): see 5333.

5385. *Rich, Ruth Anne. "Selected Piano Recitals in Carnegie Hall, the Seasons of 1895, 1920, 1945, 1970: A Record of Changing Musical Tastes" D.M.A. diss., Performance and Literature (Piano), Eastman School of Music, University of Rochester, 1973. vi, 367 pp. ill., fig., notes, works list. Study of these 4 seasons shows that 19th century works account for more than 50% of programming. Includes statistical tabulations for all composers and each work performed. Brahms is part of a consistent grouping of 6 composers (Chopin, Beethoven, Liszt, Schumann, Debussy) within the 8 composers most performed. [from S102]

5386. Romberg, Ute. "Zur Geschichte der Brahms-Rezeption im deutschsprachigen Raum" *Beiträge zur Musikwissenschaft* 29/1 (1987) pp. 49–58. notes. Reviews from 1853–1983, looking at Brahms reception as grouped into periods, the various streams of thoughts, writings on him; also looks at the popularity of the music and Brahms as a romantic or classic composer.

5387. Saint-Pulgent, Maryvonne de. "Brahms et les français. Histoire d'un malentendu" *Diapason* (Paris) no. 283 (5.1983) pp. 31–32. ill. Discusses what Brahms means to the people of France today and reviews what French composers and critics say about Brahms.

5388. Schenker, Heinrich. *Heinrich Schenker als Essayist und Kritiker. Gesammelte Aufsätze, Rezensionen und kleinere Berichte aus den Jahren 1891–1901.* Herausgegeben und mit einem Vorwort versehen von Hellmut Federhofer. (Studien und Materialien zur Musikwissenschaft 5) Hildesheim, Zürich, New York: Georg Holms Verlag, 1990. ix, [1], 375 pp. mus., ind., notes. 7 writings on Brahms in all, 1 new to this volume of Brahms Bibliography; also includes concert reviews (new references).
"Johannes Brahms. Fünf Lieder für eine Singstimme mit Pianoforte, Op. 107, N. Simrock": pp. 2–8. Reprint of 2158 (H. Schenker. *Musikalisches Wochenblatt* (1891)).
"Johannes Brahms. Fünf Gesänge für gemischten Chor a capella, Op. 104. Berlin, N. Simrock": pp. 14–26. Reprint of 2340 (H. Schenker. *Musikalisches Wochenblatt* (1892)).
"Ein Gruβ an Johannes Brahms. Zu seinem 60. Geburtstag, 7. Mai 1893": pp. 43–44. Reprint of 5314.
"Johannes Brahms. Phantasien für Pianoforte, Op. 116. Berlin, N. Simrock": pp. 64–66. Reprint of 1678 (H. Schenker. *Musikalisches Wochenblatt* (1894)).
"Johannes Brahms. (Geb. am 7. Mai 1833, gest. am 3. April 1897.)": pp. 224–30. Reprint of 516 (H. Schenker. *Neue Revue* (Wien) (1897)).
"Johannes Brahms.": pp. 230–36. Reprint of 2425 (H. Schenker. *Die Zukunft* (Berlin) (1897)).
"Johannes Brahms hat das Ehrenzeichen . . .": p. 349. Reprint of 2939 (H.Sch. *Die Zeit* [Wochenschrift] (Wien) (1896)).

5389. Scherliess, Volker. "Brahms-Wirkungen" in *Johannes Brahms: Leben und Werk* [for full citation see 3215] pp. 101–02, 106. Reviews Brahms's worth over the years.

5390. *Schick, Robert. *Classical Music Criticism.* (Garland Reference Library of the Humanities 1879; Perspectives in Music Criticism and Theory 2) New York: Garland, 1996. 350 pp. ind., notes.

5391. *Schmidt, Chr[istian]. M[artin]. "Die Brahms-Rezeption bei Schönberg und seinem Kreis" *Jahrestagung der Gesellschaft für Musikforschung Marburg* (1983).

5392. *Schubert, G[iselher]. "Ablehnende Brahms-Rezeption durch jüngere Komponisten der zwanziger Jahre" *Jahrestagung der Gesellschaft für Musikforschung Marburg* (1983).

5393. Schubert, Giselher. "Komponisten rezipieren Brahms. Aspekte eines komplexen Themas" *Musik und Bildung* 15/5 (Bd. 74) (5.1983) pp. 4–9. mus., notes. Summary: p. 2. Quotes 7 composers' comments on Brahms.

5394. *Schubring, [Adolf]. "Von Beethoven bis Brahms" *Musikalisches Wochenblatt* [9]/25, 27, 44, 45 (14. and 24.6.; 25.10.;1.11.;1878) pp. 301–03, 321–22, 527–29, 539–41.

5395. *Shaw, see 5396.

5396. Shaw, [George] Bernard. *Shaw's Music. The Complete Musical Criticism.* Dan H. Laurence, ed. New York: Dodd, Mead, 1981. 3 vols. Includes concert reviews and comments on Brahms's music. Text of work includes all collections included in 2935 ([G.] B. Shaw. *The Great Composers. Reviews and Bombardments by Bernard Shaw.* (1978)), Shaw's *The Perfect Wagnerite* (London: Constable and Company Limited, 1930?) plus a large amount of uncollected writings. Arrangement is chronological by date of publication/writing, 1876–1938 is range covered.
  also: (The Bodley Head Bernard Shaw) London [et al.]: Max Reinhardt, The Bodley Head, 1981.
  2nd rev. ed.: (The Bodley Head Bernard Shaw) London: The Bodley Head, 1989. Adds more writings, makes corrections in text and index and adds annotations.
  (d) *Shaw, [George] Bernard. *Shaw on music.* Eric Bentley, ed. New York: Applause, 1995. ix, 307 pp.

5397. *Siegmund-Schultze, Ute. "Zur Geschichte der Brahms-Rezeption im deutschsprachigen Raum von 1853 bis 1914" Ph.D. diss., Musicology, Martin-Luther-Universität, Halle-Wittenberg, 1982. 303 pp. Focuses on the changing evaluations of Brahms's music and the reasons for these changing views. Identifies the different stages in the growth of Brahms's popularity. [from S102]

5398. "Stimmen zum 100. Geburtstag von Johannes Brahms (7. Mai 1933)" in *Verteidigung des musikalischen Fortschritts*. [for full citation see 3931] pp. 53–56. Excerpts from 2921 (A. Einstein. *Berliner Tageblatt* (1933)), 2931 (W. Furtwängler. "Johannes Brahms" (1933)), 5357, 5375, 5400, 5403, 5407 and Alban Berg. *Briefe an seine Frau*. Helene Berg, ed. (München, Wien: Albert Langen Georg Müller Verlag, 1965).

5399. Storey Smith, Warren. "Why Mahler, Too?" *Chord and Discord* 2/2 (11.1940) pp. 13–15. Remarks on the pairing of Bruckner and Mahler, pairing used to be Brahms and Bruckner versus Mahler and Strauss. Now Bruckner and Mahler are obscure, while stature of Brahms and Strauss is on the rise.

5400. *Strobel, Heinrich. *Berliner Börsen-Courier* (?.5.1933). (c) excerpt: in 5398.

5401. Tuck, Lon. "Brahms, With Reserve" *The Washington Post* 106/154 (8.5.1983) pp. H1, H6-H7. ill. Discusses Brahms as a reserved, subdued man whose impact is made through his craft as a composer.
   (a) reprint: Tuck. *Symphony Magazine* 34/3 (6./7.1983) pp. 28–31. adds facsim., notes.

5402. *"Two Views of Brahms" *Musical Courier* 30 (30.1.1895) pp. 22–23.

5403. *Unger, Hermann. *Völkischer Beobachter* (4.5.1933). (c) excerpt: in 5398.

5404. Watson, Derek. "Brahms" in *Chambers Music Quotations*. Edinburgh: W & R Chambers Ltd., 1991. pp. 125–27. notes. 19 quotes about Brahms; some from letters, most from other people on Brahms, including some contemporaries. Also et passim.

5405. Weber, Horst. ""Brahms, der fortschrittliche"? Zu Wirken und Wirkung in Wien" *Österreichische Musikzeitschrift* 40/6 (6.1985) pp. 300–06. notes. Reviews Brahms's reception from 1889–1933. Includes comment on Brahms's receiving the Ritterkreuz des österr-kaiserlichen Leopold Order, Brahms's influence on Viennese musical life, his leading on to newer music.

5406. Werker, Gerard. "Hugo Wolf als muziekcriticus" *Mens en melodie* 15/3 (3.1960) pp. 73–77. A discussion of Wolf's thoughts on Brahms's music, includes excerpts of writings.

5407. *Wörner, Karl. "Wir Jüngeren zu Brahms" *Deutsche allgemeine Zeitung* (Berlin) (?.5.1933).
(c) excerpt: in 5398.

5408. Youngren, William. "Aimez-vous Brahms?" *Fanfare* 7/1 (9./10.1983) pp. 74–81, 375–76. ill. In the context of a review of 3338, discusses how we view Brahms today; reviews the history of Brahms's reception.
(d) reworked: in 5058.

See also 3216, 3217, 3249, 3256, 3258, 3267, 3278, 3287, 3289, 3290, 3385, 3438, 3464, 3465, 3468, 3506, 3533, 3535, 3539, 3540, 3546, 3550, 3579, 3581, 3597.d., 3598, 3623, 3628, 3646, 3692, 3774, 3796, 3811.c., 3812, 3822, 3855.d., 3858, 3860, 3867, 3896, 3904, 3912, 3919.d.i., 3922, 3928–30, 3937, 3950, 3951, 3983, 3988, 3989, 4033, 4040, 4052, 4055, 4102, 4129, 4131, 4139, 4158, 4177, 4231, 4233, 4234, 4243, 4257, 4298, 4301, 4321, 4439, 4453, 4478, 4479, 4481, 4519, 4532, 4541, 4543, 4574, 4585, 4587, 4592, 4599, 4617, 4619, 4627, 4655, 4660, 4761.5, 4781, 4805, 4812, 4822, 4904, 4956, 4992, 4994, 5003, 5017, 5020, 5024, 5025, 5029, 5044, 5054, 5058, 5169, 5214, 5223, 5249, 5271, 5295, 5307, 5311–13, 5315, 5316, 5440, 5462.
See also "Bruckner", "Bülow", "Tschaikovsky", "Wagner" and "Wolf" in Part III.B.2.
See also I42 in Appendix A.

D. Memorial Activities

Contains materials that report on the commemoration of Brahms and his music by the building of memorials, founding of Brahms societies, assembling exhibits, etc.

Archives: 5409, 5429, 5430, 5432, 5436, 5441, 5448, 5459, 5473.

Concerts and Competitions: 5437, 5440, 5450.
Conferences, Colloquiums and Symposiums: 5421, 5422, 5424, 5425, 5428, 5431, 5434, 5438, 5453, 5458, 5462, 5472, 5476.
Exhibits: 5414, 5416, 5417, 5419, 5435, 5452, 5454, 5471, 5474.
Houses and Museums: 5439, 5447, 5457, 5465, 5466.
Memorials and Monuments (Hamburg or Wien): 5426, 5449.
Memorials and Monuments (other than Hamburg or Wien): 5451, 5461.
Plaques: 5415.
Publications and Studies: 5427, 5463, 5469.
Scholarships: 5433, 5445, 5446, 5455, 5456, 5475.
Societies (North America): 5410–12, 5423, 5444.
Societies (not North America): 5418, 5420, 5423, 5442, 5443, 5460, 5464, 5477.

5409. *Hamburger Abendblatt* [43] (1.3.1990).
   (b) English translation: "New Brahms Archive in Lübeck" *The American Brahms Society Newsletter* 8/1 (Spring 1990) p. 5. Announces establishment of the Brahms-Institut.

5410. "American Brahms Society Celebrates Tenth Anniversary" *The American Brahms Society Newsletter* 11/1 (Spring 1993) p. 7. An overview of the Society's activities.

5411. "American Brahms Society Founded" *The Triangle of Mu Phi Epsilon* 78/2 (Winter 1983–84) p. 2. Announcement.

5412. "American Brahms Society Officially Founded" *The American Brahms Society Newsletter* 1/2 (Autumn 1983) p. [1]. Describes the first full meeting of the Board of Directors, presents a summary of activities to be undertaken.

5413. Barter, Christie. "More Brahms and Other Anniversaries" *Stereo Review* 48/8 (8.1983) p. 106. Comments on sesquicentenary activities and reviews new recordings. Other "dead" composers with anniversaries in 1983 (Frescobaldi, Gibbons) have no new recordings, but living composers with anniversaries (Gould, Carter, Messiaen, L. Berkeley) have some.

5414. Bartlitz, Eveline. "Brahms in Berlin—einst und jetzt. Gedenkausstellung in der Deutschen Staatsbibliothek" *Musik und Gesellschaft* 33/7 (7.1983) pp. 422–24. ill., facsim. Describes memorial exhibition; also describes a visit by Brahms to the Deutsche Staatsbibliothek in 2.1868.

5415. Bernstein, Kenneth. *Music Lover's Europe: A Guidebook & Companion.* New York: Charles Scribner's Sons, 1983. [4], 202 pp. ind., appendixes.
Brahms: pp. 17, 18. Describes Brahms's grave and final dwelling in Wien.
Brahms: pp. 53–55. ill. Describes Brahms's childhood haunts, Brahms Memorial Rooms, and Brahms plaques.

5416. Biba, Otto. "Brahms-Ausstellung in Mürzzuschlag" *Österreichische Musikzeitschrift* 40/10 (10.1985) p. 533. Reports on exhibition, also comments on Brahms's connections with Mürzzuschlag.

5417. Biba, Otto. *Johannes Brahms in Wien. Ausstellung. Archiv der Gesellschaft der Musikfreunde in Wien. 19. April bis 30. Juni 1983. Katalog.* Wien: Gesellschaft der Musikfreunde in Wien, 1983. 80 pp. ill., facsim. 277 items. Catalogue of items with background and description of each. Exhibition covers time period 1862–97.
(e) report: Biba, Otto. "Ausstellung "Johannes Brahms in Wien" im Musikverein" *Österreichische Musikzeitschrift* 38/4–5 (4.–5.1983) p. 254. Reports on exhibition and its contents.

5418. Bozarth, George S. "The ABS [American Brahms Society] wishes to convey . . ." *The American Brahms Society Newsletter* 4/2 (Autumn 1986) p. [10]. Notes founding of Johannes-Brahms-Gesellschaft Schweizer Sektion in June 1986. Comments on Brahms's connections with Thun and reports on Sektion's founding festivities.

5419. Bozarth, George S. "Brahms Exhibits in the United States and Europe" *The American Brahms Society Newsletter* 1/2 (Autumn 1983) pp. [3–4]. Describes exhibits in Washington, DC, Austria (Wien, Gmunden), Germany (Karlsruhe, Ulm), England (London) and Switzerland. Includes comment on Brahms's connections with location, if relevant.

5420. Bozarth, George S. "A new Brahms Society . . ." *The American Brahms Society Newsletter* 6/1 (Spring 1988) pp. [9–10]. Reports on founding of Schleswig-Holstein Brahms-Gesellschaft and its proposed activities.

5421. Bozarth, George S. "On 11 December 1986 a Brahms Colloquium . . ." *The American Brahms Society Newsletter* 6/1 (Spring 1988) p. [10]. Reports on this Greek Colloquium and its presentations.

5422. Bozarth, George S. "Our colleagues in the Brahmsgesellschaft Baden-Baden . . ." *The American Brahms Society Newsletter* 4/2 (Autumn 1986) p. [10]. Reports on the Spring 1986 Brahms Symposium and announces the 1987 event.

5423. Bozarth, George S. [et al.] "Brahms Societies, Past and Present" *The American Brahms Society Newsletter* 2/2 (Autumn 1984) pp. [3–6]. ill. Details in chronological order the nature, history and accomplishments of the societies, includes addresses for those currently active. Particulars on 6 societies provided.
(d) see: 5284.

5424. "Brahms Conferences in London, Vienna, and Hamburg" *The American Brahms Society Newsletter* 1/1 (Spring 1983) p. [5]. Announcing the conferences and their themes.

5425. "Brahms Conferences, 1983" *The American Brahms Society Newsletter* 2/1 (Spring 1984) pp. [5–8]. ill. Reports on papers given, and any related musical activities.
Musgrave, Michael. "Brahms in Florence": p. [5].
Wolff, Christoph. "Kiel Symposium": pp. [5–6].
Ostwald, Peter [F.]. "Leipzig Conference": pp. [6–7].
Goertzen, Valerie [Woodring]. "Brahms-Kongreß Wien": pp. [7–8].

5426. "The Brahms Monument in Vienna" *Musical Courier* 45/20 (Whole no. 1181) (12.11.1902) p. 40. ill. Announces that Rudolph Weyrs's design has been picked, also shows Klinger's proposal.

5427. [Bozarth, George S.] "Brahms Studies: A Call for Papers" *The American Brahms Society Newsletter* 8/2 (Autumn 1990) p. 6. Announces continuation of series, with details on its content.
(d) Brodbeck, David [Lee]. "Brahms Studies: A Call for Papers" *The American Brahms Society Newsletter* 9/1 (Spring 1991) p. 4. Calls for contributions for the 1st volume.
(d) "Brahms Studies" *The American Brahms Society Newsletter* 11/1 (Spring 1993) p. 7. Announcement of 2nd volume.

5428. *Brahms und seine Zeit. Symposion Hamburg 1983.* Peter Petersen, Schriftleitung. (Hamburger Jahrbuch für Musikwissenschaft 7) Laaber: Laaber-Verlag, 1984. 279 pp. Contains 3 additional papers not given at the actual Symposium ('*'d in list). Contains:

3305, 3441, 3455, 3628*, 3692, 3762, 3866, 3950, 4022, 4179,
4226, 4329*, 4822, 4878, 4885*, 5008, 5343, 5367.d.ii.
(e) review: Spies, Claudio. *The American Brahms Society
Newsletter* 3/1 (Spring 1985) pp. [7–8].

5429. **Brahms-Institut an der Musikhochschule Lübeck. Die Sammlung
Hofmann.* Annegret Stein-Karnbach, ed. (Patrimonia 18) Berlin:
KulturStiftung der Länder, 1992. Contains listing of major hold-
ings and 5441, 5473.

5430. [Bozarth, George S.] "The Brahms-Institut in Lübeck . . ." in
[George S. Bozarth] "Communications" *The American Brahms
Society Newsletter* 10/1 (Spring 1992) p. 9. Reports of recent acquisition of Op. 115 manuscript by Institut and reviews its other
activities to date.

5431. *Brahms-Kongress Wien 1983. Kongressbericht.* Susanne Antonicek and Otto Biba, eds. Tutzing: Hans Schneider Verlag, 1988.
519 pp. Includes an assemblage of music criticism of contemporary appearances of Op. 68 by Ingrid Fuchs (see 4541), and a list
of the musical programmes held around the Congress. Papers by
Maria Párkai-Eckhardt on Goldmark; and Hartmut Wecker on
Brüll not cited. Contains: 3359.d., 3441.d.iii., 3456, 3468, 3471,
3473, 3533, 3645, 3679, 3741, 3775, 3812, 3820, 3832, 4031,
4167, 4250, 4253, 4292, 4365, 4428.d., 4541, 4634.d., 4672,
4862, 4947, 4965, 5027, 5130, 5143.d.v.d., 5342, 5359.

5432. *"Brahms-Sammlung in Lübeck" *Neue Musikzeitung* 39
(4.–5.1990) p. 2.

5433. Brodbeck, David [Lee]. "First Geiringer Scholarship Awarded"
The American Brahms Society Newsletter 9/1 (Spring 1991) p. 4.
Announces award to Heather Platt [see 5101].
(d) "Second Geiringer Scholarship Awarded" *The American
Brahms Society Newsletter* 10/1 (Spring 1992) p. 4. Announces award to Margaret Notley [see 4131].
(d) see: 5475.

5434. [Bruckner Symposion (5th: 1983: Linz, Austria).] *Bruckner Symposion: Johannes Brahms und Anton Bruckner. Im Rahmen des
Internationalen Brucknerfestes Linz 1983, 8.–11. September
1983. Bericht.* Othmar Wessely, ed. Linz: Anton Bruckner-
Institut; Linz: Linzer Veranstaltungsgesellschaft; Graz: Kommis-

sionsverlag, Akademische Druck- und Verlagsanstalt, 1985. 250 pp. Not all papers are cited. Contains: 3609.e.ii., 3621, 3642, 3725, 3732, 3737, 3740, 4239, 4433, 4545, 5016, 5026, 5066, 5350.

5435. Carr, Jay. "Brahms 'Fanatic' Collector has even a lock of his hair" *The Detroit News* 107/193 (2.3.1980) pp. 1C, 7C. ill. Reports on exhibition during Detroit Brahms Festival, describes some items; includes comment on Kurt Hofmann, his interest and the extent of his collection of Brahmsiana. [Exhibition catalogue is 3109 (K. Hofmann and J. Fürst. *Johannes Brahms. The Man and His Work.* (1980))]

(a) reprint: Carr. *Johannes Brahms. The Man and His Work.* Detroit: n.p., [1980]. 4 pp. Includes details on where materials were borrowed from and the exhibition's hours.

5436. Clayton, Alfred. "The Brahms House" *Musical Times* 132/1781 (7.1991) p. 360. Reports on the official opening of the Brahms-Institut (Lübeck), describes the collection and its provenance from the Hofmanns, and reports on proposed activities.

5437. "Concert in Music Hall on the Sixteenth (sic) Anniversary of his Birth" *Presto* (Chicago) 9 (11.5.1893) p. 13.

5438. "Conferences Mark Brahms Sesquicentenary" *The American Brahms Society Newsletter* 1/2 (Autumn 1983) pp. [1–2]. ill. Summarizes conferences held up to early October 1983.

Frisch, Walter [M.]. "Washington Brahms Conference": pp. [1–2]. Summary of types of papers presented and details on Festival performances.

Hiebert, Elfrieda F. "England Honors Brahms": p. [2]. Summary of conference proceedings and performances.

5439. Dane, Jeffrey. "Remembering Brahms" *Classical Music Magazine* 17/2 (4.1994) pp. 18–22. ill., facsim. Describes a visit to the Brahms Museum in Mürzzuschlag, describes what's there. Includes comment on Brahms's visits to the town and Brahms the man.

5440. Dawson, Eric. "City will pay own tribute to Brahms" *Calgary Herald* (30.9.1983) p. F1. ill., facsim. Announces chamber music series to celebrate the sesquicentenary. Includes comment on Brahms the composer, his place in music history, his early years.

(d) "Brahms concert series lineup" *Calgary Herald* (30.9.1983) p. F2. Presents the programme for the series.

5441. *Debryn, Carmen. "'. . . und plotzlich hatte mich das Sammelfieber gepackt . . .': Der Sammler Kurt Hofmann und die Entstehung der 'Sammlung Hofmann'." in 5429.

5442. *"Dokumente der Geschichte der Wiener Brahms-Gesellschaft in Xerokopie" Wien: Archiv der Gesellschaft der Musikfreunde, n.d.

5443. Fellinger, Imogen. "Die Brahms-Gesellschaft in Wien (1904–1938)" in *Musikkulturgeschichte. Festschrift für Constantin Floros zum 60. Geburtstag.* [for full citation see 4342] pp. 573–86. ill., notes. Presents a history of the group, its commemorative activities, where its materials are today.

5444. "Foundation of the American Brahms Society" *The American Brahms Society Newsletter* 1/1 (Spring 1983) p. [1]. Reports on its founding, its purpose and goals, its activities both proposed and to date.

5445. "The Geiringer Scholarship Fund. One Last Step!" *The American Brahms Society Newsletter* 13/2 (Autumn 1995) p. 6. ill. Reports on latest total with exhortation to reach its stated financial goal. For earlier see 5446.
    (d) "The Geiringer Scholarship Fund. The Last Step Taken!" *The American Brahms Society Newsletter* 14/1 (Spring 1996) p. 5. ill. Reports that the goal is reached, reviews history of the fund's establishment.

5446. "The Geiringer Scholarship Fund. Our Goal is in Sight!" *The American Brahms Society Newsletter* 12/1 (Spring 1994) p. 4. Reports on latest total. For earlier see 5456.
    (d) "The Geiringer Scholarship Fund" *The American Brahms Society Newsletter* 13/1 (Spring 1995) p. 4. ill. Reports on progress.
    (d) continued by: 5445.

5447. *Hausa, Otto. "Das Brahms-Museum in Mürzzuschlag" *Musikerziehung* 47 (12.1993) pp. 83–85.

5448. *Hofmann, Kurt. "Die Sammlung Hofmann im Brahms-Institut an der Musikhochschule Lübeck" in *Almanach 1991: Schleswig-Holstein Musik Festival.* Christoph Caesar, ed. Kiel: Schleswig-Holstein Musik Festival, 1991. pp. 72–81.

5449. Imbert, Hugues. "Elle est fort éloignée de nous . . ." *Le Guide Mu-*

sical 44/23–24 (5 et 12.6.1898) pp. 488–89. Brahms: p. 489. Announces that a committee has been struck in Vienna to raise a monument.

(d) Imbert. "Monument a la mémoire de Johannes Brahms" *Le Guide Musical* 44/40 (2.10.1898) pp. 711–12. Exhorts the French to buy subscriptions for the monument and explains why.

(d) Imbert. "Le Monument a la mémoire de Johannès Brahms" *Le Guide Musical* 44/48 (27.11.1898) p. 901. Includes list of subscribers to date, and more background on Brahms the composer.

5449.5. [International Brahms Congress. (1980: Detroit, MI) *Proceedings*. Presented by the Detroit Symphony Orchestra, Wayne State University, and the University of Michigan School of Music; Ellwood S. Derr, Congress Program Chairman.] Congress proceedings not published to date [1996], however many presenters have published on their topic elsewhere: (296, 5111) (M.L. McCorkle on research in Brahms studies), (995.d., 5027) (S. Kross on Brahms and E.T.A. Hoffmann), 1187 (P. Susskind Pettler on Brahms and Clara Schumann), 1457 (P. Gülke on Schoenberg transcribing Brahms), (1485, 2145, 3410) (I. Fellinger on Brahms's compositional process), (2040, 4037, 4714) (G.S. Bozarth on Brahms's sketches), 2353.d. (P. Mast on *Oktaven und Quinten* [McCorkle Anhang Va, nr. 6]), 3455, 4092, 4564, 4575, 4833, 4835, and 4970. Papers by R. Bailey, W. E. Benjamin [referred to in 4863], C. Burkhart, H. Haack, G. Lazarevich, R.T. Oliver, E. Sams, not published to date. [from 5255.5 pp. [95–96] and compilor]

5450. [Zinnow, Ingrid.] "Die Internationalen Brahms-Wettbewerbe. Eine Dokumentation" *Brahms-Studien* Bd. 10 (1994) pp. 61–73. Lists the details for the first 6, 1983–1994.

5451. "Johannes Brahms" in *Die Großen Deutschen im Bild*. Alfred Hentzen and Niels v. Holst, eds. Berlin: Propyläen-Verlag, 1936. p. 349. ind. Illustration of the Bronze-Sitzbild from Berlin Sing-Akademie, created by Reinhold Felderhoff in 1916.

5452. *Johannes Brahms in Baden-Baden und Karlsruhe. Eine Ausstellung der Badischen Landesbibliothek Karlsruhe und der Brahmsgesellschaft Baden-Baden e.V.* Ausstellungskatalog herausgegeben von der Badischen Landesbibliothek Karlsruhe unter Mitarbeit von Joachim Draheim, Ludwig Finscher, Frithjof Haas, Klaus Häfner, Jeannot Heinen, Brigitte Höft and Ekkehard Schulz. Klaus Häfner, Redaktion. Karlsruhe: Badischen Landesbibliothek, 1983. 184 pp. ill., facsim., fig., notes. Exhibition catalogue: 192 items, focuses on Brahms's times in Baden-Baden, his circle there. Includes Zeittafel (Draheim). Contains: 3551, 3555, 3573, 3620, 3753, 3851, 4542, 4846, 5215.

5453. *Johannes Brahms: Leben, Werk, Interpretation, Rezeption. Kongressbericht zum III. [Internationales] Gewandhaus-Symposium anlässlich der "Gewandhaus-Festtage 1983."* Kurt Masur, ed. (Dokumente zur Gewandhausgeschichte 4) Leipzig: Gewandhaus zu Leipzig, Edition Peters, 1985. 116 pp. ill., notes. Contains: 3441.d.ii., 3550.d., 3616, 3650, 3656, 3959.d.ii., 3961, 4012.d., 4085, 4153, 4929, 5024, 5377.

5454. **Johannes Brahms: 1833–1897.** *Sonderausstellung der Kammerhofmuseum der Stadt Gmunden. Ausstellungsdauer: 16. April–26. Oktober 1983.* Elfriede Prillinger, ed. Gmunden: Eigenverlag des Kammerhofmuseum der Stadt Gmunden, 1983. 43 pp. ill. Exhibition catalogue; also includes a biographical outline and a chronology. Exhibition is based on the collection of Victor and Olga von Miller zu Aichholz. [from S102]

5455. [Bozarth, George S.] "The Karl Geiringer Scholarship in Brahms Studies" *The American Brahms Society Newsletter* 7/1 (Spring 1989) p. 6. Reports on scholarship being established, its purpose and the criteria for application.
(d) Bozarth, George S. "The Geiringer Scholarship Fund: A Progress Report" *The American Brahms Society Newsletter* 9/1 (Spring 1991) p. 4. Advises current fund total.
(d) continued by: 5456.

5456. "The Karl Geiringer Scholarship in Brahms Studies" *The American Brahms Society Newsletter* 9/2 (Autumn 1991) pp. 4–5. Includes a progress report on fund total, and a call for applications for 1992. For earlier see 5455.
(d) "A Progress Report on the Geiringer Scholarship Fund" *The American Brahms Society Newsletter* 11/1 (Spring 1993) p. 8. States current total and encourages additional contributions.
(d) continued by: 5446.

5457. Laude, Maria Elena. "The Beautiful House on the Hill: Summer at the Brahms house Baden-Baden" *Music Clubs Magazine* 71/4 (Summer 1992) pp. 12–13. ill. (also on cover). Author describes her experience as artist-in-residence in the house, describes the house and its contents. Includes comment on Brahms at Baden-Baden, Brahms and Clara Schumann, also Brahms the man.

5458. "The Library of Congress will host..." *Notes* 39/3 (3.1983) p. 592. Announcement of International Brahms Conference, includes information on related events, sponsors, topics to be discussed.

5458.5. *Linzer Musikinstrumente der Brucknerzeit. Johannes Brahms und Anton Bruckner. Konkurrenten.* (ABIL [Anton-Bruckner-Institut Linz]—Information[en(?)] 2) Linz: Anton-Bruckner-Institut Linz, 1983. Exhibition catalogue. Includes 3733. [from S102]

5459. Meyer, Martin. "Ein Besuch im Lübecker Brahms-Institut" *Brahms-Studien* Bd. 9 (1992) pp. 29–35. Describes the facility and holdings and presents Hofmann's background on how he got started as a Brahms collector.

5460. *Miller zu Aichholz, Eugen von. "Brahms-Gesellschaft in Wien. Jahresberichte 1904–1919" Wien: n.p., n.d.

5461. *Müller-Dombois, Richard. "Die Brahms-Plastik im Brahms-Saal der Musikhochschule Detmold: Eine Dokumentation ihrer Vor- und Entstehungsgeschichte" *Lippische Mitteilungen aus der Geschichte und Landeskunde* 61 (1992). Documents this project. [from S102]

5462. Musgrave, Michael. "Brahms: Sesquicentenary Reflections" *Musical Times* 124/1690 (12.1983) pp. 746–47. Compares interest in Brahms now to back in 1933. Reviews conferences held, particularly those in Washington, DC, and London.

5463. Obermair, Walter. "Ein geplantes Brahms-Album 1922" *Brahms-Studien* Bd. 5 (1983) pp. 169–79. notes. Background to a Viennese proposal for an album of Brahms reminiscences in 1922. Only 6 items were submitted, 3 of them published here for the first time: "Josef Kromnitzer: Johannes Brahms und der »rote Igel«": pp. 170–74. Describes the tenor of the place, the type of customers, the food and Brahms as a guest.
"Edmund Reim": p. 174. In 1889 he asked Brahms to write a piece for the Wiener Männergesangverein. Brahms refused.

"Adolf Kirchl: Eine kleine Erinnerung an Brahms": pp. 175–77. March 1895 he was involved in a performance of Op. 50. He visited Brahms at this time, they discussed the performance.

5464. [Bozarth, George S.] "On 2 December 1991 . . ." in [Bozarth, George S.] "Communications" *The American Brahms Society Newsletter* 10/1 (Spring 1992) p. 9. Records the 25th anniversary of Brahmsgesellschaft Baden-Baden, with a note of its current and proposed projects.

5465. Prillinger, Elfriede. "Johannes Brahms und Gmunden. (Die Sammlung Miller-Aichholz im Gmundner Kammerhofmuseum)" *Brahms-Studien* Bd. 5 (1983) pp. 181–95. ill., notes. A history of Miller zu Aichholz's founding of a Brahms-Museum, with some background on him, and how it joined the Gmunden Kammerhofmuseum der Stadt. Presents an overview of the inventory.

(d) continued: Prillinger. "Johannes Brahms und Gmunden. (Die Sammlung Miller-Aichholz im Gmundner Kammerhofmuseum). II. Teil" *Brahms-Studien* Bd. 6 (1985) pp. 75–87. A detailed look at the portraits section (Brahms and his family, Brahms's circle of friends).

5466. Rich, Maria F. "A Brahms Museum Discovered" *American Record Guide* 56/3 (5./6.1993) pp. 26–27. ill. Describes the museum and its history. Includes comments on Brahms's links to Mürzzuschlag, and the Brahms society there.

5467. Richter, Christoph. "Das Jahr 1983 bietet reiche Gelegenheit . . ." *Musik und Bildung* 15/5 (Bd. 74) (5.1983) p. 3. Discusses Brahms Sesquicentenary and compares him to Ligeti as to how appropriate either might be as a school lesson subject.

5468. *Rohnacher, Ilse. "Wie aus einem Brahms-Klavier ein Fronleichnamsaltar wurde" *Stadtteil-Rundschau Ziegelhausen Peterstal* Woche 24 (15.6.1984).

5469. Rueter, William. "Johannes Brahms. Detmold, September 1859. Eigen war's mir . . . = I was overcome . . . " [Limited edition] Yvonne Kotin, trans. William Rueter, printer. Toronto: The Aliquando Press, 1983. broadsheet: 8 1/2" x 14"; one side only. Produced for the sesquicentennial, consists of this letter [Brahms to ?; source of letter is ?] in parallel translation, illustrated by a drawing of Brahms's head superimposed on a landscape background.

5470. *Sanders, Paul F. "Brahmsherdenking" *[De] Muziek* (Amsterdam) 7 (5.1933) pp. 337–42.

5471. Stefan, Paul. "Seeing Brahms Through Mementos of His Life" *Musical America* 53/10 (25.5.1933) p. 66. facsim. Reports on A-Wgm exhibition and its contents. [Exhibition catalogue is 3093 (Gesellschaft der Musikfreunde in Wien. Museum. *J. Brahms Zentenar-Ausstellung* . . . (1934))]

5472. *Steinbeck, W[olfram]. "Brahms-Symposion 1983 in Kiel" *Der Landesmusikrat Schleswig-Holstein informiert* no. 5 (1983).

5473. *Struck, Michael. "Struktur, Inhalte und Bedeutung der 'Sammlung Hofmann'." in 5429.

5474. Szomory, György. "Brahms Bécsben" *Muzsika* [26]/10 (10.1983) pp. 37–38. ill. Report on the A-Wgm exhibition; includes comment on Brahms and Vienna.

5475. "Third Annual Geiringer Scholarship Awarded" *The American Brahms Society Newsletter* 11/1 (Spring 1993) p. 8. Announcement of award to Daniel Beller-McKenna [see 5080]. For earlier awards see 5433.

(d) "Fourth Annual Geiringer Scholarship Awarded" *The American Brahms Society Newsletter* 12/1 (Spring 1994) p. 4. Announcement of award to Dillon Parmer. [see 5188]

5476. Zimmermann, Werner G. "Ein Brahms-Symposium in Assisi. Referate und Konzerte in der umbrischen Stadt" *Neue Zürcher Zeitung* no. 200 (29.8.1983) [2 pp.] Reports on papers given and musical events.

5477. Zinnow, Ingrid. "25 Jahre Johannes Brahms-Gesellschaft Hamburg" *Brahms-Studien* Bd. 10 (1994) pp. 57–59. Reports on Gesellschaft's purpose and its activities.

See also 3299, 3302.d., 3303, 3432.5, 3441.d.i., 3445, 3457, 3470, 3475, 3530, 3539, 3545, 3551, 3559, 3576, 3646, 3838, 3840, 3884, 4231, 4993, 5236, 5277, 5282, 5289–94, 5297, 5299, 5348, 5480, 5481.
See also I12, I30, I32, I44 in Appendix A.

E. Publications

1. Brahms Festschriften

See 5428, 5431.

a. Monographs

5478. *Brahms and His World.* Walter [M.] Frisch, ed. Princeton:

Princeton University Press, 1990. viii, [2], 3–233 pp. ind., appendixes.

paperback edition: 1990. Includes English translations of contemporary remembrances of Brahms and analyses of Brahms works. Appendix lists works of art, books, and musical compositions that were dedicated to Brahms. Contains: 3459, 3605.d.d., 3632, 3650.d.i., 3802, 3827, 3959.d.i.d., 4032, 4074, 4084, 4480, 4595, 5116.d.

(e) i) report: Bozarth, George S. "New Books on Brahms" *The American Brahms Society Newsletter* 8/2 (Autumn 1990) pp. 8–9. 3 items, focuses on *Brahms and His World.*

(e) ii) *review: Holloway, Robin. "A World of Private Meanings" *Times Literary Supplement* no. 4612 (23.8.1991) p. 16. Includes review of 5480. [from S083]

5479. *Brahms: Biographical, Documentary and Analytical Studies.* Robert Pascall, ed. Cambridge [et al.]: Cambridge University Press, 1983. viii, 212 pp. Contains: 3647, 3871, 4387, 4481.b., 4582, 4622, 4714, 4743, 5113, 5143.d.vi.

5480. *Brahms Studies: Analytical and Historical Perspectives. Papers delivered at the International Brahms Conference Washington, DC 5–8 May 1983.* George S. Bozarth, ed. Oxford: Clarendon Press, 1990. xvii, [3], 472 pp. ind. A collection of studies based on papers delivered at the 1983 International Brahms Conference. Only 22 of 24 papers are represented here, papers by Gordana Lazarevitch and Otto Biba are not included. (See 5289 for all abstracts) "Few appear essentially as presented, most have been expanded, a number into full-length research studies." Preface contains an overview of Brahms research and descriptions of the papers included. Contains: 3625.a., 3927, 4429.d., 4430, 4581, 4590, 4605, 4654, 4895, 4910, 4929.b., 4954, 4959, 4971, 4978, 5030, 5089, 5112, 5143.d.i., 5147, 5160, 5185.

(d) continued by: 5481.

(e) i) announcement: [Bozarth, George S.] "ABS's Brahms Studies Due for Publication This Spring" *The American Brahms Society Newsletter* 8/1 (Spring 1990) p. 5. Includes detail on contents and work's background.

(e) ii) review: Daverio, John. "Themes and Variations" *19th Century Music* 15/3 (Spring 1992) pp. 246–54. notes.

(e) iii) review: see 3325.

(e) iv) *review: see 5478.e.ii.

(e) v) report: see 5380.

(e) vi) review: Rink, John. *Music & Letters* 73/2 (5.1992) pp. 301–07.

5481. *Brahms 2: Biographical, Documentary, and Analytical Studies.* Michael Musgrave, ed. Cambridge [et al.]: Cambridge University Press, 1987. x, 252 pp. ind., appendixes. Continues 5480. This collection publishes the papers of the 1983 London Brahms Conference. Contains: 3383, 3489, 3535, 3539.a., 4232.a., 4234, 4236, 4618, 4860, 4982, 5009, 5143.d.iv., 5369.

(e) report: Braus, Ira [Lincoln]. *Journal of Music Theory* 34/1 (Spring 1990) pp. 108–19. mus., fig., notes. Essentially a critique of this work, but focuses on 4232.a., 4618, 4982.

See also 3215.

b. Periodical Issues

5482. *Allgemeine Musikzeitung* 64/13/14 (26.3.1937) pp. 177–211. Brahms: pp. 177–87. ill. (on cover).
"Brahms=Sonderheft": Contains 812.d.ii.a. (E. Behm. "Studien bei Brahms"), 1996.a. (K. Huschke. "Vom Wesen der letzten Brahms-Symphonie"), 2467 (W. Furtwängler. "Johannes Brahms"), 2518 (R. Tenschert. "Zur Frage der Brahmsschen Instrumentation"), 2888 (W. Abendroth. "Brahms' Bedeutung . . .").

5483. *The American Organist* 17/5 (5.1983) pp. 40–48.
"Johannes Brahms 1833–1897. 150th Anniversary": Contains: 3687, 4431, 5143.d.iii.

5484. **L'Avant-scène opera operette musique* no. 53 (1983). 157 pp. ill., mus., notes.
"Johannes Brahms. Les Symphonies" Contains: 3379, 4455, 4869.5.

5485. *Diapason* (Paris) no. 283 (5.1983) pp. 31–36, 38–39. ill. (on cover).
"Brahms a 150 ans": Contains: 3347, 3624, 4312, 4569, 5387.

5486. *Musica* 37/1 (1./2.1983) pp. [1]–39. [100 pp. total].
"Wagner und Brahms": Contains: 4012, 4017, 4147 + other articles only on Wagner.

5487. *Musical Quarterly* 69/4 (Fall 1983) pp. 463–621. Brahms: pp. 463–542. Contains: 4232, 4575, 4835, 5142.

5488. *The Musical Times* 124/1683 (5.1983) pp. 284–94. ill. (on cover). [Section title:] "Johannes Brahms born 7 May 1833": Contains: 3934, 5111, 5145.

5489. *Musik und Bildung* 15/5 (Bd. 74) (5.1983) pp. 1–72. Brahms: pp. 1–16. ill. (on cover). "Johannes Brahms zum 150. Geburtstag": Contains: 3329, 3653.5, 4500, 5393, 5467.

5490. *Musik und Gesellschaft* 33/5 (5.1983) pp. 257–320. Brahms: pp. 257–85. "Johannes Brahms zum 150. Geburtstag": Contains: 3567, 4014, 4492, 5021, 5048.

5491. *Die Musikforschung* 36/4 (10.–12.1983) pp. 177–211. Contains: 4542.d., 4634.

5492. *Neue Zürcher Zeitung* [Literatur und Kunst Beilage] no. 106 (7/.8.5.1983) pp. 65–70. Brahms: pp. 65–68. ill. Includes short summary of Brahms's life and 3338.e.i., 3597.d.i., 3667, 3818, 4011, 4592, 5042.

5493. *19th Century Music* 18/1 (Summer 1994) 84 pp. Brahms: pp. 10–45. "Brahms-Liszt-Wagner": Contains: 4233, 4966.

5494. *Österreichische Musikzeitschrift* 38/4–5 (4.–5.1983) pp. 218–54. "Johannes Brahms zum 150. Geburtstag": Contains: 3299.b., 3302.d.ii., 3442, 3457, 5123, 5417.e., 5370.

5495. *Sovetskaia muzyka* [47]/8 (8.1983) 144 pp. Brahms: pp. 98–107. "Otmechaia 150-letie so dnia rozhdeniia Johannesa Bramsa": Contains: 4486, 4508.

See also 4455.

2. Brahms Serials

5496. [American Brahms Society, The.] *The American Brahms Society Newsletter.* 1– . (1983–). ill.

5497. "Bisher erschienene Brahms-Studien" *Brahms-Studien* Bd. 9–
(1992–). A cumulative listing of contents for all *Brahms-Studien*
Bände.

5498. *Brahms Studies*. 1– . (1994–). "In affiliation with the American
Brahms Society."
(e) i) announcement: Brodbeck, David [Lee]. "Brahms Studies"
The American Brahms Society Newsletter 12/1 (Spring 1994)
p. 5. Announces publication of vol. 1 by University of Nebraska Press.
(e) ii) report (on vol. 1): see 4561.b.e.
(e) iii) report (on vol. 1): see 3317.

5499. *Nihon Brahms Kyokai [Japan Brahms Society]. *Akai harinezumi*
= *Zum roten Igel*. no. 1– . (1973–). The Society's annual publication.

5500. *Nihon Brahms Kyokai [Japan Brahms Society]. *Botschaft*. no.
1– . (197?–). The Society's newsletter publication.

Appendix A

Brahms and the Internet

I. Johannes Brahms in Cyberspace*: an informal survey of Brahms on the Internet

by Thomas Quigley and Mary I. Ingraham
(with thanks to Virginia Hancock for her advice and comments)

While the thought of juxtaposing Brahms with the Internet (a.k.a. the Information Superhighway) may cause sharp intakes of breath among some of our readers, the authors hasten to assure you that Brahms and new technologies are wholly compatible. Indeed, if we look at the man himself, there are a number of instances in his life where his own interests in new discoveries are apparent: for example, his interest in the Edison phonograph. Brahms's friend Joseph Widmann writes that the composer was delighted with "even the smallest discovery, every improvement in any sort of gadget for domestic use; in short, every sign of human reflection, if it was accompanied by practical success."[1]

Cyberspace is such a juncture of progress (it's fast and pervasive) and practicability (it's easy, and it works). The purpose of this article is to report on your intrepid authors' routing in the Internet in quest of Brahmsiana. We have returned—not unaffected, but unscathed, and somewhat surprised by our findings. Let us begin, then, with a short review.

---

*Words followed by an asterisk are defined in the Glossary following the notes.

There are many ways to access information on the Internet, depending on your equipment and interests:

1. one-to-one: direct E-mail* correspondence;
2. one-to-several: subscribing to a Listserv*;
3. one-to-no one in particular: downloading* databases, graphics or text files, computer software programs, etc. from a remote computer;
4. one-to-thousands: accessing public computer Bulletin Boards*;
5. one-to-the-world: World Wide Web*—fast, graphic, sophisticated; accesses ANYTHING on the Internet.

We found the most common invoking of The Master's Name occurs wherever two or more people have gathered together for electronic conversation in Usenet* groups. Usenet groups like REC.MUSIC.CLASSICAL and REC.MUSIC.CLASSICAL.RECORDINGS are peppered with references[2]; a survey in the former of most-talked-about composers in that particular group showed Brahms to be in the Top 5.

So what is everybody talking about? Many of the postings express opinions on his music. Some positively, such as the person who wrote on the beauty of the late solo piano works, others negatively, such as one who wrote comparing Brahms's First Symphony to a "constipated elephant." Others are just as strongly convinced of the merits of a particular recording or interpretation of Brahms's music. We also found that Brahms has not been missed in the "flame* wars" arena, particularly in respect to his standing versus that of his musical contemporaries.

Brahms the man also surfaces as a topic in postings to Usenet groups. One thread* in particular dealt with his personal relationship to Clara Schumann and included reference to the theory first put forward in the 1920's that Felix Schumann was their "love-child." Sadly, this thread was short-lived.

A review of Listservs shows similar types of postings, but can also include more serious ruminations. For example, in a thread on AMSLIST that speculates on possible winners of a hypothetical Nobel Prize in Music, Brahms was put forward as a possible candidate for the prize; on PIANO-L Brahms was mentioned in the context of commemorative anniversary piano recital programming.[3]

Announcements of performances of Brahms's music appear "etherwhere," too. Surfing* these waves uncovers sites for the complete programmes for commemorative 1997 Brahms Centenary Festivals in Hamburg and New York, as well as pages for smaller regional and local annual events. Listings for orchestral seasons worldwide can be reviewed to see who's playing what, where and when; the why is never in question!

Many public and academic library catalogs are now available on the

Internet, making preliminary research simpler and easier. Periodical indexing services like CARL and FirstSearch can also be found in various Gopher* sites, enabling Brahms researchers to keep abreast of what's being published. Brahms turns up in MLA-L[4] occasionally, usually in relation to library cataloguing practices, or where to buy, or borrow through inter-library loan, particular editions of his music.

We've noted references to Brahms throughout Usenet and Listservs; your authors were particularly interested in whether there were any Internet sites that contained Brahms information, exclusively or otherwise. The list of resources that follows this article demonstrates that there are numerous sites whose owners have either created and now maintain Brahmsiana or provide links to it in other parts of the Internet. Currently there are several sites exclusive to Brahms, the most extensive having been developed by coauthor Ingraham. The "Johannes Brahms Web-Source" includes biographical information and a works list; as well as an "Image Gallery"; information on Brahms Societies, Scholars, Festivals and Special Events; plus audio clips from recordings, and an annotated "Webography" of Web resources.[5] Will there be more? Undoubtedly. Will they be easy to find? Certainly. Possible strategies for keeping abreast include periodically searching Kovacs's "Directory of Scholarly Electronic Conferences"[6], checking on the Gopher at the Library of Congress Internet site[7], or utilizing one of the more comprehensive search engines* to sweep the entire Internet for Brahms information.[8]

This then concludes our quick look at Brahms on the Net. If you have any comments or questions, we invite you to contact us at our e-mail addresses: Thomas Quigley (thomqui@vcn.bc.ca) and Mary I. Ingraham (icrmdpo@istar.ca)

Notes

1. Joseph Widmann, *Johannes Brahms in Erinnerungen* (Berlin, 1898), p. 58; cited in English by Leon Botstein, "Time and Memory: Concert Life, Science, and Music in Brahms's Vienna," in *Brahms and His World,* ed. by Walter Frisch (Princeton, 1990), p. 3.

2. Because of the ephemeral nature of most Internet discussions, and the fact that most discussions in Listservs and Usenet groups are not archived, no attempt has been made to provide documentation of our observations.

3. AMSLIST and PIANO-L are the names of two Listservs. AMS-LIST is for the discussion of items of interest to the membership of the

American Musicological Society and anything on the topic of music history in general. PIANO-L is a list for pianists and piano teachers to discuss topics of interest to them. To subscribe to AMSLIST send an e-mail to <listproc@ucdavis.edu>; to subscribe to PIANO-L send an e-mail to <piano-l-request@uamont.edu>. In both cases the e-mail should have a blank subject line, and the only thing in the message should be "subscribe <name of listserv> <your firstname lastname>."

4. MLA-L is a Listserv for discussing topics of interest to members of the Music Library Association, and for discussing topics of interest to the music library community in general. To subscribe to MLA-L send an e-mail to <listserv@iubvm.ucs.indiana.edu>. See endnote 3 for what to put in the e-mail.

5. Ingraham, Mary I. "Johannes Brahms WebSource" <http://web20.mindlink.net/a4369/brahms/> January, 1997. [Information inside <>'s is the URL*.] See the Webography following the Glossary for reference to the other exclusive sites.

6. Kovacs, Diane K. and The Directory Team (sic). 9th Revision. 1995. Accessible through the World Wide Web at: <gopher://una.hh.lib.umich.edu/inetdirs>.

7. Accessible through the World Wide Web at <gopher://marvel.loc.gov>.

8. There are many search engines available. Three of the more familiar (and their respective URL's) are: Alta Vista at <http://www.altavista.digital.com/>; Webcrawler at <http://webcrawler.com>; and Yahoo at <http://www.yahoo.com>. Metasearch* engines are also appearing on the World Wide Web. Two examples (with URL's) include: Inference Find at <http://www.inference.com/ifind>; and Metacrawler at <http://www.metacrawler.com/index.html>.

Glossary

Bulletin Board: a local distribution point for electronic data and files, usually accessed by dialing in with your computer, via modem, to a local access telephone number. Actually the precursor of the Internet, Boards provide many of the same resources and functions, albeit on a much smaller scale.

Cyberspace: the operating environment of networked computers. The term "Internet" refers to the overall network of the networks, "Cyberspace" is the term used to describe where all the activity takes place.

Downloading: copying something from one computer to another, from a remote computer to your personal computer.

E-mail: electronic mail; the sending and receiving of these messages over a network. E-mailing is not exclusive to the Internet.

Flame: an angry or rude response posted to a Usenet group or Listserv. A "flame war" occurs when users rant at each other.

Gopher: a tool on the Internet that allows users to select network resources from an on-screen menu, thereby eliminating the need to know individual Internet addresses, site-specific passwords and commands. A Gopher's presentation and content is unique to the individual site that creates it.

Listserv: an e-mail discussion list on a particular topic. Listservs are joined by subscribing to them, all messages posted to the Listserv are received by all subscribers.

Metasearch engine: a program which attempts to help its user find desired information or resources on the Internet by sending queries to a group of World Wide Web search engines. Metasearch engines differ from search engines in that they do not maintain their own database of keywords or concepts. Rather, they rely on the databases of other Web-based sources. For example, the program MetaCrawler sends its queries to a group of search engines that includes Lycos, Infoseek, WebCrawler, Excite, Alta Vista, and Yahoo. In a typical Metasearch engine result, findings are organized into a uniform format, and ranked by relevance. (See also Search engine)

Search engine: a program which attempts to help its user find desired information or resources, by searching the Internet for keywords or concepts that the user specifies. Examples include Lycos, Infoseek, WebCrawler, Excite, Alta Vista, and Yahoo. (See also Metasearch engine)

Surfing: browsing on the Internet, going wherever your fancy leads you. The term seems to have acquired negative connotations these days, perhaps because of close ties to mindless TV "channel surfing," which is made possible courtesy of the television remote control.

Thread: the ongoing discussion of a topic in a Listserv or Usenet group. Threads are identified by the continued use of the "subject:" line of the original e-mail in any response.

URL: Uniform Resource Locator; phrase used to designate addresses for sites on the World Wide Web.

Usenet: an area in the Internet that contains public discussion groups on thousands of topics. Each group "lives" on a particular computer. In contrast to Listservs, Usenet groups are public domain—they can be read by anyone, can be posted to by anyone. Access to Usenet groups is controlled by the "Internet Service Provider" that one uses to access the Internet.

World Wide Web: a.k.a. the Web, WWW, W3, an area in the Internet that contains information organized by subject; the information is created in a format called hypertext, which allows for document text to serve as a link to other related information sources. Users "jump" from one document to another by using these created links. The World Wide Web is currently the fastest growing area in the Internet.

II. Internet Sites

The purpose of this selected list of sites is to show the range of what is available on the Internet in regards to Brahms. As is the nature of this technology, what there is, is always in flux.

A. Selected Internet Sites for General Music Resources

I1. URL: http://musdra.ucdavis.edu/Documents/AMS/musicology_www.html
Brill, Mark and Rhio H. Barnhart. "[American Musicological Society] WWW Sites of Interest to Musicologists" December 20, 1996.

I2. URL: http://www.klassik.com/
"Klassik Online—Sprungbrett in die Welt der klassischen Musik" 1997.

I3. URL: http://www.sun.rhbnc.ac.uk/Music/Links/index.html
"Royal Holloway Music [University of London] Music Department's Golden Pages: Links for Musicians on the WWW" July 17, 1996.

I4. URL: http://www.music.indiana.edu/music_resources/
William and Gayle Cook Music Library. [Indiana University] "World-wide Internet Music Resources" November 30, 1996.

See the "Checklist of Examined Indexes and Other Bibliographic Aids" for other Internet sources.

B. Brahms Internet Sites

I5. URL: http://www.his.se/ida/~a94johal/music/brahms.html
Alkerstedt, Johan. "Johannes Brahms" in Alkerstedt. "Classical Music."
1996. Discusses Brahms's life and works.

I6. URL: http://www.radio.cbc.ca/schubert-brahms/index.html
[CBC [Canadian Broadcasting Corporation] Radio and CBC Stereo] ""An die Musik": The 1997 CBC Schubert-Brahms Celebration" Complete schedule of broadcasts of their music, interviews, documentaries, and a series of unique broadcast events, Spring 1997. Site also includes information on concert performances, audioclips of both composers' music, recipes for Viennese cuisine and links to resources on both composers.

I7. URL: http://www.music.yale.edu/research/brahms/brahms1.html
Berger, Jonathan, and Ronald Coifma, Maxim Goldberg, Charles Nichols. "Brahms at the Piano: Denoising, Transcribing and Analyzing the 1889 Cylinder Recording of Johannes Brahms" (CSMT [=Center for Studies in Music Technology at Yale] Research Report Abstracts) n.d. Analysis and reconstruction of recording using denoising procedures, in attempt to understand late nineteenth century performance practices. A complete description of the preliminary findings is published in Berger and Nichols. "Brahms at the Piano: An Analysis of Data from the Brahms Cylinder," *Leonardo Music Journal* 4 (1994). (see I8)

I8. URL: http://www-mitpress.mit.edu/Leonardo/isast/journal/berglm4.html
Berger, Jonathan, and Charles Nichols. "LMJ Berger Abstract" Abstract for article "Brahms at the Piano: an Analysis of Data from the Brahms Cylinder"; the full text of this article can be found in *Leonardo Music Journal* 4 (1994). (see I7)

I9. URL: http://www.classicalmus.com/composers/brahms.html; or
URL: http://www.primenet.com/~byoder/artclass.htm [links to]
BMG Classics World. "Johannes Brahms" 1995. Overview of Brahms's life and works; includes recommended recordings.

I10. URL: http://w3.rz-berlin.mpg.de/cmp/brahms_pic.html
Boynick, Matt. "Johannes Brahms—Picture Gallery" February 1, 1996. Contains 2 photographs and 3 drawings of Brahms, 1860–1890's, and a portion of a page from the manuscript of Op. 45. (See also I29)

I11. URL: http://www.residentieorkest.nl/brahmdui.htm
"Brahms Festival Den Haag. April–Mai 1997" Contains program for
event, put on in The Hague, Netherlands, by the Nieuwe Kerk Residen-
tie Orkest.

I12. URL: http://sun1.rrzn.uni-hannover.de/musicweb/musicweb/re-
source/institu/luebeck/index.htm
"Brahms-Institut an der Musikhochschule Lübeck, Das" n.d. Background, hours and summary of holdings.

I13. URL: http://www.chamberlinc.org/concert/brahms.htm
"A Celebration of Titans: Franz Schubert and Johannes Brahms" Pro-
gramme guide to this Schubert/Brahms celebration held in New York at
Lincoln Center, Jan.–Apr. 1997.

I14. URL: http://www.ddc.com/~decoy/brhm.htm
Coy, David E. "Johannes Brahms" n.d. Life and works; portion of article
is excerpted from *Grolier Encyclopedia.* 1993 ed.
de Jong, K.; See Jong, K. de

I15. URL: http://www.geocities.com/Vienna/7710/brahms.html
Deutsch, Wilhelm Otto. "Der Tod und Johannes Brahms. Zu Brahms'
100. Todestag am 3. April 1997 (mit Empfehlungen zum Hören)" n.d.
Discusses the theme of death in relation to Brahms: his personal feelings
on death and his musical treatment of death.

I16. URL: http://www.recmusic.org/lieder/
Ezust, Emily. "Brahms" in Ezust. "The Lied and Art Song Texts Page"
n.d. — includes public-domain texts for Opp. 33, 103, 121, as well as 163
other songs.

I17. URL: http://music.nv.cc.va.us/~nvfayxj/http/bibl.htm
Fay, James S. "Brahms Clarinet Works Bibliography" 1991. A selected
bibliography taken from Fay's dissertation. [see I18 for dissertation's ab-
stract]

I18. URL: http://music.nv.cc.va.us/~nvfayxj/http/abstract.html
Fay, James S. "[Brahms] Dissertation Abstract" [1991]. Abstract of au-
thor's dissertation, "The Clarinet and Its Use as a Solo Instrument in the
Chamber Music of Johannes Brahms, (DMA (Clarinet), Peabody Con-

servatory of Music, 1991). [see I17 for selected bibliography from this dissertation]

I19. URL: http://www.tiac.net/users/lpaul/music.html
Geffen, Paul. "Paul Geffen's Mostly Classical Music Index" n.d. Primarily made up of discographies in classical and popular music. Recordings of works by Brahms are included in the following:
"Works by Johannes Brahms" (http://www.tiac.net/users/lpaul/brahms. html)
"Sviatoslav Richter" (http:// . . . /lpaul/richter.html)
"Recordings by Vladimir Ashkenazy" (http:// . . . /lpaul/ashkenazy.html)
"Recordings by Martha Argerich" (http:// . . . /lpaul/argerich.html)

Grolier; See I14 and I27

I20. URL: http://sun1.rrzn.uni-hannover.de/musicweb/musicweb/ demos/texts/app1.htm
Hempel, Christoph. "Brahms Haydn Variations" (Weblication No. 1) General analysis of Opp. 56a and 56b.

I21. URL: http://www.hnh.com/composer/brahms.htm
HNH International Ltd. [Naxos]. "Brahms, Johannes (1833–1897)" in HNH. "Composers' Biographies and their Works" n.d. Overview of life and works; includes recommended recordings

I22. URL: http://web.calstate/a.edu/centers/Wagner/brahms.htm
Horgan, Sally. "The Spirit of Folk Song in the Lieder of Johannes Brahms" n.d.

I23. URL: http://www.hyperion-records.co.uk/catalog.html
Hyperion Records. "The Hyperion Catalogue" n.d. Brahms recordings cited

I24. URL: http://www.prs.net/midi.html
ID LOGIC [=PRS Corporation]. "Brahms, Johannes (1833–97)" in ID LOGIC. "Classical MIDI Archives" n.d. Includes MIDI arrangements of Ungarische Tänze [McCorkle WoO 1] nos. 3, 6, 7 (by B.Travis); and MIDI arrangements of excerpts from Opp. 45 (by M.Petri), 49 (by A.Kitisa), 56b (by F.Raborn), 68 (by F.Raborn), 77 (by A.De Brandt), and 118 (by R.Finley)

I25. URL: http://web20.mindlink.net/a4369/brahms/
Ingraham, Mary I. "Johannes Brahms WebSource" Ingraham Cultural
Resources Management Corp., January 1997. Includes biographical information and a works list; as well as an "Image Gallery"; information
on Brahms Societies, Scholars, Festivals and Special Events; plus audio
clips from recordings, and an annotated "Webography" of Web resources.

I26. URL: http://www.biography.com/cgi-bin/biography/biography-
request.pl?page=/biography/data/B/B.2203.txt.html [last segment con-
tains a zero]
InterActive8. "Brahms, Johannes" in InterActive8. "Biography.com"
A&E Television Networks, 1997. Life and works; reprinted from *The
Cambridge Biographical Encyclopedia*. David Crystal, ed. Cambridge,
New York: Cambridge University Press, 1994.

I27. URL: http://weber.u.washington.edu/~acamp/music/ romantic2.
html [links to]
"Johannes Brahms" Grolier Electronic Publishing, n.d. Encyclopedia article: life, works, significance

I28. URL: http://www.ubl.com/artists/010394.html [last segment con-
tains zeros]
"Johannes Brahms" n.d. Web page with links to I9, I19, I29 and CDnow
[Internet source for purchasing compact discs]

I29. URL: http://w3.rz-berlin.mpg.de/cmp/brahms.html
"Johannes Brahms" by Matt Boynick [et al.]. in "The Classical Music
Pages." February 1, 1996. Discusses Brahms's life and includes detailed
information on his works. Material is excerpted from *The Grove Concise
Dictionary of Music*. [=Norton/Grove Concise Encyclopedia of Music]
Stanley Sadie, ed. [? ed.] London: Macmillan, 1994? [see also I10]

I30. URL: http://sun1.rrzn.uni-hannover.de/musicweb/musicweb/re-
source/
Jong, K. de. "Materials for the Brahms Weblications (1996)" (Weblication No. 2) [1996?] In addition to the listings that follow, this Web site
also contains links to study aids for Opp. 56a and 56b. Includes:
http://sun1.rrzn.uni-hannover.de/musicweb/musicweb/resource/biblio/
bbib.htm

"A Brahms Bibliography" A selected listing of older standard Brahms resources, 31 items.
http://sun1.rrzn.uni-hannover.de/musicweb/musicweb/resource/institu/
instit.htm
"Brahms Institute in Deutschland" Directory of societies, museums, festivals, includes listing for the new Gesamtausgabe; information given includes respective societies' and museums' publications on Brahms.
http://sun1.rrzn.uni-hannover.de/musicweb/musicweb/resource/texts/
"Texts" Includes excerpts from Brahms correspondence and recollections of Brahms on the topic of Brahms the composer. Mostly taken from English translations of original German materials <http://. . ./resource/texts/primary/>; and excerpts from writings on Opp. 56a and 56b <http://. . ./resource/texts/secondar/>.

I31. URL: http://www.myo.inst.keio.ac.jp/wagner/120th/brahms.html
Kiesewetter, Peter. "Brahms" Richard Sterling, transl. n.d. Discusses the influence of pre-classical music in Brahms's works for chorus and orchestra.

I32. URL: http://www.austria-info.at/personen/brahms/index.html
Kokits, Zsigmond. "Johannes Brahms 1833–1897. Johannes Brahms um 1883=Johannes Brahms around 1883" n.d. Discusses life and work, life up to 1883 only; includes information on Brahms's Viennese circle, his summer vacations in Austria, memorials and museums, and Brahms exhibitions in Austria in 1997.

I33. URL: http://www.classical.net/music/rep/lists/rom.html
Lampson, L.D. [Dave Lampson] "Basic Repertoire List—Romantic Repertoire" 1995. Includes Brahms recordings.

I34. URL: http://www.classical.net/music/recs/latkey.html
Lampson, L.D. [Dave Lampson] "Recommended Recordings. Late Keyboard Music" Revision 2. August 5, 1992. Includes Brahms recordings.

I35. URL: http://www.classical.net/music/recs/latorch.html
Lampson, L.D. [Dave Lampson] "Recommended Recordings. Late Orchestral Music" Revision 2.2. January 6, 1994. Includes Brahms recordings.

I36. URL: http://www.classical.net/music/recs/conc.html
Lampson, L.D. [Dave Lampson] "Recommended Recordings. Late Concertos" Revision 2. August 5, 1992. Includes Brahms recordings.

I37. URL: http://www.classical.net/music/recs/latcham.html
Lampson, L.D. [Dave Lampson] "Recommended Recordings. Late Chamber Music" Revision 2.1. January 15, 1993. Includes Brahms recordings.

I38. URL: http://www.rhic.bhl.gov/export1/brahms/WWW/the_other_brahms.html
Lee, J.H. "Johannes Brahms (May 7 1833–April 3 1897)" n.d. Web Page that includes links to I10, I19, I25 and I45; also contains 2 audioclips from RCA Victor recordings and a picture of Brahms's grave. <http://www.rhic.bhl.gov/export1/brahms/WWW/figures/brahms_grave.gif>

I39. URL: http://fsinfo.cs.uni-sb.de/~hobbes/brahms.html
"Lieben Sie Brahms? Eine Initiative der Hamburgischen Kulturstiftung" [December 1996?] Presents the program for the year-long 1997 Hamburg Festival commemorating the centennial of Brahms's death.

I40. URL: http://members.aol.com/Orquesta/earlyromantic.html
Mata, Eddy. "Johannes Brahms" June 8, 1997. Web page with links to programme notes on Op. 68 and various biographies.

Naxos; See HNH

I41. URL: http://www.cl.cam.ac.uk/users/mn200/music/composers.html#brahms
Norrish, Michael. "Brahms, Johannes," in Norrish. "Classical Composer Biographies" n.d. Author's thoughts on Brahms as composer and his works.

I42. URL: http://members.aol.com/abelard2/davids.htm
"On the Centennial of the Death of Brahms" in "Davidsbündler Home Page." n.d. Contains:
[Furtwängler, Wilhelm] "Brahms and the Crisis of Our Time" (http:// . . . / abelard2/furt.htm) English translation of 2467.a.iii. (?) (W. Furtwängler. "Brahms und die Krise unserer Zeit")
"Gustav Jenner: Brahms as Man, Teacher and Artist" (http:// . . . / abelard2/jenner.htm) Excerpts in English translation from 694 [periodical article (?), book (?)] (G. Jenner. "Brahms als Mensch, Lehrer und Künstler")

"The Socratic Method of Johannes Brahms" (http:// . . . /abelard2/geist.htm) Analyses the text setting in Op. 91, no. 2.
"Eusebius7's recommended recordings" (http:// . . . /abelard2/records.htm) Includes Brahms works.

I43. URL: http://www.philclas.polygram.nl/class/ca-b/brahms.htm Philips Classics Productions. "Johannes Brahms" n.d. Discography of Brahms works on Polygram Recordings.

PRS Corporation; See ID LOGIC

I44. URL: http://www.rrz.uni-hamburg.de/Hamburg/praktisch/Museum/joh_bra.html Robertson, Struan. "Johannes-Brahms-Museum" n.d. Background and visiting information.

I45. URL: http://www.odyssey.net/subscribers/scior/jb.html Sciortino, Michael A. "Johannes Brahms (1833–1897)" n.d. Contains 14 MIDI files of Brahms music: Op. 45, 77, 107 no. 5, 117, 118 nos. 2 and 6, Ungarische Tänze [McCorkle WoO 1] no. 1.

I46. URL: http://pubweb.acns.nwu.edu/~jas923/brahms.html [Stevens, Jacob] "Tidbit About Brahms, A" n.d. Life, links to other Brahms sites; includes synopsis from Bill Parker's *Building A Classical Music Library*. 3rd ed. Minneapolis: Jormax Publications, 1994 on building a CD collection of Brahms's works.

I47. URL: http://www.unitel.classicalmusic.com/ucatalog/composer/brahms.htm Unitel. "Johannes Brahms. May 7, 1833–Apr. 3, 1897" in Unitel. [*Production Catalog*]. Includes 32 performance videos of 18 Brahms works.

I48. URL: http://www.ukonline.co.uk./UKOnline/Music/biogs/brahms.html Valentine, Ted. "Johannes Brahms (1833–1897)" October 1996. Life and works.

I49. URL: http://www.music.indiana.edu/musicref/brahms.htm William and Gayle Cook Music Library [Indiana University] "Johannes Brahms: Collections of Songs" n.d. Provides contents information for a number of Brahms song collections held by the Music Library.

Appendix B

Hunting for Hedgehogs: The Search for Brahmsiana

If the search for information on Johannes Brahms was as everyday as the composer walking from his Karlsgasse No. 4 apartments to his favorite Viennese restaurant "Zum roten Igel" (the red hedgehog) for midday and evening meals[1], there would be little reason for this appendix. However, notwithstanding today's relative ease in accessing information and the profusion of technology that can assist the accessing, the search is not a predictable one. One can be led down many different search routes: some look forward to the future, and some look back into the past; and for this reason I find myself, in the age of the Internet, search engines and World Wide Web pages, writing about collections of 3″ × 5″ cards housed in cabinet and catalogue drawers. This, then, is about one aspect of my Brahms research, focusing on experiences I had in the United States in Fall 1995, working with the Works Project Administration Music Periodical Index at Northwestern University and the Music Division's Periodical Index at the Library of Congress.

The Works Project Administation Music Periodical Index (hereafter noted as WPA) was an American make-work project for the white-collar sector during the 1930's Depression. As Dena Epstein relates in her 1989 article on this index, project "selectors" went through periodical runs, choosing articles that would be of the "greatest value to the research worker in the field of music." Articles were omitted if they were not of a scholarly nature or if they didn't deal with contemporary trends and changes. From the selectors the card went to the "transcribers" and from them to the "indexer". The indexer didn't see the item but relied on the information that had been provided by the selector, which could include subject headings if the selector thought that the article title was so vague, short or misleading that the indexer would not assign an appropriate heading. The Project ran from 1938–1942 under the aegis of Chicago Public Library, stopped, was then kept in storage at various institutions in the Chicago area, and in 1985 was taken by Northwestern University Music Library.[2] The index is currently housed in a storage room next to the Music Library, in a series of filing cabinets and card catalogue drawer units. My other subject, the Library of Congress Music Division's Periodical Index, (hereafter noted as LC) was started about 1902 by Oscar Sonneck, the first Chief of the Division. It was continued at least until 1942 (although references dated later have been found); it is housed in card catalogue drawers in the Performing Arts Reading Room of the Library of Congress.[3] Both indexes cover a period in the publication of music literature when comprehensive indexing for music literature did not exist; both indexes were initiated in attempts to fill that gap.

The LC is alphabetical by author and subject in one interfiled sequence; in contrast, the WPA, in its current state, is not. The WPA is a subject index only, with cards, for the most part, grouped according to the individual magazine title and then alphabetically arranged within that title; magazine titles are arranged in a sequence of rough alphabetical ranges, e.g. e-m, a-z, m, b-d. There is also one portion of the WPA in which subject cards for four different magazines have been interfiled alphabetically by subject heading. The WPA contains over 400,000 cards and indexes 111 journals—61 (55%) completely, 50 (45%) partially.[4] In the time that I had at Northwestern, I went through indexing for 99 titles. Fifty (50%) of these 99 titles had no references to Brahms at all. In only 6 (12%) cases was this because of their dates or scope, i.e. titles either from the 1830's and 1840's, before Brahms became known as a composer, or on subjects not usually associated with Brahms, such as Gregorian Chant. Additionally, 1 other title's indexing may have had references to Brahms but was unusable in its current state, because there was no apparent order to the index cards.[5] The remaining 48 titles containing Brahms references were evenly divided into 24 completely indexed and 24 partially indexed journals. Length of journal run seems to have been the factor that led to thoroughness of indexing; publication language (English vs. non-English) does not appear to have been a consideration. The run of the Brahms citations was from 1863 to 1938.

The LC index has 160,000 cards and contains selective indexing for its chosen titles. It is my understanding that no one knows for certain how many periodicals it covers, but based on Gillian Anderson's investigations, a minimum of 215 titles are present in the whole index[6]; in the

Brahms indexing I found reference to 74 titles with 4 (5%) of them being from nonmusic areas.[7] The run of the Brahms citations here was from 1896 to 1939. In addition to periodical references, some indexing of Symphony Program notes and book materials was also present.

Although routing through both these indexes for Brahms references hitherto unknown to me was my main objective in pursuing this phase of research,[8] I had two other goals:

1) since the time period for both indexes put them inside the time frame for my own published bibliography[9] (hereafter noted as TQ), I wondered how the citations I found in the indexes for a particular periodical, compared to the citations I had listed in TQ for the same periodical; and
2) I was also interested in whether the indexing in WPA and LC overlapped to any degree.

All together, the two indexes included Brahms citations from 95 different periodicals. In TQ there were 1,069 citations for those of the 95 periodicals that were within TQ's scope[10]; there were 495 references for those of the 95 periodicals indexed in WPA; and 355 references for those of the 95 periodicals indexed in LC. In regards to overlapping, 244 (49%) of the 495 WPA references were already in TQ; LC had a much higher overlap rate: 312 (88%!) out of 355 references were duplicates of either TQ or WPA.[11] I suspected that most of the overlapping references between WPA and LC would be derivative literature, i.e. articles reporting on new publications, or reporting on periodical literature published elsewhere. This was not the case. They were unique materials; they did not duplicate, or relate in some other way to writings elsewhere.

Another point discovered when crosschecking the indexes against TQ was that the number of citations that turned up in WPA and LC for a particular periodical title did not always match the number of citations for same title in TQ. For example, the periodical *Music* (published in Chicago) showed 18 citations in TQ for the time period 1895–1901; WPA had 8 citations, and LC had 11.[12] I also looked at the source of citations unique to TQ for 12 of the 95 periodicals and found that in most cases, the sources were bibliographies compiled after 1942 or published periodical indexes contemporary to WPA and LC.[13] An interesting pattern emerged, in that unique-to-TQ English language references were generally found in the indexes, unique-to-TQ German language references in the bibliographies. This finding was unexpected; I had thought that unique references in TQ were solely the result of serendipitous browsing in the periodicals themselves.

Some additional overall comments on the 95 periodicals are appropriate. There are 7 languages represented in the periodicals. Not surprisingly, German and English are the top 2 in the ranking.[14] As to which magazines are indexed where, LC indexes 47 (50%) of the 95 titles, WPA 21 (22%) with the other 27 (28%) being indexed in both sources.[15] Again duplicate indexing of the English and German language titles tops the list, but the amounts of duplication bear no relation to the numbers of titles in the total collection: English language titles have 25% overlap in titles vs. 47% of total holdings; German language titles have 30% overlap in titles versus 24% of total holdings.

Epstein makes reference in her article to concerns regarding the quality and consistency of the WPA indexing. I found both to be appropriate, relative to the index's times. Epstein also points out that Library of Congress subject headings were the authority used for WPA[16]; I also saw a range of p-slips that looked like name authority records. Table 1 shows

Table 1.—Examples of Subject Headings used in WPA

Gaz[z]ette musicale [=musicali] di Milano	*Allgemeine Musikzeitung*
Brahms, Biography	Brahms, Anniversaries
Criticism and Interpretation	Biography
Obituary	Chamber Music Reviews
Works	Compositions
	Criticism and Interpretation
	Exhibitions
	Influence of
	Instrumentation
	Piano trio, A minor
	Personality
	Reminiscences
	Symphonies
	Symphony—Style
	Triumphlied
	Ungarische Tänze
	Wills
	Works, musical
	General

representative subject headings from Brahms sections of the WPA indexing for two periodicals; they seem straightforward enough. Cross indexing is also consistent. Spot checks show, for example, that an article on a Brahms monument would be indexed under the general heading of "Monuments" as well as the more specific "Brahms Monuments." Ultimately, though, the "proof of the pudding" for an index is whether users can locate what's being cited. Table 2 compares index citations with the actual physical items they cite and shows little that would lead one into blind corners.

In references unique to WPA only 4 (3%) of 128 were 'ghost' entries, meaning that they couldn't be located at all[17]; LC, on the other hand, varied greatly in the recording of citation information, with 14 (93%) of 15 new references being 'ghosts'. But in the overlapping citations, 21 (9%) of 244 that overlapped between TQ/WPA have problems, whereas in those that overlapped between TQ/LC only 9 (6%) of 159 couldn't be

**Table 2.—Citation vs. Seen Brahms References
from both WPA and LC**

CITATION	*SEEN*
From WPA:	
Erb. J. Lawrence. "Rubinstein on the Playing of Brahms" *Etude* 27 (1.1909) p. 71.	"Rubinstein on the Playing of Brahms" *The Etude* 27/1 (1.1909) p. 71.
De Eisner. "Johannes Brahms" *Gazetta* musicale di Milano 52 (4.1897) pp. 220–21.	De Eisner. "Giovanni Brahms" *Gazzetta musicali di Milano* 52/15 (14.4.1897) pp. 220–21.
From LC:	
Kramer, A. Walter. "The Piano Music of Brahms" *Musical America* v. 16, n. 14 (1912) p. 27.	Kramer, A. Walter. "The Piano Music of Brahms" *Musical America* 16/14 (10.8.1912) p. 27.
Bülow, Marie v. "Hans v. Bülow und der Brahms-biograph" *Musikpädagogische Blätter* v.19, n.19,20 (1914)	Bülow, Marie v. "Hans v. Bülow und der Brahmsbiograph" *Musikpädagogische Blätter* 37/19,20 (1.,15.;10.1914) pp. 366–67, 379–81.

found. Perhaps this last point is a reflection of WPA's broad group effort versus LC's more focused one-man approach.

In addition to the references I found in the 2 indexes, there were others that didn't fit my criteria. WPA, in particular, contained a wealth of additional information, with illustrative material, all musical supplements, and reviews of performances and music editions being included in the indexing. It was refreshing to be referred to illustrations of Brahms that didn't have the ubiquitous hedgehog sauntering through them.

In closing, I note that both the Epstein and Anderson articles[18] argue for the importance of the Works Project Administration Music Periodical Index and the Library of Congress Music Division's Periodical Index respectively, and I add my voice to theirs. Based on my own experience, both WPA and LC are important tools, and efforts should be made to preserve them and make them more widely available. The value of their coverage far outweighs concerns that have been raised regarding their methodology or representation. While the new references I found did not lead to bold new revelations or pivotal information on Brahms the man and musician, they did provide further information, and further insight into the work of an important individual. I see no reason why this shouldn't be so for other composers, as well as for other topics in the field of musicology.

Table 3 provides further details on the 95 periodicals.

Table 3.—Number of Brahms References in TQ compared to WPA and LC (includes breakout of overlapping citations).

	Periodical	Lang	WPA/TQ	WPA/Total	LC/TQ	LC/Total	LC/WPA TQ	Overlap
1				0	Overlap	0		Overlap
2	Aeolian Quarterly, The	eng		0		1		
3	Allgemeine deutsche MZ/Allg. Musikzeitu.	ger	147	44	43	20	4	16
4	Allgemeine musikalische Zeitung	ger	20	7	6	0		
5	American Music Lover	eng	1	0		2	1	
6	American Organist	eng	2	1		0		
7	Anbruch/Musikblätter des Anbruch	ger	12	4	4	3	2	
8	Art musicale L'	fre		1		0		
9	Auftakt, Der	ger	7	0		2	2	
10	Baton	eng		1		0		
11	Bollettino bibliografico musicale	ita	1	1	1	1	1	
12	Bulletin français de la S.I.M. Société Intern.	fre	1	0		1	1	
13	Caecilia (Utrecht)	dut	18	0		5	5	
14	Chesterian	eng	4	1	1	0		
15	Clef	eng		1		0		
16	Correo musical sud-americano	spa		0		1		
17	Courrier musical, Le	fre	6	0		2	2	
18	Deutsche Militär-musikerzeitung	ger	5	0		1		
19	Deutsche Musiker-zeitung (Berlin)	ger	7	0		2	1	
20	Deutsche Musikkultur	ger	3	0		1	1	
21	Deutsche Volkslied	ger	2	0		1		
22	Diapason	eng	2	2		0		

No.	Title	Lang.						
23	Disques (Philadelphia)	eng	1	0		1		
24	Dominant	eng		0		1		
25	Dwights Journal of Music	eng	7	6		0		
26	Etude	eng	45	33	8	9	4	5
27	Gazetta musicale di Milano	ita	1	4		0		
28	Gesangspäda-gogische Blätter	ger		0		1		
29	Guide du Concert	fre	1	4		1		1
30	Guide musicale (Bruxelles), Le	fre	7	10	2	0		
31	Harvard Musical Review	eng	1	0		1	1	
32	Jacobs' Orchestra Monthly	eng		0		1		
33	Jahrbuch der Musikbibliothek Peters	ger	3	3	3	1		1
34	Kunst	dut		0		1		
35	Lookeron	eng	2	4	2	0		
36	Masters in Music	eng	18	0		18	18	
37	Melos/Der Weihergarten	ger	4	3	3	3	1	2
38				0	Overlap	0	Overlap	
39	Metronome	eng		0		1		
40	Monthly Musical record	eng	30	22	17	8		6
41	Music	eng		0		1		
42	Music (Chicago)	eng	18	21	9	14	3	10
43	Music and Letters	eng	14	4	3	1		1
44	Music News	eng		1		0		
45	Music Review	eng	15	3		0		
46	Music Student	eng	1	0		2		
47	Music Teacher	eng	15	0		1		
48	Musica	ita		0		1		
49	Musica d'oggi	ita	2	0		2	2	
50	Musical America	eng	14	13	2	6	2	1
51	Musical Courier	eng	22	64	8	8		8
52	Musical Items	eng		2		0		
53	Musical Leader	eng		0		1		
54	Musical Mercury	eng	1	0		1	1	
55	Musical News (London)	eng	4	6	2	1		1
56	Musical Observer	eng	2	0		7	2	
57	Musical Opinion/Musical Opinion and Mu.	eng	30	28	17	10		10
58	Musical Quarterly	eng	19	9	9	6	2	3
59	Musical Record	eng		3		0		
60	Musical Review	eng		1		0		
61	Musical Standard	eng	7	4	1	3	3	
62	Musical Times	eng	63	24	20	26	6	19
63	Musical World (Boston)	eng	1	0		1	1	
64	Musician (Boston)	eng	7	9	3	3	2	1
65	Musik (Berlin), Die	ger	93	81	50	39	3	36
66	Musik-Kultur	swe		2		0		
67	Musikalisches Wochenblatt/ Musikalisches.	ger	45	0		3	3	
68	Musikbuh aus Österreich	ger	2	0		1	1	
69	Musikpädagogische Blätter	ger	3	0		1		
70	Muziek, De	dut		3		0		
71	Neue Musikzeitung	ger	68	0		19	18	
72	Neue Zeitschrift für Musik/ Zeitschrift für Mu.	ger	97	8	6	23	17	6
73	New Music and Church Music Review/ N.	eng	10	2	1	7	6	1
74	Pianoforte, Il	it	3	0		1	1	
75				0	Overlap	0	Overlap	
76	Presto	eng		19		0		
77	Proceedings of the Musical Association	eng	3	3	2	3	1	2
78	Rassenga musicale, La	ita	2	3		2		2
79	Revista de musica	ita		1		0		
80	Revista musical catalana	spa	4	0		4	4	
81	Revue blanche, La	fre		0		1		
82	Revue bleue	fre	2	0		1	1	
83	Revue internationale de musique	fre	1	0		1	1	
84	Revue musicale (Paris), La	fre	4	3	2	2	1	1
85	Rheinische Musik- und Theaterzeitung (Kö.)	ger	23	0		2	2	
86	Rivista musicale italiana	ita		3		0		
87	Sackbut	eng	4	0		4	4	
88	Schweizerische Musikzeitung und Sängert.	ger	12	0		4	2	
89	Signale für die musikalische Welt	ger	52	0		14	14	
90	Stimme, Die	ger	1	0		1	1	
91	Strad, The	eng	10	6	5	6		5
92	Svensk musiktidring	swe		0		1		
93	Symphonia	dut	11	0		8	8	
94	Symphony, The	eng		0		1		
95	Vie musicale, La	fre	2	0		1	1	
96	Weekblad voor musiek	dut	2	0		1	1	
97	Zeitschrift für Musikwissenschaft	ger	9	7	7	8	1	7

Notes

1. For a description of a typical Brahms Viennese day, see Karl Geiringer, in collaboration with Irene Geiringer. *Brahms: his life and work.* 3rd ed., revised and enlarged, with a new appendix: "Brahms as a Reader and Collector". Da Capo Press Music Reprint Series (New York: Da Capo Press, 1982) pp. 164–65.

2. Dena Epstein. "The Mysterious WPA Music Periodical Index," *Notes* 45/3 (3.1989) pp. 463–82. See pp. 467–68 for the indexing process.

3. Gillian B. Anderson. "Unpublished Periodical Indexes at the Library of Congress and elsewhere in the United States of America," *Fontes artis musicae* 31/1 (1.–3.1984) pp. 54–60.

4. Epstein, p. 468.

5. I believe in this case that I was looking at original indexers' p-slips; the periodical was *Le Ménestrel.*

6. Anderson, pp. 54–55.

7. Of the 215 periodicals in LC, 29 (13.5%) were from nonmusic areas.

8. In all I spent 12 hrs working with the WPA, 4 hrs with LC, including time spent crosschecking in TQ (see note 9) for references already seen.

9. Thomas Quigley. *Johannes Brahms: an annotated bibliography of the literature through 1982.* With a Foreword by Margit L. McCorkle. (Metuchen, NJ & London: The Scarecrow Press, Inc., 1990).

10. Twenty-five (26%) of the 95 magazines weren't within TQ's scope.

11. The number of overlapping references between LC and TQ, and LC and WPA is practically equal (159 vs. 153, respectively).

12. All WPA citations overlapped LC's.

13. Two examples are "Zeitschriftenschau" in *Zeitschrift der Internationalen Musikgesellschaft* vols. 1–15 (1899–1914); and "Musikalische Zeitschriftenschau" in *Zeitschrift für Musikwissenschaft* vols. 1–17 (1918–1935).

14. In order of quantity: English (45 periodicals), German (23), French (10), Italian (8), Dutch (5), Spanish (2), Swedish (2).

15. Twenty-five (26%) of the 95 periodical titles are not in TQ.

16. Epstein, pp. 467, 470–73.

17. This is not to say that citations were error free; 35 (22%) of 128 citations had some vaguery about them, but not to the point of actually being detrimental to locating the referenced material.

18. Epstein, pp. 473–74; Anderson, p. 56.

Brahms's Works Index
for Part IV

The purpose of this index is to help the user locate information on individual works in Part IV. The index is divided into 3 sections: Works with Opus Number; Works without Opus Number and Literary and Theoretical Works; and Works by Other Composers Edited or Arranged by Brahms. Reference is made to entry numbers.

A. Works with Opus Number
(arranged in ascending numerical order)

Op. 1, Piano Sonata no. 1 in C major 4321–4324.3

Op. 2, Piano Sonata no. 2 in F sharp minor 4324.7

Op. 3, Six Songs for Tenor or Soprano 4698.2

Op. 4, Scherzo for Piano in E flat minor 4325–4327.5

Op. 5, Piano Sonata no. 3 in F minor 4328–4329.5

Op. 6, Six Songs for Tenor or Soprano 4698.3

Op. 7, Six Songs for Solo Voice 4698.4

Op. 8, Piano Trio no. 1 in B major 4139–4151.5

Op. 9, Variations for Piano on a Theme by Robert Schumann 4330–4338.5

Op. 10, Ballades for Piano 4339–4340.5

Op. 11, Serenade no. 1 in D major for Orchestra 4512.9

Op. 12, Ave Maria for Women's Choir 4781.6

Op. 13, Begräbnisgesang for Choir and Wind Instruments 4781.8

Op. 116, Seven Fantasies for Piano 4386–4389.5
Op. 117, Three Intermezzi for Piano 4390–4397.5
Op. 118, Six Piano Pieces 4398–4404.5
Op. 119, Four Piano Pieces 4405–4413.1
Op. 120, Two Clarinet (or Viola) Sonatas: No. 1 in F minor and No. 2 in E flat major 4200–4221.6
Op. 121, Four Serious Songs for Bass 4730–4744.5
Op. 122 [posthumous], Eleven Chorale Preludes for Organ 4445.5–4452.3

B. Works without Opus Number and Literary and Theoretical Works (arranged alphabetically by distinctive name of work or by uniform title designation)

Brautlied [Song] [McCorkle Anhang IIa, nr. 29] 4745.7
Chorale Prelude and Fugue for Organ on "O Traurigkeit, o Herzeleid" [McCorkle WoO 7] 4452.6–4462.9
Concerto for Violoncello [speculated] 4631.3
Counterpoint Exercises with Joachim 4342, 4855.5, 4864, 4867
Dein Herzlein mild [Song for 4 part Women's Choir] [McCorkle WoO posthum 19] 4861.2
Deutsche Sprichworte [Literary Collection] 4868
Du bist wie eine Blume [Song] [McCorkle Anhang IIa, nr. 12*] 4747.4
Exercises for Piano [McCorkle WoO 6] 4417–4420.5
[Folksongs—Entries begin]
Children's Folksongs for Solo Voice (1858) [McCorkle WoO 31] 4746–4746.5
Forty-nine German Folksongs for Solo Voice and 4 part Choir with Soloist (1894) [McCorkle WoO 33] 4747–4747.2
Fourteen German Folksongs for 4 part Choir (1864) [McCorkle WoO 34] 4861.25
Twelve German Folksongs for 4 part Mixed Choir (1926/27) [McCorkle WoO posthum 35] 4861.3
Eight German Folksongs for 3 and 4 part Women's Choir (1938) [McCorkle WoO posthum 36] 4861.35

Symphonies [speculated] 4631.2, 5037

Töne lindernder Klang [Canon] [McCorkle WoO 28] 4861.7

Trio, Piano, in A major [McCorkle Anhang IV, nr. 5] 4222–4222.3

Wann? [Canon] [McCorkle WoO posthum 29] 4861.75

Zu Rauch muβ werden [Canon] [McCorkle WoO posthum 30] 4861.8

C. Works by Other Composers
Edited or Arranged by Brahms
(arranged alphabetically by the composer's last name)

Ahle, Johann Rudolf, Es ist genug [McCorkle Anhang Va, nr. 4 (26)] 4865

Bach, Carl Philipp Emanuel, Concertos for the Cembalo, Wq 43 [McCorkle Anhang VI, nr. 1] 4631.9

Bach, Carl Philipp Emanuel, Violin Sonata in B minor, Wq 76 [McCorkle Anhang VI, nr. 2] 4250

Bach, Carl Philipp Emanuel, Violin Sonata in C minor, Wq 78 [McCorkle Anhang VI, nr. 2] 4250

Bach, Johann Sebastian, "O ewiges Feuer", Cantata BWV34 [McCorkle Anhang Ib, nr. 5] 4861.95

Bach, Wilhelm Friedemann, Sonata for 2 Pianos in F major, Falck Nr. 10 [McCorkle Anhang VI, nr. 3] 4250

Beethoven, Ludwig von, Cadenzas for First and Third Movements of Piano Concerto No. 4 in G major, Op. 58 [McCorkle WoO posthum 12] 4631.5

Bihari, János, Racoczi March, arranged for Piano [McCorkle Anhang III, nr. 10] 4632

Chopin, Frédéric, Gesamtausgabe [McCorkle Anhang VI, nr. 5] 4428

Händel, Georg Friedrich, Seven Duets and 2 Trios for Solo Voices [McCorkle Anhang Ia, nr. 10] 3798, 4863

Händel, Georg Friedrich, Six Duets for Solo Voices [McCorkle Anhang Ia, nr. 11] 3798, 4863

Händel, Georg Friedrich, Saul [Oratorio] [McCorkle Anhang Ib, nr. 26] 4862

Joachim, Joseph, Overture to Hermann Grimm's Demetrius, Op. 6, arranged for 2 Pianos [McCorkle Anhang Ia, nr. 4] 4632.5

Joachim, Joseph, Overture to Shakespeare's Hamlet, Op. 4, arranged for Piano 4 hands [McCorkle Anhang Ia, nr. 3] 4632.5

Titles, Monographic Series, and Degree-Granting Institutions Index

Information in this index is interfiled in one alphabetical sequence, word by word. A reference to a citation number includes appearances in all applicable sections within that number.

Alphabetization follows the general principles used in the body of the work, with the following refinements:

a) A title in quotation marks files before the same title underlined.
b) The only points of punctuation that affect filing are closing punctuation marks, e.g. periods, question marks.
c) Symbols file before letters, except when they have a word equivalent. In that case, they file by their spelled-out form.
d) Initials in a title file according to their full word spelling.
e) Acronyms and initialisms file as words.
f) Cardinal numbers in a title file as if they were a cardinal number spelled-out in English. 3 files as three, 1833 as one thousand eight hundred and thirty-three. Ordinal numbers file according to their spelling in the respective language. If the ordinal number is the first element in the title, the user will need to check for all possible language options; for example, first, erste, première. Numbers used as chapter or section designations are ignored in filing.
g) Initial articles as the first word in a title are disregarded in filing.

h) Uniform titles have been derived in order to standardize the collocation of information. For example, all titles that begin with Brahms's name in the possessive file as [Brahms's], regardless of their original spellings; all entries that consist of "Brahms" and his dates are filed as [Brahms 1833–1897].

"Authentic Brahms, The" 5155
[Autobiography] (Schnabel) 3919
"Autographe, Drucke und Ausgaben" 3410

"B wie Brahms" 5323
"Bach als Inspirationsquelle" 3682
"Bach and The Piano: Editions, Arrangements and Transcriptions from Czerny to Rachmaninov" 4414
Bach, Beethoven, and The Boys. Music History As It Ought To Be Taught 3236
"Bach, Beethoven, Brahms and Bovines" 5336
Bach Chaconne for Solo Violin, The. A Collection of Views 4415.d.b.
"Bach und Brahms fünfte Sommerakademie in Stuttgart" 5287
"Bach und Brahms von früh bis spät. Helmuth Rillings Sommerakademie in Stuttgart" 5288
"Bachs Werke in ihren Bearbeitungen 1750–1950" 4415
"Back to the Future" 4460.e.ii.
"Baden-Baden: Symposium der Brahms-Gesellschaft" 5247
Bärenreiter Hochschulschriften 3986, 4061.a.
Ball State University 3813, 3874, 4123. 4124, 4128, 4164, 4168, 4172, 4173, 4210, 4218, 4328, 5095
"Balzac, Turner and Brahms" 3630
"Band Transcription of Brahms' Variations on a Theme by Haydn, A" 4523
"Baroque and Romantic Stylistic Qualities in Brahm's Variations and Fugue on a Theme of Handel, Op. 24" 4347
Basic Classical and Operatic Recordings Collection for Libraries, A 3371
Basic Classical and Operatic Recordings Collection on Compact Discs for Libraries: A Buying Guide 3372
Basic Facts about UBC's Faculty of Arts 3424.e.a.ii.
Basic 50, The 3345
Basic Library of the World's Greatest Music. Master Volume 4546
Basic Music Library, A. Essential Scores and Books 3382
Basic Music Library, A: Essential Scores and Recordings 3382
"Basic Repertoire, The" 3346.5
"Basic Repertoire, The—And Beyond" 3294
Baylor University 4418
BBC Music Guides 4083, 4103
"BBC PO/Berio" 4214

1989–3367.d.d., 4717
1993–3436
1995–4546
"Brahms, Johannes . . ." 3559
"Brahms, Johannes 1883 (sic)—1897" 3427
"Brahms, Johannes 1833–1897" or "Brahms, Johannes, 1833–1897" or
    "Brahms, Johannes (1833–1897)" or "Brahms, Johannes (1833–97)"
    or "Brahms, Johannès (1833–1897)" or Brahms, Johannes [[1833–
    1897]]
1955–3358, 3365, 3373
1960–74–3351
1964–4107
1965–4107.a.
1968–3376
1970–3376.d.
1972–3376.d., 3423, 4041
1976–3376.d.d.
1979–3348, 3598
1981–3339, 4297.5
1984–3376.d.d.d., 3644
1985–3361, 4636
1986–4054
1987–3371, 3433, 3622
1988–3377
1989–3285
1990–3372
1994–4262.d.i.
"Brahms, Johannes (1833–1897) Germany" 4278
"Brahms, Johannes/1833–1897/Germany" 3428
"Brahms Legacies" 3491
"Brahms Liebeslieder Walzer" 4692
"Brahms Manuscript Discoveries" 3399
"Brahms Manuscripts" 3492
"Brahms maradandósága. 150 éve született Johannes Brahms" 5233
"Brahms—mit individueller Note" 5243
"Brahms Monument in Vienna, The" 5426
"Brahms Museum Discovered, A" 5466
"Brahms, musicista postumo" 5227.b.
"Brahms negyven éve halott" 5308
"Brahms News" 5246

"Buffalo observes Brahms Centennial; Election by Guild" 5254

Building A Chamber Music Collection. A Descriptive Guide to Published Scores 4097

Building A Classical Music Library 3369

Building A Classical Music Library. A Concise Guide To Building Your Personal Record Collection 3369

"Building a Repertoire: Brahms and Liszt" 4437

Buramsu: susung ui anae Kullara yosawa ui yonjong 3222

Buramusu wa osuki 5211.b.v.

"Burns Lieder and Other Matters. Schumann—Franz—Brahms—Bruch" 5091

Butler University 4216, 4594

By the Way. Being A Collection of Short Essays on Music and Art in General taken from the Program-Books of the Boston Symphony Orchestra 3279

"Cadenza by . . ." 4571.e.ii.

"Cadenzas: A Survey" 4571.e.iv.

California State College, Long Beach 4318

California State University, Chico 4722

California State University, Fullerton 4145, 4205, 4347, 4356, 4410, 4752, 4891, 5180

California State University, Long Beach 4211, 5126

California State University, Sacramento 5003

California State University, San Francisco 4933

California Studies in 19th Century Music 4094.b., 4909, 5002.b., 5204

Cambridge [University] 5140

Cambridge Companion to the Clarinet, The 4461

Cambridge Companions to Music 4461

Cambridge Music Handbooks 4812

"cantos folklóricos, Los: ¿Lo auténtico contra lo bello? Un nuevo concepto de música folklórica" 4686

Carl Maria von Weber. A Guide to Research 4023

"Carlo Maria Giulini on Brahms" 5166

"Carnival Music. An Introduction to the Piano Music of George Rochberg" 5117

"Cat in Music, The" 3653.9

"Cat in Music (October 1920), The" 3653.9.a.

Cat Who Played Brahms, The 5207

"Crosscurrents: Schubert, Schumann, Mendelssohn, Brahms" 4269
Cuadernos do Rio Grande, Sec. cão 4: Estudos de arte 4923
Cultura, La 4302
"Cultural World of Brahms, The" 3647
"Cyclic Tendencies in Brahms's Song Collections" 4654
Cykle pieśni ery romantycznej 1816–1914. Interpretacje 4705

Da Beethoven a Boulez: il pianoforte in ventidue saggi 4265
Da Capo Catalog of Classical Music Compositions, The 4039
Da Capo Paperback 3207, 4462
Da Capo Press Music Reprint Series 3207, 3764.b.i.a., 3811.a.
Dampfkonzert, Das. Musik und Musikleben des 19. Jahrhunderts in der Karikatur 3670
"Dangerous Liaisons: The Literary Text in Musical Criticism" 4409.d.
De editione musices. Festschrift Gerhard Croll zum 65. Geburtstag 3569
De la Wagner la contemporani, volumul 1: muzica germană si austriacă in a doua jumătate a secolului al XIX-lea 3255
De l'Italieto 5043.b.
"De mortuis nihil nisi bene" 4291
De ratione in musica. Festschrift Erich Schenk zum 5. May 1972 4826
De vocale muziek van Brahms 4638
Dead Get By With Everything, The. Poems 4379.a.
"Death Bed and Funeral of Brahms" 3499
"Death of Brahms" 3500
Death Set To Music: Masterworks by Bach, Brahms, Penderecki, Bernstein 4811
"Debate about Consecutive Fifths, The: A Context for Brahms's Manuscript 'Oktaven und Quinten'" 4869
"Debussy, Brahms et Carmen" 3748
Décalques et empreintes: Autour de R. Schumann et J. Brahms 4900
Decca Music Guides 4507
"Definitive Classical Library" 3345
"Delight for the Solo Singer: Brahms' Gypsy Songs" 4726.5
"[Delight] Reflecting: The Nature of Comparison" 4954
"Delius and Brahms" 3749
"Denkmal für Johannes Brahms, Ein" 5312.a.i. and ii.
Denkmal für Johannes Brahms, Ein. Versuche über Musik und Literatur 5312.a.ii.
Dent Concertgoer's Companion, The 4476.d.
Dent Master Musicians, The 3217

"Endlich inthronisirt. Johannes Brahms und das musikalische München" 3568.d.

Enfants célèbres 3446.b.

"England Honors Brahms" 5438

"Enharmonic Trompe-l'oreille: Reprise and the Disguised Seam in Nineteenth-Century Music" 4371

Ensayistas 3653.b.ii.

Ensemble! A Rehearsal Guide to Thirty Great Works of Chamber Music 4227

Entendre la musique; sémantique psychologique de la musique 4286

"Enter Brahms, Exit Schumann" 3952

Entstehung und Entwicklung der Instrumentalmusik. Vol. 2: Von Beethoven bis inklusive Johannes Brahms 4089

"Entwicklung des Klavierkonzerts von Liszt bis zur Gegenwart, Die" 4506

Entwicklung des Klavierkonzerts von Liszt bis zur Gegenwart, Die 4506.a.

"Epigone oder gescheiterter Reformer? Richard Heuberger in historischer Sicht" 3812

"Epistolario di musicisti" 3822.e.

EPTA Kongress. Dokumentation 4080.d.i.

"Er heiβt Johannes Brahms . . ." 5384.c.i.

Erdfélyi tudományos füzetek 5134

"Ereignisse und Gestalten" 3619

"Erforschung der deutsch-tschechischen musikalischen Wechselbeziehungen, ihre Methoden und ihre Aufgaben" 3761

Erinnerungen (Koelle) 3846

"Erinnerungen an Brahms" 3549, 3830.a.

"Erinnerungen an Hans von Bülow" 4000

"Erinnerungen an Johannes Brahms" 4020

Erinnerungen an Johannes Brahms. Ein Beitrag aus dem Kreis seiner rheinischen Freunde 3879

Erinnerungen an Johannes Brahms in Briefen aus seiner Jugendzeit 3755

Erinnerungen an Robert Fuchs 3774

"Erinnerungen an Wilhelm Kempff" 4080

"Erinnerungen aus meinem Musikerleben" 3792

"Erinnerungen der Baronin Maria von Kulmer an Eusebius Mandyczewski" 3864

"Erinnerungen eines Wiener Philharmonikers an Johannes Brahms" 3847

"Frühling am Gardasee (1897)" 3506.a.
"Führer durch die neueste Claviermusik, Der" 4293
"". . . für das Pianoforte gesetzt". Die zweihändigen Klavierbearbei-
tungen von Johannes Brahms" 4986
*Für Heinz Tiessen 1887–1971. Aufsätze, Analysen, Briefe, Erinnerung-
en, Dokumente, Werkverzeichnis, Bibliographie* 4007
"Fuga organowa w epoce romantyzmu" 4440
Fugue and Fugato in Rococo and Classical Chamber Music 4926.b.
"Fugue in As-Moll" 4454
Fuge und Fugato in der Kammermusik des Rokoko und der Klassik 4926
"Fugen und Fugatosätze in der Kammermusik bis 1882 (Brahms)" 4926
["Full Index to the Brahms-Hermann Levi Correspondence"] 3849
Fun With Music 3446
"Funeral of Brahms, The . . ." 3503
"La funzione pianistica" 4649
"Fuori dall'ansia: Brahms e Verdi sull acqua" 4009
Furtwängler and the Art of Conducting 5174
Furtwängler on Music. Essays and Addresses 5346
Furtwängler Record, The 3334

Gamma jeunesse 3446.b.
Garbe, Die 3298
*Garbe, Die. Vom Leben und Schaffen deutscher Musiker. Musikkunde für
höhere Lehranstalten Klasse 4–8* 3298
Garland Composer Resource Manuals 4023
Garland Library of the History of Western Music, The 3386, 4117,
4833.a., 4896, 4996
Garland Reference Library of the Humanities 4023, 4262.d.i., 4636,
4771, 5390
"Gasthaus der Berühmtheiten, Das" 3472
"Geburtstag von Johannes Brahms" 3619
"Gedanken über Brahms und Bruckner" 3726
"Gedanken über Brahms und Pfitzner" 3883
Gedenkschrift für Jens Peter Larsen 1902–1988 3798
Gedenkschrift Hermann Beck 3998
"Geiringer Scholar Awarded National Grants" 3466
"Geiringer Scholarship Fund, The" 5446.d.
"Geiringer Scholarship Fund, The. One Last Step!" 5445
"Geiringer Scholarship Fund, The. Our Goal is in Sight!" 5446
"Geiringer Scholarship Fund, The. The Last Step Taken!" 5445.d.

Storia della musica. L'Ottocento 3235

"Streichquintett in F-Dur im Œuvre von Anton Bruckner und Johannes Brahms, Das" 4239

String Quartet, The 4225

"String Quartets of Brahms, The: an analysis" 4228

"String Quartets Op. 51 no. 1 in C minor and No. 2 in A minor, The: a preface" 4234

Strom der Töne trug mich fort, Der. Die Welt um Richard Strauss in Briefen 3999.a.

"Strophenlied, Das" 5087

"Structural Analysis of Johannes Brahms' Piano Sonata op. 5, no. 3 in F minor" 4328

Structural Functions in Music 4533

"Structural Role of Orchestration in Brahms's Music, The: A Study of the 'Third Symphony'" 4604

Structure and Style. The Study and Analysis of Musical Forms 4529

"Struktur, Inhalte und Bedeutung der 'Sammlung Hofmann'" 5473

"Strutture pianistiche autonome" 4685

"Student Interpreter, The" 4326

"Student-Interpreter, The" 4675

Student's Music Library, The 4394

Studi e testi musicale. Nuova serie 4198

Studien und Materialien zur Musikwissenschaft 5388

"Studien zu Brahms' frühesten Komponisten. Sein Interesse an Alter Musik und dessen Niederschlag in seinem Frühwerk" 4061.d.

"Studien zur Brahms's Klaviermusik" 4272

Studien zur Wertungsforschung 5124

Studienbuch 4275

Studies in Music 4466

Studies in Musical Genres and Repertories 4274, 4658

Studies in Musicology 5143

Study in Musical Analysis, A 4976

"Study of Brahms' Songs, Opus 59, A" 4715

"Study of Brahms' Treatment of the Clarinet in His Chamber Music and in his Orchestral Works, A" 5076

"Study of Chromatic Elements in Selected Piano Works of Beethoven, Schubert, Schumann, Chopin and Brahms, A" 4974

"Study of Ferruccio Busoni's Transcriptions of Six Organ Chorale Preludes by Johannes Brahms" 5194

"Study of Four Representative Piano Quintets by Major Composers of

University of Illinois at Urbana-Champaign 4526, 4987, 5193
University of Kentucky 4475
University of London, Goldsmiths College 4142, 4191
University of London, King's College 4385
University of Maryland, College Park 4376
University of Melbourne 4258, 4902
University of Melbourne. Grainger Museum. Catalogue 3788
University of Michigan 4267, 5082
University of Minnesota 4495, 4510, 4767
University of Mississippi 4922
University of Missouri 4304
University of Natal 4195
University of New Mexico 4344
University of New York 5101
University of North Carolina 4471
University of North Carolina at Chapel Hill 4263, 4906
University of North Texas 4237, 4750
University of Nottingham 4831, 4893
University of Oklahoma 4228, 4413, 4427, 4779, 4927
University of Oregon 4695
University of Oxford 3697
University of Pennsylvania 4429, 4482
University of Pittsburgh 4736
University of Queensland 5072
University of Redlands 4741
University of Rochester 4149, 4171, 4245, 4248, 4256, 4314, 4383, 4446, 4600, 4621, 4628, 4692, 4707, 4780, 4938, 4973, 4984, 5060, 5067
University of Rochester, Eastman School of Music 4261, 4361, 4871, 5188.d., 5385
University of South Dakota 4579
University of Southern California 4370
University of Tasmania 5063
University of Tennessee, Knoxville 4936
University of Texas at Austin 4350, 4612, 4664, 4908, 5119
University of Texas at El Paso 4182, 4645, 5182
University of Texas at San Antonio 4311, 4330
University of Ulster 4242, 4521
University of Utah 4563
University of Victoria (British Columbia, Canada) 4081, 4452, 4665

"V klasse professora Evgenija Malinina: Rabota nad proizvedenijami Bramsa i Prokof'eva" 4294

Vă place Brahms? 5211.b.vii.

Variaciones psicoanaliticas sobre un tema de Mahler 3653.b.ii.

"Varianti d'autore e varianti di trasmissione nel Trio op. 114 di Johannes Brahms. Osservazioni sui testimoni manoscritti e a stampe" 4198

"Variation Forms in Piano Music from Brahms to the Present" 4277

"Variation Principles in Selected Piano Works of Johannes Brahms" 4313

"Variationen" 3668

Variationen für zwei Klaviere über ein Thema von Joseph Haydn Opus 56b. Faksimile-Ausgabe nach dem Originalmanuskript im Besitz der Musiksammlung der Wiener Stadt- und Landesbibliothek 4368

"Variations for Solo Piano by Johannes Brahms, Op. 9, Op. 21, Op. 24; A Structural Analysis" 4314

"Variations on a Theme by Robert Schumann Op. 20 by Clara Schumann: An Analytical and Interpretative Study" 4336

"Varied Thing, The: A Study of Continuity in the Variations of Brahms' Fourth Symphony" 4612

"various journeys, The . . ." 3583

"Various Versions of Hebbel's 'Vorüber', The" 4714

"Varying Schumann's Theme" 4333

Verbalisierung und Sinngehalt: Über semantische Tendenzen im Denken in und über Musik Heute 5124

"Vereint" 4552

"Vergänglichkeit als ästhetische Kategorie und Erlebnis in Liedern von Johannes Brahms" 5093

Verlags-Nr. (Musikverlag Helbing) 4050

Veröffentlichung der Deutschen Akademie der Kunste zu Berlin 3754

Veröffentlichungen des Beethovenhauses in Bonn 3690

Veröffentlichungen zur Zeitgeschichte 5295

Versi d'amore e di gloria-I 5213.a.iv.

"verstellte Frühwerk, Das. Zum H-dur Trio op. 8 von Johannes Brahms" 4147

Verteidigung des musikalischen Fortschritts. Brahms und Schönberg 3546, 3682, 3922, 3928, 3931, 3976, 4028, 4094.a., 4153.d., 4155, 4914, 5046, 5398

"Vertical Sonorities in the Piano Styles of Schumann, Chopin and Brahms" 4973

Victor Borge's My Favorite Comedies in Music 3240

Newspaper and
Magazine Index

Information in this index is interfiled in one alphabetical sequence, word by word. A reference to a citation number includes appearances in all applicable sections within that number.

Alphabetization follows the principles used in the Titles, Monographic Series, and Degree-Granting Institutions Index. Arrangement within each newspaper or magazine title is chronological by publication year.

Personal Name Index

The Personal Name Index contains references to persons or bodies who are responsible for the content of the citations included in this work—not only authors, but also editors, translators, and illustrators. Persons who are the subject of commemorative volumes, or festschriften, are also indexed here. Authors who are cited in this volume as a result of references to my previous volume, are also indexed here.

Alphabetization follows the general principles used in the body of the work, except that acronyms and initialisms file at the beginning of each letter. A reference to a citation number includes appearances in all applicable sections within that number.

ab. 3338.e.i., 3597.d.ii.e., 4011
AB 4478
A.S. 5241
A.W.K. 5278; See also Kramer,
  A. Walter
Abbiati, Franco 3235
Abbott, William Walter, Jr. 4870
Abdy Williams, Charles F.; See
  Williams, Charles F. Abdy
Abell, Arthur Maynard 3661, 4991,
  5004.b.
Abendroth, Walter 5482
Abraham, Gerald 4059
Absolon, Karel B. 3698; See also
  K.B.A.
Ackere, Jules E. van 3600; See also
  Van Ackere, Jules
Ackermann, Felicitas 3424.e.i.

Acosta, Leonardo 5029.b.
Adaïewsky, E. 5249
Adamski, Ursula 4787; See also
  Adamski-Störmer, Ursula
Adamski-Störmer, Ursula 4787.d.;
  See also Adamski, Ursula
Adorno, Theodor W. 4992
Adrian, Jack; See Adrian, John
  Stanley
Adrian, John Stanley 4871
Ahrens, Rüdiger 3972
Aichholz, Eugen von Miller zu; See
  Miller zu Aichholz, Eugen von
Aigner, Günter Weiss- ; See Weiss-
  Aigner, Günter
Albini, Eugenio 3601
Alexander, David Charles 4752
Allanbrook, Wye J. 4935

Bartlett, Kenneth Walter 5307
Bartlitz, Eveline 5414
Baruch, Gerth-Wolfgang 5287, 5288
Basart, Ann P. 3336
Basel. Musik-Akademie; See Musik-
   Akademie der Stadt Basel
Baser, Friedrich 3543, 3772; See
   also B.
Basso, Alberto 3248, 3249
Bastien, James William 5107
Batisti, Alberto 4018
Baud, Jean-Marc 4877
Bauer, Harold 4255
Baum, Günther 5078
Bayne, Pauline Shaw 3382
Beach, Thelma 4628
Beadle, Jeremy J. 4036, 4570
Beaufils, Marcel 4641
Beaujean, A. 3280
Bechert, Paul 5294
Beck, Hermann 3998, 4579
Beck, Julius 3685
Beck, Robert L. 4579
Becker, Heinz 3237, 4878, 4993
Becker, Peter 3295
Becker, Warren 4098
Beckerath, Willy von 3661, 3686,
   5099
Beckerman, Michael 3758, 3759
Beechey, Gwilym 4431
Beggs, Hugh Harlan 4256
Behm, Eduard 5482
Behne, Klaus-Ernst 3284.d.i.
Behrmann, Martin 5230
Bejinariu, Mircea 3864
Bekker, Peter O.E., Jr. 3238
Belan, William Wells 5152
Bell, A. Craig 4633.5, 5079
Bell, Carol Ann Roberts; See Roberts
   Bell, Carol Ann
Beller-McKenna, Daniel 4458, 5080
Bellman, Jonathan 4879, 5127
Beltrandi-Patier, Marie-Claire 4661
Benary, Peter 4583, 4592

Ben-Chorin, Schalom 4789
Benecke, Heike 5081
Benedict, Emil von 4090
Benjamin, Thomas 4880
Benjamin, William E. 5449.5
Bennett, Jory 3979
Bent, Ian 4566
Bent, Margaret 4926.b.
Bentley, Eric 5396.d.
Bentley, Nelson 4169
Benzi, Manlio 4881
Bereczky, János 4423
Berg, Alban 5398
Berg, Helene 5398
Bergengruen, J. 5243
Berger, Francesco 4257, 4355
Berger, Jonathan 3603
Burger, Lili Fehrle- ; See Fehrle-
   Burger, Lili
Berger, Ludwig 3231
Berger, Melvin 4065, 4091, 4459,
   4753
Bergheim, Gaigg von 3488
Berke, Dietrich 3717, 4351, 4867
Berkefeld, Henning 3522
Berkowitz, Freda Pastor 5184
Bernstein, Kenneth 5415
Bernstein, Leonard 3463.b., 3604
Berron, Linda 3281
Berry, Corre 4642
Berry, Wallace 3292, 4372, 4533,
   4833, 4882
Bertol-Raffin, Elisabeth 5219.b.
Bertram, Hans Georg 4445.5
Beuerle, Hans Michael 4851.1, 4754
Beujean, Alfred; See AB
Beveridge, David R. 3759, 3763,
   4593, 4883
Bialyï, I. 4119
Bianchetti, Egidio 5213.a.iv.
Biba, Otto 3455–58, 3460, 3464, 3489,
   3609.e.i., 3793, 3805, 3809, 3997,
   4003, 4012, 4433, 4434, 4717, 4755,
   4854, 5416, 5417, 5431, 5480

Francisc, László 4341.d.; See also
   Ferenc, László
François-Sappey, Brigitte 4661
Frank, Tibor 3580
Franken, Franz Hermann 3501
Fraser, Donald 3617
Freed, Richard 3346.5
Fribberg; See Fridberg
Fricke, Jobst Peter 4928
Fridberg, Franz 3465
Friedel, Lance 4540
Friedländler, Max 4696
Friedrich, Annegret 3838, 3839
Frisch, Walter M. 3303, 3623, 3811.a.,
   3923, 4032, 4085, 4274, 4473,
   4834, 4909, 4910, 5116, 5238,
   5242, 5344, 5345, 5438, 5478
Fröhlich, Hans J. 3945
Fronzo, Luigi Di; See Di Fronzo,
   Luigi
Frye, Louise 4347
Fuchs, Anton 3526
Fuchs, Ingrid 4541, 5066
Fuchs, Ronald 3527
Fürst, Juta 5435
Fuller-Maitland, John Alexander
   3227, 5162
Funk, Addie 5296
Furtwängler, Wilhelm 5346, 5398,
   5482
Fusner, Henry 3687
Fuszek, Rita M. 3427

GE 4478
Gädor, Agnes 3577
Gätjen, Bram 4928
Gal, Hans 3381, 3700, 3702, 3713
Galand, Joel 4911
Gallois, Jean 3624
Galston, Gottfried 4275
Gander, Irina von Kempski-
   Racoszyna- ; See
   Kempski-Racoszyna-Gander, Irina
   von

Garcia, Ana Lucia Altino 4162
Garden, Neville 3285
Gardenal da Silva, Fabio Roberto
   4141
Gardiner, John Eliot 4792
Garlington, Aubrey S., Jr. 4835,
   4842.d.
Garrett, Lee 4442.b.
Gatti, Guido Maria 3248
Gay, Peter 5347
Geck, Martin 5232
Gehring, Philip 4447
Geiger, Joachim 4847
Geiringer, Bernice 3777
Geiringer, Irene 3207
Geiringer, Karl 3207, 3332, 3625,
   3712, 3777, 3850, 4856, 4865,
   5142, 5348
Gemeentemuseum; See Hague.
   Gemeentemuseum
Geng, Veronica 5348.5
Germane, Sydney L. 4276
Gersoni, Annalisa 3249
Gerstmeier, August 5092
Gervink, Manuel 4928
Geschäftsstelle der Johannes-Brahms-
   Festwoche 5307
Gesellschaft der Musikfreunde 3380
Gesellschaft der Musikfreunde.
   Museum 5471
Geyer, Alan F. 5229
Giannini, Antoinette Frances 4277
Gibbs, W. Wayt 3626
Gieseler, Walter 4072, 4912
Gilardoni, Bruno 3347
Gilbert, Christopher Michael 4598
Gilbert, Michael 3954
Gilbert, S. Price 4556.a.
Gilder, Eric 3428
Giles, Eric 5217
Gill, Dominic 4269
Gillespie, Susan 3632, 3802, 3947,
   4074, 4480
Gilling, Graeme 4184

Stahmer, Klaus Hinrich 3861,
  4096.d., 4179
Stanford, Charles Villiers, Sir 3988
Stark, Lucien 4693
Starker, Janos 4181.d.
Steakley, James 3954
Steane, John B. 3375, 3971, 4821
Stearns, David Patrick 4460.e.ii.
Stearns, Ruby Godwin 3653.4
Stearns, Theodore 3882
Stedman, Preston 4502
Steel, Matthew C. 4400
Stefan, Paul 3478, 4742, 5471
Stegemann, Michael 4836; See also
  M.St.
Stein, Deborah 5104
Stein, Erwin 4152
Stein, Fritz Wilhelm 3893
Stein, Leon 4529
Stein, Leonard 5045
Steinbeck, Susanne 4503
Steinbeck, Wolfram 4565, 4888, 5472
Steinberg, Michael P. 4504, 5051
Steiner, Adolf 3595
Stein-Karnbach, Annegret 5429
Stellfeld, Bent 4190, 4505
Stengel, Theophil 4506
Stepanov, A. 4305.5.d.i.
Stephan, Rudolf 4144, 4626, 5011
Stephenson, Kurt 3881
Sterling, Eugene Allen 4974
Steuermann, Clara 4309
Steuermann, Edward 4309
Stevens, Agnes 3424.e.viii.
Stevens, Denis 3254, 3351
Stevens, Henry Charles 4507
Stevenson, E. Irenaeus 3482.a.
Stevenson, Robert 4775
Stewart, Jimmy Dan 4413
Stockhem, Michel 3540
Stockmann, Bernhard 4822
Störmer, Ursula Adamski- ; See
  Adamski-Störmer, Ursula
Stokes, Charles Frank 4586

Stokes, Richard 5090.b., 5165
Stokowski, Olga Samaroff 4557
Storey Smith, Warren 5399
Strack, Otto 3575
Strajnar, Julijan 4699
Straus, Joseph N. 3930
Strauss, Alice 3999.a.
Strauss, Franz 3999.a.
Strauss, Johann (Sohn) 3993
Strauss, John F. 3885
Strauss, Richard 3999, 4000
Streicher, Elizabeth 3841
Strobel, Heinrich 5400
Strohl, E.L. 3707
Struck, Michael 3966, 3967, 4148,
  4342, 4823, 5473
Stuart, Lila 3821
Stucken, Frank, van der; See Van der
  Stucken, Frank
Stuckenschmidt, Hans Heinz 3275
Sullivan, Jack 4609
Sulzer, Peter 3596, 3898, 3900, 3901
Sunderman, F. William 3708, 4235
Superchi, Romano 4685.d.
Suppan, Wolfgang 4746
Surace, Ronald Dominic 3868
Svejda, Jim 3377
Swafford, Jan 3276
Swain, Joseph Peter 4975
Swalin, Benjamin F. 4576
Swan, Howard 4669
Swartz, Melinda 4721
Sweeney, Valentine Wheeler 5178
Swickard, Alice Jayne 4353
Szeskus, Reinhard 3768, 5139
Szklarska, Kamilla F. 4324
Szomory, György 5474

Takeuchi, Fumiku 4398.b.
Tănăsescu, Dragoş 3854
Tapper, Thomas 3447
Taruskin, Richard 5120.e.
Taylor, Marilyn Gail 4311
Taylor, Ronald 5346

About the Author

Thomas Quigley (B.Mus., MLS) is the head of the Joe Fortes Branch in the Public Library System in Vancouver, BC. He was research assistant for the McCorkle Brahms Thematic Catalogue Project. He has written for *Fontes artis musicae* and *The Newsletter of the American Brahms Society*. Most recently he has spoken at conferences of the Music Library Association and the Canadian Association of Music Libraries, Archives and Documentation Centres; and Chapter Meetings of the American Musicological Society.